Accession no.
36186352

Understanding Sustainable Development

This new and expanded edition builds upon the first edition's powerful multi-perspective approach and breadth of coverage. A truly comprehensive introduction to sustainable development, it is designed specifically to allow access to the topic from a wide range of educational and professional backgrounds and to develop understanding of a diversity of approaches and traditions at different levels.

This second edition includes:

- a complete update of the text, with increased coverage of major topics including ecosystems; production and consumption; business; urban sustainability; governance; new media technologies; conservation; leadership; globalization and global crises; sustainability literacy and learning;
- more examples from the Global South and North America, while retaining its unique coverage of first world countries;
- chapter aims at the start and summaries at the end of each chapter;
- glossary of key terms;
- a new chapter on conservation with a focus on behaviour change and values;
- a brand new website, which includes discussion of how projects are done on the ground, additional exercises and online cases, test questions and recommended readings and films.

Offering boxed examples from the local to the global, *Understanding Sustainable Development* is the most complete guide to the subject for course leaders, undergraduates and postgraduates.

John Blewitt is the Director of the MSc Social Responsibility and Sustainability, Aston Business School, Aston University, UK.

'Synthesizing the broad array of ideas, debates and approaches to "Sustainable Development" is no easy task. This book does an excellent job of covering the critical issues, and in a very readable form. It moves deftly from theory to practice, touching down in different parts of the world, from China to South America, from the U.S. to the U.K. The inclusion of up-to-date topics like the role of the internet, computers, television and film in sustainable development is most welcome, indeed.'

Lawrence Herzog, San Diego State University, USA

'John Blewitt's revised and updated edition is truly a bridge – elegantly and comprehensively connecting theory with practice, socio-economic and political understanding with environmental performance, and the reader to a vast solar system of ideas, solutions and real world examples of sustainability.'

Jeff Loux, University of California, Davis, USA

'A very comprehensive, resourceful and user-friendly book for developing an understanding of sustainable development and of its interpretation in different policy areas, contexts and sectors; this textbook is essential for both students and teachers.'

Paola Gazzola, Newcastle University, UK

'This is a comprehensive, authoritative and accessible contribution to sustainable development which can only come from an author who has decades of experience in the field. John Blewitt combines meticulously researched chapters with deeply reflective questions and a clarity of argument that makes this book essential reading for all.'

Daniella Tilbury, University of Gloucestershire, UK and Chair of the UN Global Monitoring and Evaluation Expert Group on Education for Sustainable Development

'*Understanding Sustainable Development* introduces students and professionals to the basic concepts of sustainability and leads them – step by step – to explore inherent paradoxes and complexity of social, economic and environmental issues. A must read for everybody interested in (critical) theory of economic development, sustainability, and related subjects of globalization, democracy and neoliberalism.'

Helen Kopnina, The Hague University of Applied Sciences, the Netherlands

Praise for the first edition:

'A significant achievement in addressing a complex contemporary issue in such a clear and optimistic way. Will it make a difference to our understanding? I think it will.'

Stephen Martin, Visiting Professor, Center for Complexity and Change, The Open University

'This is an immensely important book that brings into a cohesive and dialogic whole, the multiple strands that do – or should – feed into understandings of sustainable development. It draws upon worldviews and perspectives often marginalized or ignored in the adrenaline rush to make sustainability a living reality. A "must read" for both those new to and those steeped in the field.'

David Selby, Director, Centre for Sustainable Futures, University of Plymouth

'Presents a comprehensive account of the sustainability territory, successfully integrating ideas from science, philosophy, sociology and cultural studies in its explication of key topics within this field. It will prove invaluable for those of us from a range of disciplines and perspectives who are trying to make sense of what "sustainability" means, and what actions we might take to realize it within our communities, organizations and homes.'

Donna Ladkin, Senior Lecturer in Organizational Learning and Leadership at Cranfield University School of Management

'*Understanding Sustainable Development* is a major work and it largely achieves a very difficult task. It comes closer than most to that elusive ideal: the comprehensive book on a broadly based interpretation of sustainable development!'

Julian Agyeman, Associate Professor and Chair, Urban and Environmental Policy and Planning, Tufts University

Understanding Sustainable Development

Second edition

John Blewitt

LIS - LIBRARY

Date	Fund
08/09/15	Shr - Xg

Order No

2646043

University of Chester

Companion website: www.routledge.com/cw/blewitt

Routledge
Taylor & Francis Group
LONDON AND NEW YORK

from Routledge

First edition published 2008
by Earthscan

This edition published 2015
by Routledge
2 Park Square, Milton Park, Abingdon, Oxon, OX14 4RN

and by Routledge
711 Third Avenue, New York, NY 10017

Routledge is an imprint of the Taylor & Francis Group, an informa business

© 2015 John Blewitt

The right of John Blewitt to be identified as author of this work has
been asserted by him in accordance with sections 77 and 78 of the
Copyright, Designs and Patents Act 1988.

All rights reserved. No part of this book may be reprinted or
reproduced or utilized in any form or by any electronic, mechanical,
or other means, now known or hereafter invented, including photocopying
and recording, or in any information storage or retrieval system,
without permission in writing from the publishers.

British Library Cataloguing in Publication Data
A catalogue record for this book is available from the British Library

Library of Congress Cataloging-in-Publication Data
Blewitt, John, 1957–.
  Understanding sustainable development/John Blewitt. – Second edition.
  pages cm
  Includes bibliographical references and index.
  1. Sustainable development. I. Title.
  HC79.E5B58 2014
  338.9'27 – dc23
  2014002638

ISBN13: 978-0-415-70781-7 (hbk)
ISBN13: 978-0-415-70782-4 (pbk)
ISBN13: 978-1-315-88645-9 (ebk)

Typeset in Sabon
by Florence Production Ltd, Stoodleigh, Devon, UK

MIX
Paper from
responsible sources
FSC
www.fsc.org   FSC® C013056

Printed and bound in Great Britain by
TJ International Ltd, Padstow, Cornwall

Contents

Illustrations

Figures

Tables

Boxes

Acronyms and abbreviations

ABCD	awareness, baseline, clear and compelling, down to action
ALS	amyotrophic lateral sclerosis
AMOEBA	Dutch acronym meaning 'general method for ecosystem description and assessment'
ANT	actor network theory
ASA	Advertising Standards Authority (UK)
BAU	business as usual
BSE	bovine spongiform encephalopathy (mad cow disease)
CAT	Centre for Alternative Technology (Wales)
CBD	Convention on Biological Diversity
CEO	Chief Executive Officer
CFC	chlorofluorocarbon
CITES	Convention on International Trade in Endangered Species
CJD	Creutzfeldt-Jacob disease
CMC	computer-mediated communications
CSR	corporate social responsibility
DCSD	Danish Committees on Scientific Dishonesty
Defra	Department for Environment, Food and Rural Affairs (UK)
DFID	Department for International Development (UK)
EM	ecological modernization
ENGO	environmental non-governmental organization
EPA	US Environmental Protection Agency
ESD	Education for Sustainable Development
FTO	Fair Trade Organization
GBM	Green Belt Movement (Kenya)
GCAR	Grupo Cultural AfroReggae (Brazil) GDP
GDP	gross domestic product
GHG	greenhouse gas
GIS	geographic information system
GM	genetic modification; genetically modified
GMO	genetically modified organism
GNP	gross national product
GPI	genuine progress indicator
GRI	Global Reporting Initiative
HDI	Human Development Index (UN)
HDR	Human Development Report (UNDP)

HPI	Happy Planet Index
IA	integrated assessment
ICT	information and communication technology
IFAW	International Fund for Animal Welfare
IMC	Independent Media Center
IMF	International Monetary Fund
IPCC	Intergovernmental Panel on Climate Change
IPPR	Institute for Public Policy Research (UK)
ISEW	index of sustainable economic welfare
IPSO	International Programme of the State of the Ocean
IUCN	World Conservation Union
LSX	London Sustainability Exchange
MEA	Millennium Ecosystem Assessment
NCWK	National Council of Women in Kenya
NGO	non-governmental organization
NIMBY	not in my backyard
NRDC	National Resources Defense Council
OECD	Organization for Economic Co-operation and Development
PR	public relations
R&D	research and development
SIBART	'Seeing Is Believing As a Replication Tool' project (EU)
SIGMA	Sustainability – Integrated Guidelines for Management project
SOFI	State of the Future Index
SPARC	Society for the Promotion of Area Resource Centres
SVTC	Silicon Valley Toxics Coalition
TEK	traditional ecological knowledge
TNC	transnational company
TNS	The Natural Step
TRIPS	Trade-Related Intellectual Property Rights Agreement
TVE	Television for the Environment
UN	United Nations
UNDP	United Nations Development Programme
UNEP	United Nations Environment Programme
UNESCO	United Nations Educational, Scientific and Cultural Organization
UNFCCC	United Nations Framework Convention on Climate Change
UN-REDD	United Nations Collaborative Programme on Reducing Emissions from Deforestation and Forest Degradation in Developing Countries
WCED	World Commission on Environment and Development
WEDO	Women's Environment and Development Organization
WMO	World Meteorological Organization
WSF	World Social Forum
WTO	World Trade Organization
WWF	World Wide Fund for Nature

Introduction

In the years since the first edition of *Understanding Sustainable Development* was written and published, quite a lot has happened. There have been a number of climate change conferences, the twentieth anniversary of the first Rio Earth summit has been and gone, the impact of the financial crash of 2007–8 still rumbles on, a near nuclear catastrophe occurred in Fukashima in Japan, we witnessed increasingly extreme weather events, and the global population continues to grow, as do cities and the level of carbon dioxide in the atmosphere. The world is quickly changing and not exactly for the better. The planet's ecosystems are more stressed than ever before and peak oil has led to the almost certain exploration of oil in regions that were formally either inaccessible ethically or physically such as the Arctic as well as a revival of interest in nuclear power and the rapid development of the fracking industry. The geopolitical climate has altered too, not least with the clear emergence of China as probably the dominant economic, and maybe political, force of the twenty-first century. One thing, however, has not changed. We have now clearly and indubitably entered the Anthropocene and few people feel capable of denying that fact. Human actions have impacted seriously and negatively on our planet's ecosystems and will continuously do so until we – that is, humanity – do something about it.

Debates over climate change now focus on mitigation, adaptation and resilience rather than whether it is happening or what is causing it. The answer to this last question is fairly simple and generally agreed. Human action is the predominant cause of the massive and rapid acceleration of greenhouse gasses, global warming and climate turbulence. Our ways of doing business, of producing goods and services, have used the Earth's resources as if they were inexhaustible. The Earth itself has been treated simultaneously as a factory, pleasure park, garbage dump, larder, market-place and war zone. It is self-evident that we, as a species, cannot continue as we are doing. Obscene poverty and fabulous wealth live side by side, and the natural world, for many, cannot be accessed at all, although poverty, inequality, injustice, environmental degradation and war are not exactly modern phenomena. We cannot simply continue in the same old way without putting the future at risk of not happening at all. Hence, sustainable development is more important than ever before, although the discussions about what it is and how it can be developed remain lively subjects for debate, negotiation and practical action.

In broad terms, sustainable development should be quite simple to understand. It is the idea that the future should be a better, healthier, place than the present and the past. The idea is not new, but the way it is understood, reflected upon, cultivated and implemented possibly is. Neither modern nor postmodern, sustainable development requires an understanding of the natural world and the human social world as being not so much 'connected' as one and the same. Sustainable development is a process that requires us to view our lives as elements of a larger entity. It requires a holistic way of looking at the world and human life. It requires a recognition that other people may not see things like this at all and will have different perceptions, values, philosophies, aims and ambitions. It requires an understanding that the world is multifaceted, fragmented and complete. This may not be easy to grasp at first, but it is a way of looking at the world and one that increasingly makes sense. That, in any case, is my view.

There are other views. Sustainable development is the product of many stories, worldviews, values, actions and perspectives which, to be fully appreciated, require a readiness to listen to others, respect differences, suspend established opinions and see with others' eyes while allowing other voices to resonate and be heard. Sustainable development requires dialogue and is a dialogue of values: that is the underpinning rationale of this book in offering a series of guides and signposts to a range of contributions to this dialogue. Of course, this view is both contestable and not particularly original, but if elements within the text motivate further thought, reflection and dialogue, then hopefully our understanding of sustainable development will have been advanced just a little bit further.

Many people are still coming to sustainable development with little understanding of the key issues and debates. They may have a deep and detailed knowledge of one specific area, but only the vaguest of inklings of anything beyond. Others may have a general but confused understanding of the theories and perspectives because they are immersed in its practice. Some people see sustainable development as essentially about the environment, and indeed sustainable development has its roots in ensuring that the planet's ecosystems are protected from the ravages of human civilization. Maybe the best way to view sustainable development is as a collage or a kaleidoscope of shapes, colours and patterns that change constantly as we ourselves change. It is for us, therefore, to make sense of the world in all its complexity. We must avoid imposing convenient conceptual frameworks which the world just does not fit but which we find comfortable or accessible. There is a need to acknowledge that we do not, and maybe cannot, understand everything, however hard we might try. Uncertainty and the incomplete nature of our knowledge do not require us to apply simple, or simplistic, solutions to problems. Complex problems require complex solutions. Sustainable development warrants an attitude of mind that welcomes change, difference, creativity, risk, uncertainty, a sense of wonder, and a desire and capacity to learn. It is a heuristic – a way of learning about life and through life. The importance of learning should never be forgotten. We can only grow, flourish and be sustainable if we learn.

Speaking personally

Having just written about values, perspectives and sustainable development, it is perhaps only right to say a little about my own understanding of sustainable development, and my own learning and journey towards it. Like so many other things, my values have evolved, taken on different hues, as I have learned more about the world, other people and myself. Having been a teacher in adult, further and higher education for over thirty years, learning is actually my business as well as my passion. I have noticed my social, political and ethical values becoming slowly greener with the years. I have a strong commitment to social and environmental justice, and a number of writers and practitioners have been significant influences on my learning journey. I have been particularly open to the social ecology of Murray Bookchin, the bioregionalism and humanism of Lewis Mumford, the urbanism of Henri Lefebrve and David Harvey, and increasingly the ancient wisdom and spiritual engagement of indigenous peoples. The work of Greg Buckman, Wolfgang Sacks and Vandana Shiva has been extremely important for me too. Finally, I have always been most at ease with an interdisciplinary or transdisciplinary approach to understanding the world around us. No one discipline can generate a holistic understanding of human beings and their relationship to the planet or each other. Having said this, I have nonetheless tried to be even handed in my selection and account of ideas, values, issues and actions discussed in this book. I have used a variety of sources and have learned a great deal from many people – friends, family, students and colleagues. Teaching is the corollary of learning, but our learning must not simply be confined to abstract academic exercises or a playing with words. Learning must be married to change, and words to action. As the American philosopher Ralph Waldo Emerson wrote in his famous 1836 essay *Nature*:

> Words are finite organs of the infinite mind. They cannot cover the dimensions of what is in truth. They break, chop and impoverish it. An action is the perfection and publication of thought. A right action seems to fill the eye, and be related to all nature.
>
> (Ziff, 1982: 61)

Outline of the book

The chapters of this book are relatively self-contained, but together make for an understanding of sustainable development that celebrates complexity and diversity. The various sections hopefully demonstrate why sustainable development is such a necessity. Theoretical discussions are interspersed with empirical case studies, the voices of numerous others and inevitably some contradictions. Chapter 1 focuses on the emergence and evolution of two related terms sustainability (a goal or condition) and sustainable development (a process). The discourse of globalization and institutionalization sustainable development are explored through the identification of four specific worldviews, the operation of a number of international organizations and agencies and the way in which the language of economics has shaped much of our understanding of what the world actually is. The second edition differs from the first in that more attention is paid to India and China than before. Europe, and particularly the United States, remain of pivotal importance in understanding sustainable development but the world is now both a bigger and a smaller place. Towards the end of the chapter the focus narrows to show how sustainable development policy has been articulated in a national context, and, using the example of the ongoing struggles to conserve the ancient temporal forests of British Columbia in Clayoquot Sound, the relationship between the local and the global is analysed. Finally, the idea of sustainable development constituting a 'dialogue of values' is outlined.

Chapter 2 explores some of the major philosophical, theoretical and ethical contributions to the evolving process of sustainable development. Each section is connected so that the reader may detect similarities and differences between the various perspectives and may gain the opportunity to learn new things or perhaps revisit previously discounted points of view. From 'deep ecology' to 'actor network theory' to 'environmental modernization' and systems thinking, this chapter maps sustainable development's intellectual terrain. Chapter 3 extends these earlier excursions by reviewing some of the major controversies, disputes and conflicts which sustainable development has stimulated. The experience of sustainability in the sometimes unreceptive environment of Russia is examined. The ideas and priorities of the Danish statistician Bjørn Lomborg, whose view on climate change and much else is hotly contested, shows how energetic the debate can be and how a certain contrariness can motivate others to develop, refine and rearticulate their own views. The role and meaning of 'sound science' and the emergence of what is now called 'sustainability science' is also discussed, as are some debates around genetic modification and nanotechnology. Some space is also dedicated to outlining the concept of the risk society and its relevance to understanding the idea that ultimately sustainability is a political act.

Chapter 4 moves towards the social and environmental spheres by discussing the growing significance of the environmental justice movement. The reality of the poor, the disadvantaged and the exploited always seeming to be the victims of corporate greed, government corruption or history demonstrates that at the core of sustainable development is a moral imperative. The decline of Detroit in the US and the emergence of grass-roots movement, particularly around food justice, indicates that even in the richest of nations cruel hardships are not to be accepted passively. Given the unavoidable and mesmerizing advances of new media technologies throughout the globe, the significance of information and communication technology (ICT) is also explored as a means towards fashioning a more just and healthy world as is the continuing relevance of public space and the idea of the cultural commons. Chapter 5 shifts the focus on to the political, looking at human agency, ecological and workplace democratization, environmental campaigning, civic action, the politics of place and community empowerment. Actions to combat violence against women in India show that democratic participation often requires strong and resolute action. The idea that sustainable development is not just environmentalism is reinforced throughout by demonstrating the complexity and interconnectedness of the issues, actions, challenges and hopes of many sustainability practitioners. Human beings have the capacity, and the capability, to right the wrongs and repair the damage they have done if they have the collective will to do so. Chapter 6 is new to the second edition. It addresses issues relating to economic development and habitat and animal conservation. The controversies around economic development, big dams, species extinction, food, urbanization and the green revolution add a wider dimension that recognizes the importance of topics that were excluded earlier for reasons of space. Chapter 7 examines the central importance of economics and business, which have been frequently viewed as a major cause of the problem but are now increasingly seen as a necessary part of the solution. Those services that the planet's ecosystems kindly offer us have to be respected rather than abused and exploited. Views differ, of course, ranging from the revolutionary dismantling of the global economic system to its restructuring and reshaping through the processes of localization, degrowth, the green economy, eco-efficiency and corporate responsibility as exemplified by such companies as Interface and such practices as fair trade. A discussion of economic growth and the hegemony of gross domestic product (GDP) frames these explorations.

Now to the future. Chapter 8 looks at how the future has been and is being conceived, by addressing the value of utopian thinking and some practical attempts to establish prefigurative ecovillages. What humans can dream, they can also create in their physical lives on Earth. Much attention is devoted to urban development and environmental design, because today over half the world's population lives in urban settlements and because the origins of our present crises can often be traced back to problems with urban design and planning. The sustainability achievements of Curitiba in Brazil are examined and critiqued. Techniques and examples of backcasting and scenario analysis are also discussed. Chapter 9 moves the focus on to the resolutely practical by exploring the connectivity between means and ends, tools and practices, indices and the nature of human well-being and human flourishing. Ecological footprinting and environmental space, the Natural Step Framework and the Global Reporting Initiative, and eco-labelling and consumption have as their aim to enable us to live on the only planet we have. The frugal innovation ideas stemming from the Indian philosophy and practice of jugaad are also addressed. Chapter 10 links communication, marketing, new media, education and learning as vehicles for, and integral aspects of, sustainable development. This immensely important field is central to fashioning a sustainable world, although here, as with so much else, there are debates and disputes as well as dialogue. Combined with action, communication and learning are ways through which many peoples, groups and communities can find their true voice and, if necessary, invite themselves to the high table of policy formulation and practical action. The final chapter, Chapter 11, explores leadership and management, with practical case-study examples, and by rooting the idea and need for leadership in some of the key values and philosophies informing the dialogue on sustainability and sustainable development. The management system Project SIGMA is rooted in the idea of environmental modernization, and the maverick businessman Ricardo Semler's leadership achievements are rooted in corporate creativity, knowledge innovation and self-organization. The practicalities of dialogue, the significance of emotional and ecological intelligence, and the capacity for understanding, being and working with others are presented as key ingredients for community development and personal engagement. The need for authenticity, trust and commitment is an implicit theme running through this chapter, which ends with a reference to the culture of aboriginal peoples, suggesting that leaders are less important than developing wisdom and respect for nature and, by implication, each other.

Sustainable development encompasses far more than can be covered in one book, so accompanying *Understanding Sustainable Development* is a website providing illustrative and complementary material, including additional case studies, exercises and recommended films and readings which will enable the reader to further explore subjects, ideas and actions. But beware, there are no magic bullets. There is no one way of squaring the circle. Sustainable development is, and probably always will be, work in progress even if in the future it goes by a different name. What we do and how we understand what we do is key to making fewer mistakes, to learning better ways and to nurturing the hope that our future will be a better place than the past for the Earth and all that lives and relies upon it.

1 Towards sustainable development

The aim of this chapter is to introduce the concepts of globalization and sustainable development, indicating the complex and often contested nature of various debates, actions and practices that have occurred in recent years. The significance of some key international agreements will be discussed, as will the criticisms and comments they have stimulated. Sustainable development has emerged through political and environmental struggles, through a business, citizen and governmental engagement with the complexity of contemporary ecological and other problems, and a vast array of perspectives, values and interests that have been applied in seeking to understand and deal with them. The chapter ends with the suggestion that sustainable development is perhaps best understood as a 'dialogue of values' – a way of encouraging people to learn, to discover and to evaluate.

The road to sustainable development

Until the industrialization of Europe in the mid-eighteenth century, wood was the primary material used for fuel, construction, smelting and shipbuilding. World trade and the great navies relied on a ready and what some believed to be an inexhaustible supply of timber. However, these people were wrong. Although timber is a renewable resource, European nations were harvesting more trees than were being planted and nurtured to maturity. Governments in Britain, France and particularly Germany slowly recognized that such a rate of timber consumption was becoming unsustainable. As Ulrich Grober (2012: 88) writes in *Sustainability: A Cultural History*, a number of foresters and enlightened government ministers such as Johan Wolfgang von Goethe of Weimar, believed that 'the true capacities of the forests' should become the basis for their use and exploitation. The science of ecology, the concept of sustainability and the practice of sustainable development was emerging. Closely aligned to its sister concept, namely conservation, sustainability became a key term for a growing body of environmentalists in the new and the old worlds. For Aldo Leopold, an American citizen of German descent and a key figure in the environmental movement in the US in the first half of the twentieth century, land use was far more than an economic problem. It was a moral and ecological issue too. 'A thing is right when it tends to preserve the integrity, stability, and beauty of the biotic community. It is wrong when it tends otherwise', he wrote (Leopold, 1970: 262). Some years later in the mid-twentieth century, the publication of Rachel Carson's (Carson, 2000) *Silent Spring* in 1962, which forensically, but with great emotion and sensitivity, analysed the devastating ecological impact chemical pesticides had on the American countryside, marked the beginning of what become known as Earth Politics and the modern environmental movement.

In Europe and America the 1960s and 1970s witnessed a growing concern that economic growth, development consumerism and related lifestyle demands were undermining the ecological balance, economic stability and security of the planet. These concerns were intensified with the publication of a single image, the lonely and luminous planet earth, taken by an astronaut from the Apollo Eight spacecraft in 1968, which revealed the beauty and fragility of the world as never seen before: *Earthrise* as seen from the moon. In 1972 a further image from the Apollo Project, *Blue Marble*, quickly became the most published image in history and an icon of, and for, the new sustainability advocates and the wider environmental movement. World-famous pressure groups were formed, such as Friends of the Earth and Greenpeace. A number of ecologically minded writers following in Rachel Carson's footsteps came to prominence such as Charles A. Reich who wrote *The Greening of America* (1970), Theodore Roszak and *The Making of a Counter Culture* (1969) and *Where the Wasteland Ends* (1972), and E.F. Schumacher's game-changing *Small is Beautiful* (1973). In 1966 Kenneth E. Boulding wrote 'The economics of the coming Spaceship Earth', in which he stated there were no unlimited reservoirs of anything and that humanity would have to recognize and find its place in a cyclical ecological system capable of continuous reproduction but which continually needed inputs of energy to maintain itself. In 1970 the first major environmental event to have any real social, public and cultural impact was held in the US. Thus, following an earlier discussion in the United Nations that there should be a global holiday, Earth Day drew attention to environmental degradation in a manner never seen before. In 1972 the editors of *The Ecologist* issued a call to action, writing, in *A Blueprint for Survival*:

> The principal defect of the industrial way of life with its ethos of expansion is that it is not sustainable. Its termination within the lifetime of someone born today is inevitable – unless it continues to be sustained for a while longer by an entrenched minority at the cost of imposing great suffering on the rest of mankind.
> (Goldsmith *et al.*, 1972: 15)

The same year, 1972, saw the publication of the landmark study *Limits to Growth* by a global think-tank known as the Club of Rome and the first serious international discussion of global environmental issues at the United Nations Conference on the Human Environment in Stockholm.

The Club of Rome (Meadows *et al.*, 1972) report attempted to combine optimism concerning human potential to innovate and transcend environmental and demographic problems with a well-evidenced warning that if contemporary trends continued there would be dire economic and ecological consequences. Their global model was built specifically to investigate five major trends – accelerating industrialization, rapid population growth, widespread malnutrition, depletion of non-renewable resources and a deteriorating environment. The authors looked to the future too, posing some key questions: What do we want our world to be like? Can we continually keep expanding production and consumption? The answer was a clear No. Achieving a self-imposed limitation to growth would require considerable effort, however. It would involve learning to do many things in new ways. It would tax the ingenuity, the flexibility, willpower, moral sense and self-discipline of the human race. Bringing a deliberate, controlled end to growth would be a tremendous challenge, not easily met. Would the final result be worth it? What would humanity gain by such a transition, and what would it lose? Thirty years later, three of the authors published an update (Meadows *et al.*, 2005). They reviewed the debates and criticisms, analysed new evidence, amended their position but firmly and clearly demonstrated that their theory of necessary limits to growth still remained vital and significant.

Concurrent with the work of the Club of Rome, the General Assembly of the IUCN (World Conservation Union), a body established in the wake of the Second World War, met in New Delhi. With the newly formed WWF (World Wildlife Fund, later renamed World Wide Fund for Nature) the IUCN was concerned to develop new strategic thinking for animal and habitat conservation and human well-being. The concept 'quality of life' became the centrepiece for IUCN thinking and policy development intelligently linking cultural diversity with ecological or biodiversity. In 1980, the IUCN published its *World Conservation Strategy* and so launched into the global public sphere the seemingly new concept, and potential future practice, of sustainable development. Humanity's relationship with the biosphere, the Strategy states, will continue to deteriorate until a new international economic order and a new environmental ethic is established. Prefiguring the more famous Brundtland Declaration of seven years later, the IUCN carefully defined its terms:

> Development is defined here as: the modification of the biosphere and the application of human, financial, living and non-living resources to satisfy human needs and improve the quality of human life. For development to be sustainable it must take account of social and ecological factors, as well as economic ones; of the living and non-living resource base; and of the long term as well as the short term advantages and disadvantages of alternative actions.
>
> (IUCN, 1980: 2)

Conservation is defined here as the management of human use of the biosphere so that it may yield the greatest sustainable benefit to present generations while maintaining its potential to meet the needs and aspirations of the future. Thus conservation is positive, embracing preservation, maintenance, sustainable utilization, restoration and enhancement of the natural environment. Living resource conservation is specifically concerned with plants, animals and micro-organisms, and with those non-living elements of the environment on which they depend. Living resources have two important properties, the combination of which distinguishes them from non-living resources: they are renewable if conserved and they are destructible if not.

In 1980 the Brandt Commission published its *North–South: A Programme for Survival*, placing the responsibility for human survival firmly in the political arena at a time when leaders seemed more concerned with Cold War ideological posturing than addressing pressing issues of global poverty, social inequality, justice, self-determination, human rights and the depletion of natural resources. The Commission did not redefine development, but duly noted:

> One must avoid the persistent confusion of growth with development, and we strongly emphasize that the prime objective of development is to lead to self-fulfillment and creative partnership in the use of a nation's productive forces and its full human potential.
>
> (Brandt, 1980: 23)

In other words, development strategy should not be predicated upon ever expanding economic growth or GDP. The whole world should not use as its model for future prosperity what has occurred in the West. The standard of life is not the same as the quality of life. Development should focus on enhancing the latter, should be more about well-being than the relentless accumulation of material products, and each region with its own ecological and cultural heritage should be able to chart its own distinct and distinctive path. In many ways the Brandt Commission Report echoed the work of the International Foundation for Development Alternatives (IFDA) which published, also in 1980, Dossier No.17, *Building Blocks for Alternative Development Strategies*, stating:

> The development *problematique* can thus be defined in an objective way: the society, its economy and polity, ought to be organized in such a manner as to maximize, for the individual and the whole, the opportunities for self-fulfillment. Developing, as the etymology suggests, means removing the husk – that is overcoming domination; liberating; unfolding. Development is the unfolding of people's individual and social imagination in defining goals, inventing means and ways to approach them, learning to identify and satisfy socially legitimate needs. . . . To develop is to be, or to become. Not to have.
>
> (IFDA, 1980: 10)

Thus wealth and development took on a qualitative as well as a quantitative aspect. Material and spiritual poverty both need to be addressed. In 1983 work started on a major study by the World Commission on Environment and Development (WCED) that would firmly establish sustainable development as the most significant concept and practice of our time. In 1987 the results were published as *Our Common Future* (the Brundtland Report). More than half of the Commission were representatives from developing countries, ensuring that global environmental concerns would not overwhelm the desire to eradicate problems of human need and poverty. Unlike Brandt, Brundtland did offer a definition of *sustainable development*: 'Development that meets the needs of the present without compromising the ability of future generations to meet their own needs' (WCED, 1987: 43).

This definition is still commonly used, despite it attracting serious criticisms for suggesting that economic growth, industrial modernization and market imperatives should be key drivers and goals for all nations. Whereas the industrialized North seemed to be, and in many ways still is, concerned with environmental impacts, the issues confronting the majority South included poverty, health, income, agricultural sustainability, food security, educational opportunity and achievement, shelter, sanitation, desertification and armed conflict. Nevertheless, the Brundtland Report did tacitly recognize the internal contradictions within the concept when it stated:

> [Sustainable development] contains within it two key concepts:
>
> 1 The concept of 'needs', in particular the essential needs of the world's poor, to which over-riding priority should be given.
> 2 The idea of limitations imposed by the state of technology and social organization on the environment's ability to meet present and future needs.
>
> (WCED, 1987: 43)

Although acknowledging that its analysis and recommendations were specifically rooted in the 1980s, *Our Common Future* concluded its outline of sustainable development by stating that its realization also required:

- a political system that secures effective citizen participation in decision-making;
- an economic system that is able to generate surpluses and technical knowledge on a self-reliant and sustained basis;
- a social system that provides for solutions for the tensions arising from disharmonious development;
- a production system that respects the obligations to preserve the ecological base for development;
- a technological system that can search continuously for new solutions;
- an international system that fosters sustainable patterns of trade and finance; and
- an administrative system that is flexible and has the capacity for self-correction.

(WCED, 1987: 65)

The 1992 Rio Earth Summit and after

Five years later, in 1992, the UN Conference on Environment and Development, the follow-up to Stockholm, was held in Rio de Janeiro. This meeting, known as the Earth Summit, produced a number of agreements, including the Rio Declaration on Environment and Development, the Framework Convention on Climate Change, the Convention on Biological Diversity, a non-binding Statement on Forest Principles, and the hugely cumbersome but nonetheless important agreement known as Agenda 21 (Grubb *et al.*, 1993).

The Convention on Biological Diversity (CBD) and the negotiations before and after the 1997 Kyoto Protocol on climate mitigation are two important examples of multilateral environmental agreements (MEAs). Maintaining biological diversity is key to maintaining the planet's overall health. Healthy ecosystems replenish natural resources, offering all creatures the dynamic equilibrium upon which life depends. If plant and animal species disappear, as they are doing at an unprecedented rate, then monocultures will emerge that are highly susceptible to disease, global warming and other damaging ecological change. Industrialized systems of agricultural production and other commercial activities are creating monocultures, and both governments and corporations officially recognize that such impacts must be mitigated and managed – biological diversity must be conserved, resources must be used more sustainably and the benefits from the planet's genetic resources shared (more) equitably. Following Rio, many national strategies have been based on these broad international agreements, although indigenous peoples and local communities have not always found their inputs accepted when the actual implementation processes are scrutinized closely. Trade and commercial imperatives have led to rather weak attachments to sustainable development. Probably most depressing have been the limited, tortuous and hesitant agreements around Kyoto – so far the only international, legally binding agreement on climate change. The parties involved agreed to a 5.2 per cent reduction by 2012 in greenhouse gas emissions relative to 1990 (8 per cent for the EU) and this was seen by many, even in 1997, as painfully inadequate, not least because developing nations like China were not included. The conversion of specific sources of pollution into tradable commodities through emissions trading was also allowed with the biggest entitlements and benefits going to the worst polluters. The biggest per capita emitter of all, the US, refused to accept even this and it was not until 2002 that Russia and Canada ratified the Kyoto Protocol, finally bringing the treaty into effect in 2005. At the 2007 G8 summit in Germany, the American administration of George W. Bush did recognize the reality of human induced climate change but nonetheless still refused to endorse international action to significantly curb emissions. However, towards the end of 2007, the US hosted its own international conference on climate mitigation and reluctantly agreed to support, albeit unspecified, climate reduction targets at the United Nations sponsored climate conference held in Bali that December.

Issues of climate change, global poverty, economic inequality and water shortage also highlight the significance of gender in sustainable development. Although much NGO attention has focused inevitably on the appalling inequalities and hardships many women experience, gender issues cannot be separated from wider social, cultural or environmental concerns, which sometimes seems to be the case. The Women's Environment and Development Organization (WEDO) has campaigned vigorously to combat the intergovernmental blindness to the gender implications of environmental policy and actions. Global climate change negotiations, including the Kyoto Protocol and the reports of the United Nations' Intergovernmental Panel on Climate Change (IPCC), concentrate almost exclusively on reducing greenhouse gas emissions, largely ignoring the wider social and gender impacts. By 2007, only:

> four out of the fourteen National Adaptation Plans of Action that have been submitted to the global climate change convention specifically mention the import-ance of gender equality. The MDGs set out global benchmarks on gender equality, poverty eradication and environmental sustainability, although national reports have so far neglected to seriously address the linkages between these areas.
>
> (WEDO, 2007: 3)

A United Nations Environment Programme (UNEP, 2006) survey, 'Gender mainstreaming among environment ministries', discovered that just two countries involved in climate change activities had incorporated a gender perspective. However, as well as arguing that women often suffer disproportionately from unsustainable development, UNEP frequently promotes women as important agents for community empowerment, social leadership and positive change. As the World Conservation Union has shown (IUCN, 2007), communities often cope more effectively during natural disasters when women play a leadership role in early warning systems and post-disaster reconstruction than when they do not. The IUCN also notes that women's local knowledge and skills offer tangible benefits such as the Inuit women of Northern Canada having a deep understanding of weather conditions because of their traditional responsibility for evaluating hunting conditions. When a drought occurs in the small islands of Micronesia, local women who have a sound knowledge of island hydrology find potable water by digging new wells. WEDO (2007: 3) adds that women tend to share information related to community well-being, choose less polluting energy sources and adapt more easily to environmental changes when their families' 'survival is at stake'.

The forty chapters of Agenda 21 offer an action plan for sustainable development, integrating environmental with social and economic concerns, and articulating a participatory, community-based approach to a variety of issues, including population control, transparency, partnership working, equity and justice, and placing market principles within a regulatory framework. Local Agenda 21 (LA21), its local realization, was and remains not legally binding, although by the end of 2000 many countries, including the UK, had policies and frameworks for sustainable development at local and regional levels, with municipal governments in many countries taking a strong lead. In those, particularly Scandinavian countries where local government has a considerable degree of autonomy to raise income locally and regulate environmental matters, LA21 has been most successful. However, throughout the world, even though local government priorities and powers may differ, global structures of economic, financial and political power, which include support for the neoliberal free-trade system, have compromised attempts to fashion sustainable development from the bottom up. The local cannot be disassociated or disconnected from the global, conceptually or practically. Nonetheless, the LA21 process continued with, from 2002, Local Agenda 21 turning into Local Action 21. In 2004 the Aalborg Commitments (CEMR/ICLEI, 2004) was published, showing many local authorities within the European Union to be firmly embracing the need for urban sustainability and good governance.

Rio was, despite all the compromises and shortfalls, a significant achievement, which over the years, has gained in stature and authority, not least, and somewhat paradoxically, because of the reluctance of the US to accept sustainable development policies, its frequent refusal to recognize the importance of the precautionary principle as a guide to environmental law, the necessity of reaching global agreements on cutting greenhouse gas emissions and its continuing support for neoliberal economic globalization. Also, again somewhat paradoxically, the fact that the Rio Declaration was seriously criticized by many radical green groups made its achievement all the more valuable and symbolic. For instance, *The Ecologist* magazine published a sharp critique, *Whose Common Future?* (*The Ecologist*, 1993), in which the Editor, Edward Goldsmith, noted that the real question is not how the environment should be managed, but *who* should manage it and in *whose* interest. We may share one planet, but we do so in an unequal and frequently unjust way. In addition, poverty is not the absence of a Western lifestyle and neither is it the cause of environmental degradation, rather it is a consequence. Globalized neoliberal economics and free trade will destroy cultural and biological diversity, not conserve it. Pollution and other externalities are caused, not cured, by modernization and development, and global environmental management, technology transfer and World Bank-financed infrastructure projects (for example, US$50 billion for 500 dams in 92 developing countries) reinforce the economic and political hegemony of the developed nations, notably the US, the big corporations and international financial agencies (Baker, 2006), while leading to further environmental and social problems. There is much evidence to support these assertions. After serious protests and much adverse publicity, in part due to the relentless campaigning of the Booker Prize-winning novelist Arundhati Roy, the World Bank reviewed its commitment to the highly controversial Narmada Dams project in Gujarat and Madhya Pradesh in India, admitting that it was likely that one million people would be adversely affected through displacement and/or loss of livelihood by the project. The Bank withdrew its support but, as will be seen in Chapter 6, this was not the end of the story.

Ten years after Rio, in 2002, the Johannesburg Summit reviewed the decade's progress. The tensions apparent in 1992 remained, with the ideas and values of market liberals and institutionalists still dominating. Although the final Declaration noted that global disparities in wealth and environmental degradation now risk becoming entrenched and that, unless the world acts in a manner that fundamentally changes the lives of the poor, these people may lose confidence in democratic systems of government, seeing their representatives as nothing more than sounding brass or tinkling cymbals, as stated in Paragraph 15 of the 2002 Johannesburg Declaration on Sustainable Development (UN, 2002a). Little was said about financing international development, although in the same year, at an International Conference on Finance for Development in Monterrey, north-east Mexico, a consensus was reached on financing sustainable development, fostering health and education, providing shelter, eradicating poverty and sustaining economic growth. The role of trade and overseas development aid, the importance of debt reduction and good governance in the developing world, and the mobilization of national economic resources and external investment were directly addressed. Economic crises underscore the importance of effective social safety nets (UN, 2002b).

For many anti-globalization protestors who had earlier demonstrated against the extension of the free trade rules of the WTO in Seattle, the Johannesburg Summit was also a disappointment, despite a few positive advances. Economic insecurity was recognized as affecting human well-being, and globalization itself was recognized as a new challenge for those advocating sustainable development. And, despite all the criticisms, disappointments and missed opportunities, the intense diplomatic activities did achieve a number of important things, not least a recognition that sustainable development at a global level has led to, and requires, policies, procedures and principles supporting intergovernmental cooperation and a global civil society that will check, monitor, promote and campaign for change in the face of official reluctance, indifference or denial, and some acute crises in the global economy.

Thus the first fifteen years of the twenty-first century has seen economic and financial crises and limited progress with regard to sustainable development. In December 2009 a major climate conference was convened in Copenhagen to decide the successor to Kyoto, but no legally binding treaty emerged from the tortuous negotiations that were frequently deadlocked. China, India and the United States were each in turn blamed for the conference failure by politicians from other nations, international NGOs and media commentators. However, delegates did agree that global warming should not exceed two degrees centigrade but set no actual targets for cutting emissions. As Benito Muller (2010: ii) of the Oxford Institute for Energy Studies wrote, the real culprits were not the negotiators at Copenhagen but 'a *lack of political will and leadership* during the months leading up to the Conference to engage in real negotiations'. However, over the next few years talks continued at Cancun, Durban, Bangkok, Bonn and in November–December 2012 in Doha, Qatar. A number of documents were produced at Doha, collectively known as The Doha Climate Gateway, which extended the Kyoto protocol to 2020 but limited the scope of global carbon emissions to 15 per cent because Japan, Russia, Canada and the US did not participate and because China, India and Brazil were classified as developing nations at Kyoto and are consequently not subject to these emissions reduction targets. Climate campaigners and others reviewing these negotiations have frequently expressed their exasperation and frustration. In 2011 Kevin Anderson and Alice Bows published a paper for the Royal Society in the UK warning that there was 'no chance' of keeping global warming below 2°C and in any case recent studies relating to the impacts associated with such a rise have been revised upwards from 'dangerous' to 'extremely dangerous'. Consequently, Anderson and Bows write: 'with tentative signs of global emissions returning to their earlier levels of growth, [the year] 2010 represents a political tipping point' (2011: 41).

Ten years further on and despite the high expectations, there were many disappointments with the Rio+20 conference too. Although progress since the first Earth Summit in 1992 was carefully evaluated, commemorated and celebrated, there were no new agreements or targets in 2012 but plenty of 'reaffirmations' and 'recognitions' in the final published document *The Future We Want* (United Nations, 2012: para 19 [p. 4]). Indeed, the clear admission expressed in the statement 'we emphasize the need to make progress in implementing previous commitments' indicates both why and how so many delegates felt so deflated with the conference outcomes. Much of the debate was polarized around the meaning of the 'green economy', which for many seemed to coalesce around the desire for green energy technologies rather than defining the need for a new economic paradigm that favoured social equity and quality of life above economic growth. UNEP, for example, clearly advocated and advocates a series of policy prescriptions characterized by the key principles of ecological modernization, the low carbon economy and eco-efficiency. At a moment when the global economy was experiencing considerable stress as a result of the serial failures of finance capitalism, the Rio+20 vision for the future was hesitant, modest and accommodative:

> In this regard, we consider green economy in the context of sustainable development and poverty eradication as one of the important tools available for achieving sustainable development and that it could provide options for policy making but should not be a rigid set of rules. We emphasize that it should contribute to eradicating poverty as well as sustained economic growth, enhancing social inclusion, improving human welfare and creating opportunities for employment and decent work for all, while maintaining the healthy functioning of the Earth's ecosystems.
>
> (United Nations, 2012: para. 56 [p. 9])

No wonder, then, that the defensive concept of 'resilience' seemed to hold centre stage, being referred to on thirteen separate occasions in the summit's outcomes document (Blewitt and Tilbury, 2013). Having said that, if progress was made at Rio in 2012 it was in acting on the recognition that no single assessment matrix for sustainable development had been previously devised and accepted. Thus it was decided that an immediate task for the future was to fashion a set of sustainable development goals (SDGs), which in effect would supersede the Millennium Development Goals (MDGs) formulated at the turn of the century (see p. 31 for a discussion on MDGs). These goals would be action orientated, concise, easy to communicate, limited in number, aspirational, global in nature and universally applicable to all countries. In January 2013 a thirty-member working group of the UN was tasked to devise a proposal on the SDGs, which would then be integrated into the UN's post-2015 development agenda. An IIED (International Institute for Environment and Development Policy Paper published in March 2013 (Geoghegan, 2013) outlined a number of possible principles and approaches to help the process move forward.

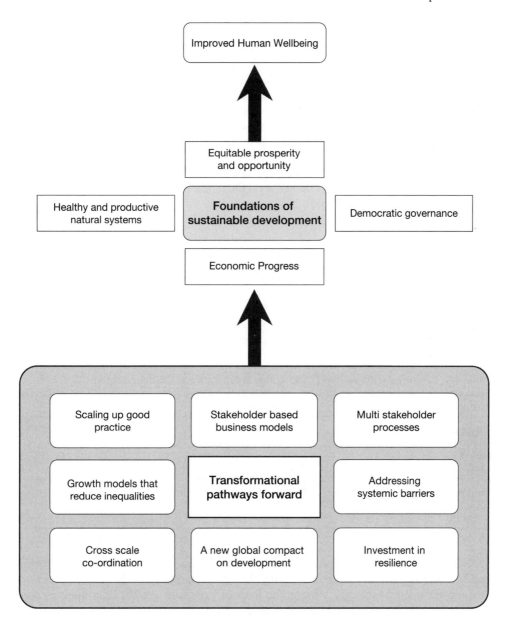

Figure 1.1 The foundations for the post-2015 sustainable development process
Source: Adapted from Geoghegan, 2013: 4.

Although there were some activist protests as well as internal disagreements among negotiators at Rio in 2012, there were little, if any, popular protests or street-based discontent with the outcomes in the world's major cities as the predominant concern for most people in the world was squarely with the economic. Financial austerity in Europe, the increase in global unemployment and in social inequality concentrated many people's minds on looking for genuine alternatives to the present order of things and ways of being. The Occupy movement and a renewed interest in alternative forms of political and economic organization did take to the streets in many of the world's global cities. As Indian activist and novelist Arundhati Roy said at the end of her 2003 *Confronting Empire* (Roy, 2003) speech at the World Social Forum in Porte Alegre, for a moment it seemed for some at least that just perhaps, 'Another world is not only possible, she is on her way. On a quiet day, I can hear her breathing.' But it wasn't breathing at Rio in 2012.

Sustainable development and the question of spatial scale

Sustainable development is about protecting and conserving the planet's natural environment and promoting social equity and a degree of economic equality within and between nations. This can be conceptualized as a process of convergence so the question of spatial scale is a necessary element in any serious thinking and action, designed to make our world a better place. It is possible to conceive of scale in ecological and socio-political terms (Grainger, 2004):

Table 1.1 Ecological and socio-political scales (adapted from Grainger, 2004)

Ecological scale	Socio-political scale
Biosphere	World
Biome-type	Supranational regions
Biome	State
Landscape	Region
Ecosystem	Locality 1: city, town
Community	Locality 2: village, community, neighbourhood
Population	Household
Organism	

Institutions and organizations operate at many different levels. The United Nations and the World Bank are large international bodies operating on the global scale and through their various projects shape the lives of people in specific communities and households. These bodies may develop and implement policies, treaties and actions that affect all ecological scales. The European Union operates at a supranational level and the Environmental Protection Agency in the USA operates at a national level but its effects may be experienced far wider. And there are countless numbers of community groups, businesses, and formally or informally structured activist organizations that operate at the very smallest scales. National or neighbourhood campaigns to reduce, recycle or reuse will ultimately rely on individual households and citizens wanting to conduct themselves in a more sustainable manner. Complementing, and perhaps complicating, this further are the various 'capitals' dispersed across the planet on a variety of spatial scales. When we consider the possible conditions – strong, weak or very weak – it may become very difficult to see some capitals applying to more than one spatial scale. Grainger suggests that under the Very Weak condition, Critical Natural Capital is meaningful at a global scale but becomes less so at lower ones. There are implications too with regard to practical action and communication. As a consequence of natural and other endowments, it may not be possible for a small town or village to be sustainable if sustainability is understood in isolation from the wider ecological or political processes, or isolated from other towns, villages and surrounding rural hinterlands. Although an individual town may strive towards being carbon neutral, this may be practically impossible although the actions of 'transition towns' may contribute to overall sustainability at higher levels and, most importantly inspire, communicate or model sustainable action for people in other localities. As towns and cities are intensive resource users, often having huge environmental footprints, any improvement will impact positively on global sustainability. Actions at local level, if multiplied, may influence policy and practice at higher levels. We can act locally and think globally. We can also act globally and nationally too, as Pontin and Roderick (2007) demonstrate in their call for a 'converging world' of equitable resource use across the planet initiated by grass-roots community-based action incorporating carbon offsetting, civic dialogue, fair trade business development, one planet living, localization and the emergence of broader solidarity movements linking North and South.

The national context: sustainable development in China

For a huge country China is surprisingly relatively poor in natural resources. It had a population of 1.344 billion in 2011 but only 20 per cent of the fresh water which is available to the US with its population of 311.6 million. Southern China may receive decent rainfall but the north of the country is looking to become the world's largest desert. Since 1979 China has introduced a number of market-orientated reforms that have transformed Chinese society and the Chinese economy. In 2010, China GDP stood at US$6 trillion but in terms of per capita income ranked 128 out of 130 countries. China is a developing country but one whose income inequalities are increasing, whose political system is largely undemocratic and whose economy needs to grow in the long term but not at the expense of its population or its natural environment. In recent decades the increases in economic production and consumption, urbanization and population movement have been immense, and these have often been accompanied by considerable social and environmental problems that have had a negative impact on the Chinese economy (Economy, 2004; Jacques, 2011; Andressen *et al.*, 2013). For instance, development has been highly resource and carbon intensive. Acid rain affects 28 per cent of Chinese territory and 300 million people lack clean drinking water. Pollution and environmental degradation accounted for 10.51 per cent of gross national income in 2008; and, since 2007 China has exceeded the US as the largest emitter of greenhouse gases in the world, although per capita emissions still fall short of those of US citizens. Public health issues ranging from respiratory illnesses to cancer are increasing. According to Guan *et al.* (2012), emissions in China may actually be up to 20 per cent higher than official statistics demonstrate. However, China has also recognized the need to implement a number of significant sustainable development policies, of which poverty reduction and population control are of primary importance, but spending on environmental protection is still largely inadequate and much tends to get diverted through local corruption.

However, the Chinese press have become more vigilant than previously in investigating environmental failings and the Chinese public have become more confident in challenging political decisions they see as being damaging to the environment and to public health. In 2011 an editorial by Environment Minister Zhou Shengxian stated the 'depletion, deterioration, and exhaustion of resources and the worsening ecological environment have become bottlenecks and grave impediments to the nation's economic and social development' (quoted in Economy, 2013). In March 2012 former Prime Minister Wen Jiabao acknowledged that the government had failed to meet many of the environmental targets in the country's eleventh five-year plan, including reductions in nitrogen and sulfur dioxide, action to combat water-pollution measures and to reduce energy intensity.

There have also been human rights concerns over China's one-child policy, and poverty eradication has often meant prioritizing economic growth at the expense of the ecological environment. The one-child policy became national policy in 1979 and the fertility rate – that is, the average number of births per woman – has fallen from 2.91 in 1978 to 1.6 in 2010. Apart from skewed sex ratios, China now has an ageing population and social security finance issues. The controversies around the construction, environmental destruction and population displacements of the massive Three Gorges Dam have received global attention. Over 120 million people live in rural poverty, and deforestation, resource degradation, overgrazing and the over-exploitation of agricultural land remain serious and unresolved problems. Around 60 per cent of the oil China uses is imported and 40 per cent of the energy China uses is to produce exports for Western markets. Much of this energy comes from coal, which in China is cheap and abundant. New environmental laws and regulations on clean production, renewable energy, environmental impact assessments and pollution control have been passed to deal with the adverse environmental impact of these market externalities and market failures, but enforcement has not yet matched the strict intentions of the law makers (Zhang, 2002). Local officials are not always very responsive to the advocacy efforts of local environmental campaigners. Air pollution in some of China's massive new cities is a major policy concern. Thus in 2012 China published a major *National Report on Sustainable Development* (Peoples Republic of China, 2012) and some Chinese economists, particularly Angang Hu (Hu, 2006, 2011), have powerfully advocated a non-traditional modernization/people-centred sustainable development, comprising green cities, green technologies, green industries and green energy. 'It is possible for China not to repeat the high resource consumption and high pollution discharge process adopted by many Western countries and go straight to the stage of "green development"' (Hu, 2006). China aims to generate 15 per cent of its electricity from renewable resources by 2020 and over 30 per cent by 2050, and has set itself the goal of becoming a global leader in low carbon technologies, including wind turbines, solar, hydro-power and batteries.

China is often presented in the West as being uninterested in combating climate change, but its National Report on Sustainable Development strongly asserts the opposite, stressing that it adheres to the principles of fairness and 'common but differentiated responsibilities', as outlined in the UN Framework Convention on Climate Change, and has made considerable progress in this area.

As of the end of 2010, China had ratified 3,241 clean development mechanism projects, of which 1,718 projects successfully registered with the United Nations

Clean Development Mechanism Executive Board. For the registered projects, the certified emission reductions are expected to be about 351 million tons of carbon dioxide equivalence, accounting for 63.78% of the global total, which is a tremendous contribution to global greenhouse gas emissions reduction.

(People's Republic of China, 2012: 85)

In 2008, China published the Circular Economy Promotion Law following those of Germany and Japan, making it the world's third. A number of pilot programmes have been introduced on resource utilization, the industrialization of remanufacturing and the recycling of renewable resources.

A total of 90 pilot cities in three batches and 11 distribution markets have been identified as pilot programs for renewable resource recycling system building. An urban renewable resource recycling system, based on recycling stations and the sorting, processing and gathering areas (bases), and supported by an information management platform, has gradually been formed. Since 2009, 110 end-of-life vehicle recycling and dismantling enterprises have been selected for pilot projects for retrofitting and upgrading, in an effort to improve the level of resource utilization. The construction of "urban minerals" model bases is being carried out in order to promote the large-scale and high-value recycling of renewable resources.

(People's Republic of China, 2012: 16)

Internationally, China has persistently argued that the developed countries should lead the world in changing unsustainable patterns of production and consumption, and that they ought to help developing countries develop a green economy through finance, technology transfer, capacity building and access to expanding markets. For developing countries, including China, green economic strategies should be designed and implemented in line with national conditions.

Many developing countries are at a stage of rapid industrialization and urban-ization, during which they are faced with both the arduous tasks of poverty eradication, economic restructuring and the transition to a green economy, and with the constraints of energy, resources and environmental factors. Developing a green economy in these countries is crucial to the global sustainable develop-ment, and they deserve the understanding and support from the international community.

(People's Republic of China, 2012: 89)

A globalizing world

Like so many other concepts, globalization has been subject to a considerable amount of debate in academic and policy circles. Although a few people dispute whether globalization is either occurring or is indeed a useful way of making sense of current trends and processes, there is a general consensus that globalization is real and characterizes the nature of our times. There are a number of definitions on offer, including notions of space-time compression and accelerating interdependence but for Held *et al.*: 'Globalization may be thought of initially as the widening, deepening and speeding up of worldwide interconnectedness in all aspects of contemporary social life, from the cultural to the criminal, the financial to the spiritual' (1999: 2).

Held *et al.* recognize the importance of various spatial attributes, suggesting that globalization can be located on a continuum that includes the local, national and regional understood as functioning clusters of states, economic relations, networks and societies. The authors continue: 'Globalization can be taken to refer to those spatio-temporal processes of change which underpin a transformation in the organisation of human affairs by linking together and expanding human activity across regions and continents' (1999: 15).

Without reference to these spatial connections there can be no meaningful articulation of globalization. This approach implies:

> A *stretching* (extensity) of social political and economic activities across frontiers such that events, decisions and activities in one region of the world have significance for individuals and communities in others.
>
> Connections across frontiers are regularized rather than occasional or random making for an *intensification*, or growth in magnitude, of interconnectedness, patterns of interactions and flows which transcend the various societies and states making up our world.
>
> The growing *extensity*, *intensity* and *velocity* of global interconnectedness relates to a speeding up of global interactions due to the development of worldwide systems of transport and communications which increase the speed of the global diffusion of ideas, goods, information, capital and people.
>
> The local and global are often deeply inter-related so that distant events may have profound local impacts in other parts of the world and very local developments may eventually have enormous global consequences. *The boundaries between domestic and global affairs are therefore likely to become blurred.*

Many globalization theorists, including most notably Manuel Castells (1996), frequently reference to:

- *Flows* – the movements of physical artefacts, people, symbols, tokens and information across space and time.
- *Networks* – regularized or patterned interactions between independent agents, nodes of activity or sites of power.

To understand globalization it is probably useful to consider issues such as climate change or transboundary pollution – for example, acid rain or the fall-out from nuclear disasters such as Chernobyl. Such phenomena do not respect national boundaries. Desertification, environmental degradation, resource depletion, world trade, global communication, new media, population movements, the refugee crisis, crime, war and security issues also rarely stay confined within states or even regional jurisdictions (Homer-Dixon, 1999; Barnett, 2001). Economic growth, industrial development and consumerism in countries such as India and China are currently having massive global impacts, influencing the wider ecological and economic environment and the everyday life experiences of citizens throughout the world. This has led geographer Doreen Massey (1993: 66) to reconceptualize the specificity of a place as 'a constellation of relations, articulated together at a particular locus' comprising many experiences and understanding of its links to a wider world. Social relations of domination and subordination are consequently stretched over space, over the whole planet, so that child labour on one continent supports consumer materialism on another, or environmental degradation or conflict in one region subsidizes politics and energy use in another (Massey, 2005).

Held *et al.* (1999: 377) posit an anthropocentric conception of *environmental degradation* which refers to 'the transformation of entire eco-systems or components of those ecosystems . . . whose consequences, whether acknowledged by human actors or not, have an adverse impact on the economic or demographic conditions of life and/or the health of human beings'. This conception recognizes the importance of the interaction between the natural and human–social worlds together with the problems and opportunities that human activity generates. Resource depletion, water shortages and, of course, climate change are again key issues. Given this, the globalization of environmental degradation may take various forms:

The exploitation and destruction of the *global commons* – the atmosphere, marine environment, hydrological cycles.

Demographic expansion and exponential economic growth that leads to increases in pollution and consumption of global raw materials e.g. oil, timber, etc.

Transboundary pollution involving the transmission of pollutants through the air, soil and water across political borders so that their environmentally degrading impact occurs in many other countries.

Joseph Stiglitz and globalization

Former Chief Economist at the World Bank and Chair of President Clinton's Council of Economic Advisers, Joseph Stiglitz (2002) has been an eloquent and constructive critic of economic globalization, suggesting that experience of the 1980s and 1990s has been at best uneven and at worst disastrous for many developing countries. As a result of IMF and World Bank policies, many saw their debts increase, their economies weaken, their environments degraded, and social injustice and economic inequality spiral downwards. Globalization has not brought the economic benefits to poorer countries which advocates of liberalization in the West promised. The developed world did not open up their markets to goods coming from the developing world, the developed world did not abolish subsidies to their own farmers, while frequently benefiting from the loosening of controls on capital flows that enabled money to easily move in and out of countries irrespective of the social consequences. Conditions attached to IMF loans undermined the sovereignty and social infrastructure of developing nations, with governments forced to privatize their assets, abandon plans for public investment in health, training and education, and lower or abolish trade tariffs. There is very little for unskilled workers to do in lesser developed countries in a globalized economy apart from live in slums and join the informal sector of beggars and casual labourers. These 'structural adjustments' have had profoundly adverse effects on many urban dwellers, increasing poverty and hardship to such an extent that researchers have wondered how the poor actually survive

(Rakodi, 1997; Potts, 1997). And it is not just the urban areas that have suffered because, as Potts and Mutambirwa (1998) have shown, the strength of rural urban economic interaction means that the destiny of the countryside is often tied to that of the town and city. The idea that economic growth, driven by the free market, would ultimately benefit everyone via the magical notion of 'trickle-down economics' has been a fiction. The hegemonic dominance of the 'Washington Consensus' forged between the IMF (on 19th Street), the World Bank (on 18th Street) and the US Treasury (on 15th Street) focused on a one-size-fits-all strategy, emphasizing downscaling government intervention in the economy, deregulation, rapid liberalization and privatization. In most cases, this strategy did not work (Africa, Latin America) but where it was tempered or ignored (East Asia, China) economic resilience and development was able to emerge from the global economic turbulence of the 1990s. The Asian Development Bank, by contrast, argued for alternatives, a 'competitive pluralism', in which governments in developing countries, although basically relying on markets, were active in shaping and guiding these markets through promoting new technologies, and by insisting private businesses seriously consider the social welfare of their employees and the wider society in which they live. Stiglitz, however, is not opposed to globalization as such, for he believes that with appropriate regulation, equitable trade laws, good nation-state and corporate governance it can be a genuine force for global good. There are alternatives to the Washington Consensus, which he develops in both *Fair Trade for All* (Stiglitz and Charlton, 2005) and *Making Globalization Work* (Stiglitz, 2006).

Stiglitz acknowledges that making globalization work 'will not be easy' (2006: 13), suggesting a number of general actions that can, and should, be initiated to produce a more comprehensive approach to global development. These include:

> Increase foreign assistance from the rich countries to the poor to the value of at least 0.7 per cent of their GDP.

> Cancellation or relief of foreign debt, with regard to the decision by the G-8 at Gleneagles in 2005 when the debts owed by the eighteen poorest developing nations to the IMF and World Bank were written off.

> Genuine fair, rather than free trade, recognizing the limitations of economic liberalization and iniquities produced by global corporate monopolies and cartels.

> Protection of the global environment on which all economies ultimately depend through a sensible and workable public management of global natural resources and regulations on their usage and on actions, giving rise to 'externalities' and costs.

> Good, democratic, government, including enhanced possibilities for democratic regulation of the economic and participation in decision-making processes at all levels.

The voice of the developing nations ought to be listened to more frequently. The fictional trial of international financial institutions that took place in Sissako's 2006 film *Bamako* is taking place in many other forums within global civil society. The USA ought to recognize, and act on, its moral obligations to emit fewer greenhouse gases, particularly CO_2, offer more aid and negotiate better trading arrangements.

Developing countries frequently do not have sufficient resources to avoid illegal logging so they should be paid to stop further deforestation, according to the Rainforest Coalition led by Papua New Guinea, by being allowed to sell carbon offsets for new forest planting. Stiglitz (2006) also believes that although global corporations frequently facilitate technology transfers, raise skill standards and develop markets that do help developing countries, their primary purpose to make money is clearly articulated by their fiduciary relationship to their stockholders. Consequently, to counteract the harmful effects of corporate actions Stiglitz believes that it is necessary to reshape private incentives with social costs and benefits to avoid environmental destruction and labour exploitation. This can be achieved through:

- A combination of corporate social responsibility supplemented by stronger regulations to prevent unfair competition.
- Limitation of corporate power through the implementation effective global anti-trust laws.
- Better corporate governance whereby companies are held accountable to all stakeholders – employees and communities as well as shareholders – making environmental destruction a crime just like fraud and embezzlement.
- International laws should be enacted against price fixing and labour exploitation.
- Reducing the scope for corruption, with bribery being viewed as an unfair competitive practice and bank secrecy eradicated so as to prevent the incentive to, or possibility of enhancing after-tax profits garnered from questionable business practices.

Stiglitz's time at the World Bank did see some changes with development priorities being refocused on poverty reduction, partnership and the creation of 'good policy environments' rather than simply economic growth. Despite these changes, limiting conditions on development loans remain, constraining the possibilities of developing nations to 'own' the preferred development policy (Pender, 2001).

Anti-globalization critiques

Activists and campaigners like Greg Buckman (2004), Vandana Shiva (2000), Walden Bello (2002) and George Monbiot (2004) criticize existing global institutions and internal trading systems. Their views have informed some of the more radical approaches to sustainability and sustainable development. They advocate alternatives that have a different value base, offering different sets of prescriptions and types of knowledge than that currently characterizing the dominant *neoliberal* discourse of economic growth, development and globalization. For Wolfgang Sachs (1999) of the Wuppertal Institute for Climate Environment and Energy, the costs and benefits of economic globalization have not been equitably globalized and nature has itself been colonized through the 1994 TRIPS (Trade-Related Intellectual Property Rights) agreement that gives corporations the right to patent genetic materials such as micro-organisms, seeds and even cells. This has helped 'modernize' agriculture, reinforcing the commercial advantages of growing cash crops in the developing world for markets in developed countries, and has effectively stolen the harvests and livelihoods of many local farmers in India and other nations (Shiva, 2000). For Bello (2002), founding director of Focus on the Global South, the IMF and the World Bank have been 'unmitigated disasters', with oligarchic decision-making defining the WTO and the centralizing tendencies of all three organizations, combined with the inordinate power of big corporations, militating against popular struggles for decentralization and democracy in many developing nations. At the very least, corporate power needs to be checked and regulated more effectively. In *Deglobalization: Ideas for a New World Economy* (Bello, 2004), he states that continuing anti-globalization action must be married to concrete proposals for an alternative system, re-empowering local and national economies, re-embedding the economy in society rather than having society driven by imperatives profit maximization, cost efficiency and other market verities. This may be accomplished as follows:

- By allowing countries to use their own internal financial resources to promote development rather than becoming dependent on foreign investment and foreign financial markets.
- Redistributing land and incomes to create a vibrant internal market that would secure economic prosperity and free up financial resources for internal investment.
- Lessen the salience accorded to economic growth in favour of emphasizing equity in order to fundamentally reduce 'environmental disequilibrium'.
- Strategic economic decisions should be made subject to democratic debate and decision-making processes and not be left to the guiding invisible hand of the market.
- Civil society organization should constantly monitor both the private sector and the state.

New approaches to production, distribution and exchange should be developed that enable the emergence of a system that includes community co-operatives, private and public enterprises and exclude transnational corporations.

For environmental activist George Monbiot, globalization refers to first, the removal of controls on the movement of what has become known as 'footloose' capital; second, the removal of trade barriers and the 'harmonization' of trading rules; and third, the growth of multinational corporations which displace local and national businesses. However, the problem is not globalization as such but the inability of people, civil society and governments to control and restrain it. Monbiot writes: 'our task is not to overthrow globalization, but to capture it, and to use is as a vehicle for humanity's first global democratic revolution' (2004: 23). His prescription or manifesto includes the establishment of a world parliament modelled in part on the World Social Forum, the establishment of an International Clearing Union, which would replace much of the undesirable work of the International Monetary Fund, many commercial banks and the World Bank whose policies and actions have increased the financial debts of the developing world. More economically sensitive and benign policies, including debt reduction and/or abandonment will replace them. Between 1980 and 1996 nations in sub-Saharan Africa paid out twice the sum of their debt in interest, thus owing three times as much in 1996 as they did sixteen years earlier. Finally, Monbiot (2003) advocates the creation of a Fair Trade Organization (FTO) to replace the iniquitous World Trade Organization whose operations seem to consistently benefit the rich nations at the expense of the poor. This would lead to greater global political and economic equality as well as a social and cultural equity only currently dreamed of.

Economic development for the poorer countries can only take place through a combination of trade and aid together with a degree of protection. Free trade rules benefit strong mature economies and not weak developing ones, which require a degree of government intervention to maintain social standards, business and economic security. For Monbiot, contemporary free trade rules are similar in effect and purpose to the imperial relationships and treaties first imposed on weaker nations – Brazil, Persia, China, Japan and the Ottoman Empire – in the nineteenth century. Poor nations are forced to grow cash crops and export raw materials to the affluent developed nations, which then 'add value' through production processes and refinement, while externalizing any environmental costs to the country of origin. 'Footloose capital' would be fettered. Multinationals would not be allowed to move from country to country seeking lower labour and environmental standards in order to boost or maintain profitability. Instead, corporations would be obliged, through incentives, to set high standards and would be punished if they did not. Producers and consumers should carry their own costs and not dump them on other people. Monbiot (2003) writes:

> The FTO would, in this respect, function as a licensing body: a company would not be permitted to trade between nations unless it could demonstrate that, at every stage of production, manufacture and distribution, its own operations and those of its suppliers and sub-contractors met the necessary standards. If, for example, a food-processing company based in Switzerland wished to import cocoa from the Ivory Coast it would need to demonstrate that the plantations it bought from were not employing slaves, using banned pesticides, expanding into protected forests or failing to conform to whatever other standards the FTO set. The firm's performance would be assessed, at its own expense, by a monitoring company accredited to the organisation. There would be, in other words, no difference between this operation and the activities of the voluntary fair-trade movement today.

The global meets the local at Clayoquot Sound, Canada

Despite the slogans, banners and protests it is sometimes difficult to see how the global meets the local, how abstract forces of supply and demand, of conflicts between the old and the new, and the cultural and economic, have broader effects. The fierce struggles, conflicts, debates and dialogues surrounding the logging of the old growth forests on Vancouver Island in western Canada from the mid 1980s onwards show how sustainable development frequently engages the local and global simultaneously, how ultimately the process is unavoidably political and unavoidably personal. At Clayoquot the interests of local businesses, the provincial government, native peoples and environmental activists combined with regional and global economic forces, with the needs and wants of individual and corporate consumers and the growing global concerns with wilderness preservation, environmental protection and the maintenance of community. The issues were (and are) far from simple and through political action, global media debate and engaged dialogue the concept of sustainable development was refined, applied and revised. Consequently, Clayoquot Sound is more than the active protests and the 800 or so arrests of 1993, the clear-cut logging practices of big corporations and the degrading of one of the most beautiful natural environments on the planet. 'Clayoquot Sound' involves networks of actors, values, spaces and places, compromises and powerplays.

Although the physical action occurred in a remote rural locality the conflict was also quite urban. The major logging company had its headquarters in Vancouver, profits and products went to Toronto and Los Angeles, the Ministry of Forests was located in Victoria and the environmentalists pitched their media messages to audiences in New York and London. It demonstrated that if rural and urban areas are to be sustainable, then linear production processes relying on a one-way extraction of natural resources and the extensive waste of unused material have to be replaced by a more circular model where waste is reused and recycled – a resource for further productive activity. Clayoquot activists launched a global campaign to save other temperate rain forests. Ecotourism was identified as the economic saviour of the area, enabling business to become aligned with the environmentalists. However, the indigenous people of the locality, the Nuu-chah-nulth, feared their place-based cultural heritage would be overrun by more outsiders. As Warren Magnusson and Karena Shaw (2002: 7–8) argue in *A Political Space: Reading the Global through Clayoquot Sound*, Clayoquot is a site where many phenomena converge:

- The globalization of political struggle through the mass media, cultural exchanges and international trade relations.
- The shift from an industrial (logging jobs) to post-industrial economy (tourism jobs) dependent on information technology and orientated toward the consumption of signs, of the aesthetic natural beauty of the Sound, in the global cultural marketplace to attract tourists and their dollars.
- Ethnonationalist resistance to the homogenizing impact of the capitalist economy and Western culture.
- The global challenge to patriarchal gender relations, as well as the norms of sexual and personal identity, e.g. female corporate spokespeople feminizing the image of an international logging company.
- The rise of indigenous peoples as credible claimants to sovereignty under international law (British Columbia was not colonized through treaty negotiations).
- The threat of environmental calamity and the concomitant rise of a globalized environmental movement.
- The continuing critique of state institutions for their political/democratic inadequacy as a result of their actions, e.g. closed meetings, exclusion of elected representatives, etc.
- The problematization of science as a contested and highly politicized way of knowing the world (whose science? in whose interests? incorporation of traditional ecological knowledge in scientific deliberations, etc.) through its differing and competing methodologies and truth claims.

Sandilands (2002) suggests the experience of Clayoquot offers lessons in the delicate move towards dialogue and the recognition of pragmatic hybridity. In seeing a future for the locality in tourism, both extractive industry and wilderness were rejected as a multiplicity of interests, interpretations, perspectives, actions and goals became entwined in the unending politics of sustainable development. A Memorandum of Understanding between the major conflicting parties was signed in 1999 and the United Nations designated the area a Biosphere Reserve in 2000. This settled some of the issues but not all. In March 2007, the Friends of Clayoquot Sound announced that environmental groups and the Tla-o-qui-aht First Nation people had won a five-year Moratorium on Logging in Clayoquot Sound's intact Upper Kennedy Valley (around 4,000 hectares) despite the provincial government's 2006 logging plan, which had included this area and where 75 per cent of the original forest had already been clear-cut. At the time of writing, this deferral allows time for the Tla-o-qui-aht to develop their own land-use plan for the entire Kennedy watershed.

The logging tenures in Clayoquot are now owned by five local First Nations who have formed the Iisaak Forest Resources. In January 2012 scientists across North

---

Box 1.1 Berlin Civil Society Center: Advancing the Post-2015 Sustainable Development Agenda

In March 2013 two hundred and seventy representatives from over two hundred civil society organizations from across the globe gathered for three days in Bonn, Germany, to discuss 'Advancing the Post-2015 Sustainable Development Agenda: Reconfirming Rights, Recognizing Limits, Redefining Goals'. With a multitude of discussions and consultation processes going on worldwide, the conference gathered key actors in the Post-2015 Sustainable Development Agenda debates, helping them to exchange information, learn from each other and identify common agendas and strategies.

The Post-2015 Agenda must address inequalities

Inequalities within and between countries in the distribution of wealth, opportunities or power are drivers of extreme poverty, conflict and violations of human rights. Therefore, addressing increasing inequalities within and between countries is a central strategic demand.

The Post-2015 Agenda must respect planetary boundaries

The realization of human rights for all and the eradication of poverty and extreme inequalities must be achieved within the limits of our planet's resources. This requires a holistic approach across all development goals and an equitable distribution of the burdens of adjustment, taking into account historic responsibilities.

The Post-2015 Agenda must aim for a transformation of global structures

This includes the regulation of financial markets, the restructuring of unfair trade regimes and of intellectual property rights regimes, the termination of tax havens, the redefinition of progress away from GDP towards measures of sustainability and well-being, and policy coherence for development. All these steps are necessary since the current global economic and financial regimes impose obstacles to poverty eradication and the full implementation of all human rights. New rules have to be created and others removed to ensure that the global frameworks do not constrain human rights and development goals.

Source: adapted from www.berlin-civil-society-center.org/shared-services/post-2015.

America signed a declaration stating that the Sound's temperate rainforests 'remain highly vulnerable to continued development'. In 2009 a Vancouver-based mining company sought and won the consent from First Nation chiefs to undertake test drilling for copper and gold on their hereditary lands. Logging continues and in the first decade of the new century the volume of timber extracted has steadily increased: in 2000, 25,000 cubic metres; in 2005, 94,000 cubic metres; and in 2008, 158,000 cubic metres (Mychajlowycz, 2010).

Perspectives and world views

Public debates, discussions and discourses on globalization, anti-globalization, sustainability and the environment reveal a wide range of perspectives and worldviews. Clapp and Dauvergne (2005) offer a fourfold categorization albeit recognizing their categories are *ideal types* and that many organizations, groups and individuals share elements drawn from two or more. Complexity and interconnectedness frequently characterize both our world and our attempts to make sense of it. The four categories and associated beliefs include the following:

Market liberals

- The main causes of global environmental problems are poverty and poor economic growth brought on by market failures and bad government polices that lead to market distortions – e.g. subsidies, unclear property rights.
- Globalization is largely positive because it fosters economic growth and, combined with the application of modern science and technology and human ingenuity, will in the long run improve the environment and people's material well-being.

Institutionalists

- The primary cause of global environmental problems are weak institutions and inadequate global co-operation, which has failed to correct environmental failures, promote development or counteract the self-interested nature of some states' actions.
- The main opportunity of globalization is to enhance opportunities for co-operation, capacity building and innovative eco-efficient technologies, which will generally enhance human well-being. The *precautionary principle* should inform the evaluation of new developments.

Bio-environmentalists

- The main causes of the environmental crisis are excessive economic growth, overpopulation, over-consumption and rampant materialism.
- Globalization is driving unsustainable growth, trade, investment and debt while accelerating the depletion of natural resources and filling waste sinks. The way forward is to create a new global economy operating within the Earth's ecological limits.

Social greens

- The main causes of the global environmental crisis are large-scale industrialization and economic growth. The main impact of globalization has resulted in the acceleration of exploitation, inequality and ecological injustice, leading to the erosion of local-community autonomy and the increase of drug-related global crime, human trafficking and the re-emergence of slavery.
- The way forward is to reject industrialism (or capitalism) and reverse or at least take democratic control of economic globalization, restore local community autonomy, empower those whose voices have been marginalized, and promote ecological justice and local indigenous knowledge systems.

The 'capitalization' of sustainable development

The discipline of Economics has had a profound influence on the conceptualization of sustainable development, sustainability and development, and much of this is due to the application and extension of the notion of 'capital' beyond the spheres of economics, business and finance. In the eighteenth century the Scottish economist Adam Smith recognized that the accumulation of fixed and reproducible capital, understood largely as productive machinery, combined with the increasing division or specialization of labour, were keys to economic growth and development. Since Smith's time, economists and other theorists have extended the capital metaphor to include Human Capital (education and skills), Social Capital (social relationships and networks) and Natural Capital (natural resources and ecosystem services), which in turn may be divided in Renewable Resource Capital and Non-renewable Resource Capital. A further concept, Critical Natural Capital, has also been developed. This refers to those aspects of the global ecosystem upon which our lives and cultures ultimately depend. Human activity consumes this natural capital relying on the ecosystem services to support our standard and quality of life. Apart from consuming this natural capital – for example, oil, timber, fish, etc. – our productive activities have frequently impaired the functioning of these environmental services. We have polluted rivers, destroyed natural habitats, rendered land toxic or air unbreathable, released greenhouse gases into the atmosphere, and consumed mineral and energy resources that cannot be renewed or regenerated. Economic growth has generally and inevitably meant more of the same, leading degrowth theorist Serge Latouche (2009) to argue that sustainable development is a pleonasm at the definitional level and an oxymoron in terms of content.

To compensate for the loss, or contamination, of this Critical Natural Capital substitutes may be sought in the form of new renewable energy technologies, in human ingenuity and future technological advances (man-made capital). A Micawber-like optimism occasionally characterizes such an approach – something will always turn up in the end. Arguments focus on the extent to which one capital stock may be substituted for another in order to maintain a constant stock of global wealth, ensuring future generations do not have a depleted inheritance. In the words of Pearce *et al.* (1989), sustainable development refers to 'non-declining natural wealth' and the maintenance of a constant stock of (natural) capital. Problems then arise over:

- Non-substitutability – what can fill the holes in the ozone layer?
- Uncertainty – what can replace the oceans' role as a climate regulator?
- Irreversibility – human-made capital cannot (yet?) replace an extinct species.
- Equity – the poor are more often disproportionately affected by environmental degradation than the wealthy.

Related to these concerns and the critical unease with conceiving the biosphere as another form of capital and one that logically can carry a price tag, the subdiscipline of Ecological Economics has explored the relationship between the scale of human productive activity and the natural environment, biosphere and 'services' the ecosystem provides. If the human productive economy grows too big with the biosphere being unable to support it, then development is literally unsustainable. The ideal condition for development is therefore 'sustainable development' – a relational concept, series of practices and processes that stay within the 'carrying capacity' of the planet. Sometimes known as the 'Strong Sustainability Condition', this idea insists that over time there should be no decline in Natural Capital, that future generations must inherit the same amount of natural resource stocks as previous ones. As with so much else, policy makers, academics, sustainability practitioners and others throughout the world rarely seem to agree – at least fully. Consequently, alternative sustainability conditions have therefore been conceptualized – namely, the 'Weak' (no reduction in Critical Natural Capital) and the 'Very Weak' (the loss of Natural Capital must not be more than the increase in Human Capital and Human-made Capital).

The substitution of natural capital with human-made capital can be quite expensive. Heal (2000) discusses how the Catskill watershed provided New York City residents with natural high-quality water for many years. Then, in the 1990s the Environmental Protection Agency (EPA) suggested that a filtration plant would soon be needed because of uncontrolled land development and intensive water consumption costing the city up to \$8 billion, with annual operating costs around \$300 million. This prompted the city to restore the watershed by improving sewage treatment and purchasing land to head off further development. Although still costly for this course of action, estimates came in at less than \$1.5 billion. There are frequently other issues too. For Norton (2005), the real problems arise when communities and professionals of various descriptions speak different languages of sustainability. He argues the need for a radical shift in attitudes, that environmental policies should be derived from long-term adaptive plans based on the values embedded in each community or locale. Too often disputes, environmental management practices and policy conflicts arise between those who wish to place a financial price on the value of nature and those who fervently do not see nature as being intrinsically valuable. An approach that reconciles these positions needs to encompass short-term goals, which may be primarily economic or employment related, medium-term goals that may need to encompass local and regional imperatives like water or land conservation, and more long-term goals that must encompass planetary survival, the health and well-being of future generations and the regulation of population increase. For Norton, adaptive management means human ingenuity and practice working as an integral *part* of nature rather than simply *on* nature, for human beings help constitute these wider ecosystems. Sustainable development projects need to articulate that. For Norton, there is not just scarcity in the economic sense but also scarcity of good ideas and effective action. In the words of Homer-Dixon (2002), there is 'an ingenuity gap'.

The 'humanization' of sustainable development: the Millennium Development Goals (MDGs)

In September 2000, at the United Nations Millennium Summit, world leaders agreed on eight measurable Millennium Development Goals to be achieved by 2015, in addition to outlining broad commitments to human rights, good governance and democracy. Official United Nations figures indicated the existence of vast inequalities in an increasingly affluent world – 113 million children do not go to school, over a billion people earn less than $1 a day, 11 million children die before they are five and preventable diseases devastate many populations. Inequality and injustice clearly go hand in hand but the Millennium Declaration, as with so many international agreements, was the product of extended dialogue, detailed negotiation and frustrating compromise (United Nations, 2000).

The Millennium Development Goals include:

- halving extreme poverty and hunger;
- achieving universal primary education;
- empowering women and achieving gender equality;
- reducing mortality for the under-fives by two-thirds;
- reducing maternal mortality by three-quarters;
- reversing the spread of major diseases, especially HIV/AIDS and malaria;
- ensuring environmental sustainability;
- creating global partnerships for development with targets for trade, aid and debt relief.

By 2006, it was also clear that progress towards meeting these goals was slow and uneven (United Nations, 2006) with Asia seeing the greatest reduction in poverty though chronic hunger was still widespread in sub-Saharan Africa and Asia. There were significant increases in universal primary education, particularly in India, although urban and gender inequalities remained serious problems. Women's position in the labour market, and child and maternal mortality rates had improved slightly, although reproductive healthcare services were very poor in many regions. The incidence of HIV/AIDS, tuberculosis and malaria was still high. The rate of deforestation had slowed down but forest loss continued. Half of all developing nations still lacked basic sanitation systems and development assistance from the more affluent nations had increased but was still below the targets set a few years earlier. Some 14 per cent of the global population had Internet access, but a digital divide was perceived as separating the developing from developed nations, with over 50 per cent of the population in developed regions using the Web as opposed to 7 per cent in developing regions (less than 1 per cent in the least developed nations). Two years earlier the Human Development Report for 2004 had also noted uneven progress, stating soberly that:

> at the current pace Sub-Saharan Africa will not meet the goal for universal primary education until 2129 or the goal for reducing child mortality by two-thirds until 2106 – 100 years away, rather than the 11 called for by the goals. In three of the goals – hunger, income poverty and access to sanitation – no date can be set because the situation in the region is worsening, not improving.
>
> (Fukuda-Parr, 2004: 132)

Despite all this, the economist Jeffrey Sachs (2005) sees no real reason why the MDGs cannot be realized in full for they are eminently achievable, requiring relatively modest amounts of aid from developed countries and alterations to trading regulations. He gives five major reasons for this thinking:

1   The numbers of the world's extreme poor have declined to become a relatively small proportion of the global population – less than 20 per cent.
2   The MDGs aim to end extreme poverty, not all poverty or to equalize incomes.
3   Low-cost interventions to improve energy generation, water, sanitation, disease control, etc. can significantly improve living standards and enhance economic development.
4   The rich parts of the world are now extremely rich and the aim of increasing overseas aid from developed countries to 0.7 per cent of GNP is fairly small. 'The point is that the Millennium Development Goals can be financed within the bounds of the official development assistance that the donor countries have already promised' (Sachs, 2005: 299).
5   Tools and information technologies can be extremely powerful and effective – potentially good communication and information dissemination, advanced agronomic practices, 'science based management of soil nutrients', new medicines biotechnology, etc.

Sachs calls for, and has faith in the idea of, an enlightened globalization of democracies, of science and technology, market economies and multilateralism with progressive public policies at national and international levels leading the way. He believes big transnational corporations have not caused the global crisis, although their past behaviour is not unblemished. The anti-globalization movement's hostility to capitalism is consequently not especially well founded. He writes:

> Too many protestors do not know that it is possible to combine faith in the power of trade and markets with understanding of their limitations as well. The movement is too pessimistic about the possibilities of capitalism with a human face, in which the remarkable power of trade and investment can be harnessed while acknowledging and addressing limitations through compensatory collective actions.
>
> (Sachs, 2005: 357)

Sachs's (2009, 2013) commitment to a mixed economy approach is reinforced in later work where he consistently argues that private sector innovation, particularly with regard to breakthrough technologies, such as cell phones, has been an essential of addressing poverty, healthcare, education, finance and agricultural value chains. Extreme global poverty, understood today as living on $1.25 per day or less, has declined markedly from 52 per cent in 1980 to 21 per cent (or 1.3 billion people) in 2010. Consequently, the public functions of disease control, public education, the promotion of science and technology, and environmental conservation must align with the dynamic of private market forces. However, 3 billion people still live on $2.50 a day or less and 40 per cent of the world's population live in countries where income and wealth differentials are worsening.

Less optimistic is Aswani Saith (2006) who notes that the MDGs owe too much to the United Nations Development Programme and for some represent a narrowing of the (sustainable) development agenda to just a few issues in what used to be called the 'Third World'. Various points are made: poverty and deprivation exist in Japan, the UK and US too; people with disability who make up around 10 per cent of the global population receive no mention and neither do the elderly who increasingly constitute a significant percentage of the global poor; and there are no goals and targets for secondary education, etc. The identification of the goals and their accompanying indicators and metrics also offer concern. For instance, feminist critics find it difficult to see how gender empowerment can be reduced to a single target or goal as this issue cuts across so many other areas – for example, universal primary education and gender inequality. Setting targets may also easily distort social and cultural behaviour, inducing governments to divert funds to meet reportable targeted areas to the exclusion of others arguably as important but not incorporated with the MDGs. Problems with data, particularly regarding malaria, tuberculosis and maternal mortality, make accurate assessment and evaluation a most important issue. There is little point in setting targets if it is uncertain which actions will produce what outcomes. The MDGs require that initiatives are costed but Saith suggests that

> This immediately reveals the futility of such exercises. One might ask: what would it cost to overcome violence against women? What might it cost to address the issue of son preference and the appalling and falling sex ratio at birth? What would it cost to get the parents to agree to send the girl child to school? How much would have to be spent to change the laws on property rights?
>
> (2006: 1178)

The global neoliberal economic agenda, structural inequality and the gap between the rhetoric and reality on human rights and environmental protection seem to go largely unchallenged and unexamined. Veteran neo-Marxist critic Samir Amin (2006b) sees the MDGs as clearly designed to shore up the North's global economic and political dominance of the South. The rhetoric of 'partnership'and the notion of 'good governance' is really about opening up commercial markets for the major economic powers. He asks cynically: what else can be expected from an initiative emanating from Japan, the USA and the European Union, and co-sponsored by the International Monetary Fund, the Organization of Economic Co-operation and Development, and the World Bank, which for Amin is little more than 'the G8's Ministry of Propaganda'?

The World Bank's emphasis is largely on the economic aspects of sustainable development, suggesting, in language reminiscent of corporate business strategies, that if human well-being is to be enhanced, then society has to carefully manage its 'portfolio of assets', recognizing that this mix of 'assets' necessary to support improvements is likely to change over time. Economic growth, at the expense of social and personal well-being or the natural environment, is not a feasible option for the future. Unchecked industrial development has led to horrifying environmental damage in some areas which, like the devastation experienced in many parts of the former Soviet Union, has led to massive human, environmental and economic costs – disease, pollution, loss of livelihoods and ecological habitats. The development of the Soviet cotton industry in central Asia led to the massive use of water for irrigation, which had the effect of reducing the level of the Aral Sea by 20 metres between 1960 and the turn of the century, with water covering just 10 per cent of the area it formerly had covered. Increased salinization led to the extinction of fish species, the destruction of the fishing and fish-processing industries, and the contamination of agricultural land up to 200 kilometres from the banks of the former inland sea (McNeill, 2000). Given this, in theory, then, global societies are confronted with three options:

1   Simultaneously addressing environmental concerns along with economic growth, even in the short run.
2   Placing higher priority on economic growth, while addressing environmental concerns that can be dealt with at relatively low cost in the short run.
3   Placing higher priority on maintaining or restoring the environment in the short run.

(World Bank, 2003: 24)

The work currently being undertaken on formulating a replacement for the MDGs with a new set of sustainable development goals is an ambitious but necessary attempt to pull all of these concerns and critiques together into an informative and motivating set of global objectives.

Sustainable development as a 'dialogue of values'

There has been no shortage of academic critiques of sustainable development. Banerjee (2003) offers a trenchant analysis of the sustainable discourse, powerfully arguing that the concept of sustainable development is subsumed under, and largely defined by, the dominant economic paradigm and is informed by colonial thought, which has resulted in the disempowerment of a majority of the rural populations in the developing world. Banerjee acknowledges that the sustainable development discourse encompasses notions of plurality and even genuine dialogue, but asserts through his analysis of biotechnology, Western science, biodiversity and intellectual property rights that there remains a very real danger of marginalizing or co-opting the traditional ecological knowledge of indigenous peoples and others who depend on their land for their livelihood. A great deal of the discussion around green business focuses on technicist solutions and eco-efficiency, with green marketing ultimately reduced to the economic bottom line at the organizational level obscuring macro-economic factors and likely ecological impacts. Conventional rationalizations of competitive advantage still pervade governmental and corporate literature. Banerjee writes:

> Current development patterns (even those touted as 'sustainable') disrupt social system and ecosystem relations rather than ensuring that natural resource use by local communities meets their basic needs at a level of comfort that is satisfactory as assessed by those same communities. What is needed is not a common future but the future as commons.
>
> (2003: 174)

Much of this is echoed in Adams (2001: 381) who, in his analysis of the environment and sustainability in the Third World, argues there is 'no magic formula for sustainable development', no easy reformist solution to poverty and that, contrary to dominant practice, development 'ought to be what human communities do to themselves' rather than what is done to them by states, bankers, experts, agencies, centralizing planners and others. A 'green development' is required for which there can be no clear blueprints or managerial strategies because of the overwhelming need to be open-ended, open-minded and democratic. Green development is about who has the power and how it is managed. It is about empowerment and self-determination.

Ignacy Sachs's (1999) concern with social sustainability is a reaction to the dominance of the economic discourse in many international organizations' approach to sustainable development. Social sustainability encompasses the absence of war or serious violence, state oppression of its citizenry and lack of meaning in one's social being. For Amartya Sen (1999), realizing human capabilities in a sustainable society means equity, democracy, human and civil rights and a continuing enhancement of people's ability to do what they have good reason to value. It means being able to conceive of alternatives, and to act and think differently, and having the capacity and opportunity to do so. It means protecting biodiversity because society is closely interwoven in a co-evolutionary relationship with the biosphere. It means conceiving and practising development holistically and systemically not one-dimensionally, not simply economically or socially, politically or anthropocentrically. Development must be synonymous with substantive and instrumental freedoms, including those relating to:

- political expression, dialogue and organization;
- economics and income sufficiency;
- social opportunity such as health and education;
- transparency and openness in government and social interaction;
- security understood in terms of welfare, food sufficiency and employment.

For Norgaard (1994), Western science, the environment and material resources are connected within mutually interactive co-evolving systems where one does not control any of the others. In nineteenth-century Europe, the application of scientific knowledge facilitated the use of coal and hydrocarbons, which in turn directed and intensified scientific activity, agricultural, technological and industrial development, and the emergence of a new social, moral and political order. Urbanization, class division, multinational business, global trade and bureaucratic management systems helped concentrate economic and political power, and the strategy of imposing this Western practice and ideology of development on non-Western others. Consequently,

> correcting the unsustainability of development is not simply a matter of choosing different technologies for intervening in the environment. The mechanisms of perceiving, choosing, and using technologies are embedded in social structures which are themselves products of modern technologies.
>
> (Norgaard, 1994: 29)

This co-evolutionary approach to historical explanation offers tremendous insights but does not lend itself to predicting the future, for in this theory there are no simple cause-and-effect relationships, so prediction becomes rather dangerous. However, Norgaard identifies five lessons from this understanding:

1 Experimentation should always be undertaken cautiously and on a small scale.
2 Experiments whose effects might be long lasting, e.g. disposal of nuclear waste, should be avoided.
3 Without cultural and biological diversity co-evolution is prone to stagnate.
4 All things are interconnected so change tends to be evolutionary rather than abrupt or revolutionary.
5 The significant exploitation of hydrocarbons has disconnected cultural evolution from the ecosystems so that the main priority of sustainable development must be to restore this connective relationship.

Working from a similar perspective, Cairns (2003, 2004) sees sustainability as being too complex to allow scientific uncertainties to be reduced to a level that many decision makers and managers would prefer. Strategies for sustainability need to be both top down and bottom up, ethically grounded in a language and literacy comprehensible to whatever the organizational level or geographical locality people find themselves living and working in. This will enable effective communication, social learning and leadership to emerge, hopefully effecting the paradigm shift in thought and action required. Cairns writes:

> The complex interactions of biology/ecology, economics, and technological and social factors must be understood and coped with in an ethical, sustainable way to save both natural systems and humankind. Ethical views must not alienate humankind from the natural world. Science has documented much of what is at risk and some of the actions needed to reduce risk. Instead of denigrating the knowledge (e.g. global warming) and placing undue emphasis on the uncertainties (which always exist in science), leaders and citizens should give attention to those areas upon which mainstream science has reached a consensus. Unsustainable practices can be halted, but, even though remedies are known, they are not acted upon. It is not too late for a paradigm shift to occur.
>
> (2004: 2)

For Ignacy Sachs, development is akin to liberation and transformation, particularly if understood as a self-organizing and intentional process freeing people from poverty and exploitation. Sachs, like the World Bank, recognizes that trade-offs will occur but some are totally, ethically, unacceptable. He writes:

> Thus, for example, whole development is incompatible with economic growth achieved through increased social inequality, and/or violation of democracy, even if its environmental impacts are kept under control. Environmental prudence, commendable as it is cannot act as a substitute for social equity. Concern for the environment should not become a diversion from the paramount imperatives of social justice and full democracy, the two basic values of whole development.
>
> (1999: 33)

Sustainable development is therefore multidimensional, encompassing social, ecological and economic goals and perspectives, and this breadth has led some critics to view the concept as vague, self-contradictory and incoherent, incapable of being put into practice. Consequently, Johnston *et al.* (2007: 61) want to 'reclaim' the concept, rooting it in a theory and set of principles, enabling development to be separated from 'the current exploitative economic paradigm' of economic growth. All that is required, suggests Johnston, is to articulate sustainability in terms of a robust set of principles and a practical operational framework relevant to both personal and organizations' actions.

Perhaps it is the sociologist, Blake Ratner's notion of sustainability as a 'dialogue of values' which constitutes the most fruitful way of engaging with, and understanding, the theories, values, perspectives and practices of sustainable development. He identifies three basic tendencies in sustainable development practice – namely, the technical, ethical and dialogic. He writes:

> The sustainability concept is meaningful, therefore, not because it provides an encompassing solution to different notions of what is good, but for the way it brings such differences into a common field of dispute, dialogue, and potential agreement as the basis of collective action.
>
> (2004: 62)

Sustainable development and sustainability are dynamic concepts and processes. Meanings and practices change as the world changes, as our skills, knowledge and capabilities develop, and as communication and dialogue improves. At every spatial scale, from the neighbourhood to the global level, different interests will come together and sometimes collide, but it is only through discussion, debate, critical reflection, learning and dialogue that agreement and action can and will emerge. The achievement of Rio and Johannesburg summits, and particularly the composition of the genuinely remarkable document known as *The Earth Charter* (Gorbachev, 2006), could only have been reached by people listening, talking and learning from one another, and being willing to do so. Thus, for Baker (2006) it is probably better to talk about 'promoting' rather than achieving sustainable development, for this enables us to attune ourselves to differing and emerging understandings, timescales and pathways across the world. The concept, then, is multifaceted because the issues, challenges and problems we confront are complex, complicated and various. Different countries exhibit different levels of development, have different values, cultures and traditions (as do people), are endowed with differing amounts of natural resources and so have, certainly according to Brundtland, differentiating responsibilities in promoting and realizing sustainable development goals. Thus, despite all the criticisms of global summits and partnership projects as being muddled compromises or lost opportunities, this very heterogeneity has allowed a coming together, and an identification of some common ground on which to build further action and agreement. In this way, sustainable development is similar to 'democracy' and 'justice' in being concepts that can be easily contested or dismissed as being rather woolly. But who would really want to throw these out?

Summary

Sustainable development is not always easy to grasp. It has a long history that relates to the care and stewardship of our Earth in the face of its continuing exploitation by human beings to make their lives materially better. This chapter has attempted to explore the evolution of the concept and practice of sustainable development by showing how, especially since the middle years of the twentieth century, environmental campaigners, sustainability educators, politicians and business people have struggled to come to terms with our negative impact on the planet's ecosystems. So, from the 1970 Earth Day to the contemporary international negotiations about climate change, sustainable development has been viewed as a necessary but elusive process operating various scales, including the global and local level. It may also take different forms in different places and at different times. It has been subject to many different interpretations but has informed the national policy goals of small and large nations alike. For some people, sustainable development is a contradiction in terms. Development means economic growth and sustainability refers to living, working, producing and consuming within ecological limitations while ensuring that economic growth continues as a way of combating poverty, disease and other hardships. Others suggest that growth is not the way and the challenge of sustainable development is to square the circle without being dismissed as hopelessly unrealistic or impractical. Thus, sustainable development requires learning and the willingness of everyone to enter into dialogue with each other to find ways by which a better life can be found for every creature on this planet.

Thinking questions

1   Examine your own everyday activities, purchases, enjoyments, work, travel, holidays and so on. In what ways is globalization part of our everyday life experience? Note down examples from your own work and life experience.
2   How would you characterize your own view on globalization and sustainability?
3   What is the lasting value of the big international conferences on sustainable development?
4   Can sustainable development occur in any one country?
5   What is the significance of devising a set of global Sustainable Development Goals?
6   What are the advantages and disadvantages of conceiving sustainable development as a dialogue of values?

Companion website

To find out more about the relationship between globalization and sustainable development, please visit the companion website for additional case studies.

2 Worldviews and ethical values
Towards an ecological paradigm

Aims

This chapter examines a wide range of academic and policy writing on sustainable development, attempting in the process to offer a critical evaluation of the significance and implications of the many worldviews, values and perspectives that inform or have emerged from it. A worldview can be understood as a set of beliefs and assumptions about life and reality that influence the way we think and behave. Worldviews help us describe the reality before us and they encompass many assumptions about such things as human nature, the meaning and value of life, society, institutional practices and much more. The German term *Weltanschauung*, from which the anglicized term 'worldview' is derived, is often translated as a total outlook on life and the universe (Koltko-Rivera, 2004). Consequently, a number of philosophical and ideological contributions to our continuing of what sustainability and sustainable development may mean or become are constitutive elements of a global dialogue on the future we want. Consequently, each *worldview*, or perspective, has its own attendant literatures and an array of subtle, and not so subtle, implications for action. Many offer an array of action-orientated normative prescriptions and proscriptions.

On sustainability and sustainable development

As noted in Chapter 1, Blake Ratner has suggested that the most appropriate way to understand the concepts of sustainability and sustainable development is as a 'dialogue of values'. Different individuals, communities, pressure groups, institutions and governments are likely to view sustainability and sustainable development from different perspectives. They will share some understandings while contesting others. For some people, sustainability will be seen as a goal and sustainable development as a process, with an underlying assumption that any equilibrium will always be dynamic and changeable rather than static and secure. For Ratner, given the complexities and debates involved, it is necessary to distinguish between trivial or populist conceptualizations and more meaningful ones:

> When advocates use the term [sustainable development] to mean 'sustained growth', 'sustained change' or simply 'successful' development, then it has little meaning, especially when development is considered as growth in material consumption. More meaningful interpretations are multidimensional, often distinguishing among social goals (including justice, participation, equality, empowerment, institutional sustainability and cultural integrity), ecological goals

(including biodiversity preservation, ecosystem resilience and resource conservation) and economic goals (including growth, efficiency and material welfare).
Such a multidimensional notion represents the mainstream in analysis and
advocacy of sustainable development. . . . It recognizes ecosystem integrity as
fundamental to the productive activities on which human society and economy
depend, acknowledges ecological limits to growth in the consumption of resources,
and assumes that the distinct goals of sustainability sometimes converge in practice
and other times require difficult tradeoffs.

(Ratner, 2004: 53–4)

Ratner is not the only one seeking clarity and a way forward. Ben-Eli (2007)
writes that if we are serious about fashioning a sustainable future, we need rigorous
concepts and key principles focusing on self-restraint, balance and a spiritual
dimension that honours the Earth and fosters compassion for non-human others by
reintroducing a sense of sacredness and reverence for all interactions making up the
planet's intricate ecology. For Pezzoli, it is the concept of political ecology that best
links ecological themes with social struggles and will help to build a radically different
and better world. These struggles may be difficult and not always successful, as
demonstrated in his study of communities of poor people who had built their own
homes, 'irregular' human settlements, resisting urban encroachment, development
and ecological deterioration in Mexico City (Pezzoli, 2000):

From the perspective of political ecology, each sphere . . . gives rise to a set of
challenges. These include the challenge to engender: (1) *holism* (an integrated,
coevolutionary understanding of social, economic and ecological interlinkages);
(2) *empowerment and community building*; (3) *social justice and equity*; and (4)
sustainable production and reproduction.

(Pezzoli, 1997: 556)

There are many other approaches to understanding sustainable development,
offering subtle but sometimes slightly dissonant variations on well-known themes.
As Robinson and Tinker (1997) note, one of the main obstacles to developing a
common conceptual framework incorporating social, economic and ecological
problems is the lack of genuine consensus among experts in each discipline as to
how ecological, economic and social systems relate to one another. The resulting
'trifocal' vision makes understanding the world, international and national policy
development, and effective action a major challenge. This is sometimes exacerbated
by occasional tendencies for one group of experts to see their approach as being
more fundamental than any other. When this happens, dialogue can become extremely
difficult. Intellectual and cultural space is needed to allow differences to be aired
and discussion to flourish. In addition, political and practical strategies, policies and
actions that facilitate the emergence of conditions allowing for possible reconciliation
between perspectives are also required. Only if this is possible can there be an effective
and sustainable engagement with the overlapping and interconnected systems making
up the biosphere, the economy and human society.

For Robinson and Tinker (1997), the intellectual basis for this engagement lies in
the processes of 'dematerialization' and 'resocialization', which uncouple economic
activity from ecological impact, substituting notions of well-being and quality of life

for the economistic and quantifying measurement of progress, development and improved standards of living encapsulated in such indices as gross national product (see Chapter 8).

In *State of the Future*, the necessity of cultural change is explicitly stated:

> Although many people criticize globalization's potential cultural impacts, it is increasingly clear that cultural change is necessary to address global challenges. The development of genuine democracy requires cultural change, preventing AIDS requires cultural change, sustainable development requires cultural change, ending violence against women requires cultural change and ending ethnic violence requires cultural change. The tools of globalization, such as the internet, global trade, international trade treaties and international outsourcing, should be used to help cultures adapt in a way that preserves their unique contributions to humanity while improving the human condition.
>
> (Glenn and Gordon, 2007: 5)

Without cultural change, without dialogue on sustainability and sustainable development, values and policies, political decision-making is liable to remain blinkered and uninformed. As Robinson notes, sustainability is a political act, but what informs that act? The rest of this chapter explores various perspectives informing this dialogue, but it should be remembered that only human action that is at once political and ethical will ultimately fashion a more sustainable world.

Deep and shallow ecology

'Deep ecologists' have the principles of ecological limits and the need for human life to harmonize with nature as their central tenet. In 1973 the Norwegian philosopher Arne Naess published in *Inquiry* a short article titled 'The shallow and the deep', which outlined the foundation of 'deep ecology', essentially an *ecocentric* value position. He later elaborated these views in a number of papers, speeches and books, and the ideas soon took root among radical activists throughout the world, particularly in the US (Ingalsbee, 1996). In many ways, largely because of its strong moral compass, deep ecology is the touchstone of the environmental movement and the conscience of sustainable development practitioners. Importantly, Naess made the distinction between *shallow* and *deep* ecology, clearly articulating the centrality of system interactions and complexity to this worldview. He writes that the differences between them can be seen by contrasting their approaches to the following (Naess, 1995: adapted from pp. 71–4).

Pollution

Shallow approach: Technology seeks to purify the air and water and to spread pollution more evenly. Laws limit permissible pollution.

Polluting industries are preferably exported to developing countries.

Deep approach: Pollution is evaluated from a biospheric perspective, not exclusively focusing on the effects on human health, but rather on life as a whole, including the life conditions of every species and system.

Resources

Shallow approach: Emphasis is on resources for humans and particularly those living in affluent countries. The Earth's resources belong to those with the technology to exploit them.

Deep approach: Emphasis is on resources and habitats for all life-forms for their own sake. No natural object is conceived purely as a resource.

Population

Shallow approach: Human 'over-population' is mainly a problem for developing countries. The issue of an 'optimum' population for humans is discussed without reference to the question of an 'optimum' population for other life-forms.

Deep approach: Excessive pressures on planetary life stem from the human population explosion. Pressures stemming from industrial societies are a major factor and population reduction must have high priority in these areas.

Cultural diversity and appropriate technology

Shallow approach: Industrialization on the Western model is held to be the goal for developing countries.

Deep approach: Industrialization and modern technologies should not be allowed to destroy the cultural identity, diversity and values of non-industrial societies. Cultural diversity is the human analogue of biodiversity.

Land and sea ethics

Shallow approach: Landscapes, ecosystems, rivers and so forth are conceptually fragmented and regarded as the properties and resources of individuals, organizations and states. Conservation is argued in terms of 'costs' and 'benefits'.

Deep approach: The Earth does not belong to humans; we only inhabit the lands and must only use resources to satisfy vital needs. If the non-vital needs of humans conflict with the vital needs of non-humans, then humans should defer to the latter.

Education and scientific enterprise

Shallow approach: The degradation of the environment and resource depletion require the training of more experts who can advise on technologies and policies designed to maintain economic growth while maintaining a healthy environment.

Deep approach: If sane ecological policies are adopted, education should concentrate on increasing human awareness and sensitivity to the natural world and combating the growth of consumer materialism.

Naess's views on deep ecology have been developed by Bill Devall and George Sessions (1985), leading to the identification of a series of ethico-political principles. They stressed that deep ecology sees humans as part of nature, rather than separate or superior to it. The idea of humanity's *dominance* over nature was one they believed the modern technocratic-industrial society had elevated to a matter of principle – humans dominating nature, men dominating women, the West over non-Western cultures, the rich over the poor, and so on – which needed to be challenged and overturned. In developing their argument, they suggested that there was no firm ontological divide between human and non-human realms, and that this *biocentric* equality was intimately related to human *self-realization*. When we harm nature, we harm ourselves. There are no boundaries and everything is related. Thus, for Naess, when viewed systematically rather than individually, maximum self-realization means the maximum realization of all manifestations of life.

The basic principles of deep ecology include:

> The wellbeing and flourishing of human and non-human life on Earth have value in themselves ('intrinsic value' or 'inherent value'). These values are independent of the usefulness of the non-human world for human purposes.
>
> Richness and diversity of life-forms contribute to the realizations of these values and are also values in themselves.
>
> Humans have no right to reduce this richness and diversity except to satisfy vital human needs.
>
> The flourishing of human life and cultures is compatible with a substantial decrease of human population. The flourishing of non-human life requires such a decrease.
>
> Present human interference with the non-human world is excessive, and the situation is rapidly worsening.
>
> Policies must therefore be changed. These policies affect basic economic, technological and ideological structures. The resulting state of affairs will be deeply different from the present.
>
> The ideological change is mainly that of appreciating life quality (dwelling in situations of inherent value), rather than adhering to an increasingly high standard of living. There will be a profound awareness of the difference between big and great.
>
> Those who subscribe to the foregoing points have an obligation to directly or indirectly try to implement the necessary changes.
>
> (Naess, 1995: 68)

Naess himself is reluctant to apply the label 'deep' or 'shallow' ecologist to anyone specifically, as the former seemed to be rather conceited and the latter too disparaging, almost offensive. Instead, applying a Ghandian perspective, he prefers the word 'supporter', believing that groups and individuals may adhere to deep ecology principles from a number of different positions and from a range of differing life experiences, cultures, technologies and practices. He therefore sees his own deep 'ecosophy' as being both didactic and dialectic, encouraging people to recognize and state their own general philosophies. Like Socrates, Naess writes, he wants to use his ecosophy to provoke questioning about basic matters of ecology, life and death, and from there to outline implications for practical situations, real-world actions and concrete issues of lifestyle: 'I believe that multifaceted, high-level self-realization is more easily reached through a lifestyle which is "simple in means but rich in ends" rather than through the material standard of living of the average citizens of industrial states' (Naess, 1995: 82).

Ramachandra Guha (1989) is less certain. Writing from the vantage point of a developing nation, India, he suggests that deep ecology, particularly in its commitment to biocentrism and wilderness preservation, is unwelcome, as it diminishes the needs of humans. The real problems are cultural and economic – over-consumption by the West and by Third World elites, growing militarization, and so on. Western conservationists, influenced by deep ecology and including organizations like the World Wide Fund for Nature (WWF) and World Conservation Union (IUCN), have sometimes, certainly in the past, failed to appreciate how the effects of environmental problems seriously impact on the poor, in the forms of, for example, water shortages, soil erosion and air pollution. The annexation of Eastern religion and mysticism to the deep ecology philosophy is also rather disingenuous, as it often serves to position the East as pre-scientific, romantic and passive, failing to recognize the active role traditional ecological knowledge has had in stable and effective environmental management. Guha's stringent critique continues by noting how the National Park Movement is intricately tied to the growing expansion of capitalism and consumerism, with wilderness areas, practically and ideologically, becoming aesthetic antidotes to the pressures of modern life while simultaneously functioning as emerging business opportunities for tourist operators, now frequently commandeering the prefix 'sustainable'. More recently, a conscientious sustainable tourism has emerged as a significant economic opportunity for many developing nations, but Guha's fundamental point about ecological concerns needing a fuller integration with people's livelihoods and work throughout the world remains pertinent. Deep ecology must not become yet another veiled form of cultural and economic imperialism.

Eco-feminism

Deep ecology has been gender blind, and a great deal of eco-feminist thought has been developed as a critique of this philosophy, which for many remains wedded to the rationalist problematic of Western thought, which additionally, as Guha notes, fails to conceptualize human beings as sufficiently social and connected. The idea that the best way to eradicate the division between humanity and nature is through a 'unifying process' is too extreme. As Val Plumwood remarks, in its over-generality, deep ecology:

> fails to provide a genuine basis for an environmental ethics of the kind sought, for the view of humans as metaphysically unified with the cosmic whole will be equally true whatever relation humans stand in with nature – the situation of exploitation of nature exemplifies such unity equally as well as a conserver situation, and the human self is just as indistinguishable from the bulldozer and Coco-Cola bottle as the rocks or the rain forest.

(1996: 165)

What is really necessary is to rethink the human side of this dualism, to understand and rearticulate the qualities that 'inferior' humans have in abundance and to see the natural world in a non-mechanistic way. For Plumwood, much of this has to do with various continuities of reproductivity, sensuousness, relationships and emotionality, rather than abstract planning and calculation. It is our relationships that make us human. Karen Warren (1996, 2004) sums up the various eco-feminist perspectives when she writes of environmental degradation and exploitation being

LIBRARY, UNIVERSITY OF CHESTER

Box 2.1 Feeding people versus saving nature?

The renowned American ecocentric philosopher Holmes Rolston III (1996, 2011) has been both highly influential and highly controversial. His approach to environmental ethics has led him to ask some direct and difficult questions, and offer answers that many within and outside of the environmental movement find discomforting. He asks whether we should save nature if it means that people will go hungry. If we always put people first, are we prepared to sacrifice every other creature? Are we prepared to see a world without rhinos? As the human population expands pressure on the land, whether it is land protected in conservation areas rich in biodiversity, or sensitively worked by indigenous peoples, or simply earmarked for 'development', will increase. Do human rights trump everything else? Should they? Environmental policy ought to and already does regulate human behaviour and there are many designated conservation areas in the world looking after cultural, ecological, scientific, historical, economic, aesthetic and religious values. Holmes Rolston III believes that every person living is already told, and knows, that he or she cannot develop some areas. They need not starve but they need and ought not to do so by sacrificing nature, and this environmental ethic needs to be communicated more fully, more effectively and more forcefully. Individuals too often look to only their immediate local concerns and interests. They deal with the pressures of the moment and do not necessarily see ahead or operate on intelligent scales that require the capacity to look deeper into the future. So . . .

> Ought we to feed people first, and save nature last? We never face so simple a question. The practical question is more complex. If persons widely demonstrate that they value many other worthwhile things over feeding the hungry (Christmas gifts, college educations, symphony concerts), and if developed countries, to protect what they value, post national boundaries across which the poor may not pass (immigration laws), and if there is unequal and unjust distribution of wealth, and if just redistribution to alleviate poverty is refused, and if charitable redistribution of justified unequal distribution of wealth is refused, and if one fifth of the world continues to consume four fifths of the production of goods and four fifths consumes one fifth, and if escalating birthrates continue so that there are no real gains in alleviating poverty, only larger numbers of poor in the next generation, and if low productivity on domesticated lands continues, and if the natural lands to be sacrificed are likely to be low in productivity, and if significant natural values are at stake, including extinctions of species, then one ought not always to feed people first, but rather one ought sometimes to save nature.
>
> (Rolston III, 1996: 265)

Saving nature is not naive. It can deepen our understanding of our place in and our duties to the world. Ethics is expanding so that what counts is not just what society does to slaves, minorities, women, children, the handicapped or future generations but to the Earth's flora, fauna, ecosystems and landscapes.

feminist issues because they are fundamentally to do with relations of oppression and as such are pertinent to the experience of women in the developing and developed worlds, where they often seem to bear the brunt of social and ecological hardships. For Warren, any conceptual framework that articulates a hierarchy of values, constructs dualisms rather than complementarities or logically leads to the justification of domination, are in themselves oppressive. She identifies eight major boundary conditions for a feminist ethic that has profound implications for understanding and engagement with nature and the environment. These conditions include:

- No 'ism' that promotes social domination is acceptable (for example classism, racism or sexism).
- Ethical discourse and practice must be *contextual*, in other words must emerge from the voices of people sited in different historical circumstances.
- A feminist ethic must incorporate a range of women's voices from different cultures and traditions, in other words be *pluralistic*.
- Ethics are always *in process*, changing over time.
- Inclusiveness is a guiding evaluative principle of a feminist ethics.
- Feminist ethics are not value neutral but offer inclusivity, a 'better bias'.
- A feminist ethics offers a central place for values that have been conventionally downplayed or misrepresented (for example, care, love, trust and friendship).
- A feminist ethic reconceptualizes what it is to be human – there can be no such thing as a gender-free or gender-neutral 'mankind', no abstract individualism.

Eco-feminism therefore should be anti-naturist, refusing to perceive non-human nature in a hierarchical or superordinate manner, with its contextual ethics based not on rights and principles but on relationships that actually define who we are. In this way, eco-feminism should deny the nature–culture divide but retain the capacity to recognize difference between peoples, and between humans and the non-human world, while maintaining a respectful attitude to both. It should refocus environmental ethics by clarifying what nature could morally mean *for* human beings.

Although there are many areas of agreement within eco-feminism, there is also considerable unease. The linguistic and philosophical feminization of nature, such as the 'Mother Earth' metaphor, culturally seems to reproduce and legitimize a range of exploitative relationships when women perform the roles of carer, life-giver, nurturer, and so on. Empirically, there is considerable evidence showing vast socio-economic inequalities and iniquities stemming from this ideological position and the way society and the economy are organized (K. Warren, 1996, 2004). It should also be remembered, as Cuomo (1992) recognizes, that women, particularly in the industrialized and developed nations, have contributed to the exploitation of the non-human world. This means that with eco-feminism there seems to be little support for a biological essentialism that goes beyond offering a feminist standpoint based on a shared understanding of cultural oppression. For Cuomo, it is not possible to talk about caring abstractly. There has to be an object for this care and a context in which it takes place. If care and caring is situation dependent, rather than a matter of principle, then what will decide the issue, what will effect equitable and sustainable change, is acute political analysis and intelligent political action.

Social ecology

Deep ecology has also been criticized by social ecologists, most notably by the anarchist writer and activist Murray Bookchin, who sees deep ecology as 'vague, formless, often self-contradictory and predominantly missing the point'. His essentialist critique of the deep greens leaves little opportunity for dialogue. In *What is Social Ecology?*, Bookchin (1993) states firmly:

> Indeed, to separate ecological problems from social problems – or even to play down or give token recognition to this crucial relationship – would be to grossly misconstrue the sources of the growing environmental crisis. The way human beings deal with each other as social beings is crucial to addressing the ecological crisis. Unless we clearly recognize this, we will surely fail to see that the hierarchical mentality and class relationships that so thoroughly permeate society give rise to the very idea of dominating the natural world. Unless we realize that the present market society, structured around the brutally competitive imperative of 'grow or die', is a thoroughly impersonal, self-operating mechanism, we will falsely tend to blame technology as such or population growth as such for environmental problems. We will ignore their root causes, such as trade for profit, industrial expansion and the identification of 'progress' with corporate self-interest. In short, we will tend to focus on the symptoms of a grim social pathology rather than on the pathology itself, and our efforts will be directed towards limited goals, whose attainment is more cosmetic than curative.

In *Toward an Ecological Society* (1980), *From Urbanization to Cities* (1995) and *The Ecology of Freedom* (2005), Bookchin develops his eco-anarchist ideas, arguing that the future is dependent on how humankind steers its relationship with the natural world. He looks in part to the experience of indigenous peoples, as well as to classic anarchist writers such as Peter Kropotkin, for guidance as to how we should 'live with' nature rather than dominate or exploit it. For Bookchin, the underlying human problem is hierarchy and inequality. So long as human beings exploit each other in terms of class, race or gender, humanity will exploit and degrade the natural world. Ecological harmony is dependent on social harmony, and the practical prescription for this entails a reversal and transcendence of contemporary capitalist arrangements – the ending of the detailed division of labour, the concentration of people and resources in massive corporations and urban developments, bureaucracy, class hierarchy, the separation of town and country, and the objectification, alienation and commoditization of nature and humankind. Cities must be decentralized in accordance with the ecosystems in which they are located, in order to establish a human-scale direct and participatory civic democracy. New kinds of flexible, versatile and productive eco-technologies must be applied to ensure that waste is recycled, reused and reduced. The leading industrialized nations must create an alternative path of development which will both address global environmental problems and eradicate the poverty blighting the developing world which the current model for 'progress' has largely caused. However, Best (1998) notes that it is sometimes difficult to comprehend the practical viability of Bookchin's anarchist politics in advanced technological societies, since he fails to address the significant role that the media and education play in socializing and acculturating people to the practices of unsustainable development. Only by fashioning a 'third nature' will the full potential for freedom, rationality and subjectivity be realized, and the media and education have an important role to play in this.

Bioregionalism

It is the nurturing of this third nature that appears in the highly engaging social philosophy of bioregional urbanist Lewis Mumford. In his early essays for the *Sociological Review* in the 1920s, and especially in the seminal texts *Technics and Civilization* (1962, first published 1934) and *The Culture of Cities* (1966a, first published 1938), Mumford clearly articulates the intricate and inextricable relationship between human social organization, economic production and ecology, stating that through sensitive regional planning an appropriate balance could be achieved between human institutions and natural, regional, resources. He saw the modern age as offering great hope in that new environmentally benign technologies could emerge to rectify the destruction wrought on the Earth through the desire to increasingly accumulate material wealth and financial profit. For this change to happen, though, a fundamental shift in human values and the human personality was needed. There could be no ecological balance without human balance, no one-sided or indefinite progress. What should emerge is a 'dynamic equilibrium', with a conservation ethic replacing the all-too-apparent 'reckless pillage'. For Mumford, this dynamic equilibrium would entail the building of *eutopias* (good places), similar to the decentralized garden cities envisaged by Ebenezer Howard (1902) in our modern world. This would encompass:

> Equilibrium in the environment: Conservation and restoration of soils; reliance on kinetic energy (sun, falling water, wind); the larger use of scrap metals; and 'the conservation of the environment itself as a resource, the fitting of human needs into the pattern formed by the region as a whole'.

> Equilibrium in industry and agriculture: A balanced industrial life in every region of the Earth; the decentralization of population into new centres; the widening of market gardening and mixed farming, with specialized farming intended for world export reduced to the essential. The *raison d'être* of capitalism will diminish as human and environmental exploitation is replaced by alternative modes of living and working.

> Equilibrium in population: The balancing of the birth rate and death rate, and of rural and urban environments and the wiping out of 'blighted industrial areas' in favour of 'a rational resettlement of the entire planet into the regions more favourable to human habitation'.

> (Mumford, 1962: 430, 432)

Visionary, practical, optimistic and frustrated in turn, Mumford is a neglected thinker, whose insights and prescience warrant greater recognition (Sale, 1991; Guha, 2006); like other bioregionalists such as Wendell Berry, Kirkpatrick Sale and Peter Berg, he emphasized the need to 'reinhabit' the places we live in but have abused ecologically and become socially alienated from. We need to recover what it means to be 'native' to a place, to refresh our relationship with the non-human environment, nurturing an ecological identity and literacy, and feeding the world upon which we depend. The sensuous world of place is more interactive, immediate and local than the world of inanimate machines. For McGinnis (1999: 75), we must embrace 'home place', through sharing our abilities to unwrap and draw on the inner expressions and experiences that expressively make up our cognitive maps of place. Returning home requires a restoration of the self. For the UK Green Party economist Molly Scott Cato (2012), it is about localization, self-reliance, land reform, the abandonment of economic growth, the recovery of craft skills and the integration of nature into economic thinking. For Berry (1990), it is about listening to the stories of the land. For Sale (1991), it is replacing the globalized abstracts and intangibles with the seen and felt, which can only be properly apprehended on a human scale. And for Peter Berg, founder of the bioregionalist organization Planet Drum Foundation and lead author of the Green City Program for San Francisco Bay Area Cities and Towns (Berg *et al.*, 1989), it is about putting regional and urban design on a natural foundation, creating and enhancing a firm sense of place, local ecology, community, culture and history through engagement, dialogue and participation. In 1986 representatives from a wide variety of green groups met to develop proposals for an overarching programme of changes that would have general appeal and which could stop and reverse the increasing ecological deterioration of the Bay region. For bioregionalists, our biggest challenge is to make cities sustainable, for city dwellers to become nature seekers and creative urban pioneers. As Berg (1992) writes:

> The first step towards reconceptualizing urban areas is to recognize that they are all situated in local bioregions within which they can be made self-reliant and sustainable. The unique soils, watersheds, native plants and animals, climate, seasonal variations, and other natural characteristics that are present in the geographical life-place where a city is located constitute the basic context for securing essential resources of food, water, energy and materials. For this to happen in a sustainable way, cities must identify with and put themselves in balanced reciprocity with natural systems. Not only do they have to find nearby sources to satisfy basic human needs, but also to adapt those needs to local conditions. They must maintain the natural features that still remain, and restore as many of those that have been disrupted as possible. For example, restoring polluted bays, lakes or rivers, so that they will once more be healthy habitats for aquatic life, can also help make urban areas more self-reliant in producing food.

Traditional ecological knowledge: the wisdom of the elders

Increasingly, the cultures, spirituality and ways of knowing of aboriginal peoples throughout the world are offering models showing that alternative ways of living and being, more in tune with the Earth, are possible. For some, this appreciation is a romantic longing for a world that the Western way of life has not so much lost but wilfully destroyed. For others in affluent post-industrial, postmodern societies, there is a rightful sense of guilt and shame. Many of those who take a more ecocentric view are therefore becoming increasingly interested in traditional ecological knowledge (TEK). The lives, cultures and well-being of many indigenous peoples have been destroyed by the relentless search for raw materials, markets, power and dominance. Part of the Western civilizing mission was aimed at deliberately disconnecting

Aboriginal peoples from their land, their history, their religion and their beliefs, and therefore from themselves. However, in this process of development, the modernizers themselves lost their own sense of connectedness, value and belonging. Environmental philosopher Jim Cheney (1989) argues that Aboriginal peoples use language and knowledge to bind the individual and community together by virtue of their roots being deeply embedded in a sense of place (Westerners should learn from this). Social relationships are reproduced through stories that reside in the land, in the geography of particular bioregions, but which in some (urban) areas are likely to be further dislocated and marred by political power and the physical manifestations of class, gender and race. Individual human and community identity, understanding and health will consequently require continual recontextualizing to achieve, or retrieve, a bioregional grounding. For Cheney, nature needs to speak to us, a complex set of images and myths of the human-land community needs to instruct us, and only when the necessary model of individual and community health has been fashioned will peoples in the 'developed' societies be able to acquire the images needed to mediate relationships with one another and to the land. A cultural language needs to grow out of and articulate this experience so that both human action and nature are jointly responsible for constructing the world, constructing the reality of bioregional, local and authentic selves and communities. It is this dual process that will produce genuine knowledge, 'the result of deep and continuous communication between humans and the more-than-human world of which they are citizens' (Hester and Cheney, 2001: 325). Western science simply offers a monologue and a knowledge based on epistemologies of domination and control. Writing about the belief systems of Native Americans, Vine Deloria, Jr *et al.* suggest, disarmingly:

> It is difficult to understand why Western peoples believe they are so clever. Any damn fool can treat a living thing as if it were a machine and establish conditions under which it is required to perform certain functions – all that is required is a sufficient application of brute force. The result of brute force is slavery.
>
> (1999: 13)

Native peoples in the Amazon have seen their bioregions, communities and selves destroyed by logging and global capitalism. The virtual genocide of Native Americans in the US and the attempted cultural annihilation of First Nation Peoples in Canada enable common stories to be told that resonate throughout the world. The lack of respect, perhaps due to fear, has led to inequalities and those inequities persisting well into the twenty-first century. A damning report on the health of Aboriginal peoples in Australia and New Zealand presented to the World Health Organization in 2007 revealed one small instance of unequal or unsustainable development and the reason why the wisdom of the elders should be retrieved (Marks, 2007). Some facts, then, which show that, compared with white Australians, the health of many Aborigines is appalling: there is a significant incidence of leprosy, rheumatic heart disease and tuberculosis among the Aborigines and Torres Strait Islanders; these peoples have a life expectancy seventeen years less than other Australians; and the average life expectancy for Aboriginal men in some parts of New South Wales is just 33. John Pilger's 2013 documentary *Utopia*, powerfully and graphically condemns the racism that Pilger believes has characterized white Australia's treatment of its native peoples. Black Australians have hardly benefited from the economic boom that Western Australia has experienced through its systematic exploitation of iron ore, gold, nickel, oil, gas and petroleum deposits invariably located on aboriginal ancestral lands. Pilger (2013) writes:

> Barely a fraction of mining, oil and gas revenue has benefited Aboriginal communities, whose poverty is an enduring shock. In Roebourne, in the mineral-rich Pilbara, 80% of the children suffer from an ear infection called otitis media, which can cause partial deafness. Or they go blind from preventable trachoma. Or they die from Dickensian infections. That is their story.

Apart from crude economics and political oppression, the loss of a connecting culture and belief has something to do with this. Aboriginal peoples are not the only ones out of joint with their times. From their perspective we all are. Bob Randall, a mixed-race Aboriginal elder and member of the 'stolen generation' who in the 1930s were taken from their families to be educated and raised as white people, has spent many years retrieving his lost culture, belief and heritage. With his remarkable book *Songman* (Randall, 2001) and documentary film *Kanyini*, he has become an educator of immense importance – a significant contributor to the dialogue on sustainable development. Through songs, paintings, dances, ceremony and stories, Randall has shown how Australian Aboriginal culture sees everything as being essentially connected, with no distinction between inner and outer worlds, material and creative forces, mind and body. *Tjukurrpa*, 'the Dreaming', is the Aboriginal knowledge of creation, of past, present and future. Sand paintings communicate this dreaming within ceremonies performed to pass on the deepest of knowledge. After the ceremonies, the paintings are dispersed, but the knowledge remains within the people, continuing to inform their ideas and ways of living and connecting. The Earth is the progenitor of everyone and everything, and as such all living creatures are part of one family. There is no 'I', just a multiplicity of 'we's. Unlike the white man and his notion of property and property rights, says Randall, the Aborigine cannot own the land, cannot own the Earth, for we all belong to the land. Everything in nature is part of the family. No one is, or can be, a stranger, for *kanyini* (connectedness) keeps the spirit alive through an unconditional love and sense of responsibility for all things.

Aboriginal people practise *kanyini* by learning to restrict 'mine-ness' and by developing 'our-ness'. Bill Neidjie (1986), another Aboriginal elder, like Bob Randall, whose poetry and wisdom have helped recover this cultural heritage, offers everyone the opportunity to share and embrace this alternative, indigenous worldview. He writes of the land, of life (Neidjie, 1986: 51):

> All my uncle gone,
> But this story I got him.
> They told me ...
> They taught me ...
> And I can feel it.
>
> I feel it with my body,
> With my blood.
> Feeling all these trees,

All this country
When this wind blow you can feel it.
Same for country . . .
You feel it.
You can look,
But feeling . . .
That make you.

Feeling make you,
Out there in open space.
He coming through your body.
Look while he blow and feel with your body . . .
Because tree just about your brother or father . . .
And tree is watching you.

Earth . . .
Like your father or brother or mother,
Because you born from earth.
You got to come back to earth.
When you dead . . .
You'll come back to earth.
Maybe little while yet . . .
Then you'll come to earth.
That's your bone,
Your blood.
It's in this earth,
Same for tree.

Gregory Cajete, a Native American educator and academic, offers a similar story. His concern is with education as the vehicle for rearticulating the intimate relationship of the American Indian to the environment, to cultural and physical survival, and to cultural identity and purpose. He writes that thinking, acting and working were traditionally played out through nature, expressed in art and through work, in hunting and respect for those animals who give their lives so human persons can live. Forests and ravens should be respected because they sustain human culture and spirituality (Nelson, 1986). Respect is again the key to life and creation. 'Indigenous people', Cajete writes (1999: 11), 'felt responsibility not only for themselves, but also for the entire world around them. The world renewal ceremonies conducted by all indigenous people are reflections of this deep ecological sensibility and responsibility.' Traditional, invariably local, ecological knowledge maintained physical as well as spiritual health through knowledge of foods, plants and medicinal herbs. Ill health grew when indigenous peoples took to eating the highly processed and refined Western foods, when their own gardens, like their culture, ceased to be nurtured, causing their nutritional and medical knowledge to wither and almost die. Gardens are important particularly to the Pueblos of New Mexico. Cajete continues:

The garden becomes not only a place to watch plants grow, but a direct way for young people to participate in the greater circle of life. As young people work the soil, plant seeds, nurture seedlings and harvest crops, they experience the fuller development of their natural connections and participate in the age-old Pueblo way of connecting to place and living a healthy life.

(1999: 53)

One logical extension of this worldview is the philosophy and practice of permaculture, where nothing is wasted, everything is used and all life is respected. This thinking has influenced a great deal of environmental education in the developed world (see Chapter 9).

TEK is therefore neither quaint nor antiquated. It is being increasingly exploited commercially by pharmaceutical and other big corporations, whose patent applications frequently conjure up property rights from life itself as well as the culture and environment that fostered it (Shiva, 2000). However, governments, the scientific establishment and the major conservation bodies have slowly recognized the significance of TEK in other ways. Indigenous peoples are now more often than not incorporated in to large-scale projects to protect areas rich in biodiversity. As people who know and work the land, they have traditionally conserved and used it wisely, and are increasingly doing so again. Only by protecting cultural diversity can biodiversity be protected too. As Mark Dowie writes in his book *Conservation Refugees*: 'Every shaman, healer, chief and elder knows that without biotic wealth there is no food security. Thus biological diversity becomes an expression of culture. They appear and disappear together' (2009: 91).

In Indonesia, since the late 1970s, there has been a revival of interest in traditional medicine and particularly herbal remedies as part of a larger campaign to promote the prevention of illness, to foster self-reliance and improve the health status of the population. Indigenous knowledge and wisdom has consequently been re-evaluated in its partial integration into primary healthcare programmes, resulting in a widening recognition and acceptance of indigenous cosmologies 'in which an equilibrium between the natural and supernatural forces is reflected in the balanced interrelationship between health and disease' (Slikkerveer and Slikkerveer, 1995). Culture, religion, wisdom and spirituality enables many Aboriginal peoples to have a direct, emotional, ethical and often personal involvement in the reasonable use and sustainable management of a variety of natural resources (Lansing and Kremer, 1995; Anderson, 1996). It also offers Western environmental philosophers an opportunity to re-evaluate the epistemological basis of Western ethical systems. Cheney, for example, argues that being able to apprehend the sacred in the Earth, as indigenous peoples do, may enable Westerners to understand existence as something more-than-human. Assuming those in the West are sufficiently mindful of such a consideration, the enduring presence of rocks will become our most important teachers: 'Once we give up epistemologies of domination and control, nature's complexity, generosity and communicative abilities, its kinship and reciprocity, come to mark our epistemological relationship with the Earth matrix' (Cheney, 1998: 274).

Latour: relations and networks

Connectedness is increasingly influencing political thought and policy making. In *Politics of Nature*, Bruno Latour (2004a) wishes to move beyond a concept of nature that sees nature as an asocial objective source of truth. For Latour, the essentially political division between this nature and the social is both subjective and contestable. 'Being' is conceived as external, with non-human actors unable to speak. Nature has been a silent partner in the development of human civilizations. It has been scientists, politicians, academics and others located in the political sphere who have consequently spoken for nature. For Latour, political ecology means critiquing, or destroying, this notion of nature, while rendering political all those practices that 'naturalize' this way of thinking, doing and being. Another aspect of Latour's project is to recognize the complexity of all those socio-natural actors, instruments and practices that address common matters of concern. Science has an important role to play here, but it is not alone. Reality is assembled more or less experimentally from the practices of both human and non-human actors. It 'grows' as new coalitions of fact, value, being and recognition are created, and this has profound ethical implications for how we conceive of politics, act politically and communicate democratically. Latour also believes (2004b) that critique has gone too far, that social constructivism has gone too far. The world should not just be understood and valued in human terms. Global warming is fact – admit it, say it, stop disputing it or asking 'What do we mean by?'. There have been too many instances where objective fact has been viewed, or represented, as ideological prejudice resulting from 'greenwashing' or the naked exercise of power by those interests who are, or feel, threatened. So if critique, dialogue and deliberation is to be renewed, critical analysis must direct itself to 'matters of concern' rather than to 'matters of fact', which are always partial, rarely revealing themselves in full to our understanding and experience. Matters of concern and matters of fact are not necessarily distinct or separate, but the former are things we care about, which are important to us, which we value, in which our past, present and future is engaged – in other words, which matter – like climate change, poverty, injustice, the future.

Latour has been influential in developing and promoting what has become known as 'actor network theory' (ANT). Not only subjects (people) are active, and not only objects are passive, in relations between (social) agents and (natural) conditions or (science-based) technologies. At least initially, all three should be considered as equal participants in a range of heterogeneously complex networks constituting the world we have shaped, know and relate to. As such, ANT is concerned with both desocialization and denaturalization, thereby either bridging, or eradicating, such conceptual divides as human vs. environment or local vs. global. Things can only be defined in relation to other things, and they become what they are, and what they mean, through those social and ecological relations and networks. Latour uses the term 'performativity' to describe this process. This network approach to understanding the world has some profound implications for sustainable development and for environmental politics. From an ANT perspective, opposing genetic modification (GM) or nanotechnology on the grounds of their not being 'natural' is neither feasible nor logically conceivable. Everything human beings help shape may be seen as 'unnatural'. Art and architecture are unnatural. So, given this, the problem really boils down to what 'unnatural' meaningfully signifies in our everyday speech and academic specialized discourse and how we understand the implications of such understandings. There are some key questions about how decisions are made, what they are, who benefits and who suffers. These questions, like the process of sustainable development itself, are themselves political, and this is probably why Latour's (2004a) intellectual journey has taken him from science to social science and specifically to the politics of nature. We often have a choice. We can think. We can act. We can say 'no'.

The philosopher Kate Soper, taking a complementary approach, articulates the political imbrications of GM, and by extension sustainable development, in this way:

> History is a transitory affair from which there is no going back, and in and through which the fate of first nature is always at any moment being decided. New technical developments, such as GM, are always arresting because of the way in which we discern in them the irreversibility of our economic and political decisions and practices. To commit to GM, for example, is to know that the pre-GM moment will not come again, and that in that sense it will create a certain fatedness, becoming part of 'second nature'. But we also know there is nothing fated about the commitment itself.
>
> (2005: 133–4)

Systems thinking and complexity

Many phenomena do not easily lend themselves to a linear, reductionist or classically scientific method of analysis and explanation. Climate change, population, global ecology, the economy and organizational management offer so many variables, uncertainties and possibilities that confident predictions of future trends and tendencies are not always easy, or even possible, to make. Many promoters of sustainable development have been influenced by the study of ecology, recognizing systems thinking as being particularly relevant to their ongoing work. Indeed, systems thinking is not confined to the work of ecologists, as its influence is felt throughout the social, human and natural sciences. Sterling (2004) applies systems thinking to his work on sustainable education and Capra (1996, 2002) has carefully rearticulated systems thinking and complexity theory to produce a 'new scientific understanding of living systems' and a new 'science for sustainable living'. Complex adaptive systems identify problems and possibilities that are simultaneously multidimensional, dynamic and evolving.

A systems approach involves examining the connections and relationships between objects and events as much as the objects and events themselves. Changes in one component of the system will lead to changes in another, which in turn may lead to changes elsewhere. Interactions occur between system components that may cause both themselves and the system itself to change. Systems theorists write of negative and positive feedback loops, emergent properties, dynamic equilibrium, hierarchy, communication, evolution, system adaptation, and system breakdown. In general, the more complex a system and the more interlocking its feedback loops, the more robust and better able they are to resist change. Emergence is a key concept in systems thinking equally applicable to the natural and social sciences. Mihata (1997) notes that it is frequently used when referring to the process by which global-level structures or patterns evolve from local-level interactions and from relatively simple rules. These 'complex adaptive systems' are 'characterized not only by a high degree of interaction among component parts, but also by the way that the particular nature of this interaction – the way the system is organized – generates outcomes not linearly related to initial conditions' (Mihata, 1997: 31–2).

Whereas linear organization is said to be in large part predictable, emergence is a property of non-linear systems whose mode of organization makes for non-obvious, and sometimes surprising, consequences. Relationships are important between levels of a system as well as between parts of the whole. It is therefore possible to view societal, group or organizational culture as each exhibiting emergent characteristics. Such an emergent culture is difficult to measure, operationalize or restrict to lower levels, since no emergent phenomenon can easily be linked in a simple manner to any one specific cause. Culture – that is, the way people make sense of their reality through their thoughts, actions, objects and values – may be conceptualized as emergent patterns occurring at multiple levels and environments affecting every individual person through their learning, experience, and social and other interactions. Industrial systems too may be likened to biological ecosystems, although as Graedel (1996) notes in his discussion of industrial ecology, the analogy is not exact, although it is to ecology that advocates of closed-loop production systems look for inspiration and guidance.

The planet's ecology is very complex and will accommodate a significant amount of stress, but there are limits and thresholds. The very complexity of the global ecology often makes human knowledge and understanding of it partial and scientific certainty improbable. Disputes over scientific findings frequently arise, and consensus occurs only after protracted debate and discussion, as the climate change issue bears witness. As Clayton and Radcliffe (1996: 34–5) write:

> It is clear that human actions are causing changes to ecosystems and other systems in the biosphere, the troposphere and the stratosphere. Some of these changes are relatively large, and some are occurring at rates that make adaptive and evolutionary response very difficult. It is possible that no combination of changes of this magnitude has occurred since the major extinction boundaries. If the levels of environmental impact, including the reduction in genetic diversity, continue at current rates, the likelihood of regional and possibly even global ecological instability must tend to increase.

Analysts frequently talk in terms of probabilities rather than certainties. With every predicted outcome there will be a margin of error that makes the calculation of risk both exceptionally important and quite difficult. This raises many challenges for policymakers, scientists, businesses, communities, peoples and nations. What are the risks associated with global warming? What are the costs and benefits? What policy options are available? Is it possible, indeed ethical, to place monetary value on such risks, particularly when lives and livelihoods are at stake? What will be the consequences and the risks involved in continuing a given pattern of behaviour – for example, the burning of fossil fuels? Ordinary people's perceptions of risk may be at variance with the technical assessments of experts, and indeed may be disproportionate. Fear and perception of a risk, as with crime, is often higher than its recorded incidence. When children are exposed to risk, adults feel particularly anxious, so citizens and politicians demand clear and direct answers, actions and solutions. However, life and science are not like that, and sometimes politicians prefer to ignore scientific evidence or political scenarios that may be electorally unpopular or which constitute, as Al Gore stated in his 2006 documentary, *An Inconvenient Truth*. Additionally, it should be remembered, as Carnap (1966), Durham (1992) and particularly Cairns (2003) have argued, that even in the 'hardest' sciences, like physics, frequently noted for their rigour and precision, uncertainty seems to be the rule. Thus, in the project to fashion a sustainable planet, uncertainty will inevitably figure greatly as experimentation is difficult when there is only one planet. There can be no control, many disciplines are involved and an ethical reluctance to experiment with human cultures, combined with a political reluctance to see beyond the next election, simply adds to the challenge. Cairns (2003: 3–4) writes that, because of continuing uncertainty, ethics and social learning will be necessarily an important part of any decision-making process. He continues:

> Humankind is now moving from the age of reductionist science to an age of synthesis or integrative science. This transition does not mean that reductionist science is no longer appropriate, but rather that as levels of complexity in any system increase, new properties emerge that were not apparent at lower levels. Consequently, one means of reducing uncertainty in this age of synthesis is determining how congruent a particular hypothesis or body of evidence is with other related bodies of evidence within the particular system being studied.

Both systems and systems-thinking continually evolve. For instance, from recent studies of natural hazards, systems thinkers write of the relationship between uncertainty, vulnerability and resilience. An ecological, social or economic system may experience some disturbance, such as an oil spill, crime rise or bank failure, but it is the resilience or capacity of the system to absorb this disturbance and reorganize itself, while experiencing change and still maintaining essentially the same function, structure, identity and feedbacks, that is truly important (Folke *et al.*, 2003; Berkes, 2007). Some disturbances, like climate change, will affect everything, and complexity theory and resilience thinking enables us to recognize that disturbances will have broad-based, non-linear consequences. A threshold point may arrive when one relatively stable state, or regime, flips into another. In social-ecological systems, such as a local neighbourhood community, adaptability and resilience will inevitably be the product of human agency, of individual and institutional leadership, of the capacity to learn from previous experience, of the strength of social and cultural networks and relationships, and of the capacity to remember past mistakes and not repeat them. Resilience is not a concept that looks back or has a single straightforward meaning. Rather it a concept that is generative of approaches that require positive, proactive change and transformation (Blewitt and Tilbury, 2013). As Jared Diamond (2005) has shown in his highly detailed examination of why some societies collapse, and why some people simply do not learn, do not see, understand, remember or care, our mechanistic conceptual frameworks have led us to underestimate or simply be blind to system effects even when they are upon us. As Diamond asks, 'What did that person think when he felled the last tree on Easter Island?' Instead of hierarchy, of seeing one thing as more important than another, there is panarchy (Holling, 2001, 2004), meaning a basic equality and connectedness between systems and subsystems. For Walker and Salt (2006) and Berkes (2007), resilience thinking offers important opportunities for fashioning new ways of coping with future surprises and unknowable risks through intentionally building up resilience in social-ecological systems. This can be achieved by:

- learning to live with change and uncertainty;
- nurturing ecological, social, economic and cultural diversity;

- combining different types of knowledge (indigenous and scientific) forlearning; and
- creating opportunity for self-organization through:
  - strengthening community-based management;
  - building cross-scale management capabilities;
  - strengthening institutional memory;
  - nurturing learning organizations and adaptive co-management.

The logic of a systems analysis is that economic activity, environmental impact, social experience, political action and cultural attitudes are not discrete and containable. Another possible implication of this approach is a policy of precaution and prudence; with knowledge being limited, decision-making on sustainability issues becomes clearly both political and ethical.

Box 2.2 Resilience and systems thinking in practice

The Millennium Ecosystem Assessment (MEA) is a clear example of resilience thinking and sustainability science (Reid *et al.*, 2006). The MEA is deeply complex, complicated and often difficult to follow in detail, particularly when one's long-held assumptions and established habits of mind and behaviour are overturned.

Strategies that have a high probability of enhancing resilience to future change

Strategies	Description
Foster ecological, economic, social and cultural diversity	Diversity provides the seeds for new opportunities and maximizes options for coping with change. By supporting and protecting diversity, countries or regions render themselves less vulnerable to adverse effects of future change.
Plan for changes that may possibly occur	By recognizing the directional nature, and drivers, of current changes, countries have the opportunity to design the institutional flexibility necessary to anticipate and adjust to change.
Foster learning	Countries, communities, non-governmental organizations (NGOs) and government agencies can learn by collaborating closely to examine patterns of response to hazards and learn which policy options show promise. Particularly effective are learning networks of public, private and civil society actors.
Communicate the societal consequences of recent changes	Societal consequences of hazards are felt at multiple levels. The communication of the consequences of perturbations is important in order to understand actual local impacts and adaptations. This communication enables a convincing case to be argued that the global nature of causes warrants global action.

Source: Adapted from Berkes (2007, p. 293).

From Gaia hypothesis to Gaia theory

The Gaia hypothesis was first formulated by James Lovelock and Lyn Margulis in the 1960s and 1970s and is a clear example of systems thinking. It has been both highly influential and quite controversial, not least in its practical implications for sustainable development. Basically, the idea is that the Earth acts as a self-organizing system, ensuring life, in its various forms, co-evolves in tandem with changes to the physical configuration of the planet's animate and inanimate components. This self-regulation is dynamic. The Earth seeks accommodation and balance in the face of a large number of internal and external factors. Some proponents of Gaia see the Earth itself as an organism, with the Earth's systems manipulating climate to ensure life continues to emerge and exist. Lovelock (1979: 10) initially conceived Gaia as a *teleological* process consisting of:

> The entire range of living matter on Earth, from whales to viruses and from oaks to algae, could be regarded as constituting a single living entity capable of maintaining the Earth's atmosphere to suit its overall needs and endowed with faculties and powers far beyond those of its constituent parts. [Gaia can be defined] as a complex entity involving the Earth's biosphere, atmosphere, oceans and soil, the totality constituting a feedback of *cybernetic systems* which seeks an optimal physical and chemical environment for life on this planet.

Following considerable criticism and debate within and beyond the scientific community, Lovelock refined his ideas, and by the turn of the century Gaia had become firmly established in the intellectual landscape of environmentalists, many scientists, sustainability practitioners and New Age travellers. In the second edition of *The Ages of Gaia*, Lovelock wrote:

> The name of the superorganism, Gaia, is not a synonym for the biosphere. The biosphere is defined as that part of the Earth where living things normally exist. Still less is Gaia the same as the biota, which is simply the collection of all individual living organisms. The biota and biosphere taken together form part but not all of Gaia. Just as the shell is part of a snail, so the rocks, the air, and the oceans are part of Gaia. Gaia, as we shall see, has continuity with the past back to the origins of life, and extends into the future as long as life persists. Gaia, as a planet sized entity, has properties that are not necessarily discernible by just knowing individual species or populations of organisms living together.
> (Lovelock, 1995: 21)

Lovelock suggests that many people may find it hard to believe that anything as large and inanimate as the Earth is actually alive. After all, most of it is rock and the centre is extremely hot. However, he argues that one way to understand Gaia is to think of a giant redwood tree. It is certainly alive, although about 99 per cent of it is quite possibly dead. The giant redwood is an ancient column of dead wood, composed of lignin and cellulose derived from layers and layers of cells built up over a long time. The tree is thus analogous to the Earth, particularly when we realize that many of the atoms of the rocks deep down in the magma were once part of the ancestral life from which we have all evolved. More recently, in *The Revenge of Gaia* (2006), Lovelock has continued to generate considerable controversy and debate by suggesting that climate change and disturbance is so severe that within a few decades the Arctic will be open sea and that the only way for human intervention to be effective is for the developing world, particularly China and India, to forgo carbon-based economic development. In the developed world there needs to be a fundamental change in energy generation and policy. The world's optimum population is probably in the region of half to one billion people. This figure would allow humans to live in diverse ways without harming Gaia. If the population exceeds this, it is likely that 'in the end, as always, Gaia will do the culling and eliminate those that break her rules' (Lovelock, 2006: 141). Lovelock is also a firm advocate of clean nuclear power. Nothing else, he argues, is likely to do the job of powering the global economy.

The Schumacher College scholar Stephan Harding (2006) has further developed Gaia theory, focusing on the need to develop a holistic understanding and practice of science and, through this, an empathic relationship with the Earth itself. Harding writes of one simple rule that has emerged from over twenty years of Gaian research: any organism destabilizing Gaia will experience feedbacks that will reduce its numbers. There are clear lessons for humans here. We cannot ultimately harm Gaia; we may destroy many species, including our own, but we cannot destroy Gaia. It will always return, re-emerge, but nonetheless, by promoting nature-destroying, climate-warming economic growth, we could initiate catastrophic Gaian feedbacks that will eliminate many future possibilities.

Ecological modernization

Ecological modernization (EM) entered the policy discourse some time in the 1980s, initially to describe technological developments with environmentally beneficial outcomes – chlorine-free bleaching of pulp for paper, more fuel-efficient cars, clean nuclear energy, and so on – fully compatible with Lovelock's Gaia theory. A little later there emerged four ecological modernization strategies, two that were remedial (compensation and environmental restoration; technical pollution control) and two that were preventative or anticipatory (environmentally friendly technical innovation; structural change). EM became seen primarily as a way of reducing costs and improving business competitiveness rather than articulating any major changes in political, public or corporate values. In the 1990s EM took on a more radical ambience, with references to ecological emancipation and the emergence of a new belief system, prefiguring systemic change and a broad transformation of social relations. However, there remain a few unresolved tensions, as Christoff (1996) identified. These include:

- Is EM economistic or ecological?
- National or international?
- Is there just one hegemonic path to modernization or are there multiple possibilities?
- Technocratic or democratic? (Should citizens participate in the planning process or should it be left simply to the 'experts'?)

Christoff also identifies weak and strong versions of EM:

The strongest or most radically ecological notion of ecological modernization will often stand in opposition to industrial modernity's predominantly instrumental relationship to nature as exploitable resource. Recognition that overproduction – the use of material resources beyond regional and global ecological capacities – must cease because of the threat of imminent ecological collapse does not allow for the self-serving gradualism of the weak forms of ecological modernization.

(1996: 495)

The 'strong' ecological modernizers feel there has been a general decline in the value and probity of industrial progress and seek to develop new ecological modernities based on human and environmental rights, social learning and a critical reflexivity that accords effectively with various, often weaker, notions of sustainable development that seek to provide a greener face to capitalist development without altering its fundamental trajectory. Thus, one key issue of contention between weak and strong EM is whether capitalism is able to reform or reorganize itself and be sustainable. Mol and Spaargaren suggest that:

mainstream modernization theorists interpret capitalism neither as an essential precondition for, nor as the key obstruction to, stringent or radical environmental reform. They focus instead on redirecting and transforming 'free market capitalism' in such a way that it less and less obstructs, and increasingly contributes to, the preservation of society's sustenance base in a fundamental/structural way.

(2000: 23)

Whatever the issues between the weak and the strong advocates, EM has succeeded in placing the environment more firmly on government, business, community and industrial agendas. However, as Mol and Spaargaren (2000) also point out, EM differs from radical ecocentrists in two significant ways: 'EM does not give environmental objectives an undisputed priority over other societal objectives. Radical proposals for environmental improvement do not automatically entail radical societal change in the sense promoted by ecocentrists.'

York and Rosa (2003: 274) are highly sceptical about whether current trends in institutional change and economic growth will enable societies to become more sustainable. EM theory needs to go beyond being largely reactive, to initiate processes leading to ecological transformation, harnessing green business models that impact lightly on the Earth, and energy and resource use that is efficient and effective:

EM theory suggests the possibility that inherent in the process of late modernization are self-referential mechanisms – such as the need to internalize environmental impacts in order to ensure future production inputs – that have the potential to lead to ecological sustainability. It argues for the potential of attaining sustainability from within – a greening of 'business as usual' – thereby avoiding such challenging alternatives as radical structural or value changes in society. The pivotal question, then, is the extent to which such expectations are justified.

The promise of new technology

Industrial ecologists are often associated with EM. They analyse flows of material and energy that connect business enterprise with the natural world in a continuous feedback loop operating in roughly three stages:

1   Natural materials are extracted from the Earth and converted into raw materials and energy.
2   These raw materials and energy flows are then worked up into usable and saleable products.
3   The resulting products are distributed, consumed or used, and disposed of by consumers.

All of these stages produce waste, which becomes pollution unless it is recycled or reused. The problem with much industrial ecology, as Hoffman (2003) notes, is that it takes an overly technical-engineering perspective that fails to accommodate the impact of individual cognition, organizational culture or social institutions on the direction of these material and energy flows. Hoffman writes of the value of analysing environmental issues from an 'open systems' perspective, recognizing that no organization operates in complete isolation, protected from external interaction and control. The application of methodological approaches from other disciplines – for example, economics, sociology, law, ethics or systems dynamics – enables industrial ecologists to make links and ask questions they would not otherwise have done. There is a need to find ways of ensuring that 'organizations think and act systematically within their social ecologies', displacing the well-established assumption that environmental protection inevitably means a loss of economic competitiveness.

Philosophers Albert Borgmann (1984), Langdon Winner (1997) and Aidan Davison (2001, 2004) see technological development as a complex social, cultural and political phenomenon. Technical innovations such as the car, cell phone or solar panel inevitably involve a reshaping of society. Change is multifaceted, so technology should not be seen as its only cause. Nonetheless, it would be unwise to suggest that new technical devices such as the car or mobile phone do not change social practices, patterns of behaviour, individual and cultural identities, or the nature of work, learning and community. We do not always perceive the influence of technology, because devices quickly become embedded into the fabric of our lives and the overall wheel of consumption, acquisition and accumulation. We soon see these devices as desirable or meaningful ends in themselves, rather than as a means to live lives in different or better ways. We may see technology as the means to combat pollution, climate change, global poverty, civic violence and alienation, world hunger, and disease without recognizing that the problems are not amenable to a simple technological fix and may, in fact, have been caused by technological innovation in the first place. For Davison (2001), ecological modernization privileges this technological fix. He suggests that the Brundtland Report's conceptualization of sustainable development, the declarations of Rio and Johannesburg, and the many eco-efficiency arguments expressed by governments and the World Business Council for Sustainable Development bear witness to the resilience of this idea. The resurrection of interest in nuclear power as a green energy source and as a means of arresting climate change is part of this discourse where faith in, or political adherence to, technology and (sound) science closes off questions and alternative possibilities. Moral and technological development and economic progress (if not growth) become aligned with instrumental policy frameworks, including measurements and quantifications that encode moral, managerial and political perspectives that deny the significance of other ways of seeing and doing things. In other words, our increasingly technological society has become integral to the way we understand and interpret the world, our proclivities and predispositions, and the structures of our thought and action, at times even shaping our tactile, sensory and aesthetic experiences of the world. Technology is not a neutral vehicle of human agency, but rather its essence. It must be fashioned to match who we are, who we want to become, and the type of world we need to build and sustain. Like sustainable development, technology is a political act. As Davison writes:

> The more we pursue goals of subjective choice, the more frantically we build a world in which means and ends are dislocated – a circular dynamic that only accelerates the processes of technological proliferation. And the more technology proliferates, the more our objective world is alien to us and opaque in our reflections. Moral inquiry is internalized into the task of self-understanding and self-expression, rather than that of world understanding and world-building. Self-expression becomes self-creation in a world meaningful only to the extent that human production creates and sustains it.
>
> (2004: 94)

Biotechnology, nanotechnology, genetic engineering, nuclear power, hybrid cars and wind turbines are all themselves expressions of human practical reason, moral choices and indeed a cultural value system (or systems). There may be no easy or readily apparent answers, but we do need to see technology (and science) as being constitutive of the ends we wish to fashion, rather than as ends in themselves.

Case study: nuclear power

In *The Revenge of Gaia* (2006), James Lovelock argues that if it had not been for the triumph of romantic idealism at Kyoto, we could all be enjoying the benign benefits of nuclear fusion technology. Nuclear power is easy to produce, creates little waste, most of which is completely harmless, and is free of CO_2 emissions, and its radioactivity has negligible effects on human health. In fact, previous nuclear disasters have been disasters in name only – few people have been killed (75 in the 20 years following Chernobyl), with contaminated areas turning into wildlife havens because they scare away hungry farmers and greedy developers. As a major element in a portfolio of low-carbon energy resources, nuclear power will enable reasonable economic development and lifestyle improvements to continue. The alternative is a Malthusian global depopulation, a serious undermining of everyone's standard of living and the ending of hope for the developing nations. This view has received support from Jesse Ausubel (2007) who, writing in the *International Journal of Nuclear Governance, Economy and Ecology*, refers to renewable energy resources as 'boutique fuels' that look good in small quantities but that, compared with nuclear power and natural gas with carbon capture, are grossly inefficient and have serious implications for land-use planning. Do you want a wind farm spoiling your view?

Furthermore, to produce energy equivalent to that generated by a 1,000 megawatt nuclear power plant would require, from biofuels, 2,500 square kilometres of good farmland or, from solar energy, 150 square kilometres of photovoltaic cells. The US would need to devote land the size of Texas if it met all its energy needs from wind power. However, for Helen Caldicott (2006) and John Turner, from the US National Renewable Energy Laboratory (McKenna, 2007), these arguments are fallacious and misleading. Land used for turbines can still be used for grazing, and the amount already paved over for roads and car parks in all major countries is immense and growing. Biofuels are problematic too, as many crops take over land that could be devoted to food production, although research on biomass thermal conversion technologies which process agricultural wastes, fast-growing wood and biogenic wastes has produced some very positive results. With carbon emissions increasing steadily, attention has once more shifted to nuclear energy, although the costs and time required for building new plants and bringing them fully on-stream mean that more extensive nuclear energy generation is a solution for the 2020s, by which time global climate change would have further worsened. There are other problems with nuclear such as the environmental costs and impact of extracting uranium from the world's dwindling supply. Large amounts of fossil fuels are often still required to mine and refine the mineral, and the link between civil nuclear power and military use is undeniable, as US critiques of the nuclear power programmes in Iran and North Korea eloquently testify. Nuclear waste includes toxic contaminants that cause leukaemia and other cancers and genetic disease. Caldicott questions both the science and politics of nuclear energy and the implicit complacency in the expectation that this technology is the 'magic bullet'. Changes will have to occur to the way we think problems through, the way we apply reasoned and moral judgements that seek alternative practical pathways, ways of living and being. Renewable energy, she writes, 'is quick to build, abundant and cheap to harvest; it is safe, flexible, secure and climate-friendly' (2006: 164); and, married to a lifestyle respectful of natural resources, human and non-human others, renewable technology will help shape a world that is sustainable and worth sustaining. This is undoubtedly the case, but with the global population certain to increase by around two billion by 2050 and with the global need to address the perennial poverty of global poverty energy, demands are anticipated to increase by around 35 per cent by 2035 with China, India and the Middle East counting for 60 per cent of the increase (IEA, 2012) nuclear energy is back on the global agenda. The current energy mix is still dominated by heavily subsidized fossil fuels – US$523 billion in 2011 or six times that of subsidies to renewables – and nuclear is a generally accepted low carbon energy source. Between 1978 and 1988, when France adopted its extensive nuclear power programme, carbon emissions fell by an average of 3.7 per cent per annum. France has one of the most carbon-efficient economies in the world. A 1GW nuclear power station can produce up to ten times more power than a 1GW solar plant because nuclear operates 24 hours a day. In addition, next generation nuclear technologies such as thorium liquid salt reactors and integral fast reactors mean that smaller, safer, plants could be built and operate, which would not go into meltdown as happened in Fukushima in 2011. These new reactors could also consume existing plutonium waste and the thorium approach, initially investigated in the US in the 1960s, is not particularly suitable for the construction of nuclear warheads – the reason why the US abandoned the thorium projects at the time. However, the

Fukushima disaster in Japan, caused by a massive earthquake and tsunami, has dampened down enthusiasm for nuclear. Radiation levels have been eighteen times higher than anticipated and decommission will take up to forty years and cost tens of billions of dollars (McCurry, 2013). In 2012, Germany decided to close down its existing nuclear power plants and invest more heavily in clean fossil fuel technologies and renewables. Germany is a global leader in solar energy and has been instrumental in stimulating the solar industries in China. For countries such as Denmark, a 100 per cent renewable energy strategy is certainly feasible (Lund, 2007) but, given the global scale of the energy issues we face, there needs to be a range of options facilitated by international cooperation, research and development. Jeong *et al.* make the following recommendations in order to increase energy sustainability:

> For countries with mature nuclear technologies it will be advantageous to deploy fast reactor systems and complete a closed fuel cycle.
>
> Governments and society need to support and promote energy efficient technologies and energy conservation.
>
> International organizations need to prepare plans that actively encourage collaboration and transfer of renewable energy technologies including those relating to carbon sequestration.
>
> (2010: 1968)

Summary

This chapter has explored how values may and often do inform the dialogue, discussion and debates around both sustainability (the goal) and sustainable development (the process). Each position, or worldview, discussed, whether deep or shallow ecology, traditional ecological knowledge, eco-feminism, social ecology, Gaia theory or ecological modernization, has within it different shades of opinion and emphases. Each worldview is not cut off from any other, for in practice people share ideas or values, holding many in common without perhaps fully realizing it. In many ways, all the worldviews have something to offer to the student and practitioner of sustainable development, although this is not to say that each worldview is equally valid. There will be conflicts and contradictions too for sustainability and sustainable development are inherently complex, sometimes inviting rather eclectic formulations and suggestions. Given this, it is probably wise to retain an open mind, a critical and questioning attitude, and a belief in, and respect for, the intrinsic value of a democratic frame of mind.

Thinking questions

1 How do politics and values inform policy choices, such as those relating to energy?
2 To what extent must sustainable development necessarily involve major cultural changes? What do you think they might be and how might they come about?
3 To what extent is dialogue the most appropriate way to promote sustainable development?
4 How might bioregionalism, deep ecology or the fundamental values of TEK influence either current Western business models or urban planning processes?

5   What worldview appeals to you the most? Why?
6   Should one always feed people first?

Companion website

To further develop and test your understanding of the key values and worldviews discussed in this chapter such as social ecology, ecological modernization and Gaia, please visit the companion website.

3 Cultural and contested understandings of science and sustainability

Aims

This chapter will explore the contested nature of science in the sustainable development process. Key illustrations will be drawn from the debates and controversies over climate change and genetic modification. The cultural and sometimes national context of these debates are also important as the discussion of sustainability in Russia demonstrates. The concept of risk, the precautionary principle and the theory of reflexive modernization will also be examined. The idea that sustainability is not a scientific concept as such, although it is, and should be informed by it is an underlying assumption of this chapter, even though in practice sustainability, and perhaps science too, is also a political act – but this, as with so much is a matter for dialogue and discussion.

From dialogue to learning: 'sustainability' as a heuristic

Professor John Robinson's perceptive commentary on sustainable development is concerned with the inherent contradictions within the concept. There is a focus on *growth* and *development* on the one hand, much appreciated by governments and business, and ecological sustainability on the other, a position taken by many NGOs, academic environmentalists and activists. Many critics consequently view the concept as being inherently contradictory and incapable of being effectively operationalized. Others have noted in response that there is a resilient compatibility within the concept and practice of sustainable development, which focuses on the ideas of freedom, of fulfilment, of being and securing what is truly valuable – the freedom to achieve, to effect solidarity with others, to develop capabilities and alternatives, and to live justly and meaningfully (Verburg and Wiegel, 1997; Sen, 1999; Stefanovic, 2000). In 'Sustainable development: Exploring the ethics of *Our Common Future*', Langhelle (1999) argues that the importance of economic growth has been overemphasized at the expense of the broadly ethical concerns of human togetherness, social justice, respect for ecological limits, and the eradication of global poverty and inequality. Social justice has much to do with the satisfaction of human needs, of securing equal opportunity between and within generations, global partnership and co-operation. It is this that defines the idea of development within sustainable development. 'Sustainable development' does not endorse 'calculative thinking' or the common managerialist desire to obsessively devise quantitative outputs, performance indicators and actions, although none of this is completely excluded. Neither is the preference for the term 'sustainability' (goal) to be used more readily than 'sustainable development' (process). There is perhaps less confusion or dispute over the former. Indeed, Robinson (2004: 370) prefers the term 'sustainability' to 'sustainable development', as it 'focuses attention where it should be placed, on the ability of humans to continue to live within environmental constraints'. Married to this, and coming from a phenomenological perspective, Stefanovic (2000) argues for more 'meditative thinking' – that is to say, more thoughts orientated towards investigating complexity and the relations between things, engaging with values, listening to the limits that our life-world brings forth, and recognizing that different cultures and histories have different rhythms of development and must therefore devise different policies. A human being, and indeed the planet, is far more than a resource. Indicators must, and will inevitably, reflect and articulate our values, enabling us to recognize that life is far more than being busy, accomplishing more and more concrete tasks, or securing more and more goods. The quality of life becomes more important than the commodities our economy produces and we consume. Human life and the environment are not two separate entities: we are on and of the world. We must think and act wisely.

By analysing many published definitions, institutional goals and established indicators, measures and values as expressed in the UN Millennium Declaration, their replacement in the SDGs or in the actions and negotiated compromises of social movements, businesses and NGOs, Kates *et al.* (2005) show there are a number of ways in which sustainable development may be understood. Some of the successes of sustainable development are the grand but workable compromises that have emerged in Rio, Kyoto and Johannesburg between competing, and sometimes ideologically opposed, environmental, economic and social interest groups. This is why many agreements on sustainable development necessarily include dialogue and open, and hopefully transparent and democratic, decision-making. It is part of the practice. Much of the power, potential and resonance of sustainable development is therefore derived from a certain, perhaps intentional, 'creative ambiguity', allowing people to engage in a multitude of ways and at a multitude of levels, from the local to the truly global. The concept is therefore adaptable. It can be, and is, applied to the planning of cities, the fashioning of a new art of living, agriculture, architecture, construction, fishing, business, education – in fact, to every field. Sustainable development also has a set of core guiding principles that will adapt and change as time passes, as people discuss and as the world inevitably moves on. Dialogue and critique must be key to such a process, although many people will inevitably find their own ideas, assumptions and ways of living being examined, challenged and contested.

Development and modernization has undoubtedly improved diets in many parts of the world, but the increase in meat eating and cattle rearing not only further stresses the environment and may lead to new problems – for example, obesity among certain more affluent groups within India – but also lead directly to increases in greenhouse gas emissions. Ruminative animals produce a lot of methane and 7.1 gigatonnes of CO_2 per annum, or 14.5 per cent of human-induced GHG emissions, as a consequence of their natural digestive processes (Gerber *et al.*, 2013). Having said that, Leiserowitz *et al.* (2005), in their thorough multinational study of global attitudes towards the environment, technology, the human–nature relationship, economic growth, income equity, consumerism and much else, concluded that in general the global public basically supports the main tenets of sustainable development. However, the authors certainly found many contradictions, not least in the differences between what people say, both as individuals and as groups, and what they actually do. For instance, science and technology generated positive attitudes, but the most technologically sophisticated individuals seemed to be the least certain about the ability of science and technology to solve global problems. Most people value the environment for both ecocentric and anthropocentric reasons, but ecosystems are in serious decline. The majority of people think something more should be done about it. Development assistance was also widely supported, but its extent was frequently overestimated, and many felt that the poor themselves were to blame. Income inequalities were often accepted as being basic facts of life. The authors also noted the barriers to pro-sustainability action as being, first, this very contradictory nature of people's consciousness; second, people's own capabilities, in that they frequently lacked time, skills, knowledge and power; and third, inadequate laws, regulations and infrastructure, perverse subsidies, the inadequacy of available technology and little political will. Explaining unsustainable behaviour seems as complex as explaining sustainable development itself, but bridging the gap between sustainable attitudes and unsustainable behaviour is essential for any transition to a fairer society. Long term, the key to this transition is probably rearticulating the meaning of human well-being, of the good life, even though socially pervasive materialist attitudes and consumerist values are often very difficult to change. In the short term, Leiserowitz *et al.* suggest that:

> leveraging the values and attitudes already dominant in particular cultures may be more practical than asking people to adopt new value orientations. For example, economic values clearly influence and motivate many human behaviours, especially in the market and cash economies of the developed countries. Incorporating environmental and social 'externalities' into prices or accounting for the monetary value of ecosystem services can thus encourage both individual and collective sustainable behaviour. Likewise, anthropocentric concerns about the impacts of environmental degradation and exploitative labour conditions on human health and social wellbeing remain strong motivators for action in both the developed and developing worlds. Additionally, religious values are vital sources of meaning, motivation and direction for much of the world, and many religions are actively reevaluating and reinterpreting their traditions in support of sustainability.

> (2005: 35)

Thus, one of the main reasons why 'sustainable development' and 'sustainability' have generated so much discussion is because they tend to reflect the political and philosophical value base of those articulating a given definition or preferred perspective. For those who want an unambiguous scientific, technical, discipline-specific and/or operationable definition, this causes problems – but not for Robinson, who observes:

> Diplomats are familiar with the need to leave key terms undefined in negotiation processes, and in much the same way the term sustainable development may profit from what might be called constructive ambiguity. Certainly the plethora of competing definitions in the literature suggests that any attempt to define the concept precisely, even if it were possible, would have the effect of excluding those whose views were not expressed in that definition.

> (2004: 374)

What is needed, and what the creative ambiguity surrounding 'sustainability' can offer, is the possibility of integration, synthesis and synergy – of a social learning process that bridges the divisions between the social and ecological, the scientific and spiritual, the economic and the political. In practice, technical fixes are necessary but not sufficient if ecological, economic and social imperatives are to be reconciled. For Robinson, this cannot be done scientifically, only politically – in dialogue and in partnership, making sustainability 'the emergent property of a conversation about what kind of world we collectively want to live in now and in the future'. Robinson concludes that within the field of sustainability multiple conflicting views exist that cannot always be reconciled.

> In other words, no single approach will, or indeed should be, seen as the correct one. This is not a matter of finding out what the truth of sustainability is by more sophisticated applications of expert understanding (the compass and ruler). Instead we are inescapably involved in a world in which there exist multiple conflicting values, moral positions and belief systems that speak to the issue of sustainability. While it is crucial to identify points of empirical disagreement and to resolve those with better research and analysis, the ultimate questions are not susceptible to empirical confirmation or disconfirmation. What is needed, therefore, is a process by which these views can be expressed and evaluated, ultimately as a political act for any given community or jurisdiction.
>
> (2004: 382)

In this way, 'sustainable development' and 'sustainability' may productively function as a heuristic, in other words a learning process by which people are enabled to find things out for themselves and to fully appreciate the contested nature of knowledge, the environment and sustainability (Macnaghten and Urry, 1998) and the impact human actions have on the Earth (Marten, 2001). Indeed, in the twenty plus years since the first Rio Earth Summit much work on sustainability has been characterized by a commitment to multidimensionality and a multi-criteria assessment, including governance, of the progress or otherwise of the sustainable development process (Hamdouch and Zuindeau, 2010).

Understanding sustainable development and the noosphere in Russia

The government of the Russian Federation declared 2013 to be the year of environmental protection, but, asked Angelina Davydova (2013), is anyone really interested? In the 1990s and the first years of the twenty-first century 'sustainable' has generally been equated with continuing economic success understood as constant GDP growth. In the Soviet era industrialization meant conquering nature, building massive industrial plants, dams and the like, although the ecologically destructive industrialization around Lake Baikal led to an environmental awakening in the 1960s, which was again supplemented by a new concern for the environment following the Chernobyl disaster in 1986 (Whitehead, 2010). Not surprisingly perhaps, the conservation and sustainable management of forestry resources was an important element of Stalin's economic and environmental policy (Brain, 2010). Nonetheless, the growth of an albeit fragile civil society movement in Russia, including a Greenpeace office in Moscow and 5,000 members within the Federation, has also meant that community-based environmental protests against massive road developments, river and air pollution or uncontrolled logging are not unknown. Community-based environmental organizations in Russia, as elsewhere, are invariably short of funds, but it should also be noted that the environmental movement did play an important role in undermining the Soviet regime in its final years, and any progress towards environmental justice or 'just sustainability' in the former Soviet Union is often limited by political and national security as well as economic concerns (Agyeman and Himmelberger, 2009). NGOs are also often consulted by the Russian Government on a formal level by the WWF, which recently calculated that only 10 per cent of environmental policy requests, recommendations or orders emanating from the prime minister or president were actually implemented. For Mol (2009) and Whitehead (2010) the emphasis on developing Russia's resource sector economy has led to a gradual loss of strategic control over Russia's natural capital, with a consequent negative impact on environmental protection. Thus for Whitehead, this

> has generated a distinctly hollow feel to the sustainable development commitments that were made in the early periods of socio-economic transition. These hollow sustainabilities exemplify socio-environmental commitments that are girded by impressive policy pronunciations and institutional architectures, but which are ultimately betrayed in the avarice of economic redevelopment.
>
> (2010: 1631)

However, to understand whether or not sustainability is actually operating as a heuristic in Russia, it is necessary to go deeper into Russia's culture and her past. Initially it seemed that sustainable development would overtly become an important element in the country's transition from socialism following the collapse of the Soviet Union in 1991. Russia participated actively in the 1992 Rio conference and a number of important presidential decrees and legislative changes followed (Oldfield, 2001). This was not followed through, however, by the formulation and implemention of a comprehensive sustainable development planning strategy or construction of the necessary infrastructure to realize it. There is no policy framework for renewable energy technologies in Russia, which means that Russia's renewable energy development is not yet firmly established (Karghiev, 2006). The sheer geographical size of Russia, and its topography and diversity, does not make things easier either for government, NGOs or the grass-roots environmental movement. A sense that Russia is a special case, a global eco-service provider, resonates loudly with Russian nationalism and a notion of Russian exceptionalism. There are also massive contradictions within Russia – a free market economy violently induced by the neoliberal shock doctrine (Klein, 2008), and a culture of political autocracy and associated elements of command-and-control economic management. There is also Russia's powerful scientific, religious and mystical heritage to factor into the equation or any dialogue of values surrounding the concepts of sustainability and sustainable development. The work of Vladimir Ivanovich Vernadsky (1863–1945) on the biosphere, and particularly the *noosphere*, has Gaia-like connotations associated in the West with James Lovelock. An underpinning assumption of the noosphere concept is that humankind is actually incapable of developing a substitute for the Earth's biota's naturally occurring regulatory mechanisms and must therefore work strenuously to avoid compromising the integrity of the biotic system. For Verdansky, the noosphere is a historical process, 'the sphere of reason', or socialized science, relating to the final evolutionary stages of the biosphere in geological history. He wrote, 'the biosphere of the 20th Century [sic] is being transformed into the noosphere which has been created above all by the growth of science, scientific understanding and the social activities of humankind based on such understanding' (Vernadsky, quoted in Oldfield and Shaw, 2006: 148). Similarly, the influence of academician Nikolai Moiseev (1902–52) still has contemporary resonances in some presidential decrees, particularly in the mid 1990s (Oldfield and Shaw, 2006). For Moriseev, the transition to the noosphere requires profound shifts in human morals and behaviours, and the ecological imperative itself requires powerful restrictions on human actions to be enforced. As the Russian news agency RIA Novosti reported following President Putin's annual report to Parliament in 2011,

> 'The country needs a decade of sustainable and calm development,' he said. 'Modernization – or in other words, consistent and quality development – is above all investment in a person, in his or her talents and abilities, in creating conditions for personal development and initiative, and in a better quality of life,' Putin said.
>
>   The premier said this was the prerequisite for rapid economic growth and technological breakthroughs.
>
> (Ria Novosti, 24.4.11: http://en.ria.ru/russia/
> 20110420/163609685.html)

For Artour L. Demtchouk (1998) of the Moscow State University, sustainable development is totally compatible with Russia's traditions and Russian culture, although he regards the everyday conservatism of the Russia people, which makes them wary of change and participation in decision-making, a potential problem. Dialogue requires participation. However, there has been an increase in academic discussion of and publications on sustainability and sustainable development in Russia, which has elicited both criticisms that sustainable development will retard the economic progress of developing nations by restricting further industrialization, and suspicions that the concept itself is a Western formulation which fails to take into account the specifics of Russian civilization. Nonetheless, there is still perhaps a faith in science and in humanity that in the Russian context at least gives contemporary significance to Verdansky's views, particularly perhaps when he suggested

> that our democratic ideals are in unison with the elemental geological processes, with the laws of nature, and are answerable to the noosphere. It is possible therefore to view our future confidently. It is in our hands. We will not let it go.
>
> (Verdansky, quoted in Oldfield and Shaw, 2006: 149)

The last sentence implies hope and optimism rather than scientific or political certainty.

The sceptical environmentalist – Lomborg's challenge

Following on from Verdanksy's optimistic uncertainty but belief in humankind's ultimate responsibility, as well as Robinson's call for a recognition that sustainability often involves a conflict of values and ultimately political decision-making and action, the controversy over the publication of Bjørn Lomborg's (2001) *The Sceptical Environmentalist* raises a number of interesting issues. With a ringing endorsement on the back cover from the distinguished British scientist Lewis Wolpert – 'at last a book that gives the environment the scientific analysis it deserves' – the book is a direct reply to the Worldwatch Institute's State of the World reports. Lomborg questions that understanding of the environment, which states that the planet is in bad shape, that resources are being exhausted, air and water quality worsening, fish stocks collapsing, and the biosphere being destroyed and human life with it. These arguments were for a time amplified by the media, becoming a conventional wisdom that, for Lomborg, needs to be overturned. To this end, Lomborg attempts to demonstrate that in many respects things have actually got better in recent years – we are not running out of energy or natural resources, food production is increasing, fewer and fewer people are starving, literacy rates are increasing, average life expectancy has increased, we are losing only 0.7 per cent of the planet's species, air and water pollution is not worsening, acid rain does not kill forests, and the total impact of global warming will not be as dire as many predict. We are not overexploiting our renewable resources – for example, global forest coverage has been more or less constant since 1945 and water is plentiful, although admittedly scarce in some places. There are not serious problems with non-renewables either, since, despite increases in consumption, supply has been increasing and many of these resources have reserves of 200 years or more. 'Consequently, there does not seem to be any foundation for the worried pessimism which claims that our society only survives by writing out ever larger checks without coverage' (Lomborg, 2001: 159–60). Indeed, early cutbacks in fossil fuel consumption will actually make people's lives worse. Problems do exist, but they are usually smaller than many environmentalists suggest. Lomborg recognizes there is room for improvement, that although many more people now have access to clean drinking water, a billion more in the developing world need this too. However, he argues that an improved environment will be the product of improved economic welfare, since, in general, higher income correlates with higher levels of environmental sustainability. Thus, when developing nations reach a certain level of economic development, as have countries in the North, these nations will be able to afford cleaner production methods, pollution controls and so forth. When Bangladesh is as affluent as the Netherlands, it will be time for Bangladesh to deal with the effects of global warming and the rise in sea levels. Environmentalists, he goes on, tend to extrapolate their pessimistic scenarios from short-term rather than long-term trends, basing their views on inadequate economic analyses and relying more on faith than reasoned judgement. By contrast, Lomborg states that his own view is based firmly on published statistics, often the official ones of the UN and its subsidiary organizations such as the Food and Agricultural Organization, the United Nations Development Programme, the World Health Organization and the United Nations Environment Programme. His book is also laden with 1,800 references, which the reader is invited to check.

Lomborg's argument continues that, by positing an ideal situation with which to compare the current state of affairs, environmentalists tend to make misguided political and moral judgements. A certain realism is required, he suggests. The Earth's resources are finite, we can't do everything and the world could be a better place, but this means that we have to prioritize our policies and actions, dealing with global warming or global poverty but not necessarily both. Avoiding this prioritization means relinquishing the opportunity of doing the best for ourselves and for future generations. The problem is that policy makers, and certainly the general public wishing to protect the environment, also want to experience constant improvements in their material well-being. They want everything, and now. Additionally, people are reluctant to prioritize, because they do not fully understand the nature of the risks involved. Hunger is a greater cause of loss of life in this world than pollution. Chemical and pesticide pollution accounts for just 2 per cent of cancers. We shouldn't worry about risks without first properly weighing them up. The media are partly to blame for this, because they focus on sensational and dramatic incidents that cause accidents or death, rather than mundane and everyday activities. Consequently, we tend to overate these statistically minor elements and underrate sizeable but more boring ones. This has led to an unwarranted hostility to genetically modified (GM) foods, despite the fact that GM foods will positively contribute to increasing the world's food supply. GM promises so much. For Lomborg, the key argument from science and economics is not the abandonment of GM research and development, the risks of which have been exaggerated wildly, but the need to establish effective regulatory systems and management practices. Indeed, as most people are readily aware, global environmental sustainability policy and action is rife with past, present and undoubtedly future controversies.

Lomborg clearly exemplifies the position of a neoliberal in his belief that the market, economic growth and development will enable rich and poor nations to improve their environmental performance in the long run. He also expresses some values shared with ecological modernizers, but Lomborg would probably describe himself as a practical realist, or as a pragmatist. Whatever the case, Lomborg does stimulate many people to think, argue and discuss the issues. It is important not to automatically dismiss views you disagree with, but to use them as a device to learn more and to understand better.

It is important to consider the context in which the debates around Lomborg take place and the use to which the arguments of the various parties are put, and by whom. Critical focus has not only been on the status of science and scientists, the value of academic refereed journals, the presentation of statistical evidence, and the role of the mass media and public communication, but also on the processes of political decision-making and political influence and, ultimately, questions of what type of world we have and think we want. Therefore, by examining the Lomborg controversy, a number of issues emerge:

- the politicized nature of the debate over the environment and sustainability;
- the soundness or otherwise of scientific knowledge, research and evaluation;
- the role of 'sound science' and statistics in policy formulation and implementation particularly, as they pertain to issues such as risk assessment;
- the role of political and economic interests in the social construction of 'sound science' and its dissemination to and understanding by a wider public; and
- public trust and understanding of science and its contribution to the ethics of the sustainable development process.

The initial response to Lomborg's first book was furiously partisan and intense. In January 2003 the Danish Committees on Scientific Dishonesty (DCSD) found that Lomborg was 'systematically one-sided'. Later in the year, however, the Danish

Ministry of Science, Technology and Innovation ruled that Lomborg had not been 'objectively dishonest', and in March 2004 the DCSD withdrew their allegations. A great deal was, and remains, at stake. The debate in *Prospect* magazine between Lomborg and environmentalist Tom Burke, the review in *Nature* by Stuart Pimms and Jeff Harvey, together with a short series of articles and a lengthy critique in *Scientific American* attacking many of Lomborg's judgements and claims, provide a clear outline of the issues. As Director of the largely US-funded Copenhagen Consensus Center, Bjørn Lomborg has turned his attention on climate change, as this issue has increased in public prominence. He has applied cost–benefit analysis to the effects of climate change, prompting a withering response from Tom Burke who, writing in *The Guardian* (Burke, 2004), stated that he was engaging in 'junk economics' and 'faith-based politics':

> Cost-benefit analysis can help you choose different routes to a goal you have agreed, but it cannot help you choose goals. For that we have politics. People disagree about priorities and they do so on a huge variety of legitimate grounds. When they do so, they are not arguing about value for money, but about the kind of world they want to live in.
>
> It is a vanity of economists to believe that all choices can be boiled down to calculations of monetary value. In the real world, outcomes are not so easily managed. A stable climate is something we might now call a system condition for civilization. That is, it is something without which civilization is impossible – though it is not, of course, itself a guarantee that there will be civilization.

Not deterred, and using the same approach that characterized *The Sceptical Environmentalist*'s critique of the environmentalist's 'litany' of disasters, Lomborg published in the *Wall Street Journal* (Lomborg, 2006) his detailed criticism of the UK Treasury's Stern Review on the economic costs of climate change. Lomborg questions Stern's calculation that doing nothing about climate change will cost 20 per cent of gross domestic product (GDP) while doing something will cost only 1 per cent, suggesting that the true cost of doing something would be nearer 3 per cent by 2100. He argues that most cost–benefit modelling shows that radical and early carbon reductions actually cost more than the good they do. What is more, it is highly unlikely that China and India will participate in any climate mitigation scheme, not least because, despite China's 2002 pledge to cut sulphur dioxide emissions by 10 per cent, they are presently 27 per cent higher and are a far more serious threat to human health and the environment than climate change. In *Cool It*, Lomborg (2007) pursues his argument that we need to find more intelligent ways of spending these billions of dollars that will genuinely enable humanity to adapt as well as mitigate the effects of climate change. Practical and pragmatic solutions are required, rather than feel-good policy statements that lead to very little.

Sustainable development is politically, economically, ethically, ideologically and scientifically charged. It will not be easy and the dialogue continues.

Science, politics and climate change

The United Nations Framework Convention on Climate Change (UNFCCC) defines climate change, in Article 1, as 'a change of climate which is attributed directly or indirectly to human activity that alters the composition of the global atmosphere and which is in addition to natural climate variability observed over comparable time periods'. The UNFCCC thus makes a distinction between 'climate change' attributable to human activities altering the atmospheric composition and 'climate variability' attributable to natural causes (IPCC, 2004: 4).

Climate change seems to be hitting the headlines more frequently than ever. The scientific, political and ethical debates about the nature and causes of the climate crisis have always been intense and sometimes fraught. A number of highly accessible and well-respected books (Flannery, 2005; Lynas, 2005, 2007; Monbiot, 2006; Pearce, 2006), together with some important and widely seen documentaries, such as Al Gore's Oscar-winning *An Inconvenient Truth*, Franny Armstrong's *The Age of Stupid* and Hollywood films such as *The Day After Tomorrow*, have helped foster general awareness and understanding. NGO campaigns like Friends of the Earth's *The Big Ask*, government-sponsored public communication strategies, and increased news and current affairs coverage of climate science and related issues, including in conservative journals such as *The Economist*, which published a special report on business and climate change in June 2007, have had their impact too. The UK Treasury's 2006 Stern Review and everyday observations and comments by ordinary people that spring is happening earlier or the expected rains are not coming and weather 'events' are seemingly more extreme have made global warming and the environment move close to the top of many national political agendas. The Inter-governmental Panel on Climate Change (IPCC) has steadily become a very significant player in this. Established in 1988 by the World Meteorological Organization (WMO) and the United Nations Environment Programme (UNEP), the IPCC's role, according to its governing principles approved in 1998, is as follows:

> The IPCC is to assess on a comprehensive, objective, open and transparent basis the scientific, technical and socioeconomic information relevant to understanding the scientific basis of risk of human-induced climate change, its potential impacts, and options for adaptation and mitigation. IPCC reports should be neutral with respect to policy, although they may need to deal objectively with scientific, technical and socioeconomic factors relevant to the application of particular policies.
>
> Review is an essential part of the IPCC process. Since the IPCC is an intergovernmental body, review of IPCC documents should involve both peer review by experts and review by governments.

The IPCC does not conduct research of its own but periodically synthesizes and evaluates the state of knowledge on climate change. It produces a range of synthesis, special, technical and methodology reports and, because of its scope and international status, its findings are critically scrutinized by NGOs, the media, businesses, lobby groups, governments and ordinary citizens. For example, the Global Climate Coalition founded in 1989, with early supporters including Amoco, the American Forest and Paper Association, the American Petroleum Institute, Chrysler, Exxon, Ford, General Motors, Shell and Texaco, organized advertising and public relations (PR) campaigns to cast doubt on scientific findings linking fossil fuel use to climate change, and lobbied aggressively at international climate negotiations to prevent meaningful agreements. By 2000, however, the Global Climate Coalition could no longer effectively deny the growing evidence of anthropogenic climate change. The IPCC published findings throughout the 1990s and 2000s and, although they have been debated vigorously, a scientific consensus has slowly emerged (though this has not stopped some governments from attempting to influence the language of its assessment reports to express a rather more cautious and conservative viewpoint). In 2002, Julian Borger of *The Guardian* reported that the US Bush administration, with the oil company Exxon-Mobil, had secretly worked to remove the head of the IPCC Robert Watson to make way for another person less likely to call for radical mitigating action. Watson was replaced by the Indian railway engineer and environmentalist Dr Rajendra Pachauri. Fred Pearce (2002), writing in *New Scientist*, reported that the US may have threatened to withdraw funding from the IPCC if there had not been change at its head, causing fears that the IPCC process had been compromised by this apparent politicization. The IPPC's conservatism was again highlighted in 2007, when Professor Stefan Rahmstorf and his team from the Potsdam Institute for Climate Impact Research in Germany suggested that the IPCC's Third Assessment Report, published in 2001, had underestimated sea-level rise by some 59 per cent. Rahmstorf used observational data, believing that computer models of the climate significantly underestimated the sea-level rises that had already taken place. The picture becomes increasingly detailed as additional reports finally reach the public sphere. According to Smith *et al.*'s (2007) climate modelling system, there may be a slowdown in global warming until about 2009, but then it will again increase, with 'at least half of the years after 2009 predicted to exceed the warmest year currently on record'.

Early in 2007 the IPCC issued the first of four major assessment reports. Significantly, its language and predictions were much stronger than six years earlier, with it concluding that it was at least 90 per cent certain that human-induced emissions of greenhouse gases (GHGs) rather than any natural variations are the cause of global warming. This was up from 6 per cent stated in the Third Assessment report in 2001. By 2013, with the publication of the Fifth Assessment Report (AR5), the level of certainty had climbed to 95 per cent, with global warming likely to exceed the generally recognized danger level of 2°C, or between 3 and 4°C in Australia, by 2100. Sea levels are likely to rise by up to 1 metre if CO_2 emissions remain below 500ppm (parts per million) but up to 3 metres if CO_2 concentration is between 700 and 1,500ppm. Many millions of people live near sea level and a sea-level rise approaching one metre would endanger many cities including London, New York, Shanghai, Venice, Sydney, Miami and New Orleans (Gillis, 2013). The risk of the Earth warming by 6°C is just 1 per cent but, as the Global Challenges Foundation noted, such a percentage risk would mean something like 500,000 fatal plane crashes every year if such a prediction was applied to the global aviation industry.

A large fraction of anthropogenic climate change resulting from CO_2 emissions is irreversible on a multi-century to millennial time scale, except in the case of a large net removal of CO_2 from the atmosphere over a sustained period. Surface temperatures will remain approximately constant at elevated levels for many centuries after a complete cessation of net anthropogenic CO_2 emissions. Due to the long time scales of heat transfer from the ocean surface to depth, ocean warming will continue for centuries. Depending on the scenario, about 15 to 40% of emitted CO_2 will remain in the atmosphere longer than 1,000 years.

(IPCC WGI AR5, 2013: 20)

The scientific consensus now suggests that impacts will be worse and are more certain than was anticipated only a few years ago (Berners-Lee and Clark, 2013). In July 2013 the Moana Loa Observatory in Hawaii, which has been monitoring atmospheric CO_2 since 1958, recorded 397.23ppm CO_2 with some daily averages for the month exceeding 400ppm. The annual average increase now exceeds 2ppm and many scientists believe near to zero emissions are now needed to stabilize the climate. Over half the permissible one trillion tonnes of carbon has already been released into the atmosphere if temperature rise is to be 2°C or less. It is likely that if present trends continue the one trillion tonne mark will be reached in about twenty five years. Dr Rajenda Pachauri, Chairman of the IPCC, argues that only a high carbon price will force power companies and manufacturers to reduce their use of fossil fuels. 'An extremely effective instrument would be to put a price on carbon. It is only through the market that you can get a large enough and rapid enough response' he said announcing the release of AR5 in September 2013 (Bawden, 2013).

There is still a great deal of uncertainty within the field of climate science and considerable discussion over measurements and models of change. Predictions and forecasts are always presented in terms of possibilities and probabilities, with recognition that findings are almost always likely to be provisional. Scientists are always learning more about the factors influencing atmospheric concentrations of greenhouse gases (primarily CO_2 and methane), the feedback effects of these gases on the climate system, the nature and extent of local and regional variations, the future use of fossil fuels (the major cause of CO_2 emissions), the rate of energy take-up by the oceans, likely global and regional temperature rise, and the rate of melting of the ice sheets in Greenland and Antarctica, and their effect on sea levels. Also in 2007, the renowned climate scientist James Hansen and his team, after reviewing the most recent scientific findings, suggested that summer ice melt in West Antarctica (and Greenland) was far greater than earlier predicted and had not been included in the IPCC projections because the panel does 'not well account for the nonlinear physics of wet ice sheet disintegration, ice streams and eroding ice shelves' (Hansen *et al.*, 2007: 1950). Referring to the palaeontologic records, Hansen *et al.*'s Royal Society paper concludes with an exceptionally bleak scenario:

> The imminent peril is initiation of dynamical and thermodynamical processes on the West Antarctic and Greenland ice sheets that produce a situation out of humanity's control, such that devastating sea-level rise will inevitably occur. Climate forcing of this century under BAU [business as usual] would dwarf natural forcings of the past million years; indeed it would probably exceed climate forcing of the middle Pliocene, when the planet was not more than 2–3°C warmer and sea level 10–25m higher. The climate sensitivities we have inferred from palaeoclimate data ensure that a BAU GHG emission scenario would produce global warming of several degrees Celsius this century, with amplification at high latitudes.
>
> (Hansen *et al.*, 2007: 1949)

Our knowledge is still limited, but the climate crisis is real and extremely serious. In 2000, Nobel chemist Paul Crutzen of the Max-Planck Institute in Germany coined a new term – the 'Anthropocene' – designating an epoch of human influence on the planet. Global, national and regional policies and actions promoting extensive mitigation and necessary adaptation are essential. The IPPC, the UN, James Hansen and campaigners like George Monbiot agree that 'business as usual' is a recipe for inevitable catastrophe. For Hansen, it is important that we find ways of taking greenhouse gases from the atmosphere. CO_2 needs to be captured at power plants, sequestered below ground, injected beneath the ocean floor; biomass needs to be developed without the excessive use of nitrogen-based fertilizers or taking out of production valuable agricultural land. The Worldwatch Institute (2007) has noted that, with the increase in world agricultural prices, biofuels could economically benefit a number of developing countries, which, instead of using foreign currency to import oil, could develop their own domestic biofuel industries and so purchase fuel from their own farmers. In *Heat*, George Monbiot (2006) notes a downside to this enthusiasm, stating that the growth of palm oil plantations has displaced many indigenous peoples and destroyed much forest land in Indonesia and Malaysia. Greenpeace has campaigned for a total end to palm oil production for these reasons and because the industry is basically 'cooking the planet' (Greenpeace International, 2007). Monbiot also argues for a number of other societal and individual actions that could reduce CO_2 emissions by 90 per cent in most sectors. These include less air and car travel, more Internet shopping, building less, installing better home insulation, using less high energy-consuming cement in construction, growing wood for heating and developing solar power. For Monbiot, civil nuclear power is not an option because of its well-documented connection with military uses, the danger of proliferation, and unresolved problems regarding waste disposal and expense. For Monbiot, we have no choice but to act now, but unfortunately governments tend to commission reports but rarely act effectively on their findings and possibilities.

Additionally, many individuals, certainly in the developed world, may be extremely reluctant to significantly alter aspects of their lifestyles, especially when it comes to cheap flights abroad. Where aviation is concerned, writes Monbiot:

> There is no technofix. The growth in aviation and the need to address climate change cannot be reconciled. . . . A 90 per cent cut in emissions requires not only that growth stops, but that most of the planes which are flying today are grounded.
>
> (2006: 182)

With perhaps growing desperation that the global situation was deteriorating rapidly and that the arguments from environmentalist and social movements were having very little impact on policy makers, George Monbiot now (controversially) believes that one technical solution, namely nuclear power, is a policy option that can no longer be ignored by Greens and governments alike (Monbiot and Goodall, 2011).

The IPCC (2007: 11) states that there is a high level of agreement and much evidence from bottom-up and top-down studies to support the conclusion that 'there is substantial economic potential for the mitigation of global GHG emissions over the coming decades, which could offset the projected growth of global emissions or reduce emissions below current levels'. These include:

> Changes in lifestyles and consumption patterns emphasizing resource conservation can contribute to developing an equitable and sustainable low-carbon economy.

Education and training programmes can help overcome barriers to the market acceptance of energy efficiency.

Changes in occupant behaviour, cultural patterns, consumer choice and use of technologies can result in considerable reduction in CO_2 emissions related to energy use in buildings.

'Transport demand management', which includes urban planning (which can reduce the demand for travel) and provision of information and educational techniques (which can reduce car usage and lead to a more efficient driving style).

In industry, management tools that include staff training, reward systems, regular feedback and documentation of existing practices can help overcome industrial organizational barriers, reducing energy use and emissions.

(IPCC, 2007: 17)

Climate change policies and the goals of sustainable development have clear synergies. Societies will need to build adaptive capacities to deal with increased risk and vulnerabilities – floods, drought, temperature extremes, which will almost certainly affect crop production, distribution and food security (Adger *et al.*, 2003; Gregory *et al.*, 2005). Other synergies clearly relate to energy efficiency and economic policy. Renewable energy can be economically beneficial, improve energy security, reduce local pollutant emissions, create jobs and improve health. (Re)forestation and bio-energy plantations can lead to restoration of degraded land, manage water run-off, retain soil carbon, reduce loss of natural habitats, enhance biodiversity, conserve soil and water, and benefit rural economies if properly designed and implemented. There are a whole host of geo-engineering solutions ranging from the bizarre to the possible, the unproven and socially questionable (Jackson and Salzman, 2010). Climate change is therefore about what we do, have done, what facts we assume we generate and most importantly the meaning we attach to these facts and actions. Climate change will take on different forms in different places and cultural values, predis-positions and political frames of understanding will generate different pre- and proscriptions, notions of citizenship and governance, corporate and other forms of responsibility, perceptions of nature, dialogues and conversation, legal obligations, and actions that bridge different geographical scales. As Sheila Jasanoff (2010) argues, the interpretative social sciences have an important role to play here in fashioning frameworks with which we can think about climate change – the social, the human and the means by which we shape our future. For Mike Hulme (2009), it is imperative that we harness our creative, psychological, spiritual and ethical imaginations to show how culture and science interrelate, and that politics and business are not the sole considerations that are important to securing the future we want. For Eileen Crist (2007), however, there are two issues that emerge from the very real and very serious threats of climate change. The first is the tendency for governments and others to look primarily to technical proposals as a means of addressing current changes and the second is that climate change seems to crowd out all the other ecological predicaments the world needs to address. She writes:

Climate change looms so huge on the environmental and political agenda today that it has contributed to downplaying other facets of the ecological crisis: mass extinction of species, the devastation of the oceans by industrial fishing, continued old-growth deforestation, topsoil losses and desertification, endocrine disruption, incessant development, and so on, are made to appear secondary and more forgiving by comparison with 'dangerous anthropogenic interference' with the climate system.

(Crist, 2007: 35–6)

Instead of swapping the *Holocene* for the *Anthropocene*, Crist suggests that it is probably wiser and more appropriate to use the term developed by the biologist, E.O.Wilson. We have now entered the *Eremozoic Era* – the Era of Loneliness and Loss rendered vividly by so many apocalyptic science fiction novels over the past four decades. However, Crist (2007: 55) concludes: 'this civilization is not beyond the reaches of radical action – and it is certainly not beyond the reaches of radical critique'.

Box 3.1 From the Arctic to the Pacific islands of Tuvalu

The National Snow and Ice Data Centre in Boulder, Colorado (USA) revealed that sea ice in the Arctic shrank by 18 per cent more in 2012 than it had the worse previous, 2007, to just 3.41m sq km. The Nobel Prize-winning climate scientist Michael Mann of Penn State University told *The Guardian* newspaper:

> We know Arctic sea ice is declining faster than the models predict. When you look at the major Greenland and the west Antarctic ice sheets, which are critical from the standpoint of sea level rise, once they begin to melt we really start to see sea level rises accelerate. The models have typically predicted that will not happen for decades but the measurements that are coming in tell us it is already happening so once again we are decades ahead of schedule. Island nations that have considered the possibility of evacuation at some point, like Tuvalu, may have to be contending those sort of decisions within the matter of a decade or so. Thousands of years of culture is at risk of disappearing as the populations of vulnerable island states have no place to go. For these people, current sea levels are already representative of dangerous anthropogenic interference because they will lose their world far before the rest of us suffer.

At their highest point Tuvalu is just 4.6m above sea level and is already experiencing flooding, saltwater intrusion that affects drinking-water supplies and increased erosion. In 2008 the Government and elders of Tuvalu held 'secret' talks with the Australian Government about the possibilities of mass evacuation to Australia in future years. New Zealand currently accepts about 75 Tuvalu islanders every year as part of a Pacific Access Countries (Fiji, Samoa, Tonga, Kiribati and Tuvalu) immigration quota which the New Zealand government states in not linked to the islands' vulnerability to the impact of climate change.

Source: adapted from Confino (2012) and Crouch (2008).

Creative policy solutions: contraction and convergence

Aubrey Meyer, musician and composer, former member of the UK Green Party and co-founder of the Global Commons Institute in 1990, is an active promoter of climate mitigation through 'contraction and convergence' – a practical and equitable approach to combating climate change. He believes that those economists who argue that climate mitigation is too expensive a policy option effectively condone the murdering of many of the world's poor. He argues (Meyer, 2000) that although greenhouse gas emissions have been accumulating in the atmosphere as a result of industrialization for over 200 years, suggesting that in principle every citizen on the planet has an equal right to emit, there must be an equitable individual allowance based on safe global emissions targets provided by the best scientific understanding available. Contraction and convergence offers a simple model on which an international agreement on greenhouse gas emissions can be based. It can be achieved in three stages:

1   securing an agreement on a cap on CO_2 concentrations in the atmosphere;
2   calculating the speed at which emissions need to be reduced to reach that target;
3   calculating the consequent total carbon budget and allocating a per capita allowance throughout the world.

The result will be that per capita emissions from each state will 'converge' at a fair level, while the global sum of emissions will 'contract'. Meyer believes that greenhouse gas concentrations should contract to 450ppm and that convergence to equal per capita emissions should be achieved by 2030. This process requires the creation of a carbon currency, which could finance clean technologies and eradicate Third World debts, combat global poverty, and minimize the economic differences between the developed and developing worlds. As Flannery (2005) notes, this 'strong medicine' could be the foundation for a new Kyoto that does away with 'free riders' but will mean definite political and economic costs for the developed nations.

Contraction and convergence is thus a vehicle for achieving global equity not only in CO_2 emissions but also in economic wealth, prosperity and human well-being. The rich nations of the North are by far the biggest emitters of greenhouse gases. Even today, Africa's accumulated emissions are a small fraction of those produced by the UK. Contraction and convergence, however, can only be realized if the participation, dialogue, debate and accommodation that is beginning to characterize global politics in major areas of environmental and sustainability policy making is developed further. NGO pressure groups, independent think-tanks, scientific organizations, and corporate and government bodies, which form 'epistemic' or knowledge-based communities, must work with rather than against each other if agreement on climate change is to be secured. As Gough and Shackley write:

> The science-policy nexus represented by the IPPC, and supporters of the UNFCCC Kyoto Protocol, with its inclusion of government officials, international organizations, scientists, NGOs, business and so on, incorporates the key features of an epistemic community. A distinctive knowledge-based approach to climate assessment and policy has emerged within the IPCC, in which NGOs have been instrumental, both as expert advisors and in providing the legitimacy

of inclusiveness needed for the epistemic coalition to have sufficient authority. The fact that environmental NGOs (ENGOs), intergovernmental and governmental actors, the scientific establishment, and even some business groups are in coalition can be a tremendously powerful influence. NGOs that have helped create the climate change epistemic community have needed to move their own terms of reference towards science and technical policy measures and responses, and away from ethical and overtly political matters: such is the price of membership of that coalition. This shut the door on the use of a range of potentially useful concepts and devices such as global equity and North–South development.

(2001: 332)

Ulrich Beck and the risk society

Climate change brings with it significant risk, particularly for those living in low-lying areas. The risks associated with GM and new developments such as nanotechnology are also hotly debated. In many ways, we seem to be living in a risk society, so the concept of 'risk' has become of primary importance in the sustainability debate. The work of the German sociologist Ulrich Beck (1992a, 1992b, 1996) has been extremely influential in this field. Although only one of many risk-society theorists, Beck has clearly identified significant issues that impact on environmental management, risk assessment, ecological politics and policy making, public communication, citizenship, intergenerational ethics, economics and finance, and scientific and technological innovation.

The key points of Beck's theory of risk include:

- Although risks are as old as human society itself, there are some associated with industrial society that are essentially new, such as nuclear power, chemical and biotechnical production, and genetic modification – all products of techno-industrial relations.
- 'People, firms, state agencies and politicians are responsible for risks' (Beck, 1992a: 98).
- Since the middle of the twentieth century, industrial society has confronted the 'historically unprecedented possibility of the destruction through decision-making of all life on this planet. This distinguishes our epoch not only from the early phase of the industrial revolution, but also from all other cultures and social forms, no matter how diverse and contradictory these may have been in detail' (Beck, 1992a: 101).
- A consequence is that political stability in risk societies comes from 'not thinking about things'. The incalculability of consequences leads to a lack of accountability.
- Lack of accountability leads in turn to 'organized irresponsibility', because mega-hazards, in particular, undermine the four principles of the risk calculus, namely:

  - Damage may not be limited or contained, so monetary compensation is inapplicable.
  - *Precautionary* after-care is excluded from the worst imaginable accident as the anticipation of effects is likely to be totally inadequate.
  - 'Accidents' are not confined to time or place, and therefore lose meaning.
  - Standards of normality, measuring procedures and comparators are no longer clear and distinct.

Beck's theory has profound consequences for the practice of science, its public understanding, and its political use and application. Scientific research often fails to allay fears, because certainty is so elusive. Acceptable risks become accepted risks, and new knowledge can turn normality into hazards overnight, as we have seen with nuclear power, holes in the ozone layer, GM contamination and, most recently, fracking. The search for secure energy supplies and extensive profits has led to a new growth industry – the hydraulic fracturing of underground rocks with a mixture of chemicals, sand and water to extract the shale gas locked within them. Although the burning of this gas will produce fewer carbon emissions than either oil or coal, there have been vigorous public protests in the United States, Canada and Europe against the fracking industry. The extractive process can lead to groundwater pollution, earth tremors, risks to health from carcinogenic chemicals, the release of radioactivity and the formation of ozone 'smogs'. The documentary films *Gasland* and *Drill Baby Drill* graphically convey both the drive for corporate profit and the very serious human and environmental risks entailed. Additionally, the production and burning of shale gas contributes nothing to the necessary transition away from the use of fossil fuels and may actually make climate change worse as the most powerful global warming pollutant, methane, is released during several stages of the fracking process (Ridlington and Rumpler, 2013; Hughes, 2013). The incredible commercial gains that are likely to accrue from the development and exploitation of synthetic biology – that is, the artificial construction of entirely new organisms from 'biobricks' (individual DNA elements) – are matched only by the potential risk. New, artificially produced bacteria may be able to break down cellulose to produce ethanol or sequestrate carbon dioxide, thereby ameliorating global warming, as the J. Craig Ventor Institute in the US has suggested (www.jcvi.org/research); but what else could they conceivably do? Bacteria are notoriously difficult to destroy, and promises of salvation could become devastating threats to many life-forms (Bunting, 2007). Science and engineering have always operated on the basis of probable safety, but when society itself becomes a scientific laboratory, testing out new technologies or theories, this type of cutting-edge activity becomes politically and ethically questionable. Given that scientific knowledge can always only be partial, always 'work in progress', complex risks need to be carefully assessed and evaluated. Political decisions will ultimately have to be made.

Unlike Lomborg, Beck believes further industrialization and wealth creation will increase global disparities in wealth and welfare, and increase human misery and ecological risk. It often seems contrary to the business logic of the financial bottom line to ignore commercial opportunities even if they may cause ecological problems:

> If it is suddenly revealed and publicized in the mass media that certain products contain certain 'toxins' (information policy is receiving a key importance considering the fact that hazards are generally imperceptible in everyday life), then entire markets may collapse and invested capital and effort are instantly devalued.
>
> (Beck, 1992b: 111–12)

Risks are therefore not simply diagnosed, predicted and ameliorated on the basis of 'sound science'; there are other factors at work. Science becomes one element of the public discourse that socially constructs the meaning and acceptability of risk – whether meat is safe to eat, the sun safe to be exposed to, nuclear power safe to generate, climate change bad for the economy, and so on. The mass media, court decisions, experts' debate, politicians' speeches, public fears, and trust in the major social institutions and big corporations will all play a part in balancing costs and benefits, risks and possibilities. With climate change comes the increasing likelihood of natural disasters in the form of floods, droughts, cyclones and hurricanes. To address these risks, issues of resilience and vulnerability need to be factored into governance and risk-management processes. As the IPCC has noted:

> The severity of the impacts of climate extremes depends strongly on the level of the exposure and vulnerability to these extremes (*high confidence*).
>
> Trends in exposure and vulnerability are major drivers of changes in disaster risk (*high confidence*). Understanding the multi-faceted nature of both exposure and vulnerability is a prerequisite for determining how weather and climate events contribute to the occurrence of disasters, and for designing and implementing effective adaptation and disaster risk management strategies. Vulnerability reduction is a core common element of adaptation and disaster risk management.
>
> (2012: 8)

Box 3.2 Global warming: health risks and impacts

Recent experience of extremes of summer heat in Europe, Asia, and North America has underscored the great threat to health when physiological thresholds are passed. Once the human body's capacity to cope with increased thermal stress is exceeded, risks of homeostatic failure, disease exacerbation, and death begin to rise rapidly. This is especially the case in older people, the very young, those with underlying cardiovascular or chronic respiratory disease, and those who are poor, uneducated, or isolated (and therefore less likely to have access to, or take, preventive action). Such effects are exacerbated by changes in air quality: ground level ozone levels rise with temperature, threatening human health. The greater absolute burden of adverse health impact from heatwaves will be in the general community, but workers in various heat exposed workplaces, both outdoors and indoors (if unventilated), are particularly vulnerable.

Climate change thus acts as a force multiplier, amplifying the negative health impacts of other environmental stressors (such as land degradation, soil nitrification, depletion of freshwater stocks, ocean acidification, and biodiversity loss). Populations with high pre-existing rates of climate sensitive diseases and conditions, such as child diarrhea, malaria, under-nutrition, asthma, atherogenic cardiovascular disease, and extreme heat exposures in workplace settings, could suffer large absolute increments in adverse health impact with relatively small changes in climate. Indeed, conservative extrapolation of estimates made for the year 2000 suggested that climate change is now causing some 200,000 premature deaths each year (from under-nutrition, diarrheal disease, malaria, and flooding), with over 90 per cent of these occurring in low income countries (especially sub-Saharan Africa and South Asia), and 85 per cent in children under 5 years of age.

Source: McMichael *et al.* (2012).

Extreme weather events will have greater impacts on those social, economic and industrial sectors which have close links to climate – for example, water, agriculture and food security, forestry, health and tourism. In many regions, the degree and nature of resultant economic losses as a result of climate extremes will be themselves influenced by political and socioeconomic factors.

The social construction of risk

For some sociologists, risk is never fully objective or knowable outside of our pre-existing knowledge and moral beliefs. All knowledge about risk is bound to the socio-cultural contexts from which it emerged. We can only know or perceive risk from a particular socio-cultural milieu or worldview. As Lupton neatly summarizes:

> Scientific knowledge, or any other knowledge, is never value-free, but rather is always the product of a way of seeing. A risk, therefore, is not a static objective phenomenon, but is constantly constructed and negotiated as part of the network of social interaction and the formation of meaning. 'Expert' judgements of risk, rather than being the 'objective' or 'neutral', and therefore 'unbiased', assessments they tend to be portrayed as in the techno-scientific literature, are regarded as being equally as constructed through implicit social and cultural processes as are lay people's judgements.
>
> (1999: 28)

The 'weak' social constructionist will see risks as cultural mediations of real hazards, whereas the 'strong' social constructionist will sees hazards and risks as existing only when people recognize and label them as such. In this way, debates in the public sphere, political activism, local campaigning, social refusal and anti-corporate feeling lead to a more reflexive, questioning society, where the constitution and generation of understanding is an ongoing process, where knowledge becomes knowledges, and where uncertainty becomes a given in contemporary life. We need to critically reflect on both our understandings and on our actions. We need to reflect on how we change the world and how the world changes us.

In our modern globalized risk society, this reflexivity, which for Beck means 'self-confrontation rather than mere reflection', manifests itself in three ways:

1   Society becomes an issue and a problem for itself at a global level.
2   Awareness of the global nature of risk stimulates the growth of cooperative international institutions and programmes.
3   State and political boundaries become less significant, as global risks require global action, for example on climate change.

For Beck, reflexivity offers both hope and danger:

> This combination of reflex and reflections, as long as the catastrophe itself fails to materialize, can set industrial modernization on the path to self-criticism and self-transformation. Reflexive modernization contains both elements: the reflex-like threat to industrial society's own foundations through a successful further modernization which is blind to dangers and the growth of awareness, the reflection on this situation.
>
> (1996: 34)

'Sound science', risk and GM

The science, business and politics of genetic modification (GM) has been a highly controversial field of activity for many years, with supporters arguing that genetic modification offers huge advances and advantages in terms of securing food supplies for the world's growing population and critics suggesting that the main driver of GM is fundamentally economic rather than ethical. The big biotechnology corporations have invested millions and expect to make millions more with terminator technology – that is, GM seeds that do not germinate, requiring increased sales of specialized herbicides and pesticides, and preventing farmers from saving seeds for next year's crop. They have done this for generations and locally harvested seeds adapt gradually and naturally to their environment. Traditional farming methods could be destroyed and environmental damage could occur if artificially produced sterile genes transfer to wild plants and non-GM crops. A single-minded approach to patenting new developments even when they are effectively based on traditional ecological knowledge could effectively 'steal' the modest harvests of many local peoples in the developing world (Shiva, 2000). This 'biopiracy' and the corporate buy-out of many small biotech companies is sometimes seen as a cynical attempt by the transnational biotech corporations to secure control of the world's food industry, estimated to be worth in excess of $2,000 billion a year (Godrej, 2002). For Pigem (2002), 'barcoding life reduces it to a commodity', inevitably leading to a loss of respect for all life-forms, including our own. The issue of what constitutes 'sound science' in such a world has consequently been hotly contested, with few firm or broadly accepted conclusions. Environmental campaigners, including many scientists, such as Mae-Wan Ho (1998), argue fiercely that there are so many uncertainties, so many possible risks to the health of ecosystems and human beings through contamination from promiscuous genes, that a principle of precaution should be strictly applied to sensitive scientific research and development. In their submission of scientific evidence presented in the defence of twenty-eight Greenpeace volunteers on trial for their non-violent removal of a GM maize crop in Norfolk in 1999, a number of scientists noted the likelihood of cross-contamination, the potential hazards of low-dose toxicity, horizontal gene transfer and genetic alteration, and possible effects on soil nutrient recycling and productivity (Greenpeace UK, 1999). In their GM Contamination Register Report for 2006, the tenth year of the commercial growing of genetically engineered crops, Greenpeace International recorded 24 incidents of GM contamination, particularly in rice and maize, making the total number 142 since 1996. The report notes that GM contamination is a serious cause for concern with serious negative consequences for those areas of countries choosing to remain GM-free. Many countries do not have a system of liability for the costs of contamination that may result from trials or clean-ups, so they may become the responsibility of the contaminated party rather than the one contaminating.

Scientific knowledge on GM is in a constant state of development, but the problem for many biotech companies and for science as an institution is the loss of public trust, particularly in the UK, that has occurred as a result of the experience of mad cow disease (BSE or bovine spongiform encephalopathy) jumping the species barrier to produce the human variant CJD (Creutzfeldt-Jacob disease). Journalists (see, for example, Brown, 2005) have reported many instances of modified genes from crops being transferred to local wild plants, resulting in herbicide-resistant 'superweeds', and other examples of cross-fertilization occurring, the probability of which corporate and government scientists had previously discounted as being too low to worry about. In the UK, government regulation has been perceived as inadequate, because private profit is seemingly given precedence over food security and ecosystem safety. Consequently, much public trust has migrated to NGOs like Friends of the Earth and Greenpeace, whose own specific agendas are not viewed as being influenced by commercial interests (Pilnick, 2002). European consumers have frequently responded to NGO campaigns against the scientific evidence presented in support of GM by not purchasing foodstuffs containing GM ingredients. For some NGO critics, government and corporate scientists seem to deliberately come up with findings supportive of their employer or funder, rather than making the impartial contributions to knowledge which Wolpert (1993) and Dunbar (1995) argue true science worth its name must do. They state that the scientific method is predominantly a dialectical process, involving detailed hard work, the generation and testing of hypotheses, experimentation, observation, measurement, deduction and self-criticism. Science proceeds through very careful assessments of new ideas and findings, and only when thorough evaluations have been completed, which may take a long time given the complexity of the problems, will scientists confirm that their theories are well founded. Regarding GM, in a circumspect article Professor Howard Dalton (2004: 11), the Chief Scientific Adviser to the UK's Department for Environment, Food and Rural Affairs (Defra), wrote:

> At present, there is no scientific case for ruling out all GM crops and their products. It would be short-sighted to decide the future of a powerful diverse new technology on the basis of its application – and in some cases violent opposition to that application – in only one area, and to ignore the analysis of risks and benefits in other areas.
>
> There are a whole host of potentially beneficial prospects for GM already in our sights. On the other hand, there are risks in any new technology, and the lessons of history tell us that sometimes we have rushed forward to exploit new technologies, only subsequently to appreciate the medical, social and environmental impacts that these may bring (thalidomide, nuclear energy, pesticides, mobile phones, and so on).

The European Union has devised and implemented fairly strict regulations concerning the assessment of possible risks and the labelling of GM produce, which mainly relates to animal feed and foods for food processing. In 2007 the UK Government, despite twenty years of protests and continued public scepticism, decided to proceed with extensive commercial planting of GM crops, irrespective of the risks and the potential negative consequences for the future of organic agriculture.

Reflexivity and the expert vs. lay knowledge divide

Professor of science studies Brian Wynne (1996) suggests that it would be a mistake to assume that the lay public have always trusted expert opinion and that only recently has there been any ambivalence. Ordinary people's trust in expert opinion has often been 'virtual' or 'as-if', with the lay public forced into a relationship of

Box 3.3 Sustainability science: birth of a new discipline

Independent scholar Robert W. Kates and others called for the development of a new discipline: Sustainability Science. In the American journal *Science*, Kates *et al.* (2001) suggested:

> A new field of sustainability science is emerging that seeks to understand the fundamental character of interactions between nature and society. Such an understanding must encompass the interaction of global processes with the ecological and social characteristics of particular places and sectors. The regional character of much sustainability science means that research will integrate the effects of key processes across scales from the local to the global. Sustainability science will require fundamental advances in our ability to address issues such as the behavior of complex self-organizing systems as well as the responses of the socio-ecological systems to multiple and interacting stresses such as climate change, population movement, economic dislocation and so on. Combining different ways of knowing and learning will permit different social actors to work in concert, even with much uncertainty and limited information.

Core questions research include:

- How can the dynamic interactions between nature and society – including lags and inertia – be better incorporated into emerging models and conceptualizations integrate the Earth system with human development and sustainability?
- How are long-term trends in environment and development, including consumption and population, reshaping nature–society interactions in ways relevant to sustainability?
- What determines the vulnerability or resilience of the nature–society system in particular kinds of places, for particular types of ecosystems and for human livelihoods?
- Can scientifically meaningful 'limits' be defined that would provide effective warning of conditions beyond which the nature–society systems incur a significantly increased risk of serious degradation?
- What systems of incentive structures, including markets and scientific information, can effectively improve social capacity to guide interactions between nature and society in a more sustainable direction?
- How can today's operational systems for monitoring and reporting environmental and social conditions be developed to provide better guidance for a transition toward sustainability?
- How can today's activities of research planning, monitoring, assessment and decision support be better integrated into systems for adaptive management and societal learning?

Source: adapted from Kates *et al.* (2001).

dependency. Scientific thinking is officially and publicly presented by politicians and scientists as the most important, if not the sole reliable source of knowledge and understanding. When proved wrong, modern expert institutions have focused on reconstructing history to communicate their own blamelessness, attributing catastrophes to acts of God or the public's own misunderstanding of the subtleties and indeterminacies of the scientific method. Furthermore, public trust is compromised, according to Wynne (1996: 27), by these institutions responding to dangers 'in the idiom of scientific risk management, tacitly and furtively' and imposing 'prescriptive models of the human and the social upon laypeople and these are implicitly found wanting in human terms'. The real world is treated as if it were a lab experiment and human and other living beings as simply among the many controllable variables.

In his analysis of the conflictual relationship between government scientific investigations into risks from radioactive fall-out and the local knowledge of Cumbrian sheep farmers following the 1986 Chernobyl disaster, Wynne clearly shows how scientific investigation consistently ignored or discounted local expert knowledge and consequently failed to appreciate the full complexity of the issues they were addressing or the inadequacy of their own methods. Lab methods cannot simply be transposed to Lakeland hills. The attempt and expectation of government scientists to predict and control failed to achieve any effective results and further succeeded in reinforcing public suspicion of the efficacy of official institutionalized knowledge processes. Wynne writes:

> After a few months, the scientists' experiments were abandoned, though the farmers' criticisms were never explicitly acknowledged. . . . Much of this conflict between expert and lay epistemologies centred on the clash between the taken-for-granted scientific culture of prediction and control and the farmers' culture, in which lack of control was taken for granted over many environmental and surrounding social factors in farm management decisions. The farmers assumed predictability to be intrinsically unreliable as an assumption, and therefore valued adaptability and flexibility as a key part of their cultural identity and practical knowledge. The scientific experts ignored or misunderstood the multidimensional complexity of this lay public's problem domain, and thus made different assumptions about its controllability.
>
> (1996: 67)

Wynne concludes that it is necessary for (indigenous) local knowledge to become part of a broader understanding of risk than has often been the case in the past. The trajectory of this line of thought appears to be that sustainable development is again perceived as a constructive consequence of a dialogue of values, methods and understandings. There needs to be a recognition of the public value of science, and a concerted and genuine effort to engage the public in scientific debate and developments, and to ask questions that scientists sometimes feel is not their job. This may mean that the institution of science, including its established role and expectations in academia and big corporations, will need to change significantly.

Characterizing global environmental risks

Risks manifest themselves on many spatial levels. Global environmental risks may be characterized in two ways:

1   Risks, like climate change, that are essentially *systemic* – environmental change at any locale can affect the environment elsewhere and even the global system itself.
2   Risks that are essentially *cumulative* – for example degradation of ecosystems, continuing deforestation, water contamination and industrial toxic pollutants.

Jeanne Kasperson and Roger Kasperson conceptualize both systemic and cumulative risk as induced by human action, arguing that many risks remain hidden from public view by ideology, competing societal priorities – for example, economic development or poverty eradication – political marginality and cultural bias. Global environmental risk analysis calls into question current approaches to knowledge, knowledge management and knowledge generation. As Kasperson and Kasperson write:

> The idea that the future is negotiable, and that affected parties are now differentially involved (or not involved) in the negotiations, brings forward considerations of power, equity and social justice – and equitable outcomes and equitable processes for getting to those outcomes. The obstacles to broad public participation in creating global futures are many, ranging from lack of access to information and expertise all the way to brute exclusionary force. Equity and the future are linked not just through reference to 'responsibilities for future generations' but by questions of who controls access to the future and who chooses the trajectories of change. Those who live in the present live, after all, in the layered remnants of a series of failed former utopias – concretized versions of earlier visions of how things might be.
>
> (2001: 7)

Kasperson and Kasperson identify five important elements in understanding contemporary global environmental risks:

- Global environmental risk is the ultimate threat.
- Uncertainty is a persistent feature both of understanding process and causation and of predicting outcomes.
- Global environmental risk manifests itself in different ways at different spatial scales.
- Vulnerability is a function of variability and distribution in physical and socio-economic systems, the limited human ability to cope with additional and sometimes accumulating hazards, and the social and economic constraints that limit these abilities.
- Futures are not given, they must be negotiated.

(2001: 4–5)

Kasperson and Kasperson schematically represent the processes involved in societal response to global environmental risk, identifying cyclical and iterative feedback loops. Their model attempts to show that failures to address environmental degradation may occur at various points in systems and may affect the driving forces by either mitigating or aggravating them. Although deliberately simplified, their model is an attempt to depict the integration and mutual interdependence of the social, political, economic and environmental. Once society has recognized the signals denoting environmental changes, risks or threats, social institutions like the media and environmental groups, journalists and the lay public can, together with the experts, evaluate their nature and scope. The way this is done, the values and methods applied, and the social and psychological assumptions exercised are likely to mean that these risk signals may be attenuated or amplified. Whatever the case, this social processing will influence the perception of risk and shape individual, group and institutional behaviour.

The precautionary principle

Principle 15 of the 1992 Rio Declaration on Environment and Development states:

> In order to protect the environment, the precautionary approach shall be widely applied by States according to their capabilities. Where there are threats of serious or irreversible damage, lack of full scientific certainty shall not be used as a reason for postponing cost-effective measures to prevent environmental degradation.

In other words, the precautionary principle suggests that it is wise to act prudently when there is sufficient scientific evidence, where action can be justified on reasonable judgements of cost-effectiveness, and where inaction could lead to potential irreversibility or demonstrable harm to people and the environment now and in the future. However, the precautionary principle takes on different hues depending on perspectives or worldviews. For example:

> *Weak sustainability* – precaution has a place as a spur to innovation and managerial adaptation to make up for losses of environmental resources. Cost–benefit analysis is consequently very important.
>
> *versus*
>
> *Strong sustainability* – precaution defines an approach to living that is in harmony with the natural world.

Risk, complexity, uncertainty and the partial nature of knowledge have led to this important guiding principle becoming central to the sustainability debate. For O'Riordan and Cameron (1994), global environmental change means that the precautionary principle ought to be understood in three ways, as:

- the requirement of collective action;
- the requirement of burden sharing; and
- the rise of global citizenship.

Three other factors are also important:

- the need to go beyond scientific understandings;
- the need to take proactive anticipatory action; and
- the need to become more averse to risk possibilities.

For O'Riordan and Cameron (1994), the precautionary principle is most likely to be applied in the following circumstances:

- where new technologies are proposed in well-regulated regimes and where public opinion is instinctively or knowledgeably risk-averse;
- where the principles of regulation allow for judgement as to what is socially tolerable;
- where there is a national culture of care for the less fortunate and the defenceless; and
- where there is openness and accountability in policy formulation and decision-taking.

One major criticism of the precautionary principle is that it is vague and often open to various legal and operational interpretations. By reversing the burden of proof, such that any activity must prove that it will not cause harm, the precautionary principle is seen by some as potentially retarding development and innovation and consequently as unscientific. Those who take this view tend to favour narrow risk assessments based on probabilities derived from available but often imperfect evidence. It is these views that have informed the design of government regulatory approaches to genetically modified organisms (GMOs). A stronger version of the precautionary principle would suggest that GMO regulation should be based to a great extent on a potential to cause harm rather than on knowledge of actual harm. In other areas, such as emissions regulations to combat climate change, devising a robust regulatory system may be even more difficult, because of the complexities of climate systems. Given this, Johnston and Santillo (2006: 6) suggest that the precautionary principle should 'be applied as a variety of precautionary approaches tailored for each issue area. Far from being unscientific or stifling progress, such approaches move towards the very highest, scientifically underpinned standards of environmental protection'. The debate will undoubtedly continue, and practice will evolve through ongoing dialogue and discussion; nonetheless, the precautionary principle is already well established, with the Commission of the European Communities within the European Union firmly endorsing the necessity of its application. In a communication issued in 2000, the Commission stated:

> The dimension of the precautionary principle goes beyond the problems associated with a short or medium term approach to risks. It also concerns the longer run and the well-being of future generations.
>
> Whether or not to invoke the precautionary principle is a decision exercised where scientific information is insufficient, inconclusive or uncertain and where there are indications that the possible effects on the environment or human, animal or plant health may be potentially dangerous and inconsistent with the chosen level of protection.
>
> (CEC, 2000)

As Montague (2004) argues, the precautionary principle does not tell people what kinds of action to take. Rather, it assumes that the overriding aim is to prevent harm, and steadily policy makers are recognizing the importance of:

- setting goals;
- examining all reasonable alternatives for achieving those goals, with the expectation that the least harmful approach will be preferred;
- shifting the burden of proof to the proponents of new activities or technologies; and
- involving those who will be affected by the decision in the decision-making process.

Like sustainability, the precautionary principle, too, is a political act.

Science, knowledge and sustainability

The interrelationship and tensions between industrial practices, business imperatives, public policy, political acceptability, social livelihoods, ways of life, cultural expectations, trust, scientific knowledge and capacity to predict are clearly apparent in many issues, whether we are talking of GM, nanotechnology or even fish farming. As Ihde (1997) notes, scientific truth often seems to be little more than scientific consensus, and the work of the Millennium Ecosystem Assessment and the Inter-governmental Panel on Climate Change demonstrates this. One problem for both scientists and non-scientists is how to acquire a perspective on scientific change that encompasses the idea of the whole Earth-as-planet. We sometimes become mesmerized by the truly amazing advances in scientific research and understanding, and we also, as Homer-Dixon (2002) reminds us, sometimes fail to realize how uneven these scientific advances are – fast and fantastic in some areas, slow and uncertain in others. This often leads to 'ingenuity gaps' between the problems we have to deal with and the scientific tools we have at our disposal, because of:

- our own limited cognitive capacity to understand highly complex systems;
- the intrinsic difficulty of some scientific problems;
- the nature of scientific institutions, funding regimes and career trajectories, which tend to make interdisciplinary research and development difficult; and
- social and cultural values which are sceptical of the methods, ethical priorities and benefits of modern science and technology.

This is often compounded by a lack of resources, including, in some developing countries, a lack of highly trained scientists. Homer-Dixon (2002: 277) concludes that 'despite all our technological and scientific prowess, it's not at all clear that we really know what we are doing in this new world we've created for ourselves'. It is this anxiety that so troubles Bill McKibben (2003) in his thought-provoking book *Enough*, which dissects the meaning of being human in an engineered age.

Given so much uncertainty and complexity, sustainable development must be participatory, democratic and inclusive in probably every sphere – knowledge generation, political decision-making and policy implementation, risk assessment, environmental management, health, public communication and so on – if it is to be anything other than a large body of warm words. If society, social norms and expectations, and major institutions are part of the problem and of any solution, Beck's notion of reflexivity as self-confrontation is undoubtedly extremely relevant to the making of green knowledge (Jamison, 2001, 2003). Contrasting forms of knowledge about nature and society derived from community, professional, militant activist and personal experiences are slowly combining to form new theories of and approaches to sustainable socio-ecological development. These forms of knowledge range from the empirically based notions of bottom-up 'citizen science' to the professionalized top-down expertise of international NGOs, universities and think-tanks, the deep ecological action-orientated militancy of activist groups like Earth First!, the meditative spiritualism of some religious people, and the knowledge management practices of business and government. There is certainly a need for a new extended approach to knowledge creation, what Funtowicz and Ravetz (2001: 178) term a 'post-normal science', where, instead of supporting what is too often presented as salvation, scientists deal mainly with managing uncertainties, so 'assuring the quality of the scientific information provided for policy decisions':

> The new paradigm of post-normal science, involving extended peer communities as essential participants, is visible in the case of AIDS. Here the research scientists operate in the full glare of publicity, involving sufferers, care-givers, journalists, ethicists, activists and self-help groups, as well as traditional institutions for funding, regulation and commercial application of pharmaceuticals. The researchers' choices of problems and evaluations of solutions are equally subjected to critical scrutiny, and their priority disputes are similarly dragged in the public arena.
>
> (Funtowicz and Ravetz, 2001: 192)

For German philosopher Martin Heidegger, tools and instruments, science and technology are the means by which human beings impact on and perceive, model, and visually and imaginatively construct our view and understanding of the planet. Technology can allow us to see. Digital modelling, computer-enhanced imaging and photographs taken by orbiting telescopes or in the lab by electronic microscopes all serve as extensions of ourselves. Science is embodied in technology, and scientific practice is embodied in much of our attitudes and behaviour, but sustainability practitioners have also highlighted the value of other more spiritual and/or sensual ways of seeing, in many ways reflecting the growing global influence of Buddhist thought and insight (Schumacher, 1974; Capra, 1991, 1996; Kumar, 1992) and the growing value of traditional ecological knowledge, dreamtime and kanyini to us all.

Case study: biotech and the state of the future

Nanotechnology has now superseded biotech as the new technological frontier, heralding amazing possibilities and potentially massive, unknowable, risks (Hunt and Mehta, 2006). Phillip Bond, the US Undersecretary of Commerce for Technology, told the World Nano-Economic Congress held in Washington in 2003 that this miraculous technology had the power to make the blind see, the lame walk and the deaf hear, could cure AIDS, cancer and diabetes, and could enable the world to be waste-free, energy-efficient and clean (Shand and Wetter, 2006). Nanotechnology is a 'platform technology' offering possibilities for low-cost solar cells and sensors, faster computers, lighter and stronger materials, crack-resistant paint, self-cleaning windows and fish ponds, odour-eating socks, anti-bacterial bandages, 'smart cell' health treatments, and so on. It also offers new toxicological risks operating at a nano-scale, with unpredictable consequences for human health, the global environment, and the economic and social well-being of developing nations, who are unable to afford or to generate nanotech research and development of their own. Whole industries and employment sectors could disappear overnight. There have been many calls for caution and further evaluative research. Many companies have undertaken toxicological studies, but these rarely make it into the public domain. For many critics, it is the dominance of corporate commercial interests that has driven the nanotech revolution, with issues of social justice, government regulation and development needs being relegated in preference to the economic exploitation of the new technology. Shand and Wetter (2006: 94) write of the need for serious and widespread public debate, a moratorium and global regulation:

> With public confidence in both private and government science at an all-time low, full societal debate on nano-scale convergence is critical. It is not for scientists and governments to 'educate' the public, but for society to determine the goals and processes for the technologies they finance.

For many critics, the same still applies to the science and commercial exploitation of genetic modification. As the International Risk Governance Council argues: 'Nanotechnology raises issues that are more complex and far-reaching than many other innovations and poses significant challenges to risk governance structures and processes' (www.irgc.org/issues/nanotechnology/nanotechnology-risk-governance).

Summary

Understanding sustainable development is perhaps best approached by viewing the concept, and by extension the practice, as an 'heuristic'. An heuristic is a guide to problem solving, a speculation that involves learning and engagement, a search for solutions that may or may not be optimal. This chapter has attempted to explore how sustainable development has operated heuristically. Consequently, it has resonances with similar and related notions, such as the noosphere in Russia, and is closely associated with questions about the nature of knowledge and the ways we seek to make use of it. Discussions of science, statistics, continuity and change, risk and uncertainty, cannot be avoided and in fact should be embraced if learning is to take place and we are to move forward towards a more sustainable world. We must therefore think carefully about what we take for granted, what we assume we know, and be mindful that sustainable development probably requires the sympathetic understanding of many different perspectives, ideas, policies and actions. Science and technology may offer some answers but it is likely that they will also create new challenges and problems as they have done so in the past. Sustainability science may be the answer, but we must wait and see.

Thinking questions

1 How might sustainability be a political act?
2 What can be learned from the work of and controversy surrounding Bjørn Lomborg?
3 What role does science play in promoting sustainable development?
4 How can the layperson best make sense of the various scientific controversies and ethical issues?
5 If you were a native of Tuvalu, how do we know whether a risk is real or imagined?
6 How should the precautionary principle be applied?

Companion website

If you would like to learn more about risk science and sustainability, please visit the companion website for additional case studies.

4 Connecting social with the environmental justice

Aims

This chapter explores the social-environmental interface of sustainable development locally and globally by critically analysing the concepts and practices associated with social and environmental justice. The role of new digital media, community development, the idea of 'the commons' together with the importance of social capital, local food initiatives and environmental justice campaigns will be examined as key elements of the sustainable development process.

Human society and the environment

In many parts of the world, there is an intellectual and pragmatic transition underway that seeks a connective, holistic and essentially ecological approach to human development, recognizing the necessity of a trans-disciplinary approach to understanding and acting in the world. Following the 1992 Rio Summit, sustainable development was frequently represented graphically as three interlocking circles standing for the economy, society and the environment, and, although there has been much critical debate about economic growth, environmental limits and eco-efficiency, the language of economics still influences much of the sustainability debate. There is now frequent reference to various 'capitals' – *natural capital, economic capital, financial capital, human capital, cultural capital, symbolic capital* and *social capital* – by organizations as diverse as the World Bank and the charity Forum for the Future. For many, the environment (natural capital) means the natural world of forests, fields, animals, rivers, atmosphere, wilderness and so on. This relatively uncomplicated understanding leads to quite serious implications for individuals, social organizations and local-to-global political arrangements. The first thing to recognize is that the natural world has been shaped for literally thousands of years by the knowledge, capabilities and skills of human beings (human capital). Our fields and woodlands are the result of agricultural transformations. Many of the world's deserts have been produced as a consequence of human activity. Our air quality, or lack of it, is often the result of changing modes and sites of industrial production, old and new technology (economic capital), and investment flows and processes (financial capital). Even the non-human animal world has literally altered shape as a result of selective breeding techniques and now genetic modification – practices inaugurated by human beings utilizing to the full their intellectual capital. Towns, cities and sprawling urban conurbations are obviously human constructs, and so is the quality of life within them, enhanced or otherwise by networks of trust and reciprocity and political arrangements (social capital). The look of the surrounding countryside is largely the product of our inter-active social relationships with each other and the 'natural' world. Consequently, what many sustainability practitioners argue is that as citizens we must start taking responsibility for our actions as they impact on the wider environment, which will necessitate moderating our behaviour and altering our ideas, predispositions and preferences accordingly.

Human behaviour has had detrimental, and frequently dire, effects on our natural capital and the ecosystem services upon which our economies, livelihoods and lives depend:

- We are using up many finite resources – minerals and fuels – which cannot be replaced, and destroying renewable ones, like our forests and fisheries, upon which our economy, our standard of living and our quality of life depend.
- Many production processes create waste, much of it toxic, causing serious pollution of rivers, land and the air we breathe. Increased CO_2 in the atmosphere, the consequence of burning fossil fuels like coal and oil, is a cause of global warming (the greenhouse effect), leading to unpredictable weather patterns, sea-level rises, floods, droughts, heat waves, freezes and so on.
- Modern methods of industrial production and technological innovation have given rise to a new range of risks, which affect people in their everyday lives but which cannot be fully known, understood or even anticipated. Thanks to the depletion of the ozone layer, sunbathing is now recognized as a direct cause of skin cancer. New 'more efficient' farming techniques have led to animal diseases which have jumped the species barrier and bring fears over food security.
- Species extinction and habitat destruction have relentlessly increased as economic development has meant more roads, more towns and more material consumption.
- Genetic modification of plants, animals and indeed of human beings exposes us to potential future harms (and benefits) which we have little understanding of and perhaps even less control over.

If we shift our focus on sustainability from the abstract or global to the local level, these implications and changes may be seen, and felt, more immediately. Many discussions of fashioning a 'sustainable society' or a 'sustainable world' are meaningless to most people if they require understanding abstract constructions that are not relevant in daily life or part of their practical consciousness. The locality, the village or the urban neighbourhood is the level of social organization where the consequences of environmental degradation are most keenly experienced and where successful intervention is most noticeable, and there tends to be greater confidence in government action at the local level. The combination of these factors arguably creates a climate of understanding more conducive to the kind of long-term political mobilization implicit in the term 'sustainable development'. Moreover, as Yanarella and Levine (1992: 769) observe, sustainable community development may ultimately be the most effective means of demonstrating that sustainability can be achieved on a broader scale, precisely because it places the concept of sustainability 'in a context within which it may be validated as a process'. By moving to the local level, the potential for generating concrete examples of sustainable development are increased and, as these successes become a tangible aspect of daily life, the concept of sustain-ability will acquire the widespread legitimacy and acceptance that has thus far proved elusive (Bridger and Luloff, 1999: 380). Many local communities have signalled their engagement by devising sustainability indicators, specifically incorporating action-related or environmental justice issues as ways of monitoring progress in ecological restoration and community participation, and even of managing urban growth and regional development (Warner, 2002). For many writers and activists, community-inspired or -led ecological restoration projects offer a 'giving back to nature' of what human beings have unjustly and damagingly expropriated from it, in the process enabling significant learning experiences that widen understanding of human society, of people's relationship to nature, to consumption and to production. Leigh notes:

> It offers the average citizen insight not only on how humans impact their immediate landscape, but on the larger biotic community as a whole, an insight that perhaps can be viewed as more valuable than the ecological restoration itself. The environmental crisis and its connections to pollution, overdevelopment, population, consumption and scarcity are strikingly realized by community volunteers when the parcel of their restored landscape is shown to be affected by these forces.
>
> (2005: 8)

A clean and healthy environment is essential for human health and well-being. It is only just and is as such a human right as the many thousands of people harmed by the 1984 disaster in Bhopal, India, know full well. About 500,000 people were exposed to toxic chemicals following a gas leak from Union Carbide's pesticide plant. More than 7,000 people died within a few days and 15,000 died within the next few years. Some 120,000 people are still suffering from chronic and debilitating illnesses for which treatment is largely ineffective and for which adequate compensation from Indian and American courts has still to be granted (Amnesty International, 2004). The existence and effectiveness of community health monitoring, research and treatment have been due to the continuing participation and action of individuals in partnership with charitable bodies such as the Sambhavna Trust (Dinham and Sarangi, 2002).

The importance of social capital: beyond self-interest

In the 1960s, ecologist Garrett Hardin illustrated the finite nature of our world and the disastrous consequences that would ensue if we all rationally pursued our own economic self-interest in the highly resonant modern parable 'The tragedy of the commons'. It offers a vivid picture of a pasture on which a number of herdsmen keep as many cattle as they can. As a rational being, each person inevitably attempts to maximize his return by adding one additional animal to his grazing herd. His gain is obvious but his loss is not, as the negative effect of grazing one extra beast will be shared by all the herdsmen. Rationally calculating the obvious benefits and gains, the rational herdsman concludes that the only sensible course to pursue is to add another animal to the herd. And then another, and another ... However, this same conclusion is reached by every rational herdsman sharing the common pasture land, and that is the basis of the tragedy. Each person is locked into a system that compels him to increase his herd without limit in a world that is inevitably and clearly limited. 'Ruin is the destination toward which all men rush, each pursuing his own best interest in a society that believes in the freedom of the commons', writes Hardin (1968: 354). Freedom is the recognition of necessity, complexity, rights and responsibilities. It is also the key to understanding the importance of social capital in the sustainable development process: it is in the long-term interest of everyone to co-operate and work to care for 'the commons' and to share its benefits.

Extending this insight in his discussion of the sustainability framework The Natural Step, David Cook, in explaining the connection between human society and nature's systems, reflects on the direct correlation and connections between the social and the ecological, and the various consequences that may ensue:

> On the one hand, social sustainability's dependence on wider ecological sustainability is becoming more evident. As we continue to undermine nature's capacity to provide humans with services (such as clean water and air) and resources (such as food and raw materials), both individuals and the social relations between them will be subjected to growing amounts of pressure. Conflict will grow and public health, personal safety and other negative social factors will increase in the face of ecological threats and decreased access to nature's services and resources.
>
> On the other hand, overall ecological sustainability has become dependent on social sustainability. If a growing number of people are living within a social system that systematically constrains their capacity to meet their needs, then participation and investment in that system will break down. The end result of such socially unsustainable development is rising violence, alienation and anger. People will place no trust at all in nature once social trust collapses and various modes of barbarism develop. Conflict, poverty and other forms of social stress will result in more environmental degradation.
>
> (D. Cook, 2004: 45)

'Social capital' is a term we can use to denote those relationships by which groups and individuals communicate, network, build trust, enter into dialogue, resolve conflicts, identify and solve problems, and realize collective and individual potential as agents of sustainable development. Just as we talk about ecological carrying capacity, perhaps there is a need, as Roseland (1998) suggests, to speak about and nurture our 'social caring capacity'. Social networking is part of this and is a key element in effective sustainable community development (Gilchrist, 2004). Although locality and a sense of place remain important in fostering community identity and belonging, social networks invariably extend well beyond one specific geographical location. The formation of communities based on interest is a means of collectively empowering oppressed or powerless groups, particularly those associated with gender, disability, ethnicity, age and/or sexual orientation. Additionally, people who experience relatively high degrees of social interaction with others often exhibit higher degrees of contentment than those who do not. The essence of community, then, is to be found in the nature and qualities of relationships as much as the qualities of a particular place. The nature of the built environment can, by turn, hinder or enable social interaction according to the existence or otherwise of places for people to meet and chat while shopping, walking, working or resting. Wide pavements, traffic-calming devices, and open but well-viewed public or urban green spaces allow for occasional, chance or intentional encounters (Barton, 2000). Many classic studies have described community in exactly these ways (see, for example, Young and Willmott, 1957; Roberts, 1971), and for those whose intention is to build (sustainable) communities, networking has become a core competence, not least because one of the most important functions of networks is their capacity to share ideas and values and develop trusting relationships and methods of co-operation and collaboration. Networks also frequently serve to facilitate reflexive and critical social dialogues, the sharing and accumulation of collective knowledge and understanding, and social and community learning, creating avenues in which common ideas and purposes can be recognized and expressed. And because cultural diversity frequently challenges dogma and prejudice, community cohesion often emerges through complex social articulations that celebrate ethnic and other difference. For diversity to be celebrated, there need to be trusted public and/or private spaces (and places) that create convivial, accessible and accommodative environments. Such spaces can be created or customized by community members themselves through project activity, community artwork, social events and gatherings. The annual Notting Hill Carnival is one spectacular example of a civic and cultural celebration of difference. As Gilchrist suggests, a community's empowerment is usually achieved through both learning and collective action or organization:

> Challenging powerful institutions and oppressive practices is a crucial aspect of community development, as is changing the flow of power through organizations and communities. Collective action is empowering in its own right, because it enables people without much power to assert their interests and influence in decision-making. Networks contribute to empowerment on a psychological level, by enabling people to compare their experiences, learn from each other's successes, and develop greater awareness of the wider politics of inequality and oppression.
>
> (Gilchrist, 2004: 44)

Empowerment doesn't simply appear as a result of a single action or event, although a transformative, life-changing experience is often a significant catalyst. Rather, as Shuftan (1996) writes, empowerment should be viewed as a continuous process that continuously enhances people's social understanding of anti-oppressive practice, developing their capacity to exercise some control over their individual and collective lives.

Building social networks

Throughout the post-war years, successive UK governments have recognized the need to reform local governance and encourage social and civic participation, devising spatial and other policies articulating many principles of sustainable development – notably, social justice, social inclusion, citizenship, equity, and sustainable environmental and economic practices (Raco, 2007). Local Agenda 21 encouraged participatory democracy, particularly when local community members deliberated upon, chose and worked to meet meaningful sustainability indicators. Civic engagement has been nurtured and social capital generated (Barton, 2000), but this is not the full story.

Box 4.1 Reflecting on the future of the commons

Radical geographer David Harvey points out that Garret Hardin's fundamental concern was population growth rather than the inherent superiority of private property relationships and the drive to maximize individual utility. If the cattle had been held in common rather than the land, Hardin's metaphor would not work. 'It would then be clear' writes Harvey (2011: 101) 'that it was private property in cattle and individual utility-maximizing behavior that lay at the heart of the problem'. By contrast, for Hardin and others who in the 1960s were concerned with the population time bomb, the crucial issue was whether the individual family should retain the right to decide whether or not to have children and if so how many. The point for Harvey is that the commons is being continuously reproduced by human action at various scales from the local to the global. He is interested in how appropriate policies and actions can maintain and extend them conceding that different actions will almost certainly be required at different spatial scales. That is, what works at the global scale may not work at the local; but whatever the case, a clear way of valuing nature and human endeavour that transcends the ethic of individual profit maximization is what is really required. Harvey writes:

> The human qualities of the city emerge from our practices in the diverse spaces of the city, even as those spaces are subject to enclosure both by private and public state ownership, as well as by social control, appropriation, and countermoves to assert what Henri Lefebvre called 'the right to the city' on the part of the inhabitants. Through their daily activities and struggles, individuals and social groups create the social world of the city and, in doing so, create something common as a framework within which we all can dwell. While this culturally creative common cannot be destroyed through use, it can be degraded and banalized through excessive abuse.

> The common is not, therefore, something extant once upon a time that has since been lost, but something that, like the urban commons, is continuously being produced. The problem is that it is just as continuously being enclosed and appropriated by capital in its commodified and monetary form. A community group that struggles to maintain ethnic diversity in its neighborhood and to protect against gentrification, for example, may suddenly find its property prices rising as real estate agents market the 'character' of the neighborhood as multicultural and diverse as an attraction for gentrifiers.

Source extracts: David Harvey (2011: 103–4 and 105–6)

Contemporary failures to engage people are often seen as resulting from a decline in membership of voluntary associations that produce the relationships and networks of reciprocity, trustworthiness, obligation and perceived mutual benefit (in other words, social capital) necessary for participation and engagement (Putnam, 2000). For James A. Coleman (1990), social capital influences the ability of people to participate in social and community affairs and is often a by-product of everyday leisure or hobby activities. There is a strong link between social activity and civic participation. Recently, Putnam (2007) has cited the US 'megachurch' phenomenon as an interesting exemplar of community-based social interactivity. Megachurches have very low barriers to entry and people can leave just as easily. Nonetheless, they generate intense commitment, often through the organization of a range of small social leisure groups – mountain bikers for God, volleyball players for God, cancer survivors for God, and so on.

Despite appearances to the contrary, members' emotional commitments are directed to other people rather than to theology. Friends and helpers are sought and gained. So, Putnam asks, can what occurs within these organizations be replicated elsewhere?

An important distinction is sometimes made between *bonding* and *bridging* social capital (Putnam, 2000; Woolcock and Narayan, 2000). Bonding social capital tends to be characterized by dense, multifunctional ties and strong, generally localized, trust, whereas bridging social capital is characterized by weak ties. Woolcock and Narayan argue that bonding social capital is an effective defence against poverty but less valuable for economic and social development – the difference between 'getting by' and 'getting on'. However, Portes (1998) also notes that strong ties and social norms may enforce a conformity that militates against working with others, leading to social exclusivity or the reproduction of such traits as ethnic prejudice, political marginalization, suspicion and xenophobia. The increasing numbers of gated communities in the US, Europe, South Africa and China is arguably one manifestation of this (Romig, 2005), since gated communities are protected, and protective spaces with delineated and defensible boundaries and rules that geographically define the existence of a 'community'. As Low (2003) notes, residents in gated communities are interested in a particular type of community – one that protects children, that keeps out crime, that looks neat and tidy, and that enjoys quality services and good amenities. For some residents, the architecture and spatial design express an ideal, a practical utopia, separating the public from private, the suburb from the city, thereby precluding a potentially rich experience of 'community' in the interests of an imagined peace of mind stemming from uniformity and familiarity. In Managua, Nicaragua, a complete layer of the city has become disembedded from the general urban fabric by a series of high-speed roads, roundabouts and the privatization of security, which, through a planned process of social and spatial segregation, has produced a fortified network of gated communities for the city's elites (Rodgers, 2004).

More progressive social initiatives do exist, but many have only short instrumentalist lifespans, with problems compounded by differential levels, capacities and predispositions to participate. The educated and materially comfortable classes tend to gain disproportionate attention, time and resources to secure their needs and wants. They have political clout, economic significance, and the skills and contacts to be effective. Unfortunately, there is sometimes a failure to connect, a resistance to the emergence of what political philosopher John Rawls (1999) terms 'a moral personality', where self-interest overrides the common or public good, where seeking the rightful redress of a grievance achieves only partial success. For example, seeking redress for the problems of traffic congestion may not necessarily facilitate the consideration of wider issues – the development of an integrated public transport system, for example. Local environmental campaigns are often characterized as NIMBYism (not in my backyard). Concluding his historical survey of urban poverty initiatives in the US, Robert Halpern (1995: 229) writes somewhat despairingly of:

our reluctance to create a somewhat larger frame of mutual interest, if not mutual responsibility, leaving us with no ways to live together as a people or to address societal problems. Our preoccupation with creating and defending boundaries tends constantly to narrow our sense of identity – as does the constant preoccupation with comparing, and with similarities and differences. . . .

Community groups historically have proven incapable of sustaining coalitions that did not necessarily address immediate community needs but might change harmful policies and practices over time.

Social capital, civic engagement and democratic renewal cannot be based solely on utility. A value change is required, which in turn perhaps points to the inadequacy of Coleman and Putnam's concept of 'social capital' if viewed largely as an exchange relationship. If something is worth doing, it should be done for its own sake as well as for any external benefit. The principle and practice of civic and community participation needs to become part of what Bourdieu (1977) termed the *social habitus* – that is, the production of systems of durable transposable dispositions, structuring structures, matrices of perceptions, appreciations, predispositions, tendencies, norms, values and actions. In her study of democratic participation in Brazil, Abers (1998: 63) suggests that a democratic habitus and collective moral personality can be constructed from virtually nothing. People learn about democratic practices through experiencing them. They gain confidence, as well as skills and habits of collective decision-making, through participating in actions that have an evidently good effect. They learn that selfishness can easily backfire, while being concerned about the needs of others does not necessarily mean losing out oneself. Nonetheless, material poverty and educational deficits need to be addressed, if people's potential for and sense of collective efficacy and personal agency is to be nurtured. Existing predispositions to exclude or to conform need to be challenged. Existing structures, relations and processes of power, systems of administration and governance, and vested interests need to be contested and reformed, so that new sustainable habits, perspectives and values can emerge – from the bottom up and dialogically. Projects that involve both social and ecological concerns but deny the importance of either are likely to falter as the initiative to build the Huangbaiyu Sustainable Village in China demonstrates. This ecovillage has houses designed and built to high ecological specifications, based on the guidance of the American green architect William McDonough, but failed to attract local buyers, largely because local people, with their limited means, prioritized social, educational and employment issues over the benefits of living in environmentally sound, comfortable and attractive dwellings. There was a lack of understanding, a lack of dialogue, between the fundamental needs of people and those of the ecosystem (Sudjic, 2006).

Public libraries: public pedagogy, democracy and sustainability

The privatization and commercialization of public space, and more generally of the public sphere, is a defining characteristic of neoliberalism's political and economic hegemony. This has been discussed fully and defiantly by many people (Low and Smith, 2006; Harvey, 2013). The future of public libraries in the age of the Internet and ubiquitous digital technologies may seem rather trivial but what makes the actual, or de facto, privatization of public libraries so important, though, is their continuing relevance to maintaining meaningful democratic processes and a moral economy that distinctly upholds, supports and realizes the notion of a cultural commons (Blewitt, 2012). Free and ready access to knowledge and information, books, journals and other cultural artefacts have been, and remain, essential to civil liberty – the freedom of expression, assembly and democratic decision-making. The continuing existence of free, safe and trusted public spaces where this knowledge and information can be pondered, discussed and questioned is thus of utmost significance. Informed judgements are only possible if free deliberation and free access to information, including assenting and dissenting voices, exists. If dissenting voices are crowded out or silenced by corporations or governments, truth and liberty, as John Stuart Mill wrote in *On Liberty* (1974: 111) 'would lose something'. The clear fact that today much of this information takes a digital form renders the need for the public library all the greater, especially as the Internet too, the cyber commons, is increasingly becoming controlled, enclosed and colonized by political and economic interests. The utopian idea that the Internet would become a global common space, almost anarchic in its egalitarian and democratic potential, is quickly fading as censorship, copyright and commerce encloses the virtual world (Lanier, 2013). By contrast, public libraries institute a civic 'right to know' (Greenhalgh *et al.*, 1995: 112). They are hubs for various networked information ecologies allowing access to materials and resources they literally hold in common but which may otherwise remain beyond the financial or other reach of users and citizens.

Public libraries also have a wider role in articulating a public pedagogy of environmental sustainability. In Helsinki, for example, the medium-sized Vallila Library became the first public institution in Finland to be awarded the EcoCompass environmental label for its green estate management processes. The library has its own environmental policy, modelled on that of the city, and displays six ecologically aware qualities encompassing image, circulation, sustainability, leadership, design and public space. Library users quickly learn that Vallila is an ecoproject. Access to environmental information has been made easier by, among other things, concentrating all eco-related books in one place. Public events such as discussions on climate change are frequently held and staff give presentations on Vallila's sustainability activities to other Finnish libraries. A new approach to library lending has also been introduced reinforcing the value of sharing and co-operation by acting as a facilitator and mediator between members of the public who wish to lend items such as skis, cameras and tools to people who may be totally unknown to them. Apart from challenging the dominant values of consumer materialism, Harri Sahavirta writes:

> The advantage of this activity is that the library does not need to buy any of these items, we only mediate the exchange. The only thing which is needed is people willing to lend their own items for the benefit of strangers. Surprisingly enough there are willing people! People wish to advance environmental sustainability and are searching for new ways to act.
>
> (2012: 242)

Networks or community in the new media age

The practice of community participation, democratic engagement, social communication and social relationships will undoubtedly be affected by the massive changes in information and communication technology (ICT) that are altering the nature of civic networks and networking, pressure group campaigning, education, urban management, leisure, politics, the labour process and social inclusivity. The relationship between social capital and the Internet is complex. Although this chapter has referred to community and social capital as being basically geographically located, rooted in actual space and place, recent attention has turned to virtual communities that are not limited spatially or indeed temporally. Bordiga *et al.* (2002) note that good existing levels of social capital in a real-world community tend to positively mediate the impact of Internet access on individual volunteering and collective community action. Hampton and Wellman (2003) note that the Internet effectively supports weak ties in suburbs, where residents are spatially dispersed, facilitating various forms of 'neighbouring' – chatting about local issues and so on. Wellman *et al.* (2001) and Wellman and Haythornthwaite (2002) suggest that it is now helpful to replace geographical notions of community with the concept of social networks. If we look at communities as networks of relationships, our picture of weakening social ties is replaced by a view of strong and weak friendships flourishing both within localities and between and across boundaries. People frequently have a much richer set of relationships than those associated with neighbourhoods. In the age of the Internet, it may be that community informatics – that is to say, computer-shaped social relations – are more important for stimulating and supporting cross-boundary relationships than (re)creating a model of community which may be flawed or may have never existed in the first place, as community informatics initiatives are often more concerned with creating spaces than maintaining places (Keeble and Loader, 2001). Rheingold (2000) warns against the 'commodification of community', but stresses the value of community networking via the Internet, citing the work of Virginia Tech and the Blacksburg Electronic Village project as a successful example of networked neighbourhoods and technologically enhanced community development. Pitkin (2006) discusses the role of ICT in building local capacity, suggesting that the quality of particular places may be improved if a reflexive and critical approach is adopted by community members/IT users. ICT and Web tools such as geographic information systems (GIS) can provide a wealth of information for local communities to analyse, discuss and use in formulating local strategies, plans and actions. Local and regional governments frequently extol the virtues of ICT in improving services, stimulating local economic development and enhancing democratic participation. However, using his own experience with the Neighbourhood Knowledge Los Angeles project, and referring to a wide range of literature, Pitkin suggests that enthusiasts and practitioners should:

- avoid being seduced by ICT into devaluing face-to-face interaction;
- not assume simple, straightforward linear effects in any application of new media and communication technologies to human social community; and
- not allow experts to usurp the role of community members in their design and application of information and communication systems.

Media and communication corporations have an interest in promoting new technology, frequently stressing in their marketing and promotion the socially connective functions this technology affords. Cisco Computers launched their Human Network with a wave of attractive, intriguing and resonant images and ideas, including a group of Buddhist monks and their trainees avidly huddled round a laptop. There is undoubted truth in the hype, but it is important to remember that ICT is still in an emergent phase, that technologies can be applied in various ways according to the social, cultural and political contexts, and that, unless information remains free and readily accessible, democracy will suffer. As Harris (2003) notes, cell phones and the Internet enhance their users' capacity to flexibly organize and control their lives, providing additional opportunities for professional contact, security, emotional bonding through informal chat, gathering information and entertainment. However, community identity and community life also depend on the nature and quality of social interaction, of how people do indeed connect. ICT may stimulate more connectivity between people who already know each other and may stimulate new connections between people who have something in common – for example, an interest in the environment or sustainability but Harris questions whether such individually orientated interactions reduce 'serendipitous connections' or devalue the weak ties that are so important in building social capital. Furthermore, people who lack the skills or confidence to use the new technologies or simply cannot afford to own or access them, may remain excluded, as will those whose interests and values simply do not fit. A sustainable community cannot be built if this occurs, since sustainability requires inclusivity, a learning culture, mutual respect and trust.

ICT, civic intelligence and green culture

New emerging media technologies affect possibilities for community development, lifelong learning, social capital, civic engagement, political activism and support for localized actions (Van der Donk *et al.*, 2004). Horton (2004) explored how the Internet is influencing environmental politics and 'green culture' in Britain, which places great value on face-to-face interaction. The local community Horton studied in the north-west of England was not especially rooted or determined by locality, but rather by a sharing of tastes, values and practices that made members somewhat distinct from mainstream society. New digital technologies were quickly and readily incorporated into everyday life, because the computer's capacity to facilitate data management, writing and, most significantly, email communication served to 'lock in' a person's position and commitment to the green movement networks. New media technologies enabled these green activists to connect easily on green issues such as the more sustainable use, reuse and recycling of what is actually a fairly environmentally unfriendly computer technology itself, through a computer 'swap shop'. Horton concludes:

> The main effect of the internet's arrival into the everyday lives of environmental activists has thus been not the eclipsing of embodied, local environmentalism by a virtual, dispersed environmentalism, but the invigoration of local green networks and an increase in face-to-face, as well as virtual, interaction between geographically proximate activists. Consequently, there is today a more complex interweaving of activists' virtual and corporeal socialities and geographies, but one that tends predominantly to result in the strengthening of activists' green identities. Overall, the new opportunities for virtual interaction provided by information and communication technologies promote a more intense sense of local dwelling among environmental activists.
>
> (2004: 749)

Horton's study illustrates how ICT can be socially appropriated by a particular group or social movement within civil society and, as Day and Schuler (2006) argue, has the potential to facilitate the emergence of a counterculture to the dominance and remoteness of the corporate generated 'space of flows' in our networked society (Castells, 1996). Day and Schuler offer an alternative conception for community and civic practice, bringing together recent developments within civil society, potential and actual opportunities afforded by new media technologies, and particular issues, like environmental degradation, that confront the contemporary world. 'Civic intelligence' posits the notion that ordinary people can help fashion and define their future, as intelligence is something possessed by groups and individuals, basically describing the capacity to make sense of information and so influencing responses to environmental and other challenges. Civic intelligence is a combination of community, civic and social networks requiring concerned people, ethical principles (inclusivity, justice and sustainability), and an enduring capacity to learn, develop and refine knowledge and understanding. New media and communication technology has an important role to play in breaching barriers that have previously maintained and reinforced social ignorance, disconnection and passivity. The technology lends itself to implementing environmental monitoring, supporting environmental justice campaigning, and enhancing communication and networking opportunities among civil society groups (Horton, 2004), and offers myriad possibilities for discovering and engaging with local–global issues such as global poverty and climate change. Although large software developers have significant power 'in setting agendas for the ways in which geographical information can be displayed and analyzed' (Dunn, 2007: 631), the potential for enhanced citizen input is also being realized in a number of ways, such as in participatory research, GIS design and environmental justice campaigning. As Montague and Pellarano (2001) have written, the development of digital resources has aided many grass-roots community groups in their attempts to alert others about the dangers associated with the irresponsible disposal of toxic materials. In some cases this has led to the formation of public policy articulating the principles of precaution, substitution and clean production. Jordan *et al.* (2011) show how citizens in Tallahassee (Florida) collaborated in collecting spatial data from Web-based software, such as Google Earth using photos, video and other sociodemographic information to oppose the installation of a biomass facility in a moderate income minority area. A permit had been issued without any prior involvement of the community or consideration of the effects of pollutants on the health of the local population and local environment. Maisonneuve *et al.* (2010) have explored how the general public could initiate a low-cost solution to measuring urban noise pollution by using just ordinary commercially purchased smart phones as noise sensors. From the data gathered collectively, annotated noise maps could be created and shared within a community and with local government. GIS and similar digital applications therefore have significant political implications for empowering particular groups, democratizing planning and enhancing the processes of local democracy. Some observers have even suggested that the utopian impulse to radical action is alive and well, and residing in digiplaces (S. Warren, 2004).

Computer hacking is a form of cyberactivism, or 'hactivism'. It has radical and democratic potential when the aim is to subvert autocratic states and other powerfully exploitative institutions and organizations, but is decidedly undemocratic when practised by those autocratic, undemocratic and unaccountable bodies themselves

(Taylor, 2005). The revolution may be digitized, but on the other hand it may not. Cottle (2011b) has shown that Facebook, Twitter, YouTube and other sites were significant factors in the Arab Spring revolution, although no clear-cut generalizations can be made. However, as Day and Schuler (2006) have suggested, the fundamental characteristic of the network society is the potential for people across the world to connect with each other. Whether active or passive, the world's various populations co-exist and interrelate within both global natural ecosystems and the global media ecology. New 'communities' can develop around new shared interests, aims, values, worldviews and concerns, and apply, adapt and/or develop socio-technical platforms to support and animate these concerns, networks and relationships. These may be local or global – or both simultaneously. We will return to this topic in Chapter 9.

Green apps

In 2012, writing for the Tree Hugger website, Alex Davies noted that

> while the 'greenness' of the iPad is debatable, and there are lots of ways to avoid ever 'needing' one, it can still be a really useful tool for living a sustainable life. From helping you get around on your bike to eating veggies to understanding climate change, these 13 awesome apps will all get you on the right path.

These apps include: Gardening Toolkit, Vegan YumYum, Bike Repair, Audubon Guide, Solar Checker, My Recycle List and Google Maps. The organizers of Earth Day in 2012 saw it as only fitting 'that we leverage the popularity of mobile phones to help further the cause of conserving planetary resources' (Steele, 2012). The Earth Day website offered all manner of green information, advice and guidance, links to social media groups of conservationists and environmental activists. The website provides details of GreenMeter, an iOS app for the iPhone and iPad Touch, which calculates a vehicle's fuel use, helping a driver assess his environmental impact while on the move. Seafood Watch is an iOS and Android app that enables consumers to make sustainable choices when purchasing wet fish or eating in fish restaurants. The Treehugger app enables people to keep up to date with sustainability-related news. Green Shine helps consumers replace many commercial cleaners with environmentally friendly, healthier and safer ones. TVE produced five short films for its contribution to Rio 2012 on how apps can assist development projects in the majority world. The US company MapCruzin offers a wide range of GIS tools, including environmental risk maps, interactive toxic facility maps and toxic-release inventory data together with online tutorials that enable community groups to locate the big polluters in their neighbourhoods, undertake ecological and habitat assessments, evaluate health risks, form toxic watch groups, publish maps indicating areas of local toxicity and conduct facility audits in the belief that they may create a more virtuous and politically green citizenry (Micheletti, 2010).

From June to November 2011 the US Environmental Protection Agency (EPA) conducted the 'Apps for the Environmental Challenge' programme asking software developers to come up with new apps which would combine and deliver environmental data. Thirty-eight apps were submitted, which are now publicly available. Among the five overall winners were: Light Bulb Finder, which facilitates the change from incandescent to energy-efficient lightbulbs empowering users to make informed decisions about their lighting needs, and the financial and environmental impact of their choices; and CGSearch – a mobile Green IT app enabling users across the United States to visually compare the air quality, energy consumption of various cites of the US using Atlanta as a base comparator. There are currently nearly 300 apps available on the EPA website. With nearly 500,000 apps available for the Apple iPhone and iPad alone – although only a small number are actually green – apps have become an important aspect of our digital culture. The evaluation of their use and usefulness is not really able to accommodate the pace of such development, but it seems that a number of green apps do have positive impact in shaping pro-sustainability behaviours (Froehlich *et al.*, 2009; Lehrer and Vasudev, 2011).

Environmental justice and sustainable development

> Environmental justice is based on the principle that all people have a right to be protected from environmental pollution and to live in and enjoy a clean and healthy environment. Environmental justice is the equal protection and meaningful involvement of all people with respect to the development, implementation and enforcement of environmental laws, regulations and policies and the equitable distribution of environmental benefits.
>
> (Commonwealth of Massachusetts, 2002, in Agyeman and Evans, 2004)

As the American environmental movement emerged in the 1970s, it was soon evident that few people of colour had participated in the various campaigns and actions of that period. It was also noted that, as some polluted areas were cleaned up, little action was taken to ensure the neighbourhoods of ethnic minorities were improved (Taylor, 1997). In response to this, the environmental justice movement emerged in the 1980s, comprising Latinos, Native Americans, Asians and African Americans. This changed the social and political complexion of the environmental movement, shifting its centre of gravity away from the primary white middle-class concerns of wildlife, wilderness and the ecologies of the 'natural world'. 'Justice' became the defining principle and rationale for this new movement, which addressed linked issues of class, ethnicity, race, gender, socio-economic inequality, and the blatant discrimination clearly evident in the distribution of environmental impacts and their costs. Environmental justice campaigners are concerned with correctional and distributive actions, taking a system-wide view that asserts, for example, that toxic waste should not be dumped in my, or for that matter anyone's, backyard. Such an approach has helped rearticulate the meaning of the term 'environmental', with homelessness, poverty, hazardous working conditions, health and safety at work and in the surrounding communities, gender inequality, and so on being significant elements of the expanded 'environmental' worldview, bringing it closer to the notion of sustainability. Women of colour have played a prominent role in the development of the environmental justice movement, with eco-feminism helping to open up many environmental debates and dialogues, if not always in practice moving much beyond the iniquities of patriarchal relations, which for Taylor have preoccupied many, though not all, white eco-feminist writers:

[Women of colour] are dominated not only by white men but also by men of colour and by white women. In addition, they work closely with men of colour who are also dominated by white men. So while eco-feminists perceive a uni-directional form of domination (in which females do not dominate and in which their dominator is not dominated), women of colour perceive sexual domination differently. The domination is multidirectional.

(Taylor, 1997: 63)

The energetic and increasingly well-documented political struggles against pollution, dumping and health inequalities have required, maybe forced, an inclusivity and holistic consciousness that has so often eluded many environmentalist philosophies and worldviews in the past. The struggles of indigenous peoples over their ancient land rights, urban minorities fighting against prejudice and discrimination, and victims of natural disasters perceiving institutional racism as a factor behind the slowness of government relief have all contributed to this development. Many interviewees in Spike Lee's 2006 documentary about Hurricane Katrina, *When the Levees Broke*, were in no doubt about this. Environmental justice campaigns are therefore not confined to any one locality, country or region. They are a truly global phenomena, as Agyeman *et al.*'s (2003) collection of empirical studies indicates, where the local and global are seen as being one and the same. For Dobson (1998), however, fundamental ethical questions regarding the general distribution of environmental goods and bads remain. Agyeman *et al.* argue:

Sustainability . . . cannot be simply a 'green' or 'environmental' concern, important though 'environmental' aspects of sustainability are. A truly sustainable society is one where wider questions of social needs and welfare, and economic opportunity, are integrally related to environmental limits imposed by supporting ecosystems.

Although the environmental justice movement emerged in the US in the 1980s and 1990s, examples of environmental justice campaigns can be found across the globe. The Chipko movement, for example, was a peasant movement in the Uttarakhand region of India aiming to prevent the logging of trees and to reclaim threatened traditional forest rights.

(2002: 78)

The movement began in 1973 and Chipko activists extended their protests to include limestone mining in the Dehradun Hills and the Tehri Dam. They later founded the Save the Seeds movement in the face of the growing encroachment of biotech corporations in their cultures, lives and livelihoods. The Chipko protests were also significant because of the mass participation of women villagers, on whose work many local economies depended. Their struggles and campaigns attracted significant attention from the international environmental movement because they successfully raised global awareness of ecological concerns. As Guha (2000) notes, the Chipko activists were seen by many academics and political commentators as being very different from environmental campaigners in the West, as they represented an 'environmentalism of the poor', seeking both justice and sustainability (Martinez-Alier, 2002). In Hindi, the word *chipko* means 'to hug' and Chipko activists would often hug trees to protect them. Indeed, the resistance to the environmental, social and economic exploitation of developing world nations by developed nations is viewed by some analysts (Agyeman, 2005; Escobar, 2006a) as primary examples of environmental justice action adamantly and articulately defending their places, environments and ecosystems. Environmental justice activists have long been dissatisfied with the narrow environmental focus of many traditional green groups, which tend also to be predominantly white, middle class and frequently anti-urban. Habitat conservation and ecological restoration are certainly important issues impacting on the quality of people's lives, but environmental justice encompasses much more – transport and access, air quality, toxic pollution, poverty, poor housing, unemployment and all the other major concerns of disadvantaged people. This has meant that the environment is broadly interpreted as denoting where people live, learn, work and play. Given this, environmental justice campaigns are inevitably quite anthropocentric in orientation, but Agyeman (2005) passionately argues for a fusion of environmental and sustainability campaigns at local, regional and national levels that clearly articulate justice and equity as central defining principles. With reference to Shutkin (2001), he notes that, although narrowly based civic environmentalism has a role, a more broadly focused civic environmentalism conceptualizing sustainability holistically through addressing gender, age and race is pivotal in fashioning a more pro-active 'just sustainability'.

In Britain the Environment Agency (Mitchell and Walker, 2003) and Defra (Lucas *et al.*, 2004) have identified environmental injustice and social deprivation as very real problems for many communities, making clear reference to transport, local services, housing, health, urban regeneration, waste, climate change, quality of life and related issues. Noting that research into environmental justice in the UK has not been as sophisticated or extensive as in the US, Lucas and her co-writers conclude that:

> Where a neighbourhood or area experiences one environmental problem, this is rarely in isolation.
>
> Ill health and reduced quality of life is usually the result of an accumulation of these problems (poor housing, inadequate local services, etc.) over an individual's lifetime or even over a number of generations.
>
> Some sectors of the population are consistently more adversely affected than others, and these are almost always those that are already recognized as the most vulnerable.
>
> Environmental ills may not only self-perpetuate, but also lead to other environmental, economic and social problems if left unaddressed.
>
> (Lucas *et al.*, 2004: vi)

Environmental justice is also about reconnecting. In an article in *Resurgence* and more fully in his book *Soil and Soul* (2004), the academic and activist Alistair McIntosh has written eloquently about the restoration, to the people living on the Hebridean island of Eigg, of their land, their community, their culture and their historical memory. For McIntosh, environmental justice means retrieving a spiritual connection to the land, to nature and through this to oneself. It refers to community members experiencing what the radical educator Paulo Freire (1996) once termed 'conscientization', a combination of conscience and consciousness, that reveals a community's and an individual's true place in the world, and the effects of unequal relations of power and wealth on lives and livelihoods. For McIntosh, heritage is not a commodity to be bought, sold and consumed, but is a living thing, and land rights are important to people across the world. On Eigg, the islanders campaigned to reclaim their heritage, raising £1.5 million to buy the island from its laird. McIntosh notes that, at 7,400 acres, Eigg represented just 1 per cent of the Scottish Highlands under private ownership. Instead of private landlordism, McIntosh advocates the establishment of community land trusts, like the Eigg Trust, where rents support community self-management and where, as in the crofting community, tenancies may be inherited, thereby allowing for both individual enterprise and communal supervision. So, like the islanders of Eigg, community members in many areas of the world may need, in order to control their futures, to re-vision, reorganize, and work to re-empower themselves and reassert their rights.

Environmental justice and social action

In London, the Mayor's Commission on the Environment noted early on in the life of the new Greater London Authority that social disadvantage and poor environmental quality should play a key role in the city's sustainable development policies and that sustainability should be central to many of London's key strategies. The capital city has over 7 million residents, over 300 languages are spoken, and although there is great wealth, there is also considerable poverty, with a disproportionate percentage of black and other minority ethnic groups experiencing the latter (Adebowale *et al.*, 2004). Poor air quality, limited access to green space, noise pollution, poor housing, fuel poverty and respiratory problems are significant issues affecting many individuals and neighbourhoods. To combat such problems, the London Sustainability Exchange (LSX), a partnership body led by the charity Forum for the Future and including Groundwork, the Mayor of London, Business in the Community and many London Councils, has called for more effective leadership, more detailed mapping of inequalities and injustices, and better water and resource management, and has worked with many local neighbourhood communities to lobby for change. They have made significant improvements themselves. In the Marks Gate community in the London Borough of Barking and Dagenham, and the Pepys Estate community in the London Borough of Lewisham, LSX is working with local residents to develop a local area map, using GIS to highlight 'trouble-spots', create an action plan to resolve environmental poverty issues, and empower 'community ambassadors' or local leaders to influence local decision-making and social behaviour. This capacity-building exercise develops experiences of earlier projects aiming to foster green lifestyles that have worked with members of the Bangladeshi and Somali Muslim community in Tower Hamlets, and with Hindu communities aiming to improve water conservation. In both areas, a cultural and particularly religious resonance was established through referencing Quranic or Hindu teachings, and offering talks and workshops in mosques and temples on the sacred nature of the environment and the need to value and conserve natural resources.

In the US, Bullard and Johnson (2000), Lerner (2005) and Bullard (2005) show how toxic pollution, health, liveable neighbourhoods, racism, and land and human rights combine in many environmental justice campaigns involving African Americans,

Native Americans, Hispanics, and other black and minority ethnic groups in the US. In what appears to be a deliberate understatement, Bullard (2005: 22) notes that 'making government respond to the needs of communities composed of the poor, working class and people of colour has not been easy'. Changes to the environmental protection paradigm have been due to the lobbying and campaigning activities of a loose alliance of grass-roots and national environmental and civil rights activists, but, as many observers have argued, the real problems are deeply rooted in the institutionalized racism that has characterized the history of land-use policy. Zoning has enabled dirty industries to infiltrate established communities. Environmental regulations have been either evaded or weakly enforced. For Wright (2005), slavery begat environmental racism and injustice, which can be seen in its purest form along Louisiana's Mississippi River 'cancer alley' or 'chemical corridor', which produces around 20 per cent of the petrochemicals in the US. Many communities have been destroyed, poisoned or relocated by this highly profitable and, in Louisiana, subsidized industry. Wright (2005) and Lerner (2005) tell the story of the residents of Diamond, a small African American mixed-income community, located within a manufacturing complex that in 1997 released 2 million pounds of toxic emissions into the atmosphere. The community subsequently lobbied Shell, whose refinery was a massive emitter of carcinogens, to buy them out and move them to an area where they would not experience the devastating health problems associated with the toxic pollution plaguing their neighbourhoods. In 2002, Shell finally agreed. The environmental justice campaigns in Diamond, and other similar communities, have an uncomfortable historical resonance, because some relocated communities were originally established by freed slaves following the Civil War. In another example, activist and academic David Pellow (2002) analyses the waste recycling industry in Chicago, developing a fourfold framework for evaluating environmental racism and injustice in the process: first, the environmental history of racism in a particular place; second, the role of multiple stakeholders in the environmental conflicts and disputes; third, the effects of social stratification – race and/or class; and fourth, the ability of the least powerful social groups to shape their struggles for environmental justice. Pellow (2002: 9) identifies a number of indicators of environmental inequality and/or racism, including:

- widespread unequal protection and enforcement against hazardous facility siting in poor neighbourhoods and communities of colour;
- disproportionate impact of occupational hazards on the poor and workers of colour;
- the abrogation of treaties with native populations, particularly with regard to mining, waste dumping and military weapons testing;
- unsafe and segregated housing;
- discriminatory transportation systems and zoning laws;
- the exclusion of the poor and people of colour from environmental decision-making;
- the neglect of human health and social justice issues by the established environmental movement.

For Pellow, industrial production and consumption is a never-ending 'treadmill' fired by the ideology of economic growth and real conflict between groups whose interests frequently vary and are often opposed. He shows how, and why, construction demolition dumps were located in many African American communities in the 1980s, how an incinerator was sited in the African American community of Robbins, and how a non-profit recycling initiative was replaced by a profit-based programme run by a big corporation. The least powerful had the least influence on policy decisions and suffered accordingly. Minority workers, including homeless and indigenous people from the poor areas where waste had been dumped, were employed as 'alley entrepreneurs' to collect contaminated recyclables to be exchanged for cash. The work was hard, of low status and hazardous to health, resulting in many workers struggling for dignity and autonomy. Recycling work is not necessarily fulfilling and, as in Pellow's study, can become just like any other exploitative and degrading business activity if the social and labour implications are excluded from environmental goals. In *The Silicon Valley of Dreams*, Pellow and Park (2002) demonstrate how the hi-tech information society rooted in California's Silicon Valley rests on a pro-duction process that is toxic to both land and people. Some 80 per cent of the production workforce are new immigrants, women and people of colour. Wages are low and jobs are tedious, and in some instances potentially injurious to health. Housing costs are high. Personal testimony bears witness to environmental injustices spreading over years, with people telling stories of chemical spillages, land and air pollution, miscarriages, birth defects, asthma, cancers, death, community resistance and labour protest. In reviewing the book, Stacey Warren states the contradictions very clearly, calling for a politically engaged scholarship:

> In short, it is almost inconceivable that this is the same Silicon Valley heralded by the media and in the popular press, or analyzed as part of the growth of hi-tech industrial landscapes. What is treated parenthetically in otherwise sound treatments such as Castells and Hall's (1994) classic examination of 'Technopoles', is brought out into the light here. The same broad, global processes inform both, but by subtly shifting the focus to the production worker herself, Pellow and Park change forever the way we think about Silicon Valley. At the outset of the book, the authors describe themselves as engaged in 'advocacy research', which they define as 'the theory and practice of making the scholarly enterprise more application-oriented, more sustainable and more relevant to communities' (p21). Indeed, this seems the only responsible way to study Silicon Valley.
>
> (2004: 402)

The Silicon Valley Toxics Coalition (SVTC) was formed in 1982, when groundwater contamination was discovered throughout Silicon Valley. Toxic chemicals had leaked from underground storage tanks formerly considered safe. Over 100,000 homes in the San Jose area were exposed to toxic chemicals emanating from the Fairchild computer chip factory. Workers and community members suffered a range of illnesses and started to campaign against this environmental injustice. The coalition of hi-tech workers, community residents, environmentalists and emergency workers campaigned successfully for state and federal legislation to monitor these types of tanks. The SVTC has also helped to mobilize and organize communities in successful campaigns to the Environmental Protection Agency (EPA) to secure a proper clean-up. The health effects of toxic contamination can be severe and long lasting, so the

SVTC has developed a local and global profile for research and advocacy, publishing a number of reports, videos and guides on pollution and environmental injustice and how to combat them. Agyeman (2005) considers the coalition to be a clear example of a 'just sustainability' organization and Ted Smith, SVTC's senior strategist and co-editor of *Challenging the Chip* (Smith *et al.*, 2006), argues forcefully that the industry's extremely harmful effects can be avoided if the will and appropriate schemes are in place. Computers quickly become obsolete, many 'old' models are simply dumped in landfills or sent to the developing world, and new chemicals incorporated into new machines have often been inadequately tested before use. However, as a result of various campaigns like 'Computer Take Back', large companies like Dell are taking back and recycling their products as well as offering free recycling of some non-Dell computers to customers who purchase a Dell.

Box 4.2 Vision for sustainable communities in Silicon Valley and around the globe

SVTC is located in Silicon Valley, the birthplace of the high-tech revolution and origin of many electronics manufacturing facilities. High-tech workers and the communities surrounding those facilities suffered from dramatic health problems from toxic exposure. Those communities came together to hold the industry accountable, create more stringent environmental protections, and move the EPA to create 29 priority Superfund sites, the highest concentration in the nation. Since then, the industry has moved much of its manufacturing oversees where labor is cheaper and environmental protections weaker. However, the industry still employs thousands of service sector workers such as janitors, gardeners and cafeteria workers. These low wage jobs are held primarily by immigrants and people of color, and because of low pay they are often forced to live in polluted areas, in sub-standard housing, far from grocery stores that sell fresh produce. SVTC works with people from those areas to create more sustainable communities that have quality air, affordable housing and access to health care and quality food.

As in Silicon Valley, similar stories have arisen from the far corners of the world about the dangers of high-tech production and the dumping of e-waste. Rice patties and groundwater supplies in China have been contaminated by high-tech manufacturing, endangering *community* food and water systems. E-waste has been sent to places like India and Nigeria where it is burned or buried. Electronics manufacturing and recycling workers often develop cancer, reproductive problems, miscarriages and illnesses. And wherever the high-tech industry exists, it often leaves a wake of unintended collateral damage. Unfortunately, it is often the most impoverished workers and communities of color who are disproportionately affected. However, by working together, communities around the globe have held the industry accountable to consider public health and our environment, and shift towards greater sustainability for high-tech communities.

Source: Silicon Valley Toxics Coalition (http://svtc.org/about-us/svtcs-mission-for-a-sustainable-future).

Case study: food justice – from Motown to Growtown

Urban agriculture is a key element in reimagining the post-industrial city. As global and urban populations grow, as food security, food safety and food miles become increasingly important, and as poor nutrition, ill health and obesity expand, the cultivation of food in cities is seen by many as a brilliant way forward. It is ecologically and socially sound, economically productive, spiritually uplifting and aesthetically pleasing. Not only can community gardens improve real-estate values but, if supported intelligently by national and city governments, they can change the nature of the urban itself. Havana in Cuba produces a considerable amount of agricultural produce per annum and has created a mode of urban sustainability and a sense of self-reliance that had previously not existed (Altieri *et al.*, 1999). In Asia, Singapore's urban farmers tend 17,300 acres of land supplying 80 per cent of the city poultry and 25 per cent of its vegetables. Urban farms and community gardens are springing up everywhere. In Kansas City, over 300 acres of land are now dedicated to urban farming, but it is to Detroit that a great deal of attention has been directed in recent years.

It is well known that since the 1950s Detroit's population has halved to today's somewhat under one million people. The car industry that once gave its name to the city and to the popular music style, Motown, has all but disappeared. Crime, drug abuse, poverty and education unattainment is endemic. Detroit also has a history of poor ethnic relations and fractious labour relations. Empty city lots, derelict buildings and trees growing on the roofs of factories have spawned numerous documentaries, books, newspaper reports and a subgenre of urban photography known as 'ruin porn'. The city's tax base has dwindled and in July 2013 the Council filed for bankruptcy – the largest municipality to do so in US history. However, Detroit's urban farmers and community gardeners have perhaps unwittingly captured the popular imagination in other ways with concepts such as 'food deserts' and 'food justice' penetrating the public policy discourse on social equity, health and urban development. *Urban Roots*, the 2012 documentary produced by Leila Conners, Mark MacInnis and Matthew Schmid, eschews the perverse attractions of ruin porn to show how Detroit's plight is motivating increasing numbers of people to grow and share their often organically grown fresh fruit and vegetables. Derelict lots are being turned over to horticulture, polluted land is slowly decontaminated and small communities are slowly regaining a sense of pride and purpose. As a number of people remarked in the film, there is a real sense of satisfaction and achievement in being responsible for creating a garden and growing one's own food. The product of one's labour is not appropriated by 'the company', as would have been the case on the production line, but clearly and distinctly remains that of the individual or community to eat, to give away or to sell.

Working the land involves learning new skills and undertaking physical exercise. It may also involve reassessing and rearticulating one's cultural identity. Some young African Americans expressed reluctance to get involved because they saw working the land as being associated with slavery, but urban farming also means improving diets and enjoying the open air, too. There is also a social equity dimension, as for many residents Detroit is a food desert – that is, access to fresh fruit and vegetables can be very limited both financially and geographically. Some 30 per cent of the city's predominantly African American population live below the poverty line and about 20 per cent lack transportation. Few if any grocery stores exist in many districts for the only places that sell food are convenience stores and petrol stations, and the food there is invariably of the processed, packaged and tinned variety. The Detroit Black Community Food Security Network, started in 2006, is a non-profit grass-roots community organization that has been instrumental in creating Detroit's Food Policy Council and runs the U-Ujamaa Food Buying Co-operative where members are able to purchase healthy foods and household items at discount prices. For Monica White (2011a, 2011b) in attempting to control their own food supply, the D-Town farmers are articulating a form of active resistance to economic deprivation that demonstrates agency, facilitates empowerment and proclaims access to decent food a human right. In fact, a loosely networked food justice movement is emerging across the United States (Gottlieb and Joshi, 2013) and beyond.

Obesity and poor nutrition is a huge problem in Detroit, as elsewhere in the USA, and increasingly elsewhere, including India and China where affluence has led to a change in diet – at least for some. Urban gardeners, horticulturalists and farmers therefore recognize that developing and tending a plot for the production of local food is as much about securing social, environmental and food justice as anything else. This is one of the key messages of *Urban Roots* as well as in reports and studies produced by journalists and academics (Gallagher, 2010). In so doing it reconnects people with the land, the source of their food and the true flavour and taste of naturally grown produce. Beans grow on vines, potatoes in the land, tomatoes on a plant, lettuce from the soil. Local food growing connects people with each other too, activities that help nurture social capital, conviviality and community development. However, small urban farming either by individuals or groups is not the only story in Detroit. John Hantz, a financial service professional and entrepreneur, runs a for-profit organization, Hantz Farms, that has a scheme to commercialize and industrialize non-organic urban agriculture. In December 2012 the City of Detroit sold to the Hantz Woodland project 1,500 lots (140 acres) below market value to plant a hardwood tree farm as part of an urban clean-up and beautification project. In March 2013 the city changed its zoning rules in order to expand farming by formally creating a classification for urban farms and community gardens but, as *Detroit Free Press* journalist John Gallagher (2013) and others have argued, urban farming is part of the solution to Detroit's problems but cannot be the sole or perhaps even the major one. However, the benefits of urban agriculture are significant socially, environmentally and economically.

There are in the region of 900 plus community gardens or small urban farms constituting about 500 or so acres in the city. Suitably scaled up to about 3,600 acres citywide with many of the farms somewhat larger than the vast majority of the existing ones, Gallagher (2010) suggests that the city could produce about 76 per cent of the vegetables and 42 per cent of the fruit the population needs for a healthy diet. As one of the participants in *Urban Roots* said, this could mean that Motown became Growtown.

Righting wrongs

A major achievement of the environmental justice movement, particularly at the policy level, has been a practice-based critique of expert-led processes of risk assessment, research and action. For Brulle (2000) and Agyeman (2005), local knowledge, perception and understanding of risks are often far richer in qualitative detail and more pertinent than expert perceptions, although this is not to deny the importance of rigorous professional and scientific analysis of environmental hazards, and so on. Collin and Collin (2005) note that the consequences of bioaccumulation and the cumulative risk suffered by many communities of colour have been invisible to environmental professionals and scientists, who are often seen as being representatives of political and economic power structures that have caused the injustice in the first place. In other words, sustainability can only be achieved if citizens – 'ordinary people' – are able to work effectively with the experts in designing and implementing proper policies, policy tools and actions. Collin and Collin (2005: 219) call for effective reparations, the designation of environmental preservation districts, insistence on clean production technologies, and so on to start righting historical wrongs, restore ecosystems and revitalize communities, asserting that 'reparations to oppressed people in a ravaged land will help the nation become sustainable'. Although absolutely central to most environmental justice campaigns, health issues have not figured prominently in many debates on sustainable development, despite the adjective 'healthy' often being used to characterize a sustainable community, society or economy. Socio-economic inequality, pollution, poverty, occupation, age, social exclusion, class and region all cause the inequitable social and spatial distribution of ill health and health risks. Wilkinson (1996 and 2005) shows that rich countries will remain dysfunctional, violent and sick if economic inequality increases beyond a certain level. Being poor and socially excluded is a cause of ill health, depression and premature death. More socially equal societies and regions have higher levels of trust and social capital than unequal ones, which have higher crime rates and poorer health. Above all, Wilkinson concludes that economic growth and material affluence may improve the material standard of life but does little or nothing for the quality of our lives. In this way, it is reasonable to equate social well-being and social welfare with sustainable economic and community development, but not necessarily, as we shall see, with economic growth. As Wilkinson writes:

> The quality of social life of a society is one of the most powerful determinants of health and this, in turn, is very closely related to the degree of income inequality. . . . The indications that the links are psychosocial make these relationships as important for the real subjective quality of life among populations as they are for their health. If the whole thing were a matter of eating too many chips or of not taking enough exercise, that in itself would not necessarily mean that the quality of life which people experienced was so much less good. You can be happy eating chips. But sources of social stress, poor social networks, low self-esteem, high rates of depression, anxiety and insecurity, and the loss of a sense of control all have such a fundamental impact on our experience of life that it is reasonable to wonder whether the effects on the quality of life are not more important than the effects on the length of life.
>
> (1996: 4–5)

A major task is finding the best way to right these wrongs. Agyeman (2005) identifies a number of valuable environmental justice policy tools, including the International Council for Local Environmental Initiatives' milestone process and the concept of 'environmental space' first developed by Friends of the Earth in Europe. Unlike the similar concept of ecological footprinting, environmental space does not aggregate resources into a single land-area based index but allows the environmental space targets for specific countries to be calculated by dividing the global environmental space for a given resource by the world's total population. In this way, each individual is allocated a 'fair share' – if people do not have the basic means and capabilities to support themselves in a dignified manner, their fundamental rights as human beings are not being met. For many of the world's people, it is basic rights and capabilities for subsistence – health, housing and nourishment – that are of immediate and imminent importance. Without access to life-sustaining ecological resources and systems, many of which are threatened by urbanization, international trading regulations, climate change and extractive industries, human development cannot be sustainable or just. For Sachs (2004), local community rights over resources must be recognized and strengthened rather than attacked or fought over. Intact ecosystems mean the poor are less vulnerable, but for this to occur people in the affluent countries must moderate their demands and expectations. As Sachs writes:

> Only if demand for oil falls will it no longer be worth launching drillings in the primeval forest. Only if the thirst for agriculture and industry abates will enough groundwater remain to supply village wells. Only if the burning of fossil fuels is restricted will insidious climate change no longer threaten the existential rights of the poor.
>
> (2004: 48)

Environmental space therefore operationalizes the notion of environmental limits in measurable terms, articulating concepts of intergenerational and environmental justice and spatial equity. The environmental space framework provides a benchmark for addressing the historic environmental justice or ecological debt issues which campaigners in the developing world see existing between the rich and poor nations of the world. As McLaren (2003) argues, the concept of ecological debt sharpens our understanding of sustainable development further by bringing sharply into focus power relations and decision-making processes, determining global resource exploitation and consumption.

Ecological debt and human development

As discussed in Chapter 1, the activities of international financial and trading organizations like the International Monetary Fund, World Bank and World Trade Organization, together with the developed world as a whole, are often held responsible for the global inequities, economic distortions and social dislocations accompanying globalization. Financial loans have been offered to developing countries on conditions that mean their national economies are liberalized and privatized while public spending on health, education and other public services is reduced. The poverty and hardship of many Third World people has increased as debts and debt repayments to the creditor nations and organizations have mounted. Criticism from NGOs like Oxfam and from publications like *The Ecologist* have been scathing. Many campaigners at Seattle in 1999 and in Prague in 2000 interpreted the failure of First World governments to eradicate Third World poverty and debt as simply maintaining

Box 4.3 Environmental justice and environmental space

In *Sustainable Europe and Environmental Space – Achieving Sustainability through the Concept of 'Environmental Space': A Trans-European Project*, McLaren (2001) explains the concept and the targets required for Europe to enjoy its fair share:

> Environmental space can be defined as the total amount of resources we can use (in a given time period), without compromising future generations' access to the same amount. Alternatively, it can be interpreted as the ability and adaptability of the environment to provide the physical and non-physical resources humans need. These resources include the provision of energy and raw materials, the absorption of wastes, genetic diversity, and fundamental life-support services such as climatic regulation. The current rate of consumption of many of these resources can be measured and compared with the sustainable rate.

We start from the premise that natural and human systems can only sustain a finite level of *impact*. Impacts must be limited (both globally and more locally) to defined levels. These levels can be termed 'sustainability constraints'. Over the longer term a range of measures, such as soil restoration and the planting of new woodlands, can effectively increase total capacity. The environmental space concept allows for this. However, our ability to enhance the capacity of natural systems to sustain greater impacts (absorb more pollution, provide a greater sustainable harvest and so on), although developing, is currently limited, and for practical purposes environmental capacity is considered as fixed in the short term.

However, the environmental space methodology recognizes that improving technology may not be adequate to reduce or keep impact below the critical levels. It implies that the level of consumption may also need to be varied. The concept of 'sufficiency' is used where reductions in consumption provide an increase in sustainable well-being as a result of bringing us within environmental space limits, even if in the short term conventional monetary measures of income fall as a result.

Table 4.1 Comparison of sustainable consumption for the UK and Europe: cuts necessary by 2050

	UK cut (%)	European cut (%)
Carbon dioxide	83	77
Timber	64	55
Cement	69	85
Pig-iron	83	87
Aluminum	84	90
Chlorine	100	100

Source: Friends of the Earth

a contemporary form of imperialist exploitation. The rhetoric and policy statements of many governments may link human rights and human development with financial, technological and economic assistance, but the reality is often quite different. In 1960, the 20 per cent of the world's population living in the richer countries were 30 times richer than the poorest 20 per cent. By 1997 they were 74 times richer. In 2006, the combined income of the 500 richest people in the world exceeded that of the poorest 416 million. About two-thirds of world trade is accounted for by just 500 companies. Many of these companies have a higher turnover than many nations, making it difficult for governments in the developing world to resist their demands and invitations. Putative global trade agreements like the abandoned Multilateral Agreement on Investment even attempted to give transnational companies the power to override national and international environmental and labour laws if they interfered with corporate profitability. Action taken by NGOs, citizen groups and individuals in opposition to these developments grew throughout the 1990s, attracting media coverage that ranged from the overtly hostile to the broadly sympathetic.

'Human development indicators' were first introduced in 1990 in the first Human Development Report (HDR) produced by the United Nations Development Programme (UNDP). They assessed the state of human development according to a variety of indicators, including life expectancy, adult literacy, enrolment at the primary, secondary and tertiary education levels, and income. In 2010 the MPI or Multidimensional Poverty Index was introduced and applied by UNDP to 109 countries. The MPI measures serious deficits in living standards, health, education and environmental factors such as cooking fuel, clean water and basic sanitation and importantly focuses specifically on the intensity of these and other deprivations experienced by certain groups of people. In developing countries roughly 60 per cent of people experience one of these deprivations and 40 per cent two or more (UNDP, 2011). Environmental deprivations are especially acute among the multidimensional poor and although life expectancy has generally increased globally, in sub-Saharan Africa it is actually lower today than it was in the 1970s. Of the 31 countries towards the bottom of the list, 28 are in sub-Saharan Africa. There, a person's life expectancy is 46 years compared with 78 years in countries with more advanced human development, due largely to HIV/AIDS, which accounts for about 20 years of this discrepancy. Although the number of child deaths has declined since 1990, 10.8 million child deaths in 2004 still directly related to inequality and were often the consequence of simply living in the wrong country, town or even street. Climate change will also significantly affect the world's poor. As dry areas get drier and wet areas wetter, the distribution of agricultural produce will worsen. Being linked to more frequent and extreme weather events, water flows will become increasingly unpredictable. The authors of the 2006 HDR suggest that:

> Agriculture and rural development will bear the brunt of climate risk – the rural sector accounts for about three-quarters of those living on less than $1 a day.

> Extreme poverty and malnutrition will increase as water insecurity increases – climate change could increase global malnutrition by 15–26 per cent, that is from 75 million to 125 million people, by 2080.

> More extreme weather patterns will increase *risk* and *vulnerability*. Susceptibility to drought and flood will increase over time.

Shrinking glaciers and rising sea levels will pose new risks for human security. The retreat of glaciers will threaten short-term flooding and long-term declines in water availability across Asia, Latin America and parts of East Africa.

The HDR concludes starkly: 'For a large share of the world's people in developing countries, climate change projections point to less secure livelihoods, greater vulnerability to hunger and poverty, worsening social inequalities, and more environmental degradation' (Watkins *et al.*, 2006: 159).

Issues relating to climate and gender justice are often tightly entwined and this is not just because of women's relatively more limited access to resources and resulting poverty compared with men. As Geraldine Terry (2009) writes, women's greater vulnerability is often related to social and cultural norms, influencing gendered divisions of labour and physical mobility, and the capability or opportunity to participate in local decision-making processes. The relationship between human rights and human development, corporate power and environmental justice, global poverty and citizen action, suggest that responsible *global citizenship* is an inescapable element of what may at first glance seem to be simply matters of personal consumer or moral choice. As Naomi Klein (2000) shows in *No Logo*, the many emotionally highly charged protests in the US against the big corporations are a direct result of people recognizing the interconnectedness of the contemporary world. Research for her book enabled Klein to see women making clothes for Gap in sweatshops in a free-trade zone in the Philippines, where rules existed preventing smiling and talking, where toilets were padlocked except for two fifteen-minute periods each day, where seam-stresses had to urinate in plastic bags under their machines, where there was forced overtime but no job security, and where wages barely reached subsistence level. Indeed, environmental justice issues are simultaneously local and global – many low-lying communities will be affected by climate change and sea-level rise, and a shortage of fresh water is expected to be a massive problem by the middle of the twenty-first century, as could be air pollution, toxic dumping and energy use. As a result, poor countries have recently argued that rich countries have accrued a large 'ecological debt' to the developing world for their over-appropriation of local and global resources in past centuries, with some claiming that this debt is larger than the 'external debt' – the financial debt which poor countries are currently having to service. A financial estimate of the size of the – 'carbon debt' – a small part of the total ecological debt – has been put at $1,500 billion. This is based on industrialized countries' historical contribution to the build-up of carbon dioxide in the atmosphere (ESRC, 2001).

Developed mainly in South America (Martinez-Alier, 2002), the concept of ecological debt includes such factors as:

- resource extraction during colonial periods;
- export of natural resources under unequal terms of trade, which do not take into account the social and environmental damage caused by their extraction;
- the historical and current intellectual appropriation of ancestral knowledge;
- the use of water, air, the best land and human energy to establish export crops, putting at risk the food, health and security of local and national communities;
- damage to the ozone layer and the appropriation of the carbon absorption capacity of the planet; and
- the export of toxic wastes and nuclear testing.

Sachs asks the key question of environmental justice: 'Who has the advantages and who the disadvantages in the use of nature?' (2004: 24). However, perhaps the ground is beginning to shift. The Human Development Report (UNDP, 2013) documented unprecedented and sustained expansion of human capabilities in the global South. In terms of pure economic output, the economies of Brazil, China and India are roughly equal to the combined GDP of France, Germany, Canada, Italy, the United Kingdom and the United States. There is now a growing middle class in the global South with expanding incomes and consumer expectations. The corollary of this development is that with income growth there has been an associated deterioration of key environmental indicators such as carbon dioxide emissions, water and soil quality and forest cover. However, a relatively new phenomenon has also emerged which has implications for both equity and sustainability. Land grabbing is seen by many as a new form of economic imperialism with the rich, both new and old, including state enterprises, Russian oligarchs and Wall Street speculators, acquiring land in poorer areas particularly in Africa, to secure their own future food security and turn a neat profit effectively at the expense of poorer communities and the natural flora and fauna of those areas (Pearce, 2013). Two million square kilometres of land was secured between 2000 and 2010, commodity prices have increased and although some commentators have suggested that such land purchases represent a welcome modernization of agriculture in underdeveloped regions, international bodies as diverse as Oxfam and the World Bank have been alarmed at human rights violations, population displacements, biodiversity loss and other negative ecological impacts. As the Human Development Report, *Sustainability and Equity*, stated:

> Recent international initiatives seek to provide a regulatory framework to spread out the benefits and balance opportunities with risks. The challenge is to implement multilevel institutional arrangements, including effective local participation, to promote sustainability and equity in this major change in land use.
>
> (UNDP, 2011: 39)

Summary

Human beings are creatures who necessarily interact with each other socially and also with the wider environment on which they depend for virtually everything. The ways in which human beings have acted and interacted has led to ecological damage, social inequality and a large number of injustices, in addition to the cultural and material wealth and well-being that has made many civilizations rich and productive. This chapter has shown that sustainable development requires all humans to connect the social with the environmental, to see where these connections are going at local, regional, national and global levels, and act accordingly. Through using physical and social networks, through harnessing the opportunities new media technologies offer, a great number of positive things can be achieved to right many of the wrongs that are evident in so many places. Sometimes it is clear that a simple and specific activity can bring people together, which make this connection between the social and the environment, such as can be seen in the growing of local food in Detroit and elsewhere. Everyone needs to eat and addressing fundamental human needs while respecting natural ecologies is a prerequisite for development that is both just and sustainable.

Thinking questions

1   How might Hardin's logic be fruitfully applied to building on greenfield sites, discharging waste into steams and rivers, fishing for endangered species, driving your car instead of taking the train, or throwing away rather than recycling or reusing?
2   How do you feel about the role and potential of digital technologies in developing socially and environmentally sustainable communities?
3   In what way could more or better information lead to transformative change?
4   What is the importance of environmental justice to sustainable development?
5   What broader lessons regarding sustainable development can be learnt from Detroit?
6   How does environmental justice bridge the gap between the local and the global?

Companion website

For further information on environmental and social justice and sustainable communities, please visit the companion website for some additional case studies.

5 Sustainable development, politics and governance

Aims

This chapter explores the connections between environmental sustainability, human agency and political participation. Some key theories, concepts and examples of practical action will illustrate both the political importance and political implications of sustainable development. Issues relating to ecological citizenship, the culture of democracy, good governance and the workplace will be examined. More broadly, the relationship between personal and societal welfare and environmental sustainability will form an underlying theme of the discussions. Recognizing the increasing importance of cities and migration, the chapter concludes with a discussion on 'the Right to the City' and the need to combat continuing phenomena of gender inequality and violence.

Human agency and perspective transformation

Sociologists tend to think of human agency – that is, the capacity of individuals to act independently and make their own free choices – in terms of external circumstances and structures. Giddens (1986) sees human beings as subject to forces beyond their control or understanding, and able to actively work and reflect on them. In doing this, people change the world and, in the process, themselves. Institutions, social rules and cultural contexts influence the fabric of human social life, community, conduct and agency. People's lives are structured by ideas, values, social habits and routines, and discourses and technologies they experience, apply and alter. Hutchby (2001) writes of social technologies and physical artefacts producing *affordances*, allowing certain behaviours and actions to flourish in preference to others. Just think what the smart phone enables people to do and how that has changed the way people relate to each other and the wider environment. By contrast, psychologists tend to think of human agency in terms of internal drivers or personality traits. For sociologists Emirbayer and Miche agency can be defined as

> the temporally constructed engagement by actors of different structural environments – the temporal-relational contexts of action – which, through the interplay of habit, imagination, and judgement, both reproduces and transforms those structures in interactive response to the problems posed by changing historical situations.

(1998: 70)

They go further to identify three different dimensions or elements of human social agency:

> *the iterational element*: the selective reactivation by actors of past patterns of thought and action, routinely incorporated in practical activity, thereby giving stability and order to social universes and helping to sustain identities, interactions, and institutions over time;
>
> *the projective element*: the imaginative generation by actors of possible future trajectories of action, in which received structures of thought and action may be creatively reconfigured in relation to actors' hopes, fears, and desires for the future;
>
> *the practical-evaluative element*: the capacity of actors to make practical and normative judgements among alternative possible trajectories of action, in response to the emerging demands, dilemmas, and ambiguities of presently evolving situations.
>
> (1998: 971)

The psychologist Rom Harre (1984) writes of people achieving *agency* through their intentions, their knowledge of social rules and their facility for 'activation', which he explains by suggesting there is within us an inner capacity to act or not to act. We tend to obey our own inner commands, just as we may obey those of others, particularly if influenced by the status or credibility of people we respect or perhaps fear, but Harre notes there is a difference between being stimulated to act and having a constraint removed, thereby enabling action to occur. Sometimes a critical incident, a significant learning experience or a disorientating dilemma, such as a major change in one's life, may lead to a change of values, attitudes and predispositions. This may constitute either a release or a stimulus. Agency is therefore a fairly complex concept that can be understood not only sociologically and psychologically but ecologically too. Thus, an 'ecology of agency' can be said to be referring to an understanding which always encompasses an actors-in-transaction-with-context – that is, people always acting by-means-of-an-environment rather than simply *in* an environment (Costall, 2000). Agency is therefore not really a possession of an individual, but something that is achieved in and through the engagement with a particular time, place and set of social relations situation. This means that an individual can be 'agentic' in one situation but not in another. Agency also has a lot to do with learning, experience and reflection.

The educational psychologist Jack Mezirow (1991) writes about transformative learning whereby our *meaning schemes* (specific attitudes, beliefs and attitudes) and *meaning perspectives* (criteria for evaluating right and wrong, good and bad) may alter as a result of experience and self-reflection. *Perspective transformation* is the process whereby people become critically aware of how and why their assumptions constrain the way they perceive, understand and feel about the world. It may involve the transformation of habitual expectations, enabling a more inclusive or integrative perspective on the world together with an enhanced capability of deciding how to act. Perspective transformation can occur slowly, through gradual changes in attitudes and beliefs, or through a shattering experience that may be highly personal or be prompted by an eye-opening discussion, film, book or article that seriously contradicts previously held assumptions. These changes often involve a questioning of beliefs, personal values, sense of self, political efficacy and cultural identity. Social movements such as feminism or environmentalism facilitate critical self-reflection and the formation of alternative meaning schemes and perspectives. They enable people to identify with causes larger than themselves, motivating them to learn and engage. People who have experienced such personal and/or wider perspective transformations frequently bring considerable energy, power and commitment to social movements. This was so for Lois Gibbs in her campaign with the residents of Love Canal in the state of New York to fight for justice and compensation after the toxic pollution caused by the Hooker Electrical Company had led to many community health problems, including cancer, epilepsy, asthma, birth defects, miscarriages and premature death (Livesey, 2003). Indeed, much policy development and political action focusing on the broader issues of sustainable development have emerged from environmental campaigning, conservation action, pollution control and environmental management practices operating at a variety of spatial levels (Doyle and McEachern, 1998; Connelly and Smith, 1999). New digital technologies, including social networking sites, seem to be further enhancing processes of political engagement and awareness. Computer-mediated communications (CMC) has facilitated globalization through its coordination of dispersed economic and political networks, but these same CMC networks have also enabled relatively inexpensive and instantaneous communication, nurturing the growth of online activist virtual communities and the formation of new counter-public spheres. New media have attracted increasing numbers of people intent on using the Internet to enhance the work of many global justice movements. The first new kind of (inter)network-based movement emerged with the anti-corporate struggles of the indigenous Mayan people, the Zapatistas, in Mexico in the early 1990s, and then, most effectively, in the Seattle, Montreal, Genoa, Miami and Cancun anti-globalization, anti-WTO protests. For the first time public street protests were supplemented and to an extent organized through the use of mobile digital technologies and the Internet. For Langman (2005), these new forms of activist organizations constitute fluid social movements united by a passionate commitment to social and environmental justice, freedom and democratic community in a networked world. Jeffrey Juris argues that transnational counter-publics have emerged as a result of grass-roots anti-corporate globalization movements developing advanced forms of computer-mediated communication and networking. Activists have integrated the Internet into their everyday routines through email lists and websites, 'building a new digital media culture through the practice of informational utopics' (Juris, 2005: 205), producing alternative values, discourses and identities effectively serving as new social, cultural and political laboratories from which new forms of empowered political agency may arise.

Towards ecological democratization

Recognizing ecological limits and planetary boundaries has led some green political theorists to argue not only for an end to economic growth but for a seemingly authoritarian politics that can curtail the relentless individual and corporate pursuit of economic self-interest and formulate appropriate political policies. These will be devised by an elite group of people who truly understand the long-term issues and can in effect articulate the general will. Thus, William Ophuls has argued for nearly forty years that this may involve measures of coercion as well as regulation and education. A market economy is incompatible with ecology and consistently fails to provide a social welfare function. Ophuls argues that human beings must learn self-restraint and respect values that are other than those of constant material accumulation before the necessary restrictions imposed by a totalitarian regime or by 'the brute force of nature' (1977: 236). An ethical and spiritual rebuilding rooted in ecological realities is necessary that, although not opposed to democracy at local levels, needs to recognize necessary limits to freedom and the need for a simple but culturally rich life (Ophuls, 2011). These views are not widely shared but they continue to resonate as ecological conditions worsen. In contrast, for the political scientist John Dryzek (1996), democratization, or the enhancement of democratic values, involves increasing the number of people participating in the political process, increasing the quality of their contributions, and extending the range of issues subject to popular control and scrutiny, and the degree to which this control is actual (substantive) rather than purely formal or symbolic. Political greening, or 'ecologization', falls into two categories:

- Politics becomes more biocentric and less anthropocentric, including recognizing the rights of nature and non-human others.
- Politics becomes increasingly sensitive to human interests in the context of a clean, safe and pleasant environment.

Some international agreements, like the Montreal Protocol restricting the manufacture and use of chlorofluorocarbons (CFCs) in order to protect the ozone layer, represent political ecologization at the global level, but generally progress has been slow at all levels, despite the growth in our ecological knowledge and our understanding of humanity's impact on the planet. Dryzek identifies four potential strategies frequently cited as potential vehicles for ecological democratization. These are:

1 *Making the most of liberal democracy*: This can be seen as a neutral platform for political outcomes and/or something that can itself be enhanced by ecological values, although economic and business imperatives have always seemed to trump ecological concerns in securing the attention of decision-makers.
2 *Crisis and apocalypse*: A view that sees liberal democracy as a major part of our ecological malaise, given the silo mentality of governments and the consequent disaggregation of policymaking and policy implementation.
3 *Reflexive development*: Collective life is now largely organized around the production, distribution and management of risks, leading to a society in which science and technology has lost much of its authority, often because new opportunities for debate and intervention in decision-making from citizens, activists and social movements have emerged.
4 *Rejection*: Whereas the risk society envisages democracy extending beyond the state, a rejectionist strategy calls for vibrant para-governmental activity and an active global and national civil society offering alternative, separate and prefigurative forms of political action, values and organization.

Dryzek places his faith in a sustainable future in a combination of reflexive development and what he terms a 'rejectionist' civil society:

A happy future for ecological democratization would involve industrial society giving way to reflexive modernization in a risk society, and the acceptance of ecological modernization as both a discourse and a set of proven claims about 'tradeoffs' between economy and environment. . . . Matters will look very different if ecology does not indeed prove good for business in general. Oppositional civil society becomes more critical in the latter case; but even in the happy scenario, such opposition is still necessary to prevent a risk-management technocracy.

(1996: 122)

Like Torgenson (1999), Dryzek sees the promise of green politics and democracy as very much relying on the green public sphere to host various discourses on environmental and sustainability issues, public education, an environmentally aware media, and public debates and investigations that change political practice. Complementing Dryzek, O'Riordan (1996) and O'Riordan and Voisey (1998), having expressed some optimism about the reshaping possibilities of Agenda 21, outline four necessary implications for a democratic and institutional transition to sustainability:

1   the need for an ecological right to know and guarantees regarding freedom of information;
2   the sharing of power in an ecological corporatist fashion;
3   controls on the movement of capital to prevent movement that would wreck economies implementing necessary ecological controls and regulations; and
4   the imposition of limits on capital accumulation that would otherwise lead to disfiguring and harmful social, economic and political inequalities (and inequities).

The adaptation of key institutions in any transition towards sustainability would need to articulate clear commitments to:

•   reflect a clear understanding of ecological limits;
•   respond to visions of a more ecologically protective and fair polity;
•   create a sustainable society by negotiated consent, understanding or agreement;
•   measure the effects of policy and actions within ecological and social parameters linked to agreed norms and targets; and
•   implement policy according to agreed norms and rules located in markets, law, social values and governmental regulation.

The transition phase will necessarily encompass a wide critical political ecology that includes an understanding of and clear political engagement with the natural environment as constituting part of the human moral community. Geography or, more specifically, the complex intersections between nature, culture, space, place, landscape, human agency, identity, knowledge, politics, power and economy are integral components of such a political ecology. In *Places and Regions in the Age of Globality*, Arturo Escobar (2006b) writes of a spatially grounded understanding and expression of 'globality' – something that is place-based, enacted and negotiated at every site or region, and not something imposed through the invisible hand of global capitalism. Local and indigenous peoples, particularly in the Columbian Pacific region, have sophisticated ecological knowledges constituting their own notions of 'globality' which frequently inform their struggles to secure their resources and livelihoods in the face of economic development, neocolonialism and political intervention. For Escobar:

> people mobilize against the destructive aspects of globalization from the perspective of what they have historically been and what they are at present: historical subjects of particular cultures, economies and ecologies; particular knowledge producers; individuals and collectivities engaged in the play of living with landscapes, living and non-living beings, and each other in particular ways. In regions such as the Pacific, people engage in the defence of place from the perspective of the economic, ecological and cultural difference that their land-scapes, cultures and economies embody in relation to those of more dominant sectors of society.
>
> (2006b: 21)

For Eckersley (2004 and 2005), ecological democratization will require revised national constitutional and multilateral arrangements, and the emergence of a new 'green state' operating as a facilitator of transboundary democratic processes and global ecological stewardship. The demand for social and environmental justice will be incorporated into the broad context of a dialogic communicative justice. It will also mean culturally embracing both human and non-human emancipatory politics, putting aside the language of prudence (economic, political and moral), even though this language may more easily travel across national cultural boundaries, in favour of realizing intrinsic non-anthropocentric values. In order to make this happen, democracy will need to be fundamentally radicalized – not a small task, you might think, but one that is currently being played out between environmental pragmatists and ecocentrists in the world of real-world democracy, with the former often forgoing the 'big picture' so as to facilitate 'interest accommodation' and the latter frequently ignoring practical criticism in favour of realizing broader goals.

Extending democracy to the workplace

It might seem a little odd that although democracy in its various forms is frequently heralded as the best form of governance (or, to paraphrase Winston Churchill, the least worst form) democratic participation and decision-making in the workplace and business has rarely captured the popular imagination except at times of acute economic and political crisis. However, democracy, in the form of producer/consumer or worker/employee co-operatives has a long history dating back at least to the Rochdale Pioneers in mid nineteenth-century England. In the Basque country of Spain, the Mondragon co-operative has expanded since its inception in the early 1940s and now involves over 100,000 people. Co-operatives can be big business and quite successful, as the United Nations recognized when it declared 2012 'The Year of the Co-operative', articulating the slogan 'Cooperative Enterprises Build a Better World'. In the vast majority of cases private business corporations are run by relatively few major shareholders, who in turn determine the composition of the board of directors who themselves tend to organize work in a highly stratified and hierarchical manner. This type of organization does not necessarily lead to either good job satisfaction or optimum company performance as high levels of job insecurity, precariousness and unemployment or under-employment in many of the world's developed and developing economies already create considerable anxiety and tension among many people. For radical economist Richard D. Wolff (2012), co-operative enterprises are the decisive alternatives to this form of undemocratic economic and stressful workplace organization. One relatively small-scale example of a successful co-operative is the Arizmendi Bakery in San Rafael, California. It is made up of seven member businesses who share ongoing accounting, legal, educational and other support services. The Arizmendi website (http://arizmendi.coop/about) offers support and information to other groups in the Bay Area who wish to establish a co-operative and on it can be read the Association mission:

- assure opportunities for workers' control of their livelihood with fairness and equality for all;
- develop as many dignified, decently paid (living 'wage' or better) work opportunities as possible through the development of new cooperatives;
- promote cooperative economic democracy as a sustainable and humane option for our society;
- create work environments that foster profound personal as well as professional growth;
- exhibit excellence in production and serving our local communities;
- provide continuing technical, educational and organizational support and services to member cooperatives;
- seek to link with other cooperatives for mutual support; and
- provide information and education to the larger community about cooperatives.

Another example is Suma, founded in 1975, and today the UK's largest independent wholefood wholesale/distributor specializing in vegetarian, organic, fairly traded, natural and ethical products. As a workers' co-operative, it is jointly owned and managed by all who work at Suma. Everyone is paid the same wage and collectively everyone does all the jobs that need to be done. This form of participation entails what Michael Albert (2004) refers to as a 'job complex' which, if scaled up to encompass the whole of a national economy, would constitute a system of participatory economics whose oversight would be provided by a network of participatory councils. However, co-operatives are a relative rarity in today's globalized market economy but there are also examples of large corporations adopting and adapting some lessons from the co-operative movement, believing these will help ensure their future own success in an increasingly harsh and competitive environment. The computer technology giant Cisco's CEO John Chambers, for example, announced in 2008 a reorganization that would spread the company's leadership and management decision capacity to working groups that at the time involved around 500 executives. Instead of the company's major decisions being made by about ten people at the top, a network of boards and councils were empowered to launch new systems, new financial incentives and new modes of employee, especially executive, co-operation. Business units that formerly competed against each other would now share responsibility for each other's success or failure. A *Fast Company* headline ironically noted that Cisco was turning into a 'socialist enterprise', with Ellen McGirt (2008) writing 'power to the people' – and profits to the company. Cisco of course, is not a socialist enterprise. It is still privately owned and still a very major player in the globally significant technology sector, but there are nonetheless some interesting lessons to draw from this.

As Ed Collom (2003) has noted in another context, increased employee participation in workplace decision-making can in certain circumstances empower workers, leading to greater commitment and satisfaction, and so improve company performance. Janice Foley and Michael Polanyi (2006) go a little further, arguing that there are sound arguments in favour of workplace democracy generally – i.e. real control over organizational goal setting and strategic planning, apart from the positive impact on 'the bottom line'. These include increasing employee morale, encouraging participation in wider democratic political processes, ethics – i.e. 'the right thing to do' – and perhaps most significantly, workplace democracy, which has clear beneficial effects on employee mental and physical health. In relation to employee well-being, such as work–life balance, job security and decision latitude or control over the nature of the work itself are of real significance. In addition, as Johnston Birchall (2003) and Nicole Goler von Ravensburg (2011) write, entrepreneurs' co-operatives can play a role in strengthening social dialogue and securing 'decent work' goals because co-operatives are invariably acceptable negotiating partners to unions, employers' organizations and governments. They also have the wider potential to raise skills, open up markets and improve working conditions in the informal economy, too.

Roberto Unger and the inspiring politics of false necessity

In an extensive series of writings and reflections, Roberto Unger, looking very much to the radicalized constitutional and democratic experiments in Brazil, offers not so much a blueprint for institutional and behavioural change but what he terms a 'music' – something that lives in sequence, that is sustained by a credible image of change, enabling the exploration of different pathways at different points, although still moving in the same direction. His argument is that institutional innovation is central to political transformation and the larger aims of radical democratic experimentation and emancipation. Attempting to avoid the pitfalls of socialism and capitalism, Unger asserts that, because everything is essentially 'just politics', human agency is paramount. The world is as it is, not as it either could or should be. 'It can always be refashioned. The result is not to deny the weight of the constraints upon transformative action', Unger (2004: 30) writes, but to recognize there is a 'negative capability', that the formative contexts of social, political and economic life can be destabilized. It requires people to change, to bring under their control and vision their institutions, practices and assumptions. In changing institutions, we change ourselves, and in doing so we reduce the distance between our ordinary everyday actions and the more exceptional ones that challenge and change them. To do this we need to understand society and ourselves; we need to develop new habits and methods of thought and marry them to action. Although Unger rarely refers to sustainability or sustainable development, his political project is an important element of the dialogue of values that informs the sustainable development process. For Unger, imagination, 'the infinity of the mind', educates radical pragmatism by recognizing the multifaceted nature of human experience. There is always 'more in us' individually and collectively. Only when we realize this will we discover what may be possibly engendered through the interaction of general ideas with particular discoveries and real-world innovations. This means, he says, that we do not need to take established social and political arrangements as the inevitable frameworks within which we develop our ideals and fulfil our interests in reconciling empowerment with solidarity, greatness with love and the strengthening of the ways we can be responsible for each other. He writes of the need for a radicalized pragmatism and an experimentalism that will 'turn society into a mirror of the imagination' (2007: 172) while recognizing the value of openness, repudiating 'the illusion of neutrality' and emphasizing a commitment to 'development through difference' (2007: 179 and 180).

Unger identifies strategies for a high-energy politics with high-energy engagement in forms of direct and representative democracy, and a self-organizing civil society. This would involve a disaggregation of consolidated property rights, a progressive redistribution of assets, a renewed relationship between economic classes, a 'jumbling' of social roles and the development of a caring economy alongside the productive one. Of primary importance is the lifting of the 'ordinary lives of ordinary people to a higher level of capacity and intensity' through new forms of human association, lifelong learning and the revaluing of labour and co-operative activity organized between small and medium-sized producers. A radicalization of competition and meritocracy would also occur. Democracy has alternative futures which, through combining insight with practice, will enable us to escape from assumptions of invulnerability. Empowerment means our opening up to others, which may cause a heightened vulnerability but will enable us to imagine, give, receive or refuse love. For Unger, empowerment and vulnerability are the guarantors of change, and the condition and possibilities for change at institutional and individual levels:

> In everyday life, the chief expression of the practice of unprotection is the willingness to endure the risks that every innovation imposes on the established form of cooperation, and the determination to press for a higher form of cooperation: one that is more hospitable to repeated and accelerated innovation and to the narrowing of the gap between the activities that take the context for granted and the activities that challenge and change it.
>
> (2004: 117)

As critics have noted, however, Unger fails to cover many things with his broad theoretical and rhetorical brush, including gender, poverty, race, militarization and the environment. He also lacks any notion of a critical or political adversary, which renders his approach to political agency, at least for Anderson (1992: 148), basically indeterminate: 'intimations of harmony discount considerations of strategy, in a reminder of the other side of the utopian tradition'. Nonetheless, Anderson continues, with Unger 'something new has occurred: a philosophical mind out of the Third World turning the tables, to become synoptist and seer of the First'.

Working on the inside: 'The death of environmentalism' and third generation environmentalism

A significant amount of political lobbying, campaigning, publishing and research is undertaken by 'think-tanks'. Some are corporate-sponsored and others funded from a variety of sources, including public-sector grants and membership subscription. In Europe and the US, Forum for the Future, New Economics Foundation, the Green Alliance/E3G, The Natural Step and the Sierra Club critically engage with environmental and sustainability issues. In 2004 the Breakthrough Institute secured a significant degree of publicity and generated considerable debate when it published

'The death of environmentalism' by Shellberger and Nordhaus (2004). The thrust of this article was that the American environmental movement had lost its edge by being increasingly obsessed with achieving incremental policy or technological changes and through constantly applying a very narrow understanding of the 'environmental'. Its importance lies in the debates it stimulated and the prescriptions it advocated. Environmentalists must act differently and forcefully. Its contribution to the sustainability project lies very much in the belief that agency must be allied with clear principles and values that go beyond pragmatism, weak sustainability or anthropocentric environmentalism. However, the fashioning of a green democracy, or ecological citizenship for individuals, community groups, business corporations and government agencies, is dependent on the politics of the possible and realizing the imperatives of a sustainable society. This has been taken up by Tom Burke of the Green Alliance, a UK-based lobby group and think-tank, with the notion of *third generation environmentalism*. The first two generations of environmentalists, he notes, were predominantly outsiders, concerned initially with environmental and habitat conservation issues, only later incorporating a more social and economic dimension, but still focusing on protecting natural resources. For Burke, the time is now right for insiders to transform the policies and practices of major institutions of government and big business. In a speech marking the 25th anniversary of the Green Alliance in 2005, Burke noted that third-generation environmentalists

> are to be found in their hundreds of thousands within the walls of bureaucracies, financial institutions, universities, trades unions, professional associations and elsewhere. They have all been infected with the environmental virus and they carry it with them wherever they work.

The need is to break out of the green ghetto and the way to do this is threefold:

1 To communicate better – 'We understand the environment better than we do people. We need to frame our arguments in terms that resonate more immediately with others. Without a stable climate, national security and economic prosperity are impossible, the world will not be fairer, communities will not be stable, families will be hurt, personal opportunities will be limited, our children's future will be stolen. But we rarely sound as if we are talking about those everyday concerns.'

2 To get real about political discourse – 'Changing environmental outcomes in the twenty-first century will require some serious money. Today, we spend just under 300 billion pounds a year on social protection, health and education. We spend about 55 billion pounds on internal and external security. We spend a fraction over 7 billion pounds on the environment. Do you really believe those are the right proportions to ensure the continued wellbeing of the British people, as our environmental problems accumulate faster than we are finding solutions for them?'

3 To build stronger institutions to defend the environment – 'We build institutions to consolidate and express our values – to make them manifest in the world. It is a strange thought that, as environmental problems have become more pressing, our national and international environmental institutions have become weaker.'

(Burke, 2005)

Luke (2005) suggests some caution. He is concerned with how private-sector interests have penetrated ecological initiatives, suggesting there is no sure guarantee that the market will result in better environmental outcomes. What is needed is a genuine 'public ecology', with new institutions, ideas and organizations that can balance the competing but often complementary insights of science and private stockholders with concerns about social equity. The socio-technical order has to be rebalanced so that commercialized private-sector beliefs and practices of commoditization do not fully define the everyday activities of governments, societies and social systems. It is important to ensure that human civilization and the biosphere on which it depends are not managed as if they were a capitalist corporate enterprise writ large. Only thus can a sustainable ecology emerge in which human and non-human life-forms can flourish.

These debates are important for green politics, since, like any other democratic practice, good communication, transparency and open dialogue on values and policies is essential. In *Rethinking Green Politics*, Barry (1999) suggests that it is harder to secure agreement on philosophical values than it is on the moral rightness of a particular course of action or policy. People may agree to the same policy for different reasons. Indeed, green activists, deep and shallow, seem for pragmatic reasons to increasingly agree on policy. For Barry, this is quite positive, not least because:

> green arguments and policy proposals would receive a better hearing by the public if environmental policies were cast in terms of extended human interests, rather than emphasizing non-human interests. A clear example of this is environmental policy based on a moral concern for future generations.
>
> (1999: 26)

The problem with deep ecology, similar in part to the expiring environmentalism referenced above, is that it gives green politics a 'fundamentalist complexion', creating a distance between believers and non-believers. So often environmentalists have been accused of not caring sufficiently about people, leading Barry to suggest that the most appropriate political approach to sustainable development is to be critical of anthropocentrism, of existing human–social–environmental relationships, without denying their significance completely. Science can be enlisted to help 'displace the arrogance of humanism', to indicate that human beings are both part of, and apart from, the natural environment. And, simultaneously, scientific knowledge has a role in fashioning agreements on the nature of ecological problems and in developing politically acceptable agreements on social-environment issues and actions. Sustainable development cannot escape politics, but it is to the politics that most attention needs to be paid even though sustainability and sustainable development may not necessarily imply any specific socio-political 'ism', such as liberalism, conservatism, libertarianism or socialism. For political geographer Erik Swyngedouw (2007: 27) 'the desired sustainable environmental future has no name and no process, only a state or condition'. Thus, for journalist Naomi Klein (2013), there is a distinct political possibility that climate change could usher in 'a disaster capitalism free for all' as corporations continue to reap the benefit of weakly constrained neoliberal economic policies. Such allegedly win–win solutions like the UN's Clean Development Mechanism, the US's Climate Action partnership or the European Union's carbon trading schemes have not resulted in a reduction in GHG emissions but have seen large amounts of public money essentially going to private corporations. Many green groups, though not necessary those like Greenpeace or Friends of the Earth, are for Klein in denial of these all too evident realities. It is by building coalitions with the more radicalized and politically aware indigenous people and other communities and not with the corporations that the true win–win solutions may emerge. Those active in the Idle No More movement of First Nation peoples in Canada argue and vigorously campaign for the oil, coal and other fossil fuels to be left in the ground. They are offering the accommodative green groups an alternative narrative that goes well beyond the political realism of Third Generation Environmentalism.

Governance, democracy and eco-welfare

Governance is not an easy concept to grasp and has been interpreted and defined in various ways. For the United Nations, governance refers to:

> the exercise of political, economic and administrative authority in the management of a country's affairs at all levels. Governance comprises the complex mechanisms, processes and institutions through which citizens and groups articulate their interests, mediate their differences, and exercise their legal rights and obligations.
>
> (UNDP, 1997: 5)

Governance occurs within corporate, local, regional, national, international and global contexts. 'Good governance' is an umbrella term denoting lasting and positive changes in accordance with the six key principles of openness, participation, accountability, effectiveness, coherence and civic peace, which may involve civil society actions as well as major public sector reforms (Batterbury, 2006). From the perspective of human development as outlined in the Human Development Report for 2002, *Deepening Democracy in a Fragmented World*, good governance means democratic governance (Fukuda-Parr, 2002: 51) – that is to say:

- People's human rights and fundamental freedoms are respected, allowing them to live with dignity.
- People have a say in decisions that affect their lives.
- People can hold decision-makers accountable.
- Inclusive and fair rules, institutions and practices govern social interactions.
- Women are equal partners with men in private and public spheres of life and decision-making.
- People are free from discrimination based on race, ethnicity, class, gender or any other attribute.
- The needs of future generations are reflected in current policies.
- Economic and social policies are responsive to people's needs and aspirations.
- Economic and social policies aim at eradicating poverty and expanding the choices that all people have in their lives.

Together with security of tenure, UN-Habitat (2000) and a number of observers (Beall *et al.*, 2000; Benjamin, 2000; Devas, 2004; Baud and Dhanalakshmi, 2007) see good governance as an 'enabling tool' in reducing urban poverty, improving service provision, combating crime and violence, fostering civic participation and enhancing economic performance.

Political ecology can act as a frame for good governance because it explicitly recognizes the multi-scaled factors that influence communities, places, local environments and human agency. It examines the human social influences on ecosystems, vulnerability to environmental hazards and scarcity, and shows how political reforms may affect human use of the land, natural resources and the overall physical landscape (Batterbury, 2006). Good governance, in needing to be inclusive, also needs to be decentralized and linked to local context. With global issues such as climate change this has led to a recognition that, in addition to the high-level international conferences, treaties and protocols, and state-based prescriptions, there have recently emerged hybrid locally focused institutional and voluntary initiatives. Thus, polycentric diversity and a dispersion of governing authority is beginning to characterize climate change governance at all scales – neighbourhood, city, federal, state, international and global – with processes combining elements of the bottom-up with the top-down (Paavola, 2011). Hoggett (2001), discussing governance and eco-welfare, sees human capacities as essentially relational, expressive, spiritual and practical–intellectual, developed through the experience of difference, conflict, participation, accommodation and transformation. Indeed, the quality of social relations depends on social conviviality and the democratization of everyday life. Hoggett argues that an eco-welfare model of society requires good governance to be green, and so differs from a consumerist or state welfare model in that:

> Green welfare would promote the utmost respect for human dependency and would champion the development of a new generation of human-scale institutions and integrated, community-based models of support in which holistic models of health, social care and education would flourish. We do not have to engage in abstract thought experiments: such an approach is already prefigured in some third-sector innovations throughout Europe and the UK, many of which are outlined in the recent ten-country European Foundation Report (Pillinger, 2000). Many such projects are experimenting with user- and worker-based cooperatives, emphasizing both user involvement and the development of a mutually respectful relationship between workers and users.
>
> (Hoggett, 2001: 615)

Governance should not be confused with government, which refers to the act and process of governing, and the organization or functional machinery through which power and authority are exercised in a political unit such as a nation-state. Too often governments work within self-enclosed silos and associated mindsets (Dale, 2001), and for many years political commentators have been arguing for more holistic government (Perri 6, 1997), which would facilitate greater effectiveness, intergovernmental communication, and understanding of issues and challenges that can no longer be administratively confined within a single departmental boundary or understood clearly by a single discipline. Joined-up government, if implemented sensitively, could empower communities by offering opportunities for meaningful participation and empowerment (Wilkinson and Appelbee, 1999). Sustainable development policies have many stakeholders and are hard to monitor and evaluate by conventional governmental methods. The risks of failing to communicate clearly to, and within, different autonomous government departments and organizational cultures increases with the complexity of the policy and approach. Writing specifically on the UK experience, Ross (2005) describes the creation of the Environmental Audit Committee as an example of merging accountability structures dealing with specific cross-cutting issues, such as green government, climate change, environmental protection, education for sustainable development and finance.

Case study: the Right to the City – a linchpin concept

The 'Right to the City' is a phrase and a concept that has its origins in the radicalism of the Paris of 1968 and the Marxist sociology of Henri Lefebvre but is now used very broadly by a range of agencies, including the United Nations. Lefebvre applied the concept to rethink the spatial structure of the city, the assumptions of liberal democracy and the social relations of capitalist society. His focus was predominantly spatial distinguishing between:

- *perceived space* – i.e. how space is experienced in everyday life;
- *conceived space* – i.e. how space is constructed by planners, property developers, politicians and businesses;
- *lived space* – i.e. space as a potentiality to re-imagine social and political relations in an alternative way.

Space is central to the way people inhabitant the city – the way they live and work, how they travel about, how they entertain themselves, where and what they eat, purchase goods and services, educate their children and themselves, and so on. For Lefebvre, to claim a Right to the City is to claim to live or experience the city fully, with dignity, co-operatively and socially. It is far more than simply seeing urban space as a site of and for making profits, of capital and property accumulation, of commodification and perhaps human dispossession. The right to the city also means the right to participate in the decision-making processes that affect how people inhabit the city, the way space is produced and used, made available and safe, lived in and enjoyed. The Make Delhi Safe Women campaign has received widespread publicity since a number of cases of gang rape received global media coverage and elicit outrage within and outside India. City planners need to make urban infrastructure women-friendly and planning processes participatory (Lama-Rewal, 2011). The claim to participate is a claim of social inclusion and as such has an explicit link to the processes of democracy. As Mark Purcell writes (2008: 96), 'participation both develops citizens' capacity for civic wisdom and produces wiser, more sustainable public decisions'. These views are expanded on at length in a wealth of inspiring material discussing various proposals and experiences in Habitat International Coalition's *Cities for All* (Sugranyes and Mathivet, 2010), which aims to strengthen the Right to the City as a conceptual and practical tool for creating a better urban world.

Some of these rights have been codified legally but although legal codification is sometimes necessary it is probably insufficient to ensure the city is inhabited well. The Montreal Charter for Rights and responsibilities and Brazil's 'City Statute' – i.e. the enactment of Federal Law 10.257 – are examples of such codifications (UNESCO, 2006). The 'City Statute' posits three key principles associated with Lefebrve's philosophy:

1   the regularization of informal settlements or *favelas* enabling residents to access basic urban services through the promotion of land tenure;
2   the social function or use value of urban land that recognizes land, space, as something more than a site for accumulating economic value thereby recognizing the cultural, social and environmental interests of groups other than those of property owners;
3   the democratization of urban land which in many instances relates to processes of participatory budgeting or the establishment of neighbourhood councils where citizens, rather than elites, decide for themselves directly how public money should be spent.

For this City Statute to exist in a practical and meaningful way requires constant political and social engagement. Groups and individuals need to be mindful of mobilizing around their specific interests but recognizing the need for commonality or equivalence. Each group – whether they are young people, the elderly, women, the homeless, small business people, and even wildlife – have an equivalent right to inhabit the city in a way that enables all to benefit and prosper fairly and equitably. Thus, the right to the city is a linchpin concept linking the interests of many different groups to the wider socio-political and ecological environment. However, as Fernandes notes:

> The increased politicization of urban law has made room for broader popular participation in the defence of social interests and collective rights, but for the same reason the enactment and enforcement of new urban laws and programmes have faced increasing resistance on the part of conservative interests and some serious backlashes have been verified. . . .
>
>   In this context, the materialization of the possibilities of the new legal-urban order will depend on several factors, but above all on the renewed social mobilization in urban areas. In the last analysis, the future of the new law will fundamentally depend on the wide mobilization of Brazilian society, within and without the State apparatus, so as to materialize Lefebvre's long claimed 'right to the city'.
>
> (2006: 51)

Global civil society and world civic politics

The last few decades have seen the growth of a number of non-governmental organizations (NGOs), such as Greenpeace, Friends of the Earth, Christian Aid, Amnesty International and Oxfam, and social movements, such as feminism, environmentalism, anti-poverty and anti-globalization, whose activities and influence on international politics, intergovernmental agencies and national governments have been significant in promoting a globalized ecological sensibility, through animating sustainable values and practices. Many of the new social movements and global civil society organizations have developed in opposition to the work of the World Bank, the International Monetary Fund (IMF), the World Economic Forum, the World Trade Organization (WTO), the European Union and the Organization for Economic Co-operation and Development (OECD), which have been perceived as insensitively, and unnecessarily, forcing neoliberalist policies and practices on developing nations.

Box 5.1 Women's safety in Delhi – realizing the Right to the City

In December 2005, the NGO Jagori (the term means 'awaken women') conducted its first stakeholder consultation on the issue, involving the police, residents' associations, Delhi government, urban planners and various vulnerable groups.

Clearly, while all categories of women (as defined by age, socio-economic status, and profession) faced problems of sexual harassment in public spaces, some were more vulnerable than others. In the Focus Group Discussions, women from lower socio-economic backgrounds – domestic workers, hawkers, homeless women and other women working in the informal sector – emerged as being acutely vulnerable as regular users of public space. The homeless women shared horror stories of how they and their children faced harassment from multiple quarters, at any time of the day or night. Students from north-eastern states reported facing discrimination due to different physical features, and misguided perceptions about their nature and character. School and college-going students were regular victims of stalking but hesitated to confront the perpetrator due to lack of confidence, or even to report the incidents at home, for fear of being stopped from pursuing their education. Women working during night hours stated that taking public transport was not an option at all; in fact, they don't feel safe in their BPO taxis or even in their own cars. Visually disabled women noted that the lack of maintenance of public spaces was a huge impediment to their mobility, and reported being harassed on the pretext of providing help.

Key infrastructure recommendations to improve women's safety include:

- good or at least adequate street lighting;
- proper maintenance of public spaces;
- clean, safe and adequate toilets for both men and women – male public toilets should be redesigned so that they don't open out on the street;
- well-designed bus stops with voice announcements;

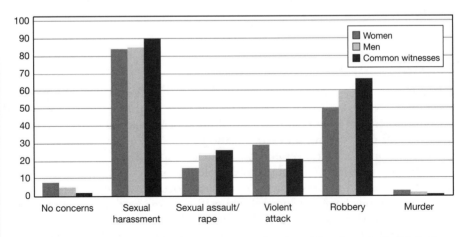

Figure 5.1 Main concerns regarding women's safety in public places in Delhi, India
Source: adapted from Suri (2010: 7).

- better and safe public transport;
- 'walkable' and disabled-friendly pavements;
- more public phone booths (some open twenty-four hours a day);
- eateries open twenty-four hours a day and allowing street vendors to trade, thereby increasing the use of space and creating 'eyes on the street';
- curtailing open drug-dealing and usage;
- concerted efforts to sensitize people on the issue;
- change of attitude of both men and women towards sexual harassment;
- sensitized and responsive redressal mechanism in which the police have a very important role to play.

Globalized protests reached a watershed in Seattle in 1999 and in Genoa in 2001, where opposition to global free trade, capitalist globalization and the self-regarding actions of the elite economic nations (the G7), spilled on to the streets in a spectacular and well-publicized fashion. The protests against globalized capitalism morphed into an opposition to the growing militarization exhibited by nations such as the US and Britain following the September 11 terrorist attack on the World Trade Center in New York, the 'war on terror', military action against the Taliban and Al-Qaeda in Afghanistan, and the highly controversial attack by the US and other national forces on Iraq in 2003. The growth of civil society activism also stimulated the formation of a counter-public sphere in the 'real' and virtual worlds, where neoliberalism, globalization, imperialism, and alternative strategies and ideas could be vigorously debated and discussed.

The World Social Forum (WSF), probably the most visible manifestation of this counter-public sphere, has expanded, since its first meeting in the democratically radical city of Porto Alegre, Brazil, in 2001, to become an important dialogic space and key intervention in world political activity. Smaller thematic Forum meetings have taken place in India, Africa, Europe, and North and South America. As Leite (2005) correctly notes, the WSF is a space and not an organization. It is a site for ideas, the sharing of experiences and intense networking among political activists from across the world. The WSF does not take a position on issues or pass resolutions. Its aim is to be, and remain, pluralist in conception and practice. As such, it should be understood as a process, rather than an event, constituting part of the larger movement opposing war, imperialism, and global economic and social exploitation. The WSF has helped create an environment that cultivates social movements, an ideological climate, and a new internationalism that offers opportunities for widespread participation and social and intercultural learning. The inauguration of the WSF in Porto Alegre was of practical and symbolic importance, because the city's radical budgetary planning process has been frequently cited as one of the best and most effective contemporary examples of large-scale and successful participatory democracy (Abers, 1998; Teivainen, 2002; Bruce, 2004). Porto Alegre demonstrates that Euro-centric knowledge structures, where the development model of the North is taught or imposed on the South, need not be applied or even be applicable. Writing of the WSF meeting in Mumbai in 2004, Smith observes that:

to a larger extent than in the past, activists from India and Asia sought to use the WSF to educate international activists and to mobilize international support for their struggles. This points to a particular advantage of the WSF process in helping raise international awareness of the plight of marginalized groups whose voices never reach international forums. Many international activists left India far more informed about the injustices of caste, class and religious conflicts in India. They certainly would have learned about the grievances of the Dalit, or the 'untouchables', who were prominent on the forum's programme. They might also have learned how the move of increasing numbers of well-paying information technology jobs from the US and Europe to India affects Indian workers. The Mumbai forum provided an opportunity for Indian hosts to honour a delegation from Pakistan and to expand a Hindu–Muslim dialogue. For their part, by interacting with a community of transnational activists well versed in the values of participatory democracy, Indian activists (and the Brazilians before them) were forced to be sensitive to some of their own exclusionary practices.

(2004: 416)

Although not without its critics, tensions and conflicts, the WSF articulates possibilities for a distributed democratic global leadership through its commitment to the belief that 'another world is possible'. Through the processes of dialogue, discussion and networking, activist groups can break free from their sometimes overwhelming sense of isolation and the seeming enormity of their aims. By 2005, the WSF had secured a prominent presence and largely sympathetic coverage by the world's news media, intrigued with its real-time/real world actions and debates, supplemented and extended by innumerable blogs, online forums, links and websites. However, as Smith (2004) notes, isolated groups still exist, and these often lack the information and creative input needed to innovate and adapt in the face of concerted repression, exclusion and ignorance. Nonetheless, the WSF's support of transnational solidarity energizes and inspires many activists unable to attend the main WSF meetings or global forum. Regional and local meetings act as focal points, expressing the unity among diverse local struggles and encouraging activist coordination at local, national and transnational levels.

The challenges of sustainable development are interlinked and politics is now central in an attempt to reframe some key debates particularly with regard to the recognition of the complexity and uncertainty that characterize the operation of socio-ecological, economic and political systems; appreciating divergent notions of progress and pathways to sustainability; and encouraging an open politics of choice around possible directions for sustainable development and their attendant distributional consequences. As Leach *et al.* (2012) write, such choices between different social, environmental and technological pathways are inevitably political, requiring top-down regulation, bottom-up mobilization, and alliances cutting across government, business and civil society organizations North and South. This will involve forging links between global science and local participation in decision-making and implementation to create a '3-D agenda' for innovation encompassing:

- the *direction* of innovation towards sustainability;
- the more equitable *distribution* of costs, benefits and risks;
- the value of *diversity* in socio-technological systems and approaches to innovation.

Box 5.2 The 2012 World Social Forum on Migration (WSFM), Manila (Philippines)

The WSFM is a space for democratic debate, reflection, formulation of proposals, exchange of experiences, and articulation of action plans among social movements, networks, NGOs and other CSOs that are opposed to neoliberal globalization and the restriction of citizenship rights, civil rights, and political/economic/social/cultural rights of migrants, displaced persons, refugees, and stateless persons.

Extracts from Walden Bello's keynote speech: Labour Trafficking as the Modern-Day Slave Trade

This gap between increasing demand and restricted supply has created an explosive situation, one that has been filled by a global system of trafficking in human beings that can in many respects be compared to the slave trade of the 16th century. The dynamics of the current system of trade in repressed labor is illustrated in the case of the Philippines. This country is one of the great labor exporters of the world. Some 10 percent of its total population and 22 percent its working age population are now migrant workers in other countries. With remittances totaling some $20 billion a year, the Philippines placed fourth as a recipient of remittances, after China, India, and Mexico.

In its effort to curb this free market in virtual slavery or to prevent workers from going intocountries where their physical security would be in great danger like Afghanistan or Iraq, the Philippine government requires government-issued permits for workers to be able to leave or it has imposed deployment bans to some countries. However, labor recruiters, which are often in cahoots not only with Middle East employers but also with the US Defense Department and US private contractors, have found ways of getting around these regulations.

The predominance of women among the workers being trafficked to the Middle East has created a situation rife with sexual abuse, and a system whereby labor trafficking and sexual trafficking are increasingly intersecting. Here is an excerpt from a report of the House Committee on Overseas Workers following the visit of some members to Saudi Arabia that I led in January 2011:

> Rape is the ever-present specter that haunts Filipino domestic workers in Saudi Arabia. . . . Rape and sexual abuse is more frequent than the raw Embassy statistics reveal, probably coming to 15 to 20 per cent of cases reported for domestics in distress. If one takes these indicators as roughly representative of unreported cases of abuse of domestic workers throughout the kingdom, then one cannot but come to the conclusion that rape and sexual abuse is common.
>
> I would go further and say that there is a strong element of sex trafficking in the migration of Filipino women into the Middle East given the expectation, especially in many Gulf households, that providing sex to the master of the household is seen as part of the domestic worker's tasks.

Source: World Social Forum (2012) (www.wsfm2012.org).

Greenpeace International and the politics of perspective change

International NGOs have helped create a global civil society, and their actions, as Wapner (1996) argues, can have a significant impact on world politics. Greenpeace International, originating in Vancouver, Canada, in the late 1960s with a small but highly visible direct protest action against nuclear testing in the Pacific, is now a large global organization operating transnationally, nationally and locally. Many of their actions have focused on securing sufficient publicity to alter people's way of looking at the world, on changing their values and perspectives, and ultimately their actions and behaviour. Greenpeace aims to broadly disseminate an ecological sensibility that can operate as a political force by changing people's meaning schemes and perspectives, influencing policy development and implementation, and changing practice. With its defining campaigns against seal culling, whaling and the proposed dumping by Shell of their Brent Spar oil installation in the North Sea, Greenpeace has helped nurture an ideational context, through the use of striking imagery, that has in turn inspired their direct and indirect supporters to act in a more pro-environmental manner. Such activism often employs a sophisticated and effective image politics (Dale, 1996; DeLuca, 1999), and Greenpeace International has become a master of the political image, the mocking vlog, and the penetrating 'spot' and subversive culture jam. As Wapner (1996) notes, people generally tend to translate experience into action through their general interpretative categories, understandings and conceptions of the world. Their experience is mediated culturally through the dominance or operationalization of certain norms, values and predispositions. Greenpeace campaigns aim to (re)align these with a clearer and deeper concern for the planet, often by 'bearing witness', stinging people's consciences by showing environmental abuse or revealing corporate disinformation, and exposing the gap between the rhetoric and the reality of public relations, news management and actual behaviour. In some cases Greenpeace activists experience concerted attacks on their physical well-being, arrests and, as in Russia in 2013, imprisonment on charges of piracy for protesting against oil exploration in the Arctic.

Defining what is meant by 'ecological sensibility' and measuring changes to societal and ideological discourses is not easy. It requires a fluid approach that accepts diffuseness and is sensitive to subtle but meaningful changes in individual, group, institutional, corporate and governmental deliberations. Despite the cyclical nature of green activity and activism, environmental and sustainability awareness is slowly becoming mainstreamed within business, government, culture and politics. We are all environmentalists now, because a generalized ecological sensibility is increasingly pervasive, perhaps even fashionable, in Western civil society. Green has become a symbol for global political action, as with the rapid expansion and globalization of new and old media, TV and the Internet, national sovereignties are being perforated by images of protest, environmental degradation and activist achievements. Globalism is now increasingly associated with the drive for a global (ecological) citizenship (Dobson, 2003a; O'Byrne, 2003) that understands and acts with regard to the fragility of the planet's ecosystems, its life-support systems, its beauty and its interdependent nature, combined with a belief in global human equality. Similarly, global civil society campaigns like Jubilee 2000, Make Poverty History, Live Eight and Live Earth have arguably functioned to extend this ecological sensibility to encompass the wide range of sustainability concerns. Paul Hawken (2007: 165) has gone a step further, suggesting that 'the insanity of human destructiveness may be matched by an older grace and intelligence that is fastening us together in ways we have never before seen or imagined'. There is a 'movement of movements', informed by a broad spectrum of ideas and values, underpinning countless citizen-based organizations, from the rich suburbs of the developed world to the poor *favelas* and indigenous communities of the developing world, which are constantly challenging political corruption and inertia, corporate greed, environmental pillage, global poverty, preventable diseases and species extinction. It is this 'blessed unrest', this human desire to change the world rather than simply interpret it, that offers hope for a sustainable future. Globalization is a fact; and, thanks particularly to new and emerging media technologies, we are all connected now (Anderson, 2001) and doing something about it.

Strong democracy

For the political philosopher Benjamin Barber, strong democracy suggests that politics is something done *by* citizens, rather than *to* them by elites, big companies, bureaucrats or any other 'other' one can think of. Citizenship in this context is active and transformative. It is also very public, in the sense that it is about creating or building community, and modes and habits of participation, deciding on public goods and public ends rather than reproducing isolated privatized lifestyles and wants. A participatory citizen democracy cannot avoid the necessity of public choice and judgement, or the interconnectedness of issues and events. Citizens think in terms of *we* rather than *me*, and to be able to choose between courses of action, recognizing the inequity of power structures and social conditions, requires the application of a critical reason, or at least a *reasonableness* and imagination, in public deliberation. As Barber writes:

> Community grows out of participation and at the same time makes participation possible; civic activity educates individuals about how to think publicly as citizens, even as citizenship informs civic activity with the required sense of publicness and justice. Politics becomes its own university, citizenship its own training ground and participation its own tutor. Freedom is what comes out of this process, not what goes into it.
>
> (1984: 152)

Strong democracy with active participatory citizenship has a close affinity with practices of community development, community empowerment and community action, all of which emphasize the importance of people having the capacity to be agents of change, capable of refashioning their social worlds and themselves. The core values informing this type of action have been identified as conviviality and culture, critical and dynamic education, free access to information and communication media, health and well-being, strong participatory involvement, economic equity, opportunity and sustainability. Socio-economic inequality, uncertainty of public purpose or vision, may consequently place serious limits on the efficacy of participatory democracy. An adversarial approach to public discussion will also harm this form of democratic process. Political or public 'talk', Barber suggests, leads to the invention of alternative futures, the creation of mutual purposes, and the construction of possible visions for the community and agreed action to transform civil society. Engagement through public conversation allows the registration of intensity of feeling and belief, of public seeing and judgement of right and wrong. Given this, genuine participation builds those affective links that bind one to another, that engender social capital and self-respect, that offer avenues for empowerment, responsible self-governance and civic education. Too great a reliance on representative mechanisms and procedures, voting for representatives to do our talking and decision-making, says Barber, deprives individuals of common activities that could turn a citizenry into a genuine political community. This view is echoed by many other political theorists who argue that democratic dialogue needs to be accompanied by the development of green institutions and the nurturing of green values. For Dryzek (2000), since democracy exists among humans and in human interactions with the natural world, what is needed for enhanced (ecological democratization is an effective integration of political and ecological communication. Nature does 'speak' to us; it does have agency, as is evident with climate change, deforestation, species extinction, Gaia, and so on. We might not hear the words, but we can certainly feel the effects. Human beings need to see themselves as ecological beings as much as social or political ones. Human beings are parts of those ecosystems and ecosystem services that our economies depend on and exploit. Democracy is therefore more than representation or the aggregation of particular interests, but to see this requires enlarged thinking and new forms of interaction and deliberation transcending the boundary of the human world. We can listen to non-human animals through the very human (and bureaucratic) practices of sustainability appraisals, human and environmental impact assessments, and environmental reporting, and our institutions and institutional responses need to be appropriately calibrated to deal with the size and scope of the problems. Central and centralized structures may not effectively hear or engage with the various messages nature is sending us. For Dryzek:

> Bioregionalism is not just about a matter of redrawing political boundaries: it is also a matter of living in place. Redesigned political units should promote, and in turn be promoted by, awareness on the part of their human inhabitants of the biological surroundings that sustain them.
>
> (2000: 157)

Discursive public spheres and political institutions will be variable, not limited by formal geographical boundaries, and debates will continue about the meaning and practice of green democracy, as without these debates a democratic society is unable to exist.

Processes and opportunities for participation are important in giving voice to those whose voices cannot be heard or whose voices are never used. The argument against the practicality of increased participation is that the socially excluded, the poor and the victimized are too apathetic, and the rich are simply too busy or too self-interested to get involved actively in civil society organizations, to join neighbourhood assemblies, forums, citizen juries, and so on. Barber disagrees:

> But of course people refuse to participate only where politics does not count – or counts less than rival forms of private activity. They are apathetic because they are powerless, not powerless because they are apathetic. There is no evidence

to suggest that once empowered, a people will refuse to participate. The historical evidence of New England towns, community school boards, neighbourhood associations and other local bodies is that participation fosters more participation.

(1984: 272)

Government and political decision-making needs to be closer to people's lives, and decentralization has been seen as necessary for improvements in democracy, environmental management and economic development (Bardhan, 2002). Arjun Appadurai (2001) writes of the activities of three civil society organizations in Mumbai: the NGO SPARC (Society for the Promotion of Area Resource Centres), the National Slum Dwellers' Federation and a co-operative group representing women's savings groups, Mahila Milan. Working together they use their own local knowledge to develop capacity to negotiate with local government and to effect changes that drastically improve the conditions of poor people. They promote micro-finance, better sanitation, organize community housing surveys and exhibitions, and the learning of key civic skills to leverage the support and recognition of other NGOs and government officials. Alliances, networks and exchanges have been organized with urban poor federations in other countries, making for 'a globalization from below' and 'a politics without parties' that has deepened democratic processes. The spread of this model elsewhere, if successful, could produce more poor communities able to enter into partnerships with powerful agencies that concern themselves with poverty and citizenship. Similarly, Pal (2006), studying grass-roots planning processes in Kolkata, India, recognizes the need for political decision-makers to design new institutional mechanisms if more people-centred politics and governance is to emerge. Goodin and Dryzek (2006) show that deliberative innovations, 'mini publics' such as citizen juries, deliberative polls, planning cells and consensus conferences, do have a real and tangible effect on the wider political scene, public debate, and policy formation and implementation. Media coverage of these mini publics may influence policy makers and other members of the public who, through listening and discussing issues, may change their own ideas and policy preferences. The authors offer an example of a mini-public conference in 1999 informing the wider public debates in Australia on genetically modified foods. Debates in the Australian legislature referred to these debates, and Monsanto was forced to alter its communication strategy, recognizing that corporate engagement with local people needed to go far beyond sophisticated public relations. Mini publics can be used as a form of 'market testing', of 'listening to the city', which may ultimately result in citizens rejecting development proposals, as the Lower Manhattan Development Corporation discovered when its plans to rebuild the area devastated in the September 11 attacks were fully and openly discussed. The UK Government also explored the market of public opinion regarding the extension of commercial GM and, despite its own stubborn refusal to heed much of the public debate, was nonetheless forced to pursue its pro-GM policies without the public enthusiasm or endorsement it had hoped for:

Thus, despite the government's insistence that all was well, the 'GM Nation?' debate – and especially its more genuinely deliberative 'Narrow but Deep' component, by which government explicitly set most store – succeeded in extracting some 'further action' from government. Those specific measures came in the areas of 'providing choice for consumers and farmers', 'mandatory labelling for consumers', and steps to ensure the 'coexistence' of GM and non-GM crops.

Beyond those specific measures, the government committed itself, first and foremost, to 'protect human health and the environment through robust regulation of GM crops on a case-by-case basis, consistent with the precautionary principle'.

(Goodin and Dryzek, 2006: 231)

Participatory processes may also promote empowerment by giving people the psychological confidence to express their views, learn from others, and challenge those in political authority or those with expert specialist (but not necessarily local) knowledge. Additionally, the experience of having participated in a debate, or on a citizen jury, may provide people with the skills and motivation to go further, mobilizing actions that apply pressure to the wider political system in other ways. Goodin and Dryzek (2006) argue that discursive forums are difficult for the established authorities to neutralize through co-option, because deliberative discussions are frequently very difficult to control, manage or predict. For instance, the scientific panel established by the provincial government of British Columbia to investigate clear-cutting in Clayoquot Sound included both logging experts and local people, including representatives from indigenous groups. The result was a report encompassing a variety of perspectives, including that of the First Nations' traditional ecological knowledge, which scientific members generally accepted without resistance. The criticism of the deliberative process has focused not so much on the report but in the failure of the provincial government of British Columbia to properly implement it. It is also interesting to recall that Gundersen (1995) conducted a series of 'deliberative interviews' with forty-six subjects about ecological issues, all of whom had previously expressed little interest in or concern about the environment. He noted that by the time the interviews finished, they possessed a stronger commitment to environmental values than previously, suggesting the persuasive power of reasoned debate and communicative action.

Civic environmentalism and the politics of place

William Shutkin (2001) takes a systems approach to public policy, local democracy and what he terms 'civic environmentalism'. He is strongly influenced by the work of environmental historians William Cronon (1983) and Carolyn Merchant (1989), who see the instability in human relations and culture as being bound up with changes in the environment. Cronon views human relations and the environment as mutually, dialectically, playing off each other, while Merchant argues that environmental change may be best understood by exploring changes in a given society's ecology, mode of production, biological reproductive processes, social relationships and forms of consciousness. Consequently, social structure, the law and demographics help determine a society's demand for natural resources, and the ways in which societies and cultures understand the natural world depend on a combination of factors – religion, myth, thoughts, feelings, ideologies, belief or otherwise in human volition, and so on. For Shutkin, real democracy is strong democracy. It is citizen participation in decision-making, co-operation, trust, common purpose, open discussion, networking and real physical (rather than virtual) places where people can genuinely interact socially and culturally. In other words, civic democracy is a combination of local environment, civil society and social capital. A sense of belonging and commitment to place, to community or localized identity, to where people physically interact with each other and may sensually experience the wider environment, is absolutely central. Acknowledging the ideas of urbanists Dolores Hayden (1997) and Daniel Kemmis (1990), Shutkin sees the power or sense of place as the capacity for everyday landscapes, towns or cityscapes to foster within local citizens, neighbourhood residents or individual householders a public memory, a sense of a shared time and territory:

> The relationship between the environment and civic life is thus not just about the physical effects of development, such as pollution or sprawl. It is also about the feelings, attitudes and sensory experiences nurtured by the environment that contribute to civic consciousness and identity. Just as civic attitudes and the 'habits of the heart' that Tocqueville saw as critical to the success of democratic communities affect the way in which physical space is developed, so too does the sense of place and experience of nature influence our civic sensibility and consciousness.
>
> (Shutkin, 2001: 49)

It is important to embrace the humble and the everyday, local solutions, to be inclusive, and to link environmental problem-solving with the building of community capacity. Shutkin explores some empirical real-world and ongoing examples of civic environmentalism, such as community conservation and conservation-based planning in Colorado, the development of a transit village in Oakdale, urban agriculture in Boston, and community planning and cooperation in a New Jersey suburb. Although inevitably incomplete, Shutkin elicits from his analysis the core concepts of civic environmentalism:

- Participatory process: meaningful and informed participation in the decision-making procedures that impact on the quality of people's lives. This means a bottom–up approach to democracy and a public recognition of the worth of all inhabitants or citizens.
- Community and regional planning: meaningful structures to facilitate involvement, multi-stakeholder participation and collaboration, and a sense of responsibility for the future of places in which citizens live and may also work.
- Environmental education: developing the recognition and understanding that the economy, society and the environment are interlinked and that local communities are able to alter their circumstances. This may mean people understanding the environmental consequences of their actions – CO_2 emissions produced by commuting by car, increased landfill use through profligate waste disposal, and so on.
- Industrial ecology: focusing on such actions as integrated pollution prevention, full-cost accounting, and ecologically sensitive development planning and economic growth.
- Environmental justice: the awareness of the social and spatial distributive aspect of environmental degradation and environmental protection.
- Place: developing a sense of place or, as Alistair McIntosh (2004) puts it, recognizing the intimate connection between soil and soul.

Civic environmentalism involves many things, ranging from the development and articulation of a place based on existential and cognitive processes of reasoning to community empowerment through participation (Friedmann, 1992) and a political literacy married to a set of political skills encompassing communication, argument, political action and 'politicking' (Flyvbjerg, 1998). The incorporation by professional planners of social with environmental impact analyses now encompasses an understanding of the hidden spheres of everyday life – for example, the domestic, 'women's' worlds of child-rearing, caring, and so on. This is particularly so in processes of collaborative and neighbourhood planning, where unless the voices and insights of marginal groups, including ethnic minorities, are recognized, community development programmes are likely to flounder by generating opposition, fear and conflict (Healey, 1997; Mills, 1998). Only an inclusive sense of community and belonging can nurture social cohesion, participation, trust and neighbourliness (Putnam, 2007).

Ecological citizenship

The sociologist Bryan S. Turner (1993: 2) defines citizenship as 'that set of practices (juridical, political, economic and cultural) which define a person as a competent member of society, and which as a consequence shape the flow of resources to persons and social groups'. The word 'practice' is important, because it encompasses the experience of everyday life, of social structure and inequality, of action and agency, and of power, social relationships, and the distribution of resources within societies and between them. Modifying Turner's argument slightly, citizenship may be said to address the following issues:

- the nature of rights, responsibilities and obligations;
- the form or type of such rights, responsibilities and obligations;
- the social and political forces that produce practices of various sorts; and
- the arrangements whereby benefits (or otherwise) are distributed among people or between peoples, or between peoples and the non-human world.

We tend to value things either weakly or strongly. Environmental activists argue that if we do not value the environment, safe food or clean air strongly, we may become lesser beings as a result. Individuals have rights, but so does the planet, which has a real claim on me to act wisely, prudently and sensibly. Unfortunately, much environmental legislation, particularly in relation to the requirement to undertake environmental impact assessments, is often based on the economic costs or benefits of specific developments – for example, a new motorway – and not on any principle of rights. It is utility or usefulness to 'society' or to the 'economy' that counts. However, underpinning the idea of ecological citizenship is active citizenship, social inclusion, deliberation, civic virtue, ecological welfare, information and political participation (Saiz, 2005). For Barry, citizenship and democratic deliberation involve social learning, perspective transformation and the internalization of others' interests – those of non-human animals, future generations, and political and environmental refugees. Ecological citizenship is democratic and is able to inform the voluntary creation and maintenance of an ecologically rational society because communicative and instrumental rationality characterizes ecological rationality (Barry, 1999: 230). For Dobson (2003b), ecological citizenship encompasses the private as well as the public realms, is more about obligations than rights, and is international and intergenerational, incorporating notions of ecological footprinting and ecological debt.

Although formal education is important – citizenship is now, after all, part of the UK's National Curriculum – it is the reflection of one's lived experience that probably has most bearing on changing human conduct.

Globalization and cosmopolitanism have affected the life experience of the individual as well as the conduct of transnational companies (TNCs), not least because of growing public awareness of global inequality and the serious problems associated with free trade and unsustainable modes of economic production. Zadek (2001) argues that TNCs should become good corporate citizens, taking due account of their employment practices and ecological footprints in local and national environments. Although others suggest that TNCs will only do this if their financial bottom line is threatened, their commitment being purely instrumental, corporate social and environmental responsibility is a practice that many large companies now engage with seriously. The expectation of gaining new consumer markets or the fear of bad media publicity, as recently experienced by organizations such as McDonald's, Shell, Nike, Nestlé and Monsanto, are strong motivators. Consequently, there have developed a number of strategic corporate/NGO alliances in recent years – Starbucks and CARE, Reebok and Amnesty International – suggesting that the responsible corporation may be something more than a PR exercise (Palacios, 2004).

Equally, it may be asked whether it is easy for citizens to be green. How can individuals, groups and businesses fashion and act on their ecological obligations when so much of our social and economic lives are structured unsustainably, or offer so many contradictory and incompatible forms of satisfaction and reward. As Paterson (2000) shows, car culture is intimately bound up with the global political economy. Cars themselves symbolize modernity, growth, success and development, as the massive expansion of car use and ownership in China testifies. Seyfang (2005), writing on ecological citizenship and shopping, notes that a major criticism of the mainstream model of sustainable consumption through market transformation argues that only purchases, not votes, really count in today's world. However, not everyone is able to influence the market. Sustainable goods may be beyond a person's price range or may be simply unavailable in local stores. People may become disempowered, disillusioned with the ideology of green consumerism, and overly suspicious of corporate greening and green marketing. They may see themselves as being part of a corporately imagined or stimulated community, identifying themselves readily with particular brands and logos. Seyfang also recognizes that people buy things for a variety of purposes that may have little to do with being a good ecological citizen. People shop for therapeutic reasons to raise their self-esteem, to buy themselves a treat, to identify with a particular cultural group, to foster a sense of belonging or to display a certain social status in the community. In developing countries, ecological citizenship may take similar forms, but frequently, when combined with direct political action, the focus is strongly on engagement, action, participation, environmental learning, gender equality, human rights, subsistence, leadership and empowerment, rather than material consumption. However, this is not to deny that issues of consumption may not also be genuine issues of survival, cultural or personal identity. Civic environmentalism, combined with practices of ecological citizenship, including grass-roots action, may therefore be firmly and literally rooted in the local ecology, generating both a sense of and a commitment to place, the land, the locality and the home (Maathai, 2004).

Box 5.3 The Green Belt Movement in Kenya

The Green Belt Movement (GBM) is a community-based, development and environmental organization focused on community mobilization and empowerment. Its vision is to create a society of principled grassroots people who consciously work for continued improvement of their livelihoods. This goal is achieved by mobilizing thousands of women's groups, who establish tree nurseries and plant indigenous trees on their farms and public lands, including forests, to prevent soil erosion, and generally protect, rehabilitate and conserve the environment. For those tree seedlings that survive, women's groups receive a financial token of appreciation, making the initiative an income-generating activity. The income earned by the women is mostly used to supplement domestic needs.

In the course of the past thirty years, the GBM has evolved a procedure that is effective at mobilizing action and has produced 30 million trees, transforming the landscapes and lives of families and communities, which are very appreciative of their achievements. One of these achievements with long-lasting impact has been the inculcation of a culture of tree-planting and environmental care. Additionally, communities have internalized the linkages between their basic needs and a healthy environment. The GBM was founded in 1977 by Wangari Maathai, who nurtured it under the auspices of the National Council of Women in Kenya (NCWK). Over the years, GBM programmes have expanded to include civic and environmental education, advocacy and networking, household food security, Green Belt Safaris and Women for Change (capacity-building for self-sufficiency).

Communities are organized into groups and networks, which engage in activities that promote primary environmental care. These activities provide communities with basic services like food, firewood, building and fencing materials, and fodder. Communities also provide themselves with security and responsible parenting by ridding themselves of illegal alcohol and drugs. This protects children, especially girls.

The mission of the GBM is to mobilize community consciousness for self-determination, justice, equity, reduction of poverty, and environmental conservation, using trees as the entry point. The overall vision of the GBM is to inculcate in our communities values such as volunteerism for the common good, love for a greener environment, action for self-betterment, accountability, transparency and community empowerment.

Source: The Green Belt Movement (2003).

Green reason

It is a common assumption that instrumental reason has been a major determinant of humankind's disregard for the environment. Nature is there to be used, quelled, dominated and subordinated to the needs of human welfare and emancipation. Ecologists of various descriptions, but particularly those of the deep green variety, have sought to replace this instrumental reason with something else – usually some form of holistic consciousness and spirituality. For John Dryzek (1990) this is not really appropriate for an environmental ethic and a political practice that needs to place humankind as part of the natural world as opposed to apart from it. Additionally, there have been societies and civilizations in the past, such as ancient Egypt, whose open spirituality and reverence for nature has actually been rather destructive. Instead of this, one alternative is to extend the democratic and discursive theories of the German philosopher Jurgen Habermas to develop a communicative ethics based on an ecological reason that encompasses nature as an actor in the communication and discursive process. Dryzek suggests that this is feasible if perception is equated with communication, and that as human impacts on ecological processes inevitably alter those processes, these changes can be perceived as nature talking/communicating with us in return. If nature is accorded value, or a kind of subjectivity, just as a human party to the communication processes would be accorded value and a subjectivity, then it becomes incumbent upon us to listen and act in an appropriate manner, which Dryzek suggests should normally be on a scale and in a way that is readily understood by all. However, there are plenty of examples of human action operating at a scale whose consequences are poorly understood, discounted or ignored. The ecological and social impact of big dams in massive development projects in India and China may be cited as evidence of this and the idea that these impacts and consequences themselves institute a form of communication or performance. The implication of this is a new form of politics and a new conception of nature – a reinscription of political ecology. Thus, Bruno Latour writes in his *Politics of Nature*:

> Within the collective, there is now a blend of entities, voices, and actors, such that it would have been impossible to deal with it either through ecology alone or through politics alone. The first would have naturalized all the entities: the second would have socialized them all. By refusing to tie politics to humans, subjects, or freedom, and [should be 'or'] to tie Science to objects, nature or necessity, we have discovered the work common to politics and to the sciences alike: stirring the entities of the collective together in order to make them articulable and to *make them speak*.
>
> (2004a: 89)

A communicative ethics for the biosphere would almost certainly entail political conversations among 'actants', to use a term Latour adopts, where human beings silently attune themselves to what the biosphere is saying and doing. Political participation and engagement then would entail a 'better listening' and a de-emphasis on the practice of speaking (Dobson, 2010). Democratic debate and communication would look very different and if the utterances of Big Dams and Economic Growth are taken into account, Green Reason would surely posit small as being beautiful and rationality as being green.

Finally, in discussing politics, agency, communication and dialogue, it is well to spend a little time considering the nature of talk. In everyday life people sometimes shy away from appearing overly political or committed to a particular point of view. One may not want to appear a zealot, or extremist, or 'greenie'. In various studies of political talk by Americans, Nina Eliasoph (1990: 487) noted that 'holding an opinion' means different things to different people and that the display of opinion varies according to context and situation. In studying the relationships people display towards their own political views when speaking among others or in public, Eliasoph (1990: 465) remarks that people literally 'do things with words'. When talking politics, people are often as concerned about how they sound as about what they actually say. Far from being a palliative, a symbolic compensation for a structural lack of power, talking politics actually gives tangible life to the public sphere, even though it may seem that many people watch or read the news to reassure themselves that the public sphere remains far from their own lives. She also notes that it is important to discover how both membership of civic associations and the media influence political discussion and political displays. In later studies, Eliasoph (1998) and Eliasoph and Lichterman (2003) show how cultural and collective representations enable groups to develop a style of interaction that acts as a social and ideological filter. Eliasoph and Lichterman studied one group of environmental activists operating in a suburban setting where engagement could be seen as socially courageous. This group consequently used the language of expressive individualism and personal empowerment 'to *affirm* social responsibility and public-spiritedness, rather than to subordinate them to self-centred expression' (Eliasoph and Lichterman, 2003: 748). By contrast, a group of Country and Western devotees, known as 'the Buffaloes', occupying a social space – a bar – that political scientist Robert Putnam would see as a potential generator of social capital, frequently appeared to be '*irrational, excitable, wild* and *passionate*' (Eliasoph and Lichterman, 2003: 760). They exhibited a group style the authors termed 'active disaffiliation', often breaking the moral code with racist or sexist jokes, teasing and often citicizing serious discussion as getting on the 'high horse'. There was to be no hypocrisy among the Buffaloes while engaged in social events, no false pretences or feigned political correctness. They were to be authentically themselves. Eliasoph and Lichterman concluded (2003: 782) that through examining culture in interaction it can be seen that 'people always make meanings in specific social settings, in relation to each other as they perceive each other'. Political talk occurs in many contexts but is tailored to context and by the culture of interaction pertaining in everyday life. Thus Eliasoph and Lichterman write:

> A study of culture in interaction offers a more systematic method for analyzing the 'tone' of these groups. Thus, the bar patrons and the suburban activist group's styles were not just not neutral, transparent conveyors of cultural meanings. Neither were they just pro- or antidemocratic. The concept of culture in interaction operationalizes an insight from students of public life such as Dewey (1927), Mead (1934) and others that meaning and practice – or 'content and form' – are intertwined, creating varied kinds of openings for members to become democratic citizens.
>
> (2003: 783)

In an interesting discussion of Eliasoph's work on political talk and everyday life, Liebes (1999) identifies various cases where people do enter into political conversations about the state of the world, without necessarily engaging in the political activist practice of trying to change it through lobbying, protest, negotiation, campaigning, and so on. Of course, discussion and reflection are a form of action, and conversation and dialogue are a core component of a healthy democracy and human sustainable development. Liebes suggests that political talk is framed or constrained by the degree to which a society is politicized. For example, Israel is a more politicized society than America, and Northern Ireland is more politicized than England. In many countries the traditional mainstream media probably reflects rather than determines the political agenda and terms of debate, although with the advent of new media this is becoming increasingly unlikely. A final and interesting thought, which may be of note to sustainability activists not wishing to seem too shrill, is that a certain depoliticization, perhaps even a political neutering of debate and discussion, occurs when the rhetoric of caring, management and personality dominates a particular discourse. For Schudson (1999), political talk is not like everyday conversation – one is instrumental with an agreed goal or action in mind and the other is largely creative and free-flowing – and they require different, but perhaps complementary, skills and interactive cultures. Political action may mean more than buying organic chocolate or saying one cares for a plant.

Summary

Human beings are political as well as social animals and sustainable development is ultimately a political act – or, more precisely, a series of political acts. How this politics is played out, how we govern ourselves, how we make decisions and act upon them, is the subject of this chapter. Politics and governance within the context of sustainable development certainly requires learning from experience, theoretical understanding, and a continuous looking for the best ways in which progress can be achieved and maintained. For many, although not all commentators, the most appropriate direction to follow is one that involves extensive democratization and participation in decision-making at all levels from the global to the local levels of the neighbourhood and the workplace. Strong democracy and green reason may become married to other concepts too, such as ecological citizenship, eco-welfare and the Right to the City. The idea that sustainable development encompasses all of humanity can, and perhaps should, be taken further still to embrace a less anthropocentric and a more ecocentric philosophy and practice. After all, human beings are not the only creatures who inhabit this planet and in many ways all of us, human and non-human, need each other in order to thrive and prosper materially, culturally and spiritually.

Thinking questions

1   In what ways can ecological democratization be achieved?
2   How important is a sense of place and ecological belonging in fashioning a green, or sustainable, political practice?
3   How important is ecological citizenship, corporate or individual, to fashioning a more sustainable society?
4   What is the value of organizations such as the World Social Forum?
5   In what ways is the concept 'the Right to the City' important to progressing sustainable development?
6   In your experience, do people feel able to discuss environmental and broader sustainability issues?

Companion website

If you would like to learn more about environmental politics and governance and test your knowledge and understanding of recent campaigns, please visit the companion website for further information.

6 Conservation and sustainable development

Aims

This chapter explores the relationship between conservation and sustainable development, revisiting issues relating to population, resource use and human beings' impact on what is often termed the natural world. More specifically, efforts to preserve the natural landscape and, more latterly, a wide range of wildlife habitats brings into focus a range of policies and practices that have seen conflicts, controversies and a considerable degree of debate. The friction induced by the imposition of Western notions of conservation and stewardship on other lands has invariably led many to address and readdress both the rights of indigenous peoples and the very nature of economic development, urbanization and sustainability. This friction is practical and political in nature and although it seems that dialogue is leading to progress and accommodation, we are witnessing, indeed causing, a sixth massive extinction of many of the species with whom we supposedly share the planet.

Here, there and everywhere

Ecologist Marc Bekoff and conservation social worker Sarah Bexell (2010) perhaps state the obvious when they write that human beings are here, there and everywhere; but importantly they add that because of our short lifespans we seem removed from the nuances of natural evolutionary cycles. We are not here long enough to see what is going on in the long term and, additionally, we can negatively affect ecosystems even when we are not physically present in them. Our penchant for technical fixes also gives us a false sense of security and perhaps of optimism, and we rarely stop to think that 'we're a species whom almost all other species could easily live without' (Bekoff and Bexell, 2010: 70). Michele Soulé (2002), a pioneer in the field of conservation biology aptly put it when he noted that human beings are certainly the dominant species but we are clearly not a keystone species, for when you remove a keystone species biodiversity itself collapses. When we humans are *added* to an ecosystem, as the history of human migration and imperialism show clearly, biodiversity collapses. Unfortunately, we can't live without these other species and our actions are a direct cause of their rapid decline and frequently their extinction. Despite captive breeding programmes, transdisciplinary research projects, conservation initiatives, including moving people and animals to different locations and an array of political and economic measures, we continue to witness an alarming decline in global biodiversity. Although these 'band aid' projects are undoubtedly quite necessary, they are clearly not sufficient because the root problems of overpopulation, over-consumption, speciesism and ignorance seem to be deeply ingrained in human psychology. Bekoff and Bexell continue:

> *Therefore, we must address the important psychological and social/cultural issues that support our poor stewardship of Earth, our only home, and psychological barriers that prevent people from facing and addressing these complex, frustrating, and urgent issues that are human-induced (anthropogenic).* ... We need to extend efforts to inform people as part of a social movement that is concerned with losses in biodiversity and the implications of these losses for animals and for us.
>
> (2010: 72)

It is probably self-evident that our disconnection from the natural world and our tendency to ignore or override conservation regulations, laws and moral imperatives are sometimes undertaken for material gain, status and/or even human survival, but this only emphasizes the need for human beings to acquire the knowledge, skills and understanding to recognize the supreme importance of maintaining a rich biodiversity. We therefore need to cultivate an ecological consciousness that will enable us to live with other creatures rather than simply kill them if they get in our way or help us make some quick money. We consequently need a paradigm shift in human thought. Communication, sustainable education and political action are ways in which the current exploitative and irresponsible paradigm of unsustainable development can be shifted. A useful starting point for this is to go beyond the limits to growth debates and to actually delineate what a safe planetary operating space for human life in concert with non-human life entails. Global planetary boundaries, such as those delineated by the Stockholm Resilience Centre, must be recognized and adhered to. These boundaries include:

climate change
global freshwater use
biogeochemical flows
rate of biodiversity loss
stratospheric ozone depletion
ocean acidification
change in land use
chemical pollution
atmospheric aerosol loading.

These boundaries are clearly interlinked and changes in one may impact on others, causing these others to exceed what the Centre firmly believes to be safe operating spaces for humanity. However, as the authors of an important paper conclude, 'the evidence so far suggests that, as long as the thresholds are not crossed, humanity has the freedom to pursue long-term social and economic development' (Rockström *et al.*, 2009: 475). In 2012 Anders Wijkman, a former member of the European Parliament, and Johan Rockström, head of the Stockholm Resilience Centre, produced a Report to the Club of Rome titled *Bankrupting Nature: Denying our Planetary Boundaries* (Wijkman and Rockström, 2012). The interconnected nature of the planetary crisis and a science-based framework for a transition to sustainability forms the core of this text. They argue that the financial crisis is not just an economic one as it involves repaying all our debts, especially those we owe to nature, the climate, ecosystems, the oceans, and so on. Many of the points Wijkman and Rockström make are now becoming generally accepted, but what remains are the politics, the policy formulation and implementation. Population, for instance, is often a key driver of environmental problems but the boundary model which states so many and no more does not offer any ready-made policy solutions. Paul Ehrlich and Anne Ehrlich (2009), in reviewing their famous demographic treatise *The Population Bomb* published forty years earlier (Ehrlich, 1968), argue that population growth retards the development of poor nations and has a disproportionately negative impact on our life-support systems. In other words, we seem to need, and consequently take, too much from the planet. Wijkman and Rockström are wary of science being drawn into political debates but, given what they argue, this is surely unavoidable. Democratic political processes invariably involve debates, dialogue and, in practice, 'trade-offs', even though many conservationists and sustainability practitioners may feel that certain values such as individual rights, species protection and cultural heritage should not actually be tradable at all. Eileen Crist (Crist, 2012: 148) takes the view that humanity is 'spellbound by the idea that Earth is our planetary real estate' and that we continually do our utmost to exploit it with increasing (eco)efficiency which could ultimately result in a completely denatured planet. The issue for Crist is not so much the potential for human self-annihilation but the 'totalitarian' conversion of the natural world to a repository of goods and ecosystem services. What we are in danger of losing is not so much resources but our own family – i.e. the richness of life on earth. Not *Resource Earth* but *Abundant Earth* and this *Abundant Earth* can and should support far fewer billions of people than it presently does and is anticipated will do as this century progresses. The political problem then becomes, as David Harvey (1996) puts it, how in a society ruled by a dominant class are those who are not dominant going to avoid material, political, economic and social repression; and how are the debates about ecoscarcity, natural limits and overpopulation going to avoid being debates about preserving the existing social order rather than nature per se.

Politics, business and scientific developments have certainly increased human food supply through the introduction of scientifically improved crops that produce high yields protected by the liberal dispensation of pesticides in areas of high population growth and evident hunger – south-east Asia, Africa, China and India. This 'Green Revolution', which had its major impact in the 1960s and 1970s, was also seen by many political elites as a way of building up economic capital through the development of an export-orientated agriculture, which would in turn facilitate the path towards industrialization and urbanization. Many developing countries introduced new strains of high-yield wheat and rice so that by the early 1990s nearly 75 per cent of land in the developing world was used to cultivate these crops. In China the cultivation figure for rice and maize was nearer 95 per cent (McNeill, 2000). Food production did certainly increase, preventing the prospect of starvation being the principal experience of the developing world's growing population, but hunger and indeed periodic famines have not disappeared entirely.

There were also other, unforeseen, consequences to the Green Revolution.

Ecologically [the Green Revolution] combined with mechanization to promote monoculture. Since farmers now had to purchase seed rather than use their own, and because they needed fertilizers and pesticides specific to a single crop, they saved money on inputs by buying in bulk for one crop. Monocultures, . . ., invites pest problems. Often even the initially pest-resistant crops eventually proved vulnerable to one or another infestation. Hence farmers turned to heavier and heavier doses of pesticides.

(McNeill, 2000: 223–4)

Many of these pesticides had little or no effect but did end up in water supplies and the human body. The World Health Organization estimated that in 1990 about 20,000 people died of pesticide poisoning and in 1985 about one million people had experienced acute but non-fatal poisoning. As Indian environmental activist and founder of the Navdanya Research Foundation for Science, Technology and Ecology, Vandana Shiva (1991) wrote, the so-called green revolution in India involved the growth of high-yield cash crops, the creation of monocultures and an increased use of pesticides which destroyed a considerable amount of biodiversity. Industrial-scale agricultural production was also a cause of rural impoverishment, local conflict, ecological vulnerability and severe water shortages. The Punjab, for example, was not transformed from being a begging bowl to a bread basket but the agrochemical industries, large petrochemical companies, manufacturers of agricultural plant and equipment, dam builders and large landowners did gain significant financial dividends. She writes:

The central paradox posed by the Green Revolution and biotechnology development is that modern plant improvement has been based on the destruction of the biodiversity which it uses as raw material. The irony of plant and animal breeding is that it destroys the very building blocks on which the technology depends. When agricultural modernization schemes introduce new and uniform crops into the farmers' fields, they push into extinction the diversity of local varieties.

(1991: 251)

In *Stolen Harvest*, Vandana Shiva (2000) further explores the impact of genetic engineering and the corporate patenting of life on local people and ecosystems powerfully advocating organic and small-scale community-based agriculture, which she believes will produce sufficient food and a decent quality of life for all rural dwellers. She believes organic farming, agroforestry and forest regeneration not only creates a major carbon sink, and thereby addresses climate change issues to a degree, but they also address issues of poverty, hunger and nutrition. Industrialized chemical-based agriculture does not. She writes:

Industrial chemical agriculture also causes hunger and malnutrition by robbing crops of nutrients. Industrially produced food is nutritionally empty but loaded with chemicals and toxins. Nutrition in food comes from the nutrients in the soil. Industrial agriculture, based on the NPK mentality of synthetic nitrogen, phosphorous and potassium-based fertilizers, leads to depletion of vital micro-nutrients and trace elements such as magnesium, zinc, calcium, iron.

Biodiverse systems have higher output than monocultures, that is why organic farming is more beneficial for farmers and the earth than chemical farming.

The increase in yields does not translate into more nutrition. In fact, it is leading to malnutrition. To get the required amount of nutrition people need to eat much more food.

The most effective and low-cost strategy for addressing hunger and malnutrition is through biodiverse organic farming. It enriches the soil and nutrient-rich soils give us nutrient-rich food.

(2012)

The loss of biodiversity is publicly most evident in the decline and loss of rich habitats such as the Amazon and the disappearance of increasing numbers of other creatures with whom we share the planet.

IUCN Red List 2009

The IUCN Red List itself is the world's most comprehensive information source on the global conservation status of plant and animal species; it is updated annually and is freely available online at www.iucnredlist.org. It is based on contributions from a large global network of scientific experts who have helped produce an objective system which assigns all species, except the micro-organisms, to one of eight Red List Categories according to various criteria relating to population trend, size, structure and geographic range. It is therefore an invaluable source of scientific data and an important policy making and campaigning tool.

Rodrigues *et al.* write:

> Vulnerability and irreplaceability are two key principles guiding systematic conservation planning. Vulnerability is the likelihood that biodiversity values in a site will be lost, and the Red List contributes valuable information that can be used to measure it. Irreplaceability is the extent to which spatial options for conservation targets are reduced if the site is lost. Measurement of site irreplaceability is thus dependent on information about population size, dynamics and distribution of species, all of which are being collected in increasing detail to support Red List assessments.
>
> (2006: 74)

One of the IUCN Red List's main purposes is to highlight those species that are facing a high risk of global extinction. However, it is not just a register of names and associated threat categories. The real power and usefulness of the Red List is the rich scientific evidence on species' ecological requirements, information on their geographic distribution and threats that they offer. It offers some indications as to how these issues can best be addressed, but it is important to realize that however full and comprehensive the IUCN data appears, the knowledge it presents is partial and uncertain. The Red List covers only 2.7 per cent of the world's estimated 1.8 million species it has assessed to date. Given this, it is more than likely that the number of reported threatened species is far fewer than the actual number at serious risk of extinction. Even so, by documenting the threatened status of so many species, the IUCN attempts to fulfil its major two goals: to identify and document those

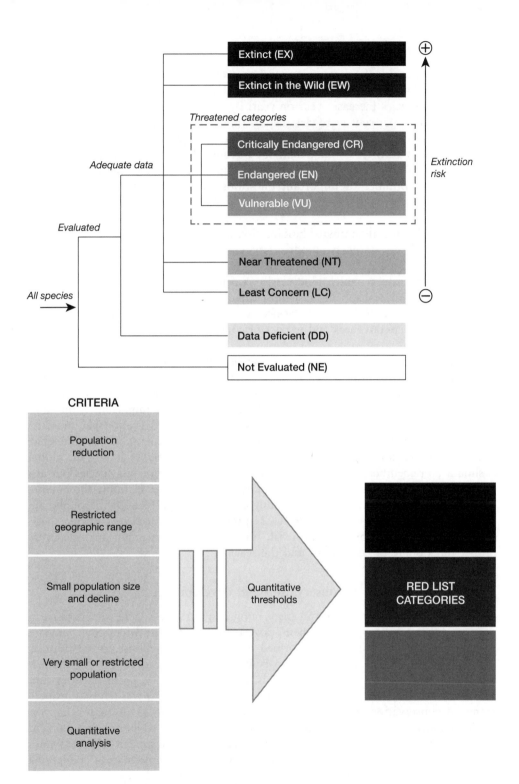

Figures 6.1a and 6.1b Wildlife in a changing world: structure of the Red List Categories and the five Red List Criteria

Source: Vie *et al.* (2009: 4).

species most in need of conservation, and to provide a global index of the state of change of biodiversity. In doing this, what the IUCN has shown is that the number of threatened species increases year on year. By 2008, 44,837 had been assessed, of which around 38 per cent were classified as threatened. Over 800 were classified as extinct. In addition, there was insufficient data to make a judgement on 5,561 species; so many of these could actually be threatened. Nonetheless, despite the fact that IUCN data represents just the proverbial tip of the iceberg, the Red List does help answer a number of important questions, which the organization usefully identifies as:

- What is the overall status of biodiversity, and how is it changing over time?
- How does the status of biodiversity vary between regions, countries and subnational areas?
- What is the rate at which biodiversity is being lost?
- Where is biodiversity being lost most rapidly?
- What are the main drivers of the decline and loss of biodiversity?
- What is the effectiveness and impact of conservation activities?

The information the IUCN produces on the distribution and ecological requirements of species are used in numerous large-scale analyses, which frequently identify gaps in threatened species coverage by the existing network of conservation or protected areas such as Important Bird Areas, Key Biodiversity Areas, Important Plant Areas and Alliance for Zero Extinction sites. This helps with conservation planning, the identification of conservation priorities and in informing specific species requirements at particular sites and at a variety of spatial scales and levels, including the global. It should be remembered that biological diversity includes not just species but also encompasses ecosystems and genetics. Species that remain are certainly the building blocks of biodiversity and they are readily comprehensible to both the public and policy makers. The information the IUCN produces is essential to ensuring that a good decision-making process can exist, for species play an important role in the proper functioning of ecosystems and the services they provide.

The political ecology of conservation and development

The IUCN's World Conservation Strategy, published in 1980, was the first mainstream document that combined development, poverty alleviation and wider environmental management. It was powerfully informed by the views of wildlife conservationists within both the WWF and IUCN who believe that conservation and development are complementary if not integrated goals. Poor communities, particularly in rural areas, do not always clearly benefit from being developed and it was felt that properly managed conservation would be better able to meet their needs than what was predominantly a Western model of modernization based on economic development, industrialization, free trade and urbanization. However, two models of conservation emerged. The one following the example of protected wilderness areas or National Parks in the US became known as 'fortress conservation' and was quite top-down, while the other was essentially bottom-up and community led (Adams, 2001).

In the late nineteenth and early twentieth centuries iconic figures such as John Muir and Aldo Leopold argued fervently to protect what they perceived as the pristine

Box 6.1 Highlights of the 2008 IUCN Red List

Some of the highlights of the 2008 update of The IUCN Red List include the following:

- A complete reassessment of the world's mammals showed that nearly one quarter (22 per cent) of the world's mammal species are globally threatened or Extinct and 836 (15 per cent) are Data Deficient.
- The addition of 366 new amphibian species, many listed as threatened, and the confirmed extinction of two species, which reaffirms the extinction crisis faced by amphibians; nearly one-third (31 per cent) are threatened or Extinct and 25 per cent are Data Deficient.
- A complete reassessment of the world's birds indicates that more than one in eight (13.6 per cent) are considered threatened or extinct; birds are one of the best known groups with less than 1 per cent being listed as Data Deficient.
- For the first time, 845 species of warm water reef-building corals have been included on the Red List with more than one-quarter (27 per cent) listed as threatened and 17 per cent as Data Deficient.
- All 161 species of groupers are now assessed; over 12 per cent of these highly sought after luxury live food fish species are threatened with extinction as a result of unsustainable fishing; a further 30 per cent are Data Deficient.
- All 1,280 species of freshwater crabs have been assessed, 16 per cent of which are listed as threatened with extinction, but a further 49 per cent are Data Deficient.
- 359 freshwater fishes endemic to Europe, with 24 per cent listed as threatened and only 4 per cent listed as Data Deficient.

Some species are much more susceptible to climate change impacts than others due to inherent biological traits related to their life history, ecology, behaviour, physiology and genetics.

- High risks of extinction occur when species experience both high susceptibility to climate change and large climatic changes.
- IUCN has conducted assessments of susceptibility to climate change for the world's birds, amphibians and warm water reef-building coral species. Based on a range of taxon-specific traits, we found that 35 per cent, 52 per cent and 71 per cent of these groups respectively have traits that render them particularly susceptible to climate change impacts.
- 70–80 per cent of birds, amphibians and corals that are already threatened are also 'climate-change-susceptible'. Given exposure to large climatic changes, these species which also have least resilience to further threat, already face the greatest risk of extinction. Of species that are not considered threatened, 28–71 per cent are 'climate change susceptible'. We identify the taxonomic groups and geographic regions harbouring the greatest concentrations of the above species and recommend that they are given high conservation priority.
- Assessments of 'climate-change susceptibility' complement IUCN Red List assessments of extinction risk and serve as a 'warning flag' highlighting the need for intensive monitoring and potentially conservation action for affected species.

Source: adapted from www.iucn.org/news_homepage/?13243/Worlds-oldest-and-largest-species-in-decline–IUCN-Red-List.

beauty of large areas of wilderness in the United States. John Muir struggled all his life to protect and preserve wildernesses from destructive development. His activism, and particularly his writing, were extremely influential in persuading many people, including President Theodore Roosevelt, that environmental conservation was a necessary element of any truly civilized nation. His work inspired the formation of many conservation agencies, including America's famous Sierra Club established in 1892, of which he became its first president. Muir, apart from being an active and effective campaigner, had a deeply romantic attachment to the natural world and many of his writings are infused with a spiritual sense of Earth's wonders. In Chapter 16 of *The Yosemite*, published in 1912, Muir explored the wonders of the Hetch Hetchy Valley:

> The making of gardens and parks goes on with civilization all over the world, and they increase both in size and number as their value is recognized. Everybody needs beauty as well as bread, places to play in and pray in, where Nature may heal and cheer and give strength to body and soul alike. This natural beauty-hunger is made manifest in the little window-sill gardens of the poor, though perhaps only a geranium slip in a broken cup, as well as in the carefully tended rose and lily gardens of the rich, the thousands of spacious city parks and botanical gardens, and in our magnificent National parks – the Yellowstone, Yosemite, Sequoia, etc. – Nature's sublime wonderlands, the admiration and joy of the world. Nevertheless, like anything else worth while, from the very beginning, however well guarded, they have always been subject to attack by despoiling gain seekers and mischief-makers of every degree from Satan to Senators, eagerly trying to make everything immediately and selfishly commercial, with schemes disguised in smug-smiling philanthropy, industriously, shampiously crying, 'Conservation, conservation, panutilization,' that man and beast may be fed and the dear Nation made great. Thus long ago a few enterprising merchants utilized the Jerusalem temple as a place of business instead of a place of prayer, changing money, buying and selling cattle and sheep and doves; and earlier still, the first forest reservation, including only one tree, was likewise despoiled. Ever since the establishment of the Yosemite National Park [in 1864], strife has been going on around its borders and I suppose this will go on as part of the universal battle between right and wrong, however much its boundaries may be shorn, or its wild beauty destroyed.

Ken Burns's remarkable 2008 documentary series for PBS, *The National Parks: America's Best Idea*, tells the story of their creation, struggles and controversies in a proud, clear but critical manner. The nature protection afforded by the national parks involved displacing the relatively few human inhabitants of these areas and protecting them for posterity from economic development, although this did not necessarily exclude tourism. In many cases human displacement meant depriving indigenous peoples of their cultural, natural and ancestral heritage (Spence, 2000). All indigenous peoples were ordered out of Yellowstone in 1877 and the Sierra Club operated a 'Whites Only' policy until 1920. It was therefore not only Native American Indians who were to be excluded from these places of natural wilderness, awe, wonder and the sublime. Those predominantly wealthy tourists who visited the wilderness went there not as producers but as consumers, as privileged spectators and sometimes as prospectors. Thus, the idea of wilderness as nature was as ripe for exploitation as it was supposedly devoid of human existence, and this notion has dominated public consciousness for years even though it is totally unhistorical and totally false. For environmental historian William Cronon (1996) this conception of wilderness, and by extension conservation, places humanity outside nature, representing an escape from human beings' real responsibility to respect it and use it reflectively and wisely now and in the future. It also leads to a clear disrespect for the rights, cultures and knowledge of many of the peoples who actually do, and have done this, for millennia. Cronon writes: 'If we set too higher a stock on wilderness, too many other corners of the earth become less than natural and too many other people become less than human, thereby giving us permission not to care much about their suffering or their fate' (1996: 84–5).

This social construction of wilderness, and by extension nature (Escobar, 1996), has been in large part responsible for both distracting attention from environmental predicaments and supporting these predicaments (Crist, 2004). When this idea of a nature and conservation model was adopted by colonial and then independent governments in Africa and other 'developing countries', local people were systematic-ally displaced too, because the dominant belief among Western conservation scientists and the big conservation organizations that dominated the late and post-colonial period was that human beings harmed the environment (Brockington, 2002; Dowie, 2009). Hunting game or wildlife in these protected areas or national parks by local indigenous people was labelled 'poaching', although licensed big game hunting by colonial whites continued in many cases and still exists today. In 2012 the news that King Juan Carlos of Spain was on safari in Botswana shooting elephants hit the news with photographs of the monarch posing proudly by his kill in the pages of many newspapers. In contrast, local Kalahari bushmen are forbidden to kill game on the same reserve.

Western conservationists have felt that the indigenous human presence was actually a disturbance to the natural equilibrium, not really appreciating that these areas, including such 'unspoiled' places as the Serengeti, were actually created by a continuous interaction of empathetic human beings with the landscape over centuries. Indeed, the whole field of human ecology and environmental history is a rich exploration of how human communities and the natural environment shape each other (Crosby, 1986; Merchant, 1989; Cronon, 1996; Diamond, 1998). In excluding humans, essentially the rural poor, in the creation, establishment and management of national parks in Tanzania, Kenya and elsewhere was tantamount to a denial of African history. Adams writes:

> Wildlife and people were to be kept apart, the animals confined to reserves and shot as 'problem animals' when they transgressed invisible administrative boundaries and raided crops, and people kept at bay by the policing of protected area boundaries and the control of incursions through paramilitary anti-poaching patrols. The plight of people evicted from protected areas is directly comparable to that of reservoir evacuees and the economic impact of such evictions can be considerable. . . .
>
> Fortress conservation therefore involved the suppression of resource use by local people.
>
> (2001: 272)

As Adams writes, 'fortress conservation' invariably reflects the values and priorities of the national and international agencies, governments, experts and businesses involved. Thus, African hunting damaged wildlife populations, and conservation strategies that excluded and pathologized local people were soon recognized by critics, as well as by local people, as contradictory, undesirable and ineffective. The BINGOs – that is, the big international conservation organizations such as Conservation International, the Nature Conservancy and the WWF – have been criticized for their exclusionary policies and for their extremely close relationships to their major funders – the World Bank, big corporations, USAID, the multilateral banks and private foundations. Such measures and their possible alternatives were also perceived quite rightly at scales ranging from the global to the local, and as extremely political too. Thus, with fortress conservation came development aid but conservation, whatever form or forms it takes, engages the political, the economic, the environmental and the social. Thus, Mac Chapin writes:

> Indigenous peoples, on whose land the three conservation groups have launched a plethora of programs, have for their part become increasingly hostile. One of their primary disagreements is over the establishment of protected natural areas, which, according to the human inhabitants of those areas, often infringe on their rights.
>
> Sometimes the indigenous people are evicted, and the conservationists frequently seem to be behind the evictions. On other occasions, traditional uses of the land have been declared 'illegal,' resulting in prosecution of the inhabitants by government authorities. Coupled to all of this has been the partnering of conservationist organizations with multinational corporations – particularly in the businesses of gas and oil, pharmaceuticals, and mining – that are directly involved in pillaging and destroying forest areas owned by indigenous peoples.
>
> (2004: 18)

An alternative approach to conservation and economic development is associated with community engagement and participation initiatives developed in response. These initiatives by contrast needed to be locally conceived, flexible and participatory, and based on sound information about the local ecology and local economy. However, participation can take many forms and, far from being a panacea to all the ills of imposed top-down solutions, can also be fraught with and plagued by political interests, power plays and vested economic and other sectional interests (Cooke and Kothari, 2001). In the 1960s, Sherry Arnstein (1969) developed the 'ladder of participation', showing that participation can in practice range from manipulation by powerful groups at one end of the ladder to, more rarely, full citizen power at the other. However, this participation/conservation from below, together with a very effective and sometimes fierce resistance from indigenous peoples, such as the Kayapo in Kenya, to forced expropriation and exclusion has led to a greater respect for traditional ecological knowledge (TEK), respect for local conditions, skills, cultures and values and respect for the rights of indigenous peoples that were acknowledged at Rio in 1992 but little acted upon until quite recently. As well as involving local people in conservation policy and practice, the community-led approach also saw the national parks being integrated into economic development planning processes, resulting in education and healthcare schemes, and local people contributing to management decisions and activities. Community rangers replaced anti-poaching patrols in some locations and, following the Fourth World Congress on National Parks held in Venezuela in 1992, partnership became a key feature in the future policy developments. As journalist Mark Dowie (2009: 266) has written: 'If we really want people to live in harmony with nature, history is showing us that the dumbest thing we can do is kick them out of it' (2009: 266).

Thus, Kent Redford (2011: 235), Director of the Wildlife Conservation Society Institute, recognizes that human beings are 'legitimate elements in nature', but as Helen Kopnina (2012a) qualifies, the traditional practices of indigenous peoples may no longer be as innocent as they are presumed to be given the inevitable influence of global capitalism. McNeely (1996) argues that, apart from national parks, other protected areas are also important to conservation and socio-economic development. The IUCN recognizes eight different types of protected areas, ranging from scientific reserves to resource reserves and multiple-use management areas, including what have become known as 'biosphere reserves', which allow for the sustained production and consumption of natural resources such as fish, water, timber, wildlife and outdoor recreation. The idea is that sustainability and development, conservation and production are compatible and complementary rather than contradictory and opposed, although in practice this is hard quite hard to achieve practically and conceptually. Erich Hoyt sums up the essence of the biosphere reserve according to three aspects or roles:

1   A conservation role including the conservation of genetic material, ecosystems and species.
2   A logistic role providing interconnected facilities for research and monitoring within and internationally co-ordinated scientific programme.
3   A development role fostering a connection with human populations near the protected area through the rational and sustainable use of ecosystem resources.

(2005: 25–6)

Nature conservation and accommodating the interests of disadvantaged groups are often quite distinct: biologists are concerned with wildlife preservation and maintaining biodiversity while local people are concerned with earning a living and protecting their crops from whoever may decide to feast on them, including elephants and gorillas or other endangered species. One way of squaring this particular circle has been to apply a market mentality to wildlife resources. The motivation behind ecotourism, for example, whether it is expensive big game safaris on the African savannah or whale watching in Alaska, is to make the wildlife 'pay their way'. This non-consumptive use of wildlife does not always pay the environmental dividends expected, as local people are not always major beneficiaries of such business ventures, and also because the tourism industry is subject to fashion, taste and the caprice of the affluent (France, 1997; Lavigne, 2006; Honey, 2008). On the other hand, wildlife may need to pay its way through 'consumptive-use', which may involve the harvesting or hunting of animals for their economically valuable tusks, meat or fur, or being the targets for vacationing European monarchs and other rich people. The most controversial aspect of this economically based conservation policy has been around the legal harvesting of elephants as opposed to the illegal poaching of them, and similarly of endangered rhinos. Controlled hunting through the sale of licences to tourists or through the distribution of licences to indigenous peoples in respect of their ancient traditions invariably causes heated discussion and considerable moral controversy. CITES (Convention on International Trade in Endangered Species) has, at various times, imposed bans on the international trade in ivory, and many countries, including the USA, have imposed a ban on the importation of hides of polar bears legally hunted by the Inuit or by commercial hunters in northern Canada.

The Canadian, Russian and US governments allow indigenous peoples to hunt a restricted number of polar bears for food and for economic gain, but only Canada permits the bears to be hunted for sport. Since the 1973 Agreement on the Conservation of Polar Bears and later conservation agreements by the range states (Canada, Greenland, Norway, Russia and the US), polar bears have not been commercially killed and harvested. Russia and Norway have not hunted polar bears since the mid 1950s. The Canadian government will pay native hunters up to $11,000 for hides. Inuit peoples sometimes supplement their income by acting as guides to trophy hunters from the US and elsewhere who may pay in excess of US$35,000 for the privilege of killing a polar bear. American hunters cannot take the hides back to the US with them but a photograph of the hunter with his kill is often sufficient. Hunters from elsewhere, such as Mexico, may import the hides if they have applied for and received the appropriate permits. The philosopher Michael Sandel (2013) raises an important ethical issue here regarding the morality of Inuit hunters selling their ancient and privileged hunting rights (or dispensation) to trophy hunters, even though the additional economic benefits are clear. Is applying market criteria so overtly to an indigenous right degrading that right through its commercialization? Referring to the killing of walrus rather than polar bears, Sandel writes: 'It's one thing to honor the Inuit way of life and to respect its long standing reliance on subsistence walrus hunting. It's quite another to convert that privilege into a cash concession in killing on the side' (2013: 84).

In 2013, a US proposal, supported by Russia, went before the CITES conference in Bangkok, Thailand, arguing that polar bears should be listed in Appendix One and that a total trade ban on polar bear products should be imposed. The Inuit Tapiriit Kanatami opposed the proposal, stating that scientific surveys suggesting the species was in decline was wrong. The proposal was defeated, with 38 countries voting in favour, 42 against and 46 abstaining. The WWF supported the Canadian Inuit whereas IFAW (International Fund for Animal Welfare) and the New York-based NRDC (National Resources Defense Council) suggested that the science was clear and that up to two-thirds of the 20,000–25, 000 polar bears currently inhabiting the Arctic worldwide would be extinct by 2050. The IUCN suggested a more accurate figure was probably closer to one third.

The oceans and global fisheries

In 2013 the International Programme of the State of the Ocean (IPSO), in association with the IUCN, issued a comprehensive report outlining a series of perils, prognoses and proposals for the marine environment (IPSO, 2013). The scientific evidence cited demonstrated a trio of problems stemming from climate change – acidification, warming and deoxygenation. Like so many other ecological indicators, the rate of ocean acidification is unprecedented in the Earth's history, which is exposing marine

Box 6.2 Polar bear hunting in the Canadian Arctic

Pongphon Sarnsamak, writing in Thailand's *The Nation*, states:

'Inuit people rely on polar bear for food and money,' Audla said [Terry Audla is the President of the Inuit Tapiriit Kanatami (ITK)]. 'We do eat polar bear meat. It is like pork and lamb.' Inuit people do not hunt polar bear for commercial trade but they do benefit from it. For them, hunting is not a hobby or a luxury but it is a source of sustenance for the millennia.

To date, polar bears are listed and protected by the CITES's Appendix II, which allowed legal hunting and international trade but with certain limitations.

Moreover, the polar bear population is managed by the Nunavut's wildlife management system.

Under this system, there is a polar bear population quota, or total allowable harvest that limits the number of bears that can be harvested each year. The total number of bears hunted in populations managed by Nunavut was approximately 460 from July 1, 2011 to June 30, 2012. In Canada, the average annual harvest is about 500.

In 2011–2012, 41 bears were killed for hunting sport and about 419 were killed for subsistence hunting and self defense. 'We have a quota to hunt about 700 polar bears a year but actually we annually hunt about 600 and 50 per cent of them go to trade,' a 42-year-old hunter said.

They also export polar bear parts like fur to China, Germany, France and Russia. Previously, they exported to the US as well but have now stopped.

To hunt polar bears, Inuit people will make a decision together about the number of polar bears that they would be able to hunt per year to ensure that they do not hunt too many.

Source: Pongphon Sarnsamak (2013).

ecosystems to what is likely to be intolerable evolutionary pressure. A number of marine creatures which build their shells and skeletons from calcium carbonate may soon no longer be able to do so. Coral reefs will be endangered and marine biodiversity generally will be threatened. The upper levels of the ocean are also warming. In the previous one hundred years this warming has been estimated at 0.6 degrees centigrade, which may not seem much but does have serious implications that include the disappearance of Arctic summer ice, local extinctions, temperature drive range shifts and species invasions and a likely 60 per cent loss of present biodiversity. The redistribution of commercial fish species through range shifts is likely to result in a significant decrease in catch potential – anything between 30 per cent and 70 per cent depending on location and species. There is already evidence of coral bleaching in the Caribbean and in the Great Barrier Reef off Australia. Oxygen depletion is the third problem and this has increased considerably since the introduction of industrial fertilizers in the 1940s. Since the 1960s the number of 'dead zones' in the oceans double every decade and eutrophication has consequently expanded sometimes at an alarming rate. Although some marine creatures will be able to adapt to these new conditions many will not and mass migrations will alter food web dynamics and increase pressure on these green marine pastures that survive.

Scientists and conservations have argued for a number of years that the global fishing industry is doing irreparable harm to the marine environment. Indeed, there have been a number of well-documented collapse of fish stocks and ongoing controversies over hunting, particularly of whales, tuna and dolphins, which have gained increased notoriety through films such as *The End of the Line* and *The Cove* (Clover, 2005; Blewitt, 2010b). Despite some optimism at the beginning of the twenty-first century that fisheries depletions were being successfully dealt with, the IPSO report suggests that such optimism is not well founded because serious depletions remain the norm, the quality of fisheries management is poor, the catch per unit continues to decline and marine pollution remains an unresolved problem. The key features of an ecosystem fisheries management has not been introduced to any appreciable degree, and illegal and unregulated fishing probably accounts for 35 per cent of the global catch (Lam and Pitcher, 2012). In any case, a quota system restricting future catches may be swamped by environmental factors. This means that the livelihood of many coastal communities are threatened or have already collapsed, and long-term prospects for food security based on harvesting the oceans is increasingly a cause for concern. However, there are solutions as the marine scientists Tony Pitcher and William Cheung clearly state:

> A fundamental solution to many of these problems is to ensure effective implementation of community and ecosystem-based management, favouring small-scale fisheries. There is sufficient scientific knowledge for developing these measures, many of them are already embedded in national, regional and international legislations and guidelines such as the FAO Code of Conduct. Examples of the broad-scale solutions ... include introducing true co-management with resource adjacent communities, eliminating harmful subsidies that encourage high fishing effort, careful spatial marine planning and protection of vulnerable ecosystems eliminating fishing gear that give rise to significant damage to marine habitats or have high bycatch, combating illegal and unreported fishing and dealing with the food web complexities of implementing ecosystem-based management. The challenge is in effective and ethical implementation of these measures, which could be fostered in several ways: provide economic incentives, foster the realization of moral obligations and improve monitoring, control and surveillance. These require effort from all levels from individual communities to international bodies.
>
> (2013: 506–16)

Capitalism and conservation

For Igoe *et al.* (2010), conservation and capitalism are shaping both the protection of nature and the sustainable development industry according to neoliberal market logics and the ideology of economic growth and capital accumulation. For a growing number of environmentalists and ecologists, wildlife conservation has become a crude exercise in materialism, economic valuation and development (Oates, 1999; Terborgh, 2004). The application of neoliberal market ideologies and policy prescriptions are in effect re-regulating nature, creating new forms of territorialization that basically excludes local people. Neoliberalism has also created new networks linking states governments, conservation NGOs and private businesses that share the same or very similar values. Becky Mansfield (2007) writes of a new political economy of the oceans that may undermine conservation imperatives, including local involvement in protected areas such as the biosphere reserves whether they are on land or in the ocean. At the core of this is the notion of the commons and that of property rights, collective or individual privatization, and the imposition of quotas in the new enclosures. What is frequently at issue is open access and the nurturing of, for example, rapidly declining fish stocks for future sustainable use. However, quotas are often set very generously and often ignored. Although the more radical policy of declaring no fish zones in certain places has seen significant benefits, they are few and far between and very difficult to establish even, perhaps especially so, in such pristine environments as the Antarctic Ocean.

Luxury ecotourism resorts define themselves as private-sector, profit-driven companies and are frequently the unstated locations for respected natural history and wildlife films (Christophers, 2006; Duffy, 2010). Brockington *et al.* (2008) argue that the conservation and tourist industries invariably work together to produce the best possible spectacle for their customers and viewers. Together with their associated merchandising, both are primarily consumptive experiences involving resource extraction, alienation and commodity fetishization. However, as Duffy and Moore (2010) write in their study of elephant back tourism in Thailand and Botswana, the tourist industry has provided alternative employment for elephants and their mahouts, and in Thailand, thanks to the god Ganesha, elephants are seen as more than just a basic commercial enterprise. They have intrinsic worth and neoliberal approaches to nature have inadvertently served to reinvent some traditional practices. In 2008, the owner of a tourist enterprise, Elephant Life Experience, organized an elephant fashion show featuring clothes with patterns taken from elephant paintings to celebrate National Elephant Day. The show was designed to draw attention to elephant conservation: the Art by Elephants Foundation and the artificial insemination programme organized jointly by the privately owned Maesa Camp and the Elephant Hospital at the Thai Elephant Conservation Centre. The event reached television newsrooms and YouTube.

No one strategy or approach is going to be effective on its own and many conservationists argue for multifaceted strategies and continuous and meaningful dialogue among all parties concerned in order to understand the challenges – illegal hunting, habitat loss, rapid human population increase, development, etc. – and to derive realistic but effective actions to arrest a generally worsening situation. Thus, in relation to promoting positive attitudes to wildlife conservation among local peoples inhabiting the Serengeti, Jafari Kideghesho argues that the following range of practical measures would produce positive outcomes:

- Balancing the costs of wildlife conservation with benefits by ensuring that the benefits are sufficient to offset the conservation-induced costs and contribute notably to poverty reduction.
- Enhancing conservation education to provide people with basic knowledge and clear understanding of the long-term consequences of their actions on species and habitats and the legal and policy aspects pertaining to wildlife conservation.

- Enhancing regular contacts with communities in order to avoid conflicts between conservation authorities and local communities that may result due to poor communication of development and conservation policies.

(2010: 238)

Kideghesho also notes that increased personal contact can be a really important factor in developing understanding and trust between wildlife staff and local people. Activities involving media-based, community-orientated storytelling, image production and filmmaking can also have significant beneficial effects, too (Blewitt, 2010b).

Conservation and development: REDD+ and the Yasuni National Park

Conservation policies and practices are often designed to meet multiple goals – poverty alleviation, economic diversity, climate change mitigation, biodiversity and species protection. This multiple benefits perspectives, sometimes referred to as win–win scenarios, sometimes lead to cycles of optimism and disappointment when the best laid plans seem to falter or fail. Paul Hirsch *et al.* (2010) argue that a realistic acknowledgement of possible losses and gains is essential and need not lead to policy paralysis. Such a recognition, combined with popular faith in win–win solutions, led to the development of the United Nations Collaborative Programme on Reducing Emissions from Deforestation and Forest Degradation in Developing Countries (UN-REDD Programme), the paramount problem being that tropical deforestation is a major contributor to the increase in global greenhouse gas emissions and losses in biodiversity, but forests and what lies underneath them may be of immense economic value too. This invites a policy framework that invites trade-offs, adaptive management procedures, continuous learning and the need for a multivariate approach to valuing the benefits of nature and ecosystems. Such a policy framework can, despite the win–win potentialities, lead to a contested terrain, including worldviews, philosophical values, indigenous rights, scientific assessments, political power and economic interests. Complexity is a fundamental characteristic of what might at first glance seem a quite simple or obvious solution to a difficult problem.

> The [UN-REDD Programme] was created in September 2008 to assist developing countries to build capacity to reduce emissions and to participate in a future REDD+ mechanism. For the purpose of this strategy, REDD+ refers to reducing emissions from deforestation and forest degradation in developing countries; and the role of conservation, sustainable management of forests and enhancement of forest carbon stocks in developing countries.
>
> The goal of significantly reducing emissions from deforestation and forest degradation can best be achieved through a strong global partnership to create a REDD+ mechanism under the United Nations Framework Convention on Climate Change (UNFCCC). Such a partnership must be based on a commitment, on one hand, by developing countries to embark on low-carbon, climate resilient development, and on the other hand, by developed countries to provide predictable and significant funding as an incentive for reduced forest-based carbon emissions.

(UN-REDD, 2011: 1)

Box 6.3 Social media vs. conservation education: the cute slow loris video

There's no doubt the slow loris looks like a cute little creature. It is an animal that could easily have been dreamed up in the studios of the Disney Corporation of the 1950s and I'm afraid that, for many YouTube viewers, the loris is seen through such a lens. How can one resist such a fluffy little thing, with its arms outstretched, enjoying a nice tickle? It seems to be the perfect toy, perfect pet, perfect plaything. One loris in particular, and her penchant for play, has now sparked a debate on the role new media plays in the illegal trade of rare animals. Millions of people have watched a YouTube video of Sonya, the loris, enjoying a tickle, but a new study of the comments the audience subsequently made has concluded that behind the emotional and sentimental reaction to these cuddly cuties there lurks – well, not much really.

Many viewers who demonstrated their own peculiar joy at Sonya's antics appear to know little about conservation issues and even less about the cuties they profess to adore. And now Anna Nekaris (Nekaris *et al.*, 2013) and the team behind the research say that viewers are indirectly responsible for the demise of the loris by fuelling the trade in this rare creature. They found that YouTube users were quick to post comments about how much they'd like to have a loris of their own but not so quick to pick up on the fact that these animals have been taken from the wild illegally, and often suffer terrible cruelty before ending up as the stars of their favourite videos. The research also found that celebrity endorsements generate hits for the videos but do little to raise awareness about conservation. The researchers argue that sites such as YouTube should take a greater responsibility for the videos they host that depict illegally traded animals.

But is the fault of social media? On YouTube and other sites, you can also see videos about endangered species, the illegal animal trade, animal cruelty and informative reports on the slow loris from ABC News, NatGeo Wild and the BBC. Unfortunately, these uploads have attracted far fewer hits than the now infamous tickling Sonya video which started the whole thing off. Nevertheless, these more informative videos still attract viewers in their tens or even hundreds of thousands. What's more, you can also find many comments posted on the cutie videos which do reveal a strong awareness of the issues and express both anger and frustration at the stupidity of some people and the cruelty of the those involved in the illegal animal trade. Like it or not, YouTube is an important part of the public sphere. It's a space for public debate as well as for action of a nature that isn't blind to the life and integrity of other living sentient creatures.

If left to market forces, illicit or otherwise, the problems of species extinction, habitat destruction, animal cruelty and illegal animal trading will not go away. In fact, they will probably get worse. People, especially in Japan and Russia, want a cuddly cute loris for a pet. The media, old and new, is a space for communication and learning. We need to listen and learn rather than to close off yet more avenues where the possibility of learning about the world beyond our own particular bubbles can conceivably occur. The real issue, then, is transforming human attitudes to nature and this is a task that needs to be undertaken everywhere. It may mean recognizing that when a home video of a cute loris being tickled appears, there should be a warning sign – 'stupid, irresponsible behaviour on show'. It might also mean that if a warning sign must appear alongside a report showing the fetid animal markets of Asia, it should not read, 'some viewers may find scenes distressing' but 'watch it and, if you don't like it, do something about it'.

Source: extracted from *The Conversation* blog – Blewitt (2013b).

In 2010 Ecuador signed an agreement with the United Nations not to exploit 850 million barrels out of an estimated 5,000 million barrels of oil reserves within the one million hectare Yasuni National Park – one of the most biologically rich and diverse areas on the planet designated by UNESCO in 1989 to be a Biosphere Reserve. The Government of Ecuador estimated that it would require US$3.6 billion from the global community to leave the rainforest unspoiled for a decade. This figure represented half the anticipated economic value of the oil in the Yasuni rainforest. Germany pledged US$836 million, and Sweden, France, Spain and Switzerland announced they would also pledge some money. This agreement seemed to represent a great victory for indigenous peoples, particularly the Waorani people, the Taromenanes and the Tagaeris who live in voluntary isolation, and was supported by 90 per cent of Ecuador's population (Lebrun, 2013). Conservationists who had been campaigning to maintain the ecological integrity of the area believed that by preventing oil exploration they would also be saving the atmosphere from an additional 410 million cubic tons of carbon dioxide.

In August 2013 President Rafael Correa appeared on television declaring 'the world has let us down', stating that Ecuador had only received $13.3 million, although the UN itself said that $376 million had been collected. However, drillings had already taken place in the park as far back as the 1990s, and 40 per cent of the area had been divided into blocks and allocated to foreign oil companies by the time Correa made his announcement. The country's poor record in conservation and preservation and the fact that 50 per cent of its exports are dependent on its oil reserves had dampened the enthusiasm of many prospective donors. Having said that, the governments of China and the US had never been particularly enthusiastic.

In an open letter to President Correa, the SOS Yasuni campaign group wrote of concessions to foreign companies, road construction and the laying of pipelines which had been granted before the August announcement:

> All of these actions, which are being undertaken in advance of any publicly-announced decision about oil exploitation in Yasuni, seem designed to ensure as quick a start to oil exploitation as possible. They are of a piece with other recent actions with high environmental costs: the growth of large-scale mining in various regions of the country, the opening of the oil frontier in the south central Amazon region, the advance of genetically-modified crops and large-scale dams, the criminalization of social protest, and the control and disciplining of critical NGOs. They can only be seen as part of a process of decision-making by stealth. . . .
>
> The Yasuni-ITT initiative was not an isolated, one-off technical proposal, but rather a pathway, a transition. It embodied a proposal for genuine civilizational change. To question oil, capitalism's fundamental commodity; to call attention to the impacts extraction has had on nature and the environment (and ultimately people); to question the commodification of nature through carbon markets; to try to map out a future without petroleum: all of these aspects of the Yasuni initiative were born out of the experience and deep reflection of the society. To traditional development, which makes one-sided reference to industrialized nations, was counterposed sumak kawsay [ancient teaching of indigenous peoples] and harmonious relations with nature. Yasuni was to be one of the first addresses of utopia – the very antithesis of what it appears to have been for your government, namely just another profit-making alternative.
>
> (SOS Yasuni, 2013)

Mines, big dams and development

Economic development and economic security frequently seem to conflict with the needs of environmental conservation and protection. Although the struggles in Amazon are well documented, such struggles with and conflicts between policy goals are apparent in many other places, too. In 2009, Greenland gained self-government from Denmark and, as global warming has proceeded, many areas of Greenland previously inaccessible to economic development have offered themselves as open for business. In 2013, the Greenland Government awarded a thirty-year licence to London Mining to build, in association with its Chinese partners, an open-cast mine which could produce up to 15 million tonnes of high quality iron-ore concentrate per annum. The same year also saw the Greenland Government ending a twenty-five year ban on digging for radioactive materials such as uranium, as well as other rare earth metals, which is expected to attract investors from Australia and China. Such policy actions are designed to promote Greenland's economic independence, but environmentalists fear that such development will be at the expense of Greenland's environment. Similarly, in southern Africa the NGO Survival International is campaigning with the Kalahari bushmen to protect their ancestral lands located in the Central Kalahari Game Reserve from an economic development which would seriously compromise the limited rights they still retain. The Botswana Government has given permission for the British company Gem Diamonds to exploit the $3.3 billion diamond deposit it bought from De Beers in 2007. Economic development is again the dominant policy priority.

In other parts of the world big dams have long been associated with economic development, environmental destruction and political protest (McCully, 1996). The O'Shaughnessy Dam, completed in 1923 in the north-western part of the Yosemite National Park, led to the flooding of the Hetch Hetchy Valley, a place of sublime natural beauty and an area inhabited by indigenous peoples for 6,000 years. The newly formed Sierra Club of America and one of the pioneers of the environment and wilderness movement had earlier protested vigorously to stop it, but in 1934 started delivering water to the San Francisco Bay Area over 160 miles away. The Hoover Dam, equally controversial but situated in the Black Canyon of the Colorado River straddling the states of Arizona and Nevada, was constructed between 1931 and 1936. At the time it was the biggest concrete structure ever built, producing hydroelectric power and providing water for the irrigation of farmland and for the city of Las Vegas. In the twentieth century big dams became synonymous with development, severe environmental impact and biodiversity loss, displacement of human populations from established settlements, vast expense and often exceedingly long periods of disruptive development. Big dams have been central to development policy and practice in India, China and Brazil. For Jawaharlal Nehru, India's first prime minister after independence, dams were 'the temples of modern India', necessities and icons of modernization and development. Between 1947 and 1982 dams accounted for 15 per cent of planned state expenditure. Between 1947 and 1992, an estimated 20 million people were displaced by dams and reservoirs (McNeill, 2000). They have also attracted a great deal of criticism and for many have been at best unwise and at worst disastrous all round. The World Bank often linked development aid to the construction of huge dams, but even the Bank in the 1990s, following a range of negative assessments regarding their efficacy, particularly in relation to the Sardar Saravor and other Narmada Dam projects in central India, became less certain of their value. However, the Narmada Dams did go ahead with financing from the state of Gujurat rather than the World Bank. Tribal peoples were displaced and lands were flooded. Protests led by former trade union activist Medha Patkar attracted the attention of people worldwide, including the Booker Prize winning writer Arundhati Roy, whose powerful essays and physical protests led to her being arrested and briefly incarcerated (Dwivedi, 2006). The drive for economic development was understandably extremely powerful, but doubts and suspicions lingered, despite in 2000 the majority ruling by Justice Kirpal and Justice Anand of the Supreme Court of India, which carefully assessed a revised plan and pronounced in favour of the project:

> Displacement of people living on the proposed sites and the areas to be submerged is an important issue. Most of the hydrology projects are located in remote and inaccessible areas, where local population is, like in the present case, either illiterate or having marginal means of employment and the per capita income of the families is low. It is a fact that people are displaced by projects from their ancestral homes. Displacement of these people would undoubtedly disconnect them from their past, culture, custom and traditions, but then it becomes necessary to harvest a river for larger good. A nature river is not only meant for the people close by but it should be for the benefit of those who can make use of it, being away from it or near by.
>
> Loss of forest because of any activity is undoubtedly harmful. Without going into the question as to whether the loss of forest due to river valley project because of submergence is negligible, compared to deforestation due to other reasons like cutting of trees for fuel, it is true that large dams cause submergence leading to loss of forest areas. But it cannot be ignored and it is important to note that these large dams also cause conversion of waste land into agricultural land and making the area greener. Large dams can also become instruments in improving the environment, as has been the case in the Western Rajasthan, which transformed into a green area because of Indira Gandhi Canal, which draws water from Bhakhra Nangal Dam. This project not only allows the farmers to grow crops in deserts but also checks the spread of Thar desert in adjoining areas of Punjab and Haryana.
>
> (Supreme Court of India Judgement, 2000)

Around 3,200 dams have now been built and the displacement of largely tribal peoples has not been accompanied by satisfactory rehabilitation or compensation. At the root of the continuing protests is a burning sense of social and environmental injustice, although supporters claimed the waters from the largest dam on the Namarda River, the Sardar Saravor, would provide sufficient water to irrigate nearly 18,000sq km of land, three-quarters of which is prone to drought, and would provide flood protection to a further 30,000 hectares and nearly 500,000 people. Drinking-water facilities would be provided for 8,215 and 135 urban centres in Gujarat, and the power generation potential would be in the region of 1,450 megawatts.

However, the biggest dam project the world has ever witnessed has been in China. The Three Gorges Dam was completed in 2006 and is the biggest producer of renewable energy, hydropower, in the world. By 2020 China intends to triple its

---

Box 6.4 Dams and the greater common good

In Kevadia Colony, the most barbaric joke of all is the wildlife museum. The Shoolpaneshwar Sanctuary Interpretation Centre gives you a quick, comprehensive picture of the Government's commitment to Conservation.

The Sardar Sarovar reservoir, when the dam is at its full height, is going to submerge about 13,000 hectares of prime forest land. (In anticipation of submergence, the forest began to be felled many greedy years ago.) Environmentalists and conservationists were quite rightly alarmed at the extent of loss of biodiversity and wildlife habitat that the submergence would cause. To mitigate this loss, the Government decided to expand the Shoolpaneshwar Wildlife Sanctuary that straddles the dam on the south side of the river.

There is a hare-brained scheme that envisages drowning animals from the submerged forests swimming their way to 'wild-life corridors' that will be created for them, and setting up home in the New! Improved! Shoolpaneshwar Sanctuary. Presumably wildlife and biodiversity can be protected and maintained only if human activity is restricted and traditional rights to use forest resources curtailed. Forty thousand tribal people from 101 villages within the boundaries of the Shoolpaneshwar Sanctuary depend on the forest for a livelihood. They will be 'persuaded' to leave. They are not included in the definition of Project Affected.

Where will they go? I imagine you know by now.

Whatever their troubles in the real world, in the Shoolpaneshwar Sanctuary Interpretation Centre (where an old stuffed leopard and a mouldy sloth bear have to make do with a shared corner) the tribal people have a whole room to themselves. On the walls there are clumsy wooden carvings – Government-approved tribal art, with signs that say 'Tribal Art'. In the centre, there is a life-sized thatched hut with the door open. The pot's on the fire, the dog is asleep on the floor and all's well with the world. Outside, to welcome you, are Mr. and Mrs. Tribal. A lumpy, papier mache couple, smiling.

Smiling. They're not even permitted the grace of rage. That's what I can't get over.

Oh, but have I got it wrong? What if they're smiling voluntarily, bursting with National Pride? Brimming with the joy of having sacrificed their lives to bring drinking water to thirsty millions in Gujarat?

Source: Arundhati Roy (1999).

---

hydropower capacity and in so doing has created a massive economic interest in dam construction and renewables among the companies responsible for their construction. There have also been massive social and environmental costs, some of which can be seen in Yung Chan's 2007 film *Up the Yangtze*. Forests were clear cut and the timber harvested before land was submerged. Over a million people have been displaced by the Three Gorges project and the flooding of lands to create a 410-mile long reservoir has submerged 13 cities, 140 towns and 1,350 villages. Financial compensation to displaced people has often been inadequate, not covering the cost of new accommodation because much of it has been appropriated by corrupt local officials. Many fragile ecosystems have been destroyed and many species such as the baiji dolphin, Chinese sturgeon and the Siberian crane are now endangered. Geologists have warned the Chinese governments that damming up so much water increases the risks of seismic activity, prolonged damage to the River Yangtze's ecology and of serious landslides. In addition, droughts have reduced river flows, affecting supplies of water to homes and industry, river navigation, worsened the effects of pollution and had a negative effect on the capacity to generate hydroelectric power. Many of the Yangtze's tributaries and lakes have been contaminated with copper, zinc, lead and ammonium, and water-treatment plants have failed to contain this growing problem. Large algae blooms often grace the reservoir. In addition, the estimated financial cost of the project has increased from US$9 billion in 1992 to possibly US$88 billion (International Rivers, 2012) leading many people within China to question whether the assumed advantages of such dams projects outweigh the clearly apparent problems. Chinese electric motors, which consume half the country's energy supply, are 10–30 per cent less efficient than those conforming to international standards, and investment in solar and wind technologies and less energy-intensive economic enterprises is set to increase markedly in the near future. This, though, does not mean the end of big dams either in China, India or elsewhere. Government delegations from Congo, Nepal, Pakistan, South Africa and other countries have visited the Three Gorges project, and in July 2013 the World Bank adopted a new energy strategy paper proposing to increase its financial support of gas and large hydroelectric power projects. The electricity produced by the expensive Inga 1 and 2 dams on the Congo River has largely been consumed by the Congo's energy-intensive consumers, although 90 per cent of the republic's population still lacks access to electricity. Big dams in Africa have led to an increase in the continent's debt burden and a hastening of species extinction rather than fostering economic development. Peter Bosshard writes:

> The World Bank has identified the $12 billion Inga 3 Dam on the Congo River – the most expensive hydropower project ever proposed in Africa – and two other multi-billion dollar schemes on the Zambezi River as key examples of its new approach. All three projects would primarily generate electricity for mining companies and middle-class consumers in Southern Africa. . . .
>
> The Lom Pangar Dam in Cameroon is an example of the World Bank's recent mid-sized hydropower projects. The project will flood 30,000 hectares of tropical hardwood forest, including part of the Deng Deng national park – a refuge for gorillas, chimpanzees and other threatened species. The project's electricity is primarily intended for the multinational aluminum industry that is by far Cameroon's biggest energy user.
>
> (2013)

Urban biodiversity

One obvious component of economic development is urbanization and the encroachments of the built environment, particularly urban areas, on the natural world. By 2050, 70 per cent of the global population will be living in cities and in the twenty-first century many new cities will be built. In Brazil, nineteen cities have doubled their populations since 2000 and of these ten are in the Amazon (Emmott, 2013).

These cities will take up more land and will impact on the overall biodiversity of the Amazon region. Manaus, a city of nearly two million people, is located in the north of the country. Surrounded by the Amazon jungle, its inhabitants would prefer not to share their lives with all the local flora and fauna, especially boa constrictors, mosquitos and piranhas. Some trees are not suitable for urban environments either, requiring too much trimming, pruning and clearing up. Biodiversity in urban environments is nonetheless extremely important but often depends on individual context. This is not to gainsay the fact that many cities throughout the world are located in areas rich in biodiversity, including estuaries, coastlines and floodplains, and urbanization is rapidly transforming many critical habitats and biodiverse hotspots. However, cities need not be barren ecological wastelands with unremitting and relentless displays of concrete and tarmac, sprawling suburbs and congested road networks. Many cities contain sites that are of major importance to conservation because they protect threatened species, natural vegetation and habitat. Many cities have encouraged biodiversity and the phenomenon of urban wildlife is familiar in many urban environments in all parts of the world as industrial agriculture has reduced the ecological richness of the countryside. A number of creatures have migrated to the city and some, like the urban fox, seem to thrive. City dwellers often encourage wildlife by deliberately creating natural habitats within urban areas – in residential gardens, parks, allotments, verges, and so on. The relative recent innovation of vertical forests and rooftop gardens, combined with supplementary feeding and watering, have created ecological niches for some threatened or novel species.

In 2008, 400 scientists, planners and sustainability practitioners from around 50 countries attended the Urbio conference in Erfurt, Germany. The delegates, recognizing the importance of the 2002 Convention on Biological Diversity in towns and cities, issued an important Declaration that further promotes the values of urban biodiversity. Part of it reads:

- Towns and cities are both important experimental areas and fields of experience in the interrelationship between humans and nature.
- The case for urban biodiversity in relation to the aims of the CBD is compelling.
- Urban ecosystems have their own distinctive characteristics.
- Urban areas are centres of evolution and adaptation.
- Urban areas are complex hotspots and melting pots for regional biodiversity.
- Urban biodiversity can contribute significantly to the quality of life in an increasingly urban global society.
- Urban biodiversity is the only biodiversity that many people directly experience.
- Experiencing urban biodiversity will be the key to halt the loss of global biodiversity, because people are more likely to take action for biodiversity if they have direct contact with nature.

Urban geographer Jennifer Wolch (1996, 2007) has argued for renaturalization and re-enchantment of cities by reintegrating people with animals. Such a reintegration, she suggests, would stimulate a rethinking of many everyday urban practices, habits of consumption and production, and urban design options. It would also restore the city's ecological integrity and go some way to realizing the goals of social and ecological justice. In the 2009 documentary film *The Nature of Cities* and the book *Biophilic Cities*, Tim Beatley (2011) writes of the ways cities can encourage biodiversity

– connected greenspaces, urban ecological networks, biophilic design, eco-planning, pavements and vertical gardens, and so on. There are increasing examples of cities becoming nature friendly, making them increasingly important as biological reservoirs and spaces for ecological restoration and repair. Singapore has been immensely successful in this regard. It is a city state of five million people and because of its geographical location has a rich natural heritage despite the fact that a great deal of it was destroyed during the period when it was a British colony. Close to the busiest shopping centre in Singapore lies the central catchment nature reserve and the Bukit Timah Nature Reserve. A network of parks, park canopies and connectors, including elevated walkways, allow easy access to varied plant and wildlife habitats throughout the island, which also has a large number of roof gardens, community-based agriculture and horticulture, and iconic examples of innovative bioclimatic architecture. In 2012, in a speech marking the opening of the Gardens by the Bay, Prime Minister Lee Hsien Loong inverted the idea of a garden city to that of a 'city in a garden'. He said:

> The next phase from being a 'Garden City' is to make ourselves into a 'City in a Garden'. It is a play on words, but it means something different, because it means connecting our communities and our places and spaces through parks, gardens, streetscapes and skyrise greenery. And we already have got 3,000 hectares of parks and we are going to add another 900 hectares, another 2 Toa Payoh New Towns, of park land. And we are going to bring the green spaces and the biodiversity closer to our homes and workplaces. Butterflies, birds, all sorts of interesting flora, fauna; once in a while a wild boar, but not here.

The City Biodiversity Index, also known as the Singapore Index on Cities' Biodiversity, is a self-assessment that encourages city authorities to conserve and enhance urban biodiversity. It is also a very useful public communication tool (Chan and Rahman, 2010). For Beatley, biophilic urban population represents huge armies of citizen scientists who can track and monitor ecosystem changes with their smart phone apps as well as actively create habitats for birds, bats and other creatures. A growing number of urban community-based action now revolves around the protection of specific wild animals and animal populations within and beyond urban environments. Many of these go beyond the issue of animal rights and welfare, looking towards rebalancing human attitudes and relationships with other creatures.

The Secretariat of the Convention on Biological Diversity (2012) have ten clear messages for urban planners and citizens alike. These are:

- Urbanization is both a challenge and an opportunity to manage ecosystem services globally.
- Rich biodiversity can exist in cities.
- Biodiversity and ecosystem services are critical natural capital.
- Maintaining functioning urban ecosystems can significantly enhance human health and well-being.
- Urban ecosystem services and biodiversity can help contribute to climate-change mitigation and adaptation.

Box 6.5 Urban biodiversity

Urban biodiversity is the variety and richness of living organisms (including genetic variation) and habitat diversity found in and on the edge of human settlements. This biodiversity ranges from the rural fringe to the urban core. At the landscape and habitat level it includes:

- Remnants of natural landscapes (e.g. leftovers of primeval forests).
- Traditional agricultural landscapes (e.g. meadows, areas of arable land).
- Urban-industrial landscapes (e.g. city centers, residential areas, industrial parks, railway areas, formal parks and gardens, brownfields).
- Diversity of plants and animals in the urban landscape shows some interesting patterns:

  - The number of plant species in urban areas often correlates with human population size – more so than it does with the size of the city area.
  - The age of the city affects species richness; large, older cities have more plant species than large, younger cities.
  - Diversity may correlate with economic wealth. For example, in Phoenix, USA, plant and bird diversity in urban neighborhoods and parks shows a significant positive correlation with median family income.
  - Twenty per cent of the world's bird species and 5 per cent of the vascular plant species occur in cities.
  - On average, 70 per cent of the plant species and 94 per cent of the bird species found in urban areas are native to the surrounding region.

Source: Secretariat of the Convention on Biological Diversity (2012: 8).

- Increasing the biodiversity of urban food systems can enhance food and nutrition security.
- Ecosystem services must be integrated in urban policy and planning.
- Successful management of biodiversity and ecosystem services must be based on multi-scale, multi-sectoral, and multi-stakeholder involvement.
- Cities offer unique opportunities for learning and education about a resilient and sustainable future.
- Cities have a large potential to generate innovations and governance tools and therefore can and must take the lead in sustainable development.

It is also important to keep in mind that just as cities influence biodiversity, biodiversity influences cities and the quality of urban life. Water supply, recreation, health, atmosphere and temperature are all influenced by the type and amount of biodiversity existing within an urban environment. Consequently, the governance of cities is an important, and in some cases, determining factor in sustaining or creating biodiversity in urban environments.

Summary

The question of whether or not human beings are a part of nature rather than separate from it characterizes much of the theories and practices around conservation, economic development and what attempts to be sustainable development. It is clear that economic growth and development has had a severe impact on the natural world, but it is not always exactly clear what the natural world is or whether it has a purpose other than just to be whatever it is. For many observers, nature's purpose is to service human wants and needs, to be, as Eileen Crist (2004: 19), puts it 'settled, paved, mined, burnt, dammed, drained, overfished, poached, and roundly used'. This has led to various attempts to manage development sustainably, and to protect and conserve habitats and species other than those that are immediately our own. In protecting or conserving nature, human beings have frequently been displaced and dominant economic arrangements have gone largely unchallenged. However, as always, there are differences of opinion, conflicts of values and interests, and the exercise of power that ignores the need for dialogue. As Helen Kopnina writes:

> The importance of the dialogue between individuals holding different gradations of biocentric and anthropocentric values is certainly not limited to conservationists and anthropologists, but also includes all communities and individuals that traditionally – and presently – strongly care about the environment – including humans.
>
> (2012a: 140–1)

Thinking questions

1   In what ways has humanity tended to perceive the earth as so much planetary real estate?
2   What arguments can be raised in favour of 'fortress conservation'?
3   Does development inevitably mean 'big dams'?
4   What is the value of the IUCN RedList?
5   Are capitalism and conservation compatible?
6   What can be done to enhance urban biodiversity?

Companion website

To learn more about conservation and development, please check out the companion website for case studies on wildlife protection and ecological restoration.

7 Beyond the imperatives of economic growth and 'business as usual'

Aims

This chapter explores some key issues relating to modernity, capitalism and economic growth, focusing on a range of arguments and opinions that see business and development as both part of the problem and part of the solution. It will critically consider the role of business in promoting sustainable development, addressing issues relating to the financial valuation of nature, 'eco' or sustainability entrepreneurship, corporate responsibility, localization and fair trade, growth and degrowth. A case study of digital media companies, carbon footprints and corporate sustainability ends the chapter.

The millennium ecosystem assessment

> The demand for ecosystem services is now so great that trade-offs among services have become the rule. A country can increase food supply by converting a forest to agriculture, for example, but in so doing it decreases the supply of services that may be of equal or greater importance, such as clean water, timber, ecotourism destinations, or flood regulation and drought control. There are many indications that human demands on ecosystems will grow still greater in the coming decades. Current estimates of three billion more people and a quadrupling of the world economy by 2050 imply a formidable increase in demand for and consumption of biological and physical resources, as well as escalating impacts on ecosystems and the services they provide.
>
> (Millennium Ecosystem Assessment, 2005: 27)

Environmental scientists Gretchen Daily, Katherine Ellison and Walter Reid *et al.* (Daily, 1997; Daily and Ellison, 2003; Reid *et al.*, 2006) have written extensively about the dependence of the human economy on the planet's natural systems. In 1999/2000, Reid initiated the Millennium Ecosystem Assessment (MEA) – a massive global study produced by 700 natural and social scientists and reviewed by 1,300 others from 95 countries. It examined the state of the Earth's natural resources, its various ecosystems, and the 'services' these ecosystems provide in facilitating human development and well-being. These services fall into four categories:

- *provisioning services* such as food, water, timber and fibre;
- *regulating services* that affect climate, floods, disease, wastes and water quality;

- *cultural services* that provide recreational, aesthetic and spiritual benefits; and
- *supporting services* such as soil formation, photosynthesis and nutrient cycling.

Despite the growth in human ingenuity, knowledge and technology, the survival and flourishing of human society is utterly and ultimately dependent on these ecosystem services. The MEA (2005) understands human well-being as consisting of:

- *basic material for a good life*, such as secure and adequate livelihoods, enough food at all times, shelter, clothing, and access to goods;
- *health*, including feeling well and having a healthy physical environment, such as clean air and access to clean water;
- *good social relations*, including social cohesion, mutual respect, and the ability to help others and provide for children;
- *security*, including secure access to natural and other resources, personal safety, and security from natural and human-made disasters; and
- *freedom of choice and action*, including the opportunity to achieve what an individual values doing and being.

However, the MEA (2005: 1) recognizes that freedom of choice and action is also influenced by education, political culture and economic well-being. It is therefore a scientific study informed by social, cultural and human contexts. There are four main findings:

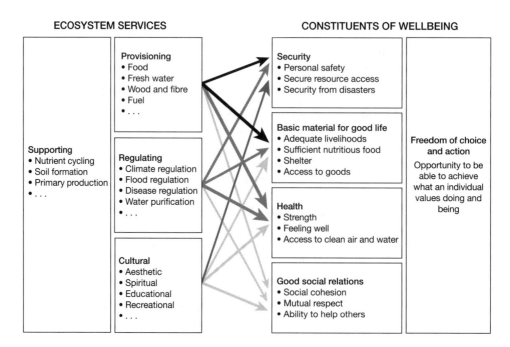

Figure 7.1 The constituents of well-being
Source: Millennium Ecosystem Assessment (MEA) (2005).

1 Over the past fifty years, humans have changed ecosystems more rapidly and extensively than in any comparable period of time in human history, largely to meet rapidly growing demands for food, fresh water, timber, fibre and fuel. This has resulted in a substantial and largely irreversible loss in the diversity of life on Earth.

2 The changes that have been made to ecosystems have contributed to substantial net gains in human well-being and economic development, but these gains have been achieved at growing costs in the form of the degradation of many ecosystem services, increased risks of non-linear changes and the exacerbation of poverty for some groups of people. These problems, unless addressed, will substantially diminish the benefits that future generations will obtain from ecosystems.

3 The degradation of ecosystem services could grow significantly worse during the first half of this century and is a barrier to achieving the Millennium Development Goals, particularly regarding the eradication of hunger, reduction in child mortality and disease control.

4 The challenge of reversing the degradation of ecosystems while meeting increasing demands for their services can be partially met under some scenarios that the MEA has considered, but these involve significant changes in policies, institutions and practices that are not currently underway. Many options exist to conserve or enhance specific ecosystem services in ways that reduce negative tradeoffs or that provide positive synergies with other ecosystem services.

Around 60 per cent of the ecosystem services that support life on Earth – fresh water, fish stocks, pests, natural hazards, regional regulation of climate – are either degraded or are being exploited unsustainably. According to the MEA, the next fifty years will probably witness the collapse of more fish stocks, the creation of dead zones around some coastal areas, the emergence of new diseases, deterioration in freshwater quality, river flooding, desertification, deforestation, increase in invasive species, general species extinction, loss of biodiversity, habitat degradation and increased pollution, especially nutrient loading due to the increases in artificial fertilizer use in agricultural production – all leading to a decline in human well-being and loss of capital assets that even the wealthiest populations will notice. In 2008, the human demand on the natural world's capacity to meet this demand exceeded the biosphere's regeneration rate by 50 per cent (WWF-Int, 2012). As a result, the WWF argue that it is necessary to significantly expand the network of global protected spaces of representative land, freshwater and marine areas necessary for food, biodiversity, energy security, climate change resilience and adaptation to 20 per cent. Of course, if we don't do this, it will be the poor who are likely to suffer the most.

The MEA report also states that the total economic value associated with the sustainable management of an ecosystem is usually higher than the value assumed to come from the conversion of the ecosystem through farming, clear-cutting or other intensive uses. Thus, the MEA (2005: 15) outlines four possible scenarios exploring potential futures for both ecosystems and human well-being. These scenarios are based on differing assumptions about the forces driving change and their interactions:

1 *Global orchestration*: A globally connected society that focuses on economic growth, global trade and economic liberalization, and takes a reactive approach

to ecosystem problems, but also takes strong steps to reduce poverty and inequality and to invest in public goods such as infrastructure and education.

2   *Order from strength*: A regionalized and fragmented world, concerned with security and protection, emphasizing primarily regional markets, paying little attention to public goods, and taking a reactive approach to ecosystem problems. Economic growth rates are low while population growth is high.

3   *Adapting mosaic*: Regional watershed-scale ecosystems are the focus of political and economic activity. Local institutions are strengthened and local ecosystem management strategies are common; societies develop a strongly proactive approach to the management of ecosystems. Economic growth rates are relatively low initially but increase with time. Population growth is relatively high.

4   *TechnoGarden*: A globally connected world relying strongly on environmentally sound technology, using highly managed, often engineered, ecosystems to deliver ecosystem services, and taking a proactive approach to the management of ecosystems to avoid problems. Economic growth is relatively high and accelerates, while population in 2050 is in the mid-range of the scenarios.

All four scenarios have a clear managerial and technicist orientation and none offer a truly radical alternative. Having said this, a number of important observations have been made:

- Past actions to slow or reverse the degradation of ecosystems have yielded significant benefits, but these improvements have generally not kept pace with growing pressures and demands.
- Substitutes can be developed for some but not all ecosystem services – for example, plastics and vinyl for wood – but the cost of substitutes is generally high, and substitutes may also have other negative environmental consequences – for example, pollution or increased economic costs.
- Ecosystem degradation can rarely be reversed without actions that address the negative effects or enhance the positive effects of one or more of five indirect drivers of change: population change (including growth and migration), change in economic activity (including economic growth, disparities in wealth and trade patterns), socio-political factors (including factors ranging from the presence of conflict to public participation in decision-making), cultural factors and technological change leading to greater eco-efficiency.
- Any effective set of responses ensuring that the sustainable management of ecosystems must also overcome a number of barriers related to:

  – inappropriate institutional and governance arrangements, such as corruption and weak systems of regulation and accountability;
  – market failures and the misalignment of economic incentives, which can in part be rectified by eliminating subsidies that promote excessive use of ecosystem services, the levying of green taxes, payment for conservation services and so on;
  – social and behavioural factors that can be rectified in part through consumer education, empowerment and awareness campaigns to reduce aggregate consumption;

- underinvestment in the development and diffusion of technologies that could increase the efficiency of use of ecosystem services and could drive ecosystem change, such as renewable energy; and
- insufficient knowledge (as well as the poor use of existing knowledge) concerning ecosystem services and management, policy, and technological, behavioural and institutional responses that could enhance benefits from these services while conserving resources.

The MEA (2005: 33–4) states clearly that the value of ecosystem services has implications for policy formation and decision-making:

Current decision-making processes often ignore or underestimate the value of ecosystem services. Decision-making concerning ecosystems and their services can be particularly challenging because different discipline schools of thought assess the value of ecosystems differently. One paradigm of value, known as the utilitarian (anthropocentric) concept, is based on the principle of humans' preference satisfaction (welfare). In this case, ecosystems and the services they provide have value to human societies because people derive utility from their use, either directly or indirectly (use values). Within this utilitarian concept of value, people also give value to ecosystem services that they are not currently using (non-use values). Non-use values, usually known as existence value, involve the case where humans ascribe value to knowing that a resource exists, even if they never use that resource directly. These often involve the deeply held historical, national, ethical, religious and spiritual values people ascribe to ecosystems – the values that the MEA recognizes as cultural services of ecosystems. A different, non-utilitarian value paradigm holds that something can have intrinsic value – that is, it can be of value in and for itself, irrespective of its utility for someone else. From the perspective of many ethical, religious and cultural points of view, ecosystems may have intrinsic value, independent of their contribution to human wellbeing.

This report, together with *The Economics of Ecosystems and Biodiversity* (TEEB, 2010a) reports published a few years later, argue clearly that the best way for governments and societies to perceive the value of nature is to calculate what it is worth in dollars or euros. Essentially, this commodification of nature is about applying market criteria and economic instruments to those services 'nature currently provides for us'. If we account for them in a set of balance sheets measuring costs and benefits, financial value, depreciation, discounts, and so on we will consequently recognize that conservation is both economically valuable and economically essential. TEEB aims to accelerate the development of a new economy where the value of natural capital and ecosystems services is fully integrated into the mainstream of private and public accounting. One example cited (TEEB, 2010b: 8) is that on average 'Swiss bee colonies ensured a yearly agricultural production worth about US$213 million by providing pollination, about five times the value of the production of honey' while the '*total economic value* of insect pollination worldwide is estimated at €153 billion, representing 9.5 per cent of world agricultural output in 2005'. It is therefore important to invest in the Earth's 'ecological infrastructure' to ensure that we get value for money which we will invariably do. Thus (TEEB, 2010b: 28), 'while it is usually cheaper to avoid degradation than to pay for ecological restoration, there are, nonetheless, many cases in which the benefits from restoring degraded ecosystems far outweigh the costs'. Such action can also be cost-effective ways of mitigating the effects of climate change. Of course, economists have been searching for ways to accurately account for nature. In a seminal article in *Nature*, after many years of research, Robert Costanza and his colleagues (Costanza *et al.*, 1997) did put a price tag on the biosphere as a whole, valuing it at a cool $33 trillion annually. With inflation, it has probably increased markedly since the time of that estimate irrespective of the arguments, debates and refinements that have been published since. Indeed, Costanza argued that the $33 trillion ought to be viewed as a low estimate and that in future years, natural capital stocks and ecosystem services would become increasingly stressed and undoubtedly more scarce. A useful comparator is perhaps global gross national product (GNP). In 1997 the minimum estimate of the global GNP total was US$18 trillion per year. In 2012, according to the *CIA World Fact Book*, nominal gross world product (GWP) was estimated to be US$71.83 trillion.

However, it is the UK's Stern Review (Stern, 2005), which quantified the likely economic effects of climate change for business and society, that has significantly caused a sharp refocusing of governmental and media interest throughout the world on environmental and sustainability issues. The Stern Review noted that if the world does not act immediately, the costs of climate change could be in the region of 5 per cent of global GDP each year from now – and for ever. If wider impacts are accounted for, the figure could conceivably rise to 20 per cent. In contrast, the costs of action, of reducing greenhouse gas emissions, are likely to be in the region of 1 per cent of GDP. Therefore, what governments, businesses and society do in the next twenty years will affect life for the rest of the twenty-first century. The Review also argued that although climate change was a clear example of market failure, necessary remedial action need not negatively affect the aspirations of either rich or poor countries and could, in fact, promote a pro-growth strategy. For instance, each ton of CO_2 emitted causes damage worth at least US$85, but emissions could be cut for less than US$25 a ton. If the world shifts to a low-carbon development pathway, this could eventually benefit the economy by US$2.5 trillion a year, and by 2050 markets for low-carbon technologies are likely be worth in the region US$500 billion. Conclusion: a new economy of nature urgently needs to be developed (Daily and Ellison, 2003) recognizing the issues that may arise from the fact that money in itself does not have a moral value, although it is through money terms that morals, human desires and passions are frequently mediated (Harvey, 1996).

The Review argues that explicit action aimed at dealing with climate change will create significant opportunities for business. There will be new markets for low-carbon energy and goods and services, producing excellent profits and opportunities for employment in these new sectors. New energy technologies will allow economic growth to be decoupled from the production of greenhouse gases, but ignoring the climate crisis will undoubtedly damage prospects for sustained growth. Pro-environmental change is both necessary and possible, and Stern's prescriptions included greater international co-operation in four areas:

- emissions trading and carbon pricing;
- innovation in low-carbon technologies and effective cooperation;
- actions to reduce deforestation; and
- adaptation (for example, new crop varieties).

Barriers to energy efficiency need to be overcome, and individuals and organizations need to be informed, educated and persuaded to act in a more sustainable fashion. That the 'business as usual' assumption is no longer tenable is, at least publicly, increasingly acknowledged. Nonetheless, Jonathan Porritt, the British environmental campaigner and former Chair of the UK Sustainable Commission, warns that although politicians may heed some (economic) warnings about climate change, many other problems, such as the build-up of toxic chemicals in the environment or the continuing loss of land to new development, are frequently ignored. This is partly because it is assumed that nature is infinitely resilient or that something is bound to turn up to offset the disasters that have beset previously civilizations (Diamond, 2005). As Porritt writes:

> The idea that we now live in an age of evidence-based policymaking is preposterous. . . . Talk of a whole host of natural limits to economic growth as presented in the Millennium Ecosystem Assessment report, and that's a completely different story. You're suddenly a radical subversive beyond the pale of intelligent discourse.
>
> (2005: 307–8)

In this context the Stern Review is perceived by many as being either highly optimistic, erring on the side of caution and conservatism. In 2012 the American campaigner Bill McKibben wrote a highly influential article for *Rolling Stone* magazine which swiftly went viral. In it he explored the economic interests involved in climate change debates and our fossil fuel addiction in the clearest of terms. He noted that if we burn all the fossil fuels – oil, coal and gas – currently held in reserve by governments and big energy corporations, we would easily and relatively quickly exceed the modest carbon budgets that international agencies have tentatively suggested that we need to adhere to. What is more, he continued, given the economic value of these reserves, US$27trillion, and the economic valuation of the companies and presumed economic growth needs of the world's nation-states, it is highly unlikely that most of these fuels will remain unspent and the economic value therefore not realized. That would mean leaving 80 per cent, or US$20trillion, in the ground. Institutional investors – pensions, insurance companies, universities – often look to fossil fuel companies for a regular return, which implicates virtually everyone in reproducing the conditions that make pro-sustainability transformative change the 'big ask' that it is. Indeed, from this perspective, it is in the economic interests of governments and corporations to resist measures to limit economic growth and fossil fuel-based energy consumption just as it remains a cultural and social want for most citizens to drive, fly and buy those carbon-based goods and services that constitute what is considered a desirable material standard of living, a sense of status and social worth. Thus, McKibben writes (2012):

> In early June [2012], Secretary of State Hillary Clinton traveled on a Norwegian research trawler to see firsthand the growing damage from climate change. 'Many of the predictions about warming in the Arctic are being surpassed by the actual data,' she said, describing the sight as 'sobering.' But the discussions she traveled to Scandinavia to have with other foreign ministers were mostly about how to make sure Western nations get their share of the estimated

$9 trillion in oil (that's more than 90 billion barrels, or 37 gigatons of carbon) that will become accessible as the Arctic ice melts.

It is therefore quite possible, as Mike Berners-Lee and Duncan Clark make plain in the *Burning Question* (Berners-Lee and Clark, 2013) that runaway climate change, and all that it entails, is a distinct possibility. Those states that have been most obstructive in the quest to curtail emissions – the US, Russia, China, Australia, Venezuela, Iran, Saudi Arabia, India, Canada and Kazakhstan – have the largest reserves of untapped fossil fuel.

Ecology against capitalism

In the early stages of capitalist economic growth, 'nature' became completely objectified as solely existing for the purposes of human exploitation and the satisfaction of human wants. Later, the major imperatives of continuing economic growth, industrialization and technological development meant the use of ever greater amounts of energy. Oil production, upon which the global economy has grown to depend, is now either near, past or actually at its peak. The future is likely to see oil prices rise, despite desperate attempts to drill in the world's last remaining wildernesses in the Arctic and Antarctic (Heinberg, 2004; Zittel and Schindler, 2007). Historically, when local environmental resources are exhausted, then industry looks further afield, extending both its geographical reach and ecological footprint, and free market liberalism, and liberalization, has become the ideological rationale for increased production and consumption, even though wealth creation has been unequally distributed socially and geographically. For Carlos J. Castro (2004), the problem with the concept of sustainable development, and particularly in the form articulated by the United Nations and the World Bank, is that it is effectively synonymous with *capitalist development*, meaning continual economic growth, the private accumulation of profit and the optimization of utility. Understood as such, sustainable development is a contradiction in terms. For Castro, the idea that the capitalist system could transform itself to incorporate a strong sustainability thesis is highly unlikely:

> The idea that economic growth is achieved by free trade, that economic growth reduces poverty and that, once poverty is reduced, environmental degradation will be reduced as well does not work out in practice.
>
> (2004: 198)

For post-structuralist and ecological Marxist writers, economic growth and the profit motive are integrally linked in theory and practice. Their criticisms are often acute, but they sometimes fail to fully develop practical proposals for sustainable change. Capitalism, with its driving logic of continuous accumulation, has privileged certain technological and economic initiatives but closed off others (Foster, 1999, 2000, 2002). For instance, the car has been central to capitalist development, and although the eco-modernist promotion of greater fuel/eco-efficiency has led to modest eco-innovation in car manufacture, there has been little significant investment in public transit systems, particularly in the US and UK, which would have had far greater societal benefits. The car is also tied to growth in rubber, glass, steel and petroleum production, trucking, highway construction, and suburbanization.

Consequently, a clear dependence on the car industry as a sure way of securing good profitability has emerged. As Foster writes:

> The capitalist class is divided when it comes to reductions in carbon dioxide emissions to slow down the rate of global warming. A significant part of the ruling class in the US is willing to contemplate more efficient technology, not so much through a greatly expanded system of public transport, but rather through cars with greater gas mileage, or perhaps even a shift to cars using more benign forms of energy. Efficiency in the use of energy, as long as it does not change the basic structure of production, is generally acceptable to capital as something that would ultimately spur production and increase the scale of accumulation.
>
> (2002: 99)

For many Marxist analysts, hope lies neither in more stringent regulation nor new technology, but in nothing less than the full transformation of the capitalist mode of production.

Indian economist Partha Dasgupta (2001) argues that globalization has led many economists to ignore the significance of geography and the local as conditions for economic development and progress, but he also recognizes that environmental damage may have some human benefit. He does not completely dismiss the value of cost–benefit analysis. A road may destroy part of a local ecosystem, but there are benefits to communication, travel and economic development. For Dasgupta, it is important to clearly understand economic signals, such as migration, price, resource scarcity and product quality that derive from human interaction with the natural environment. However, he does not wholeheartedly dismiss the possibility and desirability of substituting one form of capital for another. People do seek alternatives to goods, services and resources when their traditional supply dries up. Necessity is the mother of invention, and with peak oil the world may invest seriously in alternative, renewable, fuel sources. For Dasgupta, then, economic development needs to be sustainable and growth needs to be measured in terms of wealth rather than crude economic activity (GNP) and understood as the value of manufactured assets like buildings and roads, human knowledge and skills, ecosystems, and civil and governmental institutions. GNP per capita may increase but overall wealth may not – for example, in India. Substitution of human for natural capital may lead to an increase in both GNP and overall wealth – for example, in China. However, there are limits to the services the planet's ecosystems provide – and limits to substitution. There is only so much CO_2 the ecosystem can accommodate before significant climatic change occurs. Thus, in examining the economic development of a large number of poor countries, Dasgupta (2007) concluded that in all cases this development was either unsustainable or barely sustainable, with Pakistan being the worst performer on the Indian subcontinent. For Dasgupta, sustainable development means:

> that an economy's wealth must not decline. But the equivalence doesn't mean that sustainable development is possible. Whether it is possible depends upon demographic behaviour, consumption patterns, and production and substitution possibilities among the myriad forms of capital assets.
>
> (2001: 142)

He also clearly argues that 'ecological truths can be introduced without fuss into economic reasoning' (Dasgupta, 2007: 11). The only problem is getting economists to embrace it.

Development is a cultural and economic process, leading many environmentalists and ecologists to look to indigenous cultures and values as a model for sustainability, but many of these are, in fact, hybrid cultures, having evolved in relationship to dominant Western economic and scientific paradigms (Agrawal, 1995; Escobar, 1995). The co-evolution of societies and cultures, and of society with nature, has caused a 'metabolic rift' in the relations between humans and nature. The universal transformation of societies and nature *is* a major feature of capitalism.

Do corporations rule the world?

A great deal of the anti-globalization market is also anti-corporate, and those who campaign for deglobalization, localization and eco-localism frequently argue that the corporation, far from being a potential vehicle for sustainable development, is irredeemably a barrier. David C. Korten, whose books *When Corporations Rule the World* (1995) and *The Post-Corporate World: Life after Capitalism* (1999) have been widely discussed by environmentalists, suggests that trans and multi-national corporations actually prevent the market – which would, other things being equal, enable more sustainable economies to emerge – from functioning in a healthy fashion. Most megacorporations are grossly inefficient. Firms should be human scale and competition should not eradicate the weak. There should be economic democracy based on stakeholder ownership, economic relations should be managed locally or nationally, and effective international agreements should regulate financial speculation as well as the activities of the corporations. A healthy market must rest on firm ethical foundations, and one major step towards realizing this is to end the legal fiction that corporations are 'persons', as they have more rights than actual persons but fewer legal, financial and moral obligations and fewer liabilities. For Korten (2000), the corporation is a legal perversion allowing for a massive accumulation of financial and economic power with the minimum of social accountability. Corporations employ millions of poorly paid workers in all parts of the world and are frequently in receipt of massive government subsidies. Only shareholders are legally entitled to benefit directly from the surpluses and profits the corporations produce, and in order to ensure the interests of shareholders are met, the needs of individual workers and whole communities are sometimes sacrificed. Capital needs to be mobile – 'footloose' – to secure the lowest possible production and labour costs. Korten also notes that corporations bankroll political campaigns in order to protect their interests and gain favour, so as to call in favours when required. Organizations like the World Trade Organization (WTO) were established specifically to serve global corporate interests, even if these run contrary to the policies and needs of democratically elected governments and their people. The WTO has given corporations considerable operational freedom, which, combined with their power and size, frequently makes it very difficult for smaller businesses to develop. This has been no accident: as Beder (2006) demonstrates in her surgically precise analysis of global corporate politics, *Suiting Themselves: How Corporations Drive the Global Agenda*, through their creation of think-tanks and business associations, the big corporations have intentionally shaped the global economic agenda to meet their own specific commercial ends at the cost of both the environment and the democratic process. The ecosystem services of the planet have been exploited for commercial corporate ends and have often been despoiled in the processes – sometimes irreparably so. For Korten, corporations have also done to people (human capital) what they have done to the environment (natural capital), and society as a whole has turned in one seamless series of commercialized and commoditized relationships. Big, for Korten, is far from being beautiful, and writers and activists like Colin Hines (2000) and Walden Bello (2002, 2004) argue that 'localization', small-scale production with local producers meeting local needs, and the 'deconstruction' of the present system of global economic governance, including the World Trade Organization, the International Monetary Fund and the World Bank, is the only true path of sustainable development.

On economic growth and sustainable development

Herman Daly (1996, 1999, 2002) has significantly influenced the debate on the relationship between economics and the environment. He believes that as *critical natural capital* is not readily substitutable by *human-made capital*, it should be preserved and conserved as a top priority. Daly argues that economic growth is not a cure-all for unemployment, inequality, environmental protection and excessive population growth. There is such a thing as *uneconomic growth* – that is to say, when the level of economic activity continues to use up precious natural resources and provides no tangible benefit to human well-being and welfare. The notion that uneconomic growth is making us poorer has informed the work of a number of think-tanks and pressure groups, such as the New Economics Foundation in the UK, particularly in the attempt to measure sustainable economic well-being and to replace the crude indices of economic growth such as gross national product. Daly also suggests that the global integration of the world economies will probably militate against opportunities for taking the radical political action necessary to combat contemporary socio-economic and environmental problems. Individual nation-states and a world 'community of communities' is the proper site for such action to develop. Only with this will his 'pre-analytic vision' of a fully functioning sustainable economy be realized and the planet's ecological limits respected:

> Ecological limits are rapidly converting 'economic growth' into 'uneconomic growth' – growth which increases costs by more than it increases benefits, thus making us poorer not richer. The macro-economy is not the whole – it is part of a larger whole, the ecosystem. As the macro-economy grows in its physical dimensions (population and per capita resource use), it does not grow into a void. It grows into and encroaches on the larger ecosystem, thereby incurring an opportunity cost of pre-empted natural capital and services. These opportunity costs of sacrificed natural services can be, and often are, worth more than the extra production benefits of growth. We cannot be absolutely sure, because we measure only the benefits, not the costs. And even if we measure the costs, we add rather than subtract them. But whatever the true benefits of economic growth, it is clear that they cannot apply to uneconomic growth.
>
> Even if growth were still economic, much of what we mean by poverty is a function of relative rather than absolute income, that is of social conditions of

distributive inequality. Growth cannot possibly increase everyone's relative income. We cannot all be above average – unlike the children of Lake Wobegon. There is a degree of inequality that is legitimate and in accord with a larger concept of fairness and incentives, but also there is a degree beyond which further inequality destroys community and social cohesion, as well as undermining incentive to work.

(Daly, 2002: 48)

Daly (2007) suggests that the growing acceptance of anthropogenic climate change has stimulated a sense of public urgency, but decision-makers still ask the wrong questions and consequently get the wrong answers. They ask 'What will be the economic damage inflicted by global warming?' 'How much will the costs of abatement be compared with expenditures?' And 'What will the discount rates be?' This leads to uncertainty, because the fine detail is not easily knowable. Instead, they should ask some fundamental questions based on first principles. For instance, can we systematically continue to increasingly emit CO_2 and other greenhouse gases into the atmosphere without causing unacceptable climate change? The answer is more certain. It is no. His next question is simple: What is causing us to do this? The answer is unequivocal: our commitment to exponential economic growth. These questions and answers imply fairly obvious policy options: heavily tax carbon extraction and compensate by lightly taxing income, which would produce climate stability and public revenue. Thus, although the uncertainties engendered by complex empirical measurements and predictions would not disappear, 'setting policy in accord with first principles allows us to act now without getting mired in endless delays' and hesitations (Daly, 2007: 19).

Paul Ekins (2000) also explores economic growth and its relationship to environmental sustainability. He identifies four types of growth:

* growth of the economy's biophysical throughput;
* growth of monetary or non-monetary production (GDP, GNP);
* growth of economic welfare measured by consumption and negative production feedbacks – for example, environmental destruction or erosion of community; and
* environmental growth measured by increases in natural capital through regeneration of ecosystem services.

Growth needs to be distinguished from development and welfare. The relationship between GNP growth and sustainable development is highly complex and not at all obvious, as perhaps exemplified in the debate over the negative climate impacts of flying and the insistence that aviation is a key to national and regional economic growth. The arguments are further complicated when environmental sustainability and economic development are linked to notions of lifestyle, and the standard and quality of life of present and future generations. Costs and benefits and decisions about 'trade-offs' shape the discussion. As Ekins (2000: 82) notes, 'sustainability guarantees certain life opportunities in the future at the cost of the modification or sacrifice of life opportunities in the present'. The difficulty is deciding on what trade-offs and how many. So, with this in mind, and by developing the work of Herman Daly, Ekins (2000: 95–6) formulates a set of sustainability principles upon which such decisions could be based:

- Destabilization of global environmental features such as climate patterns or the ozone layer must be prevented.
- Important ecosystems and ecological features must be absolutely protected to maintain biodiversity.
- The renewal of renewable resources must be fostered through the maintenance of soil fertility, hydrobiological cycles and necessary vegetative cover and the rigorous enforcement of sustainable harvesting.
- Depletion of non-renewable resources should seek to balance the maintenance of a minimum life-expectancy of the resource with the development of substitutes for it.
- Emissions into air, soil and water must not exceed their critical load – that is, the capability of receiving media to disperse, absorb, neutralize and recycle them, thereby preventing the build-up of toxins that could damage human health.
- Landscapes of special human or ecological importance should be preserved.
- Risks of life-damaging actions and technologies should not be undertaken.

Ecological economists argue that the economy is a subset of the environment. Attention therefore needs to be paid to that which adds value. For Douthwaite (1999b), as all growth involves the use of natural resources, it would be best if production levels remain stable and resource use be halved. He believes that the eco-efficiency Factor Four notion (Von Weizsacker *et al.*, 1997) is a myth because living better in a materialist society still means producing more. Thus the only sustainable society Douthwaite envisages is one where population, energy, material production and conception are maintained in constant equilibrium, with the total value of social, human, natural and fixed capital passed on to future generations not being less than that presently existing. A steady-state economy requires sustainable developments rather than sustainable development. From this analysis Douthwaite draws three main principles:

- The interests of present and future generations must be given equal weight.
- Other people's interests must be valued as highly as one's own.
- Not everything is tradable (can be sold off for money or increased production).

Some economists believe the general focus on economic growth and the satisfaction of individual wants is now slowly being displaced by an ethic rooted in the concept, principles and practices of sustainability, which offers a new approach to economic organization and a new model for business decision-making (Balakrishnan *et al.*, 2003). Rampant individualism has given way to a focus on society. The financial bottom line has been joined by social and environmental concerns to make up a *triple bottom line* (Henriques and Richardson, 2004). Opportunity cost no longer becomes exclusively identified with economic or financial matters, as factors other than utility need to be considered. The 'best use' of resources is being replaced by an adherence to 'minimal use', and, instead of seeing growth as the perpetual driver of economic development, other drivers are coming into view – for example, perfecting products, earning customer loyalty, providing human enrichment and maintaining natural ecosystems. As Balakrishnan *et al.* (2003: 312) write:

Opportunity-cost decision-making is never neutral. Something and/or someone is always hurt. Ascribing those same underlying assumptions to sustainability, ethical analysis forces an examination of all potential costs. That tree in the yard has value. Cutting it down to construct a chair offers many benefits, among them money in the pockets of the carpenter and comfort for the individual purchasing it. Yet, letting it stand offers other benefits to humanity and nature, though not readily measurable monetarily or definable economically.

For Economists like David Pearce, putting a price tag on the environment could help. For many years he has argued that without placing a monetary value on environmental gains and losses, we will continue to treat natural resources as if they were free. Quantifying how much people will pay to preserve or improve their environment will enable decision-makers to see how much people value it. The more they are willing to pay, the more they appreciate the resource or amenity, enabling economists, using a form of cost–benefit analysis, to calculate the net worth of various options. As David Pearce *et al.* (1989: 81) write, 'by trying to value environmental services we are forced into a rational decision-making frame of mind'. Writing from a Marxist perspective, geographer David Harvey (1996) is extremely wary of a number of positions promoted by ecological economists and others who continually emphasize eco-scarcity and what amounts to an arbitrary financial valuation of nature independent of market prices. Harvey notes that what exists in nature is and always has been in a constant state of transformation and to declare that a state of eco-scarcity exists is tantamount to suggesting that human societies lack the capacity, knowledge and capability to modify either our material practices, our social goals, our economic arrangements, our technologies or nature itself. He writes:

> To say that scarcity resides in nature and that natural limits exist is to ignore how scarcity is socially produced and how 'limits' are a social relation within nature (including human society) rather than some externally imposed necessity.
> (1996: 147)

On sustainable development and degrowth

The ambiguity of the concept of sustainable development has long been a subject of criticism and although the concept has many defenders and many advocates most of the global indicators have not been favourable. The Copenhagen Climate Conference in 2009 and the Rio+20 conference in 2012 have increased academic and policy interest in an idea that goes beyond sustainable development, natural capitalism and the steady state economy. In the early 1970s the economist and mathematician Nicholas Georgescu-Roegan produced a paper titled 'The Entropy Law and the Economic Problem' (Georgescu-Roegan, 1994) which explored the laws of entropy in the context of economics. For Georgescu-Roegan, the economic process is an immaterial flux referring to the enjoyment of life rather than a never-ending material flow of production, consumption and waste. Indeed, the economic process depends on using material and energy resources that, however much we recycle or freecycle, cannot ensure industrial abundance in the long term. Economic growth, even zero growth, cannot exist forever in a finite environment, although population control and new technology may enable the steady state economy to exist for quite some time albeit subject to fluctuations, challenges and stresses. Thus the truly desirable state is not a steady one but a declining one. These rather bleak but logical ideas were taken up by others in the 1980s, particularly Serge Latouche who, together others has questioned the veracity of 'Third World development', and in the process has fashioned the emergent theories of *decroissance* (sustainable degrowth) and post-development. For Latouche (1997) any economic or political system predicated on growth is problematic. The fetishization of technological innovation and creativity and a business ethics exalting an egotistical will to power, is close to totalitarianism because it inhibits any fundamental questioning. Thus, 'there is no alternative' as UK Prime Minister Margaret Thatcher often repeated. For Latouche, though, the idea that growth will lead to greater affluence for all is both a misnomer and an ideological mask for increasing incidence of social and economic inequality and widening income disparities. In most development models inequality is actually a necessary precondition for accumulation, for profit. In addition, ecologically it is an impossibility for there are not only limits to growth but limits to what the planet will provide for over time. Consequently, for Latouche, downscaling is a necessity but this downscaling, or in French *decroissance*, also means progress but *progressing backwards*, for which the nearest words in the English language seem to be *sustainable degrowth*, or perhaps the phrase 'prosperity without growth', which is the title of Tim Jackson's (2009) book of the same name and which outlines very similar ideas to Latouche.

Downscaling, however, only makes sense in a non-growth society. It could start with calling a halt to those activities whose environmental impact brings no satisfaction – for example, reducing the amount food travels from producer to consumer, relocalizing the economy and curbing advertising. The disposability of certain products could be questioned and reversed by their being reused or in the future not produced at all. Mindsets, work patterns, workloads and social expectations will need to change, too. An ethics of voluntary systems of co-operation will need to be developed that will challenge and ultimately transcend the psychological bases for growth, production, material wealth and their links to social status and conceptions of personal worth. There are resonances here with the ideas of the Ghandhian economist J.C. Kumarappa (Govindu and Malghan, 2005) as well as more obviously E.F. Schumacher (1974) who stressed the importance of the freedom and autonomy of the individual, economic decentralization and good meaningful work for all. Quality will transcend quantity, voluntary simplicity will transcend addictive consumerism, co-operation and conviviality will transcend competition, and sanity will overcome the lunacy of continual economistic growth. This does not mean the end of profit or the market, but it would mean the end of its overweening dominance. Degrowth would not just be a policy for the global North. It would also apply to the South. Latouche (2004) writes:

> if there is to be any chance to stop Southern societies from rushing up the blind alley of growth economics. Where there is still time, they should aim not for development but for disentanglement – removing the obstacles that prevent them from developing differently. This does not mean a return to an idealized version of an informal economy – nothing can be expected to change in the South if the North does not adopt some form of economic contraction. As long as hungry Ethiopia and Somalia still have to export feedstuffs destined for pet animals in the North, and the meat we eat is raised on soya from the razed Amazon rainforest, our excessive consumption smothers any chance of real self-sufficiency in the South.

All this would mean major institutional changes – delinking income from work, the reform of financial services, taxes at the origin of extraction, and the reduction of energy and material resources by societies in the North, and the refusal of the South particularly to be the supply ground for cheap commodities for the consumption of the already affluent. For some analysists (Kerschner, 2010; Martínez-Alier *et al.*, 2010) degrowth in the North combined with a decrease in world population might actually be a path towards a global steady state economy. We know how much energy we have used in the past to create what we have now and we also know what energy we can use in the future to ensure, as Odum and Odum (2001) put it, 'a prosperous way down'. In *Farewell to Growth*, Latouche (2009) outlines a political programme showing how degrowth will improve people's quality of life, restore a degraded environment, create free time, conviviality, better health, social equity, encourage community participation and enhance cultural wealth. The process of civilized contraction will revolve around the '8 Rs' of: Re-evaluate, Reconceptualize, Restructure, Redistribute, Relocalize, Reduce, Reuse, Recycle. For this degrowth to occur, knowledge and information will need to be shared, and decision-making become transparent and inclusive. For Joan Martínez-Alier (2009) these are feasible propositions and would find allies among progressive groups in the North and environmental justice movements in the South. He writes:

> There could be a confluence among conservationists concerned with the loss of biodiversity, the many people concerned with climate change who push for solar energy, the socialists and trade unionists who want more economic justice in the world, urban squatters who preach 'autonomy', agro-ecologists, neo-rurals and the large peasant movements (as represented by Via Campesina), the pessimists (or realists) on the risks and uncertainties of technical change (post-normal science), and the 'environmentalism of the poor' that demands the preservation of the environment for livelihood.
>
> (2009: 1117)

However, despite the repeated failures of development to be sustainable and the obvious problems confronting contemporaries' societies, not least of which is climate change, *decroissance* (degrowth) is not a concept that inspires the world's economic, political and business leaders. There is no 'incentive' in a degrowth policy. Thus, perhaps like sustainable development or at least an ecologically compatible capitalism – 'the Green Economy' – degrowth is conceivable in theory but unrealistic in practice. However, continual economic growth is not realistic either.

Capitalism for ecology

Paul Hawken (1994), Hawken *et al.* (1999), Lester Brown (2001, 2006), Jonathan Porritt (2005) and many others have argued that business in a modified capitalist environment is part of the solution. Brown offers a vision of an eco-efficient economy and ecological modernization. There is a need for more accurate accounting procedures that fully recognize environmental and financial costs. Hunter and Amory Lovins of the Rocky Mountain Institute in Colorado have vigorously promoted the need for an eco-efficient 'natural capitalism'. This approach to economic and business development protects the biosphere and improves competitiveness and profitability by making 'simple changes' to the way businesses are run. The idea is to make more productive use of resources and to increase energy efficiency four- to tenfold ('factor four' or 'factor ten') through sustainably enhanced technological design. This may also enable the trappings of the Western lifestyle to be preserved. For instance, the institute has developed the 'Hypercar' – an ultra-light vehicle with a hybrid-electric drive and low-drag design, which on its first release was heralded as up to five times more efficient than conventional cars. To reach its full potential and virtually eliminate pollution, the Hypercar needs to be powered by hydrogen fuel-cells. Richard Welford (1998) argues that sustainability must fully inform the design of every product, building and service, as 80–90 per cent of a product's life-cycle costs, and waste resulting from the production process, are committed at the final design stage. Edwin Datschefski (2001) reinforces this, noting that just one in around 10,000 products is usually designed with the environment in mind. In *Biomimicry*, Janine Benyus (2002) demonstrates the benefits to designers and businesses from learning from natural systems, processes, shapes and forms. In *Cradle to Cradle*, McDonough and Braungart (2002) argue that creative sustainable design essentially means eliminating waste completely through the application of human ingenuity. Once a product has reached the end of its useful life in one form, it serves as the raw technical material, or biological nourishment, for another. Closed-loop industrial cycles will see recycling being replaced by downcycling, as exemplified by the plastic material from which the actual *Cradle to Cradle* book has been manufactured. From all this, Lovins *et al.* (1999) identify four necessary interlinked shifts in business practices:

- dramatically increase the productivity of natural resources;
- shift to biologically inspired production models;
- move to a solutions-based business model; and
- reinvest in natural capital.

The US carpet manufacturer Interface, whose Chief Executive Officer (CEO) Ray Anderson experienced an epiphany after reading Hawken's *Ecology of Commerce*, is frequently cited as an adventurous corporation adopting these necessary and interlinked shifts, and committing to developing an ecologically sustainable business practice. In his autobiography, *Mid-Course Correction*, Anderson (1998) writes of his billion-dollar corporation first becoming sustainable and then restorative. Instead of just taking materials from the Earth it will put things back. Carpet tiles will no longer be sold, used and then discarded but, in this 'age of access' (Rifkin, 2000), will be leased, reused and recycled. The production and consumption process will become cyclical rather than linear. Destructive technologies will be replaced by new ecologically sensitive ones and, most important, Interface will model a new, sustainable and successful mode of doing business that could be emulated by others.

The world is a complex and complicated place. The Finland-based company Neste Oil has entered the increasingly controversial field of producing new forms of low-emission biofuels. Neste Oil's NExBTL Renewable Diesel reduces greenhouse gas emissions by between 40 and 60 per cent compared with conventional diesel, but is derived from palm oil, viewed by Greenpeace International (2007) and other NGOs as a major environmental problem. However, Neste Oil prioritizes sustainable development in all its policies and operations, and expects similar from its suppliers. The organization is a member of the Roundtable on Sustainable Palm Oil and is one of the main sponsors of WWF Finland. Indeed, the WWF is an adviser to the Roundtable, working closely to ensure that this renewable energy source is sourced sustainably. It should be noted that the WWF and palm oil production continues to be subject to continuous scrutiny and often fierce criticism. For Greenpeace many of the companies that subscribe to the Roundtable have taken few if any steps to avoid the worst practices, such as wholesale forest clearance and the continuing eradication of the orang-utan and the Sumatran tiger, associated with the industry. Their campaigns have produced considerable negative publicity for many well-known companies, including Nestlé, Proctor & Gamble, Neste Oil, Unilever, Tesco, Cadbury and Colgate Palmolive, many of whom are associated with Wilmar International which controls 45 per cent of the global palm oil trade. As a result of this persistent campaigning, and perhaps triggered by Greenpeace International's report *Licence to Kill* (Greenpeace International, 2013), which demonstrated that the expansion of palm oil and pulpwood plantations was responsible for the destruction of over two-thirds of the habitat of the critically endangered Sumatran tiger, Wilmar International announced in December 2013 that it would now pursue a No Deforestation policy and that by the end of 2015 it would no longer buy or sell oil from companies that are involved in forest destruction.

There is no shortage of models, of management systems, frameworks, guidelines, toolkits, manuals, books, academic readers, and training and coaching opportunities offering advice to organizations wishing to become socially responsible and environmentally sustainable (McDonagh and Prothero, 1997; Mellahi and Wood, 2002; Dunphy *et al.*, 2003; BITC, 2006; Hitchcock and Willard, 2006). Two of the most significant are The Natural Step (Nattrass and Altomare, 1999) and the SIGMA Project (2003). Neither is there a shortage of media-friendly business gurus and futurists who see economic and business lessons being delivered in the fast-developing world of cyberspace. Chris Anderson (2006) sees the Internet as offering an infinite number of niche opportunities for all types of businesses to satisfy the most arcane, and potentially the most ecologically sensitive, of consumers' needs and wants. For others, the Net may simply create unlimited and unconstrained consumer demand. If you look hard enough you can buy virtually anything on the Internet. Tapscott and Williams (2007) see the Wikipedia phenomenon as prefiguring new forms of economic arrangements and production processes characterized by collective intelligence, social collaboration and self-organization. 'Wikinomics' is the future and the Chinese motorcycle industry is a sign of things to come. The Internet is also giving many people the opportunity to be more professional in the way they interact with each other and with larger collectivities such as big corporations. InnoCentive is a Web forum of about 1.5 million full-time, retired and amateur scientific experts. A company can post its requirements on the forum, offer payment (usually less than US$100,000) and immediately tap into this community of 1.5 million scientists spread over 170 countries. In 2004, Prize4Life, a non-profit group established by a group of Harvard Business School graduates and based in Cambridge, Massachusetts, offered a US$1 million prize for the successful identification of a biomarker for amyotrophic lateral sclerosis (ALS). In 2006, Netflix, a mail-order movie company, offered US$1 million for an algorithm that will perform 10 per cent more effectively

Table 7.1 The sustainability spectrum

1st Wave Organization		2nd Wave Organization		3rd Wave Organization	
Rejection	Non-responsive	Compliance	Efficiency	Strategically Proactive	Sustaining Corporation
Elite seeks profit maximization, treating all resources as means to that end.	More ignorant than oppositional.	Focuses on reducing risk of being penalized for not complying with minimum standards.	Introduces human and environmental policies to reduce costs and increase efficiency.	Seeks to be employer of choice.	Reinterprets the nature of the corporation as an integral self-renewing element of the whole of society in its ecological context – and attempts to renew this.
Pays lip-service to health and safety.	Prefers business as usual.	Reactive to community and legal requirements.		Seeks stakeholder engagement to innovate safe, environmentally friendly products and processes.	
Opposition to government and green campaigners.	Ignores negative environmental impacts.	Prefers compliance but proactive in developing good public image.		Advocates good corporate citizenship to maximize profits.	
Community claims regarded as illegitimate.					
Value Destroyers	Value Limiters	Value Conservers	Value Creators	Sustainable Business	

Source: adapted from Kemp et al. (2003: 34).

than its current system for predicting whether a customer will enjoy a film. This does not replace corporate R&D but may encourage 'ways to spur innovation crucial to improving how well we – and our children and grandchildren – live' (Wessel, 2007).

Drawing on the work of Dunphy *et al.* (2003), Kemp *et al.* (2003) have added four value concepts to the three waves a business organization may pass through to become fully sustainable. Kemp *et al.* state that those activities designed to control business impacts and risks *conserve* value and can be seen in any well-managed company. Those activities that generate additional revenue or improve cost-efficiency *create* value. There are, of course, also actions that may *destroy* or *limit* business value. At the final stage, companies pioneer alternative interpretations of business value and success, and aim to develop restorative business practices that nurture natural and social capital. The task is challenging, but many corporations are on this journey, with many in the second but few, apart from Interface, in the third wave.

Box 7.1 Plan B update: creating new jobs, cutting carbon emissions in the US

The US goal for Detroit should be not merely to save it but to make it the world leader in producing high-efficiency plug-in hybrid cars. Replacing one gas-guzzling SUV with a plug-in hybrid will, over the car's lifetime, reduce oil imports by 200 barrels, saving $20,000 of oil imports. Such an initiative multiplied across the fleet would keep hundreds of billions of dollars at home for job-creating U.S. investments.

In terms of job creation, investment in retrofitting buildings creates more than seven times as many jobs as a similar investment in coal-fired power plants. One of the early leaders is Houston, which plans to retrofit each of its 271 government buildings, thus simultaneously reducing energy use and operational costs. As Houston Mayor Bill White says, "It makes good business sense."

Building the new energy economy creates jobs in the construction of wind farms or the retrofitting of buildings, and also indirectly in the supply lines that provide, for example, the parts for wind turbines or the thermally efficient windows for retrofitting. These investments also generate jobs outside the energy sector. For example, the construction of a wind farm in a Great Plains community generates jobs in local businesses such as restaurants and home improvement outlets.

The government's role in this vast job creation initiative is to use public funds as incentives to leverage far greater investments of private capital. We estimate that $100 billion of federal funds used strategically over the next 12 years would leverage $400 billion of private capital investment. If this $500 billion is allocated evenly between renewable energy development (wind, solar, and geothermal) and retrofitting, and if every two jobs created in the energy sector creates one job elsewhere, this would quickly generate 600,000 new jobs that would last through 2020.

Source: Lester R. Brown (2008) Creating New Jobs, Cutting Carbon Emissions, and Reducing Oil Imports by Investing in Renewable Energy and Energy Efficiency (www.earth-policy.org/plan_b_updates/2008/update80).

UNEP Green Economy Report 2011

The UN's conception of a green economy is not a fundamental rethink of the current system of production and consumption, ownership and control, but an exercise in ecological modernization and state-assisted development of the global market economy. The Green Economy Report clearly defines its terms of references as:

> A major challenge is reconciling the competing economic development aspirations of rich and poor countries in a world economy that is facing increasing climate change, energy insecurity and ecological scarcity. A green economy can meet this challenge by offering a development path that reduces carbon dependency, promotes resource and energy efficiency and lessens environmental degradation. As economic growth and investments become less dependent on liquidating environmental assets and sacrificing environmental quality, both rich and poor countries can attain more sustainable economic development.
>
> The concept of a green economy does not replace sustainable development; but there is a growing recognition that achieving sustainability rests almost entirely on getting the economy right.
>
> (UNEP, 2011: 17)

The report notes that investments in renewable energy have grown considerably in the major emerging economies of Brazil, India and China, which account for about 90 per cent of the same investment undertaken by developing countries. In 2006, Brazil accounted for around 50 per cent of the world's production of ethanol. In 2008, China was the second heaviest investor in renewable energy after Spain. Brazil ranked fourth and India seventh. In 2011, global investment in renewables was in the region of US$160 billion. There is considerable opportunity for expansion in these countries and with it the growth of green jobs. Currently, China employs the largest number of people in the renewable energy field, followed by Germany, Brazil, Japan and the US.

UNEP argues that there needs to be both international and national policy commitments to renewable energy growth, which would need to include an enabling policy framework, establishing long-term targets for investment in additional capacity and penetration rates within the current energy mix. Such targets can powerfully communicate intent and security to potential investors. Among the developing countries, Brazil, China, Egypt, India, Kenya, the Philippines and Thailand have set targets for 2020 or later. Some significant financial reform, green regulations and positive incentives will be required to promote the necessary public and private investing, if a green economy is to emerge. The UNEP report argues:

> Analysis and modeling conducted for the *Green Economy Report* suggests that the level of additional investment needed is between 1 to 2.5 per cent of global GDP per year from 2010 to 2050. Currently, green economy investment is well below 1 per cent of global GDP. . . .
>
> If a robust business case can be created and properly demonstrated, for example, by governments fully implementing the 'polluter pays' and 'user pays' principles agreed by OECD countries, then arguably some of this re-deployment of capital will occur naturally as investors pursuing enlightened self-interest shift their assets from less attractive brown economy (based on fossil fuels) activities.
>
> (2011: 622)

By contrast, according to the Stockholm International Peace Research Institute, world military expenditure in 2012 was US$1,753 billion, the equivalent to 2.5 per cent of world GDP. According to the World Bank, Brazil spent 1.4 per cent, India 2.5 per cent, China 2 per cent and the US 4.7 per cent of their GDP on the armed forces.

There is another dimension to the green economy, too, and that is in the all-important area of job creation. The International Labour Organization (ILO, 2012) estimates that around 600 million new productive jobs will need to be created in the global economy within a decade in order to secure sustainable economic development and social cohesion. Since the financial and economic crisis of 2008 there has been a continuous crisis in global labour markets. Even so, by 2020 there will still be something like 900 million workers living with their families and earning US$2 a day or less. Optimistically, the UNEP believes that up to 60 million of these could be 'green jobs'. However, UNEP also offers some cautionary words:

> a transition towards a green economy does not automatically lead to more decent work. The implementation of adequate policies and strong labour market institutions will be required. These policies and institutions need to promote a just and inclusive transition. A broad social acceptance for such a transition is also required and this is only possible if peoples' livelihoods and working conditions are taken into account by policy-makers.
>
> (2012a: 3)

Not surprisingly, most economists on the Left believe that aligning profit seeking with environmental goals, meaningful work and employment remains basically an illusion (Foster, 2002; Smith, 2011). The privatization of the commons and the further commodification of nature will simply continue. Thus, as the UNEP (2012b) Briefing Paper 'Valuing Nature' reported, a valuation exercise for Kampala, Uganda, demonstrated that the economic value of Nakivubo Swamp could be estimated as between US$1 million and US$1.75 million per annum, because of the nutrient retention and wastewater purification services it provides for the nearby city.

Corporate social responsibility

In *Corporate Social Responsibility: Making Good Business Sense* (Holme and Watts, 2000: 6), published by the World Business Council for Sustainable Development, corporate social responsibility (CSR) is defined as 'the continuing commitment by business to behave ethically and contribute to economic development, while improving the quality of life of the workforce and their families as well as of the local community and society at large'. The UK Government advocates CSR as a way of meeting the challenge of more ethical, resource-efficient, sustainable consumption and production, and it is increasingly promoted by the World Bank, the UN, multinationals and many national governments. Its advocates view it as a private sector development that incorporates the goals of inclusivity, equity, environmental sustainability and global poverty reduction. Despite its growth and support by some high-profile business leaders, such as Richard Branson, Stuart Rose and the late Ray Anderson, however, neoliberal economists like Milton Friedman view CSR as a distraction from the core business of business – developing new markets, making a profit for shareholders, and so on.

Given this, it is important to make a distinction between the fiduciary rights of shareholders from the moral and social rights of stakeholders. Max Clarkson (1995) defines stakeholders as persons and/or groups who have, or claim, ownership, rights or interests in a corporation and its activities, past, present or future. He distinguishes between:

- *primary stakeholders* – including shareholders, investors, employees, customers;
- *suppliers, government and communities*, without whom business infrastructure, markets, laws and regulations would not exist; and
- *secondary stakeholders* – including the media and a wide range of social interest groups, who may affect or influence the work of the business or corporation.

CSR, often shortened to CR and explicitly incorporating environmental and wide-ranging sustainability concerns, addresses the putative rights, interests and expectations of the stakeholder. It becomes imperative to see the business of business as being far more than the 'bottom line', although the bottom line ultimately colours everything a corporation does. Consequently, Hart (1997, 2005) writes of the need for corporations to go beyond cosmetic greening by creating a vision for sustainability that will include product stewardship, clean technologies and pollution prevention. For Hart, there is a difference between being eco-efficient and eco-effective. The latter means that corporations will simultaneously deliver economic, social and environmental benefits to the whole world. To do this, corporations must become indigenous to the places where they are located, developing 'native capabilities' that respect local culture, and address the broad sustainability challenge and natural diversity. Apart from technological advances, new adaptable business models and innovations are required that go beyond continuous improvements to search for, foster and develop new markets, new (unconventional) partners and new emerging technologies. Hart writes of the 'great leap to the bottom', which essentially means that corporations can meet the needs of the world's poor and make a good profit in the process. As C.K. Prahalad (2009) and Prahalad and Hammond (2002) have written, it is misleading to write of the 'global poor', as together they constitute a significant and untapped global market. By 2015, nearly 1,300 cities in Asia, Africa and Latin America will have populations of over 1 million. A total of 27 cities will have populations in excess of 8 million, half of whom will be 'bottom of the pyramid' (BOP) consumers. In Rio de Janeiro, Johannesburg and Mumbai, the poor have a purchasing power of around US$1.2 billion. Slums in these cities have their own ecosystems, informal economies and range of different businesses. Some companies are adopting a shared access model, where poor people hire or lease their computers, fridges, Internet connections, mobile phones, cars, and so forth, on a pay-per-use basis from the providers of such services, who gain considerably more revenue per investment dollar than they would normally. Obviously, new skills, new synergies and new management practices are required to make this work, but, as Prahalad shows, the benefits are real and tangible. In certain circumstances, consumption can, and does, alleviate poverty:

> Consider healthcare. If you are legally blind with cataracts, you can't work and neither can the family member who cares for you. But if you get access to inexpensive cataract surgery, now you can see and both of you can work. Have

you consumed eye surgery or increased the family's earning power? You've done both. It's two sides to the same coin.

(Prahalad, quoted in Green, 2007)

This market-driven solution to poverty alleviation has been criticized, though many non-market-driven development policies have themselves failed to completely meet the needs of the poor. For Jaiswal (2007), BOP investments can only succeed if there is a significant invent in education, too, for education has a marked impact on economic development, income generation and quality of life. In a later work, Prahalad (2009) addresses education and information more directly using another positive motivational case study as illustration. Harnessing the affordances of digital technology and the Internet, the e-Choupal system, an initiative of ITC Ltd, a conglomerate based in Kolkata in India, enables rural farmers to access market prices in real time, allowing them to make better informed decisions. Thus, as Hahn (2009) and Payaud and Martinet (2010) have concluded, BOP initiatives can certainly contribute to alleviating poverty but they need to be inventive and move beyond conventional CSR goals and perspectives to fashion and enforce, in effect, citizenship as well as producer and consumer rights.

New media companies can make an important contribution to human and economic development. People in low- and middle-income countries make up more than 20 per cent of the world's mobile-phone users, with the growth of mobile-phone subscribers in developing countries twice that of developed countries. Research conducted for Vodaphone in South Africa and Tanzania, *Africa: The Impact of Mobile Phones* (Coyle, 2005), demonstrated that the greatest impact of mobiles has been in reducing the need for travel. People have saved time and money by avoiding expensive and unreliable transport, have substantially improved business performance through providing better access to information and by creating new commercial opportunities, have helped nurture social capital, and have helped the poor in remote areas find employment. Mobile phones have provided farmers with weather and market information, helping them to decide which crops to plant, or when to harvest. Businesses have reduced costs by using mobiles to search for lower prices or by replacing more expensive services such as post. Vodafone has also participated in a project in Kenya and Tanzania (in partnership with Safaricom and Vodacom, and supported by the UK's Department for International Development) to develop ways in which mobiles can deliver financial services to 'unbanked' customers. Access to financial services is crucial to the success of micro-entrepreneurs and small businesses. Although the links between mobile-phone technology and broad economic performance are complex, the section authored by Leonard Waverman, Meloria Meschi and Melvyn Fuss in the report noted that the impact of mobile growth on gross domestic product (GDP) in thirty-eight low-income and lower-middle income countries between 1996 and 2002 had a strong positive impact on economic development.

CSR needs to accommodate a wide range of stakeholders. Hopkins (1999, 2006) argues that it is essential for businesses to carefully manage their relations with society and the natural environment. Collins and Porras (1994) suggest that those managers who reflect a real concern for their stakeholders produce superior results for their shareholders. De Gues (1997) goes a little further, arguing that although the average life expectancy of a company is less than twenty years, those that have lasted longest, two hundred years or more, share four fundamental characteristics:

- conservatism in financing;
- sensitivity to the world around them;
- awareness of their identity; and
- tolerance of new ideas.

Porter and Kramer (2006), however, argue that CSR, and certainly CSR reporting, rarely seems to express a coherent strategy, often being more concerned with publicly demonstrating a company's social sensitivity than being genuinely forward-looking. Philanthropic activities are usually quantified in terms of volunteer hours and/or dollars, rather than in overall social or ecological influence, with CSR largely being justified in terms of moral obligation, sustainability, licence to operate and reputation. These are all very important for many businesses, but fall short of properly integrating business activity with those social issues that may foster and produce a healthy society. For Porter and Kramer (2006: 85), social issues affect a company in three specific categories:

- *generic social issues* that are not significantly affected by a company's operations nor materially affect its long-term competitiveness;
- *value chain social impacts* that are significantly affected by a company's activities in the ordinary course of business; and
- *social dimensions of competitive context*, where social issues in the external environment significantly affect the underlying drivers of a company's competitiveness in the location where it operates.

It is important that a corporate social agenda simultaneously achieves social and economic benefits, that employees take pride in what their employer does, and to realize that CSR needs to be responsive, strategic – in other words, doing things differently from competitors – and able to articulate a clear and meaningful value proposition. All businesses should have a social, ecological and moral purpose, should seek to create shared value, recognizing that there will be some issues best left to NGOs and governments. Porter and Kramer continue:

> Supporting a dance company may be a generic social issue for a utility like Southern California Edison but an important part of the competitive context for a corporation like American Express, which depends on the high-end entertainment, hospitality and tourism cluster. Carbon emissions may be a generic social issue for a financial services firm like Bank of America, a negative value chain impact for a transportation-based company like UPS, or both a value chain impact and a competitive context issue for a car manufacturer like Toyota. The AIDS pandemic in Africa may be a generic social issue for a US retailer like Home Depot, a value chain impact for a pharmaceutical company like GlaxoSmithKline and a competitive context issue for a mining company like Anglo American that depends on local labour in Africa for its operations.
>
> (2006: 85)

Criticisms of corporate social responsibility

Many NGOs and some academics are critical of CSR, suggesting there is a thin divide between CSR from PR (public relations), with companies more:

concerned with their own reputations, with the potential damage of public campaigns directed against them, and, overwhelmingly, with the desire – and the imperative – to secure ever greater profits. None of this necessarily means that companies cannot act responsibly if they choose too. But it does mean that their attempts to do so are likely to be partial, short-term and patchy – leaving vulnerable poor communities at risk.

(Christian Aid, 2004: 5)

Other critics of CSR suggest that there is no proven link between CSR, economic growth and poverty reduction, given that CSR's focus is usually on environmental, labour and human rights issues (Jenkins, 2005). In their controversial book *The End of Corporate Social Responsibility?* Peter Fleming and Mark Jones (2013) argue that in many ways both the policy and practice have acted to mask some of the iniquitous consequences of a deregulated global economy and that in the last twenty years, a period when CSR has become more prominent publicly, many social and environmental indices of global progress have actually worsened. What it may have done, however, is help to incorporate workers into the ideology of the commercialism, particularly when there is likely to be a breach or non-alignment between progressive personal values and an unsustainable business environment. Similarly, the United Nations' Global Compact initiative, which is an attempt to motivate big business to adhere to a range of social, environmental and human rights principles, has also been criticized as lacking significant achievements. There is also evidence that large corporations, often with the tacit acceptance of governments, do not always respect the environmental and other rights of indigenous peoples, or maintain their interest in the sustainable community development activities over time even though they may feature prominently in corporate public communications. Kimerling (2001), writing of Occidental's activities in Ecuador, states that the language of sustainable community development was basically appropriated by the big corporation to serve its own economic ends, helping it to reproduce and perpetuate an environmentally dubious and potentially dangerous model of development. Local people were not informed or consulted effectively and in many instances were deliberately fed false or misleading information which, combined with pressure tactics and sheer economic power, simply wore down the local Qyicha communities. Their consent for Occidental to work in their localities was tricked out of them. Outside the area of oil exploration, Occidental used its PR machine to communicate a sound and responsible image to deflect potential criticism from environmentalists and journalists. In this way, as Doane (2005) warns, the CSR agenda becomes undermined if it serves corporate interests at the expense of its stakeholders. This may variously take the form of simplistic cause-related marketing, or more sophisticated and Machiavellian risk-management actions:

> On the former side, we find programmes in the UK like a supermarket's (Tesco) computers for schools, or a confectionary corporation's (Cadbury) sports equipment voucher programme, which gets children collecting chocolate wrappers in return for sports equipment for their schools. Both are aimed at providing community benefits through increased sales. Neither does anything to tackle the larger questions that CSR should have been confronting, that is, the very way that companies directly impact on communities through the ways in which they do business. What of Tesco's opening of big-box shops on green-field sites, and

the additional implication that, by doing so, they have led to increased traffic and a closing down of local shops, leading to what some have called 'food deserts'? Or Cadbury's role in sourcing their cocoa through commodity markets, which effectively keeps market prices low, resulting in poor labour standards in cocoa production? What too of the ethical issues associated with promoting chocolate consumption on the one hand and buying sports equipment to alleviate obesity on the other?

(Doane, 2005: 218)

Others have argued that stakeholder engagement continues to be more a way of pacifying communities than really engaging. BP (British Petroleum, rebranded as 'Beyond Petroleum' and then quietly dropped), well known for its stakeholder dialogue programmes, has been criticized by civil society groups, including Amnesty International, for displacing local communities in Turkey or Azerbaijan. BP promotes its CSR to shareholders while passing on any relevant risk to the host government, thereby avoiding any direct responsibility as, according to legal convention, only governments and individuals acting on behalf of governments can commit human rights abuses. These and other criticisms led BP to review its approach, issuing a human rights 'guidance note' to project leaders and reaffirming its commitment to the Universal Declaration on Human Rights in its 2006 Sustainability Report (verified by Ernst and Young), noting that a company can 'demonstrate leadership in supporting and promoting international human rights norms' (BP, 2006: 3), which it is doing by helping to provide for the world's energy needs. Doane and the pressure group Corpwatch also note that BP has essentially bought itself into the renewable energy business by taking over smaller, more ethically motivated firms, making it difficult for some highly innovative small green businesses, the 'ethical minnows', to place their model of a more sustainable business practice on to a larger, possibly global, scale. These minnows are invariably swimming against the tide of ferocious competition from less ethically motivated corporate competitors. Doane concludes:

The ethical minnows, however, seem to offer a gem of inspiration. One could foresee a future wherein big business no longer exists at all. What the ethical minnows have is an ability to innovate: to be closer to the people that produce and consume their products and develop products that serve, rather than drive, human need. They tend to drive out the middle-man and make new rules that satisfy a social end. The New Economics Foundation, amongst others, has called this 'social innovation'.

(2005: 228)

A positive future for minnows will require boldness in effecting individual and institutional change. It will probably require a system of sympathetic global govern-ance that is unlikely to emerge in the very near future, and will require businesses to go beyond the bottom line and seek out the changes to practices, regulations and organizational culture that are being developed in the more progressive organizations. If this happens, CSR could easily and genuinely become synonymous with sustain-ability. Wal-Mart, like BP, have publicly adopted pro-sustainability practices, partly to rescue their brand reputation as a result of serious public criticism of their social and economic impact, as exemplified in Robert Greenwald's excoriating documentary feature *Wal-Mart: The High Cost of Low Prices*, and partly in recognition of the fact that large companies can do much to help restore some balance to climate systems by reducing greenhouse gases and dependence on oil, while still saving money for customers. Finally, as Mirvis and Coocins (2004) suggest, one way to distinguish companies that talk about social responsibility from those that live it is to observe what employees are doing about it.

Moving beyond business efficiency

Some business commentators have suggested that eco-efficiency is just one aspect of creating a sustainable business, for the real challenge is to ensure that social, economic and environmental aims are integrated under a single sustainability objective. This integration will involve understanding both production and consumption, including the nature of entrepreneurship, marketing and the generation of consumer wants (Young and Tilley, 2006). A pro-sustainable business practice requires a pro-sustainable entrepreneurship and this too requires an integrative approach as seen in Figure 7.2.

For Young and Tilley, the hope is that sustainability entrepreneurship will become more than the sum of its interrelated parts and 'the only "entrepreneurial" route to fulfilling sustainable development' (Tilley and Young, 2009: 86). Thus, sustainability entrepreneurs will need to be, among other things, life-style motivators, as well as being concerned to maintain the sustainability of their company. Such advocates will also need to look beyond not only efficiency but the profit motive, too. As Lux (2003) has argued, companies need to be motivated by the common good rather than private gain: common good – non-profit – sustainability as opposed to self-interest profit motive – growth. However, there are problems. A major one is that, as Tilley and Young (2009) acknowledge, the sustainability entrepreneur is still very much an abstract construct and that in capitalist society, despite all the various forms of entrepreneurship emerging and developing, the dominant bias is still towards economic self-interest.

There are models of business activity, such as social enterprise, that although not yet 'business as usual' could conceivably prefigure how businesses could operate to secure a more sustainable future. In *Social Enterprise in Anytown*, John Pearce (2003) argues that social enterprise should be defined as:

- having a social purpose or purposes;
- achieving the social purposes by, at least in part, engaging in trade in the market-place;
- not distributing profits to individuals;
- holding assets and wealth in trust for community benefit;
- democratically involving members of its constituency in the governance of the organization; and
- being independent organizations accountable to a defined constituency and to the wider community.

Bill Drayton (2003), Chairman of Ashoka: Innovators for the Public, writes that social entrepreneurs focus their entrepreneurial skills and talents on solving social problems such as underachievement in children, the digital divide, environmental

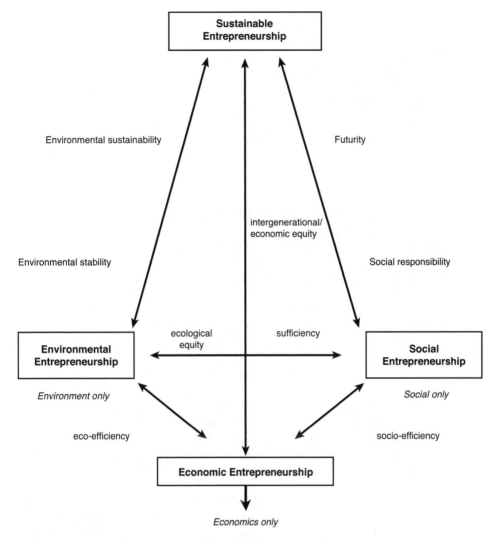

Figure 7.2 The sustainable entrepreneurship module
Source: adapted from Tilley and Young (2009: 86).

pollution and homelessness. It doesn't matter whether an entrepreneur is concerned solely with making money or effecting a social good, the skills required for both are roughly the same or at least very similar. Each entrepreneur can envisage ways of identifying and leveraging change to build up sufficient momentum to cause a tipping point, making for significant, systemic change. Leadbeater and Miller (2004) write of the *pro-am revolution* and pro-am power, which basically means harnessing the interests, enthusiasms and skills people develop outside (as well as inside) their professional lives for the public good. As Leadbeater and Miller write:

> An outstanding example is Bangladesh's Grameen Bank, founded in 1976 by Muhammad Yunnus, a Bangladeshi economics professor, to provide very poor

people with access to micro-credit to allow them to improve their houses and invest in businesses. Traditional banks, reliant on professional expertise, regarded poor people seeking small loans as unprofitable. Grameen built a different model, based on pro-am expertise. It employs a small body of professionals, who train an army of barefoot bankers. Village committees administer most of Grameen's loans. This pro-am workforce makes it possible to administer millions of tiny loans cost-effectively. By 2003, Grameen had lent more than US$4 billion to about 2.8 million Bangladeshis, including 570,000 mortgages to build tin roofs for huts to keep people dry during the monsoons. Had Grameen relied on traditional, professional models of organization it would only have reached a tiny proportion of the population.

(2004: 1)

In 2006, Mohammed Yunnus and the Grameen Bank were jointly awarded the Nobel Peace Prize for their work.

The adoption of environmentally and socially responsible business practices can open up an additional range of opportunities for entrepreneurs. The move to a sustainable business framework provides numerous niches that enterprising individuals and firms can successfully identify and service. These include the development of new products and services, improvements to the efficiency of existing firms, new methods of marketing, and the reconfiguration of existing business models and practices. Green entrepreneurship, writes Schaper (2002), provides new opportunities for first movers who are able to spot and exploit opportunities, gaps in the market and new ideas. Green entrepreneurship can also act as a change agent within the wider business community, particularly when this wider business community recognizes that green business is good, profitable and rewarding. Green entrepreneurs will then exert a 'pull' that motivates others to become more proactive in their developments, which, if additionally supported by the 'push' factor articulated through revised government regulation, green taxation, and stakeholder and pressure-group lobbying, could make a considerable impact. As Robert Isaak writes:

> Businesses that are not designed to be sustainable decrease our health, shorten our time on Earth and destroy the heritage we leave for our children, no matter where we are located globally. In contrast, green-green businesses are models that can help show the way to increase productivity while reducing resource use in a manner that is harmonious with human health and the sustainability of non-human species as well. Green start-ups make it easier to 'fix' environmental components and processes from the outset. Green subsidiaries of larger firms can foster innovation and bring back the heightened motivation of social solidarity to businesses where it may be all too easy to slip into cynicism in an era of global economic crises.

(2002: 81–91)

But if sustainability or green entrepreneurship requires integration, then so does the creation and implementation of a corporate sustainability strategy. From a business development perspective, it also goes beyond Henry Mintzberg's five 'Ps' of strategy – plan, ploy, pattern, position and perspective (Mintzberg, 1987). As Michael Blowfield (2013: 111) has written, many companies who decide they need to position themselves as sustainable business cannot stop at producing or marketing a few specialized goods or services – 'it is impossible to be a little bit pregnant'. As Blowfield remarks, there are different ways of interpreting sustainability strategy. Some companies see it as about the company itself dealing with a vast array of potential threats to reputation, brand and market share. Therefore, if a company is suffering from sourcing its materials from degraded ecosystems, or from sweatshops employing child workers, then it is best to deal with any possible blowback before it occurs. Another interpretation sees sustainability become part of how a business actually does business. PepsiCo's business sells soft drinks but, given the health and obesity concerns affecting many societies, it also needs to sell soft drinks that are healthy, too. A company can prosper if it can identify these types of sustainability sweet-spots (Savitz, 2006). A third interpretation is to posit sustainability and the company itself as a sustainable change agent – that is, through it product design, procurement, production, financing, technology, logistics, marketing and training, aiming to and actually working towards increasing the stock of the planet's stock of natural capital. This is at least taking the ideas of cradle to cradle, if not degrowth to its corporate heart. Blowfield writes:

> Sustainability issues only begin to have meaning for a company in strategic terms when they are integrated into high-level strategy. This will normally mean moving beyond defensive or offensive tactics, and treating sustainability as a factor in competitive strategy.
>
> Thus sustainability should be synonymous with the three value disciplines of business strategy theory and practice, namely: operational excellence, customer intimacy and product leadership.
>
> (2013: 123)

Fair trade

One aspect of creating an honest global market is the development of a fair-trade system, which in recent years has seen considerable expansion, developing far beyond coffee and tea, to fresh fruit and other products. The market is currently worth in the region of US$1.5 billion and is growing, particularly in the UK and US. Many large supermarket chains are now developing their own fair-trade brands to meet and nurture this demand, as well as to communicate their own commitment to CSR. However, when considered as a percentage of total sales, even 'big' sellers like fair-trade tea still constitute only a small percentage (2 per cent) of the total, and fair-trade sales as a whole in the UK make up just 0.2 per cent of all grocery sales. There is an important difference between increasing the commercial profile of a brand and the aims of the fair-trade movement to impact positively on broader development goals. However, Mike Gidney, policy director at Traidcraft and chairman of the Fairtrade Foundation, notes that the influence of fair trade is not easy to quantify. Consumers are more aware of development issues and frequently factor these into purchasing decisions. In 2007, Oxfam reported the results of a survey of more than 1,700 UK residents and discovered that although 92 per cent of British consumers buy their food and drink at major supermarkets, just 11 per cent actually want to do so. Instead, most preferred to buy directly from farmers (69 per cent), local independent retailers (54 per cent) or even to grow their own food (47 per cent).

Some 14 per cent of British consumers buy fair-trade products at every possible opportunity, 57 per cent shop fair-trade on a regular basis and 80 per cent feel very clear about why people should buy fair-trade goods (Oxfam, 2007). Roughly 25 per cent of Traidcraft's 120,000 customers are active development campaigners. Oxfam has also noted that fair trade has undoubtedly helped generate interest in its own Make Trade Fair campaign (Oxfam, 2002) and has given the developing world more influence at global trade negotiations (Kelly, 2007). Additionally, a growing number of towns in the UK have been certified as Fairtrade Towns by the Fairtrade Foundation. The first was Gastang in Lancashire, and by early 2007 there were over 230 others.

Some new businesses are directly applying fair-trade principles in establishing ethically based but commercial social enterprises. In Luton, north of London, fair-trade tea is being sold directly from Indian tribal communities in Tamil Nadu to the deprived multicultural working-class housing estate of Marsh Farm. A forty-bag pack of tea is sold door to door, on market stalls and in a few local shops. The retail price is at 75 pence, compared with £1.20 for regular tea and £1.60 for fair-trade tea at the major supermarkets. Stan Thekaekara, a trustee of Oxfam UK and fellow at the Saïd Business School at Oxford University, brought the Indian growers together. He suggests that ethics should not just be for the well-off – fair trade should benefit deprived producer and consumer communities more than the big chains. He told John Vidal of *The Guardian* that the experiment with tea is the first of a number of other intended initiatives involving rice, oils, spices and cloth:

> Fair trade is more expensive. The supermarkets make the most profit out of it and nothing really changes in the trading system. Tea does not become a penny cheaper for the people who drink it by the gallon on British housing estates, and workers' children still face starvation and malnutrition on tea estates everywhere. It has to become a brand. If poor people cannot drink fairly traded tea, then it seems wrong.
>
> (2007a)

Fair-trade certification and the influence of a number of alternative trading organizations have led some observers to see in this movement a new type of globalization, a reframing from below, where marginalized workers and producers in the Global South benefit in clear ways (Nicholls, 2002; Raynolds *et al.*, 2007):

- producers enjoy guaranteed prices that are above those in conventional markets, which is most important for those trading in tropical commodity markets, which are often volatile;
- organized capacity-building for democratic groups – for example, producer co-operatives or worker unions, is supported;
- the development of marketing and other skills of fair-trade producers;
- provision of market information to consumers;
- transparent and long-term trading partnerships; and
- a social premium is provided in that community, so that healthcare, schools, roads, sanitation and other services can be financed.

As fair trade becomes increasingly popular, the movement will confront a number of challenges, not least in how it intersects with the dominant conventional market sector, while still enabling consumers to promote sustainability through their ability to consume more ethically. Some retailers and multinationals have attempted to enhance their own corporate brand value through 'clean-washing' – in other words, misleading consumers by using fair trade as a simple public relations tool to upgrade a company's reputation to that of a responsible and socially concerned organization (Pierre, 2007). Many criticisms of Nestlé's launch of its own fair-trade coffee, Partners' Blend, ran along these lines. Additionally, with the increase in demand, the future of small-scale producers may become precarious, as supermarkets will demand both volume and perhaps quality, and aesthetic standards and accreditation far beyond the purse of small growers and producers. This may lead fair-trade producers to pursue competition rather than co-operation strategies in order to secure and maintain contracts with the major retailers, thus jeopardizing the fair-trade movement's capacity to mediate and reshape local global relations and socio-ecological concerns in the interests of trade, social and environmental justice.

Case study: digital media companies, carbon footprints and corporate responsibility

With the number of mobile and other digital devices rapidly expanding and the ever-increasing amount of data being being transmitted via the Internet, there is clearly a downside to the ubiquitous nature of new media technology. This not only relates to a degree of government surveillance, corporate colonization of the cyber commons and destructive hacking, but also the burgeoning ecological footprint and the discernible trend towards the sheer size of the global digital infrastructure being too large for appropriate human monitoring and control. A report by the International Telecommunications Union, an agency based in Geneva, has suggested that by 2014 there will probably be 7.3 billion devices in the world compared with a global population of around 7 billion (ITU, 2012). Russia and Brazil have more cell-phone accounts than people, and China already accounts for around 25 per cent of the world's cell-phone users. It is, then, no wonder that the earnings from digital communication services and technologies has been estimated at about $1.5 trillion in 2010 – i.e. 2.4 per cent of global GDP (ITU, 2012). The ecological footprint of this digital technology, including its voracious consumption of rare earth metals that go into the device's manufacture, and the energy used to run the devices and increasing numbers of huge data services, is already equivalent to that of global aviation – i.e. about 2 per cent of global carbon emissions (Maxwell and Miller, 2012). In 2013, a series of system crashes affected Google, Amazon, Apple and Microsoft, and on one quiet Thursday in August the Nasdaq stock market shut down for three hours, caused by a communication failure between its platform for processing quotes and trades and that of allegedly the New York Stock Exchange. This resulted in about one-third fewer shares being traded that day than expected. These outages are likely to continue in the future (Garside, 2013). According to Cisco, the major digital media manufacturing company, the amount of data being transmitted in 2017 will be calculated in terms of zettabytes – about one trillion gigabytes (Cisco, 2013). Overall, IP traffic will grow at a compound annual growth rate of 23 per cent from 2012 to 2017, with traffic from wireless and mobile devices exceeding that from wired devices by 2016 and the monthly Internet traffic in North America generating around 7 billion DVDs' worth of data every month. There will inevitably be more data servers and although these are likely to be up to 25 per cent more environmentally efficient in the future, the energy consumption for IT is bound to increase.

As Cubitt *et al.* (2011: 155) have written, 'sustainability will only be achieved once the larger population realizes that the internet is not weightless and information is not immaterial'. This has meant that the major hi-tech and Internet companies have come under increasing scrutiny from environmental campaigners and to a lesser extent public opinion. Facebook has committed itself to reducing its carbon footprint and publishing a green energy target that states its commitment to becoming fully powered by renewable energy. In response Google, Apple and other companies seem to have worked hard to reduce their ecological footprint and demonstrate a degree of responsible corporate citizenship that was neither expected nor demanded only a few years ago. In August 2013, Google released data regarding its carbon footprint for 2012, claiming that for the previous six years it has achieved carbon neutrality through the purchasing of high quality carbon offsets. In the near future it will go beyond carbon neutrality by committing over $1 billion to renewable energy projects. The company has won an award from the US Environmental Protection Agency and praise from both Greenpeace and *Fortune* magazine. Although emitting 1.5 million metric tons of carbon dioxide in 2012, its total level of carbon emissions declined by 9 per cent in 2011, representing a declining level of carbon emissions relative to income. The company has also contracted over 330 MW of wind power from the US and Europe, and argues that its services are often greener than those of its competitors (Google, 2013). The company argues that Gmail is more energy efficient than using email hosted on local servers, because Gmail is hosted in the cloud and more efficiently allocates resources among many users. Additionally, Google's cloud-based services are engineered to run on efficient software and hardware housed in data centres across the world (Google, 2011). Interestingly, many of the larger data centres, also known as 'farms', generate a considerable degree of heat and the amount of energy required to cool them is huge. Around 72 per cent of Facebook's carbon emissions are generated by its data centres in the US. Facebook opened a new data centre in the small Swedish town of Lulea, just 100km south of the Arctic Circle, in 2013. Using 100 per cent renewable energy its Power Usage Efficiency rating is an impressive 1.07. Google, too, has recently located a data centre in the cold remote region of Hamina in the frozen Gulf of Finland. Apple has also responded to serious criticism of it operations, products and procurement strategy, particularly from Greenpeace International. In 2012, Apple launched the redesigned iMac, which uses 68 per cent less material and generates 67 per cent fewer carbon emissions than earlier generations. In addition, the aluminium stand on the iMac is made using 30 per cent recycled content. Apple has also achieved 100 per cent renewable energy use in its corporate facilities in Austin, Elk Grove, Cork and Munich as well as many other sites in the US and Australia. The company's iPad 2 Environmental Report states that the tablets exceed the European Directive on the Restriction of the Use of Certain Hazardous Substances in Electrical and Electronic Equipment by avoiding mercury in its display, arsenic in its glass as well as BFRs (brominated flame retardants) and PVCs (polyvinyl chloride). In 2011, Apple experienced its own 'Nike moment' when it was revealed that factories in China supplying the company were using underage labour and that there had been a number of suicides. Apple reacted by introducing stricter hiring and verification practices, and quickly became the first technology company to join the Washington-funded Fair Labor Association set up by Bill Clinton in 1999 to monitor workplace environments globally (Apple, 2012; James and Satariano, 2012). This has led Cary Krosinsky (2012), Senior Vice President of the environmental data company TruCost, to speculate whether, given Apple's record in innovation, its recent transparency, improvement in the labour practices of its Chinese subsidiaries, and its potential to further scale up sustainable change, the company is becoming a model sustainable company.

However, there are also other issues to consider when reading corporate communications and perhaps overly sympathetic interpretations. As Greenpeace noted in their report *How Green is Your Cloud?* (Greenpeace, 2012), Apple's huge $1 billion data centre in North Carolina, one of the world's largest, draws only 10 per cent of its energy from onsite renewables with the rest coming from the local grid, which is predominantly based on coal supplemented by nuclear. This led the NGO to remark:

> Apple has been incredibly selective about the energy related details of its iCloud in North Carolina, offering those nuggets of detail and data that it feels are most favorable, such as the size or scale of onsite renewable energy investment, but refusing to disclose the size of the energy demand of the facility itself, or the environmental footprint associated with the iCloud.
>
> (Greenpeace, 2012: 38)

Additionally, as the Green Computing Report stated in its report on Google:

> The 9 percent drop reflects the 2012 decision to include power purchase agreement (PPA) deductions. If PPA deductions are omitted (as they were in 2011), the total gross emissions for 2012 add up to 2,024,444 metric tons.
>
> (Trader, 2013)

The report also noted that Google had hosted a fund-raising dinner for the climate change denier Republican Senator James Inhofe and contributed '$50,000 for a fundraising dinner for the ultra-conservative Competitive Enterprise Institute, which attempts to discredit climate change scientists by suing them for fraud'.

Summary

All economic development and the pursuit of economic well-being requires a healthy environment with fully functioning ecosystem services that enable us to produce, to consume and to breathe. The idea that the planet's ecosystems provide human beings with services is one clearly derived from an economistic perspective, but then sustainable development emerged through the desire to reconcile economic processes with ecological ones. For an increasing number of economists and ecologists, this involves questioning and indeed overturning the ideological dominance of continuing economic growth. There are, it is argued, ecological limits to growth and this has led to a range of theoretical and practical explorations of what a green economy would involve. Eco-efficiency is one aspect of that exploration, but there have also been calls for more radical systemic transformations that would see the end of capitalism as we know it. This has led to discussions around degrowth, sustainable business and non-alienating work, green entrepreneurship and a corporate responsibility that extends ways beyond a company's financial stockholders.

Thinking questions

1   To what extent does the Millennium Ecosystem Assessment set the parameters for future business activity?
2   Is it feasible that economic growth might no longer be an acceptable policy goal?
3   In what ways can all businesses become social or eco-enterprises?
4   How might a green economy create more jobs?
5   What makes an ethical minnow innovative?
6   In what ways may big corporations not necessarily be a bad thing?

Companion website

If you are interested in learning more about the role of business in sustainable development and would like to further explore ideas and policies relating to the green economy, please visit the companion website.

8 Envisioning sustainable societies and urban areas

Aims

This chapter explores various methods and approaches to envisioning a sustainable society, making particular reference to past and present examples of utopian thinking. In relation to this, the potential and significance of practical experiments, strategies and plans that focus largely on sustainable design and urban development will be discussed. Finally, the possible relationship between utopian thinking, scenario analysis and practical action will be addressed.

The value of utopian writing

Many writers, from Plato (*The Republic*) and Sir Thomas More (*Utopia*) onwards have offered sophisticated and detailed visions of future utopian, and sometimes *ecotopian*, societies. Some have been fictional romances and others more non-fictional planning blueprints or intricate philosophical works. Lewis Mumford produced an enlightening critical study in 1922, *The Story of Utopias*, at a time when the modern world had been devastated by a world war. For those concerned with fashioning a more ecologically sustainable and socially just society, the anarchist ideas of William Morris (*News from Nowhere*), the futurist musings of Edward Bellamy's *Looking Forward* and, more recently, the bioregionalist extrapolations of Ernest Callenbach (*Ecotopia*) are possibly the most interesting and influential. There are also a large number of political dystopias, with Aldous Huxley's *Brave New World*, George Orwell's *1984* and Margaret Atwood's *The Handmaid's Tale* probably being the most famous. There are also a large number of green apocalyptic science fiction novels too, such as John Brunner's *Stand on Zanzibar*, Octavia Butler's *Parable of the Sower* and Geoff Ryman's *Child Garden*, that are becoming increasingly less like fiction and more like the world we inhabit, but it has been those panoramic visions of a future designed for clean, efficient living supported by speedy car travel, circular airports, eleven-lane highways and elevated walkways allowing more space for urban road vehicles, that until recently have been perceived by many as the true image of the future. General Motors's popular *Futurama* exhibit at the 1939 World's Fair in New York, devised by industrial and Hollywood set-designer Norman Bel Geddes, articulates the power of the corporate imagination. The social ecology of Murray Bookchin (*The Ecology of Freedom, From Urbanization to Cities*) is grounded in historical and social scientific analysis that looks to a different future. For Bookchin (1980), if utopian thinking has any power and significance at all, it is as a vision of a new society that brings into view all the pre-given assumptions of contemporary society while offering the opportunity to radically rethink new forms and values. It addresses qualitative changes to the way people live their lives and the deep-seated processes that govern our personal selves and relationships with nature. Utopias are, or must be, essentially libertarian, bioregional and ecological to warrant the name:

> We must 'phase out' our formless urban agglomerations into eco-communities that are scaled to human dimensions, sensitively tailored in size, population, needs and architecture to the specific ecosystems in which they are to be located. We must use modern technics to replace our factories, agribusiness enterprises and mines with new, human-scaled ecotechnologies that deploy sun, wind, streams, recycled wastes and vegetation to create a comprehensible people's technology. We must replace the state institutions based on professional violence with social institutions based on mutual aid and human solidarity.
>
> (Bookchin, 1980: 284–5)

In a wide-ranging discussion, de Geus (1999) identifies eight metaphors found in eco-utopian writing that facilitate the envisioning of a sustainable society:

- *Utopia as a kaleidoscope*: providing an array of philosophical reflections on the relationship between humanity and nature, the economy and ecology, consumer materialism and environmental degradation.
- *Utopia as coloured glasses*: providing alternative interpretative frameworks and reference points by which we can recognize processes that degrade the quality of living and environment.
- *Utopia as a mirror*: providing a mirror to society showing up injustices and short-comings that may have become invisible in the living of our day-to-day lives, such as increased consumption, road transport, bland design, draughty housing, air and water pollution.
- *Utopia as a CT-scan*: providing an analysis of how far social and environmental problems are rooted in the current organization and structure of society, political governance and the economy.
- *Utopia as an interactive medium*: providing stimulus to engage in debate and discussion about desirable futures, potential barriers and means by which an ideal may be realized.
- *Utopia as a microscope*: providing an opportunity to envisage how future scenarios could have consequences for the minutiae of social life, of conduct, of energy use and of forms of pro-environmental behaviour.
- *Utopia as a telescope*: providing a detailed, credible and broadly encompassing model of social, political and economic organization making for a clean and ecologically balanced society.
- *Utopia as a magic lantern*: providing vivid graphic and verbal images of possible futures.

For Pepper (2005), utopian thinking is not confined to radical environmentalism, but can also be readily found in the statements, theories, expectations and reformist policies of environmental modernizers. He suggests that practical ecological reforms usually associated with ecological modernization are frequently found in utopian writings if they are read carefully. Political scientist Ruth Levitas (2010: 540) argues that utopian thinking is therefore inherently practical and political because a 'utopia may be understood as the expression of the desire for a better way of being or of living'. Thus, the true value of utopias is in providing *transgressive* and *heuristic* spaces. To be of value, he writes, they 'must be rooted in existing social and economic relations rather than being merely a form of abstraction unrelated to the processes and situations operating in today's – real world' (Pepper, 2005: 18). If not, they would be nothing more than intellectual exercises – 'mere utopias of escape' (Mumford, 1966a: 390). On the other hand, in emphasizing the influence of the physical environment, whether it be built or natural, some utopian, and certainly nature, writing, such as the recent work of Richard Mabey (2006) and Roger Deakin (2007), is able to sharpen our capacity for individual and collective understanding and sensuous understanding (Buell, 2001).

Practical utopias: ecovillages

As Dawson (2006) shows in his Schumacher briefing on ecovillages, the history of alternative communities can be traced back to a small settlement, developed by Pythagoras, called Homakoeion in ancient Greece. Since then there have been many experiments that have endured for varying periods of time, differing in size and

---

Box 8.1 Carless living in Ecotopia's new towns

San Francisco, 7 May. Under the new regime, the established cities of Ecotopia have to some extent been broken up into neighbourhoods or communities, but they are still considered to be somewhat outside the ideal long-term line of development of Ecotopian living patterns. I have just had the opportunity to visit one of the strange new mini-cities that are arising to carry out the more extreme urban vision of this decentralized society. Once a sleepy village, it is called Alviso, and is located on the southern shores of the San Franciso Bay. You get there on the interurban train, which drops you off in the basement of a large complex of buildings. The main structure, it turns out, is not the city hall or courthouse, but a factory. It produces the electric traction units – they hardly qualify as cars or trucks in our terms – that are used for transporting people and goods in Ecotopian cities and for general transportation in the countryside. (Individually owned vehicles were prohibited in 'car-free' zones soon after independence. These zones at first covered only downtown areas where pollution and congestion were most severe. As minibus service was extended, these zones expanded, and now cover all densely settled city areas.)

Alviso streets are named, not numbered, and they are almost as narrow and winding as those of medieval cities – not easy for a stranger to get around in. They are hardly wide enough for two cars to pass; but then there *are* no cars, so that is no problem. Pedestrians and bicyclists meander along. Once in a while you see a delivery truck hauling a piece of furniture or some other large object, but the Ecotopians bring their groceries home in string bags or large bicycle baskets.

Source: Callenbach (1975: 24–5).

purpose. Some have been overtly political and intentionally prefigurative; others have been mainly meditative or mainly spiritual. Robert Gilman (1991), one of the main founders of the Global Ecovillage Network, suggests an ecovillage community must encompass the following:

- *Human-scale*: the upper population limit is about 500 persons, although many contemporary communities have 100 persons or less.
- *Full-featured settlement*: all major functions of normal living – residence, food provision, manufacture, leisure, social life and commerce – are present in a balanced proportion, making the ecovillage a microcosm of a future society.
- *Human activities harmlessly integrated into the natural world*: humans do not dominate nature but live within it alongside other creatures. Ecovillages adopt a cyclic use of material resources – for example, renewable energy, the composting of organic wastes and other strategies to minimize their ecological footprint.
- *A way that is supportive of healthy human development*: a balanced and integrated development of the physical, emotional, mental and spiritual elements of individual life and community living.
- *Able to be successfully continued into the indefinite future*: through the application of the sustainability principle and incorporating a commitment to fairness and non-exploitation of human and non-human persons and the natural world.

Gilman argues that we have the understanding, awareness, technological capacity and knowledge to live sustainably, for cities to be sustainable by being composed of a constellation of ecovillages and for these to last over time. To do so, putative eco-communities must have the capacity to successfully negotiate a number of challenges, including:

- *the biosystem challenge*: living in an ecologically sound manner;
- *the built environment challenge*: minimize transportation needs, always using environmentally friendly building materials, balance of private and public space, and so on;
- *the economic system challenge*: economically and ecologically efficient business enterprise, equitable forms of property ownership or common use, and so on;
- *the governance challenge*: decision-making processes, leadership roles, conflict resolution mechanisms, and so on;
- *the 'glue' challenge*: vision, internal and external social relationships, closeness and cohesion, and so on; and
- *the whole system challenge*: 'to get an honest sense of the scope of the undertaking and then develop an approach that allows the community to develop at a sustainable pace'.

Many ecovillages, alternative and/or intentional communities have evolved and developed. Rarely do they exist in a complete bubble isolated from the wider society, and in many cases community members do not want or intend them to. However, for many people living within these communities, a spiritual and ethical motivation dominates, which contests the materialism of contemporary culture and its abstraction from the natural environment. Ecovillages tend to reflect their cultural and ecological environment – some are extremely small, residing discretely and quietly in woods and forests (like Tinkers Bubble in Somerset, UK), being concerned predominantly with living simply with the smallest environmental impact possible (Fairlie, 1996), while others may be more fashionable, consciously modern settlements (and perhaps not strictly ecovillages) whose eco-values have been tempered by a market-orientated pragmatism, planning restrictions and desire to blend easily into the mainstream (Crystal Waters in Australia). Some sustainable community developments have been informed by innovative green architectural design (BedZed, London) and exemplary urban eco-planning and spatial development (Kronsberg, Germany). For Dawson, ecovillages mostly share five common features:

- the community is of primary importance;
- their origin as citizen initiatives;
- self-reliance;
- the sharing of a strong set of values; and
- they frequently act as centres of research, demonstration and training.

The Findhorn Community in the north of Scotland is one of the best-known ecovillages in the UK, if not the world. It has been established for over forty years, is spiritually based, with a profound commitment to living in harmony with the natural world, is largely democratic in organization and structure, and aims to be self-sufficient in food. Over the years it has been exceedingly enterprising in its approach to green building and design, developing external consultancy, fund raising and investment, and education and communication. In October 1998, Findhorn's Ecovillage Project was awarded a UN Habitat Best Practice citation and in 2006 an independent study concluded that the community had the smallest ecological footprint of any comparably sized settlement in the industrialized world (Tinsley and George, 2006). People who live in ecovillages, and intentional communities with an ecological ethos, usually fashion a holistic lifestyle, where the domestic situation becomes part of an overall project of social transformation, where residents live their beliefs, and where the communities provide safe places to experiment with different forms of living, behaving and acting. Many communities have open days or offer interested people the opportunity to join for a short while to see if they could live the life. In this way, ecovillages act as showcases for alternative and ecological living. Political values become infused in both the private/domestic and public spheres – shared living and working, organic permaculture production, communal decision-making, co-operative ownership, recycling, and so on. As Sargisson (2001: 88) notes:

> Intentional communities form part of individual change: this includes patterns of behaviour, processes of communication, the integration of personal spirituality, work and ecology, and, importantly, the opportunity to bring all of these changes into everyday life. Change, paradoxically, becomes part of daily routine. In some communities, such as those associated with the Findhorn Foundation, these changes are consciously desired and cultivated. In others this occurs subliminally as part of the background and as an effect of participation. Intentional communities are an ideal space in which to effect and sustain personal transformation through practice and practical experience as compared (or in addition) to intellectual engagement with proselytizing texts or ideology. They

lack dogma and seek rather to find better ways of living sustainably. The key, I suspect, is in the unselfconscious and unpretentious 'being' of ecological citizenry.

(2001: 88)

Other examples include Ecodyfi in west Wales, essentially a regeneration project inspired and emerging from the alternative community that is part of the Centre for Alternative Technology (CAT) just outside of Machynlleth. Specialist agencies, local government and community groups are engaged in a range of activities, in which CAT has developed considerable expertise – for example, community-based water, wind, solar and wood fuel schemes, and sustainable land management. The overall aim is to regenerate the Dyfi Valley in a sustainable fashion, building on its local attributes and engaging local people. Projects include horticulture, ecotourism, new green business start-ups, affordable housing and community amenity developments. The Dfyi Biosphere Area is the only accredited United Nations Educational, Scientific and Cultural Organization (UNESCO) biosphere reserve in Wales.

In southern India, the spiritual community of Auroville has the largest concentration of alternative and appropriate energy systems in the subcontinent, is self-sufficient in milk and produces half its fruit and vegetables, has reforested many acres, has an extensive seed bank, and works with other local communities in cataloguing medicinal plants. In 2003 Auroville won an Ashden Award for Sustainable Energy. The community also hosts the well-respected Centre for Scientific Research and a Graduate School for the Environment housed in a the splendid Wales Institute for for Sustainable Education running with its rammed earth constructed lecture theatre, wi fi and a range of externally accredited courses on sustainable architecture, energy and the environment.

Ecocity development: towards an ecopolis

Although a great deal of ecological and bioregionalist thought focuses on the small scale and the rural, the majority of the global population now lives in cities. If anything, the most important development in the twenty-first century will be to ensure that urban development is sustainable – environmentally, socially, economically and politically. In the second half of this century up to 70 per cent of the global population will reside in urban settlements. Sustainable urban design is extremely important, and the utopian, and increasingly the sustainable, city has captured the imagination of artists, architects, planners and urbanists of various descriptions. The twentieth century witnessed practical utopian schemes by major architect-planners – Ebenezer Howard (*Garden Cities of Tomorrow*), Lewis Mumford's and Clarence Stein's Radburn in New Jersey (USA), Le Corbusier's Radiant City, Frank Lloyd Wright's Broadacre and, more modestly, Usonia (Hall, 1996). From Paolo Soleri's 'urban laboratory', Arcosanti, in the Arizona Desert, to the Prince of Wales's retro-new urbanism of Poundbury in Dorset (UK), to the super-modernism of the massive ecocity developments in China, Masdar in Abu Dhabi, the integration of architecture, ecology and the planning of communities has seen no shortage of ideals and visions for those seeking alternative inspiration. However, it is important to make a distinction between the impractical and sometimes bizarre imaginings of some self-appointed prophets and visionaries and the more reasoned explorations of designers, architects, artists and planners who at their core have significant lessons to communicate. Thus, for Fishman (1982), Howard, Le Corbusier and Wright's utopianism represents coherent bodies of thought that transcend the immediate situation and whose realization would break the bonds and cultural restrictions imposed by conventional wisdom. Their utopian visions were the three-dimensional expressions of social philosophies advocating human peace, beauty and harmonious living with nature. For Howard, the emphasis was on healthy, co-operative and compact communities of no more than 30,000 people. His garden cities would relieve pressure on the big cities, combat urban alienation and reconnect people to the natural world. In the twenty-first century Philip Ross, a former mayor of Letchworth, one of the original garden cities, has revitalized interest in the garden city ideal. He argues that the garden city is not about architecture or new developments but community, where the measure of success is the happiness of the people who live within them and the harmonious and just balancing of town and country. In *21st Century Garden Cities of Tomorrow: a Manifesto*, Philip Ross and Yves Cabannes, Professor of Urban Planning, have identified twelve principles or doorways to creating a 'Garden City' which for Cabannes can include any town, city or neighbourhood (Ross and Cabannes, 2013). These principles include common ownership of the 'city', carbon neutral, urban agriculture, participatory budgeting, egalitarianism, participatory design and citizen rights for all. While Mayor of Letchworth, Ross developed and implemented many of his ideas and since then he has attracted growing interest from NGOs, think tanks and political parties in the UK, China and the US. As Pindar (2005) concludes in his *Visions of the City*, utopian visions of future cities should not be so easily dismissed as authoritarian and irrelevant distractions or fantasies, for it is possible to learn a great deal if we allow them to effectively challenge the conditions and contradictions of the present. A number of contemporary ecological visions, ecovillage experiments, design scenarios and actually existing developments continue to demonstrate how the future could work (Manzini and Jegou, 2003; Beatley, 2004; Downton, 2009; Girardet, 2010, 2012), and major international exhibitions such as 'Future city: Experiment and utopia and architecture 1956–2006' demonstrate the excitement as well as the need for continual exploration, conceptual creativity in project design that transcends disciplinary boundaries (Alison *et al.*, 2006).

American architect Frank Lloyd Wright conceived of human settlements where each domestic unit or homestead would have plots of between one and five acres, with at least one acre for tillage. He rejected the big city, finance capital and landlordism. His Broadacre City was an attempt to realize in imagination and practice the reconnection of people with the land by merging town and country. He advocated a form of living influenced by the *transcendentalism* of Whitman, Emerson and Thoreau, with a Jeffersonian notion of democracy. He believed in a trenchant individualism, currently evading people in the densely inhabited and polluted cities like that 'fibrous tumour' he called New York. Modern communications, particularly the automobile and telephones, would make the Broadacre concept possible, overcoming limitations of space and place. For Wright (1958), new building materials and techniques made the verticality of the city 'unscientific' and unnecessary. However, his 'Usonian' vision, powerful in itself, was realized in another form that would not have won his wholehearted approval, even though Wright was one of the first architects to design houses with integral garage space – a post-war suburban sprawl, a numbing automobile culture that arguably inhibits the development of community social relationships, degrading the natural environment with tract housing, billboards,

strip malls, and so on. As Lewis Mumford (1966b: 564) lamented, the suburb represented a childish view of the world, serving largely 'as an asylum for the preservation
of an illusion. Here, domesticity could flourish, forgetful of the exploitation on which
so much of it was based', undermined by a social and psychological emptiness.

Another twentieth-century architect whose utopian vision misfired was Le
Corbusier, whose Contemporary City and Radiant City seem to be a high point of
modernism, emphasizing clean lines, high densities and efficient living – a synthesis
of collective order and individual freedom, geometry and nature. For Le Corbusier,
homes, or cells, were machines for living in, and, although he too felt the car was
a liberator, he took no account of garaging or the effects of pollution. Nevertheless,
Le Corbusier was drawn to what he considered to be organic and biological designs,
although his schemes, reflecting the era of assumed fossil fuel abundance, were far
from being environmentally sustainable. Jencks writes:

> His general scheme for the Radiant City develops on the biological analogy with
> the business centre as the head, housing and institutes as the spine, and factories,
> warehouses and heavy industry as the belly. The biological analogy leads of
> course to the separation of functions, or 'organs'. Le Corbusier makes this his
> keynote. A plan arranges organs in order, thus creating an organism or organisms.
> Biology! The great new word in architecture and planning.
>
> (1987: 123)

Although very different from Wright's vision, and sometimes associated with
dehumanizing urbanism, some city planners, particularly in Japan and China, are
relatively comfortable with marrying neo-Corbusian solutions to the very pressing
problems of urban growth and development. However, Le Corbusier's and Wright's
visions offer both negative and positive lessons about utopian thinking, planning for
the future and sustainability. Both contrast significantly with the eco-anarchist
communities advocated by Bookchin and Callenbach, the ecological architecture and
building at Findhorn, and the grader schemes of ecological master planners and
architects.

For Australian ecoarchitect Paul Downton (2009: 21) an ecocity is a city that
recognizes itself as being part of the overall biosphere and one that 'generates health
and dynamic ecological stability'. Designing and developing an ecocity involves
ensuring that the biophysical environmental processes of a region are sustained
through active and sensitive management by citizens who seek to fit their activities
within the constraints and limitations of the biosphere while building environments
that support and nurture human culture. In other words, an ecopolis is about process
– always a work in progress, always working in co-operation rather than in conflict
with nature, always promoting a design for living that maintains cycles off water,
nutrients, atmosphere biology in health and in balance. It also encompasses social
equity, empowerment, participation and democracy. Inevitably, developing an ecopolis
and a sustainable way of living and working will entail major cultural and political
changes of which access, mobility and transportation are of key importance. For
many people private cars are essential to contemporary living, to social status,
economic progress and even to a sense of political freedom. In the year 2012–13,
3.23 million passenger vehicles were produced in India and production is expected
to grow at a rate of 13 per cent during 2012–21 according to the Automotive

Component Manufacturers Association of India (ACMA). The percentage of luxury cars in the Indian car market is expected to increase to 4 per cent by 2020 (IBEF, 2013). According to BP's *Energy Outlook 2030* (BP, 2012), the global fleet of commercial and passenger vehicles will grow by 60 per cent from 1 billion in 2012 to 1.6 billion in 2030, with most of the growth occurring in non-OECD countries. It is anticipated that vehicle density per 1,000 population will grow from around 50 to 140 in China (5.7 per cent growth per annum) and in India from 20 to 65 (6.7 per cent, per annum).

Around one million people die on the roads globally each year, the car is an immense consumer of resources, including metal, rubber, land and oil, and although the car is a symbol of freedom, progress and modernity in both the developed and developing worlds, its effects on our quality of life are frequently negative – gridlock, personal frustration, atmospheric pollution, expense, and so on. Although there has been considerable research on fuel-efficient cars, the hypercar, the hybrid car and increasing commercial development of such hybrids as the Toyota Prius and, more recently, the electric car, the car remains both a problem and a major attraction. As Kingsley Dennis and John Urry write (2009: 64), 'a post car system will need to be at least as effective as the current car at meeting people's economic, aesthetic, emotional, sensory and sociability requirements. This is a tall order'. This has not deterred the likes of J.H. Crawford (2000) who has analysed the possibilities of car-free cities, or rather cities where priority is afforded to other means of transportation, and has sketched out the urban design requirements, public transit alternatives and so on, that would facilitate the practical utopia of such an environment emerging. In 1994, the city of Amsterdam organized the 'Car-free cities?' conference, the result of which was the formation of the Car-Free Cities Club to promote policies that discourage private car use. As Crawford (2000: 33) suggests, 'car-free cities can offer rich human experience, great beauty and true peace. . . . Car-free cities are a practical alternative, available now. They can be built using existing technology at a price we can afford'. The Vauban district of the city of Freiburg in Germany is a primarily car-free eco neighbourhood development, that could be a model for future developments elsewhere.

Cities like Copenhagen, Denmark and Portland in Oregon, US, are developing a clean economy of place. Portland has an efficient public transport system and has encouraged its green business and construction sector with a system of green investment grants. In Copenhagen 36 per cent of all commutes to work or to school are by bicycle and 32 per cent of Copenhagen's citizens walk or use the public bus or train systems. Cycling improves health and reduces the city healthcare bill by as much as £236 million per year. The city's environmental business sector grew by 77 per cent between 2004 and 2009. As the European Green Capital of 2014, following Stockholm in 2010, Hamburg in 2011, Vitoria-Gaseiz in 2013, Copenhagen aims to be carbon neutral by 2025. The city has nurtured public support for wind turbines by encouraging community ownership, sophisticated technological innovation and the development of local green skills and green jobs. By 2025 it is anticipated that 50 per cent of the city's energy will come from wind and when its current population of just over 534,000 will be over 600,000. A key issue that needed resolution was improving the ability of the power grid to accept and balance increased levels of intermittent energy from wind turbines, but this has now been achieved. Following initial investment, wind turbines have low running costs and collectively the Danish wind-turbine industry is a multibillion euro industry, with more than 350 companies producing turbine towers and blades, gear-boxes, generators and control systems (City of Copenhagen, 2012). Most importantly, the city's people have orientated themselves to sustainable change and their democratic values have given the city a reputation for being socially inclusive. In recent years there has been a shift from managerialism to entrepreneurialism that, in addition to public and private partnerships, has also seen the re-emergence of a democratic and communicative planning discourse on public participation in the planning processes. However, participation is not always particularly high, invariably due to lack of time and interest on the part of citizens as well as official attempts to diffuse antagonism, the stuff of democratic debate, through seeking permanent consensus and rational solutions (Ploger, 2004). Nevertheless, the global design and lifestyle magazine *Monocle* named Copenhagen as the 'Most Livable City' and 'Best Quality of Life for 2013' in its global quality of life survey.

Urban development in China is proceeding at an unprecedented rate. There are more than 170 cities in China with more than one million people, and in recent years construction firms have built more than two billion square metres of apartments, offices and skyscrapers. New infrastructure development consumes a considerable amount of steel, aluminum, cement and energy. However, as David Biello (2012) writes,

> The Chinese government and various organizations are beginning to come to grips with the challenge, however. The central government has eliminated real estate as a priority industry in the latest Five Year Plan in a bid to restrain this unsustainable growth. It has also begun to consider mandated efficiency measures for new construction. China's central government hopes ultimately to build an "ecological civilization" via a "circular economy" of recycling and sustainability. Tianjin Eco-City, scheduled to be completed by 2018, exemplifies many of the proposed attributes: minimal waste, wise water use, and power generated mainly from renewable sources such as the sun, wind, and geothermal wells.

Case study: Curitiba (Brazil)

Curitiba is the seventh largest city in Brazil with a population of 1.8 million people and with a global reputation for being one of the most successful eco-cities in the world thanks to the efforts of former mayor Jaime Lerner and his colleagues. Over a forty-year period dating back to the early 1970s when Brazil was ruled by a military dictatorship, Lerner and a relatively small group of planners, architects and business people have transformed the city. Using essentially technocratic and somewhat autocratic methods that have ignored the democratic participation processes that occur in Europe and North America, Curitiba has become an award-winning icon of urban sustainability and Lerner himself a much sought after lecturer on the global conference circuit. Advocates of 'natural capitalism' such as Bill McKibben (1995), Paul Hawken *et al.* (1999) and the ICLEI (2002) have been ardent admirers of the entrepreneurialism and sustainability achievements of the city technocrats. In getting the job done, Lerner and his colleagues have, according to observers (Moore, 2007; Macedo, 2004, 2013), implemented five innovative strategies:

- the creation of new green space through rezoning, property condemnation and public works projects;
- the implementation of structural axes to facilitate the flow of traffic and create access to decentralized mixed use centres along these axes of development such as sports and recreational centres, commercial outlets and lifelong learning 'lighthouses', including libraries and public Internet facilities;
- the introduction of an Integrated Transportation Network using speedy bi-articulated buses and iconic tubular bus shelters and a clearly designated route managed by a public–private company. Car traffic has declined markedly and atmospheric pollution is lower than in all the other major Brazilian cities. Transportation access has been a major plank in the city's employment and economic development programmes.
- the design and development of the Cicdade Industrial de Curitiba in the south-western part of the city which, thanks to attractive financial incentives, from the mid 1970s on attracted a considerable amount of industrial relocation;
- the implementation of small-scale incremental quick-return projects projects, most famously the pedestrianization of Rua das Flores over the course of one weekend, thanks to the help of armed police and the employment of vagrants to keep the new mall clean. Other projects have included 'cohab' infill housing and decentralized medical care through the creation of six outpatient clinics open twenty four hours a day.

Lerner has articulated a form of whole systems thinking that is far from being apolitical. For Moore, Curitaba's regime of sustainability has been based on a clientlist system that has often been occluded by the effective marketing and publicity strategies the city has initiated. Unlike Porto Alegre, Curitiba has not garnered a reputation of citizen democracy, participatory budgeting or socio-economic equality though efficiency is something that does stand out, although for Macedo this has been at the expense of the wider city region:

> Curitiba has always been planned as if it were an 'island', which contributed to endemic problems in the other municipalities of the metropolitan region. A regional approach to planning is long overdue. As long as Curitiba is surrounded by poverty, it cannot be held as a model of successful planning nor called a 'social capital'. Until there are no families settling in riparian areas within the water supply watersheds of metropolitan Curitiba, it cannot be dubbed 'the ecological capital.'
>
> (2004: 548)

Although elements of the Curitiba experience, such as the articulation of a strong set of core values, integrated planning processes, the creation of an independent municipal planning authority and the establishment of a close relation between transport planning and land use legislation are probably replicable elsewhere, the context and the culture in which this occurred are perhaps not. For North American commentators such as Robert Brulle (2000), environmental problems are social problems requiring social learning and democracy rather than an enlightened despotism; for Joseli Macedo, 'the institutional and political structures that made it possible for Curitiba to become a symbol of sustainable planning are not easily replicable' (2013: 17). At a particular historical moment a group of talented, creative and innovative technocrats and professionals came together and remained together for a considerable time, implementing changes that were largely unchallenged because they did not have to contend with the unpredictable vagaries of democratic participation. Sustainability takes time and Lerner had this time. Ingenious marketing, city branding and by consistent political campaign, promises have helped create a collective urban imaginary among Curitiba's citizens which has clearly informed the city's success.

Environmental design and the sustainable community

Environmental design seeks to create spaces that will enhance the natural, social, cultural and physical environment. The relationship of people to place, their identification with specific neighbourhoods, and their use of particular spaces for social, political and cultural activities may be influenced by design and may be renewed through environmentally sensitive planning processes. Designers must understand social psychology, human behaviour and ecology. Café society, culturally vibrant street life, pedestrianized shopping precincts, crime prevention and community safety through natural surveillance, the construction of children's play areas, accessible street furniture and resting places for the elderly and infirm, and open public spaces that support the practice of social and political democracy are all aspects of good environmental design, as they promote and support social sustainability. Environmental design is therefore about helping to fashion human experience through a created physical space. Many see the high-density compact city as a solution to many environmental problems, combating suburban sprawl by building at higher densities, encouraging walking, cycling and social interaction, and discouraging car use, aided by congestion charging, fewer parking facilities and the provision of reliable public transport systems, particularly light rail and trams (Jenks *et al.*, 1996; Williams *et al.*, 2000).

Architects and engineers may exploit solar and wind power, choose environmentally sound building materials, recycle old brick and concrete as aggregate, install double or triple glazing, insulate effectively, use natural ventilation to provide thermal comfort and healthy air circulation, design roof gardens or even turf roofs, allow for the recycling of grey water, minimize noise pollution through effective sound absorption, and be open to unconventional built forms. However, without co-operation between architects, engineers and planners, a great deal of environmental design will never be seen. In many parts of Europe, wood has become the sustainable building material of choice, this going far beyond the visible tokenism of external cladding. As a result, craft traditions have been revived, with carpentry enjoying renewed popularity. Computer technology, including computer-aided design, combined with glue-laminated timber technology, has enhanced the possibilities of timber engineering and construction, with many keynote designs consciously emulating natural forms, as with 'the core' at the Eden Project in Cornwall. So long as forest sources are managed sustainably, the fit between wood construction and sustainable development is near perfect. In energy terms, timber uses 190kWh per cubic metre compared with 8,500kWh for steel and 11,000kWh for plastics (Lowenstein and Bridgood, 2007). The 'passive houses' developed in Sweden, Denmark and Germany are designed to need no active heating – they can be kept warm 'passively' using internal heat sources such as the inhabitants, solar energy admitted by the windows, and by heating the supply of fresh air. The first prototype passive houses were built in Kranichstein in the city of Darmstadt in 1991, with the emphasis on thermal insulation and heat recovery ventilation. Since then, design improvements have been made, and by 2006 over 6,000 of these very comfortable, ecologically sound and warm houses had been built in Germany alone. As Lockward (2006: 130) writes in the *Harvard Business Review*, building green is 'no longer a pricey experiment'. It is now the sensible option for businesses and communities. Environmental design and construction may also aim to reduce greenhouse gas emissions through energy-efficient buildings, combined heat and power systems, water recycling and waste minimization. Large household gardens, trees and turf roofs all reduce high temperatures as well as increasing the potential for domestic food production and composting. Parks and gardens, the city's 'urban lungs', provide healthy recreational areas. The acquisition of land for nature reserves, town trails, community gardens, urban farms, allotments, widespread tree planting and urban agriculture (a tool for transforming urban organic wastes into food and jobs, improving public health and land, and saving water and other natural resources) offers ways in which urban dwellers can build mutually supportive social relationships and reconnect to the larger ecosystems.

Urban environments have hitherto been shaped by economic rather than social and environmental goals. Hough (1995), McLennan (2004) and Low *et al.* (2005) argue that designers must ensure that urban developments positively influence the environments they change. Stefanovic (2000) remarks that the ways in which we spatially and operationally structure and construct our human settlements, inform how we envision social and community relationships and our relationships with the natural world. Architecture can help us articulate and find our place in the world. And being rooted in a place provides a sense of belonging, nurtures an ethic of care, and perhaps promotes a more efficient and ecologically meaningful use of resources than would a more mobile and transient habitation. Natural processes need to become incorporated into human activities through the creation of multifunctional, productive and working spaces that integrate people, economic activity and the environment, and where design is more intimately connected to the changing nature of our climate. For Low *et al.*, the key to good green urban design is the ability to bring people back into contact with nature, whether it is in the home, work environment or local neighbourhood. It is important to make transparent the processes by which nature is turned into the goods and services we use for our convenience, our lifestyle and our homes, and there are general green design principles that can, and should, be applied to the construction, maintenance or refitting of our homes, apartments and housing developments. These include:

- design for local climate;
- orientating the house so the main windows face the sun (north in the southern hemisphere and south in the northern hemisphere);
- optimizing the use of thermal mass; providing good insulation;
- design for good ventilation, minimizing leakage of heat and air;
- good water management;
- using localized energy systems with the national grid as back-up; and
- aiming at zero greenhouse gas emission for everyday use of the dwelling.

(Low *et al.*, 2005: 53)

Green housing developments should:

- minimize the use of resources – atmosphere, water, land and rare or toxic materials;
- be responsive to local environment, make open space useful and accommodate for the lives of non-human others;
- minimize the need for travel, maximizing low-energy modes of transportation – for example, bicycles, walking and public transport;
- keep space public and as far as possible occupied and socially inclusive;
- design for public safety, with walkways open to view; and
- be affordable, with sufficient dwellings available for those with special needs.

(Low *et al.*, 2005: 70)

Hugh Barton (2000: 89–90) argues that places, neighbourhoods, are best conceived as open ecosystems, if sustainable living environments are to be achieved and maintained, and a community's ecological footprint reduced without compromising choice and opportunity.

The inventor and designer Stewart Brand (1997) has written on 'low-road' buildings and spaces that people make their own – where they feel free and in fact are free 'to do their own thing'. These spaces become places of personal significance because of the freedom and psychological warmth they offer as a result of their customization. Low-road space can become part of the self. Similarly, the anarchist writer Colin Ward (2002) has written warmly of individuals and movements of people who also occupy space to build or construct their own places of leisure and respite away from or in opposition to planning regulations, social conventions, political and economic power, and mainstream cultural expectations. In many ways, squatter settlements make homes and place out of necessity; but then, isn't necessity the mother of invention and cannot the converted garage be a place of immense creativity because of the freedom it affords? Some alternative communities such as Christiana in Copenhagen can be interpreted as urban laboratories, testing and demonstrating new ideas, values and social structures. In November 2006 Christiania's collaboratively designed *Green Plan* was awarded the Initiative Award of the Society for the Beautification of Copenhagen. It received positive endorsement from the Local Agenda 21 Society because of its sustainable goals and democratic, participatory design process and although alternatives themselves may not necessarily be superior to existing structures and institutions, '*the process of constructing an alternative* in itself provides a critical benchmark against which to reflect on taken for granted mainstream assumptions' (Jarvis, 2011: 159).

Self-build more generally has been an important part of many people's desire to create their own space, often articulated with ecological principles, aims and values. However, self-build has its own issues and problems, not least with the need for self-builders to have the requisite time, skills, finances, and understanding of building techniques, building regulations and planning processes. Nevertheless, creating one's own space is something that all animals need to do. It is what we call home, and feeling at home in a space or place is surely the key to caring for it and feeling one belongs to it. As geographer Yi-Fu Tuan (1977) writes, home is a place that offers security, familiarity and nurture, and can take many forms. Architect and teacher

Samuel Mockbee once said that 'everybody wants the same thing, rich or poor – not only a warm, dry room, but a shelter for the soul'. Working at the College of Architecture at Auburn University in Alabama, Mockbee established the Rural Studio in the 1990s for his students to gain real-world experience of architectural and building projects. Unlike many architectural education programmes, Mockbee's aim was to work constructively with the rural, usually black, poor, providing them with decent, well-designed, beautiful and innovative homes and community buildings at low cost. Much of the work is in Hale County, made famous in the 1930s by the documentary photographs of Walker Evans and James Agee's book *Let Us Now Praise Famous Men*. Materials are often recycled or reused, his students' designs are sympathetic to the local environment and vernacular style but totally fashioned to meet their client's needs, whose views and practical requirements fully inform the students' learning and evolving architectural knowledge. As Mockbee said, the community is the students' classroom and frequently their first intimate experience with 'the smell and feel of poverty' (Dean and Hursely, 2002: 3). Aesthetics and ethics, honesty and spirituality, combine in a pedagogy and practice that demonstrate to usually middle-class students that they, and their chosen profession, can make a genuine difference for the good.

Box 8.2 Transitioning from green to regenerative design

Understanding and engaging with 'place' permeates the whole regenerative design paradigm. The framing of the discussion of building design as inseparable from place carries the implication that it is equally, if not more important, to understand how building design, construction and use positively influence the social, ecological and economic health of the places they exist within. This is clearly different from green building practice that focuses on the performance of the building as a separate entity.

Regenerative design prioritizes the understanding and engagement in the unique qualities of place and continues the bioregionalist commitment to developing communities integrated with their surrounding ecosystems. What distinguishes bioregionalism from other movements and theories is its firm base in the right of a group to self-determination and decision-making.

The development of design frameworks and tools must spur innovative design solutions as a priority for architectural design practitioners. Apart from the building of capability, there are three potential implications emerging from shifting from green to regenerative design:

1   Re-establishing regional design practices to accommodate the richness of architectural diversity, vernacular practices and regionally specific solutions.
2   Establishing common ground with diverse stakeholders, through creating an expansive social dialogue as central to the design process.
3   Changing responsibilities and skills of designers in order to gain familiarity with a host of environmental strategies that blur professional boundaries positioning them within a whole system setting.

Source: adapted from Cole, 2012.

Applying the Hanover Principles at Kronsberg

A development of another sort is that of the city district of Kronsberg, south-east of Hanover in Germany. This area has been recognized by the European Union as a model of ecological optimization and human-scale development. In 1992 the City of Hanover had commissioned William McDonough and Michael Braungart (1992) to devise a comprehensive set of sustainability principles (the Hanover Principles) for urban designers, planners and architects that would inform the international design competitions for the EXPO 2000, whose themes were to be humankind, nature and technology. Kronsberg was a World Exposition exhibit in 2000. The plan allows for 6,000 homes, 15,000 people and more than 3,000 jobs. Ecological objectives had overriding priority in planning and construction, and no single developer was given ultimate authority. In fact, thirty developers were involved in the building of the residential area, and this necessitated close consultation and co-operation with the local authority to ensure that high standards of soil, water and waste management, energy provision and natural resource conservation were attained. Residential dwellings were required to emit 60 per cent less CO_2 than conventional housing units, this being achieved by a combination of solar, wind turbine and super-insulation projects. All rainfall on built-up and paved areas is absorbed, collected and gradually released, making for efficient water management. Ponds and other open spaces make water a design feature of the development that is constantly in the public eye. Waste separation and garden composting schemes address waste-management issues, and excavated soil from the development has been reused to establish local biotopes, to raise two hills that act as a noise buffer against a nearby motorway and to seal a local landfill site. Public transit and high residential densities, but with open green spaces and varied architecture, also figure prominently. The City of Hanover has since published *The Hanover Kronsberg Handbook* (Rumming, 2004) as part of the European Union's SIBART ('Seeing Is Believing As a Replication Tool') project, which, aimed at planners, developers and investors, addresses all aspects of the design, planning and construction of this exemplary sustainable urban district.

The Hanover Principles have formed the basis of other similar declarations throughout the world, including The Shenzhen Declaration on EcoCity Development in 2002. As the world's urban population increases, as economic development and foreign direct investment fuel urban growth in China (Zhang, 2002) and other parts of Asia, and as the relatively new phenomena of mega-cities of 10 million or more people become more common, environmental and social problems, ranging from air pollution to drug-related crime and unemployment, are likely to increase (Fuchs *et al.*, 1994; Davis, 2006). In 2000 there were 18 mega-cities, but by 2025 Asia alone could have 10 'hyper-cities' with populations in excess of 20 million, including Jakata, Dhaka, Karachi, Mumbai and Shanghai. By 2004, 183 of China's 661 cities had plans to become 'internationalized' cosmopolitan metropolises like New York, Paris or Tokyo, and by 2020, the Chinese urban population will be in the region of 900 million (Li, 2006). By 2050, 6 billion out of an estimated 9 billion global population will be urban dwellers, 80 per cent of whom will be living in the developing world. As researchers on sustainable mega-cities at Bauhaus-Universität Weimer in Germany have noted, steering such urbanization 'is a central challenge in the pursuit of the goal of global sustainable development' (Bauhaus-Universität Weimar, 2004: 4). As Janice E. Perlman (2000), founder of the Mega-Cities Project, clearly states:

No precedent exists for feeding, sheltering, employing or transporting so many people. No precedent exists for protecting the environment from the pollution and resource consumption required by such multitudes. Urban regions, entire countries and ultimately the entire Earth could be affected by cities improperly managed.

Within cities, poor citizens face the worst environmental consequences. In low-income settlements, services such as water, sewage, drainage and garbage collection are often non-existent. Lacking the resources to purchase or rent housing, between one-third and two-thirds of urbanites in developing countries become squatters on dangerously steep hillsides, flood-prone riverbanks and other undesirable lands.

The solution does not lie in simply scaling up solutions that work in small urban regions or directly transferring technologies from mega-cities in the developed world, but rather in creatively devising new solutions, urban management practices and modes of governance based on sound sustainability principles. Thus, as Haughton (1999) states, the fates of cities are intimately tied to the fates of their broader hinterlands, and with global economic trading, global exchanges of environmental resources and wastes, it will not be possible, or desirable, to create a sustainable city in total isolation from the rest of the planet. Satterthwaite (1997) discusses how the environmental costs of consumers in many growing cities are increasingly being transferred across national boundaries or into the future, although 'the scale and severity of environmental problems in cities reflect the failure of governments' (Hardoy *et al.*, 2001: 7). The sustainable city model which Haughton prefers is one that combines bioregional self-reliance with the values of environmental justice or 'fair shares', where basically environmental assets should be traded between cities and regions on the understanding that any damage or degradation should be adequately repaired or compensated.

In praise of cities

In a short article entitled 'Environmental heresies', the futurist Stewart Brand writes that environmentalists need to rethink many of their ideas. Brand (2005) writes that environmentalists tend to overvalue the rural ideal and despise cities even though life in many rural locations is far from idyllic, particularly for the poor. Hardoy *et al.* (2001) also argue that cities offer many potential opportunities for promoting sustainable development, not least through economies of scale and proximity of infrastructure and services, water reuse and recycling, reduced heating and motor vehicle use, the funding of environmental management, and the establishment of good governance, participation and democracy. Following Hurricane Sandy, which hit the east coast of the US in 2012, a number of high-profile American urban planners and politicians started to talk more enthusiastically about how cities could be at the forefront of dealing with the impacts of climate change. As David Biello (2013) wrote in *Scientific American*, cities are responsible for about 70 per cent of global greenhouse gas emissions and about 75 per cent of this is under the direct control of city governments adopting measures that reduce the energy costs of sanitation, constructing buildings that are energy efficient, developing green municipal power stations and acquiring private land necessary to build light rail lines which

Box 8.3 The Hanover Principles

1   *Insist on the rights of humanity and nature to coexist* in a healthy, supportive, diverse and sustainable condition.
2   *Recognize interdependence*: The elements of human design interact with and depend upon the natural world, with broad and diverse implications at every scale. Expand design considerations to recognize even distant effects.
3   *Respect relationships between spirit and matter*: Consider all aspects of human settlement, including community, dwelling, industry and trade, in terms of existing and evolving connections between spiritual and material consciousness.
4   *Accept responsibility for the consequences of design decisions* upon human well-being, the viability of natural systems and their right to coexist.
5   *Create safe objects of long-term value*: Do not burden future generations with requirements for maintenance or vigilant administration of potential danger due to the careless creation of products, processes or standards.
6   *Eliminate the concept of waste*: Evaluate and optimize the full life-cycle of products and processes, to approach the state of natural systems, in which there is no waste.
7   *Rely on natural energy flows*: Human designs should, like the living world, derive their creative forces from perpetual solar income. Incorporate this energy efficiently and safely for responsible use.
8   *Understand the limitations of design*: No human creation lasts forever and design does not solve all problems. Those who create and plan should practice humility in the face of nature. Treat nature as a model and mentor, not as an inconvenience to be evaded or controlled.
9   *Seek constant improvement by the sharing of knowledge*: Encourage direct and open communication between colleagues, patrons, manufacturers and users to link long-term sustainable considerations with ethical responsibility and re-establish the integral relationship between natural processes and human activity.

The Hanover Principles should be seen as a living document committed to the transformation and growth in the understanding of our interdependence with nature, so that they may adapt as our knowledge of the world evolves.

Source: McDonough and Braungart (1992: 6).

would take people out of their cars. China is currently building 40 different metrolines in 40 different cities, each one covering around 1,000 kilometres, but many of its new houses are poorly constructed using poor quality materials. Many cities, particularly in the developing world, offer the poor few opportunities for work, housing and education, although, as can be seen in Jeremy Seabrook's *In the Cities of the South* (1996), Richard Neuwirth's *Shadow Cities* (2006) and Mike Davis's *Planet of Slums* (2006), even in the slums and shanties there is sometimes a sense of community solidarity not present elsewhere, which can be enhanced by innovative government schemes, as operating in Thailand, Nicaragua and Mexico, and more community-driven projects operating in India, South Africa and Brazil. These initiatives strive to reduce urban poverty and degradation through empowering the 'squatter citizen' (Mitlin and Satterthwaite, 2004). For many people, urban areas in the developing and developed world signify hope and possibility, making the need to ensure these urban environments are socially and environmentally sustainable all the more imperative. Thus, despite the many problems associated with the contemporary urban environment – pollution, alienation, overcrowding, violence, and so on – Amin (2006a) argues that at the centre of the good city must be 'four registers of solidarity' which are feasible, desirable and necessary:

1   *Repair*: The trans-human material culture of telecommunications, water, transport, social ritual, software systems, and so on that prevents cities from collapsing under the strain of horrifying events like terrorist attacks on the underground.
2   *Relatedness*: Welfare, healthcare, public service activities, ethical tolerance and other measures like returning a city's public spaces to public use have the capacity to deal with alienation, inequality and disaffection.
3   *Rights*: Through participation, the right and entitlement of all citizens to shape urban life and to benefit from it – civil liberty, community planning, local political engagement, and a fair and equitable representation of all social and ethic groups.
4   *Re-enchantment*: The celebration of urban life through good design, good services, adequate housing, clean environment, public art, enjoyable leisure amenities and meeting places, and an urban life not predominantly based on a consumerist ethos.

Civic politics can facilitate urban living, thicken democratic processes, support social relationships, celebrate difference and diversity, and so restore a sense of hopefulness to cities. For Amin, a civic ethic of care based on a politics of recognition is needed far more than any attempt to foster a community of communities or joined-up urban governance. Herbert Girardet has been an advocate of sustainable urban living for decades and differs a little from Amin. His work with the UN's HABITAT Human Settlements Programme clearly outlines the key dimension of urban sustainability in a series of highly detailed and substantial reports on global urbanization, the challenges and problems relating to the growth of slums, and urban safety and security. It also addresses the ecological loops and flows of urban consumption, waste minimization and recycling, organic composting, resource use and budgeting, energy conservation and efficiency, renewable energy technology, economic expansion, green architecture and planning, durable construction, good public transport systems, local supply of staple foodstuffs, good quality housing, and proximity of work to home, which all help improve the quality of urban life by staying within ecological limits. Girardet (1996) writes that contemporary cities need to conceptualize their relationship to the rest of the world, and that for this to be realized new forms of governance and organization will have to develop. Joined-up, or holistic, city government, with each department working to an environmental brief, is required. Cities need to be multi-centred and their built inheritance needs to be reused, renovated and rearticulated. They need to become places people want to be proud of – an end and not simply a means. Giddings *et al.*'s contribution to Jenks and Dempsey's excellent *Future Forms and Design for Sustainable Cities* (2005) emphasizes the need for the city economy to be inextricably linked to the livelihoods of its inhabitants, to be essentially local and ecologically sensitive to their region, thus enabling both urban and rural environments to re-establish their own distinct identities and purpose. City regions need to be diverse, vibrant and organic:

> While getting food, energy and water from their surroundings, they in turn provide other vital components of sustainability, including health services, festivals, education and manufactured goods. Often the best way to strengthen the centre of cities is to support the existing local people, business, activities and culture. They enhance the quality of the environment without gentrification, encourage walking, and support public places and buildings and design for people.
>
> (Giddings *et al.*, 2005: 26)

William J. Mitchell, author of *City of Bits* (1996), *E-topia* (2000) and *Me++* (2003), sees tremendous potential in the application of emerging media technologies to urban public and private spheres. He is not alone in developing the notion of 'the intelligent city', defined simply as an urban environment incorporating a degree of digital infrastructure responding autonomously to a range of stimuli (Briggs, 2005). Cities and the buildings in them can be 'smart', although the digital infrastructure is just one element in a city's physical fabric, its 'hardware'. What really animates the city is the social and cultural interactions, its politics and sociality, its economic and commercial transactions, and so on. Consequently, Briggs argues that the broader understanding of the intelligent city allows us to see the city holistically and therefore sustainably. City intelligence will assess the capability to adapt to an array of pressures and impacts – global trade, technological developments, new skill and knowledge requirements, investment flows and climate change – while maintaining the quality of life and work and without negatively affecting the wider environment. Mitchell sees the developing digital infrastructure as affecting public policy, planning and politics, suggesting that intra-urban digital networking potentially offers a contemporary version of the agora, revitalizing democratic debate and participation. Online communities could complement physical ones, stimulating new social relationships, entrepreneurial and employment opportunities, economic markets, and informational connections. Rural telecommunications infrastructure could deliver numerous educational, health and business services. The disturbing divisions between rural and urban living may gradually fade. Virtualization and miniaturization could alter our sense and use of space. Digital sensors will help us monitor our consumption of renewable and non-renewable resources. An electronically managed vehicle rental and distribution service could lead to the rejection of the two- or three-car household by creating highly efficient information, booking and tracking systems. Work could become more flexible, more mobile and connected. Living and working spaces may no longer require separate zoning, with leisure, learning, living and working spaces being more intricately interwoven than before.

Transition towns: powering down

Starting with a group of further education college students in Kinsale, south-west Ireland, permaculture teacher Rob Hopkins initiated the 'transition town' movement in 2005. The aim is that any locality – a village, town, city or district – can reduce its consumption of fossil fuels. The transition town movement is above all about articulating an ethical but practical vision that local inhabitants can support, develop and identify with. As Hopkins (2005) writes:

> The continual decline in the net energy supporting humanity [is] a decline which mirrors the ascent in net energy that has taken place since the Industrial Revolution. It also refers to a future scenario in which humanity has successfully adapted to the declining net fossil fuel energy availability and has become more localized and self-reliant. It is a term favoured by people looking towards peak energy as an opportunity for positive change rather than an inevitable disaster.

The idea was provoked by the notion of 'peak oil' and the work of Richard Heinberg, particularly *Powerdown* (2004), and inspired by the social and economic changes that have taken place in Cuba since 1991, following the drastic reduction in its oil supplies, food and trade economy following the fall of the Soviet Union (Quinn, 2006). Limited petrol supplies have transformed Cuban agriculture, with much food now grown in urban neighbourhoods, and permaculture design principles applied widely. Small-scale renewable energy and energy-saving mass transit systems have been developed. Educational and healthcare provision has been localized. The Cuban national slogan is now 'A Better World is Possible', replacing 'Socialism or Death'. The first decade of the twenty-first century will probably see the maximum extraction of oil from the Earth, after which oil supplies will steadily diminish while the need for processing will increase as the oil extracted decreases in quality. It is therefore imperative for all communities to develop alternative energy sources and reduce energy consumption, while maintaining and enhancing the quality of individual and collective living. To do this, it is necessary to establish a path of 'energy descent', applying permaculture design systems and relocalizing the economy. The anticipated benefits include:

- healthier food;
- more active lifestyles;
- greater self-reliance;
- a sense of connection to place and products;
- the re-emergence of local identity;
- an emphasis on quality over quantity;
- a means of overcoming addictive behaviours such as over-consumption; and
- a meaningful common goal and sense of purpose.

In 2005 Hopkins, working with students and colleagues, devised the first energy descent plan, *Kinsale 2021*, with Kinsale Town Council in Ireland a little later officially adopting it as council policy. Energy descent is about *living* a post-carbon future rather than preparing to *live in* a post-carbon future. It is about changing everyday habits, behaviours, proclivities and perceptions. It means rooting transitional change in individual and community action. The transition process involves community education and networking; food mapping; community arts activities and craft workshops; research, natural building, renewable energy and permaculture projects; the creation of community gardens; and local political lobbying, dialogue and clear media communication. The idea has caught on. By 2007, a number of towns in the

UK, including Totnes, Ivybridge, Falmouth and Stroud, had become 'transition towns', with others, like Lampeter in Wales, showing considerable interest. The Transition movement now has roots in the major cities throughout the world and is seen as quite the small town, middle-class activist movement it once was. In Totnes, community working groups focusing on healthcare, energy, food, local government, livelihood, economics, the arts, the psychology of change, housing, transport, education, youth and community have been established. A pilot local alternative currency, the 'Totnes pound', was launched in March 2007 to engage a wider number of local people and businesses. Inspired by regional alternative currency models developed in Germany and the southern Berkshire region of Massachusetts in the US, the aim is to strengthen the local economy by keeping money circulating within a geographically bounded locality, which in effect is the same as attracting new money and owes much to the theories of economic localization or local protectionism (Crowther *et al.*, 2002) and that of the New Economics Foundation (Ward and Lewis, 2002). As Douthwaite (1999a: 1) has written, local and alternative currencies are nothing new. In the past they have helped fashion different types of societies and cultures by establishing an ecology of money: 'if we wish to live more ecologically, it would make sense to adopt monetary systems that make it easier for us to do so'. Transition also has shifted much of its promotional and campaigning emphasis away from peak oil and energy to sustainable local economic development and social issues, thereby attracting new supporters who were initially not particularly attracted to the more narrowly defined or conventional green activities (Blewitt and Tilbury, 2013). As Rob Hopkins writes:

> Transition may well be most successful if it retains its broadness rather than focusing too closely at any one facet of the process. It will do best if based on practical action, community appeal, inner Transition, social entrepreneurship, social justice, careful attention to deep engagement, using the best evidence, creating new economic models for inward investment, and finding ways to involve local businesses and local government. Its strength and resilience will be in its breadth; in its ability to keep moving forward on all those fronts.
>
> (2011: 290)

New urbanism

The recent development of 'urban villages' may offer environmental benefits, high-quality and affordable neighbourhoods, and mixed-use urban space with stable and diversely populated communities. 'New urbanism' (Katz, 1994) has set about redefining the American Dream, replacing suburban sprawl with higher densities, open space, less pollution and:

> neighbourhoods of housing and parks, and schools placed within walking distance of shops, civic services, jobs and transit – a modern version of the traditional town. The convenience of the car and the opportunity to walk or use transit can be blended in an environment with local access for all the daily needs of a diverse community.
>
> (Calthorpe, 1993: 6)

Talen (2002) assesses how the physical design principles of new urbanism, as stated in the Charter of New Urbanism (Congress for the New Urbanism, 2000), relate to realizing the goals of community, social equity and the common good for the new urbanism movement as a whole, rather than just in a few high-income developments. There is a general agreement that good design can contribute to residents' commitment or attachment to a place, foster localized social interaction, and help nurture a sense of community. New urbanism expresses community abstractly, referring generally to the promotion of social identity and civic bonds, although Talen admits that good design can foster genuine sociologically informed neighbourhood level interaction. New urbanist planning provides for pedestrian, bicycle as well as motor vehicle access to physical resources and civic amenities, thereby clearly contributing to social equity. As for the common good, this can be interpreted as referring to the protection of the environment, historical buildings and farmland, the provision of public transport, and the promotion of a place-based, neighbourhood identity through the provision of spaces for public gathering. Furthermore, new urbanism is committed to participatory design, making physical improvements a public matter, building in a capacity to develop a community as well as a series of buildings. New urbanism therefore recognizes that social and environmental problems need to be dealt with together and has explicitly linked a variety of social goals with optimum urban form.

In the UK, the Prince of Wales's new development of Poundbury in Dorset is based on the principles of new urbanism, particularly regarding the emphasis on traditional architecture, walkability, and 'car-unfriendly' and community values (Hardy, 2006). The master plan was designed by Leon Krier and construction started on the 400-acre site in 1993. Many of the commissioned architects are local and many of the building materials, like the stone and slate, distinctive of the area. There is a strong sense of heritage in many of the buildings' design, which has led some critics to perceive the Poundbury vision as somewhat kitsch. Nonetheless, new houses have been built to the EcoHomes 'excellent' standard (the highest rating) with 20 per cent domestic properties designated for affordable housing. By October 2006, 1,250 people were living and 750 working in Poundbury. In 2011, West Dorset District Council approved plans for a further 1,200 homes, with an agreement that 35 per cent would be 'affordable', as well as a new primary school and the likelihood of more jobs being created by businesses located in the town.

Ezio Manzini and the sustainable everyday

For the Italian designer Ezio Manzini (Manzini and Jegou, 2003; Manzini, 2004 and 2005), everyday urban living is influenced by population density, technical functions and networks (water, transport, energy, waste), the quality of the built environment, human social connectivity and interaction, and the quality of localized services. In addition, the size and role of the family or household, social expectations regarding human social welfare, opportunities for democratic participation, and the distribution of wealth and knowledge are other more social influences. Cities are complex places, and so is the experience of living in them. Frequently, what adversely affects urban dwellers' lived experience may have no obvious or direct cause; if it does, that cause has its origins in opaque and distant decision-making, or vaguely defined economic or market forces. Given this, grass-roots changes to everyday living might seem doomed to insignificance, and Manzini agrees that changes to an individual's lifestyle choices, actions and behaviour will not in themselves alter the urban physical and social forms. On the other hand, Manzini argues that any transformation of a complex system requires that it is put under some tension from within at the micro-scale as a preparation for wider systemic change. This is what urban dwellers can do by changing their everyday habits, routines and actions. Things can be done differently, new and old skills can be learned, and alternatives to 'business as usual' can be sought out and developed. New practical pathways can be supported and reinforced by the generation of new cosmopolitan ideas, business opportunities, applied research and technological innovation. It is possible to learn from the diversity within cities across the globe to produce a dynamic catalogue of new urban possibilities – new scenarios for everyday living, new opportunities for communication, sustainability projects and the diffusion of a new design culture. Manzini's initial research led to seventy-two proposed scenarios, which together exhibit a number of common traits and recurrent ideas:

- *Multiple aims*: Each proposal has more than one aim, representing an emerging heterogeneity and a culture of complexity.
- *Local–global link*: Each proposal is open to communication flows between the local and global and, although place-based, is not rooted in a nostalgic search for a golden past.
- *Individual–community link*: Both individuals and communities are able to benefit from and develop each proposal.
- *Ecology of time*: Each proposal will move at a different speed and rhythm, creating islands of slowness within faster-paced city flows.
- *Enabling technology*: Each proposal accepts the potential role of technology, but none posits technology as the sole or simple solution.

The scenarios emerge from a growing social consciousness and everyday sustainable development practice. Based on actual innovations from countries across the world – in China, Canada, Italy, India, the US and Japan – they include:

- *the extended home*, including a kitchen club, sauna network, net shopping service and clothes-care service;
- *localized activities*, including neighbourhood office space, optimal management and multifunction use of city work spaces, and combined telework and recreation areas;
- *alternative mobility*, including systems of local delivery services, use of light vehicles and personalized public transport;
- *advanced natural food*, including the prevention of ill health through the consumption of traditional food and eating seasonal fresh and local foods;
- *symbiotic nature*, including greenhouses, community gardens and allotments allover the city and community eco-landscaping projects;
- *socio-bio-technological building construction*, including green roofs, communal spa and bathing facilities, and efficient municipal water management; and
- *sustainable micro enterprises*, including small green businesses, 'fix it shops', etc.

The realization of sustainable everyday living will require social learning, co-operation between urban designers and communities, social experimentation, and the modelling of new project ideas and actions. It will also require urban planning systems to facilitate the emergence of open and lively cities with significant centres of local cultural diversity, a new and dynamic fluidity to everyday life, and the development of new types of services and empowered places that exhibit a form of ambient intelligence, harnessing the possibilities afforded by emerging media technology. As Manzini and Jegou write:

> Given the complex, hybrid nature of these local-global, real-virtual services, they could in fact become catalyzers for other, wider phenomena. Particularly in the perspective of a multi-local city, they could be engines for a strategy of 'bottom-up' change where, by operating on a neighbourhood scale while being highly connected on a global scale, they could activate new dynamics in the economic and social fields, leading to the generation of new forms of community and identity. In short, if appropriately planned, they could contribute to the birth of a new sense of place and consequently to a new idea of the city.
>
> The sustainable city will be created by a change in outlook, a critical and reflexive mindset, and a million and one small changes to the living of our everyday lives.
>
> (Manzini and Jegou, 2003: 223)

Manzini offers various pictures, or scenarios, for future and present sustainable living. Some involve a degree of technological problem solving, but the technical fix is only part of the process and you don't have to be a writer, designer or architect to envision a sustainable future. There have been many local regional and global initiatives involving various groups of stakeholders who have undertaken various forms of visioning, scenario-building, forecasting and backcasting. However, as Barr *et al.* (2011) point out, although promoting and embedding a more sustainable lifestyle within the home is clearly quite feasible, there is a real tension, particularly in relation to carbon emissions and consumption, between other lifestyle choices such as overseas tourism and air travel.

Scenario analysis

Economic forecasters, weather forecasters and scientific forecasters use very similar methods of building models based on the collection, description and analysis of vast quantities of often quantitative data, leading to a presentation of future behaviour as a product of carefully calculated mathematical probabilities. But, as the authors of the Stockholm Environment Institute's report *The Great Transition* (Raskin *et al.*, 2002: 13) state, 'predictive modelling is inadequate for illuminating the long-range future of our stunningly complex planetary system'. Global futures evade prediction because of three factors:

1 *Ignorance*: Incomplete information on the current state of the system and the forces governing its dynamics leads to a statistical dispersion over possible future states.

2   *Surprise*: Complex systems are known to exhibit turbulent behaviour, extreme sensitivity to initial conditions and branching behaviours at critical thresholds; the possibilities for novelty and emergent phenomena render prediction impossible.
3   *Volition*: The future is unknowable because it is subject to human choices that have not yet been made.

Scenarios outline contexts and situations in which possibilities unfold – issues, actors, events, processes, flows, images, actions, and so on. Global scenarios particularly are based on the combination of science and the arts, of hard facts and flights of the imagination, the description of current trends, the extrapolation of likely future consequences, and the construction of alternatives for human and non-human beings and the natural and the social environment. Utopian and dystopian thinking may be part of this, just as practical possibilities and desires may be. As Raskin *et al.* (2002: 14) write, 'rather than prediction, the goal of scenarios is to support volition and rational action by providing insight into the scope of the possible'. This is what Manzini has done on the everyday neighbourhood scale and what the Stockholm Environment Institute has done on a macro-level.

Three archetypal scenarios of the future have been developed – *Conventional Worlds*, *Barbarization* and *Great Transitions*. The Conventional Worlds scenario assumes that current trends will play out without producing major disturbance to the evolution of contemporary institutions, environmental systems and human values. In the Barbarization scenario, fundamental and unwelcome social change does occur, causing significant human misery and the destruction of civilized norms. In the Great Transitions scenario, fundamental social transformation also occurs, but this leads to a new and arguably higher stage of human civilization. Raskin *et al.* (2002: 15) explain in some detail:

> Conventional Worlds assume the global system in the 21st century evolves without major surprise, sharp discontinuity or fundamental transformation in the basis of human civilization. The dominant forces and values currently driving globalization shape the future. Incremental market and policy adjustments are able to cope with social, economic and environmental problems as they arise. Barbarization foresees the possibilities that these problems are not managed. Instead, they cascade into self-amplifying crises that overwhelm the coping capacity of conventional institutions. Civilization descends into anarchy or tyranny. Great Transitions, the focus of this essay, envision profound historical transformations in the fundamental values and organizing principles of society. New values and development paradigms ascend that emphasize quality of life and material sufficiency, human solidarity and global equity, and affinity with nature and environmental sustainability. For each of these three scenario classes, we define two variants, for a total of six scenarios. In order to sharpen an important distinction in the contemporary debate, we divide the evolutionary Conventional Worlds into *Market Forces* and *Policy Reform*. In Market Forces, competitive, open and integrated global markets drive world development. Social and environmental concerns are secondary. By contrast, Policy Reform assumes that comprehensive and coordinated government action is initiated for poverty reduction and environmental sustainability. The pessimistic Barbarization perspective also is partitioned into two important variants, *Breakdown* and *Fortress*

World. In Breakdown, conflict and crises spiral out of control and institutions collapse. Fortress World features an authoritarian response to the threat of breakdown, as the world divides into a kind of global apartheid with the elite in interconnected, protected enclaves and an impoverished majority outside.

There are also two variants of Great Transitions: *Eco-communalism* and the *New Sustainability Paradigm*. Eco-communalism offers a bioregional, localist, participatory democracy supported by economic autarky. Raskin and his co-authors find it difficult to envisage a plausible path from today's globalizing trends to eco-communalism without involving some form of Barbarization. Thus the Great Transition becomes identified with the New Sustainability Paradigm, which would change the nature of global civilization, encompassing global solidarity, cross-cultural interaction and economic connectedness, while aiming for a liberating humanistic and ecological politics rather than relying on mainly localist anarchistic-style solutions. The authors base their scenario analysis and 'history of the future' on a detailed interpretation of current drivers, including demographics, economics, social issues, culture, technology, environment and governance. There are moments, 'branch points', when opportunities arise and when development may take different directions. Leadership for change may come from different quarters, linking and influencing change in other areas. Globalization is presented as a process that expands categories of consciousness and is not something that should be opposed outright, as if it is civilized, then it offers significant new potentialities for corporations, civil society, technological development and application, and governance. In the great transition taking place after 2025, Raskin *et al.* suggest that a new social movement, 'the accountability movement', will emerge, encompassing increasing numbers of business leaders accepting the legitimacy of many social and environmental demands and leading newly creative business initiatives to meet them. Countless global manufacturing firms will adopt 'zero impact' goals – producing no waste, releasing no pollution, and accepting responsibility for post-consumer product recovery and recycling. Many corporations will have cut costs dramatically as a result and are providing affordable basic goods, services and jobs in poor communities, which in the process creates large new markets. Other corporations will harness nanotechnologies to produce products using less raw materials and energy. Consequently, sustainable development will mean a new form of ecologically based 'reindustrialization', providing the material basis for the continuance of human civilization.

Summary

Being able to envision a future sustainable society is an important element in the sustainable development process. Utopian thinkers and writers have wondered what a future good society, or a good place, would be like and although it is clearly mistaken to see utopian thinking as a guide to all things sustainable, it does certainly free the imagination. And it is the imagination, as well as the intellect and knowledge, that has been employed in developing sustainable communities, towns and cities across the world. Indeed, many people have argued that the key to global sustainability lies with the way we manage our existing urban environments and build our future ones. The last few decades have witnessed many sustainable urban initiatives at a variety of scales from grand new ecocities in China and in the deserts of the Middle

East, to the regeneration of specific neighbourhoods in some ancient cities in Europe, to a new urbanism in the United States. As the world's population steadily expands towards nine billion, and as more and more people are born in or migrate to cities, the everyday experience of urban life is going to be the dominant experience of sustainability . . . or unsustainability. If we are to be sustainable, then it is essential that we start with where most people live and work.

Thinking questions

1   In your view, what is the value of utopian thinking to sustainable development?
2   Does each separate worldview imply a specific vision of the future?
3   In what ways do sustainable architecture, planning and design benefit from utopian thinking?
4   Are ecovillages practical utopias?
5   What is an ecopolis?
6   What is the relationship, if any, between utopian visioning, and scenario analysis and backcasting?

Companion website

So what does sustainable development look and feel like? Please visit the companion website for additional case studies on sustainable design and urban sustainability.

9 Tools, systems and innovation for sustainability

Aims

This chapter will examine a range of tools and measurements designed to assess the progress made towards realizing sustainability goals. The relationship between the Natural Step Framework and the development of sustainability indicators, and the theory and application of ecological footprinting analysis and ecological space will be discussed. Apart from specific tools, management systems and instruments, moving towards sustainability also involves unleashing creativity, doing things in different ways, experimentation and changing mindsets. Finally, the chapter will evaluate the role and applicability of various sustainability tools and indicators in the broader process of communication and social learning accompanying sustainable development practice.

Achieving sustainable development

For the economist Paul Ekins (2000), sustainable development means that economic, social, environmental and other benefits must be delivered. Human beings need to live and produce within ecological limits. Human social welfare needs to be enhanced for all, with equity and justice defining a sustainable society, but the benefits of living in a sustainable society need to be clearly and distinctly communicated in a series of measures or summaries of relevant information. The problem for Ekins is that, although numerical indicators may exist for certain areas – for example, finance or economic capital – combining them all into one index of sustainable development is extremely difficult to achieve as many potential indicators are not commensurable. Ekins also notes that, in public policy terms, standards for sustainability are usually set by government, becoming, through the governmental process, motivating targets and indicators. Turnhout *et al.* (2007) suggest that although many ecological indicators are based on scientific knowledge and understanding, they cannot be purely scientific in their practical application. Ethical issues are invariably involved too, as they inform the policy process, help define the policy problem, and are frequently used strategically, or tactically, to effect socio-political, economic and environmental change:

> This means that the idea of a 'chain of knowledge' needs to be reconsidered. The overlap between science and policy in the boundary area means that it is not only knowledge translation and transfer that takes place here, but knowledge production and use as well. In the case of ecological indicators, science and policy enter into some kind of joint knowledge production. Scientific knowledge

is used in ecological indicators, but so is political knowledge. Ecological indicators are shaped by political preferences and considerations to protect certain species, certain types of nature, and so on. Development and use of indicators go hand in hand and are hard to distinguish empirically. Clearly, ecological indicators cannot be unproblematically labelled as scientific. Labelling it as solely political, on the other hand, does not acknowledge the scientific input that is required.

(Turnhout *et al.*, 2007: 221)

Science can inform and ecology can serve as a model for sustainable development, but sustainable development cannot be reduced to either. Ethical and political considerations will always be part of the picture; this is clearly seen, perhaps, in their influence on the development of good governance indicators. Stewart (2006) argues, in his discussion of political participation in the Greater Vancouver region, that social justice and inclusion need to be operationalized by applying the theory of 'persistent losing'. Community members may be committed to collective decision-making but may persistently lose out in the decision-making process. In this context, they would be acting quite reasonably if they rejected the rules that persistently cause this to happen. In this way, the interests of marginal, perhaps aboriginal groups, can be factored in. For Stewart (2006: 203), both the World Bank (World Bank, 2006) and UN Habitat (UNDP, 2006) have failed 'to include an adequate assessment of citizen participation in their good urban governance indicator sets, nor do they provide much guidance as to why their indicators are essential and, most importantly, how these indicators should be assessed'. The most appropriate and effective indicators are developed dialogically, working at the interface of (social) science and their specific socio-cultural, political and economic contexts. Unfortunately, but perhaps inevitably, this may occasionally lead to some necessary vagueness in order to necessarily and diplomatically accommodate different perspectives, values and interests.

Carbon capture and storage: geosequestration or biosequestration

Carbon Capture and Storage (CCS), or geosequestration, is an intermediate technical solution that is seen by many governments as a way of limiting the amount of CO_2 emitted in to the atmosphere. The idea is that the CO_2 produced by burning fossil fuels – for example, coal should be captured and stored within the Earth's crust. In this way power companies can burn 'clean coal'. However, to perfect this process requires massive investment and technological developments that have had successes in small-scale trials but have yet to be proven at a large commercial scale anywhere in the world. Storing large amounts of carbon underground could possibly lead to unwanted environmental effects, may not actually be permanent and could result in some loss of efficiency. The International Energy Agency (2007) has noted that for CCS to make a tangible contribution to global climate mitigation by 2050 there would have to be in the region of 6,000 projects on stream each sequestering and storing a million tons of CO_2 or more per year. However, there is an alternative.

The Ecological Sequestration Trust is a participant in the United Nations Global Compact, which is a global network bringing together businesses and other bodies to help make mainstream the Compact's ten universally accepted principles relating to labour, human rights, the environment and anti-corruption. Biological sequestration

Table 9.1 UN Habitat Urban Governance Indicators: project categories and measures of 'good urban governance' in developing world cities

Effectiveness	Equity	Participation	Accountability	Security
Major sources of income	Citizen's charter	Elected council	Contracts, tenders, budget and account publications	Crime prevention
Predictability of local budget transfers	Percentage of women councillors	Elected mayor	Protection from higher levels of government	Police services per 100,000
Published performance delivery standards	Pro-poor pricing policies for water	Voter turnout	Codes of conduct for officials	Conflict resolution
Consumer satisfaction surveys	Incentives for informal businesses	Public forums	Facility for citizen complaints	Violence against women policies
Vision statement		Civic associations per 10,000	Anti-corruption commission	HIV/AIDS policy
			Disclosure of income and assets	
			Independent audit	

Source: Stewart (2006: 197).

prioritizes biological carbon capture and storage through deliberate measures relating to forest protection and management, afforestation and soil improvement through the addition of biochar. It also involves restoring ocean vegetation by addressing problems of overfishing and the destructive trawling of the seabed. Marine ecosystems are finely balanced and they have evolved over millions of years both to generate oxygen and to safely absorb carbon dioxide. Governments and energy corporations seem to be less interested in this ecological approach even though some countries, such as China, do complement their economic, industrial and urban developments with massive ecological projects such as tree planting, which aim to arrest the very serious problems of desertification and deforestation. Unfortunately, it seems, insufficient research attention has been applied to many ecologically sensitive areas, particularly to hydrological, pedological and landscape matters, which has meant that not all afforestation schemes in China have been as successful as originally hoped (Cao *et al.*, 2011). Nonetheless, 40 billion trees have been planted since 1981 and there have clearly been gradual improvements in some areas with a modest positive impact on mitigating the effects of increased carbon emissions.

Biosequestration is arguably beneficial to both human society and the environment, for it is a proven way of absorbing carbon. It does offer genuine opportunities for nurturing biodiversity, preventing soil erosion, potentially enhancing food production and in some areas rural poverty by reducing the need for rural dwellers to seek work in the cities (Girardet and Mendonca, 2009). This type of work requires visioning and the establishment of generative conditions for a structured collaboration and partnership among professional groups, researchers in universities, corporations and politicians. These groups need to develop and share knowledge of capacity-building tools which would accelerate the development of biosequestration projects and, where possible, scale up the development of integrated low-carbon technologies.

Ecological footprint analysis

The continuing design, application and revision of sustainability indicators, and other similar tools, is often an attempt to manage the sustainability process by gently questioning the notion that only what is measurable is valuable. We need to move to a position where we seek to measure what we value. Developing a sustainable indicator is an attempt to point out both what we value and how we intend to measure it. The problem arises in selecting a reasonable and manageable number of indicators that effectively serve to organize information into specific categories and showing the interconnections and possible trade-offs among them. Apart from being resonant, valid and motivational, for Chambers *et al.* indicators must also be:

- organized around a sharp purpose (for example, building municipal sustainability);
- captured in an effective framework for organizing the indicators that explains the challenges and trade-offs (for example, economic quality of life and maintaining Earth's biocapacity);
- imaginative and realistic about possible intervention points (public planning); and
- specific about the next steps beyond the indicator project (for example, new green taxation and regulation).

(2000: 18)

Ecological footprint analysis, as defined and developed by Mathis Wackernagel and William Rees (1996), refers to the total area of productive land and water required continuously to produce all the resources consumed by a region (or city) *and* to assimilate all the wastes produced by a particular population, wherever on Earth that land is located. The ecological footprint is therefore a land-based substitute measure of the population's demands on natural capital. It assumes that it is possible to accurately measure a given population's resource consumption and waste production, and that these flows can be converted to a biotically productive area. It should not be confused with the related concept of 'environmental space', designed by the pressure group Friends of the Earth in the 1990s (McLaren *et al.*, 1998). Environmental space methodology identifies the ecological capacity of a particular resource used by people and sets a target of what consumption of it ought to be if everyone has a fair share (of, say, CO_2) – that is to say, a share that allows everyone to live within the Earth's carrying capacity. Environmental space sets normative sustainability targets and, through setting such targets, the methodology articulates a philosophy of environmental justice as well as providing a useful policy tool for governmental and corporate decision-makers. However, space targets do not always readily appeal to individuals or adequately express how different resource uses and material substitutions interact with one another. Environmental footprint analysis, on the other hand, although it too has certain disadvantages, is arguably easier to understand and communicate to a broad non-specialist public. The major strength of the footprinting approach is its conceptual simplicity – it is accessible, intuitive and easily communicable in graphic forms, making the idea of ecological restraint more meaningful or acceptable to those reluctant to embrace pro-sustainability behaviour change. The footprint aggregates ecological flows associated with consumption and production, translating them into an appropriate land area serving as the key indicator and ready comparator between demand for ecological space and its finite supply.

A moderate business-as-usual approach to using the planet's ecosystem services is likely to lead to complete ecosystem collapse during this century, but there are also currently differences in individual nation's environmental impacts. The WWF (2006) states that, given the world's present population, the average biocapacity per capita is 1.8 hectares. The actual per capita ecological footprint is 9.6 hectares for the average American, 5.6 for the Briton, 1.6 for the Chinese and 0.8 for the Indian, with the economies of the latter two states growing quickly and massively. However, the rapid economic expansion of the BRIICS group of countries – Brazil, Russia, India, Indonesia and China – combined with their population growth and increase in average consumption, each person is adding further pressure on the planet's biocapacity, leading to more losses in biodiversity. As the richer countries continue to purchase import resources from poorer ones and development occurs at the expense of the environment, the situation of the poorest countries rapidly worsens. The 2012 WWF International's Living Planet Report states:

> The trend in low income countries is potentially catastrophic, not just for biodiversity but also for the people living there. While everyone depends ultimately on the biodiversity that provides ecosystem services and natural assets, the impact of environmental degradation is felt most directly by the world's poorest people, particularly by rural populations, and forest and coastal communities. Without

access to land, clean water, adequate food, fuel and materials; vulnerable people cannot break out of the poverty trap and prosper.

(WWF-Int, 2012: 57)

By focusing on the tension between the standard and quality of life and the ecological integrity of the planet, ecological footprinting effectively captures the primary sustainability notion that the economy is a means to an end and not an end in itself. People's lived experience, life satisfaction, and social and human development are at the root of much of the work that has gone into developing ecological footprint analysis. For example, Wackernagel and Yount (1998: 513) define sustainability as 'the continuous support of human quality of life [in other words, people's subjectively perceived well-being] within a region's ecological carrying capacity [or the ecological or biotic capacity within a region to regenerate used resources and assimilate waste]'. The tension between living well and living sustainably, and the reality of the interconnected nature of the world, where even renewable resources like forests can disappear if we exploit them without a thought for tomorrow, is clearly brought to the fore. For Stuart Hart (1997), today's businesses need to go beyond greening their processes and practices. They need to make a positive impact. 'Ironically, the greatest threat to sustainable development today is depletion of the world's renewable resources' as soils, water, forests and fisheries have all been pushed beyond their limits by industrial development, economic growth and human population increase (Hart, 1997: 69). It also makes trade imbalances and the eco-ameliorating effects of new technology visible, while expressing the first and second laws of thermodynamics. These laws state, respectively, that mass is neither created nor destroyed but just gets rearranged and energy is neither created nor destroyed but is just transformed, and that everything ultimately runs down. Despite all the advantages, ecological footprinting has three significant drawbacks: it is not a dynamic modelling tool, has no predictive capacity and does not factor in the needs of non-human species. It is not a forecast of the future or even an analysis of socio-political issues, but simply a means of indexing biophysical impacts, of evaluating the present state of affairs and providing some tools for understanding possible alternative 'what if' scenarios. Furthermore, it does not prescribe what an individual or country's ecological footprint should be. It also tends to underestimate overall impacts and may overestimate the planet's carrying capacity, although it remains a very useful tool, as Rees and Wackernagel argue:

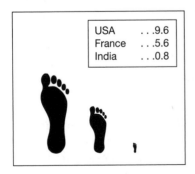

USA   . . .9.6
France   . . .5.6
India   . . .0.8

Figure 9.1 National ecofootprints (to scale)

Ecological footprinting acts, in effect, as an ecological camera – each analysis provides a snapshot of our current demands on nature, a portrait of how things stand right now under prevailing technology and social values. We believe that this in itself is an important contribution. We show that humanity has exceeded carrying capacity and that some people contribute significantly more to this ecological 'overshoot' than do others. Ecological footprinting also estimates by how much we have to reduce our consumption, improve our technology or change our behaviour to achieve sustainability.

(Rees and Wackernagel, 1996: 231)

Additionally, ecological footprinting does not indicate how trade may reduce incentives for material resource conservation by facilitating and reinforcing urban dependences on other territories, as resources are basically sought further afield. This becomes especially apparent when trade and natural flows in contemporary relationships between the North and the South are examined:

Much of the wealth of urban industrial countries comes from the exploitation (and sometimes liquidation) of natural capital, not only within their own territories, but also within their former colonies. The energy and material flows in trade thus represent a form of thermodynamic imperialism. The low-cost essergy [essential energy] represented by commodity imports is required to sustain growth and maintain the internal order of the so-called 'advanced economies' of the urban North. . . . Colonialism involved the forceful appropriation of extraterritorial carrying capacity, but today economic purchasing power secures the same resource flows. What used to require territorial occupation is now achieved through commerce.

(Rees and Wackernagel, 1996: 239)

The authors conclude that urban policy should aim to minimize disruption of ecosystem processes and reduce energy and material consumption. For McManus and Haughton (2006), as an indicator of impact, ecological footprinting decontextualizes place and natural diversity, by suggesting that everything can be reduced to one common metric, and may actually narrow our understanding of sustainable development, despite raising our general awareness. The same may actually be said for the current emphasis on carbon reduction. For Newman (2006), it may help frame environmental management and sustainable development policies, but has difficulties in assessing detailed priorities as to what needs to be reduced first or even by how much – for example, a city's use of water, energy or land. However, since the work in the early 1990s, methods of ecological footprint analysis have been refined and the extent to which the world's population is overshooting the biosphere's capacity is becoming clearer. Ecofootprinting does provide possibilities for comparing a variety of sustainability options and project choices in business, technological and industrial production processes, policy scenarios for development, population and consumption, urban design and regeneration, and so on. It can be applied to testing such things as the role of efficiency gains in reducing resource consumption, the relationship between income and ecological impact, dematerialization of economies, the relationship between economic and ecological debt, the link between population health and resource throughput, and transition to a solar economy, and provides a practical and expressive education tool in schools, colleges, universities, community groups, business and the professions (Wackernagel and Yount, 2000). The same type of analysis can be done for local communities, small businesses, transnational corporations, cities, city regions and nation-states by both specialists and non-specialists. It is an organizing, educational and analytical tool. The method's repeatability enables the development of comparisons, debate and discussion. Finally, although there is evidence that a smaller ecological footprint does not necessarily mean a reduced quality, or even lower standard of living, Wackernagel and Yount suggest that ecological footprinting could be more socially embracing if it were linked to, or complemented by, measures of human satisfaction or happiness.

Environmental management systems: Life Cycle Assessment (LCA)

One particular tool commonly applied by businesses, governments, NGOs and campaign groups is Life Cycle Assessment, whose processes, principles and procedures have been standardized by the ISO (the International Organization for Standardization). The ISO, a global private sector organization, aims to standardize a wide range of products and services. Its LCA standards include both technical and organizational aspects with one of the key aims of its 9000 series being to integrate quality aspects into business practice. The ISO 14000 series includes the 14001 Environmental Management Systems and the 14040 series relate to LCA, first published in 1997–8 and revised in 2006 and defines LCA as the 'compilation and evaluation of the inputs, outputs and potential environmental impacts of a product system throughout its life cycle' (Guinée, 2002: 7). It is a tool with which to analyse the environmental impact of products at all stages in their life cycle – extraction of resources, production of materials, the product itself, the use of the product, its afterlife – where it may be reused, recycled or disposed. The environmental burden of a product may encompass many different environmental impacts, including emission of hazardous substances and different types of land use. The term 'product' may refer to physical goods as well as services at both operational and strategic levels. In comparative LCA studies, it is the function provided by these products rather than the products themselves that are the subject of comparison.

There are four main stages in LCA methodology (Welford, 1998):

- *Inventory*: gathering mainly quantifiable data which may involve extensive research for some companies who have long supply chains.
- *Impact analysis*: consideration of how this inventory impacts the environment in each area documented under the inventory.
- *Impact assessment*: the measuring of impacts is usually broken down into three stages:
    - *classification*: e.g. human health, natural resources, etc.;
    - *characterization*: aggregation of data and creation of impact profiles;
    - *valuation*: the weighting of different impact categories using quantitative and qualitative data.
- *Improvement*: an appraisal of where and how the product or service can be further improved.

Box 9.1 The ecological footprint of Greater London

The data and trends below provide a picture of the capital's environment, to help assess the sustainability of London. This is part of the London State of the Environment Report for 2010. The environment is important for London. It enables the city to function as it does by providing key ecosystem services – water, air, land and natural resources.

What is an ecological footprint?

The ecological footprint measures the area of land needed to both:

- provide all the resources and services consumed;
- absorb all the waste produced.

The data on London's ecological footprint has been sourced by using the Resource and Energy Analysis Programme (REAP) model. This model was produced by the Stockholm Environment Institute. The calculation uses expenditure data – the higher cost of living in London may impact on the final footprint. This means that London's footprint may be potentially lower than reported below.

Trends on London's footprint

London's ecological footprint is 4.54 global hectares (gha) per person (2006). This is slightly lower than the UK average of 4.64 gha per person.

Although London's footprint is lower than the UK average, the high consumption of resources means it is just under twice the size of the global average footprint of 2.6 gha per person (Global Footprint Network). When divided equally between the world population, it is 2.5 times bigger than the bio-capacity of the land (1.8 gha per person), which is the area of land available to supply natural resources.

The total ecological footprint for London in global hectares is over 34 million. This amounts to an area over 200 times the city itself.

The affluent City of London, Kensington and Chelsea, Westminster and Richmond upon Thames have the highest footprints in London – they are all over 5 gha per person.

The less affluent Barking and Dagenham, Tower Hamlets and Newham have the lowest ecological footprints in London, along with Hackney, Southwark and Brent.

The main contributors to the ecological footprint in London are:

- Housing – mainly electricity and fuel use.
- Food – fruit and vegetables, and catering services.

London's ecological footprint is higher than the UK average for housing, food and private services.

The capital's footprint is lower than the UK average for transport. This could be due to the higher cost of living in London, compared with the rest of the UK, plus the high use of public transport in London, and so the fewer miles that people drive.

The percentage of the ecological footprint made up by consumer items, public services and capital investments is the same for London and the UK.

Source: adapted from Environment Agency, available at: www.environmentagency.gov.uk/research/library/publications/115654.aspx.

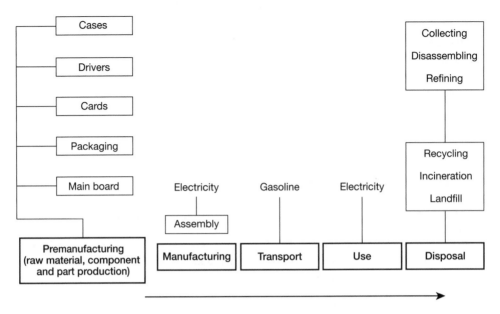

Figure 9.2 Personal Computer life-cycle assessment structure
Source: adapted from Choi *et al*. (2006: 123).

In their life-cycle assessment of the Personal Computer (PC) and its effective recycling rate in Korea, Choi *et al.* (2006) found the pre-manufacturing stage to be the largest contributor to all environmental impact categories, excluding those relating to human toxicity. At this stage in the PC's life cycle, a substantial amount of materials and energy is consumed to manufacture a range of small electric parts and electronic components, which in turn causes significant greenhouse gas emissions, waste water and solid waste. The disposal stage, which included collection, disassembly, recycling, landfill and/or incineration, was found to be a potentially serious contributor for human and ecological toxicity. Leakage from landfill sites was a leading factor in human toxicity and the use of chemicals during the recycling/ refinery process was a major element in ecotoxicity – i.e. land contamination.

Based on their detailed study, the authors recommended a more environmentally friendly PC design, which would be thinner, lighter and more energy efficient. A greater emphasis was also placed on green supply-chain management enacted through stricter procurement guidelines, and the urgent need to develop and implement better recycling technologies. Product recovery was identified as key to efficient recycling, but for this to occur in a cost-effective and efficient manner, recovery infrastructure would need to be constructed. Many countries and regions are now doing this.

Sustainability assessments and appraisals

Cities are massive consumers of resources and many are literally getting bigger by the day. Newman (2006) looks into reducing the ecological footprint of Sydney by applying the more finely grained tool of *sustainability assessment,* which simultaneously considers social, economic and environmental issues, and has the potential to encourage integrated policy initiatives suitable for the urban management of specific factors, such as energy, transport, waste, employment, access, governance, population/housing density and land use. A sustainability assessment requires any new development to produce a 'net benefit' in the three areas of environment, social and economic performance, with no trade-offs between any, by promoting positive outcomes from development. Ravetz (2000), working on similar and related concerns, has developed an integrated sustainability appraisal process in his work on the Greater Manchester city region. His discussion of complexity, systems, flows, stocks, limits, dynamics and externalities complements the work of Rees and Wackernagel by highlighting the practical/programme, planning and policy dimensions of city governance. The problems Ravetz confronts are essentially the complex interdependencies of ecosystems, the intangible qualities of environmental capital, the tangibility of material resources, and the dynamic evolutionary nature of physical and human systems over time. Ravetz also explores the possibilities of integrating the social and the economic (although not the political) into the development of sustainability indicators and the evaluation of their likely future directions. He recognizes that virtually any approach to sustainability appraisal, integrated or not, of corporations or urban municipalities will be value-laden, and will require linking up different forms of professional expertise, knowledge and opinion. So, given this, the application of a systems perspective is valuable in putting together multiple factors from environmental, economic and social dimensions:

> For integration of environmental and socio-economic assessments in an IA [integrated assessment] framework, there is an important distinction between weak and strong approaches. Weak integration leaves different sets of impacts to be balanced by stakeholders and decision-makers, or in effect integrated through a political process. Strong integration aims to carry out the integration within the technical process, whether multi-criteria or economic, and thus requires comprehensive frameworks, which are more vulnerable to indeterminacy and multiplicity. Integration via community impact evaluation relies on the expert definition of costs and benefits for different stakeholders, which again has difficulty with cumulative effects, multiple values and contested boundaries. Integration via the criteria of futurity and equity also struggles to define these in practical terms where different actors have multiple perspectives and the line between costs and benefits is often fuzzy.
>
> (Ravetz, 2000: 57)

In practice, Ravetz continues, indeterminacy and multiplicity mean that any sustainability appraisal is never a final and true answer – it is always work in progress – but it is more likely to be viable if holistic system principles guide the methods and context of investigation.

Sustainability indicators can also be translated into an array of league tables seeking to compare the performance of one business or city with another, and in the process to motivate changes and improvements. League tables are notorious for their oversimplification of highly complex issues, but they often produce a picture that demonstrates the effectiveness or otherwise of policy and action. However, there is always a difference, it seems, between rhetoric or appearance and reality, as even though league tables may be based on sound and generally accepted criteria, they frequently operate on a range of political and ethical levels. What city government wants to preside over a dirty city? Who wants to live there and what business will want to invest there? In 2007, the charity Forum for the Future produced a league table or index of twenty sustainable cities in the UK, applying a range of specific measures and official data sets offering both specific environmental, quality of life and 'future proofing' (assessing the way in which cities are preparing for future social and environmental impacts) indices and one aggregate ranking. The results were enlightening. The greenest city in the index was the former textile town of Bradford in West Yorkshire, which, thanks to a long process of industrial and commercial decline, has seen the environmental quality of its degraded land and rivers slowly improve. However, due to a range of social problems and lack of economic opportunities, Bradford figures less well in terms of quality of life, safety and security. The overall leader in Forum for the Future's index is the affluent town of Brighton and Hove on England's south coast, just an hour on the train from central London. Affluent cities, particularly service cities, are able to devote significant resources to sustainability issues and usually do not have to deal with the lingering effects of deindustrialization. They sometimes have a sizeable and growing green vote. Interestingly, the report, 'The sustainable cities index', questions the efficacy of a major element in British urban regeneration strategy, namely, the emphasis on iconic architecture and grand projects evident in Glasgow, Manchester, Liverpool and Birmingham, whose grand designs seem relatively incapable of significantly improving the local environment or people's quality of life 'and may distract from a broader set of criteria of what makes a successful, sustainable and liveable city' (Forum for the Future, 2007: 13). The report concluded that the English cities that performed best were those, like Leeds, Bristol and Plymouth, which have not pursued the iconic 'trophy-collecting' regeneration pathway but engaged in a range of varied, smaller-scale projects and initiatives.

The Natural Step Framework – socio-ecological indicators

The Natural Step (TNS) Framework is a methodology that has been developed to enable organizations and communities to plan their activities in a more sustainable fashion (The Natural Step, 2000). The TNS Framework outlines a set of system conditions, developed over time by an international network of scientists that must apply if a sustainable society is to be achieved. TNS focuses on the initial causes of problems, rather than the environmental effects. It supports proactive rather than reactive environmental planning, with investments and measures selected specifically to foster a sustainable trajectory offering long-term flexibility and short-term profitability. The TNS process lends itself to both graphic and numeric formulations (see Figure 9.3).

TNS System Conditions are summarized as follows: in a sustainable society, nature is *not* subject to systematically increasing:

- concentrations of substances extracted from the Earth's crust;
- concentrations of substances produced by society; or
- deradation by physical means;

  – and in that society:

- human needs are met worldwide.

As anything can be done within the above constraints, TNS aims to nurture positive and creative solutions-based thinking, brainstorming, sharing knowledge and ideas, and social and organizational learning. TNS consists of the following five levels:

1   *Principles of ecosphere* (social and ecological constitution): historically, resource availability, productive ecosystems, purity, trust and equity in society decline while simultaneously population, resource demand and competitiveness increase.
2   *System conditions* (principles of sustainability): this may be considered the success or achievement level.
3   *Strategy* (principles for sustainable development): particularly backcasting from principles.
4   *Activities* (concrete actions): these could include phasing out fossil fuel use, switching capacity to renewable energy, or substituting metals that are naturally abundant in the biosphere or benign for ones that are scarce or potentially harmful.
5   *Tools* (management): such as environmental management systems, ISO 14001, life-cycle assessment, Factor 10, ecological footprinting, zero emission or TNS's own ABCD analysis (see below).

TNS originator Karl-Henrik Robèrt argues that to create a sustainable society, and for groups and organizations to be successful in complex systems, all participants must articulate the same mental models in their economic and business practices (Robèrt, 2000; Robèrt *et al.*, 2002). Each individual, group, institution and business will be able to contribute their own special skills and talents, but the real challenge

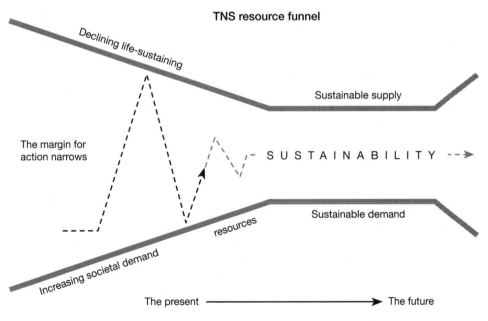

Figure 9.3 The funnel as a metaphor
Source: www.naturalstep.ca.

is for stakeholders to think in a systems-like way. TNS is designed to facilitate and lead this necessary learning process through its application of core principles and values, including such methods as backcasting ('What do we need to do now to get where we want to be?'), while offering the freedom to creatively harness energy and enthusiasm at an operational or local level. In an interview with Julian Gold, Robèrt (2004) notes:

> Focusing on the basic principles of complex systems is not only a methodology for individual intellectual performance; it is a way of leadership. Clarity, a shared understanding of what we are trying to achieve, and a framework to use in moving forward are tremendous sources of hope and inspiration. In my mind, this is where the solutions are going to come from – by people becoming engaged in the process, more so than by people being told what to do and what not to do.

TNS practitioners recognize that the core principles must not be violated, even though they will not know exactly what a future sustainable organization will look like. TNS is a strategic approach that maintains a clear motivational and ethical vision, as can be illustrated in Holmberg and Robèrt's discussion of renewable energy (2000: 304–5):

> Transformation into renewable energy is a measure to meet the four system conditions. The rationale for renewable energy is that:
>
> - Compounds from the Earth's crust, such as fossil carbon, forming carbon dioxide and radioactive elements must not accumulate in the ecosphere (system condition 1).
> - Compounds that are produced in energy conversion, such as nitrogen oxides or plutonium, should not accumulate in the ecosphere (system condition 2).
> - The exploitation of energy sources must not destabilize the conditions which support the life processes of Earth, for example degradation of ecosystems in the sea due to drilling for and transportation of oil or degradation of ecosystems on land due to mining for uranium (system condition 3).
> - We must not waste resources and eventually run out of our potential to meet human needs further ahead (system condition 4).
>
> Thus the four system conditions form the *core rationale* of what TNS founder refers to as ABCD analysis.

The TNS management and development framework has been widely taken up in many countries and by a number of very well-known businesses, including IKEA, Interface, Nike, Starbucks and McDonald's, and by many public and voluntary sector organizations. In the case of the Swedish company IKEA, TNS initiated the emergence of a successful corporation that continues to develop and enhance its commitment to sustainability through introducing green travel plans, providing bus services to customers in some locations, giving gifts of bicycles to employees, and introducing waste-to-energy technology and geothermal heating techniques in some stores. In the UK, charging for plastic bags reduced customer bag use by 95 per cent or 32 million bags (Webb, 2007).

In a technical article, Azar *et al.* (1996) identified a range of socio-ecological indicators that they feel could aid the planning and monitoring process in corporations, governments and other bodies. Unlike many other indicators, they argue, TNS focuses on the relation between society and ecosystems, rather than simply the state of the environment, concentrating on processes early in the causal chain:

There are two aspects that are important in the construction of our indicators:

(i) There are in many cases long time delays between a specific activity and the corresponding environmental damage. This means that indicators based on the environmental state may give a warning too late, and in many cases only indicate whether past societal activities were sustainable or not; and

(ii) The complexity of the ecosystems makes it impossible to predict all possible effects of a certain societal activity. Some damages are well known, but others have not yet been identified. Most of the sustainability indicators suggested so far are formulated with respect to known effects in the environment. We suggest that indicators of sustainability should be formulated with respect to general principles or conditions of sustainability.

(Azar *et al.*, 1996: 90)

The authors identify four socio-ecological principles upon which the indicators are based. Indicators for Principle One refer to society's use of elements from the lithosphere and will measure such things as carbon dioxide in the atmosphere, sulphur dioxide and acid rain, phosphorous in lakes, heavy metals in soils and in human bodies. In practice, this means restrictions on the extraction of metals and fossil fuels combined with increased recycling and the substitution of abundant elements for scarce ones. Principle Two deals with restricting emissions of anthropogenically produced substances with measures/indicators for CFCs, DDT, radioactive inert gases, etc. Principle Three addresses the anthropogenic manipulation of nature and will monitor deforestation and desertification, animal and plant extinctions, exploitation of productive land for waste landfill sites and other activities that injure the long-term functioning of global ecosystems. Principle Four relates to the efficiency of society's use of natural assets recognizing that limited assimilative capacity and available resources, human needs will have to be met more efficiently and equitably, including a just distribution of resources to eradicate poverty, disease and hunger.

As public awareness about the world's ecological problems grows, it is becoming increasingly incumbent on business corporations to be ecologically responsible. However, as Keeble *et al.* (2003) remark, the sustainable development agenda has brought to the boardroom many issues that lie outside the direct control of business, are difficult to characterize and are often based on value judgements rather than hard data. This sometimes makes it very difficult for business decision-makers, who require sets of indicators that reflect the commercial realities of business and the culture and values of the organization. Large corporations may have an organizational structure that may also cause problems, particularly as the sustainability performance of individual divisions may be obscured by generalized statements about the accomplishments of the organization as a whole. TNS consultants usually advise that time should not be wasted on looking to develop *ideal* indicators but rather attempt to create indicators that are dynamic and negotiated, encourage debate, involve external stakeholders and transparently inform the decision-making process.

Table 9.2 TNS's ABCD analysis

Step A	In ABCD analysis (or backcasting) the **four system conditions** define the frame for all planning. It is also important to identify the **need** of the product, service or organization and **key stakeholders**.
Step B	The **present situation** is analysed – What is doing well and what needs to change? This involves a review against the TNS four system conditions.
Step C	**Future scenarios** that work within the frame are envisioned.
Step D	Strategies are identified and adopted that will create a more **sustainable future**.

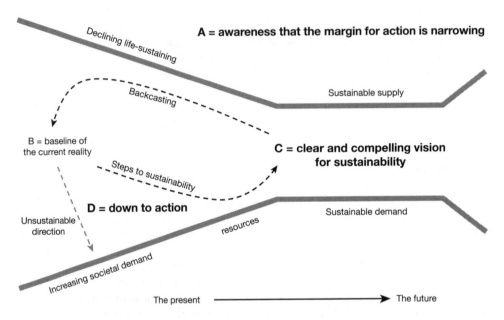

Figure 9.4 The Natural Step Framework: The ABCD process

Additionally, indicators need to be 'owned' by the organization and functionally adhere to recognizable standards for measurement and comparison.

In offering a scientific grounding, a vision and a practical method for creating a more sustainable world, TNS may help to change the dominant 'business-as-usual' mindsets still existing within many organizations.

The Global Reporting Initiative

It is also becoming increasingly necessary to communicate sustainable development practices internally to employees and stockholders and externally to the general public.

For some businesses, maintaining or improving market share may depend on how green the company is and appears to be. The Global Reporting Initiative (GRI) is a not-for-profit foundation with funding derived from voluntary donations and support in kind. It is a collaborating centre of the United Nations Environment Programme and has produced a widely used sustainability reporting framework setting out principles and indicators which organizations may use to measure and communicate their economic, environmental and social performance. This framework has been developed, and is regularly reviewed, by a wide range of business, civil society, trade union and professional stakeholders. The major aim of the GRI is to promote a standardized approach to reporting, to stimulate demand for sustainability information, and facilitate the implementation of sustainability reporting through the provision of learning materials and the accreditation of partner organizations. The GRI network consists of around 30,000 stakeholders, including more than 1,000 companies, among which are many leading brands who have adopted the guidelines. The third version of the centre's sustainability reporting guidelines (G3) was developed with the financial assistance of BP, Shell, GM, Microsoft, Alcan, Ford and the RBC financial group and published in 2006 as a free public good available on the Internet. The G3 framework includes 'sector supplements' (specific indicators for industry sectors such as finance, telecommunications, mining and metals, transportation, and the automotive industry), 'protocols' (detailed reporting guidance on content, quality, boundary-setting, performance and management disclosure) and 'national annexes' (addressing country and/or regional sustainability issues). Although the multi-stakeholder approach was welcomed by many sustainability practitioners, not all were satisfied with the unwieldy range of indicators included, the degree of information companies were required to produce that may or may not have been relevant to their market sector or the assumptions underlying some of them. In May 2013 GRI issued its fourth-generation guidelines (G4), which took many of these criticisms into account with an increased emphasis on the need for businesses to concentrate the reporting process and final report on those topics that are materially relevant to the business itself and its key stakeholders. G4 therefore seems to be more streamlined, easier to use and more straightforward than previous guidelines. A few new standard disclosures have been introduced too, including one on 'Ethics and Integrity'. Sustainability reports based on the GRI framework from major companies such as BMW and Coca-Cola are freely available and may be used to benchmark and compare organizational performance, demonstrating as well as communicating organizational commitment to sustainable development.

The GRI also undertakes research with partners on sustainability. In 2007 it published the results of a survey conducted by itself and KPMG, 'Reporting the business implications of climate change in sustainability report' (GRI, 2007). It discovered that most companies reported on the potential opportunities of climate change, such as new products, services and trading, rather than the financial or legal risks. The reasons for this included the desire to seek new profits so the perception or even identification of long-term risks and the need for a new ecological paradigm for business organization and activity was largely beyond business planning and reporting horizons. However, greenhouse gas emissions and emissions trading were frequently reported on, and for nearly one-third of the companies surveyed climate change was presented as a major issue of stakeholder dialogue and engagement. For the oil and gas sector, climate change issues are becoming linked with organizational reputation and brand value, but many other companies did not explicitly make the same connection.

The GRI focuses on corporate external communication of sustainability in business and requires the publication of qualitative and quantitative, systemic micro and macro, and some cross-cutting indicators. The GRI's sustainability reporting guidelines encompass three connected elements:

- *Economic*: For example, wages and benefits, labour productivity, job creation, expenditures on research and development, and investments in training and other forms of human capital.
- *Environmental*: For example, impacts of processes, products and services on air, water, land, biodiversity and human health.
- *Social*: For example, workplace health and safety, employee retention, labour rights, human rights, and wages and working conditions in outsourced operations.

Data gathering and ecological frameworks

In a careful consideration of the relationship between measuring progress (performance management) in sustainable development and numerical data, Hardi and DeSouza-Huletey (2000) suggest that accurate econometric and statistical analysis is essential for long-term planning, monitoring and reporting. Effective performance measurement and meaningful data interpretation depend on the interrelationship between the empirical (the real-world context) and numerical models (the transformation of sustainable development issues into measurable entities). Hardi and DeSouza-Huletey offer a number of recommendations which they argue will improve data collection and interpretation, for example:

- Data assessment should be carried out before the final selection of indicators.
- A mechanism should be designed for local authorities to collect and monitor their own data. Each data-collection method should use the kind of information needed for the study since there is no single method that is superior to others.
- Data analysis based on statistical and econometric techniques should be applied to all models.
- The definition of the geographic scale and time range for a study should depend on the context and accessibility of data.
- Linking different data sources and creating a database to archive all existing sources of sustainable development data will provide a new opportunity for a historical perspective on the systematic review of existing work.

Finally, Becker (2005: 88) suggests that 'educating stakeholders about the process of achieving sustainable development may be the most important result of the indicator selection process' and that education should not be divorced from communication and dissemination. Bell and Morse (1999) apply a soft systems approach as a way of understanding the progress being made by sustainable development activities and projects. They suggest a pictorial presentation of sustainability progress, the 'AMOEBA' (a Dutch acronym meaning 'general method for ecosystem description and assessment'), as being an appropriate way of developing in a participatory fashion and fully comprehending a sustainability project (Bell and Morse, 2003). Others, notably Clayton and Radcliffe (1996), have written of the advisability of adapting Sustainability Assessment Maps that similarly represent in pictorial form progress towards sustainability along a number of selected ordinal axes. With due recognition given to weightings and the value of given indicators, Bell and Morse suggest that the closer the AMOEBA is to a perfect circle, the more balanced and so more sustainable the activity is.

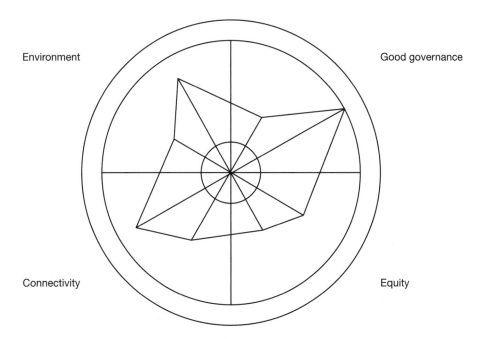

Figure 9.5 Illustration for a neighbourhood or community

Graphic representation and coding are simple ways of communicating a message and changing mindsets. Eco-labelling may help raise awareness about the nature and impact of consumption. Who now buys a D-rated fridge? And, although there may be many issues to do with product labelling, particularly regarding foodstuffs, where nutritional value as well as origin may be important, the idea of the label or kite mark signifies the use of indicators as key elements in communicating sustainability. The European Ecolabel Scheme was launched in 1992, aiming to establish a credible and generally recognized sign across the European Union. The flower emblem can be applied to both goods and services and can be seen in all twenty-seven EU countries as well as in Norway, Iceland and Liechtenstein. Its basic aims are:

- to promote the design, production, marketing and use of products which have a reduced environmental impact during their entire life-cycle; and
- to provide consumers with better information on the environmental impact of products.

Making indicators, kite marks and logos resonate with everyday life experience enables them to be readily recognized and understood. The Cradle to Cradle product certification programme, started in 2005 by William McDonough and Michael Braungart, and since 2010 administered by the non-profit Cradle to Cradle Products Innovation Institute, takes a comprehensive approach to the design and manufacturing practices of products. The materials and manufacturing of a product is assessed according to five categories: material health, material reutilization, renewable energy use, water stewardship and social responsibility. The Fair Trade Association, Soil

Association, Forestry Stewardship Council, and many other organized and regulated labels communicate trust, authority and transparency because they come with a clear explanation of the criteria informing them. This serves to undermine the rather vague and usually meaningless green claims some manufacturers place on their products. What, after all, does 'environmentally friendly', 'simple' or 'natural' mean unless there is a clear explanation? In the US, progress has been made regarding food labelling, but there are still no clear standards for household products. As Beth Daley (2005) of the *Boston Globe* noted, 'to find out what's really inside a cleaner, consumers must decipher label claims or request documents the company must publish that list federally named hazardous substances'.

Occasionally, changes to policy can lead to widespread critical discussion. In October 2007, the Soil Association, Britain's most important campaigning and certification organization for organic food and farming, announced that it was recommending that only organic food air-freighted into the country that had been produced according to the Association's own ethical trade standards, or those of the Fair Trade Association, would qualify for the Soil Association label. The reasoning behind the decision was to help minimize the use of air freight, since this mode of transportation generates 177 times more greenhouse gases than shipping. It is clear that increasing fossil fuel use worsens the effects of global warming, and Africa is already suffering particularly badly from climate change. Less than 1 per cent of organic food comes into the UK by air, but 80 per cent of this is produced by farmers in low- or middle-income countries who otherwise have a very low carbon footprint. Recognizing the moral difficulty of this recommendation, Anna Bradley, Chair of the Soil Association's Standards Board, said:

> It is neither sustainable nor responsible to encourage poorer farmers to be reliant on air freight, but we recognize that building alternative markets that offer the same social and economic benefits as organic exports will take time. Therefore, the Soil Association will be doing all it can to encourage farmers in developing countries to create and build organic markets that do not depend on air freight. We also want the public to have clear and meaningful information about both the environmental and social impact of air-freighted organic food.
>
> (Soil Association, 2007)

Similarly, *Ethical Consumer Magazine* provides consumers with information on the ethical and sustainability performance of companies and products, rating them against five ethical criteria based on information from a variety of sources, including NGO reports, corporate communications and daily news. The resulting 'ethiscore' enables users to quickly differentiate between companies, monitor corporate ethical performance, and benchmark companies within product or market sectors. The five categories are:

1   *Environment* (environmental reporting, nuclear power, climate change, pollution and toxics, habitats and resources).
2   *People* (human rights, workers' rights, supply chain policy, irresponsible marketing, armaments).
3   *Animals* (animal testing, factory farming).

4 *Politics* (political activity, boycott call, genetic engineering, anti-social finance, company ethos).
5 *Product sustainability* (organic, fair trade, positive environmental and/or sustainability features).

There are two types of ethiscore. For companies the score can range from 0 (bad) to 15 (excellent) and for products 0 (bad) to 20 (excellent), based on combining the company ethiscore with a score for product sustainability. Points are deducted for criticism of company performance – for example, on workers' rights or animal testing – and added for positive product attributes – for example, fair trade or organic. An example of the value of such a system can be found in a study of the effects of large corporate takeovers on the performance of smaller ethical enterprises such as Ben and Jerry's, Pret a Manger, Green and Black's, The Body Shop and Rachel's Organic. In each case, the bigger corporation wants to improve its brand image by incorporating the ethical business, but in each case reviewed, the smaller organization's company and product ethiscore dropped, in some cases quite considerably. The rating of the ice-cream manufacturer Ben and Jerry's, for example, fell from its pre-takeover rating of 13 to 1.5 following its capture by Unilever (Teather, 2007). Significantly, possibly as a result of this type of criticism, many large companies, including Unilever, have considerably revised and reformed their social responsibility and sustainability practices and some, such as Nike, are successfully moving towards developing more ecocentric transformational business and marketing strategies (Borland and Lingreen, 2013).

Jugaad: creativity, frugal innovation and resilient ingenuity

Jugaad is a Hindi term meaning an improvised solution born from ingenuity. For the authors of *Jugaad Innovation* (Radjou, Prabhu and Ahuja, 2012) this translates further to mean doing more with less, seeking opportunity from adversity, seeking simple solutions and believing in what you are doing. Jugaad is closely associated with an improvised solution, but since the 2008 financial crash the idea seems to have gone global, attracting major corporations from all over the world. The basic idea is that at the root of these improvised solutions is a creativity that should not be systematized or made rigid by management systems that identify and prescribe specific steps, stages and actions. There is a flow and naturalness to jugaad that resonates with the more creative juices of the sustainability debate and the need to conserve resources rather than to flagrantly expend them in high-status R&D exercises. Total Quality Management systems such as Six Sigma and similar were, and are, designed to deliver predictability to organizations. For instance, the Six Sigma website states that 'it is a disciplined, data-driven approach and methodology for eliminating defects ... in any process – from manufacturing to transactional and from product to service'. There is now a need to go beyond this if the uncertainties and risks of unsustainability are to be addressed effectively. Predictability in such circumstances, especially when major changes can occur swiftly, can impede action, development, creativity and learning. There needs to be a greater degree of flexibility, fluidity and creativity than a more prescriptive process can offer. Social media has democratized innovation and communication to some extent and this in turn has led to a greater degree of flexibility and a changing of mindsets, of thinking and perception.

To illustrate the jugaad concept, Radjou *et al.* have drawn on their extensive fieldwork in India and one example is frequently quoted as exemplifying the reality and spirit of resilient ingenuity. Mansukh Prajapati lives in a hot desert region of India where electricity is yet to come to the village and, even if it did, most villagers are too poor to purchase it. In order to keep food cool he wanted a refrigerator but one that did not use electricity which, if such a thing could be created, would significantly improve the quality and standard of life of the village. He came up with an innovative solution constructing a biodegradable refrigerator called Mitticool that can store fruit and vegetables for up to five days and dairy products for two days, by harnessing the natural cooling effects of clay from which the refrigerator is made. Composed of two compartments one above the other, water runs down the walls and so cools the lower chamber through evaporation. This invention now sells throughout India and markets for it are now developing in the Middle East, the US and even parts of the UK. There have been other low-cost improvised innovations too, including the means to retrofit motor vehicles to make them more fuel efficient and sustainable, and the creation of a low-cost computer tablet, similar to the iPad, but retailing at 10 per cent of the price. These Aakash tablets are now being used in Indian schools and even in the heart of hi-tech innovation itself – Silicon Valley. A new company called Embrace developed an affordable infant warmer that looks rather like a tiny sleeping-bag, employed by doctors and nurses primarily in rural areas within developing countries. Embrace piloted the product in India where 1.2 million premature babies die every year and, retailing at US$200, it costs about 5 per cent of what an incubator would cost in the US.

Jugaad innovators tend to work quickly, pay considerable attention to prototyping techniques, technologies and attendant behaviours, and place great value in harnessing the collective endeavours and wisdom of networks. Anil Gupta and his colleagues (Gupta *et al.*, 2003; Gupta, 2006) have helped create the Honey Bee Network, a loose platform to bring together creative but otherwise unco-ordinated individuals across a number of Indian states, with a view to transforming the way resources such as knowledge, practices and skills are used by rich and poor alike. Ecological ethics and collaborative learning have been integrated into the work of this network, which has profound implications for the future of sustainable development processes generally. Gupta *et al.* write:

> The democratic development of multiple futures in different parts of the world hinges considerably on the possibility of polycentric spurs of innovations. Unless a hundred flowers bloom and we create legitimacy for diversity and autonomy for each flower to blossom, there is no future for democratic development with human dignity. . . . Forces of globalization tend to homogenize the human taste and preferences, constricting in the process the space for articulating ethical capital, particularly from the grassroots' green innovators. The major institutional gaps in the developmental thinking and action around the world prove the sterility of conventional wisdom in overcoming the massive problem of poverty, unemployment, iniquity and discrimination. . . . The development process can become sustainable only when it has an intrinsic source of revitalization, self-renewal and self-criticism. . . . For a polycentric development in future, we need to look for multiple spurs of entrepreneurial growth.

(2003: 984–5)

This growth entails respecting traditional ecological knowledge, recognizing the importance of widespread diffusion of knowledge and understanding about the new innovation and a democratic system in which learning and communication can occur freely. Finally, for Radjou, Prabhu and Ahuja (2012), jugaad is something that can help conventional companies too in their mainstream activity and in intensifying their commitment to corporate responsibility. This can take place though the delivery of economies of scope, when companies need to customize solutions to the needs of specific but multiple market segments in varied and diverse environments; by providing 'soft' capital through releasing the enthusiasm and creative instincts of employees, business partners and customers; and by enhancing flexibility, adaptability and versatility, and by enabling the improvisational use of limited resources.

Production and consumption: the logic of sufficiency

For Thomas Princen (2002, 2005), one major problem confronting contemporary society in any attempt to become more ecologically sustainable is the emphasis placed on production rather than consumption. If cars pollute, then we produce catalytic converters and more fuel-efficient engines. If traffic is congested, we produce more road signals and more roads. If suburban growth becomes too extensive, we promote 'smart growth'. If flooding destroys property, we produce better flood defences. If aquifers are depleted, we sink deeper wells. And so on. The alternative is to develop an ecological conception of economic activity that incorporates environmental consideration as integral to both the analysis of economic practice and the practice itself – 'goods may be good but cautious consuming is better' (Princen, 2002: 27). People need to produce goods and services in order to live, to engage with others in society, and to secure a decent standard and quality of life, but not all of people's needs have to be met through the purchase of commercially produced goods and services. One problem is that the simple consumption of material goods, particularly consumer goods, does not satisfy socially constructed wants and needs for any length of time. Advertisers promise more than the goods are able to deliver, and many are instantly disposable, not least because of fashion, but also because their functionality is either superseded by new developments or they just break down. For design critics like Jonathan Chapman (2005), the problem is partly one of design: users and purchasers rarely relate emotionally to the product. Design does not generally elicit an emotionally durable commitment or connection. We dispose of things, of stuff, because we basically do not care about what we throw away. Non-purchase decisions also need to be factored in, as it is quite possible for many people to secure a healthy diet by growing some produce themselves, to enjoy music by playing an instrument with others rather than buying a CD or purchasing a download. It is quite possible to meet some needs without increasing economic and material throughput. In other words, it is quite possible to develop an ecological economics that relates biophysical conditions with human behaviour by simply focusing on various aspects of the appropriation and application of energy resources and materials for production and consumption.

Obviously, consumption is necessary for the survival of any and every species on the planet. There is clearly a necessary background level of consumption. But ecological economics suggests that human consumption can lead to problems if there is too much of it (over-consumption, excessive throughput) or where consumption is misdirected (misconsumption). Unlike other species, humans can reflect on their actions and offer moral judgements on what they do (or don't do), both at a macro-aggregate (society/planet) and an individual (personal) level. We can simply buy something to make us happy and when that happiness wears off we can buy something else, throwing the first purchase away. But in doing so, we can cause both societal and individual psychological problems, and producers will continue to produce more if consumers and the market demand it. For Princen, it is therefore incumbent on producers and consumers to develop restraint if further ecological damage is to be avoided. Simple living, micro-renewable energy generation and local currencies as used in local exchange and trading schemes, and in some 'Transition towns' are self-limiting behaviours that place ecosystem services ahead of ongoing material production, capital accumulation and resource depletion. Consequently, a consumption perspective highlights the nature of demand. Do we need more houses because of population increases? Do new housing developments reflect their full ecological costs and impacts? Is car use facilitated by subsidized road building? Does easy credit encourage undesirable consumerism? Tied to all this, as Maniates (2002) argues, is the individualization of responsibility for living lightly and reducing environmental impacts. Apart from ignoring larger institutional responsibilities, eco-living has itself turned into a consumer product growth industry, as the publication of green lifestyle magazines and features seems to confirm. Capitalism is capable of incorporating and commoditizing alternatives and ideological dissent, such as 'No Zone like the Ozone' T-shirts or buying into tree-planting schemes to offset carbon emissions simultaneously with your e-ticket cheap flight weekend break in Copenhagen, leading to little more than building 'a better mousetrap' – unless organized social and political power, the control and guidance of economic development, and technological innovation is confronted through collective action (Winner, 1989). Maniates argues that the very processes that individualize consumption can be addressed by revising the familiar environmental formulation 'IPAT':

$$\text{Impact} = \text{Population} \times \text{Affluence} \times \text{Technology}$$

Maniates sees IPAT as naively obscuring an understanding of political power and, as such, being quite disempowering. In its place, a convenient and more accurate formulation might be 'IWAC':

$$\text{Environmental Impact} = \text{Quality of Work} \times \text{Meaningful Consumption} \\ \text{Alternatives} \times \text{Political Creativity}$$

For many people, work is deeply unsatisfying, arduous and insecure. Corporate downsizing, restructuring and permanent change is not compensated for by either salaries or the relentless search for consumer commodities, foreign holidays or the soon-to-be-obsolete new media devices. This means that consumers will need to ensure they extract the full benefit from their purchases, that what people need is not more 'stuff' but more satisfaction. Manno (2002: 67) has devised the concept of 'consumption efficiency' to help this process of challenging commoditization, replacing the primary emphasis on the maximization of a good or service's potential to be sold in a competitive marketplace with establishing economic arrangements that foster an economy of care and connection.

The private car, plastics and the new media technology industry are prime examples of this, with considerable amounts of research and development being invested in ensuring that use value is secondary to exchange or commodity value. Obviously, a different form of rationality, an ecological rationality, needs to come into play.

Money makes the world go around?

It has long been established with tools such as the Index of Sustainable Economic Wellbeing (Ekins, 2000) and major studies like those of Robert E. Lane (2000) that more goods and increasing demand through advertising does not necessarily mean greater human happiness and contentment. As Lane writes:

> Although it is said that the function of the market is to satisfy human wants and so maximize various satisfactions, it is not true that the function of advertising is to maximize satisfaction; rather, its function is to increase people's dissatisfaction with any current state of affairs, to create wants and to exploit the dissatisfactions of the present. Advertising must use dissatisfaction to achieve its purpose.
>
> (2000: 179)

Hamilton (2003) writes of a growth fetish, which has basically failed to improve the quality of people's lives in the more developed countries. Crime, drugs, environmental destruction, job insecurity, family breakdown, rampant and conspicuous consumerism, economic inequality, feelings of political impotence, and corruption are identified as key factors that are wrong with contemporary Western society. 'Social democracy is being superseded by a sort of market totalitarianism,' he writes (2003: 21). Robert Frank (1999) has shown that our satisfaction with our materialistic way of life depends very much on how we see ourselves in relation to others – and not just those similar to ourselves. Kasser (2002) examines a number of psychological studies into the effects of consumerism on everyday happiness and psychological health. People who are highly motivated by materialistic values seem to have lower personal well-being than those who believe a materialistic way of life is relatively undesirable. What increases psychological health and well-being are feelings of safety, security, autonomy, authenticity and connection to others. Those people who tend to watch a great deal of commercial television have materialistic values reinforced through advertising and popular TV programming on celebrity lifestyles, leading to a tendency to (over)idealize possessions and wealth, to buy themselves out of unhappiness (retail therapy), and to enter less into community and other social activities. Freedom of choice and an overabundance of goods and services comes at the cost of feeling pressured and compelled to keep up. Materialistic people also tend to show little interest in environmental and ecological issues, and exhibit little empathy or intimacy in their relationships. It seems that many of us are not happy and, in the present cultural circumstances, are unlikely ever to be so. One recognition and reaction to this has been the growth of the voluntary simplicity movement – the intentional personal downsizing of wants and commodity needs, the reduction in working hours or the search for more fulfilling and less stressful employment, and the desire perhaps to live with a much reduced environmental impact (Durning, 1992; Andrews, 1997; Schor, 1998; Maniates, 2002). Those who adopt this simplified lifestyle, usually middle class but not necessarily wealthy or privileged, tend to use their time in more socially, culturally and community-orientated activities. Voluntary simplifiers are not dropping out, but becoming more engaged at a time when, because of various pressures, many people are disengaging from civic and community life. Others have emphasized the need for and importance of personal growth, reconnecting with nature and doing something 'meaningful' instead of seeking short-term gratifications in the marketplace.

Well-being and human flourishing

This dissatisfaction has also led critics to develop alternative measures of progress and development. GNP and GDP measure the level of economic activity expressed in monetary terms so that, for example, the money spent on clearing up an oil spill will mean an increase in economic activity, irrespective of the social and environmental harms incurred. The index of sustainable economic welfare (ISEW) (Daly and Cobb, 1989) and the genuine progress indicator (GPI), on the other hand, are two, albeit contested alternatives attempting to incorporate a range of factors that influence human well-being into a single aggregate index. Costs and benefits are included in the calculus. Jackson and Marks (1998) revised the ISEW, basing it explicitly on Manfred Max-Neef's (1991) characterization of human needs (subsistence, protection, affection, understanding, participation, idleness, creation, identity, freedom) and exist-ential satisfiers (being, having, doing, interacting). They demonstrate that consuming economic goods and satisfying human needs are not the same thing, because the relationship between the consumption of an economic good and the satisfaction of an underlying need is complex. For example:

> In their most functional capacity, cars provide mobility. But mobility itself is neither a satisfier nor a need. Rather it is a structural element within the attempted satisfaction of many needs. Mobility allows us to travel to work, where we can earn a living (subsistence) and to shop so that we can buy, for example, food and clothing (subsistence and protection). But use values for cars are now well-established in relation to a wide variety of other needs. Cars are associated in the prevailing Western culture (and increasingly in other cultures) with social status (participation and identity), with sexual success (affection), with personal power (identity), with recreation and leisure (participation, idleness), and with freedom and creativity.
>
> (Jackson and Marks, 1998: 430)

Over the years, consumer expenditure aimed at satisfying material and non-material needs, such as travel, sports and recreation, electrical goods, communications, clothing, alcohol, leisure and entertainment, has increased significantly, but Jackson and Marks's conclusions (1998: 439) are salutary: increased needs-satisfaction cannot be inferred from increased expenditure, with material consumption probably offering no more than 'a pseudo-satisfaction of non-material needs' and possibly actually inhibiting the satisfaction of those needs. In other words, 'wellbeing does not consist in the accumulation of material possessions'.

The GPI will evaluate job losses against economic growth, attempting to value the full psychological as well as financial costs of unemployment, will assess activities that enhance well-being but which fall outside of the marketplace, like housework and community volunteering, and will deduct the costs of crime-related expenditure, environmental pollution and the depletion of non-renewable resources. According to the GPI, the costs of economic growth now significantly outweigh the benefits. Distaso (2007) applies Sen's theory of well-being as the basis for making the concept of sustainable development operational, through the construction of a multidimensional index of sustainability that also addresses the inadequacies of both GDP and some multi-attribute indices like the ISEW and the UN's Human Development Index (HDI), which stress such factors as longevity, literacy and maternal mortality rates. Sen (1999) posits qualitative analytical categories such as functionings (personal achievements), capabilities (achievable functionings) and freedom (actual opportunities). Meaningful variables relating to sustainability, such as consumption, income distribution, life expectancy, health, education, employment, pollution, and aesthetic and cultural values, were selected. Various weightings were then decided and, using a standardized deviation methodology, Distaso applied the index to the countries of the European Union. The method allowed relationships between natural capital and quality of life, social well-being and environmental and economic conditions, and environmental well-being and issues relating to inter- and intra-generational equity. Irrespective of the sustainable development ranking, however, Distaso (2007: 178) concluded that each country 'should implement policies which are specifically aimed at reaching a development more careful to the environment, notwithstanding the well known economic implications'.

Lawn (2003) notes that many critics of multidimensional indices argue that they lack a robust theoretical foundation, particularly with regard to their valuation methods, which may be rather crude and involve some massive assumptions. However, Lawn argues that, although these methods can be improved upon, they are basically sound, if warranting a continual refinement over time. Better standardization and better welfare comparisons between nations will improve the likelihood of these alternative indices to GDP being more broadly accepted and applied. However, a note of caution is expressed by Stapleton and Garrod (2007), who, examining whether the equal weights assumption informing the HDI should be relaxed or not, conclude that only limited, if any, gains in validity may be achieved by increasing the complexity of an already highly complex system.

Another alternative index that has attracted considerable recent interest has been developed by the New Economics Foundation. The Happy Planet Index (HPI) attempts to express the average years of happy life or well-being produced by any given society or nation compared with the consumption of the Earth's finite resources. The HPI incorporates three separate indicators relating to a country's ecological footprint and people's life expectancy and life satisfaction. Data from 178 countries have been compiled to produce a global happiness league table. The G8 countries do rather poorly, with Britain in 108th place, France 129th, the US 150th and Russia 172nd. The Foundation's HPI Report (Marks *et al.*, 2006) makes the following points:

- *Countries classified by the United Nations as 'medium human development' fair better than* both *low and high-development countries* because, beyond a certain level, vastly increasing consumption fails to lead to greater well-being.
- *Well-being is not based on high levels of consumption:* for example, Estonia, with high consumption, rates poorly on well-being, while the Dominican Republic enjoys consumption at an equitable global (lower) level, but well-being is high.

- *Life satisfaction varies wildly country by country*: 29.4 per cent of Zimbabweans rate their life satisfaction at the lowest level, while 5.7 per cent rate it highly. In contrast, 28.4 per cent of Danes rate their life satisfaction highly, with less than 1 per cent rating it poorly.
- *Life expectancy varies wildly*: Life expectancy in Japan is 82 years, in Swaziland it is just over 32.
- *Social, cultural and political structures are strongly associated with life satisfaction*, with high levels being found in those nations where more people belong to community groups, where government is open and democratic, and where concepts of adventure, creativity, meaningful work and loyalty are valued highly.
- *Overall, we are overburdening the Earth's currently available biocapacity* by consuming 22 per cent above our ecosystems' ability to regenerate.

NEF's 2012 HP1 report indicated that our planet is still fairly unhappy with only 9 out of 151 reaching high and sustainable levels of well-being. Eight of these are in Latin America and the Caribbean. The highest ranked European country is Norway coming in at 29 with the USA trailing at 105 (Abdallah *et al.*, 2012).

This will come as no surprise to readers of Helena Norberg-Hodge's powerful study of Ladakh, *Ancient Futures* (Norberg-Hodge, 2000), before and after its modernization. A settled, spiritual and traditional culture was displaced by a

Table 9.3 EU sustainable development ranking

Issue: Protect and enhance the environment	Examples of popular community indicators
Use energy, water and other **natural resources**	Number of buildings measured for energy efficiently and with care efficiency
	Water leakage (in litres/property/day)
	Value and protect the **diversity** of nature
	Wildlife in rivers and streams
	Wildlife diversity
Protect human **health** and amenity through safe, clean, pleasant environments	Number of asthma cases
	Skin cancer incidence
	Number of bronchodilator asthma treatments prescribed
Meet local needs **locally** wherever possible	Percentage of shops selling locally produced or processed foods
	Basic services within walking distance Alternative means of transport: kilometres of dedicated cycle lanes
Ensure access to good **food, water, housing** and **fuel** at reasonable cost	Homelessness: number of households applying to local authorities
	Average house prices
	Availability of a healthy food basket

Source: McGillivray *et al.* (1998).

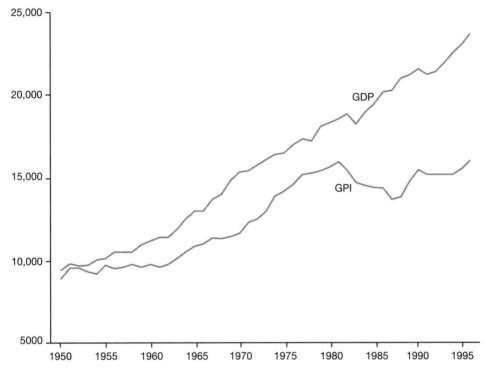

Figure 9.6 Australia: GDP and GPI, 1950–96 (constant 1990 prices)

consumer-driven one that led to dissatisfaction, disruption and an alienation from both past and present. The need for change and the need to live equitably on one planet without destroying its ability to sustain human and other life-forms is now recognized globally as of the utmost importance. Footprinting, environmental space methodologies, corporate sustainability indicators, and broader schemes such as the WWF's One Planet Living are elements of a wide social and cultural movement to change minds and behaviours. The survey *State of the Future*, produced by the World Federation of United Nations Associations (Glenn and Gordon, 2007), offers considerable statistical information: the global economy grew at 5.4 per cent in 2006 to US$66 trillion, although income disparities remain huge, with 2 per cent of the world's richest people owning more than 50 per cent of the world's wealth, while the poorest 50 per cent of people own just 1 per cent. Despite many violent clashes, the vast majority of the world is living in peace, with the number of conflicts falling, dialogues among differing worldviews growing and the number of refugees decreasing. Gender equality is growing too, with the legislative, senior official or managerial positions held by women slowly increasing from 25.6 per cent in 1995 to 28.3 per cent in 2006. Gender equality in primary education has virtually been achieved, although 781 million adults (two-thirds women) still lack basic literacy skills, and violence against women by men continues to cause more casualties than wars. There are more slaves in the world today than at the highest point of the African slave trade, with estimates varying from 12.3 million to 27 million (the majority are Asian

Table 9.4 State of the future index 2007: where humanity is winning and losing

Sweden	1	Belgium	9
Austria	2	UK	10
France	3	Spain	11
Germany	4	Greece	12
Denmark	5	Luxembourg	13
Netherlands	6	Ireland	14
Finland	7	Portugal	15
Italy	8		

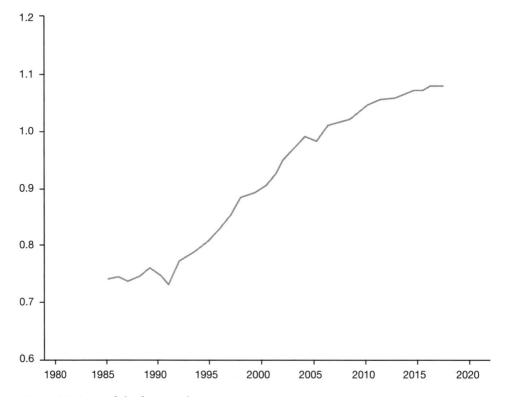

Figure 9.7 State of the future index

women). The shortage of fresh water is acute in some regions. The incidence of AIDS in Africa is levelling off. Computer power is increasing, as is climate change awareness. And the list goes on.

   With so much data available, it is extremely difficult to know whether the general state of the future is improving or not, but the 2007 report helpfully offers a revised state of the future index (SOFI), including twenty-nine variables, attempting to give a general indication of how we are likely to do.

   The conclusion: the SOFI is improving, but not as rapidly as it did in the previous twenty years. However, as the renowned Cambridge economist Partha Dasgupta (2001) notes, different indicators indicate different things, and very few offer a holistic and informed understanding of sustainable development.

Case study: the guiding principles of one planet living

To achieve a sustainable future, we need to design communities that enable people to live sustainably, that is, within the limits of the biosphere. Clearly, the situation in different countries will vary. Factors such as the commuting distance between home and work, where the food comes from, and how waste is dealt with will be as important as, if not more important than the energy performance of buildings. The NGOs BioRegional and WWF aim to build on their work to promote the concepts of sustainable development and ecological footprinting, notably by establishing a set of sustainable communities in diverse contexts across the globe. Projects are intended to be delivered via partnerships with private developers, community groups and the public sector, and must commit to and adopt the guiding principles of One Planet Living. Via these communities and associated initiatives, the programme aims to have a transformative effect on the surrounding region and inform policy changes at national and international levels. The One Planet Living programme is based on ten guiding principles, which act as a framework to highlight the sustainability challenge in a given situation and as a mechanism for developing and presenting solutions. The principles – zero carbon, zero waste, sustainable transport, local and sustainable materials, local and sustainable food, sustainable water, protection of natural habitats and wildlife, culture and heritage, equity and fair trade, and health and happiness – offer a clear direction, and although actions to realize them may vary according to context or organization, it is clearly possible to develop indicators identifying and communicating progress in all these areas.

Summary

This chapter examines some of the practical ways in which we can work towards achieving a greater degree of sustainability in our social and economic practices. Most of these tools invariably take a systems and a systemic approach to societal or organizational change, although they may vary in their degree of prescription to follow a set of steps or in their freedom to innovate and extemporize. Thus, the practical tools and practical action should not be seen as being divorced from the values and knowledge that actually informs them for both theory and practice are reflexively related. They work on each other and we can learn from how the tools are applied, whether they succeed or fail, in different contexts and specific circumstances. Ecological principles come to have a practical importance as do ideas and conceptions of sufficiency, innovation and well-being for without understanding, these tools and toolkits would be literally meaningless. It is, therefore, important that we understand what the ideas and concepts refer to and how best to measure or assess the effects of their implementation. However, measurement can take different forms and should not be automatically associated with quantification. Not everything that existed can be weighed or counted.

Thinking questions

1   What are the important advantages and disadvantages of the ecological footprinting and environmental space metaphors?

2   How do indicators relate to frameworks such as The Natural Step or One Planet Living?
3   What can be learnt from jugaad?
4   In what ways are indicators more than communication tools?
5   What value do aggregate quality of life or happiness indices have in promoting sustainable development?
6   What is the significance of product labelling?

Companion website

To test your understanding of sustainability tools and frameworks, please visit the companion website for further case studies and some test questions.

10 Communication and learning for sustainability

Aims

This chapter will examine various aspects of communication and learning for sustainability. The role of marketing, public communication campaigns, the Internet, cyberspace, film and television will be explored using a range of examples. In many ways, the mediascape can be seen as being an environment through which we make sense of the world and of ourselves. The chapter will close with a brief discussion of the main features of Education for Sustainable Development, referencing both the formal learning taking place within institutions like schools, colleges, universities, etc., and the informal learning occurring outside the classroom in the community and in everyday life.

Mediascapes, the mediapolis and the public sphere

The anthropologist Arjun Appadurai (1996: 33) has written of the global cultural economy and the interrelationship of five global cultural flows: ethnoscapes, mediascapes, technoscapes, financescapes and ideoscapes. He uses the suffix 'scape' to highlight the variability of these environments and to 'indicate that these are not objectively given relations that look the same from every angle of vision, but rather, that they are deeply perspectival constructs shaped by language, politics, space and place:

> Mediascapes refer both to the distribution of the electronic capabilities to produce and disseminate information (newspapers, magazines, television stations and film-production studios), which are now available to a growing number of private and public interests through the world, and to the images of the world created by these media. These images involve many complicated inflections, depending on their mode (documentary or entertainment), their hardware (electronic or pre-electronic), their audiences (local, national or transnational), and the interests of those who own and control them. What is most important about these mediascapes is that they provide (especially in their television, film and cassette forms) large and complex repertoires of images, narratives and ethnoscapes to viewers throughout the world, in which the world of commodities and the world of news and politics are profoundly mixed. What this means is that many audiences around the world experience the media themselves as a complicated and interconnected repertoire of print, celluloid, electronic screens and billboards.
>
> (Appadurai, 1996: 35)

From these mediascapes, people are able to construct scripts of others' imagined lives and of events beyond their direct experience, to gain information communicated by big global corporations, public broadcasters, international agencies or small groups of indigenous peoples harnessing the opportunities of new media technology to tell their stories to whoever will listen in the rest of the increasingly 'wired-up' world. Related to the concept of mediascape is that of ideoscape, which refers to chains of ideas, concepts, images and values like freedom, democracy, growth and perhaps sustainability that constitute individual and group worldviews and perspectives. There are many debates and discussions about the economic and ideological power of global media corporations, with fears that global culture is being standardized, simplified, homogenized and Americanized. Ritzer (2000) writes of social, cultural and business practices suffering from 'McDonaldization' and Bryman (1999) sees the 'Disneyization' of much of our cultural leisure practices. A form of cultural imperialism is often evident through the ubiquity of Hollywood movies and the Hollywood-style, adaptable reality television and game-show formats and global sales of popular entertainments like *Friends* and *Big Brother*. However, this argument is contested by those who see consumers as being producers too – of meaning and interpretation that culturally mediates alien ideas and values, and also of media artefacts such as films, video shorts, blogs and advertisements that increasingly find distribution in the still largely unregulated globalized cultural commons known as the Internet (Tomlinson, 1991; Ginsburg *et al.*, 2002; Couldry and Curran, 2003; Roth, 2005; Parks, 2005; Thussu, 2006). The advertising, marketing and public relations industry is also viewed by many as a direct influence, or even cause, of the insatiable growth in global consumerism (Schiller, 1989). However, as Silverstone (2007) states, the mediated space of appearance he calls the 'mediapolis' is important because ultimately its degree of freedom from corporate or government restrictions will influence not just the free flow of communication – our access to others' worlds and worldviews, ideas and ideologies – but the very possibility of social dialogue, human growth and development. To enable this, we need global standards for media practice that will combat the pollution of the global media environment – the mediascape – by powerful corporations and reactionary governments. Securing the future of our physical environment, Silverstone argues, will in the end be of limited value if we allow our symbolic one to be fatally eroded or destroyed. We need both eco-sustainability literacy and media literacy, combining knowledge and skills with morality and ethics from both cognate fields: 'For without an adequate expression of the plurality of the world which the mediapolis must provide, both on the screen and in the interaction of screen and spectator, then there is little to look forward to' (Silverstone, 2007: 55).

Indeed, the concept 'mediapolis' updates the work of Jurgen Habermas (1974) whose earlier notion of 'the public sphere' – a site (or sites) where free, rational, popular and passionate debate can occur, where political understanding and engagement can be nurtured and where learning can continually take place. For Habermas the public sphere is an essential component of any democracy worth its name and the media, both traditional and new (analogue and digital), is central to its maintenance or (alternatively) its erosion. Thus the public sphere exists whenever individual citizen voices come to share, question or communicate 'in an unrestricted fashion – that is, with the guarantee of freedom of assembly and association and the freedom to express and publish their opinions – about matters of general interest' (Habermas, 1974: 49). Fears that governments, corporations and other bodies are increasingly limiting these freedoms or that some groups consistently fail to get their voices heard have led to numerous discussions about counter-publics, alternative media forms and counter public spheres (Fraser, 1990; Dahlberg, 2007; Downey and Fenton, 2003).

Box 10.1 Greenpeace international media analyst reflects on communicating climate change

In normal times the public sphere is dominated by economically and politically powerful actors but at times of perceived or actual crisis campaign groups and counter publics have greater opportunities to influence public opinion. It is at these times that the public sphere becomes more discernibly public.

Q: Please describe a few successful GI campaigns. What factors made them successful?

A: There are many campaigns/actions that come to mind that were successful from a media viewpoint, so I will share only a few illustrative examples. In 2006, we launched a digital campaign with a parody version of the Apple website called 'GreenMyApple,' which encouraged Mac lovers to push Apple to review its recycling policies and use of toxic chemicals. After having received thousands of reactions online, Apple finally decided last year to start to comply with a more responsible regime of environmental stewardship. Our anti-whaling campaign over the past years has also been increasingly successful in isolating Japan internationally on its defense of its inappropriate use of 'scientific' whaling on a commercial scale. In 2008, we decided to focus on Japanese youth to support Japan's cessation of all whaling activities via a 'whale love' bus tour and online campaign, as well as cartoon adverts in cinemas. For the first time in years, we were able to generate significant media attention in Japan itself, where the media were questioning the validity of the whaling industry's actions. Late last year, two of our Japanese activists were unjustly arrested and charged for exposing corruption and scandal in the whaling industry. They had intercepted a box of whale meat being improperly transferred from the whaling ship Nisshin Maru to the private home of a crew member. Our Japanese colleagues took this box directly to the Tokyo public prosecutor as evidence of this improper transfer. The following press conference received major media coverage in Japan and has discredited the whaling industry. The public prosecutor actually dropped the charges against the Nisshin Maru whilst our activists are still under investigation. Another direct Greenpeace action with a high media impact took place in January 2006 and actually resulted in the return of an asbestos-laden French aircraft carrier from France bound for ship-breaking in Alang, India. Greenpeace volunteers intercepted and boarded the Clemenceau off the coast of Egypt and the resultant ongoing international media attention ultimately forced the governments in France and India to react.

Source: extract from DeLuca (2009: 266–7).

Media communications and the environment

The media and communications enable us to actively shape our understanding of the world beyond our own immediate direct experience. They help us create meaning and so orientate us in some way to the world we inhabit. In terms of symbolic action, Robert Cox (2013) uses the term environmental communication in two ways:

- *As pragmatic*: educating, alerting, persuading and helping audiences and users to deal with environmental problems.
- *As constitutive*: helping audiences and users to compose and construct representations of sustainability, nature and environment challenges as subjects for people's understanding.

Thus media communications may evoke certain perspectives, articulate certain values, define certain problems and offer particular references for attention, denial and/or action.

Images have been particularly important from both perspectives. In mid nineteenth-century America, the landscape photography of Carleton Watkins helped define the term 'wilderness' and establish a new resonance for the term 'environment' and in so doing became an important factor in persuading Congress to establish the Yosemite and Marisopa areas in California as the world's first national parks in 1864 (DeLuca and Demo, 2000). In the twentieth century the documentary films of Pare Lorentz and the photography of Walker Evans and Dorothea Lange helped shape the emotional response to the American Dust Bowl, just as the photography of Ansel Adams and the series of coffee-table books produced by the Sierra Club continued the work of the early wilderness pioneers such as John Muir (Dunaway, 2005). Of course, nature photography and wildlife filmmaking have been massively important to the world conservation movement, more generally creating symbols that can both mobilize and motivate action for positive change, with NGOs such as Greenpeace, PETA and WWF particularly adept in their use of images (Blewitt, 2010b). In other contexts, some photographers such as Edward Burtynsky whose twenty-five project photographing devastated and contaminated industrial landscapes across the world has led to a series of images that tend to elicit a sublime but negative response to toxicity which, rather than aestheticizing the landscape, serves to move the viewer 'beyond paralysis or indifference to the active contemplation of the self in relation to the object' (Peeples, 2011: 387). A sense of complicity that moves beyond indifference leads Jennifer Peeples to suggest:

> The recognition of a connection to these toxic places is the important step to understanding the need for alternative resource and waste protocols and decision making. In addition, the improbability of the sublime also allows for audacious thinking as one grapples with solutions to the difficult and abstruse problems of contamination. The toxic sublime, then, confronts two of the most damning barriers to dealing with contamination: (1) a lack of a visual presence leading to people not knowing the extent of the environmental damage and (2) a sense of impotence when facing the omnipresence and destructive capacity of the toxins.
>
> (2011: 388)

In an increasingly image-saturated cultural environment, image communication can play an important part in promoting social learning and even in motivating significant policy, technological and life-style changes. For Stephen Shepherd, realistic future landscape visualizations in 3D and 4D offer important advantages in rapidly advancing people's environmental awareness by enabling people to see in a vivid manner the possible consequences of climate change in a way that they can relate to personally and experientially. They can see and feel what may happen to their own backyards (Shepherd, 2012). However a spectacular visualization of climate change may be, however much they may galvanize sentiment, or even mobilize a more cosmopolitan perspective and local-global solidarity, still or moving images, whether in an art gallery or on a television news broadcast, 'cannot entirely substitute for the processes of political debate and deliberation which must also inform the politics of climate change' (Lester and Cottle, 2009: 933). The politics of climate change, of the environment and of sustainable development is not the same as the associated image politics or visual rhetoric, although one does closely inform the other (Lester, 2010).

The United Nations Decade for Education for Sustainable Development, 2005–14 (ESD) identifies the media as an important vehicle for promoting learning about the global environment and the developing world. The draft implementation guidance for the ESD Decade states:

> Journalists and media organizations have an important role to play in reporting on issues and in helping raise public awareness of the various dimensions and requirements of sustainable development. Their involvement can contribute to reinforcing access to information, communication and knowledge, as well as access to the know-how and capacities necessary for effective use of ICTs in the framework of development programmes. This can include, for instance, the production of radio and television programmes with local content and on themes such as gender equality and universal basic education.
>
> (UNESCO, 2005: 25)

Contemporary debate about sustainability and the environment is dominated by corporations, governments, NGOs, universities and other organizations which often have, or hire, sophisticated Public Relations outfits which often represent particular interests, values and perspectives in sometimes open and in sometimes covert ways. The use of PR companies and techniques has increased phenomenally since the 1990s, with the big corporations often able to outspend other groups by wide margins. In the period preceding the Climate Change Conference in Copenhagen in 2009, the powerful oil and gas industry in the United States increased its PR budgets by 50 per cent (Lester, 2010). As news organizations cut their expenditure on investigative reporting, many journalists become increasingly reliant on detailed and ready-to-use media releases, which has arguably compromised journalistic values, the public sphere and the public interest (Lewis *et al.*, 2008; Reich, 2010). Richard Heede (2013), a researcher at the Climate Accountability Institute at Colorado, has shown that just ninety major companies or state-owned entities, such as Chevron, BP, Gazprom, Exxon Mobil and Saudi Aramoco, have been responsible for nearly two-thirds of the world's historical global greenhouse gas emissions, and a number of the biggest emitters have been active funders of climate disinformation campaigns. In such a context, the concerned citizen, oppositional group or counter public may find it difficult to get her voice heard within the traditional press and broadcasting media, leading commentators such as Anabela Carvalho (2007) to suggest that it is imperative that we read media output, whether an interpretation of a scientific report or a major environmental conference, politically, ideologically and critically, recognizing not only being said but what is also being left out. The struggle for a mediated visibility that is to be heard and seen is therefore of critical importance for the future of sustainable development. John B. Thompson writes:

> To achieve visibility through the media is to gain a kind of presence or recognition in the public space, which can help to call attention to one's situation or to advance one's cause. But equally, the inability to achieve visibility through the media can confine one to obscurity – and, in the worst cases, can lead to a kind of death by neglect. Hence it is not surprising that *struggles for visibility* have come to assume such significance in our societies today. Mediated visibility is not just a vehicle through which aspects of social and political life are brought to the attention of others: it has become a principal means by which social and political struggles are articulated and carried out.
>
> (2005: 49)

CARMA's 2006 report on Western media coverage of humanitarian disasters included analyses of media reporting on Hurricane Katrina in the US, Hurricane Stanley in Central America, famine in the Sudan, the Boxing Day tsunami, and earthquakes in Kashmir and Iran (CARMA, 2006). The conclusion is stark: Western self-interest is the major precondition for any significant coverage of an overseas humanitarian crisis. Economics was discovered to be a far more important motivator of media interest than the loss of human life, human suffering or displacement, and overt Western political interests determined the timing and extent of the coverage. Too often, as the BBC's Developing World Correspondent David Loyn (2006) has written, the mainstream media's and even NGOs' interest in 'compelling pictures' of dying babies or famine to promote or document a cause becomes little more than 'disaster-porn'. TV news and NGO marketing is unable to articulate the full story of a complex emergency into a simple visual narrative. Misguided development policies, war and long-term climate change, rather than locusts or short-term drought, are often the real culprits of sudden disasters.

Recently, there have been an increasing number of television and film documentaries (*An Inconvenient Truth, Darwin's Nightmare, The Corporation, Ghosts, Black Gold, The Age of Stupid, The Cove, Gasland, The Last Mountain*), feature articles in popular magazines, and Hollywood blockbusters (*The Constant Gardener, The Day After Tomorrow, Erin Brockovich, Avatar*) addressing some of the principal elements of sustainable and unsustainable development. Leiserowitz's (2004) impact study of *The Day After Tomorrow*, essentially a disaster movie/melodrama about climate change, suggests that the film did alter audience attitudes, although it was difficult to tell whether attitudes would remain changed. The film was seen by 21 million Americans (10 per cent of the US adult population) at the box office and by many more on television and DVD, mainly because people enjoy blockbuster disaster movies. Leiserowitz concludes:

The Day After Tomorrow had a significant impact on the climate change risk perceptions, conceptual models, behavioural intentions, policy priorities and even voting intentions of moviegoers. The film led moviegoers to have higher levels of concern and worry about global warming, to estimate various impacts on the US as more likely, and to shift their conceptual understanding of the climate system towards a threshold model. Further, the movie encouraged watchers to engage in personal, political and social action to address climate change and to elevate global warming as a national priority. Finally, the movie even appears to have influenced voter preferences. These results demonstrate that the representation of environmental risks in popular culture can influence public attitudes and behaviours.

(2004: 33)

Another impact study, in Germany, had slightly different results, but the authors concluded that the film:

raised awareness of the problem and stimulated the willingness to act, or at least to support government action. At the same time, the film has had a remarkable effect, having stimulated a more complex and enriched view of the Earth system in general and the climate system in particular.

(Reusswig *et al.*, 2004: 40)

Similarly, Morgan Spurlock's *Supersize Me*, released in 2004, addressed the problem of the fast-food industry's contribution to obesity and ill health, focusing specifically on the huge portions and poor nutritional value of McDonald's burgers. For thirty days, Spurlock, the Director, subjected himself to a diet of nothing but McDonald's, resulting in significant weight gain, increased cholesterol levels and other health ailments, including mood swings, liver damage and sexual dysfunction. The surrounding publicity, particularly after its screening at the Sundance Film Festival, combined with the long-running 'McLibel trial' in London, seriously tarnished McDonald's' reputation. Although denying that the decision had anything to do with the publicity the film generated, McDonald's soon started to phase out its supersize option, introducing healthier menu options while maintaining that health problems were largely the result of consumers overeating. In Australia, the company even offered to pay cinemas if their staff were allowed to distribute apples to audiences watching the film. In 2005, the medical journal *The Lancet* published a study (Pereira *et al.*, 2005), arguing that fast food could increase risk of obesity and diabetes through excessive portion size, emphasis on primordial taste preferences for sugar, salt and fat, and high glycemic load and trans-fatty acid content. More generally, it can be argued that in recent years a clear trend has developed which has seen the production, distribution and exhibition at festivals and increasingly on the Internet of films that have a clear consciousness raising and activist intention. Some of these tentatively suggest a trend towards eco-centrism and a critical public pedagogy (Willoquet-Maricondi, 2010; Blewitt, 2011). As Willoquet-Maricondi writes: 'Ecocinema overtly strives to inspire personal and political action on the part of viewers, stimulating our thinking so as to bring about concrete changes in the choices we make, daily and in the long run, as individuals and as societies, locally and globally' (2010: 45).

Reading new films politically, or engaging with ecocinema sympathetically, are elements of a wider project to develop a synergy between media and sustainability literacy. Online film festivals such as Green Unplugged and associated sites line www.cultureunplugged.com are making a considerable contribution to promoting this synergy. For media educator Antonio Lopez (2012) who, influenced by Bill

---

Box 10.2 Communicating climate change

In 2006 a study conducted by the Institute for Public Policy Research (IPPR) in London found that the climate change discourse in the UK was 'confusing, contradictory and chaotic' (Ereaut and Segnit, 2006: 7). Although there is today a recognized scientific consensus supporting the theory of anthropogenic climate change, popular responses consequently veered between 'everything is too big even to consider doing something about it' to 'climate change is so familiar that there's no point doing anything now'. The IPPR's advice to climate change and other sustainability communicators is to treat the fundamental facts as self-evident and use deep-seated cultural norms to galvanize interest and action. Possible actions need to become part of people's practical consciousness. They need to be valued personally, willingly, and understood and accepted in culturally meaningful terms. 'The answer is not to try to change their radar but to change the issue, so it becomes something they willingly pick up, because it means something valuable in their own terms', with communicators marketing 'climate-friendly everyday activity as a brand that can be sold' (Ereaut and Segnit, 2006: 28). Climate-friendly behaviours must therefore feel normal, natural, right and 'ours'. Uncertainties about the future need not lead to negative responses if these uncertainties are framed with caution, highlighting the ways in which loss may be avoided or mitigated (Morton *et al.*, 2011).

The National Center for Atmospheric Research's Institute for the Study of Society and Environment in Colorado hosted a three-day conference on climate change communication in June 2004. From this emerged the Boulder Manifesto, which significantly encapsulates a dialogic approach to climate change communication and social change which its authors believe will nurture efficient, adaptive, resilient and sustainable understanding and action. Its five propositions state that climate change communication:

- will stimulate a dialogue on hopeful visions of future everyday life through democratic means;
- will create a future vision that addresses immediate societal issues and needs while linking them to larger, systemic climate change issues;
- will acknowledge and incorporate the diversity of local cultures and practices that contribute to a sense of place;
- will be concerned with the design of institutions that promote adaptive and resilient, life-enhancing practices and lifestyles;
- will embody the change, demonstrating that personal climate-friendly lifestyles can eventually lead to change in the system as a whole.

(Harriss, 2007)

McKibben's idea of creating a media equivalent of a farmer's market, this means drawing on the educative potential of small and slow media such as discussion groups around specific films and books, peer-to-peer sharing of user-generated content on the Internet, practical media workshops, community-based radio stations and the creation of meaningful public dialogues on certain media messages, thereby helping to contextualize corporate media with a more localized situated knowledge.

Digital media

The Internet is the media platform of the twenty-first century, and is the focal point for the convergence of virtually every other traditional and familiar media of communication – speech, still and moving image, news and information, political debate and campaigning, environmental monitoring, community access, public art, and, of course, advertising and marketing. It is potentially a 'smooth' way of spreading ideas in a virus-like fashion (Godin, 2002). For public communicators, including public relations specialists and marketers, the Internet allows global reach to be achieved at relatively low cost. Website visits, clicks on ads, products purchased and others recommended, and documents or videos downloaded can be counted and campaigns evaluated. Direct sales and customized marketing are now virtually ubiquitous: 'customers who have bought X may also be interested in Y' or 'welcome, we recommend . . .'. Despite this, websites can be impersonal and invisible to those not looking for them, which means that Internet search engines are becoming increasingly important, commercially valuable and ideologically influential.

The Internet has also been used effectively by radical activists and campaign groups as new technology and open-access publishing of pressure group material has improved, and facilities for digital interaction, communication, debate and dialogue have expanded. The real possibilities of the Net as an organizing tool became clearly apparent at the time of the anti-capitalist protests in Seattle in 1999 (Bennett, 2003; de Jong *et al.*, 2005). Bennett (2003) argues that the integration and growth of Internet communications has influenced the form and perspective of political campaigns – from being ideologically based to being more personal and with looser modes of association. Political issues that tend to be relatively ignored by government or traditional media, such as food standards, environmental issues, labour relations, human rights and cultural identity, are picked up, often to the clear discomfort of corporate and government bureaucracies and politicians. Communication practices become almost inseparable from organizational and political capabilities and, to a significant degree, serve to constitute many contemporary protests, forms of activism and social movements (Cottle, 2011a). For example, patterns of digital communication allow the following:

- Campaigns can change shape and continue over considerable lengths of time.
- Digital communication campaigns are frequently quite rich in addressing identity and lifestyle issues.
- Digital hub organizations often become resources for other, emerging, campaign groups.
- New media can influence information flows and agendas in mainstream mass media news outlets.

Digital communication can also nurture connectivity, a sense of ownership, peer-to-peer as well as people-to-people relationships and a sense of empowerment, and have acted to counter stereotypes. However, just as visibility is mediated, there is also a tendency for invisibility to be mediated too. Major participants to a dispute such as the one over the highly divisive and seemingly intractable deforestation in Tasmania described by Lester and Hutchins (2012), may ominously lead to a deliberate decision to become invisible, to stop communicating digitally, thereby removing politics from public screens and the public sphere, and consequently the range of potential inputs into the decision-making process. The authors conclude: 'In a multimodal, multichannel and multi-platform environment, the ability to *not* be seen at strategically significant moments should be recognized as a sign and source of power' (Lester and Hutchins, 2012: 860).

Corporate identity, brand positioning and logo awareness have made many corporations vulnerable to net-based anti-globalization and pro-democracy campaigns. Microsoft, Nike, Shell and BP have all experienced highly effective cyber campaigning. Greenpeace International have been particularly adept at harnessing the mobilizing power of new media and exploiting its affordances in effectively disseminating its vivid image based communications. Peretti (2003) has shown how an individual culture jammer working on a small scale can swiftly unleash a communication 'virus' that can have serious and widespread effects. For Haiven (2007), the Vancouver-based Adbusters groups have adopted a set of tactics reminiscent of the French Situationists of the 1950s and 1960s, which might not have a major measurable impact on public consciousness, but certainly do invite different and often radical apprehensions of contemporary consumerism and so, in a way, act as a form of critical public pedagogy. They have also been credited with inspiring the Occupy Wall Street phenomena and its various spin-offs in major cities throughout the world. Thus, for a number of years, as Bennett (2003: 35) has suggested, the Internet has been emerging as 'a core resource for the growth of new global publics'. But this global politics, which is as likely to manifest itself in a local as a global form, is also increasingly complex and complicated. Counter-publics of both a progressive and reactionary varieties use the Internet to engage in counter-publicity and engage in campaign activities that some commentators see as little more than a slactivist clicktivism (Shulman, 2009) and others recognize as being functionally equivalent to earlier offline forms of protest – photocopied petitions, letter writing, and so on (Karpf, 2010).

YouTube, MySpace, Facebook, Twitter and many other social networking sites offer many opportunities for personal expression, information sharing, dialogue and action. YouTube has become a major outlet for NGO video promos, announcements from international agencies, governments and corporations, and even though tweets, blogs and vlogs may not in themselves create meaningful engagement or action on the ground, they do significantly increase participation of a type (Gladwell, 2010; Morozov, 2012). Digital-based communication such as 'eco-blogging' may have a clear pedagogic function, especially if the Internet's technological affordances move beyond the superficial in order to pose deeper questions about established cultural and historical values (Tinnell, 2011). Facebook offers an e-deliberation platform that has been used successfully by some activist groups and some progressive municipalities. Facebook's affordances tend to enable dialogic and open-ended modes of discourse, integrating various forms of expression and supporting wide-ranging conversation that does not necessarily seek consensus as the end goal. To an extent, participants may refashion discursive space and actually help change established political cultures to allow for differences and dissent to emerge productively. In this way, democracy and sustainable development practice may find common ground and a means of effectively reaching sound decisions collectively (Bendor *et al.*, 2012). Mainstream journalists may also find themselves writing more freely in their blogs and micro-blogs than in their set piece articles and reports (Lasorsa *et al.*, 2012). Paul Mason (2013), a journalist with the BBC, has suggested that different platforms serve different functions. For instance, Twitter tends to be used for updates, social media sites like Facebook are used for forming groups or finding like-minded people, YouTube and photo-sharing services such Flickr or Picasa are used for sharing evidence, blog for analysis, while traditional broadcast media often take on a curatorial function collecting and collating different sources and informing the public who are not active Internet users.

The wiki phenomena is a further example of Web 2.0-based collaboration, interactivity and participation generating a collective knowledge and intelligence that has much in common with the fan cultures studied by Henry Jenkins (2006), but with a clearly enhanced educational purpose. In *Confronting the Challenges of Participatory Culture: Media Education for the 21st Century*, media theorist Henry Jenkins writes:

> A growing body of scholarship suggests potential benefits of these forms of participatory culture, including opportunities for peer-to-peer learning, a changed attitude toward intellectual property, the diversification of cultural expression, the development of skills valued in the modern workplace, and a more empowered conception of citizenship. Access to this participatory culture functions as a new form of the hidden curriculum, shaping which youth will succeed and which will be left behind as they enter school and the workplace.
>
> (Jenkins, 2007: 3)

Educators and critics tend to ask the wrong question when they assert that Wikipedia is inaccurate, because this implies a conception of Wikipedia as a finished product rather than a work in progress. Users can edit articles and monitor how these articles have been altered. They can discuss and argue about the changes and in so doing gain new skills, knowledge and understanding about the subject at hand, politics and the media itself. This means that wiki articles are indeed open to intellectual and other vandalism, but it also means that users may generate both content and a sense of responsibility for maintaining the integrity of their contri-butions, interests and concerns. In 2004, Wikipedia published its 500,000th article and has continued to expand. As Weinberger (2002: 69) suggests, we ought to embrace this new emergent way of looking and learning. The Web may be distracting and open to abuse but, like the world, it is potentially so interesting that 'when set free in a field of abundance, our hunger moves us from three meals a day to day-long grazing'. In other words, we often can't leave it alone. Similarly, for Jenkins (2007), developing the work of Pierre Levy (1997), wikis offer an important learning environment whose processes and possibilities seem constitutive of a sustainable education itself:

- *collective intelligence* – the ability to pool knowledge and compare notes with others often working towards a common goal;
- *judgement* – the ability to evaluate the reliability and credibility of different information sources;
- *networking* – the ability to search for, synthesize and disseminate information; and
- *negotiation* – the ability to travel across diverse communities, discerning and respecting multiple perspectives, and grasping and following alternative sets of norms.

Indeed, the number of wikis is continually growing and, like the World Wide Web more generally, their application and significance has been recognized by many sustainability educators, political activists and media practitioners, although it does seem that Wikipedia tends to be dominated by a small class of editors who are not particularly diverse culturally. Sunstein (2006) also suggests that, unlike blogs, which tend to be highly personal, often cocooning information, wikis are freer to challenge assumptions, values and predispositions. In the Net-based global information society, the overall amount of non-expert knowledge exceeds that of specific experts so long as the many minds engaged in an issue do not get bogged down in clumsy, irrelevant and time-consuming deliberation, and when the majority of those engaged feel they are more right than wrong and are unwilling to compromise or concede a point. Finally, it is now commonplace to argue that the Web offers an infinite wealth of possibilities, most of which cannot be known in advance, and some of which will be undoubtedly be good but others less so. TreeHugger, a 'green CNN', founded by social entrepreneur Graham Hill, fully utilizes the Web 2.0 platform, offering articles, vlogs and space for user-generated content on a global range of sustainable development issues. Striving to be 'a one-stop shop for green news, solutions and product information', it is structured into a series of 'departments' – design, technology, business, living, transportation, science, energy, social and slideshows. TreeHugger also directly encourages interactivity, participation and action, making considerable use of social media sites, such as Twitter, Facebook, Tumblr, Pinterest and Instagram. Its Stumbleupon channel enables users to quickly explore their own interests by searching for reports and articles on specific topics. Now part of the Discovery Communications media empire, Treehugger retains an alternative focus without being oppositional or particularly radical.

Planetark.com is a Web-based non-confrontational, not-for-profit environmental organization established in Australia in 1992 and sponsored by Reuters News Agency. MediaLens is a UK-based indymedia site offering alternatives to the corporate owned and shaped news output of traditional media and the activist orientated PRWatch and CorpWatch maintain a critical scrutiny of big business and corporate communications. It works in partnership with businesses, local government bodies and community groups on campaigns that range from ink-cartridge recycling, tree planting and low carbon construction. It offers photos, videos and newsletters, and has produced education packs for use in primary schools. There are many other sites too of varying quality, and which vary in purpose, politics and intent. For some critics, the generally unregulated nature of the Web produces so much uncorroborated rubbish that some users will mistake prejudice for knowledge and fiction as fact, with the sheer multitude of sites, hyperlinks and imagery resulting in a distracted, dumbed-down, sub-intellectual culture. This fear is probably unfounded for as Jenkins (2007) argues in a discussion of ongoing research at the University of Southern California. He notes that young learners often exploit the emerging digital tools to the full, going far beyond cut and paste, and are likely, because of their collaborative experience of digital knowledge production, to be highly critical consumers of information garnered from wikis and elsewhere. This means that the digital divide really concerns the uneven access to new digital technologies, which leads to inequalities in the acquisition of new media literacies – Net-based social skills and cultural competences.

The virtual world of Second Life (Web 3.0), established by the San Francisco-based Linden Lab in 2003, is still one of the best known cyberworlds in operation. Its popularity has declined markedly in recent years as virtual worlds have clearly not realized all the creative communication and networking possibilities that many expected of them. In 2007, the University of Southern California Center on Public Diplomacy ran an iCommons Summit in Second Life. Its aim was to mix the real and virtual worlds for both actual attendees of the summit in Dubrovnik and those who could not be there. By doing this, the global diversity of the conference was enlarged, enabling participants to more broadly learn, collaborate, and share knowledge and experiences. Unlike the conventional diplomacy operating between states and international organizations, public diplomacy starts from the premise of a two-way dialogue involving the shaping of messages a country wishes to present overseas and understanding the ways the messages are interpreted by diverse cultures and societies. Public diplomacy helps develop the tools of listening, conversation and persuasion. Second Life has been used by activist groups as a resource for public education and campaigning. The United Nations, Greenpeace International and Better World Island offered users the opportunity to view global problems relating to war, environmental degradation and human suffering, and seek ways to rectify them. A parallel event to the Live Earth concerts was held in the Center for Water Studies in July 2007, and in December the NGO OneWorld hosted a virtual meeting of the UN Climate Conference in Bali on Second Life. Research has suggested that virtual engagement with the world's real-life problems could positively enhance social understanding and stimulate political action (Davis, 2007), although more attention now seems to be applied to the possibilities afforded through gamification.

Empowerment through communication, fun and games

The relatively new phenomena of citizen journalists, online newsrooms and independent media centres are a potentially liberating force in the mediapolis. The increased potential for participation, direct action, free expression, dialogue and engaged critique is a welcome alternative to the dominance of corporate and state media, of Fox News and the failure of traditional editorial policy to cover issues not meeting the narrow criteria of newsworthiness or the ideological restrictions of 'due impartiality'. Citizen media projects may not always be commercially successful, but blurring the distinction between producer and audience is a useful antidote to the blurring of editorial and advertising/funding criteria in many commercial operations. A citizen journalist does not need a great deal of technical skill to post a comment or upload an image from a camera phone, though to set up a site does require significant technical knowledge and understanding. One famous example of this is the Independent

Media Center (IMC). Established by a number of independent and alternative media organizations and activists in 1999 to provide grass-roots coverage of the World Trade Organization (WTO) protests in Seattle, the IMC is a network of collectively run media outlets with the common purpose of creating and disseminating radical but accurate reportage. It acted as an Internet clearinghouse of information for journalists, offering the latest reports, photos and audio and video footage. The IMC produced a series of five documentaries, uplinked daily to satellite and distributed to public-access TV stations throughout the US. In the year following the Seattle protests, decentralized and autonomous networks of media activists established other independent media centres in London, Canada, Mexico City, Prague, Belgium, France and Italy. For Pickard (2006) and Downey (2007), Indymedia activists have succeeded in actualizing radical democratic practices in unprecedented ways, although in the long term the corporate colonization and state censorship of the Internet may not only lead to a greater fragmentation of the public sphere and a real erosion of its democratic potential. For the moment, though, sites such as PR Watch, Corp Watch, Indymedia UK, EcoFirms.org and Alternativemedia.org seem to be surviving if not thriving. Bowman and Willis (2003) suggest voice and personality are also key hallmarks of participatory media.

However, some journalists and academics have questioned the quality and therefore the effectiveness and credibility of vlogs, blogs and various other components of the indymedia/citizen journalism phenomenon (Grubisich, 2005, 2006). Many see the Internet as undermining established, high-quality editorial control and trusted investigative journalism. Similarly, public-access television such as Deep Dish TV in the US and community media, including television, video, radio and the Internet also aim at empowering non-professionals through engaging interest, and developing skills through constructing reports, news items, artworks and entertainments that would not be transmitted by mainstream media (Halleck, 2002). Accompanying websites and production activities are always subject to the constraints and restrictions of uncertain funding, but links with education institutions, particularly media schools, often provide access to facilities, important contacts and influential networks. There has also been a considerable growth of, particularly, Internet TV, with NGOs, corporations and government departments establishing their own sites and an increasing number of small enterprises such as GreenTV assiduously working to raise awareness of environmental, social and other issues – and not just climate change. Big Picture TV streams free video clips of leading experts, thinkers and activists in environmental and social sustainability, and Al Gore's ambitious cable and Internet-based Current TV project that aimed to screen mainly viewer-generated contact was brilliant in conception but failed to develop into the major media player Gore had hoped for it. It was sold to Al Jazeera in January 2013, which closed the channel seven months later.

However, it is to the fast expanding world of digital gaming, particularly what is known as serious games and the use of apps for mobile devices such as the smart phone or tablet, that much informal learning, communication and value-based behaviour change may be initiated and reinforced. The visual rhetoric, narrative force and immersive qualities of many games render them powerfully persuasive as well as highly enjoyable. Their value in and for education is now rarely disputed (De Freitus and Maharg, 2011), although some critics correctly pointed to the violent, sexist and hyper commercial import of some of the most successful and popular games (Dyer-Witheford and de Peuter, 2009). A serious alternative reality game such as *World Without Oil*, funded in the US by the Corporation for Public Broadcasting for ITVS, gained considerable media attention and acclaim was the first game of its type drawing over 60,000 visitors and 1,900 registered in one month in the spring of 2007. Jane McGonigal (2012) has argued that computer games play an important role in making life for many people a more emotionally and creatively rich experience. Around three billion hours are devoted by the world's gamers each week to playing computer games. For McGonigal, who was largely responsible for creating *World Without Oil*, they can help people work collectively and collaboratively, maintain optimism in the face of major global challenges and point to what a better world might actually look and feel like. Used within an educational context, serious games such as energy planning/conservation game *Enercities*, can be highly effective in changing behaviour and values (Knol and De Vries, 2011). Paula Owen (2012) has shown how gamification has been successfully used to improve the sustainability performance of companies and cities. In Bangalore, Infosys Technologies has used gamification techniques to alter the commuting behaviours of their employees, which has reduced average daily travel to work time by almost twenty minutes, saving up to 2,600 person hours per day at their main factory. In the US, a start-up software business has worked with utility companies to foster competition among neighbouring householders to lower their utility bills. On average, a 2 per cent reduction in energy costs was achieved by every participating household. Such examples have led Katsaliaki and Mustafee (2012) to review how the increasing availability of serious games can become major communication and learning tools supporting sustainable development. They suggest that the most popular profile for serious sustainable development games include the following characteristics: they are accessible online, are sandbox simulation games with 3D graphics, are played by an individual, and target a young people who act as decision-makers solving environmental problems by using alternative technologies and considering economic consequences. Game-like elements are often incorporated into interactive exhibits at museums, science parks, galleries, heritage and other learning centres.

Television for the Environment (TVE '*Inspiring Change*')

Established in 1984, Television for the Environment (TVE) is an independent non-profit-making organization contributing to non-formal development education across the globe. Its core funders and major donors include the European, ITV, the WWF-UK, the UN Environment Programme (UNEP), Islamic Relief, Oxfam Novib, IFMR (Centre for Development Finance), the Engineering company ARUP, the US financial services company Bloomberg, the Indian new media technology Handygo, Friends of TVE and the Web design company, Chapter Eight. Specific project funders range from Astra Zeneca, BBC World News, the European Union, the Open University and the World Bank. TVE productions ranging from public service announcements and shorts to half-hour documentaries in the long-running documentary series *Earth Report* and *Life*. *Hands On* reports are divided into five or six items, providing broad coverage of serious problems and people's successful attempts to remedy them. Empowerment, participatory action and efficacy are the dominant motifs. A series of six 25-minute programmes were produced as part of the *Future Food* series which explored key questions of global food security using Peru, Kenya, India, Nigeria,

China and the US as specific case study examples. TVE has embraced the opportunities afforded by digital technologies. It has its own YouTube Channel and has created multimedia platforms, such as *Reframing Rio*, that have been specifically focused on major global events like the Rio+20 summit. TVE's editorially independent films have been broadcast across the world on global, regional and national TV such as PBS in the US, including international channels such as Al Jazeera English, MTV International, BBC World, Canal Futura in Brazil, ETV in India and over thirty-two regional channels across Indonesia. 'Joined-up communications' to inspire and report on change is TVE's basic aim. Porter and Sims (2003) argue that ending poverty, improving living standards, and protecting the environment and human rights are internationally agreed goals and the media has a duty to be objective but not necessarily neutral.

In 1995, TVE helped co-ordinate a global network of women broadcasters, producers and filmmakers in the long-running project Broadcasting for Change. Snapshots for Change, 32 short films made in 31 countries, were made to support the tenth anniversary of the Fourth World Conference on Women held in Beijing. Topics included women campaigning against sex trafficking in Nepal and HIV/AIDS prejudice in China, Fiji and Kenya. Issues such as education, domestic violence, trafficking and women's rights were addressed, and in 2005/6 a copyright arrangement allowed each individual member's five-minute short to be available to the whole network. For the price of making one short, broadcasters would have access to forty-four others. TVE filmmakers have also collected a number of awards: Sandra Mbanefo Obiago from Nigeria won Best Director Award for her documentary *Cash Madam* at the Biennial Africast conference in 2004 and Aarti Chataut won the Nepalese 2006 Women's Empowerment Journalism Award for her film *Shakti – Empowerment*. The series *Earth Report* and *Life* forcefully explore broad thematic issues such as health, global warming, the race to the bottom, development education, urban violence, pollution, environmental destruction, indigenous land rights, sustainable construction, fair trade, grass-roots activism, world trade and gender inequality. Two *Life* programmes, *Holding Our Ground* and *Balancing Acts*, have specifically given women in the developing world an international voice to tell their important and necessary stories.

Occasionally, TVE influences filmmakers through screenings at environmental or human rights film festivals, or by screening films to delegates and decision-makers at the UN, European Union or World Bank conferences. Significant resonance is achieved when a major broadcaster is inspired by a TVE report to use a report as a basis for a much larger and ambitious production. Deputy Director Jenny Richards says:

> What fascinates me about what we do is how our low budget regular pro-gramming is being used by all these people out there, in many different ways; and what you then find is some of these story lines reappearing in soaps or in other people's programmes like, I shouldn't really claim this, *The West Wing*, which tackled intellectual property rights after we had covered it in four programmes. TVE has catalyzed other productions around the world. We know we've done this with *Panorama*.
>
> (Blewitt, 2007: 29–30)

BBC *Panorama's Dead Mums Don't Cry*, broadcast in 2005, focused on the Millennium Development Goal to cut maternal mortality by two-thirds by 2015. The report featured the work of Dr Grace Kodindo, an obstetrician in Chad, who showed viewers the problems she confronts working in a hospital with little equipment, few basic drugs and no blood supplies. The programme was available for download from the BBC website in the week following its initial screening and TVE secured funding for it to be translated into French so it could be rebroadcast in Chad, Somalia, Ethiopia, Sudan and elsewhere. TVE retained the rights to distribute *Dead Mums* for broadcast in other developing countries and for non-broadcast educational use elsewhere. Some TVE films have been re-edited and used on mobile video vans in Namibia, in public education and communication campaigns aimed at halting the spread of HIV/AIDS. Others, like *Dead Mums* and the *Life* programmes on health and sanitation, have revisited areas to monitor and assess changes taking place since the time of the first production. Many of TVE's films use a human interest story as a way into broader social, environmental, political and economic issues. The central figures in such stories often represent or symbolize changes that would otherwise seem abstract and overwhelming – industrialization, urbanization, immigration, rapid economic growth. With the term 'inspiration' as part of TVE's promotional strapline, many stories seek to cautiously emphasize the positive as with the story of *Kay Kay: The Girl from Guangzhou*, a 47-minute documentary first broadcast as part of the Witness series on Al Jazeera in November 2012, whose life story has been documented by filmmaker Bruno Sorrentino since her birth in 1992 at the time of the first Rio Earth Summit.

In 2009 *tvebiomovies* competition was launched. Open to anyone in the world with access to a camera, entrants were asked to choose a category from among seven sponsored by such groups as European Bank for Reconstruction, UNEP, WWF, YouTube, Biodiversity International, the Lighthouse Foundation and the Inlaks Shivdasani Foundation, and submit a proposal to make a one-minute film about the environment which might be an animation, drama, documentary, comedy, or whatever. Fourteen finalists were then chosen and given US$300 to make a film. The winner in each category was based on the number of views the film attracts on TVE's YouTube channel and received a US$1500 prize. The winning films in 2013 were also screened at the UN COP19 conference in Warsaw in November. Another competition was launched in 2012. TVE's Global Sustainability Film Awards is in large part a fund-raising event, but is also aimed at encouraging the corporate sector and regional and local governments to showcase their pro-sustainability actions and CSR policies in short films of no more than ten minutes. Films can be entered in any one of three categories: the environment, community investment, inspiring good governance. The award ceremony is hosted by BAFTA and takes place in London in October. In 2012 winner was the Mexican-owned global baking company Grupo Bimbo.

The United Nations Environment Programme's (UNEP) *Talk the Walk*

Marketing techniques can be applied in a range of settings for a wide variety of social, environmental or commercial purposes. They can be community- or neighbourhood-based, aimed at changing everyday behaviour in a given locality (McKenzie-Mohr, 2000), or less obviously aiming to shift opinion or cultural predispositions regarding sustainable consumption (Collins *et al.*, 2003; Jackson, 2005). A 2002 report produced by the consultancy firm McCann Erikson asked the simple question 'Can sustainability sell?' The answer is yes, but it needs to be effectively promoted. Advertising and marketing clearly influence consumer patterns linking producers with consumers, and the advertising, marketing and PR industries are renowned for employing exceptionally gifted creative talents. Even so, Ries and Ries (2002) suggest in *The Fall of Advertising and the Rise of PR* that advertising is in crisis. Consumers know that advertisers are trying to sell you something and are automatically sceptical as a result. The authors believe that advertising has lost public credibility and that, if an organization wishes to build a brand or spread an idea, public relations activities, third-party endorsement, positive accounts in the press or other media, and word-of-mouth communication are probably more effective. Advertising is best for keeping a product or service in the public eye once it has been established.

The issue for sustainability practitioners is finding ways of harnessing advertising, marketing and public relations talents to produce attractive and engaging ways of encouraging people to buy sustainable products and adopt sustainable lifestyles. Agencies like Futerra, a busy London-based communication and public relations company, specializes in innovative and creative ways of promoting sustainable development. Its *Communicating Sustainability* (UNEP, 2005) gives clear practical advice and guidance on how sustainability practitioners should seek to understand what motivates audiences, how to address them, and ways the big vision can be turned into personally meaningful and practical messages that also inspire a response. In recent years there has been a growing concern to integrate sustainability with marketing (Grant, 2007, 2010; Belz and Peattie, 2012). As Franz-Martin Belz writes:

> Sustainability marketing aims at creating customer value, social value and ecological value. Similar to the marketing concept, sustainability marketing analyses customer needs and wants, develops sustainable products that provide superior value and prices and distributes and promotes them effectively to selected target groups.
>
> (2006: 139)

There is a growing imperative for producers to meet consumer needs sustainably, and many consumers are increasingly exercising discretion over what and from whom they buy. Many consumers state that they would buy green if they had sufficient information about functionality and pricing to enable them to do so. The growth of fair trade and organic markets is testimony to this. The United Nations Environment Programme (UNEP, 2005) argues that some of the most heavily advertised products are often highly resource-intensive, particularly food, personal transportation and to some extent household goods. For UNEP, sustainable lifestyle marketing covers three aspects:

- *Responsible marketing*: procedures and management systems developed to avoid promoting unsustainable behaviours.
- *Green marketing*: the design and promotion of goods and services with an environmental value added, which might include improvements over the life-cycle of a product such as environmentally friendly sourcing, clean production process, improved impact during use, reduced packaging, recycleability, reusability or existence of take-back schemes.

- *Social marketing*: programmes and campaigns raising public awareness in order to introduce more sustainable action, such as energy or water-conservation, waste reduction, reducing car use, and promoting sensible driving.

In order to successfully promote sustainable products, services and lifestyles, organizations will need to carefully associate green selling points with traditionally orientated purchasing criteria, such as overall economic benefit, social status and environmental safety; embrace corporate responsibility goals that enhance product responsibility (no more gas-guzzling SUVs); and, most important, strengthen their credibility and green credentials to avoid successful accusations of greenwashing.

Many corporations have used their marketing and PR departments to manage reputations following public criticism, and many media and environmental critiques which have highlighted expensive-looking PR, advertising and marketing campaigns as being deliberately deceptive (Beder, 1997). Indeed, some companies have invested disproportionate amounts of their advertising budgets on promoting relatively modest green initiatives. BP, for example, developed its new Helios logo to convey its commitment to going 'beyond petroleum', with its growing interests in solar energy, even though BP's investments in oil and gas were actually increasing. It spent $7 million developing its new green brand image while planning to spend a further $200 million on rebranding its facilities between 2000 and 2002, and $400 million on advertising petrol and its new logo. BP continues to explore for oil in environmentally sensitive areas such as the Atlantic Frontier, the foothills of the Andes and Alaska (Beder, 2002). As Chief Executive John Browne was reported by the BBC as saying, 'It's all about increasing sales, increasing margins and reducing costs at the retail sites' (BBC News, 2000). Some advertisers have inflated the green credentials of their clients. In December 2006 the Advertising Standards Authority (ASA) in the UK ruled that a national newspaper advertisement gave a misleading impression regarding the 'low emissions' of the Golf GT TSI. In June 2007 the ASA upheld a complaint against a television commercial for misleading information exaggerating the environmental benefits of the Toyota Prius. A number of brands, particularly in the travel sector, seem to be making green claims without being able to substantiate them, prompting the Committee of Advertising Practice to prepare additional environmental guidelines. In such a context, the United Nations Environment Programme's concern to develop and disseminate approaches to marketing and advertising that effectively and properly promote sustainable development is truly to the point. Part of this project involved producing an educational 'toolkit' to be used by businesses, marketing professionals and sustainability practitioners to learn more about sustainability and promote sustainable lifestyles and responsible business practice. This toolkit (UNEP, 2007) suggests that the most important determinants of effective communications from a marketing and social perspective include:

- *Sincerity and transparency*: the organization needs to be legitimate, relevant and authentic in its commitments to sustainability, rather than simply instrumental.
- *Consistency*: business practice needs to match the public image and communications; it needs to be proactive and anticipatory rather than reactive to sustainability issues. Sustainability has to pervade the whole organization.
- *Analysis*: Knowledge of the target audiences' perceptions and behaviours needs to be understood.

- *Credibility*: Sustainable marketing communications must:

    - be integrated with a broad-based sustainability strategy at an operational as well as policy level;
    - engage with credible NGOs working in the field of sustainable development;
    - use green labels or certifications awarded by independent and respected bodies.

Art, activism and the public interest

Visual metaphor or backgrounds in advertising imagery are frequently used to suggest particular associations – natural, energetic, fresh, powerful, cool, sexy, and so on. However, much media and advertising research demonstrates that there is no guarantee that visual metaphors will be either recognized or interpreted by audience members in the way that advertisers or producers intended. A number of factors here are important, including how media consumers read an image, and their gender, age, cultural values and perceptions, political interests, visual literacy, and personal experiences and motivations. As Proctor *et al.* write:

> Arguing that human-engineered communication systems are purposive in nature, we assume there is intentionality in consumer communication and accept the inevitability of a polysemy of interpretations because of the 'member resources' of the interpreter. However, in examining advertisements where metaphors may be perceived, it is interesting to consider the possibility of the intended message never reaching the consumer because of the ambiguity of the message, which may lead to a plethora of interpretations. It is therefore interesting to explore what consumers do take from these messages.
>
> (2005: 55–72)

Phillips and McQuarrie (2004) suggest that visual figures can be effectively differentiated in terms of their visual structure, defined terms of the physical arrangement of image elements and their meaning operations, and understood in terms of the instructions for the inference they suggest. Visual structure and meaning operation are fundamentally rhetorical ideas. They are rhetorical because they distinguish and bring out the available possibilities for creating a deviant visual interpretation. Some photojournalists straddle the worlds of fine art and political activism, thereby giving their work both cultural and political capital. Green architectural designs may operate in a similar fashion to inspire and prefigure future possibilities. The aerial photographs of Yves Bertrand communicate both the Earth's beauty and the impact of human activity on the planet, offering a personal aesthetic that is more emotive than the remote sensing images produced by orbiting satellites and published in such works as the United Nations's *One Planet, Many People* (Singh, 2005) or even Andrew Johnston's (2007) glossy *Earth from Space*. Sebastiano Salgado combines a high art photographic style with an incisive reportage that brings out the cruelty and human costs of economic globalization, but people from every walk of life are creators of their own images with their camera phones or with their bodies. Powerful, cinematic design can enhance a coffee-table book from being a piece of interior decoration to being a stimulating and disturbing learning tool. The book design for *An Inconvenient Truth* (Gore, 2006) mimics that of the feature documentary, with striking colour photographs and diagrams creating a powerful montage of attraction. People communicate with each other in many ways. Virtually everything we do gives off 'signals' of some description, whether we like it or not – our manner of dress, lifestyle, body language, choice of interior or exterior decor, car, and so on. Some of this communication is intentional and some not. Some occurs within private spaces and others in the public sphere. Marketing, advertising, public relations, radio and television broadcasting, theatre, music, photography, cinema, architecture and fine art are all elements of a communication process that may, or may not, facilitate debate, dialogue, discussion, knowledge, and understanding of sustainability, justice and peace. Art is not necessarily for art's sake – and never has been.

The American art critic Suzi Gablik (2002) believes that it is necessary to re-enchant art by breaking down the barriers between the individual and the wider world, showing how artistic creativity may serve a wider purpose than self-expression. For Gablik (2000), her writing simply puts down what is already 'in the air':

> Ours is a 'doing' culture, however, which means that there is unrelenting pressure to produce, and to produce something visible, a saleable product, or you will get left behind. Thinking of art as an essentially social-dialogical process – as improvised collaboration or relational activity – definitely steps on the toes of those who are deeply engaged with the notion of self-expression as the signal value of art's worth. Often, in my lectures, I would talk about artists who had shifted their work from the studio to the more public arenas of political, social and environmental life. They looked at art in terms of its social purpose rather than its aesthetic style. Many of them were exploring a more 'feminine' and responsive way of working, opening up spaces for 'deep listening' and letting groups that had been previously excluded speak directly of their own experience.

Creative artists are frequently concerned with stimulating reflection, thought and action on specific issues, events and experiences. Environmental artists, for example, tend to work with nature, natural forms and natural materials to produce works of aesthetic value and beauty, but also, perhaps, to invite the spectator to meditate on human, social and natural relationships. Such meditation requires contemplative time and maybe an immersion in the spatial, spiritual and emotional experiences the artworks afford. Art can foster dialogue and conversation about culturally sensitive and politically controversial issues (Kester, 2004), empower disadvantaged communities by harnessing latent talent and repressed creativity (Cockcroft *et al.*, 1998), and even physically transform a local ecology through a process of 'ecovention' – artists working in collaboration with local communities (Spaid, 2002). The cultural geographer Ian Cook (2000, 2004), taking a lead from Gablik, looks at what the aesthetic connections and stories, photographs, paintings and installations may offer the engaged spectator. Lowenstein (2001) refers to the Scottish environmental artist Andy Goldsworthy's primary concerns being simplicity and process – with making connections tracing the journey from the leaf to the tree, to growth, to the resonance of place. It is this that animates Goldsworthy's use of natural materials. The Canadian multimedia artist Janet Cardiff has produced 'audio walks', replicating three-dimensional (binaural) sound that enables the listener to explore external and interior worlds and relationships to place, memory and imagination. For example, Cardiff's *Her Long Black Hair* is a 35-minute soundscape journey beginning in Central Park South, which turns a simple walk in the park into an engrossing psycho-geographical experience. Listeners are guided on a twisting journey through nineteenth-century pathways which follows the footsteps of a mysterious dark-haired woman, producing a complex exploration of location, time, sound and physicality through stream-of-consciousness observations that merge fact, fiction, local history, opera, gospel music and other cultural elements. In an image-soaked universe, Cardiff's audio excursions and other works, including films and installations, are simultaneously liberating and disconcerting (Egoyan, 2002). Gallery exhibitions often have an afterlife online. The Permaculture exhibition at the NeuroTitan Gallery in Berlin in 2011 featured seven international artists. If science measures, then art disturbs. Natalie Holmes reported for *New Scientist* magazine (2011),

> A video installation by the European art collective Neozoon drew some laughs from the crowd as it showed an earlier project at the Münster Zoo. The artists had made mechanical animals from old fur coats and filmed visitors' reactions to this 'new species'. The puzzlement and incredulity of the visitors, children and adults alike, was both funny and thought-provoking – particularly when one person asked, 'Don't they make fur coats from these animals?'

Other art projects may be more closely associated with specific campaigns, protests or issues. The group Platform London has combined art, activism, education and communication for thirty years promoting social justice and environmental sustainability in the city. The 10th Annual Environmental Art Show at the North Water Street Gallery in Kent, Ohio, took environmental destruction as its theme, featuring Vince Packard's 'Fukishima Anniversary'. The artist also set up an online anti-nuclear art show, *Earth Art/Fukishima 3/11* on Facebook to commemorate the near meltdowns in the former Soviet Union and Japan. The open group has 338 members sharing artwork, comments, ideas and news. Murals may protest against ethnic inequality or environmental injustice as well as asserting cultural heritage and identity. Indigenous and aboriginal art forms frequently express the interconnected relationship of human beings to all aspects of the living landscape – rock, trees, birds, plants, rivers and the infinite cosmos – and within this living landscape are encapsulated the great myths of creation known as 'the Dreamtime' (Morphy, 1998). This has inspired artists, writers and filmmakers throughout the world to creatively articulate a sense of place and belonging, and may be seen clearly in the experimental, meditative and mesmerizing video art of Bill Viola's *Hatsu-Yume* (Viola, 1981). Art may inhabit public spaces as well as elite art galleries and can continue its life in the virtual world of the Internet. Community murals, poster and graffiti art, guerrilla theatre and performance may form a constellation of personal and community expression, social empowerment, ideological critique and political action. Many NGOs – for instance, Greenpeace and Friends of the Earth – frequently use street theatre and/or performance stunts to gain media and public attention. One of the most infamous street performers and culture jammers with an explicit eco-political message is the Rev. Billy of the Church of Stop Shopping, whose act, including preaching to shoppers outside major stores against the evils of consumerism, has often gained considerable publicity and the occasional spell in jail for disorderly conduct or obstruction. The now internationally renowned street artist Banksy has produced a striking array of stencilled images that are both politically pointed and creatively daring. His work is presented on the street, in art galleries and on the Web. Banksy muses:

> Imagine a city where graffiti wasn't illegal, a city where everybody could draw wherever they liked. Where every street was awash with a million colours and little phrases. Where standing at a bus stop was never boring. A city that felt like a party where everyone was invited, not just the estate agents and barons of big business. Imagine a city like that and stop leaning against the wall – it's wet.
>
> (2005: 85)

Graffiti and community art, street theatre, fine art and architectural exhibitions, the anti-globalization activists, and new media technologists are teaming up, producing exciting, creative and innovative communications and many new political possibilities. A number of art schools are now offering electives in sustainability-focused topics such as, in the US, Maryland Institute College of Art's Sustainability and Social Practice elective, which was offered for the first time in the autumn 2012.

Education for sustainable development

The UN Decade for Education for Sustainable Development (DESD), which ran from 2005 to the end of 2014, applied to all areas of education – formal and informal sector, schools, colleges and universities, adult and work-based learning, learning throughout life, from cradle to grave and in effect beyond. The UN Decade clearly identified the main ESD tasks as to:

- act as the primary agent of transformation towards sustainable development, increasing people's capacities to transform their visions for society into reality;
- foster the values, behaviour and lifestyles required for a sustainable future;
- become a learning process, facilitating decision-making that considers the long-term future of the equity, economy and ecology of all communities;
- build the capacity for such futures orientated thinking.

The education systems in different countries and regions tackle sustainable development issues in relation to the nature and the extent of their knowledge, cultural values, languages, worldviews and ideological perspectives in different ways. Indeed, the UN Decade suggested that culture, understood in a broadly anthropological and connective sense, would in large part predetermine the way issues of education for sustainable development are addressed in specific national contexts. The findings of two DESD evaluation reports (Tilbury, 2009; Wals, 2012) indeed show that ESD manifests itself differently in different regions. In some areas, ESD may be about cultural survival or intelligent living; in others, such as Latin America, it may be more overtly politically contesting existing institutions that are perceived as being barriers to sustainable development. Underpinning the continuing development of ESD is the perennial question about education itself. Is it about social reproduction or social transformation? Wals (2012) notes that the answer invariably correlates with a nation or region's interpretation of democracy, inclusiveness and participation. There is also a danger that a more technical interpretation of sustainability, combined with the naturalization of environmental degradation and poverty – that is, an education that does not critique to socio-economic structures that have largely been responsible for them – will not engender the transformative learning and actions required. Given that education, certainly higher education, is or at least should be about free enquiry and debate the notion of sustainability as a heuristic dialogue of values is all important. Indeed, in their critical discourse analysis of various ESD declarations and the steady accommodation of neoliberal ideologies within them over the last thirty years, Sylvestre *et al.* state: 'contestation around the concept should be seen as an opportunity to develop a plurality of divergent position in interaction with one another from out of which the potential for premise reflection and deep social learning may occur' (2013: 1369).

In *Earth in Mind*, the American educator David Orr (1994) notes that, with climate change, environmental degradation and species extinction, a great deal of that on which our future health, livelihood and prosperity depends, is under serious threat. Significantly, he continues, this is not the work of ignorant people but of highly educated ones, often holding highly desirable and well-respected qualifications. It is therefore logical to deduce that there is something wrong with the education systems dominating the advanced and developed nations of the world. One cause may lie with the root metaphors and assumptions informing our scientific worldviews – the world is like a machine, the mind is separate from the body, the planet and all its wonders are just there for humankind to exploit and destroy. Orr also suggests that it is imperative to confront a number of common myths. First, that ignorance is a solvable problem. It isn't; it is part of the human condition and so it is something we have to live with. Second, that with sufficient knowledge and technology we can manage the Earth and all the problems we have given it. However, the ultimate complexity of the Earth's natural systems means that the best we can manage are our own desires, emotions, policies, economies and communities. We must reshape ourselves, not the planet. Third, that our stock of knowledge is increasing. However, in fact, with the information explosion, much traditional and local knowledge is actually being lost or discounted under an avalanche of new data. Fourth, that contemporary unreformed higher education can restore what we have lost. Unfortunately, progress in developing trans-disciplinarity has been slow, uneven but nonetheless discernible (Blewitt and Cullingford, 2004; Jones *et al.* 2010; Sterling *et al.*, 2013) and, despite the positive and growing actions of staff and students alike, higher education sector impacts have been modest (Bartlett and Chase, 2004; Corcoran and Wals, 2004). Fifth, the purpose of education is to provide its students with the means for upward mobility and economic success, however defined. What the planet really needs, however, are 'more peace-makers, healers, restorers, storytellers and lovers of every kind' (Orr, 1994: 12). Finally, the arrogant and misinformed myth that Western culture is the highest achievement of humanity. Learning to live well and sustainably is not a once-and-for-all activity. Orr, like Sterling (2001), considers that education's response ought to be a major rethink, a paradigm shift, offering a combination of humility and reflexivity, creativity and renewal. To this end, Orr identifies six possible principles to guide such a rethink:

* All education should in effect be environmental education.
* The goal of education should be self-mastery rather than mastery of subject matter.

- With education and knowledge comes the duty to see that the planet is well used.
- Knowledge can only truly be said to exist when we can understand the effects of knowledge on people and their communities.
- Educational institutions together with their staff should be models of care, mindfulness, integrity and responsibility.
- Learning should be active, enquiring, sensitive and sensual, formal and informal.

Without this, learning, and certainly formal education, can be a dangerously abstract, instrumental and amoral thing. Education needs to reconnect people with their environments, with their experiences and with themselves. It needs to recover the importance and value of the senses and their inter-relationships, of their feelings and intuitions, seeking to embody an engagement with the world of which we are all a part (Abram, 1996).

Curriculum change is just one necessary part of this paradigm shift, for it also requires a major shift in the wider cultural values, dispositions and proclivities informing modernization and (post-)industrial development that currently define the purpose of 'education'. In many countries, not just the UK or US, primary/elementary education has driven ESD, inspired in large part by the belief that adults are 'saving' the world for their children. This is a notion often referencing Native Americans, such as Chief Seattle's 1855 'Manifesto for the Earth' (the authenticity of which is disputed by some), in which he asserts that the Great Chief in Washington who wants to buy 'Indian' territory cares nothing for the land and once, having conquered it, will surely move on, forgetting 'his father's grave and his children's heritage' (Chief Seattle (2000), quoted in Benton and Short, 2000: 12). The idea that we should teach children to care for the natural world and non-human inhabitants has long been popular, reasonably funded from public and private sources, and politically quite acceptable (Palmer, 1998). Over the years there have been innumerable pedagogic approaches, educational theories, toolkits, curriculum packs, teaching aids, lesson plans and so on, produced by the likes of the IUCN, the WWF, UNESCO, and even some of the major oil and chemical companies like Shell. There have also been numerous conservation, wildlife and outdoors environmental education programmes, such as Project Wild, which have aimed to nurture awareness, action and responsible citizenship among young children. Steve van Matre's *Earth Education* (1990) and Joseph Bharat Connell's *Sharing Nature with Children* (1998) have been particularly influential, although it should be remembered that environmental education is only one aspect of ESD.

Scott and Gough (2003) have identified three approaches to thinking about sustainable development, learning and change. The first approach sees the problems we face as being primarily environmental, to be understood and solved through science and the application of appropriate technologies. The second approach sees our current problems as primarily social and political, in which the environmental issues are relegated to the status of symptoms rather than causes. Solutions can be found through the application of social scientific, local and indigenous knowledge, where learning facilitates choice between perceived alternatives and futures. The third approach sees our knowledge and tools as essentially inadequate, requiring learning to be inevitably open-ended and lifelong. Uncertainty and complexity characterize our life-worlds, necessitating reflective social and co-operative learning.

Institutionally based education must facilitate change through promoting skills development, behaviour change and, importantly, by fashioning a learning *for* sustainable development. But this too is insufficient, because our learning, our technologies, our emergent understandings help shape our moral universe, our social and political worlds, and the very possibilities for, and of, sustainable living. Given this, Scott and Gough write of learning as sustainable development, the building of capacity to think critically about (and beyond) expert knowledge enshrined in the conventional wisdoms and nurturing capabilities for individually and collectively exploring the contradictions inherent is sustainable living. Blewitt (2006) complements this analysis through his emphases on the importance of informal learning, social practices, cultural mores and the experience of everyday life – the antimonies and joys of consumption, travel, leisure, food, work, the media and life itself – and Dyer (2007) suggests that, despite the steady increase of cultural heritage, ecology and sustainability in formal education, there is still lacking the holistic energy that will effectively transform facts into feelings, understanding into personal action, or professional development into corporate responsibility. The major reason for this is the absence of a certain magic and enchantment, the 'wow' factor, that would render learning a truly memorable, meaningful and life-enhancing experience. Building on the work of Chet Bowers (2001), David A. Gruenewald (2003: 9) has persuasively argued for a critical pedagogy of place which 'aims to (a) identify, recover, and create material spaces and places that teach us how to live well in our total environments (reinhabitation); and (b) identify and change ways of thinking that injure and exploit other people and places (decolonization).' There are consequently no shortages of ideas, theories and, thankfully, practical examples of education for sustainable development, though perhaps less so for education as sustainable development. Tilbury and Wortman (2004) have offered their contribution to the debate by arguing that ESD should consist of the processes described in the following sections.

Imagining a better future

Learners are encouraged to envision their ideal, preferred or possible futures, which in the process reveals their underlying beliefs and values. Envisioning can be deeply motivating, not least because it enables people to develop their own interpretation and understanding of sustainability, to share and enter into dialogue with others:

> In education for sustainability, all people need to share knowledge and partici-
> pate in working towards a sustainable future. For such participation to effectively
> take place, people need both the time and freedom to articulate their ideals
> and dreams and to share them in a learning space that sees each of them as
> equally valid and meaningful. Such a process values every person's vision of
> what a better future might look like, regardless of their background, knowledge
> or expertise. The process of envisioning facilitates an understanding of what
> sustainability is in their context and how it relates directly to their lives. Visioning
> is also a process that is inclusive to all cultures, and one that begins a dialogue
> which *strengthens intercultural understanding*. It can act as a bridge to incorporate
> intercultural and indigenous perspectives and knowledge. Every individual's vision
> can have direct or indirect implications for future action and provokes further

questions. In some cases, strategic partnerships can help people to address questions, obstacles and opportunities for action.

(Tilbury and Wortman, 2004: 25)

Critical thinking and reflection

Critical thinking and reflection means exploring questions and the answers and actions they elicit. Critical thinking invites a questioning of information sources, of social behaviour and community relationships, of the nature of political power and governmental decision-making, and of the role of technology, big business and science in our society. It invites us to investigate and understand the basis of our pre-given assumptions, ideas and values. Critical thinking helps us to understand the systemic causes of problems and avoid simplistic or misconceived solutions. Critical thinking enables us to explore the cultural and/or religious influences shaping our worldviews. Self-reflection and critical thinking can facilitate values clarification and participation in the sustainable development processes.

Participation in decision-making

Participation in decision-making is a key element in sustainable development, ranging in practice from cursory consultations more akin to the manipulation of the weak by the powerful to genuine full stakeholder engagements empowering communities and individuals. Learners are therefore at the centre, building skills, increasing confidence, and developing knowledge and understanding in a free and democratic manner, with the professional educator acting as a facilitator rather than 'expert'. Participation helps learners self-organize to develop greater self-reliance and a stronger sense of personal, cultural or community identity, which in turn can deepen a commitment to lifelong learning and long-term sustainable actions.

Multi-agency partnership working

Multi-agency partnership working is a key means of effecting sustainable, structural change at global, societal and community levels. ESD partnerships frequently involve formal education institutions, businesses and community groups working to create a shared vision and common ground for action. Partnerships can seek synergies, share knowledge and skills, and develop capacity to lever vital private and public sector project-funding. Ideally, partnerships should nurture long-term commitments and predispositions for sustainable learning and change. The Johannesburg Summit suggested two main types of partnerships for sustainability:

- Type l: government partnerships aiming to fulfill agreed commitments.
- Type ll: voluntary and self-organizing partnerships of government, international organizations and major civil society groups.

Systemic thinking

Systemic thinking encourages us to think outside of our familiar boxes. It is a relational way of thinking, enabling us to focus on processes rather than things, dynamics rather than static states, and wholes rather than parts. Systems or holistic thinking crosses disciplinary boundaries and eschews either/or dichotomies or mechanistic cause and effect metaphors. Most sustainability issues, such as climate change, are indeed highly complex, requiring new knowledge and approaches to problem identification and understanding that are not reducible to simple analyses or single disciplinary solutions. For Sterling (2004), systems thinking is related to three dimensions:

- *perception* – extending our viewpoint and boundaries of concern;
- *conception* – helping us recognize connections and patterns of relationship; and
- *action* – helping us to design and act in a holistic and integrative way.

Underpinning ESD is the aim to encourage people to become eco-literate. This involves being able to comprehend the world holistically and developing the knowledge and capacity to perceive its overall interrelatedness. It must fully engage with a set of ethical values embracing notions of care or stewardship, environmental justice, and community (Bowers, 2001). An eco-literate person is not just a person who thinks and feels; at the base of his or her ecological perspective must be a practical competence that enables action and the generation of knowledge derived from the experience of doing. To this end, eco-literacy is more likely to be developed non-formally in community-based action-orientated learning activities than in formal settings like schools (Wharbuton, 2006). So, as David Orr (1992: 92) notes, 'knowing, caring, and practical competence constitute the basis of ecological literacy', with Earth-centred education constantly seeking to nurture that quality of mind that seeks out connections. ESD must therefore broadly ensure that cognitive, affective and aesthetic domains of learning are not compartmentalized. An understanding of the signs and symbols, metaphors and stories, tools and technologies (traditional and emerging) that bind people into networks of understanding and which constitute new relationships between self and others, and self and the 'natural world' are required.

The Foundation for Environmental Education (FEE) established the Eco-Schools International Programme as a response to the needs identified at the 1992 Earth Summit. Officially starting in 1994 with the support of Germany, Denmark, Greece and the United Kingdom, by 2013 it runs in fifty-three countries linking up over 40,000 schools. Participating schools work towards certification in nine areas, including: energy, water, biodiversity, school grounds, healthy living, transport, litter, waste and global citizenship. This work, the programme claims, enhances the National Curriculum and can save money, too. In England, 11,358 schools have either gained bronze, silver or Green Flag awards. Local Education Authorities in the London Borough of Southwark and in Wigan, Lancashire, have registered over 85 per cent and 95 per cent of their schools with the scheme. In the United States, the Sustainable Schools Project aims to work with schools and communities to cultivate responsible and informed future citizens. The campus and community are in effect extensions of the classroom. The K-5 Sustainability Academy, an elementary school at Lawrence Barnes in Burlington, Vermont, US), is a collaborative partnership involving families, educators and the wider community including other educational bodies and the University of Vermont. The Academy's Schoolyard Transformation Project started in 2009, with a series of design charettes that identified outdoor learning, food cultivation and community gathers as key elements required for future development. Each classroom has a raised garden bed used to cultivate flowers and vegetables, and the school kitchen has an additional herb and vegetable garden for school lunches. In the years since 2009, considerable progress has been made in realizing these aims, and in late 2012 an accessible trail and amphitheatre were identified as future big projects. For Michael Stone (2009) of the Center for Ecological Literacy, it is important for schools to be smart by nature and this involves applying four guiding principles:

- Nature is our teacher.
- Sustainability is a community practice.
- The real world is the optimal learning environment.
- Sustainable living is rooted in a deep knowledge of place.

Furthermore, sustainable schools recognize the overwhelming importance of being embedded in and committed to the local are. Fritjof Capra and Michael Stone (2010) write:

> *Sustainable living is rooted in a deep knowledge of place.* When people get to know a particular place well, they begin to care about what happens to the landscape, creatures, and people in it. When they understand its ecology and diversity, the web of relations it supports, and the rhythm of its cycles, they develop an appreciation for and a sense of kinship with their surroundings. Well-known, well-loved places have the best chance to be protected and preserved so that they may be cherished and cared for by future generations of students.

Sustainable schools must directly involve and engage pupils. Ideally, many initiatives should be pupil-led, as this develops a sense of possibility and encourages practical learning, teamwork, group dialogue and decision-making, and action and a pre-disposition to care. Developing a sustainable school can transform that school into a creative and innovative learning environment for the pupils, raise standards of attainment and put it at the heart of a vibrant cosmopolitan community. Through school it is possible for children to become eco-literate citizens and members of a community that values and respects the wider environment. Krasny and Tidball (2007) refer to the civic ecology aspects of ESD in their discussion of garden mosaics of cultures, plants and planting practices within urban community greening activities in South Africa and the US. These community garden projects empower learners through building community resilience, enhancing existing individual, social and environmental assets, and nurturing the experience of inclusion and co-operation, skills of social learning, and the capacity to grow in a world of change and uncertainty. Education is therefore supremely important, with a great deal to do.

Worldwide, there are literally thousands of ESD projects. Some can be categorized as essentially 'add ons' to existing school structures, curricula and pedagogies and others may be characterized by their attempt to develop and implement a 'whole system redesign strategy' which looks to challenge traditional approaches to disciplinary-based educational content, teacher-centred learning processes and hierarchical school organization. Those whole-school approaches to ESD are an attempt to operationalize a systemic redesign. Schools wishing to become 'eco-schools' or 'green' or 'sustainable' schools act on a range of different elements often simultaneously using networks of recognized schools, school labels and certification schemes as their guides. However, for ESD to become truly embedded within the formal education system of a nation or region, whether at primary, secondary or tertiary level, it is often the case that the educators must themselves first be educated. To this end, some higher education institutions are working with NGOs and other international bodies to develop generic sustainability competences, educational toolkits and guides that can be applied, with suitable modification, to both formal and informal community-based learning environments (de Hann, 2010). The United Nations University project to establish a global network of Regional Centres of Excellence in ESD can be seen as a part of this process although its success to date has been rather uneven (Wals and Blewitt, 2010). In addition, ESD is beginning to be recognized as an important component of economic development and well-being, skills development, job and knowledge generation (Blewitt, 2010a; UNECE, 2011). Some universities, such as those in Melbourne (Australia) and British Columbia (Canada), have identified a set of graduate attributes that students should acquire through their studies in order to act effectively, sensitively and sustainably in our increasingly stressed world. Building very much on the Delors report on Lifelong Learning (Delors, 1996; Blewitt, 2004) the United Nations Economic Commission for Europe has outlined an array of ESD competences that educators need to develop in order to advance ESD effectively in their respective spheres. The competences are based around the three major characteristics of ESD.

There is still a long way to go before sustainable education becomes mainstream. As Wals writes, although there has been progress in recent years, 'learning processes and multi-stakeholder interactions that engage in deep change involving developing alternative values are still scarce' (2012: 71). The growing global recognition that a transition to a green economy is urgently needed may foster future interest in sustainability and transformation, but for this to occur and to be meaningful, ESD needs to retain its critical focus and arguably take a more challenging approach to

Table 10.1 Summary of UNECE competences in ESD for educators

A holistic approach integrating thinking and practice.	The educator understands the fundamentals of systems thinking, is able to work with different perspectives, engage with different groups across disciplines and cultures and is therefore inclusive.
Envisioning change, exploring an alternative future and inspiring engagement in the present.	The educator understands the root causes of unsustainable development, is able to evaluate potentially different consequences of specific actions and decisions, can encourage consideration of alternatives and is motivated to make a positive difference to people's lives and environments.
Achieving transformation in the way people learn and in the systems supporting learning.	The educator understands why the education systems should be transformed, is able to assess learning outcomes in terms of their contribution to sustainable development, can help to clarify different worldviews through dialogue and is personally a reflective practitioner.

Source: adapted from UNECE (2011).

the shibboleths of the market economy and increasingly marketized societies of this world (Blewitt, 2013a). It may also need to recover some of the urgency around environmental and ecological matters, which for Helen Kopnina (2012b) have been too much ignored by many ESD advocates. If we are to live in harmony with the planet, we need to learn and to teach from a clear and distinct commitment to ecocentrism.

Summary

Communication and learning are discussed in many places in this book, but this chapter strives to identify more precisely why learning and communication are important and how they connect with each other. We can learn through good communication and communicate through learning and both need to resonate with the transformative practices that affect both self and others. Learning can be informal or formal. It is possible to study formal college or university programmes on sustainable development or watch serious documentaries or become immersed in exciting Hollywood movies, and an increasing number of computer games, which take sustainability, or more likely crises emanating from unsustainability, as their central theme. Fine art, theatrical performances on stage or in the street, marketing and advertising, photography and blog posts on the Internet, can all play a part in spreading pro-sustainable messages and entreating people to think and act differently. Indeed, media literacy is itself a form of citizenship education for all of us who now inhabit the global mediapolis. Education for Sustainable Development (ESD) has gradually increased its influence on teaching and learning practice, but it is not yet mainstream or even universally applauded. All education is, in effect, environmental and sustainable education is, by design or by default, here to stay.

Thinking questions

1   When does sustainability communication end and education for sustainable development begin?
2   How important are feature films and television in raising ecological awareness?
3   In what ways can images be more powerful than the spoken or the printed word in promoting sustainable development?
4   What is the likely influence of new and emerging media technologies on communication, learning and sustainability?
5   In your view, what skills and knowledge does an eco-literate person need to develop?
6   How can schools and colleges best promote sustainable development?

Companion website

Learning and communication are of vital importance in creating a more sustainable world. If you want to learn more about communicating sustainability, visit the companion website for some additional case studies and some pointers on how to communicate more effectively.

11 Leading the sustainability process

Aims

This chapter aims to develop an understanding of the theory and practice of leadership in organizations and society, highlighting the need to explore different dimensions of leadership within sustainable development. An important aspect of this is the relationship between learning, knowledge management and innovation, and by examining the views of a number of writers who place leadership within a systems or ecological perspective, the clear relevance of leadership to sustainable development practice will be outlined. Finally, by identifying a number of traits and characteristics frequently associated with leaders and leadership, it may be possible for readers to discern their own personal and professional development needs and the means to realize them.

Looking for leaders?

In 2007, the authors of the Human Development Report, *Fighting Climate Change: Human Solidarity in a Divided World* (Watkins *et al.*, 2007), called on developed nations to immediately take the lead in combating climate change by cutting carbon emissions by up to 30 per cent by 2020 and 80 per cent by 2050. Unless this is achieved, at least 40 per cent of the global population will suffer immensely. Stephanie Draper (2006) of Forum for the Future has discussed a business leadership model based on competitive advantage, that may promote more responsible and sustainable behaviour by inspiring and motivating others to adopt ecologically sound businesses practices. However, this may not work in other sectors, cultures or times. Underpinning all leadership activity is human agency, sometimes acting independently but almost always acting collectively in groups or in networks. A town can only embark on the road to transition if the people within choose to act in certain ways. The Isle of Wight, just off the southern coast of England, can only become the world's largest eco-island, as is planned (Vidal, 2007b), if its inhabitants, its politicians, its business people and others work to make it so, linking the local inevitably to the global. The world's future eco-cities will have smart and green housing, local organic farms and perhaps space-saving vertical gardens, eco-friendly transport, renewable energy, opportunities for social learning and democratic participation. Individual states and cities can only shift political awareness and the will to act sustainably if its political leadership makes and implements certain policies offering the possibility of change that will engage both supporters and sceptics. City governments can do a lot, and in many cases have done so but, as Andrew Ross (2011) has argued, it is fast-growing and low-density places like Phoenix in Arizona that major, almost inconceivable cultural and economic, changes have to occur. Ross sees possibilities for spaces of hope in the community activism of the indigenous people as evidenced by the Gila River Indian community's successful campaign against further 'development'. Hope needs to be fed by action at many levels and often simultaneously. If the former Governor of California, Arnold Schwarzenegger, had not signed the Executive Order capping greenhouse emissions in 2006, or announced publicly with former Prime Minister Tony Blair his commitment to environmental action, or given pro-environmental speeches at the University of Georgetown in April 2007 and to international bodies like the United Nations on the imperative need to combat climate change; and if former Vice President Al Gore and the whole Intergovernmental Panel on Climate Change had not acted as they did to be jointly awarded the Nobel Peace Prize, then there would not have been the debate or shift in attitudes that occurred in the US during 2007. Schwarzenegger argued that courageous goal-setting makes industries innovative and creative problem-solvers that can address economic and environmental issues simultaneously and effectively. He argued that sustainability and the environment needs to be seen as sexy and inspiring. He used his own business and movie background as a way of directly communicating the message so that it resonates in the media, appearing on the front cover of *Outside* magazine and *Newsweek*, and among voters in their communities. A field poll released soon after the governor's speech at the University of Georgetown showed that 81 per cent of Californian voters said global warming was a very serious or somewhat serious problem. Only 21 per cent believed the federal government was positively addressing it. Of course, as commentators have noted, there is a danger in suggesting that politicians and businesses may not have to make fundamental changes, particularly if technical solutions like biofuels or hydrogen cells fail to provide the hoped-for environmental benefits. However, that is what makes sustainability a political act and not a scientific concept.

In 2007 Forum for the Future conducted a poll of 262 'green movers and shakers' on sustainable leadership. Over 80 per cent of respondents voted for Al Gore and, although voters had three votes, the female Indian environmentalist Vandana Shiva garnered just 14 per cent. As Roger East (2007), Editor of Forum's *Green Futures* magazine, noted, the female half of humanity was hugely under-represented in the poll. He could also have added the people from the Third World and all those who are not in elite positions in the First. For Vandana Shiva (1993), writing specifically of the Chipko Movement, it is the unsung heroes, and particularly women, rather than the well-known charismatic leaders who frequently deserve the credit for initiating change and debate in contexts far wider than their own; but they rarely receive it. The publicly applauded achievements of the most visible leaders are often due to the achievements of the invisible many. The Forum poll, then, certainly articulated a certain type of leadership and leader, but there are other possibilities, including the idea that sustainable development does not need leaders, and certainly not charismatic ones, but simply people who simply do, who guide, who advise, who nurture, who innovate and who embrace the natural world. Our knowledge has increased, although will always remain provisional and analytical approaches to both sustainability and sustainable development have clearly gained depth and sophistica-tion in the years following *Our Common Future*'s publication in 1987. However, formally constituted strategies and institutions are often quite constrained and limited with issues of implementation often remaining problematic to say the least. Sometimes top-down and sometimes bottom-up approaches to sustainable development are advocated, but their value will depend on many things – time, culture, geography, learning, resources, politics, the economy, and so on. Economic interests and sustainability demands may (or may not) be opposed, but it is clear that many major and minor changes too are needed in the way that we live, work and produce. Genuinely transformative changes to thinking and behaviour are required and leadership is needed to help discover what these are. For American leadership expert Benjamin Redekop (2011), a major issue to overcome is human short-sightedness. Applying an integrative psychologically based personality model known as the CFC or 'Consideration of Future Consequences', Redekop notes that those people low in CFC focus on the immediate consequences of their behaviour while those high in CFC are able to look more constructively into the future. It is therefore incumbent on leaders 'to induce positive emotional states if constituents are to engage in future-orientated behaviours' (Redekop, 2011: 57). When people are less hopeful they become more short-sighted. Future-orientated behaviour is a sign of hope. Good communication is essential in this context. It must not be perceived as manipulative. It must elicit co-operation and must be realistic rather than pessimistic about the resources at hand to initiate change. Thus, Redekop writes using a current debate as an example of our leadership which may come into conflict with 'environmentalism' (Redekop's quotation marks):

> [M]any environmentalists are opposed to nuclear power as an alternative to carbon-intensive forms of power generation. Nuclear waste is just another form of pollution to be avoided and nuclear accidents are potentially very dangerous. Yet, it may be necessary for those wanting to exercise leadership on global warming, for example, to let their constituents decide if they are willing to accept the risks of nuclear power in order to avoid the severe disruptions that will likely be the result of unchecked climate change. If not, then they are going to need to be very good at explaining why nuclear power is unacceptable, and they are going to need to demonstrate clear and practical alternative pathways towards independence from fossil fuels.
>
> Recognizing alternatively, seeing them modeled in practice such as with the Transition movement leads to a sense of self-efficacy which can be further enhanced if clearly associated with issues of equity and social justice.
>
> (2011: 61)

For green activist and co-founder of Forum for the Future, Sara Parkin (2010), unsustainable development has been produced by too many people making too many wrong decisions every day. For her, the true sustainability leader is a 'positive deviant' – that is, someone who brings together different types of leadership ideas and skills in an effective and generative manner. This may involve systems thinking, asking the right questions, having a moral compass, resilience, the capacity for self-reflection and criticism, and the ability to communicate across disciplines, cultures and professions well. Everyone in this sense can be a leader in some way and to some degree. As Hamdouch and Zuindeau write:

It is vital that the impetus should come both from 'above' (states and the multilateral governance authorities) and from 'below' (citizens, social organizations and the mechanisms of the 'grassroots democracy') so that the 'intermediary' actors (firms, territorial authorities) are included and make a real contribution to the required institutional change in order to promote SD on a long-term basis.

(2010: 436)

So just as sustainable development may be conceived as a dialogue of values encompassing a myriad of perspectives and worldviews, approaches to leadership for sustainability may be equally diverse and multifaceted, embracing even a denial of the importance of leadership as conventionally understood itself.

On leadership

Management theorists have invested a great deal of energy in analysing leaders and leadership. They frequently draw lessons from politics, history and war as well as business. The focus is frequently on the individual and his or her relationship to situation or contingency. There has been relatively little work on the type of leadership required to fashion a more sustainable world, although recently sustainability practitioners have begun to think about this quite seriously. There is no longer a reluctance to see leadership negatively as inevitably hierarchical, linear or a danger to equity and democracy, although it can be that and may even be conceived and promoted as such. The business theorist Peter G. Northouse (2007: 3) defines leadership as being principally 'a process whereby an individual influences a group of individuals to achieve a common goal', pointing to four key elements.

- Leadership is a *process*, an interactive transactional event that takes place between a leader and his or her followers and is as such open to everyone – not just the great, special or worthy.
- Leadership involves *influence* or the ways in which a leader affects followers. Without influence there can be no leadership.
- Leadership occurs within a *group context*, involving influencing people who have a common goal or purpose. These groups can be small or large, task-orientated or ideologically motivated.
- Leadership involves *goal attainment*, achieving a desired aim, end or task collectively.

For many, this may be too restrictive and too individualized, but it nonetheless does offer a starting point. Whatever the approach or theory, leadership almost inevitably involves consideration of political power, personality traits, institutional and organizational culture, motivation, inspiration, emotion, intelligence, visioning, skills, ethics and learning. Mumford *et al.* (2000) developed a capability model of leadership, relating a leader's knowledge and skills with the leader's performance. Leadership capabilities can be learned and developed through experience. They consist of various competencies, including problem-solving and social judgement skills, and the ability to acquire and process information into knowledge. For many environmentalists, however, the most important element of any leader must be the values that he or she has and is able to successfully communicate to others so that we can achieve. As Egri and Herman write:

Transformational leaders are needed to effect transformations in the way humankind relates to the natural environment. The importance of human agency in this endeavour cannot be overstated. Just as human agency has contributed to ecological degradation, human agency will play an essential role in advancing long term environmental sustainability. Although this role may seem daunting to many, modern society will need more people like this leader of a for-profit environmental retail organization to take on the challenge.

(2000: 60)

The most appealing part is being able to take a group of people, an organization, a concept, an idea or a mission from one place to another. You can dream and then make it happen. Nothing is more exciting to a leader than to hear 'You can't do it'. Perfect! That's just what I want to hear. So now we are going to do it. I think that's what I enjoy the most. Trying to get to places that we didn't think we could go.

Leadership is perhaps above all an *intervention* primarily rooted in the imagination. This involves having a *vision* of when, why, where and how something will be achieved, invariably leading to self- and organizational transformation. The former CEO of Interface, the late Ray Anderson, may be perceived as a transformational leader, a man who changed himself through serious reflection and through a series of motivating, inspirational, pragmatic, learning and empowering actions that altered the nature and purpose of his company and his employees. Interface is frequently cited as a commercial organization that has come closest to realizing the goals of sustainability. In his autobiography, Anderson (1998) wrote that the new sustainability thinking now permeates everything Interface does, particularly product design and development. He says that one person can make a difference but leadership is not a solitary activity – transformation cannot be dependent on one person as it takes place in social, community and organizational settings involving many others:

I believe one person can make a difference. You can. I can. People coming together in organizations like yours and mine can make a big difference. Companies coming together, for example customers and suppliers uniting in recycling efforts, can make a vast difference. Harnessing wind, current solar income and hydrogen can make a monumental difference. . . . 'The power of one' has become a recurring theme in our company, as many of our customers, as well as our people, recognize.

(Anderson, 1998: 140–1)

Anderson recognizes that Interface, and indeed society, has a long way to travel before anything approximating sustainability can be realized. He sees the journey as taking place on three levels:

- the level of *understanding* – learning the what and where of sustainability, including the methods, approaches, technologies, practices and attitudes required;
- the level of *achieving* sustainability – bridging the resource, technical, ingenuity and knowledge gaps between envisioning and doing; and
- the level of *influence* – extending sustainability beyond the point of doing no harm to being positively restorative ecologically and socially.

Transformational leaders, and organizations, have a strong set of internalized values and ideals which raise the game emotionally and intellectually for all concerned. The overarching goal of leadership is to motivate, to inspire and sometimes to be morally uplifting (Avolio, 1999). Anderson seemed to perfectly fit the model of the transformational leader – offering a vision, shaping an organization, creating trust and creatively deploying his personal strengths.

However, this may not be enough. Julia Middleton (2007), founder and Chief Executive of the leadership training enterprise Common Purpose, argues that in virtually every sector, conventional boundaries are dissolving, with traditional forms of authority becoming less clear and less relevant. Unfortunately, many organizations still operate in silos, with leaders focusing exclusively on their own responsibilities. In an increasingly interconnected world, however, this occurs at the expense of context, which renders leaders vulnerable to threats or unable to see opportunities. For Middleton, leaders must understand the value of diverse networks that extend beyond their zones of comfort, familiarity and even competence. In these new circumstances, they must rely on influence rather than power because they are in effect operating beyond their authority. In a world where partnership, collaboration and co-operation is becoming increasingly necessary, leaders and decision-makers of all descriptions cannot afford to operate in isolation. By working in what Middleton terms 'the outer circles', leaders are able to detect small but significant changes in the environment that may sooner or later impact seriously on their immediate sphere of influence, control and responsibility. This 'environmental scanning' is essential for being able to move forward in a dynamic and proactive manner. However, leaders need to maintain an independence of mind that combines self-confidence with a degree of humility. In a complex, complicated, changing, connected and uncertain world it is quite easy to be wrong. So what becomes really important is the ability to communicate effectively across different cultural fields and to supplement traditional leadership tools with others. A corollary of this, following on from the work of Wielkiewicz and Stelzner (2005), is that there needs to be a balance in most organizations between vesting power in a positional leader – the person at the top – and having a diverse selection of organizational members who can influence and inform the leadership process. Thus, drawing on an ecological system they write: 'leadership occurs in a web of interdependent social and biological systems' and 'adaptability is determined by the richness and variability of feedback loops allowed to influence leadership processes' (2005: 332).

For Heifetz (1994), *followers* are important too, because just as good leaders may reflect the problems back to where they have to be solved, it is the followers who also rectify the consequences of mistakes that leaders must inevitably sometimes make. Heifetz (1999) feels that students of leadership have spent too much time examining resistance to change, because change is frequently welcomed and when it is not, it is usually the result of change representing the possibility of loss, appre-hension, fear and anxiety. Changes representing gains of some description are usually most welcome, but the past must not be forgotten or dismissed in its entirety. Leadership involves mobilizing people's capacity, whether in business, the community or wider society, to select and carry with them what is essential from their past, enabling them to adapt better to the present and emerging future than they would have otherwise. And the better people adapt, the more innovative they become and the more able they are to fashion an active or creative consciousness. When this occurs, people become increasingly willing to engage with different or opposing ideas and values without fearing they will be accused of being inconsistent. This nurturing frequently means applying an ethic of care or raising followers' awareness and understanding to a higher level, which may emphasize values such as liberty, justice, equality and now certainly sustainability (Cuilla, 2003). Ladkin (2006) suggests that leaders need to be attentive both to their own values and responses to a given situation, and to those of others. They need to be able to influence others and in turn be influenced. They need to be able to apply what the German philosopher Heidegger termed a sense of 'dwelling' – a staying or being with a problem, particularly when ethical issues dominate. To dwell means to open up to possibilities by letting go of preconceived assumptions, interpretations, analyses and judgements. Others are then more likely to open up themselves, because they perceive leadership to be caring and sensitive to complexities, rather than enacting a stereotypical leadership role that rushes to judgement with speedy prefabricated actions. All this takes time, but the potential benefits may be immense. This slower, more meditative approach to leading, according to Ladkin, requires three specific adjustments to the conventional wisdom on leadership.

- In practicing 'staying with', the leader attends to the present and the factors which have shaped that present rather than focusing his or her energies solely on the future. This noticing of the present enables new contours of the given situation to be revealed and, through that, new understanding to be gleaned.
- The leader is influenced as well as influencing, and actively seeks out information which will help him or her to understand the situation more fully. Through their comportment, they suggest to others that they are willing to be moved and influenced by others' ways of being in the world and their understanding of a given situation.
- The leader is not required to have a clear vision of the 'right' course of action or decision, but instead, through a process of engagement, enables a space to be created wherein a resolution which 'fits' the situation emerges.

(2006: 96)

Authenticity and sustainability leadership

Authenticity is often seen as a guarantor of genuine leadership, more so in the field of sustainability than possibly any other given the growing distrust of national political leaders and justified scepticism of many of the claims emerging from the major corporations. Even those organizations whose business is the production and selling of lethal products often promote their good citizenship and sustainability credentials, and those corporations that are collectively known as 'Big Oil' invariably pay a great deal of attention to publicly promoting their questionable commitments to sustainability (Beder, 2006). Additionally, as Boltanski and Chiapello (1999, 2005) have shown through their exhaustive study of management texts published (mainly in France) in the 1980s and 1990s, business leaders seem to have co-opted many of the values, or perhaps rather expressions of value, of its radical critics instituting what they term a 'new spirit of capitalism'. This, essentially, ideological justification of capitalist accumulation and appropriation is aimed to foster commitment and make it culturally attractive to wage earners and others. Thus ideas of fairness,

---

Box 11.1 Innovating to zero: philanthropy, innovation and business leadership

Microsoft founder and former CEO Bill Gates and his wife Melinda, through their Foundation established in 2000, have become one of the world's most important leaders in corporate philanthropy and sustainability. They have funded a range of research and development projects across the world, including Internet access in libraries, research on malaria, family planning, sanitation, nutrition, agricultural development and financial services for the poor. The Gates Foundation's work is globally integrated and emphasizes the importance of leadership through innovation. Millions of dollars of grants are awarded every year on a proactive basis to primarily US tax-exempt organizations from its Asset Trust Endowment of over US$38 bn. Gates has also been an active promoter of low to zero carbon energy. To do this at a global scale, Gates believes, 'we need energy miracles'. With his former Chief Technology Officer at Microsoft and co founder of one of the world's largest patent holding companies *Intellectual Ventures*, Nathan Myhrvold, Bill Gates's mission led energy company *TerraPower* aims to develop 'a sustainable and economic nuclear energy technology' through worldclass privatesector leadership, supercomputer modeling, durable metallic fuels and safe, clean and secure nuclear innovation.

> Nathan Myhrvold and I actually are backing a company that, perhaps surprisingly, is actually taking the nuclear approach. There are some innovations in nuclear: modular, liquid. And innovation really stopped in this industry quite some ago, so the idea that there's some good ideas laying around is not all that surprising.
>
> The idea of *TerraPower* is that, instead of burning a part of uranium – the one percent, which is the U235 – we decided, 'Let's burn the 99 percent, the U238.' It is kind of a crazy idea. In fact, people had talked about it for a long time, but they could never simulate properly whether it would work or not, and so it's through the advent of modern supercomputers that now you can simulate and see that, yes, with the right materials approach, this looks like it would work.
>
> And, because you're burning that 99 percent, you have greatly improved cost profile. You actually burn up the waste, and you can actually use as fuel all the leftover waste from today's reactors. So, instead of worrying about them, you just take that. It's a great thing. It breathes this uranium as it goes along, so it's kind of like a candle. You can see it's a log there, often referred to as a traveling wave reactor.
>
> (*TED Talk* by Bill Gates, 2010, available at: www.ted.com/talks/bill_gates.html)

Source: adapted from TerraPower: www.terrapower.com/

---

meritocracy, excitement, achievement, partnership, responsibility, communal benefit and, more recently, citizenship and sustainability have become important elements of the discourse of business which have at least in part disarmed the impact of businesses detractors. Authentic leadership has become a major element in discussions of business development where a renewal of the ancient Greek axiom of being true to oneself is seen as a foundation for authenticity, which is not necessarily to be confused with sincerity. Authenticity is often quite self-referential and does not therefore have to take others into account. Thus, authentic leadership, particularly in organizations, can be characterized as 'a process that draws from both positive psychological capacities and a highly developed organizational context, which results in both greater self-awareness and self-regulated positive behaviors on the part of leaders and associates, fostering positive self-development' (Luthans and Avolio, 2003: 243). It is thus multifaceted, operates at many different levels and is in large part constituted by the following (Avolio and Gardner, 2005):

- positive psychological capital;
- positive moral perspective;
- leader self-awareness;
- leader self-regulation;
- leadership processes and behaviours;
- follower self-awareness/regulation;
- follower development;
- organization context;
- veritable and sustained performance beyond expectations.

Leadership theory often comes with a number of prefixes such as transformational, charismatic, spiritual, servant as well as authentic. Given the significance of digital technology and the Internet, it is no surprise that E-Leadership has also received a considerable amount of attention recently together with virtual teams (Zigurs, 2003). A key issue here is the influence of technology on traditional leadership functions and whether the degree of media richness impacts positively or negatively and at what level.

Global social inequality, climate change and environmental degradation is still perceived by many as a consequence of the capitalist model of development that has promoted a culture of wants, demands and greed. Scott Prudham (2009) writes in his highly critical study of the entrepreneur business leader Richard Branson, that the legitimacy of green capitalism and its leaders rely on an image of ethical and innovative dynamism and highly publicized expressions of commitment to global challenges such as climate action. Prudham argues that Richard Branson's entrepreneurial successes, his high media profile and his much publicized green announcements conceal more than they reveal. In 2006 he pledged that all the profits from Virgin Atlantic and Virgin Trains would be used to fight global climate change by diverting the money to investments in carbon sequestration and the production of (highly problematic) biofuels through his own company Virgin Fuels. This would invariably produce new ecological conditions that may in themselves be highly destructive. Prudham writes:

> Here, a private entrepreneur proposes to invest money from companies he controls into new, private, profit-seeking ventures which ostensibly redress an existing set of environmental dilemmas (i.e. climate-change-inducing effects of fossil fuel combustion) by introducing a new set of fuels for profit-driven transportation services and an attendant set of new environmental problems, many as yet unspecified or not well known. Hardly an example of the harnessing of capital to the green cause.
>
> (2009: 1604)

A renewed search for authenticity has also accompanied this new spirit, which has sometimes enticed researchers to seek examples of genuinely transformative and inspiring leaders from the recent and sometimes quite distant past. In India, Mahatma Gandhi is often cited as a leader whose moral integrity, critiques of industrialism and colonialism, and advocacy of equality, decentralized power and small-scale local economic development was summed up by the term 'sarvodaya' or 'welfare for all' (Rath, 2010). There are earlier figures from India's history, particularly Kautilya, author of *Arthasastra* and the *Edicts* of King Ashoka, who has received some attention recently as an exemplar or guide for a sustainability leadership whether in business, society or government that can be trusted and valued (Alexander and Buckingham, 2011; Narayanan, 2013). The 'common good' is central in their philosophy and teachings but it often has to be cultivated and taught for it does not always come naturally to people. From this, Alexander and Buckingham (2011) draw three important leadership lessons especially relevant to contemporary business practice:

- the need to cultivate inner qualities such as self-discipline through education;
- the need to empathize and listen to people at all levels;
- the need to reflect upon the consequences of decisions and actions and alter them if necessary.

In addition to the above, authentic leaders will need to develop and articulate a positive moral framework of values and processes by which these values can be demonstrated and implemented. Thus, leading by example becomes an important element of authentic leadership – 'walking the talk' – which will enable leaders to nurture emotional, cognitive and moral development among others whose own growth in self-awareness will render their 'followship' purposive, informed, knowing, relational and transparent (Avolio and Gardner, 2005). Authentic leaders for sustainability will also need to work by definition with complexity and uncertainties, which for Metcalf and Benn (2013) will require them to acquire 'extraordinary abilities'. They write:

> These are likely to be leaders who can read and predict through complexity, can think through complex problems, engage groups in dynamic adaptive organizational change and can manage emotion appropriately. In essence, leaders and leadership is a key interpreter of how the complexity of the wider complex adaptive systems environment of the organization 'links' internally to the organization, and this link is a powerful mediator for successful implementation of sustainability, or may even be an expression of it. Leaders that do this will have to use the ability to navigate through complex environments, an element of complex problem solving that we are still endeavouring to describe.
>
> (2013: 381)

Leadership and the upside of down

The Canadian political scientist Thomas Homer-Dixon (2002, 2006) argues, like many others, that the world is currently facing a convergence of multiple stresses, which is leading to changes that could quite possibly engulf us. It is in these threats of catastrophe, however, that opportunities for change and renewal lie, if only we

Box 11.2 GlobeScan/SustainAbility Leadership Survey (2013)

Question: Please rate the overall performance of each of the following types of leaders in advancing sustainability over the past year.

Performance on Sustainability Leadership by Different Types of Leaders

Table 11.1 Total percentage rated as 'excellent' by region (2013)

Leaders in	Asia	Europe	North America	Africa/ Middle East	Latin America/ Caribbean	Oceania
Science	35	40	47	55	47	47
Social enterprise	59	54	62	45	51	47
Multilateral organizations	29	20	20	23	30	9
NGOs	33	35	46	52	49	43
Corporations	32	20	20	32	22	9
Government	3	3	3	3	3	4

The survey sampled considered leaders in 73 countries. Of the 1,173 sustainability experts who returned the online questionnaire, between 2010 and 2013, 53 per cent had more than ten years' experience; respondents with less than three years' experience were excluded. They were drawn primarily from the corporate, government, non-governmental, academic/research and service/media sectors.

Source: The 2013 Sustainability Leaders: A GlobeScan/SustainAbility Survey (p.10): www. sustainability.com/library/the-2013-sustainability-leaders#.UitKG-A3SvS.

can engage and fashion a resolution that fits as the situation emerges. Homer-Dixon identifies five tectonic shifts:

1   *Differential demographic growth*, with populations increasing in poor areas and remaining static or in decline in richer areas.
2   *Climate change*, for example increase in greenhouse gas emissions and global warming.
3   *Environmental degradation*, particularly in the developing world, which is reducing economic capacity and weakening institutions.
4   *Energy*, for instance peak oil and natural gas production is occurring with no clear plans for alternatives.
5   *Global income and wealth inequality*, with massive global poverty co-existing with massive wealth, causing anger, resentment and conflict.

The effects of these stresses are being multiplied by the increased connectivity and speed with which materials, energy and information move around the planet, leading to cascading failures among the world's ecological, economic and social systems, and a power shift down the social hierarchy from states and large organizations to various subgroups and individuals, enhanced by the analytic power of new information technologies and possibilities of terrorist action. The danger is increased by the possibilities of convergence and simultaneity, with all the shifts happening in one place at the same time. Additionally, in the future we may not have sufficient high-quality energy to run our complex systems as the energy return on investment is declining (more energy is needed to produce energy). One of the deep drivers of our contemporary crisis is the desire to increase economic growth, resulting in increased material throughput, and based on the assumption that more means a better quality of life. These drivers counteract attempts to improve efficiency and lessen our impact on the environment and, although it is not possible to predict the future, for Homer-Dixon, systems breakdown and increasing systems volatility seem ever more likely. However, this grim scenario does have a brighter side, as a number of opportunities lie between the twin poles of living harmoniously and sustainably and complete catastrophic breakdown. Complex systems are able to adapt, and adaptation to moments of breakdown offers possibilities for creativity and for leadership to push society down one path rather than another. Adaptation will depend on the extent to which we are able to increase our social, economic, political and technological resilience, accomplished in large part by the development of a 'prospective mind' that recognizes that sharp and hurtful discontinuities are an inevitable part of our future. We must embrace the unexpected and expect surprises. For Homer-Dixon (2006: 283), scientific knowledge remains the best tool people have to distinguish between 'plausible and implausible futures'. This may mean new localized and sustainable forms of energy production, more time to deal with shocks, abandoning the system of 'just in time' production, and embarking on a proactive process of advanced planning and thought which focuses on how future crises could be dealt with in a 'non-extreme', dialogic, networked and collective manner. Open-source approaches that have been used to develop computer software need to be applied ferociously to hard social, political and environmental problems. The seeds of rebirth will therefore be found in the reality of present problems, with the possibilities of future breakdown breaking down denial and inertia to produce something new, useful and hopefully sustainable. As Homer-Dixon writes, we therefore need to be:

> open to radically new ways of thinking about our world and about the way we should lead our lives. We need to exercise our imaginations so that we can challenge the unchallengeable and conceive the inconceivable. Hunkering down, denying what's happening around us and refusing to countenance anything more than incremental adjustments to our course are just about the worst things we can do. These behaviours increase our rigidity and dangerously extend the growth phases of our adaptive cycle. When a social earthquake eventually occurs, we'll have no new concepts, ideas, or plans to help us cope and no alternative ways of seeing our future.
>
> (2006: 282)

Is this not a task for us all? Is this not a task for us all to be leaders in, whatever the spheres in which we lead our lives?

Box 11.3 The change leadership sustainability demands

Many [business executives] make the mistake of treating sustainability like any other large corporate initiative; it's actually different in several crucial ways. Or they assume that it will require a steady, constant effort over years. In fact, it entails three distinct phases, each requiring different leadership skills.

Phase 1: Making the case for change

When an organization is largely unprepared to address sustainability, the key challenge is to make a clear and compelling case for change. Because the organization is at best reactive to the challenges of sustainability (and usually unaware of the opportunities), the sustainability leader must be adept at collaborating and influencing others in the course of the transition from unconscious to conscious reactivity. At the end of Phase 1, sustainability emerges as a powerful mandate that is pervasive throughout the organization.

Phase 2: Translating vision into action

When companies emerge from Phase 1, commercial orientation becomes the key competence in aligning sustainability initiatives and value creation, a point that cannot be emphasized strongly enough. Now the task is to translate high-level commitments into a comprehensive change program with clearly defined initiatives and hard commercial targets. To make this happen, sustainability leaders in Phase 2 must excel at delivering results, and they must have a strong commercial awareness. At the end of this phase, the organization is consciously proactive on sustainability across its footprint and tracks economic, environmental and social metrics over the business planning cycle.

Phase 3: Expanding boundaries

The need for commercial orientation continues unabated but is now matched by a strong strategic orientation. As the organization continuously raises the bar and leverages sustainability to create competitive advantage, it increasingly views sustainability as a strategic opportunity and gauges its progress with metrics that reach beyond the short and medium term. The sustainability leader must be adept at anticipating and evaluating long-term sustainability trends, spotting new opportunities and developing strategies to reposition the organization to benefit from them. The goal is to embed sustainability in the organization's DNA such that it is a core value and the organization is unconsciously proactive about it.

Source: extracted from: Lueneburger and Goleman (2010).

Leading change for sustainability

As an ecological sensibility begins to pervade Western culture, government and business leaders are increasingly looking to ways in which they can embed sustainability into their business practices. Hitchcock and Willard (2006: 121) state that 'sustainability can be a powerful framework for harnessing employee commitment and energy; and that senior management teams can apply five clear strategies:

- *assessing threats, opportunities and constraints* which can be incorporated through processes of strategic planning, scenario planning, stakeholder management and backcasting, perhaps using the Natural Step Framework;
- *choosing terms and communication frameworks* such as business-friendly 'zero waste', high-performance building, triple bottom line, smart growth, corporate responsibility and product stewardship;
- *devising an implementation strategy and enlisting support*, involving selecting the best entry point for new sustainability practices (for example, capital investment, energy saving and green transport plans) and establishing the best organizational structure to effect this;
- *aligning business systems* through strategic and operational planning, budgeting, performance appraisals, orientation and training, and environmental management systems;
- *providing for transparency and stakeholder engagement* through the publication and public dissemination of corporate responsibility reports and partnership working with green consultancies and possibly NGOs like the WWF, Friends of the Earth or even Greenpeace.

In *Leading Change for Sustainability*, Bob Doppelt (2003) analyses the processes whereby private and public sector organizations may successfully realize sustainability goals. He offers a theoretical framework and a methodology that managers may use to transform and orientate their organizations towards sustainable development. According to Doppelt, discussions about new technologies and policy instruments have dominated public dialogue on sustainability, with relatively little attention paid to how organizations may change their internal thinking, values and assumptions, and conduct. For Doppelt, organizational and cultural change is key to the effective and successful operationalization of sustainable development. Avoiding 'sustainability blunders' and achieving a more sustainable organization will require interventions in the following.

- *Governance* – organizations that have made good progress towards sustainability see their internal and external stakeholders as important parts of an interdependent system. In leading sustainability organizations, a sensitive distribution of information, power and wealth among employees and stakeholders enables all to feel valued and meaningfully involved in the core vision and purposes of the organization.
- *Leadership* – effective sustainability leaders keep their organization focused on achieving this core vision while dealing with numerous, sometimes contradictory, demands and pressures. Intelligent leaders inspire and mobilize employees and stakeholders to embrace change as a significant learning opportunity. In exemplary organizations, leadership may be found at all or most levels of the organization.

Table 11.2 Sustainability solutions and blunders

Blunder	Solution
1 Patriarchal thinking that leads to a false sense of security	Change the dominant mindset through the imperative of achieving sustainability
2 A 'silo' approach to environmental and socio-economic issues	Rearrange the parts by organizing sustainability transition teams
3 No clear vision of sustainability	Change the goals by crafting an ideal vision and guiding sustainability principles
4 Confusion over cause and effect	Restructure the rules of engagement by adopting new strategies
5 Lack of information	Shift information flows by tirelessly communicating the need, vision and strategies for achieving sustainability
6 Insufficient mechanisms for learning	Correct feedback loops by encouraging learning and rewarding innovation
7 Failure to institutionalize sustainability	Adjust the parameters by aligning systems and structures with sustainability

Source: Doppelt (2000).

Doppelt bases his analyses and prescriptions on detailed research and explains his finding with the help of many case studies, interviews and checklists. After identifying seven major sustainability blunders, he discusses seven interventions, 'the wheel of change', that should correct them (see Table 11.2).

Although recent research and debate concludes that leadership and management in an organizational context are not totally distinct, that a good manager often exhibits leadership qualities or is able to work with others in order to motivate colleagues and initiate and adapt to change, for many, there remains an underlying feeling that leadership is separable from management. Kotter (1996) offers some clarification here – managers are concerned with planning, budgeting, organizing, staffing, controlling and problem solving, and leaders with establishing direction, aligning people, and motivating and inspiring people. Rost (1991) sees leadership as being concerned with developing mutual purposes in multidirectional relationships, while management is basically a co-ordinating function, operating in a unidirectional authority relationship. Leadership is a contradictory, dynamic or paradoxical art with a strong relational aspect, frequently rooted in the context in which it emerges or is practised. It may be that this dynamic nature of leadership is fully suited to the changing realities, pragmatics and dialogues surrounding the theories, hopes and practices of sustainable development.

Project SIGMA: environmental management and leadership combined

Project SIGMA (Sustainability – Integrated Guidelines for Management) was launched in 1999 by the UK Government's Department for Trade and Industry in partnership with the British Standards Institution, the NGO Forum for the Future and AccountAbility (the international professional body for accountability). The overall aim was to provide clear, practical advice to organizations, enabling them to contribute significantly to the process of sustainable development, helping businesses to become more ecologically responsible through the adoption and development of an alternative business model. Consequently, the SIGMA project developed guidelines for organizations to:

- effectively meet challenges posed by social, environmental and economic problems, threats and opportunities; and
- become change agents for a sustainable future.

SIGMA's guiding principles consist of:

- the holistic management of the natural, social, human, manufactured and financial capital that reflect an organization's overall impact and wealth;
- the exercise of accountability, by being transparent and responsive to stakeholders; and
- complying with relevant voluntary and statutory rules and standards.

Project SIGMA's management framework (see Table 11.3) identifies a basic four-phase cycle, together with various sub-phases, designed to manage and integrate sustainability issues within an organization's core activities.

Management phase

Complementing the principles and management framework is the SIGMA toolkit, which consists of a number of targeted tools and approaches to help with specific management challenges illustrated by a range of practical real-life case studies; a 'SIGMA guide to sustainability issues', relating to everything from directors' pay to ozone depletion; and guidance on designing a business case through which an organization can develop, promote and communicate its commitment to sustainable development by detailed information on the reporting of its sustainability practice and performance in accordance with the SIGMA guidelines and management framework.

Although this is a management system, Project SIGMA should not be confused with the similar sounding Six Sigma, which the advocates of *jugaad*, discussed earlier, are so critical of.

Leadership, complexity and self-organization

As noted earlier, the idea of complexity is associated with ecology, with living beings, usually manifesting itself at the level of the system itself. Complexity and systems thinking has had a profound effect on many thinkers and activists promoting sustainability values and practices in a wide variety of fields – business, community, politics, society and the economy. A complex system comprises many elements which interact physically and communicatively in relation to the transfer of information and other factors. These interactions are fairly short range, with each element operating in ignorance of the overall nature of the system itself. However, they may have consequences far in excess of their localized existence. The effects are therefore non-linear in scope and not necessarily predictable. Feedback loops may enhance or stimulate development, or alternatively hinder or inhibit it. Most importantly, complex systems are not closed, as they constantly interact with the external environment,

Table 11.3 Project SIGMA management framework

Management phase		Activity
LV1	Business case and top-level commitment	Developing a business case to address sustainability.
		Securing top-level management understanding and commitment to integrate sustainability and stakeholder engagement into core processes and decision-making.
		Identifying stakeholders and opening dialogue on key impacts.
LV2	Vision, mission and operating principles	Formulating long-term sustainability vision, mission and principles and high-level strategy, which will be reviewed periodically.
LV3	Training and communication	Establishing and delivering the organization's training requirements.
LV4	Culture change	Ensuring organizational change supports sustainability.
Planning phase		Activity
P1	Performance review	Ascertaining current sustainability performance.
		Identifying and prioritizing the organization's key sustainability issues.
		Involving stakeholders in review.
P2	Legal and regulatory analysis and management	Identifying and understanding regulatory requirements and voluntary commitments.
		Developing means to ensure future compliance and related improvements.
P3	Actions, impacts and outcomes	Identifying, evaluating and managing significant sustainability actions and outcomes.
P4	Strategic planning	Developing strategic plans to deliver the organization's sustainability mission.
P5	Tactical planning	Developing short-term plans to deliver sustainability strategy together with appropriate objectives, targets and responsibilities.

Source: adapted from Project Sigma Management Framework, available at: www.projectsigma.co.uk/Guide lines/Framework.

adjusting or not adjusting according to their degree of internal flexibility and capacity to accommodate, manage or mediate the variety of flows they experience. The behaviour of a complex system is not determined primarily by the priorities of the individual components or elements of the system, but is the result of complex patterns of interaction. Complex systems only achieve equilibrium when the possibility of change is exhausted. Hence the whole is greater than the sum of a system's constituent parts, and its structure is not so much designed and imposed as emerging from the various interactions taking place between the system and its relation to the wider environment. This does not deny the significance of human agency, but does qualify any notion of purely voluntaristic action or planned management outcomes. A self-organizing or autopoietic system selects flows of information or influence, enabling it to develop or change its internal structure spontaneously and adaptively. What it integrates is not so much a product of conscious decision-making, but rather the system's capacity to make sense of, and rearticulate or redesign, itself in accordance with what it encounters. A self-organizing system is not determined by an established series of specific goals or targets. Rather it may be said to have a function shaped by and within the overall context in which it operates. This is a lesson for leaders and managers of the sustainability process.

It is also the basis of James Lovelock's highly influential Gaia hypothesis and the work of Fritjof Capra (1996), who argues that a basic set of principles derived from our understanding of ecosystems as self-organizing networks and dissipative structures may serve as guidelines for building sustainable human communities of practice, experience and hope in business, the community and elsewhere. These principles include interdependence and networking, non-linear relationships, cyclical processes, flexibility and partnership, implying democracy, enrichment and personal empowerment. Management theorist Peter Senge (1990, 1999) argues that our focus must be on generative and creative learning that sees systems as shaping events. When we fail to grasp the systemic source of problems such as economic growth, we are left to 'push on' symptoms rather than eliminate underlying causes. Adaptive learning is simply about coping, but coping is not enough. To create a learning organization and sustainable human communities, non-hierarchical, lateral and co-operative leadership is needed. As Senge writes:

> Leadership in learning organizations centres on subtler and ultimately more important work [than simply energizing the troops]. In a learning organization, leaders' roles differ from that of the charismatic decision-maker. Leaders are designers, teachers and stewards. These roles require new skills: the ability to build shared vision, to bring to the surface and challenge prevailing mental models, and to foster more systemic patterns of thinking. In short, leaders in learning organizations are continually expanding their capabilities to shape their future – that is, leaders are responsible for learning.
>
> (1990 [2008]: 489)

In *Leaders and the New Science* (Wheatley, 1999) and *A Simpler Way* (Wheatley and Kellner-Rogers, 1999), Meg Wheatley develops an approach to leadership and organizations that is deeply rooted in systems thinking and eco-philosophy. Life, she writes, is about invention, creativity, self-organization, order, functionality (what works), relationships and networks. All manner of possibilities emerge when people connect with one another, when there is freedom to experiment in a playful way or to see the world differently and to fashion something new and exciting. Much emphasis is placed on co-evolution, collectivities and interdependencies. For Wheatley, there can be no heroes or visionary leaders and little place for individuals in a world perceived as so many interweaving systems, networks and webs:

> We make the world lonelier and less interesting by yearning for heroes. We deny the constant, inclusionary creating that is going on; we deny our own capacity to contribute and expand.
>
> (Wheatley and Kellner-Rogers, 1999: 44)

However, the sense of individual purpose is not absent from Wheatley's writings. We all seek meaning in our lives, and sometimes, though not always successfully, in our work, because most people are creative and often quite passionate. The ethical and spiritual dimension is aptly summarized when she writes that in 'a systems-seeking world, we find wellbeing only when we remember that we belong together' (Wheatley and Kellner-Rogers 1999: 64). In other words, systems are part of us, systems influence us and, by extension, we influence systems, enabling them to 'self-organize' to higher levels of complexity so as to deal more effectively with present contingencies, dangers and other influences. Many sustainable development practitioners draw on this insight by recognizing the significance of the concept of 'emergence' and elevating it to the level of principle. Interactivity leads to the emergence of new structures, possibilities and properties that stand outside and beyond the explicit knowledge and formal configuration of every organization. For the new to emerge, we need to participate openly and trustingly rather than just strategize, action plan, work plan and implement. We may need to visualize things differently – metaphorically, visually, poetically – to arrive at understanding, adaptation and the adoption of new capacities and capabilities. For Capra (2002: 107), 'the ability to express a vision in metaphors, to articulate it in such a way that it is understood and embraced by all, is an essential quality of leadership'. Building on this, Wheatley (1999) argues that a vision is a power and not place or destination. It is essentially an influence rendering congruent the messages and values we care about and the behaviours needed to realize them. Visions can offer and nurture clarity and integrity, but organizations need to be open to new ideas and new knowledge in order to facilitate emergence, and leaders must create this openness by nurturing a learning culture through encouraging questioning and rewarding innovation. Such a culture will value diversity and tolerate marginal and sometimes maverick activities that provide stretch, difference and novelty. It is not just about speedily applied new technologies, information processing or instant sticking-plaster solutions. It is often the product of long reflection, meditation and thought.

For Wheatley and Capra, people and organizations do not resist change unless they are treated as non-living, non-creative and irresponsible things. In nature, change never happens in a directed, top-down, preconceived fashion. Change begins at quite low and localized levels, often simultaneously and in many places. And the levels will remain localized unless, or until, they are connected in some way, and when they do, change emerges powerfully on a larger scale (or scales). Organizational and human relationships, communities of practice, and social and knowledge networks are the ways in which knowledge is created, learning generated, innovation diffused and new practices implemented. Relationships open up a variety of potentialities, serving to close off expectations that the world is ultimately predictable. For Wheatley (1999), what gives power its charge, and people and organizations their creative force, is the quality of these relationships. People become different persons in different places, they become surprising and more interesting, they stop arguing about the nature of truth and look to what works. In engaging with their environments, they help fashion those environments in creative ways. Change occurs and change can be directed because of the critical connections between and among these relationships. Thinking should be strategic and should displace the desire to plan and to learn 'skills'. The ability to analyse and predict should be replaced by a capability to understand what is happening now 'and we need to be better, faster learners from what just happened. Agility and intelligence are required to respond to the incessant barrage of frequent, unplanned changes' (Wheatley, 1999: 38).

Knowledge is often linked with power. Perhaps it would be more appropriate to link it to life and sustainability. As Wheatley (2001b) writes:

> Although we live in a world completely revolutionized by information, it is important to remember that it is knowledge we are seeking, not information. Unlike information, knowledge involves us and our deeper motivations and dynamics as human beings. We interact with something or someone in our environment and then use who we are – our history, our identity, our values, habits, beliefs – to decide what the information means. In this way, through our construction, information becomes knowledge. Knowledge is always a reflection of who we are, in all our uniqueness. It is impossible to disassociate who is creating the knowledge from the knowledge itself.

Adaptability to change within communities, organizations and societies will largely depend on their relationship to new and possibly disturbing information. Wheatley concludes:

> Information must actively be sought from everywhere, from places and sources people never thought to look before. And then it must circulate freely so that many people can interpret it. The intent of this new information is to keep the system off balance, alert to how it might need to change. An open organization doesn't look for information that makes it feel good, that verifies its past and validates its present. It is deliberately looking for information that might threaten its stability, knock it off balance and open it to growth.
>
> (1999: 83)

Open access to information contributes to self-organized effectiveness. Innovation is nurtured by seeking and securing information and developing knowledge from a variety of connections that cross disciplinary or institutional boundaries, cultural spaces and physical and virtual places, from actively participating in a variety of professional and other networks, and so on. Knowledge will therefore grow within relationships shared, made meaningful and developed through dialogue, debate and interaction. Indeed, a living network will only pass on what it believes to be meaningful.

Changing minds

The process of sustainable development often involves changing attitudes and values as well as behaviours. The American psychologist Howard Gardner (2006: 1) writes that, almost by definition, leaders can be understood as people who change minds. He reviews a number of ways and contexts in which minds change directly within organizations, intimate family situations or other personal relationships or indirectly within a culture or within nature. Whatever the case, the key to changing minds is changing people's mental representations – in other words, the way a person conceives, perceives, codes, retains and accesses information. This may occur through speech, discussion, art, scientific discovery or lived experience. It may involve sound, image,

---

Box 11.4 Ricardo Semler and the Semco way

Semco has no official structure. It has no organizational chart. There's no business plan or company strategy, no two-year or five-year plan, no goal or mission statement, no long-term budget. The company often does not have a fixed CEO. There are no vice-presidents or chief officers for information technology or operations. There are no standards or practices. There's no human resources department. There are no career plans, no job descriptions or employee contracts. No one approves reports or expense accounts. Supervision or monitoring of workers is rare indeed.

It's our lack of formal structure, our willingness to let workers follow their interests and their instincts when choosing jobs or projects.

It's our insistence that workers seek personal challenges and satisfaction before trying to meet the company's goals.

It's our commitment to encouraging employees to ramble through their day or week so that they will meander into new ideas and new business opportunities.

It's our philosophy of embracing democracy and open communication, and inciting questions and dissent in the workplace.

Even though our workers can veto a deal or close a factory with a show of hands, Semco grows by an average of 40 per cent a year and has annual revenue of more than US$212 million.

We need to first walk through the seven-day weekend that is the metaphor for the Semco way. . . . It's about creating an atmosphere and culture that grants permission to employees to be men and women in full for seven days a week. Why should the fun, fulfillment and freedom stop first thing Monday morning and be on hold until Friday night? . . . I believe no one can afford, can endure or can stomach leaving half a life in the parking lot when she or he goes to work. It's a lousy way to live and a lousy way to work.

Source: adapted from Semler (2004).

---

touch – indeed, all of the five senses. Mind changing will also encompass, in one form or another, one or a combination of the following:

- the use of reason, analysis and evaluation;
- the collection of relevant information in one or more forms;
- the appeal to the emotions as well as the intellect;
- the redescription or representation of a particular state of affairs or viewpoint in different ways – linguistic, numeric, graphic – recognizing the significance of people's multiple intelligences;
- encouragement, enticement or motivation to change;
- the impact of real-world events or, to put it simply, life; and
- personal, social or cultural resistance to change or difference.

For Gardner, an intelligence is the biophysical potential enabling people to process information in certain kinds of ways, and people have many of them. He first outlined his theory that human beings possess multiple intelligences in his *Frames of*

Mind (Gardner, 1993). Intelligences include the linguistic, logico-mathematical, musical, spatial, bodily-kinetic, naturalist (about the natural environment), inter- and intra-personal, emotional and existential (addressing the big meaning of life-type issues). Intelligence involves fashioning products and solving problems. The more of a person's intelligences a leader is able to engage or appeal to in fashioning an argument, the more likely that leader will change minds and behaviour. And although it is harder to change minds when views and perspectives are held strongly and publicly, it is far easier when individuals find themselves in new or relatively unfamiliar environments, when surrounded by people with different ideas and values, or when confronted with transformative, perhaps shattering experiences. Being with persuasive and charismatic others also helps. Leaders who tend to address large and diverse audiences will frequently use a story 'serene in its simplicity' (Gardner, 2006: 88) to explain or paint a picture of an issue, problem or aspiration. Leaders working with smaller, more uniform groups will tend to use theories, or maybe stories, exhibiting a high degree of complexity to enlist listeners' attention, interest and appreciation. A form of dialogue will always be present. Leaders need to use their linguistic skills, but also to avoid accusations of hypocrisy by actually embodying in their actions the changes they seek to induce in others. For Gardner (2006), the key attributes of an effective leader include:

- excellent linguistic, emotional and existential aptitudes – they can fashion good stories, understand people, and articulate the big questions or vision;
- excellent instinct, intuition or 'gut feeling', meaning they are able to perceive, and put into words, resemblances between present and past situations and experiences; and
- excellent integrity – usually the consequence of having the capacity for deep analysis, reflection and self-knowledge.

Excellent leaders are often highly creative people, not necessarily artistically or scientifically, but in the ways and means they deal with people and events. They may initiate new strategies for change, like the Indian political leader Mahatma Gandhi's advocacy of non-violent political action, relating the practical to the spiritual, or, like Muhammad Yunus, developer of the Grameen Bank, devising a new micro-finance model to encourage community engagement and business development among poor people in India, or, like Al Gore perhaps, communicating a complex issue simply, graphically, resonantly and powerfully in conference speeches, academic seminars or political writings, or on film or popular television.

On the practice of dialogue

Sustainability leaders need to bring about ecological and sustainable *learning* that is both social and dialogic. They need to communicate and persuade people with all manner of backgrounds, understandings and experiences. This may mean acting beyond one's authority, operating in the outer circles, moving out of familiar comfort zones, challenging opposing views and starting up a conversation. As Bocking (2007) notes, both Al Gore, with his film documentary and book *An Inconvenient Truth*, and Rachel Carson (2000), with *Silent Spring*, first published in the US in 1962, are regarded by many as two writers who have produced foundational texts of the environmental movement, and they have sought to communicate complicated science to non-scientists in the public sphere. Carson did so through the use of detailed evidence and having the social authority stemming from being a scientist. Gore does so by visually representing scientific knowledge in stunning photographs, and video and computer graphics. Both present a clear moral view of the human–nature relationship as one where human action disrupts the underlying harmony and balance of nature, and both have demonstrated how ecological damage affects our very selves. Gore is quite personal in his discussion of his own experiences, while Carson writes more dispassionately about the effects of DDT on our bodies. What is common to both their lives and their commitments is passion. And passion is, in many instances, an important aspect of leadership and a key ingredient of being taken seriously. Both have also been criticized, but, most importantly, both initiated a widespread and wide-ranging public dialogue and debate.

Sustainability leaders and practitioners in less visible public arenas frequently need to persuade others to think differently. This usually means entering into a conversation or dialogue in the community, at work, in the pub, in the home or in the classroom, and when misunderstandings or disputes occur, the problem often lies not so much in a failure to communicate but in a failure to learn to think together. When confronted by novelty or the need to be creative, innovative or to 'think outside of the box', we resolutely stay inside because of feelings of safety and familiarity and from habit. As William Isaacs notes, we cling to and defend existing views 'as if our lives depended on them' (1999: 6). However, for Isaacs, we can learn to go beyond this by nurturing a conversational spirit that can penetrate and dissolve the most inflexible and intractable of issues and problems. This can occur in close personal relationships, at the workplace within large organizations, within government, and between governments and peoples. Dialogue is the key and, to borrow an ecological metaphor from David Bohm (1996), if we remove what pollutes our thinking upstream, then we can avoid all sorts of problems and difficulties further down. 'The whole ecological problem,' writes Bohm, 'is due to thought, because we have thought that the world is there for us to exploit, that it is infinite, and so no matter what we did, the pollution would all get dissolved away' (1999: 10). Similarly, our thoughts, pre-conceived and pre-given assumptions often prevent us from talking freely, from sharing our fears, worries, thoughts and expectations. This affects the whole meaning of what we do, what we say and how we act. Conversation is never static. It must always be in motion, for there are times when people will fight, contest, be polite or nice, engage creatively or simply argue. Leaders have the responsibility to fashion the space, or 'container', in which these conversations emerge and change, where dialogues may embrace wider ideas and pressures, where the experience of interaction may be enriched and enhanced, and where a variety of styles and approaches may secure recognition and acknowledgement. Dialogue is therefore as much about learning as communication, but it does not just happen. It is, like the creation of new knowledge, the responsibility of everyone, a collective, community activity. Drawing on Bohm, Isaacs identifies four fields of conversation constituting a fruitful dialogue:

- *Field one*: Instability of the field – politeness in the container. Participants do not say what they think or feel, do not share as a result of convention, expectation, politeness, insecurity or just a lack of familiarity with the process.

- *Field two*: Instability in the field – break-down in the container. Participants seek dominance, battle with each other, oppose or withdraw, get angry. The leader's task is to fashion new ways of acting that allow people to think, reflect and be together differently.
- *Field three*: Enquiry in the field and the flowering of reflective dialogue. People express their own thoughts, admit not knowing and exhibit a spirit of curiosity. Meaning unfolds through conversation, exploration and the free flow of ideas. From fragmentation emerge new creative spaces and possibilities.
- *Field four*: Creativity in the field – generative dialogue. A rare space where participants are aware of the significance of the whole, where new rules for interaction are fashioned and where people experience synchronicities, connections, and individual and collective 'flow'.

Having experienced the fourth field, problems may arise when participants leave the dialogic space and return to their 'real' worlds. The key to this re-entry is for people to learn to let the meaning of this familiar world change, observing critically, evaluatively and sensitively the frames and spaces in which others operate most of the time. As Isaacs notes, 'leadership emerges when an individual or a group understands the shape of the world, and so is not deceived or overly intoxicated by any particular arrangement of its features' (1999: 287). The task of the leader is to ensure that people come together so that talk does not drive people apart, enabling them to learn to listen to others and to suspend preconceptions and assumptions so as to encourage flexibility and creativity in thought and expression. Thus, people are able to genuinely enter into dialogue when they demonstrate qualities of:

- *listening*, not only to others, but to ourselves, dropping our assumptions, resistance and reactions;
- *respecting* different viewpoints;
- *suspending* our opinions, stepping back, changing direction and seeing with new eyes; and
- *voicing*: speaking genuinely, discovering our own authority and relinquishing any need to dominate.

Different leadership skills are required within each field. For example, in field one, the leader or convener needs to relate to each person differently in order to draw them out, develop a predisposition to deep listening and to suspend judgement; in field two, the leader needs to help people learn by facilitating conversation between different perspectives; in field three the leader must model reflective enquiry and listen out for emerging themes; and in field four the leader must become the servant to the group, encouraging deep reflection and seeking paths and possibilities for future action and resolution. In field four the leadership function may change, but the essence is for all to see the whole as primary – the sum is greater than its individual parts. Dialogue facilitates participation and the development of richer and potentially wiser interpretations of the world and ways to change it. Indeed, through dialogue and participation new possibilities are not only created and made real, but those who have facilitated their emergence may sense among group members a growing commitment and ownership of the process. Knowledge management theorists Ikujiro Nonaka and Ryoko Toyama call the phenomenological time and space where new knowledge is created and where new learning occurs and problems are posed and solved 'ba':

> Ba can emerge in individuals, working groups, project teams, informal circles, temporary meetings, virtual spaces such as email groups and at the front line contact with the customer. Ba is an existential place where participants share their contexts and create new meanings through interactions. Participants of ba bring in their own contexts, and through interactions with others and the environment, the contexts of ba, participants and the environment change.
>
> (Nonaka and Toyama, 2004: 102)

Dialogue is central to the sustainable development process because it facilitates collective and different ways of thinking, learning and communication. Before this process is initiated, sustainability practitioners ought to ask questions about themselves, about the deep sources of their own thoughts, beliefs, assumptions, values and feelings. It is useful to know who you are.

Developing emotional and ecological intelligence in sustainability leadership

Good communicators and effective leaders need to understand people. This is particularly important when discussing issues and values, listening to others, and making sense of their and one's own experiences and feelings. Daniel Goleman (1996, 2002a) has formulated a theory of *emotional intelligence*, which essentially refers to how individuals effectively relate to self and others. This intelligence, or capability, may be broken down into a series of elements or competencies, which for Goleman are major prerequisites for effective leadership. Leaders must therefore exhibit the qualities described in the following sections.

Self-awareness

- Emotional self-awareness – attuned to inner feelings and convictions.
- Accurate self-assessment – aware of strengths and limitations and welcoming constructive criticism.
- Self-confidence – providing presence and self-assurance.

Self-management

- Self control – the ability to manage disturbing emotions and impulses and channel them in productive ways.
- Transparency – leaders *live* their values, are open and *authentic.*
- Adaptability – flexible, able to adjust to changing circumstances and uncertainties.
- Achievement – high personal standards, constantly seeking improvements in performance and continuous learning opportunities.
- Initiative – a sense of efficacy.
- Optimism – a positive attitude.

Social awareness

- Empathy – able to attune to a wide range of emotional signals in other people or groups.
- Organizational awareness – politically astute, able to detect crucial social networks and read key power relationships.
- Service – foster a supportive emotional climate.

Relationship management

- Inspiration – create resonance and motivating vision, making work exciting.
- Influence – build 'buy-in', persuasive communication, and engage others.
- Developing others – cultivate people's skills, interests and capabilities, giving timely and constructive feedback.
- Change agent – challenge the status quo, advocate change even in face of opposition, producing compelling arguments, and overcome barriers.
- Conflict manager – understand different perspectives, able to draw out all parties, redirecting energy towards shared ideals.
- Teamwork and collaboration – collegial, team players, models of respect and co-operation, drawing out others' commitments and enthusiasm.

Table 11.4 Leadership styles for resonant organizational teams

Leadership style	How it builds resonance	Impact on climate	When appropriate
Visionary	Moves people toward shared dreams	Most strongly positive	When change requires a new vision, or when a clear direction is needed
Coaching	Connects what a person wants with the team's goals	Highly positive	To help a person contribute more effectively to the team
Affiliative	Creates harmony by connecting people to each other	Positive	To heal rifts in a team, motivate during stressful times or strengthen connections
Democratic	Values people's input and gets commitment through participation	Positive	To build buy-in or consensus or to get valuable input from team members
Pacesetting	Sets challenging and exciting goals	Frequently highly negative because poorly executed	To get high-quality results from a motivated and competent team
Commanding	Soothes fears by giving clear direction in an emergency	Often highly negative because misused	In a crisis, to kick-start a turnaround

Source: Goleman (2002b).

Goleman also discusses how particular leadership styles may be appropriate for specific situations and particularly in developing teams. Allied to emotional intelligence is what Earley and Mosakowski (2004) call cultural intelligence – a capability that helps people engage with others from different occupational, national or ethnic cultures. Goleman has also extended his views on intelligence to encompass the ecological. This enables us to learn and understand how what we know about human activity can impact on ecosystems more sensitively and gently. This intelligence, Goleman (2009: 43) argues is something that existed for centuries in pre-modern 'simpler' societies. It has since been lost but can be regained. Ecological intelligence today means that in recognizing the hidden web of connections that make up our world, we are in desperate need for 'a collective eye opening, a shift in our most basic assumptions and perceptions'. He continues:

> Just as social and emotional intelligence build on the abilities to take other people's perspective, feel with them, and show our concern, ecological intelligence extends this capacity to all natural systems. We display such empathy whenever we feel distress at a sign of the 'pain' of the planet or resolve to make things better. This expanded empathy adds to a rational analysis of cause and effect the motivation to help.
>
> (2009: 44)

Given the highly connected nature of sustainability, both cultural and emotional intelligence are clearly significant. As Earley and Mosakowski remark:

> A person with high emotional intelligence grasps what makes us human and at the same time what makes each of us different from one another. A person with high cultural intelligence can somehow tease out of a person's or group's behavior those features that would be true of all people and all groups, those peculiar to this person or this group, and those that are neither universal nor idiosyncratic. The vast realm that lies between those two poles is culture.
>
> (2004: 140)

Educationalists write of *intercultural learning*, finding common values and common ground, and cultural intelligence is a tool that may allow this to be realized:

> The people who are socially the most successful among their peers often have the greatest difficulty making sense of, and then being accepted by, cultural strangers. Those who fully embody the habits and norms of their native culture may be the most alien when they enter a culture not their own. Sometimes people who are somewhat detached from their own culture can more easily adopt the mores and even the body language of an unfamiliar host. They're used to being observers and making a conscious effort to fit in.
>
> (Earley and Mosakowski, 2004: 140)

Community leadership can also take many forms, but invariably involves dialogue, group facilitation, empathy, emotional intelligence, conflict negotiation, leading by example and inspiration, and may be symbolized by the action and energy of a single individual, group or of a cultural initiative. In the favelas of Rio de Janeiro, where gun crime and drug trafficking have blighted many poor communities and distorted the life chances of many young people, the activist Anderson Sa, himself a former drugs trafficker turned musician, by detaching himself from his host culture, became a leader of a cultural and social movement based around music – the community-based Grupo Cultural AfroReggae (GCAR), formed in 1993. The group opened its first Núcleo Comunitário de Cultura (cultural community centre) in a slum area called Vigário Geral favela in 1993 and quickly organized workshops in dance, percussion, garbage recycling, soccer and *capoeira* (a cross between a martial art, a dance and a game). Four years later, in 1997, the GCAR opened the Centro Cultural AfroReggae Vigário Legal (Vigário Legal AfroReggae Cultural Centre), which had better facilities to run social, educational and cultural programmes. The vibrant hip-hop sounds of the Banda AfroReggae inspired many young favela residents to participate in the 'Centro', which soon offered previously unknown possibilities for collective engagement and individual and group creativity. The GCAR has since mobilized and empowered many slum communities. In *Favela Rising*, a documentary directed by Jeff Zimbalist released in 2005, Anderson Sa can be seen reasoning with street kids, organizing events and community actions, performing his music, and bravely recovering from serious injury following a terrible accident. The film, together with the book *Culture is Our Weapon* (Neate and Platt, 2006), explores and clearly demonstrates how leadership is both complex and social and also intensely personal. The GCAR and the street kids of Rio could not respond to managerial or bureaucratic initiatives – only something that truly emerges from their own lived experiences will resonate with their needs and desires for a life cleared of the false and temporary excitements, and rewards, of drugs, violence and aggression. Anderson Sa personalizes and personifies the possibility and reality of change, leadership and sustainability. Similar energetic cultural initiatives can be seen in many other cities in both the developing and the developed worlds, sometimes running parallel with a range of other community regeneration projects.

Leadership lessons from indigenous cultures

In order to learn from other cultures, it is necessary to be open to different ideas and experiences, even those which might at first seem odd or alien. In order to lead by example, there need to be those who are willing to follow, to learn and to act on that learning. Indigenous cultures in many parts of the world offer opportunities for learning and for leadership. Whether in Australia or North America, storytelling is central to indigenous culture. The way human beings are part of nature is passed on through the generations by stories told by the elders. Human beings talk of being with or becoming animals, of the wind whispering, and of the spirits communicating knowledge of the sacredness of the Earth. Life is part of a natural cycle and is itself inherently cyclical. The indigenous worldview is essentially connective, with under-standings of both time and space frequently expressed in oral and visual metaphors. Spirituality is timeless, and linear time – beginning, middle and end – is but part of the aboriginal person's circular understanding of a time continuum. Stories are retold, become acknowledged, and, through the experience of time, place, character, event and purpose, are shared communally and made real. As Fixico (2003) writes in *The American Indian Mind in a Linear World*, the logic of the Native American's worldview combines the physical with the metaphysical, the conscious with the subconscious. This is real, this is profound and knowledge of it only becomes truly meaningful if it is used to help the community.

To learn from this, people in the developed world will require a change of mindset, including the desire and capacity to rethink, re-evaluate and challenge their long-held and fundamental assumptions about the world, about the nature of intelligence, about leadership and about themselves. As environmental educator Chet Bowers (1995, 2003) says, unintelligent behaviour is really any action, way of thinking or moral view that degrades the environment. We therefore need to think and understand relationships in similar ways to that of many indigenous peoples, applying ecological principles of interdependence, sustainability, ecological cycles, energy flows, partnership, flexibility, diversity, complexity and co-evolution. We need to rethink the mechanistic linear root metaphors we live by and recognize that the dominant target-driven, goal-directed managerialism is neither realistic nor effective. It has disconnected humanity from the source of its meaning and, if the process of sustainable development needs leaders, then these leaders should perhaps best be perceived as actors, as agents, as people with the wisdom to create and to conserve. As Swedish management theorist Karl Erik Sveiby and Australian aboriginal artist Tex Skuthorpe (2006) write in their book *Treading Lightly: The Hidden Wisdom of the World's Oldest People*, the Aboriginal people of Australia have a sophisticated culture that has enabled them to live sensitively with the rhythm and dynamics of the Earth for 40,000 years, and they have done so without leaders.

Or rather, they have done so by recognizing the value of respect for all of nature, that knowledge is embedded in nature and the way we tread upon the Earth. It is through the wisdom of the elders that a human social environment may be nurtured, enabling consensus and the empowerment of all people through sharing. The elders have no power as understood in the developed world, but they do have a responsibility to empower by fostering participation, discussion, dialogue and agreement. Survival requires balance. We need balance. Instead of looking ahead, we need to look around us, for only by examining our environment and all our relations, our 'context', will we be able to see what is to come. As Black Elk noted, if the buffalo disappears, then the people do too:

> Moving around the lodge in a sun-wise manner, the mysterious woman left, but after walking a short distance she looked back towards the people and sat down. When she rose the people were amazed to see that she had become a young red and brown buffalo calf. Then this calf walked farther, lay down and rolled, looking back at the people, and when she got up she was a white buffalo. Again the white buffalo walked farther and rolled on the ground, becoming now a black buffalo. This buffalo then walked farther away from the people, stopped and, after bowing to each of the four quarters of the universe, disappeared over the hill.
>
> (Fixico, 2003: 58–9)

The moral lesson offered is that in studying and reflecting upon indigenous ways of life, we must recognize that other, quite different, and probably better, ways of understanding the world and the human condition are possible. We need to examine our present situation at the most fundamental level, recognizing the harm we have done to the planet and being determined to change our ways, if we are to have any

---

Box 11.5 A story of leadership, hope and achievement: Gaviotas

In 1966, Colombian activist Paulo Lugari and a group of scientists, artists, agronomists and engineers took a fifteen-hour journey along a tortuous route from Bogotá to the Llanos Orientales (eastern plains) bordering Venezuela. They wanted to immerse themselves in the ecosystem and develop alternative technologies that could meet the basic needs of any community. They chose Gaviotas, where the soil is 'like a desert', where employment prospects were poor and where a high level of violence existed.

Soon the Gaviotas pioneers were planting trees and digging gardens to grow food for their day-to-day needs. The soils of the river banks were too poor for vegetables, so they grew tomatoes, cucumbers, lettuce and eggplants in containers made out of rice husks, washed by a manure tea. By the late 1970s, they had created a square kilometre of hydroponic greenhouses and set up co-operatives to sell and exchange produce with villages in the region.

By 2003, many of the indigenous Guahíbo people and rural peasants living in Gaviotas were riding to work on Gaviotas-designed savannah bicycles. The settlement has a decent school and a solar and wind-powered hospital, where patients enjoy the aesthetic pleasure of shrubs and benefit from the 250 species of tropical medicinal plants cultivated in its greenhouses. In the wards, indigenous hammocks alternate with traditional hospital beds.

The electricity needed to run Gaviotas comes mainly from the winds of the savannah. Around fifty-eight types of windmill were tried and tested before the pioneers came up with one that functioned best in the plains. That is how the gigantic 'sunflowers', so characteristic of Gaviotas, came into being. Originally manufactured at Gaviotas, there are now thousands throughout Central and South America as their creators are determined not to patent their invention.

Around 8,000 hectares of forest were planted, in ever-increasing circles. As the pine forest grew, it provided shade for other seeds dropped by birds. The rainforest started to return – as did its creatures – deer, anteaters, capybaras and eagles. The resin harvested from the trees made eco-friendly turpentine, replacing imported petroleum-based products. And the pollution-free factory built to refine the resin won Gaviotas the 1997 United Nations World Zero Emissions Award.

Source: adapted from Pilar and Marin (2003).

---

hope of achieving a fulfilling, equitable and sustainable existence. The leadership task within sustainable development processes should therefore be clearly apparent, but how is it to be done?

Summary

The final chapter explores the concept and practice of leadership for sustainability. Much of the academic and professionally orientated work on leadership seems to have its roots in either the experience of business, the military, and to a lesser extent politics and government. This is reflected in the ideas and the writers discussed here, but it also accounts for a tendency for some sustainability practitioners to eschew the concept of leadership altogether or to interpret leadership very powerfully as an extension of facilitation, guidance and spiritual learning. Sustainability leadership and learning may look for role models outside the world of politics, business and government, and see the most significant teacher and leader to be the natural environment itself or those indigenous peoples who have over time co-evolved in respectful sympathy with the natural rhythms, affordances and gifts nature frequently bestows. Leadership may need to be positively deviant or basically accommodative. It may also need to be inspiring, but good sustainability leadership requires an ecological intelligence, a respect for non-human others and an understanding of sustainable development that we have yet to fully achieve.

Thinking questions

1   In what ways might systems theory inform the development of leadership in sustainable development practice?
2   How closely should dialogue be associated with leadership for sustainability?
3   Where are leaders for sustainability to be found?
4   How significant is the idea of leadership to the creation of a more sustainable future?
5   What is meant by authenticity?
6   What can we learn from indigenous cultures?

Companion website

Leadership in sustainability can clearly take many forms. Would you like to be a sustainability leader? Check out the companion website to learn more about leading for sustainability and see how you might develop your own leadership potential.

LIBRARY, UNIVERSITY OF CHESTER

Glossary

Biocapacity   The capacity of ecosystems to produce useful biological materials and to absorb waste materials generated by human production and consumption.

Biosphere   The global sum of all of the Earth's ecosystems.

Capitalism   An economic system in which the means of production, trade and industry is based on private ownership and the accumulation of private profit.

Climate change   A significant and long-term change to global weather patterns.

Complexity   An arrangement characterized by intricate and connected linkages and connections.

Conservation   A process, practice and movement aimed to protect flora and fauna at a variety of scales.

Corporate (social) responsibility   A policy and practice whereby private and public corporations operate responsibly in relation to their social, economic and environment impacts.

Degrowth   A political and economic philosophy and potential strategy based on anti-consumerist and ecological principles.

Democracy   A political system where all citizens have the right to participate in government through the election of representatives.

Development   A process that refers to actions and polices that are designed to enhance and improve the economic, social and environmental well-being of a country's or region's inhabitants.

Earth summit   A series of United Nations sponsored conferences on sustainability, conservation and development.

Ecoefficiency   An economic management strategy aimed at minimizing environmental impact, optimizing resource use and increasing product or service value.

Ecofeminism   A movement and philosophy linking ecological with feminist principles and values.

Ecological debt   The environmental liabilities of 'developed countries' such as resource extraction, greenhouse gas emissions, etc. incurred during the process of economic growth and development.

Ecological footprint   A measure expressing the human impact on the planet's ecosystems.

Ecological modernization   A belief in a process whereby innovation and reform will lead to greater economic efficiency and sustainable economies and industries.

Ecology   A scientific study of organisms as they interact with the environment.

Economic growth   The increase in the market value of goods and services produced by a given economy or economies over time.

Ecosystem   A community of living organisms living in relation to non-living elements in a given environment.

Ecosystem services   The ways in which natural biological processes enable and support the continuous enjoyment of a range of economic and other benefits required by human society.

Education for sustainability   An holistic approach to education and learning that enables people to develop the knowledge, skills and values necessary for sustainable living.

Environmental justice   A social movement and philosophy that posits the need for an equitable distribution of environmental benefits and burdens.

Gaia   A term closely associated with the scientist James Lovelock which likens the Earth to a living organism.

Globalization   A process relating to the global integration of economic, communication, trade, cultural and other factors.

Governance   The act and manner of governing relating to practices of expectations, verifications and scrutiny.

Greenhouse gas   A gas in the atmosphere, such as carbon dioxide, that absorbs and emits radiation.

Indigenous people   Groups of people native to a particular locality or bioregion who are usually vulnerable to marginalization, exploitation and oppression.

Localization   A process whereby decision-making and economic development is focused at a local level such as town, village or neighbourhood.

Media ecology   The study of media environments and the idea that technology, modes of information and codes of communication play a major role in human society.

Resilience   Within ecology, the capacity of an ecosystem to respond to a disturbance by resisting damage and recovering effectively within a given time frame.

Rio   A shorthand term referring to the Earth Summits held in Rio de Janeiro in 1992 and 2012, the latter often called Rio+20.

Risk society   A term associated with Ulrich Beck, denoting the manner in which a society organizes its response to natural or human-induced risks, dangers and uncertainties.

Social capital   Relationships of and resources for human social reciprocity and co-operation existing with a society or community.

Social ecology   A critical social theory developed by Murray Bookchin relating issues of social and economic equality with environmental justice.

Sustainability   Often referred to as goal relating to living and producing within the Earth's biological and ecological limits.

Sustainability science   A new largely applied academic discipline designed to advance understanding of the dynamics of human–environmental systems.

Sustainable development   A concept and a practice aiming to reconcile the goal of sustainability with that of continuing economic development and well-being.

Systems thinking   Seeing the world holistically as an arrangement of interconnected and co-operative components, structures and processes.

Urban sustainability   The capacity of a city or urban settlement to be organized with view to limiting or reducing its environmental impacts in a progressively positive manner.

Worldview   A fundamentally cognitive and value-laden orientation of an individual, group or society to understand the nature of the world and universe beyond.

References

Abdallah, S., Michaelson, J., Shah, S., Stoll, L. and Marks, N. (2012) *The Happy Planet Index: 2012 Report*. New Economics Foundation, London, available at: www.neweconom ics.org/publications/entry/happy-planet-index-2012-report.

Abers, R. (1998) 'Learning democratic practice: Distributing government resources through popular participation in Porto Alegre, Brazil', in M. Douglass and J. Friedmann (eds) *Cities for Citizens*, John Wiley, London, pp. 39–66.

Abram, D. (1996) *The Spell of the Sensuous*, Vintage, New York.

Adams, W.M. (2001) *Green Development: Environment and Sustainability in the Third World*, Routledge, London.

Adebowale, M., Church, C. and Shepherd, P. (2004) 'Environmental justice in London, London Sustainability Exchange, London', available at: www.lsx.org.uk/whatwedo/communities_ page2604.aspx.

Adger, W.N., Huq, S., Brown, K., Conway, D. and Hulme, M. (2003) 'Adaptation to climate change in the developing world', *Progress in Development Studies*, vol. 3, no. 3, pp. 179–95.

Agrawal, A. (1995) 'Dismantling the divide between indigenous and scientific knowledge', *Development and Change*, vol. 26, pp. 413–39.

Agyeman, J. (2005) *Sustainable Communities and the Challenge of Environmental Justice*, New York University Press, New York.

Agyeman, J. and Evans, B. (2004) 'Just sustainability: The emergence of environmental justice in Britain', *The Geographical Journal*, vol. 170, no. 2, pp. 155–64.

Agyeman, J. and Himmelberger, Y.O. (eds) (2009) *Environmental Justice and Sustainability in the Former Soviet Union*, Cambridge, MA, MIT Press.

Agyeman, J., Bullard, R. and Evans, B. (2002) 'Exploring the nexus: Bringing together sustainability, environmental justice and equity', *Space and Polity*, vol. 6, pp. 77–90.

Agyeman, J., Bullard, R.D. and Evans, B. (eds) (2003) *Just Sustainabilities: Development in an Unequal World*, Earthscan, London.

Albert, M. (2004) *Parecon: Life after Capitalism*, Verso, London.

Alexander, J.M. and Buckingham, J. (2011) 'Common good leadership in business management: An ethical model from the Indian tradition', *Business Ethics: A European Review*, vol. 20, no. 4, pp. 317–27.

Alison, J., Brayer, M.-A., Migayrou, F. and Spiller, N. (2006) *Future City: Experiment and Utopia and Architecture 1956–2006*, Barbican Art Gallery, London.

Altieri, M.A., Companioni, N., Cañizares, K., Murphy, C., Rosset, P., Bourque, M. and Nicholls, C.I. (1999) 'The greening of the "barrios": Urban agriculture for food security in Cuba', *Agriculture and Human Values*, vol. 16, pp. 131–40.

Amin, A. (2006a) 'The good city', *Urban Studies*, vol. 43, nos 5/6, pp. 1009–23.

Amin, S. (2006b) 'The millennium development goals: A critique from the South', *Monthly Review Press*, vol. 57, no. 10, available at: www.monthlyreview.org/0306amin.htm, accessed 10 June 2007.

Amnesty International (2004) *Clouds of Disaster: Bhopal Disaster 20 Years On*, Amnesty International, London.

Anderson, C. (2006) *The Long Tail*, Random House Business Books, London.

Anderson, E.N. (1996) *Ecologies of the Heart: Emotion, Belief and the Environment*, Oxford University Press, Oxford, UK.

Anderson, K. and Bows, A. (2011) 'Beyond "dangerous" climate change: Emission scenarios for a new world', *Philosophical Transactions of the Royal Society A*, vol. 369, pp. 20–44.

Anderson, P. (1992) *A Zone of Engagement*, Verso, London.

Anderson, R.C. (1998) *Mid-Course Correction*, Peregrinzilla Press, Atlanta, GA.

Anderson, W.T. (2001) *All Connected Now: Life in the First Global Civilization*, Westview Press, Boulder, CO.

Andressen, C., Mubarak, A.R. and Wang, X. (eds) (2013) *Sustainable Development in China*, London, Routledge.

Andrews, C. (1997) *The Circle of Simplicity: Return to the Good Life*, HarperCollins, London.

Appadurai, A. (1996) 'Disjuncture and difference in the global cultural economy', in A. Appadurai (ed.) *Modernity at Large*, University of Minnesota Press, Minneapolis, MN, pp. 27–47.

Appadurai, A. (2001) 'Deep democracy: Urban governmentality and the horizon of politics', *Environment and Urbanization*, vol. 3, no. 2, pp. 23–43.

Apple (2012) 'Apple Supplier Responsibility 2012 Progress Report', available at: http://images.apple.com/supplierresponsibility/pdf/Apple_SR_2012_Progress_Report.pdf.

Arnstein, S. (1969) 'A ladder of citizen participation', *Journal of the American Institute of Planners*, vol. 35, no. 4, pp. 216–24.

Audit Commission (2005) 'Local quality of life indicators – Supporting local communities to become sustainable', available at: www.audit-commission.gov.uk.

Ausubel, J.H. (2007) 'Renewable and nuclear heresies', *International Journal of Nuclear Governance, Economy and Ecology*, vol. 1, no. 3, pp. 229–43.

Avolio, B. J. (1999) *Full Leadership Development: Building the Vital Forces in Organizations*, Sage, Thousand Oaks, CA.

Avolio, B.J. and Gardner, W.L. (2005) 'Authentic leadership development: Getting to the root of positive forms of leadership', *The Leadership Quarterly*, vol. 16, no. 3, pp. 315–38.

Azar, C., Holmberg, J. and Lingren K. (1996) 'Socio-ecological indicators for sustainability', *Ecological Economics*, vol. 18, pp. 89–112.

Baker, S. (2006) *Sustainable Development*, Routledge, London.

Balakrishnan, U., Duvall, T. and Primeaux, P. (2003) 'Rewriting the bases of capitalism: Reflexive modernity and ecological sustainability as the foundations of a new normative framework', *Journal of Business Ethics*, vol. 47, pp. 299–314.

Banerjee, S.B. (2003) 'Who sustains whose development? Sustainable development and the reinvention of nature', *Organization Studies*, vol. 24, no. 1, pp. 143–80.

Banksy, R. (2005) *Wall and Piece*, Century Books, London.

Barber, B. (1984) *Strong Democracy*, University of California Press, Berkeley, CA.

Bardhan, P. (2002) 'Decentralization of governance and development', *The Journal of Economic Perspectives*, vol. 16, no. 4, pp. 185–205.

Barnett, J. (2001) *The Meaning of Environmental Security*, Zed Books, London.

Barr, S., Gilg, A. and Shaw, G. (2011) '"Helping people make better choices": Exploring the behaviour change agenda for environmental sustainability', *Applied Geography*, vol. 31, no. 2, pp. 712–20.

Barry, J. (1999) *Rethinking Green Politics*, Sage, London.

Bartlett, P.F. and Chase, G.W. (eds) (2004) *Sustainability of Campus: Stories and Strategies for Change*, MIT Press, Cambridge, MA.

Barton, H. (ed.) (2000) *Sustainable Communities: The Potential for Eco-Neighbourhoods*, Earthscan, London.

Batterbury, S.P.J. (2006) 'Rescaling governance and the impacts of political and environmental decentralization: An introduction', *World Development*, vol. 34, no. 11, pp. 1851–63.

Baud, I. and Dhanalakshmi, R. (2007) 'Governance in urban environmental management: Comparing accountability and performance in multi-stakeholder arrangements in South India', *Cities*, vol. 24, no. 2, pp. 133–47.

Bauhaus-Universität Weimar (2004) 'The urban transition: Research for the sustainable development of the megacities of tomorrow', Federal Ministry of Education and Research, Berlin, available at: www.uni-weimar.de/Bauing/ abfallw/downloads/Megacities_long-paper.pdf.

Bauman, Z. (2000) *Liquid Modernity*, Polity Press, Cambridge.

Bawden, T. (2013) 'IPCC report: The financial markets are the only hope in the race to stop global warming', *The Independent*, 27 September, available at: www.independent.co.uk/environment/climate-change/ipcc-report-the-financial-markets-are-the-only-hope-in-the-race-to-stop-global-warming-8843573.html.

BBC News (2000) 'BP goes green', available at: http://news.bbc.co.uk/1/hi/business/849475.stm.

Beall, J., Crankshaw, O. and Parnell, S. (2000) 'Local government, poverty reduction and inequality in Johannesburg', *Environment and Urbanization*, vol. 12, no. 1, pp. 107–22.

Beatley, T. (2004) *Native to Nowhere: Sustaining Home and Community in a Global Age*, Island Press, Washington, DC.

Beatley, T. (2011) *Biophilic Cities: Integrating Nature into Urban Design*, Island Press, Washington, DC.

Beck, U. (1992a) *Risk Society*, Sage, London.

Beck, U. (1992b) 'From industrial society to the risk society: Questions of survival, social structure and ecological enlightenment', *Theory, Culture and Society*, vol. 9, pp. 97–123.

Beck, U. (1996) 'Risk society and the provident state', in S. Lash, B. Szerszynski and B. Wynne (eds) *Risk, Environment and Modernity: Towards a New Ecology*, Sage, London, pp. 27–43.

Becker, J. (2005) 'Measuring progress towards sustainable development: An ecological framework for selecting indicators', *Local Environment*, vol. 10, no. 1, pp. 87–101.

Beder, S. (1997) *Global Spin: The Corporate Assault on Environmentalism*, Green Books, Totnes, UK.

Beder, S. (2002) 'BP: Beyond Petroleum?', in E. Lubbers (ed.) *Battling Big Business: Countering Greenwash, Infiltration and Other Forms of Corporate Bullying*, Green Books, Totnes, UK, pp. 26–32.

Beder, S. (2006) *Suiting Themselves: How Corporations Drive the Global Agenda*, Earthscan, London.

Bekoff, M. and Bexell, S. (2010) 'Ignoring nature: Why we do it, the dire consequences, and the need for a paradigm shift to save animals, habitats, and ourselves', *Human Ecology Review*, vol. 17, pp. 70–6.

Bell, S. and Morse, S. (1999) *Sustainability Indicators: Measuring the Immeasurable*, Earthscan, London.

Bell, S. and Morse, S. (2003) *Measuring Sustainability: Learning By Doing*, Earthscan, London.

Bello, W. (2002) 'Future of global economic governance', in H. van Ginkel, B. Barrett, J. Court and J. Velasquez (eds) *Human Development and the Environment: Challenges for the United Nations in the New Millennium*, United Nations University Press, Tokyo, pp. 161–82.

Bello, W. (2004) *Deglobalization: Ideas for a New World Economy*, Zed Books, London.

Belz, F.-M. (2006) 'Marketing in the 21st century', *Business Strategy and the Environment*, vol. 15, pp. 139–44.

Belz, F.-M. and Peattie, K. (2012) *Sustainability Marketing: A Global Perspective* (2nd edn), Chichester, John Wiley & Sons.

Bendor, R., Lyons, S.H. and Robinson, J. (2012) 'What's there not to "like"? The technical affordances of sustainability deliberations on Facebook', *Journal of E-Democracy*, vol. 4, no. 1, pp. 67–88.

Ben-Eli, M. (2007) 'Defining sustainability', *Resurgence*, no. 244, pp. 12–14.

Benjamin, S. (2000) 'Governance, economic settings and poverty in Bangalore', *Environment and Urbanization*, vol. 12, no. 1, pp. 35–56.

Bennett, W.L. (2003) 'Communicating global activism: Strengths and vulnerabilities of networked politics', available at: http://depts.washington.edu/ccce/research/ WorkingPapers. htm.

Benton, L.M. and Short, J.R. (eds) (2000) *Environmental Discourse and Practice: A Reader*, Blackwell, Oxford.

Benyus, J.M. (2002) *Biomimicry: Innovation Inspired by Nature*, HarperPerennial, New York.

Berg, P. (1992) 'A metamorphosis for cities: From gray to green', available at: www.planetdrum. org/metamorphosis_for_cities.htm.

Berg, P., Magilavy, B. and Zuckerman, S. (1989) *Green City Program for San Francisco Bay Area Cities and Towns*, Planet Drum Foundation, San Francisco, CA.

Berkes, F. (2007) 'Understanding uncertainty and reducing vulnerability: Lessons from resilience thinking', *Natural Hazards*, vol. 41, no. 2, pp. 283–95.

Berners-Lee, M. and Clark, D. (2013) *The Burning Question*, London, Profile Books.

Berry, W. (1990) *The Dream of the Earth*, Sierra Club Books, San Francisco, CA.

Best, S. (1998) 'Murray Bookchin's theory of social ecology', *Organization and Environment*, vol. 11, no. 3, pp. 334–53.

Biello, D. (2012) 'Can smarter growth guide China's urban building boom?', *environment360*, 13 February, available at: http://e360.yale.edu/feature/can_smarter_growth_guide_chinas_ urban_building_boom/2494/

Biello, D. (2013) 'Can cities solve climate change?' *Scientific American*, 9 October, available at: www.scientificamerican.com/article.cfm?id=cities-as-solutions-to-climate-change.

Birchall, J. (2004) 'Cooperatives and the millennium development goals', Geneva: ILO/COPAC, available at: www.copac.coop/publications/2004.birchall-mdgs.pdf.

BITC (2006) 'Looking back, moving forward: Building the business case for environmental improvement, business in the community, London', available at: www.bitc.org.uk/resources/ publications/looking_back_moving.html.

Blewitt J. (2004) 'Sustainability and lifelong learning', in J. Blewitt and C. Cullingford (eds) *The Sustainability Curriculum*, Earthscan, London.

Blewitt, J. (2006) *The Ecology of Learning: Sustainability, Lifelong Learning and Everyday Life*, Earthscan, London.

Blewitt, J. (2007) 'Television for the environment: Communicating for change', *Development Education Journal,* vol. 13, no. 2, pp. 29–30.

Blewitt, J. (2010a) 'Higher education for a sustainable world', *Education + Training*, vol. 52, no. 6/7, pp. 477–88.

Blewitt, J. (2010b) *Media, Ecology and Conservation: Using the Media to Protect the World's Wildlife and Ecosystems*, Green Books, Totnes, UK.

Blewitt, J. (2011) 'Critical practice and the public pedagogy of environmental and conservation media', *Environmental Education Research*, vol. 17, no. 6, pp. 719–34.

Blewitt, J. (2012) 'The future of the public library: Reimagining the moral economy of the "people's university"', *Power and Education*, vol. 4, no. 1, pp. 106–15.

Blewitt, J. (2013a) 'EfS: Contesting the market model of higher education', in S. Sterling, L. Maxey and H. Luna (eds) *The Sustainable University*, Routledge, London, pp. 51–70.

Blewitt, J. (2013b) 'Cute slow loris videos should come with a health warning', 14 August, *The Conversation*, available at: http://theconversation.com/cute-slow-loris-videos-should-come-with-a-health-warning-17029.

Blewitt, J. and Cullingford, C. (eds) (2004) *The Sustainability Curriculum: The Challenge for Higher Education*, Earthscan, London.

Blewitt, J. and Tilbury, D. (2013) *Searching for Resilience in Sustainable Development*, Routledge-Earthscan, London.

Blowfield, M. (2013) *Business and Sustainability*, Oxford: Oxford University Press.

Bocking, S. (2007) 'The silent spring of Al Gore', *Alternatives Journal*, vol. 33, no. 1, available at: www.alternativesjournal.ca/index.phpoption=com_content&task=view&id=284.

Bohm, D. (1996) *On Dialogue*, Routledge, London.

Boltanski, L. and Chiapello, E. (1999) *Le nouvel esprit du capitalisme*, Gallimard, Paris.

Boltanski, L. and Chiapello, E. (2005) 'The new spirit of capitalism', *International Journal of Politics, Culture and Society*, vol. 18, no. 3–4, pp. 161–88.

Bookchin, M. (1980) *Toward an Ecological Society*, Black Rose Books, Montreal, Canada.

Bookchin, M. (1993) 'What is social ecology?', available at: http://dwardmac.pitzer.edu/Anarchist_Archives/bookchin/socecol.html.

Bookchin, M. (1995) *From Urbanization to Cities*, Cassell, London.

Bookchin, M. (2005) *The Ecology of Freedom: The Emergence and Dissolution of Hierarchy*, AK Press, Oakland, CA.

Bordiga, E., Sullivan, J.L., Oxendine, A., Jackson, M.S. and Riedel, E. (2002) 'Civic culture meets the digital divide: The role of community electronic networks', *Journal of Social Issues*, vol. 58, no. 1, pp. 125–41.

Borgmann, A. (1984) *Technology and the Character of Contemporary Life*, University of Chicago Press, Chicago.

Borland, H. and Lindgreen, A. (2013) 'Sustainability, epistemology, ecocentric business, and marketing strategy: Ideology, reality, and vision', *Journal of Business Ethics*, vol. 117, no. 1, pp. 173–87.

Bosshard, P. (2013) 'World Bank returns to big dams', *World Rivers Review*, vol. 28, no. 3, available at: www.internationalrivers.org/files/attached-files/wrr_sept_2013_6.pdf.

Boulding, K.E. (1966) 'The economics of the coming Spaceship Earth', in H. Jarrett (ed.) *Environmental Quality in a Growing Economy*, Johns Hopkins Press for Resources for the Future, Baltimore, MD, pp. 3–14.

Bourdieu, P. (1977) *Outline of a Theory of Practice*, Cambridge University Press, Cambridge.

Bowers, C.A. (1995) *Educating for an Ecologically Sustainable Culture*, State University of New York Press, Albany, NY.

Bowers, C.A. (2001) *Educating for Eco-Justice and Community*, University of Georgia Press, Athens, GA.

Bowers, C.A. (2003) *Mindful Conservatism: Rethinking the Ideological and Educational Basis of an Ecologically Sustainable Future*, Rowman & Littlefield, Lanham, MD.

Bowman, S. and Willis, C. (2003) 'We media', available at: www.hypergene.net/wemedia/weblog.php.

BP (2006) 'Human rights: A guidance note', available at: www.bp.com/liveassets/bp_internet/globalbp/STAGING/global_assets/downloads/BP_Human_Rights_2005.pdf.

BP (2012) 'Energy Outlook 2030', London, BP, available at: www.bp.com/en/global/corporate/about-bp/statistical-review-of-world-energy-2013/energy-outlook-2030.html.

Brain, S. (2010) 'Stalin's environmentalism', *The Russian Review*, vol. 69, no. 1, pp. 93–118.

Brand, S. (1997) *How Buildings Learn*, Orion, London.

Brand, S. (2005) 'Environmental heresies', *Technology Review*, vol. 108, no. 5, pp. 60–3, available at: www.technologyreview.com/Energy/14406.

Brandt, W. (1980) *North–South: A Programme for Survival*, The Brandt Commission, Pan Books, London.

Bridger, J.C. and Luloff, A.E. (1999) 'Toward an interactional approach to sustainable community development', *Journal of Rural Studies*, vol. 15, pp. 377–87.

Briggs, G. (2005) 'The intelligent city: Ubiquitous network or humane environment?', in M. Jenks and N. Dempsey (eds) *Future Forms and Design for Sustainable Cities*, Architectural Press, London, pp. 31–54.

Brockington, D. (2002) *Fortress Conservation: The Preservation of the Mkomazi Game Reserve, Tanzania*, James Currey, London.

Brockington, D., Duffy, R. and Igoe, J. (2008) *Nature Unbound: Conservation, Capitalism, and the Future of Protected Areas*, Earthscan, London.

Brown, L.R. (2001) *Eco-Economy: Building an Economy for the Earth*, Earthscan, London.

Brown, L.R. (2006) 'Plan B 2.0: Rescuing a planet under stress and a civilization in trouble, Norton, New York, available at: www.earth-policy.org/Books/PB2/pb2ch12.pdf.

Brown, P. (2005) 'Modified rape crosses with wild plant to create tough pesticide-resistant strain', *The Guardian*, 25 July.

Bruce, I. (2004) *The Porte Allegre Alternative: Direct Democracy in Action*, Pluto Press, London.

Brulle, R. (2000) *Agency, Democracy and Nature: The US Environmental Movement from a Critical Theory Perspective*, MIT Press, Cambridge, MA.

Bryman, A. (1999) 'The Disneyization of society', *The Sociological Review*, vol. 47, no. 1, pp. 25–47.

Buckman, G. (2004) *Globalization: Tame it or Scrap it?*, Zed Books, London.

Buell, L. (2001) *Writing for an Endangered World*, Harvard University Press, Cambridge, MA.

Bullard, R.D. (ed.) (2005) *The Quest for Environmental Justice: Human Rights and the Politics of Pollution*, Sierra Club Books, San Francisco, CA.

Bullard, R.D. and Johnson, G.S. (2000) 'Environmental justice and its impact on public policy decision-making', *Journal of Social Issues*, vol. 56, no. 3, pp. 555–78.

Bunting, M. (2007) 'Scientists have a new way to reshape nature, but none can predict the cost', *The Guardian*, 22 October.

Burke, T. (2004) 'This is neither scepticism nor science – Just nonsense', *The Guardian*, 23 October, available at: www.guardian.co.uk/comment/story/0,3604,1334209,00.html.

Burke, T. (2005) 'Address to Green Alliance 25th anniversary', available at: www.e3g. org/index.php/concept/concept-articles/address-to-green-alliance-25th-anniversary, accessed 25 July 2007.

Cairns, J. Jr (2003) 'Integrating top–down/bottom-up sustainability strategies: An ethical challenge', *Ethics in Science and Environmental Politics*, vol. 3, available at: www.int-res. com/articles/esep/ 2003/E26.pdf.

Cairns, J. Jr (2004) 'Future of life on Earth', *Ethics in Science and Environmental Politics*, vol. 4, available at: www.int-res.com/articles/esep/2004/E41.pdf.

Cajete, G. (ed.) (1999) *A People's Ecology: Explorations in Sustainable Living*, Clear Light Publishers, Sante Fe, NM.

Caldicott, H. (2006) *Nuclear Power is Not the Answer*, The New Press, New York.

Callenbach, E. (1975) *Ecotopia*, Banyan Tree Books, Berkeley, CA.

Calthorpe, P. (1993) *The Next American Metropolis: Ecology, Community and the American Dream*, Princeton Architectural Press, New York.

Cao, S., Chen, L., Shankman, D., Wang, C., Wang, X. and Zhang, H. (2011) 'Excessive reliance on afforestation in China's arid and semi-arid regions: Lessons in ecological restoration', *Earth-Science Reviews*, vol. 104, no. 4, pp. 240–5.

Capra, F. (1991) *The Tao of Physics* (3rd edn), Flamingo, London.

Capra, F. (1996) *The Web of Life*, Anchor Books, London.

Capra, F. (2002) *The Hidden Connections*, Flamingo, London.

Capra, F. and Stone, M.K. (2010) 'Smart by nature: Schooling for sustainability', *Journal of Sustainability Education*, 25 May, available at: www.jsedimensions.org/wordpress/content/ trial-author-change_2010_05.

CARMA (2006) 'Western media coverage of humanitarian disasters', available at: www.carma. com/research.

Carnap, R. (1966) *Philosophical Foundation of Physics*, Basic Books, New York.

Carson, R. (2000 [1962]) *Silent Spring*, Penguin Books, London.

Carvalho. A. (2007) 'Ideological cultures and media discourses on scientific knowledge: re-reading news on climate change', *Public Understanding of Science*, vol. 16, no. 2, pp. 223–43.

Castells, M. (1996) *The Rise of the Network Society* (3 vols), Blackwell, Oxford, UK.

Castells, M. and Hall, P. (1994) *Technopoles of the World: The Making of 21st-Century Industrial Complexes*, Routledge, London and New York.

Castro, C.J. (2004) 'Sustainable development: Mainstream and critical perspectives', *Organization and Environment*, vol. 17, no. 2, pp. 195–225.

CEC (2000) 'Communication from the Commission on the precautionary principle', EU, Brussels CEMR/ICLEI.

Chambers, N., Simmons, C. and Wackernagel, M. (2000) *Sharing Nature's Interest: Ecological Footprints as an Indicator of Sustainability*, Earthscan, London.

Chan, L. and Rahman, M.A. (2010) 'A model for assessing biodiversity conservation in cities: The Singapore Index on Cities' Biodiversity', *CityGreen*, vol. 4, pp. 78–87.

Chapin, M. (2004) 'A challenge to conservationists', *WORLDWATCH*, November/December, pp. 17–31.

Chapman, J. (2005) *Emotionally Durable Design: Objects, Experiences and Empathy*, Earthscan, London.

Cheney, J. (1989) 'Postmodern environmental ethics: Ethics as bioregional narrative', *Environmental Ethics*, vol. 11, no. 2, pp. 117–34.

Cheney, J. (1998) 'Universal consideration: An epistemological map of the terrain', *Environmental Ethics*, vol. 20, Fall, pp. 265–77.

Chief Seattle (2000, original *c.* 1855) 'How can one sell the air? A Manifesto for the Earth', in L.M. Benton and J.R. Short (eds) *Environmental Discourse and Practice: A Reader*, Blackwell, Oxford, UK, pp. 12–13.

Choi, B.-C., Shin, H.-S., Lee, S.-Y. and Hur, T. (2006) 'Life cycle assessment of a personal computer and its effective recycling rate', *International Journal of Life Cycle Assessment*, vol. 11, no. 2, pp. 122–8.

Christian Aid (2004) 'Behind the mask: The real face of corporate social responsibility, Christian Aid, London', available at: www.globalpolicy.org/socecon/tncs/2004/0121mask.pdf.

Christoff, P. (1996) 'Ecological modernization, ecological modernities', *Environmental Politics*, vol. 5, no. 3, pp. 476–500.

Christophers, B. (2006) 'Visions of nature, spaces of empire: Framing natural history programming within geometries of power', *Geoforum*, vol. 37, no. 6, pp. 973–85.

CIA World Fact Book, available at: www.cia.gov/library/publications/the-world-factbook/geos/xx.html.

Cisco (2013) Cisco Global Cloud Index: Forecast and Methodology, 2012–2017, available at: www.cisco.com/c/en/us/solutions/collateral/service-provider/global-cloud-idex-gci/Cloud_Index_White_Paper.pdf.

City of Copenhagen (2012) *Copenhagen: Solutions For Sustainable Cities*, City Hall, Copenhagen.

Clapp, J. and Dauvergne, P. (2005) *Paths to a Green World: The Political Economy of the Global Environment*, MIT Press, Cambridge, MA.

Clarkson, M.B.E. (1995) 'A stakeholder framework for analysing and evaluating corporate social performance', *Academy of Management Review*, vol. 20, no. 1, pp. 92–117.

Clayton, T. and Radcliffe, N. (1996) *Sustainability: A Systems Approach*, Earthscan, London.

Clover, C. (2005) *The End of the Line*, Ebury Press, London.

Cockcroft, E., Weber, J.P. and Cockcroft, J. (1998) *Toward a People's Art: The Contemporary Mural Movement*, University of New Mexico Press, Albuquerque, NM.

Cole, R.J. (2012) 'Transitioning from green to regenerative design', *Building Research & Information*, vol. 40, no. 1, pp. 39–53.

Coleman, J.A. (1990) *Foundations of Social Theory*, Harvard University Press, Cambridge, MA.

Collin, R.M. and Collin, R. (2005) 'Environmental reparations', in R.D. Bullard (ed.) *The Quest for Environmental Justice: Human Rights and the Politics of Pollution*, Sierra Club Books, San Francisco, CA, pp. 209–21.

Collins, J. and Porras, J.I. (1994) *Built to Last: Successful Habits of Visionary Companies*, HarperBusiness, New York.

Collins, J., Thomas, G., Willis, R. and Wilsdon, J. (2003) 'Carrots, sticks and sermons: Influencing public behaviour for environmental goals', Demos/Green Alliance report produced for Defra, available at: www.green-alliance.org.uk.

Collom, E. (2003) 'Two classes and one vision?: Managers' and workers' attitudes toward workplace democracy', *Work and Occupations*, vol. 30, no. 1, pp. 62–96.

Confino, J. (2012) 'Climate change may force evacuation of vulnerable island states within a decade', *The Guardian*, 4 October, available at: www.theguardian.com/sustainable-business/blog/polar-arctic-greenland-ice-climate-change.

Congress for the New Urbanism (2000) *Charter for New Urbanism*, CNU, Chicago, IL, available at: www.cnu.org/charter.

Connell, J.B. (1990) *Sharing Nature With Children* (20th anniversary edition), Dawn Publications, Nevada City, CA.

Connelly, J. and Smith, G. (1999) *Politics and the Environment: From Theory to Practice*, Routledge, London.

Cook, D. (2004) *The Natural Step: A Framework for Sustainability*, Schumacher Briefings, Green Books, Totnes, UK.

Cook, I. (2000) 'Social sculpture and connective aesthetics: Shelley Sacks's exchange values', *Ecumene*, vol. 7, no. 3, pp. 337–43.

Cook, I. (2004) 'Follow the thing: Papaya', *Antipode*, vol. 36, no. 4, pp. 642–64.

Cooke, B. and Kothari, U. (eds) (2001) *Participation: The New Tyranny*, London, Zed Books.

Corcoran, P.B. and Wals, A.E.J. (eds) (2004) *Higher Education and the Challenge of Sustainability: Problematics, Promise and Practice*, Kluwer Academic Publishers, Dordrecht, The Netherlands.

Costall, A. (2000) 'James Gibson and the ecology of agency', *Communication & Cognition*, vol. 33, no. 1, pp. 23–32.

Costanza, R., de Groot, R., Farber, S., Grasso, M., Hannon, B., Limburg, K. Naeem, S., O'Neill, R.V., Paruelo, J., Raskin, R.G., Sutton, P. and van den Belt (1997) 'The value of the world's ecosystem services and natural capital', *Nature*, no. 387, pp. 253–60.

Cottle, S. (2011a) 'Transnational protests and the media: New departures, challenging debates', in S. Cottle and L. Lester (eds) *Transnational Protests and the Media*, Peter Lang, New York, pp.17–38.

Cottle, S. (2011b) 'Media and the Arab uprisings of 2011: Research notes', *Journalism*, vol. 12, no. 5, pp. 647–59.

Couldry, N. and Curran, J. (eds) (2003) *Contesting Media Power: Alternative Media in a Networked World*, Rowman & Littlefield, Lanham, MD.

Council of European Municipalities and Regions)/Local Governments for Sustainability (2004) *Final Version of The Aalborg Commitments*, available at: www.aalborgplus10.dk/default.aspx?m=2&i=307.

Coyle, D. (ed.) (2005) 'Africa: The impact of mobile phones', Vodaphone Policy Paper no. 3, available at: www.vodafone.com/etc/medialib/ attachments/cr_downloads.Par.78351.File.dat/GPP_SIM_paper_3.pdf.

Cox, R. (2013) *Environmental Communication and the Public Sphere*, Sage, Los Angeles, CA.

Crawford, J.H. (2000) *Carfree Cities*, International Books, Utrecht.

Crist, E. (2004) 'Against the social construction of nature and wilderness', *Environmental Ethics*, vol. 26, no. 1, pp. 5–24.

Crist, E. (2007) 'Beyond the climate crisis', *Telos*, 141, Winter, pp. 29–55.

Crist, E. (2012) 'Abundant Earth and the population question', in P. Cafaro and E. Crist (eds) *Life on the Brink: Environmentalists Confront Overpopulation*, University of Georgia Press, Athens, GA, 141–53.

Cronon, W. (1983) *Changes in the Land: Indians, Colonists and the Ecology of New England*, Hill & Wang, New York.

Cronon, W. (1996) 'The trouble with wilderness': Or, getting back to the wrong nature', in W. Cronon (ed.) *Uncommon Ground: Rethinking the Human Place in Nature*, Norton, New York, pp. 69–90.

Crosby, A.W. (1986) *Ecological Imperialism: The Biological Expansion of Europe, 900–1900*, Cambridge University Press, Cambridge.

Crouch, B. (2008) 'Tiny Tuvalu in save us plea over rising seas', *The Adelaide Avertiser*, 4 October, available at: www.adelaidenow.com.au/news/save-us-islands-climate-plea/story-e6frea6u-1111117655755.

Crowther, D., Greene, A.-M. and Hosking, D.A. (2002) 'Local economic trading schemes and their implications for marketing assumptions, concepts and practices', *Management Decision*, vol. 40, no. 4, pp. 352–62.

Cubitt, S., Hassan, J. and Volkmer, I. (2011) 'Does cloud computing have a silver lining?', *Media, Culture & Society*, vol. 33, no. 1, pp. 149–58.

Cuilla, J.B. (2003) *The Ethics of Leadership*, Wadsworth/Thomson Learning, Belmont, CA.

Cuomo, C.J. (1992) 'Unravelling the problems in ecofeminism', *Environmental Ethics*, vol. 14, pp. 351–63.

Dahlberg, L. (2007) 'The corporate colonization of online attention and the marginalization of critical communication?', *Journal of Communication Inquiry*, vol. 29, no. 2, pp. 160–80.

Daily, G.C. (1997) *Nature's Services: Societal Dependence on Natural Ecosystems*, Island Press, Washington, DC.

Daily, G.C. and Ellison, K. (2003) *The New Economy of Nature: The Quest to Make Conservation Profitable*, Shearwater Books, Covelo, CA.

Dale, A. (2001) *At the Edge*, UBC Press, Vancouver, Canada.

Dale, S. (1996) *McLuhan's Children: The Greenpeace Message and the Media*, Between the Lines, Toronto, Canada.

Daley, B. (2005) 'Eco products in demand, but labels can be murky', *Boston Globe*, 9 February, available at: www.boston.com/news/nation/articles/2005/02/09/eco_products_in_demand_but_labels_can_ be_murky.

Dalton, H. (2004) 'The science of GM agriculture', *The Journal of the Foundation for Science and Technology*, vol. 18, no. 3, pp. 9–11.

Daly, H.E. (1996) *Beyond Growth: The Economics of Sustainable Development*, Beacon Press, Boston, MA.

Daly, H.E. (1999) 'Uneconomic growth in theory and in fact', First Annual Feasta Lecture, Dublin, available at: www.feasta.org/documents/ feastareview/daly1.pdf.

Daly, H.E. (2002) 'Reconciling the economics of social equity and environmental sustainability', *Population and Environment*, vol. 24, no. 1, pp. 47–53.

Daly, H.E. (2007) 'What is the question?', *Resurgence*, vol. 244, pp. 18–19.

Daly, H.E. and Cobb, J. (1989) *For the Common Good*, Beacon Press, Boston, MA.

Dasgupta, P. (2001) *Human Wellbeing and the Natural Environment*, Oxford University Press, Oxford.

Dasgupta, P. (2007) 'The idea of sustainable development', *Sustainability Science*, vol. 2, no. 1, pp. 5–11.

Datschefski, E. (2001) *The Total Beauty of Sustainable Products*, RotoVision, Hove, UK.

Davis, L.S. (2007) 'Click here to create a better world', *On Earth*, Spring, available at: www.nrdc.org/onearth/07spr/livgreen.asp.

Davis, M. (2006) *Planet of Slums*, Verso, London.

Davison, A. (2001) *Technology and the Contested Meaning of Sustainability*, State University of New York Press, Albany, NY.

Davison, A. (2004) 'Reinhabiting technology: Ends in means and the practice of place', *Technology in Society*, vol. 26, pp. 85–97.

Davydova, A. (2013) 'Sustainability and civil society engagement in Russia: A gain for democracy?' 11 April, Friedrich Ebert Stiftung Sustainability, available at: www.fes-sustainability.org/esp/nachhaltigkeit-und-demokratie/sustainability-and-civil-society-engagement-russia.

Dawson, J. (2006) *Ecovillages: New Frontiers for Sustainability*, Green Books, Totnes, UK.

Day, P. and Schuler, D. (2006) 'Community practice in the network society: Pathways towards civic intelligence', in P. Purcell (ed.) *Networked Neighbourhoods: The Connected Community in Context*, Springer-Verlag, London, pp. 19–46.

Deakin, R. (2007) *Wildwood: A Journey through Trees*, Hamish Hamilton, London.

Dean, A.O. and Hursley, T. (2002) *Rural Studio: Samuel Mockbee and an Architecture of Decency*, Princeton Architectural Press, New York.

Defra (2005) *Sustainable Development Indicators in Your Pocket*, HMSO, London, available at: www.sustainable-development.gov.uk/performance/indicatorsindex.htm.

De Freitus, S. and Maharg, P. (2011) *Digital Games and Learning*, London, Continuum.

De Geus, M. (1999) *Ecological Utopias: Envisioning the Sustainable Society*, International Books, Utrecht, The Netherlands.

De Gues, A. (1997) 'The living company', *Harvard Business Review*, March–April, pp. 51–9.

de Haan, G. (2010) 'The development of ESD-related competencies in supportive institutional frameworks', *International Review of Education*, vol. 56, nos. 2–3, pp. 315–28.

De Jong, W., Shaw, M. and Stammers, N. (eds) (2005) *Global Activism, Global Media*, Pluto Press, London.

Deloria, V. Jr, Deloria, B., Foehner, K. and Scinta, S. (eds) (1999) *Spirit and Reason: The Vine Deloria Jr Reader*, Fulcrum Publishing, Golden, CO.

Delors, J. (1996) *Learning: the Treasure Within. Report to UNESCO of the International Commission on Education for the Twenty-first Century*, UNESCO, Paris.

DeLuca, K.M. (1999) *Image Politics: The New Rhetoric of Environmental Activism*, Lawrence Erlbaum, Mahwah, NJ.

DeLuca, K.M. (2009) 'Greenpeace international media analyst reflects on communicating climate change', *Environmental Communication: A Journal of Nature and Culture*, vol. 3, no. 2, pp. 263–9.

DeLuca, K.M. and Demo, A.T. (2000) 'Imaging nature: Watkins, Yosemite, and the birth of environmentalism', *Critical Studies in Media Communication*, vol. 17, no. 3, pp. 241–60.

Demtchouk, A.L (1998) 'Sustainable Development: new political philosophy for Russia?', paper presented at the Twentieth World Congress of Philosophy, Boston, MA, available at: www.bu.edu/wcp/Papers/Poli/PoliDemt.htm.

Dennis, K. and Urry, J. (2009) *After the Car*, Polity Press, Cambridge.

Devall, B. and Sessions, G. (1985) *Deep Ecology: Living as if Nature Mattered*, Gibbs M. Smith, Salt Lake City, UT.

Devas, N. (2004) *Urban Governance, Voice and Poverty in the Developing World*, Earthscan, London.

Dewey, J. (1927) *The Public and its Problems*, Henry Holt & Co., New York.

Diamond, J. (1998) *Guns, Germs and Steel*, Vintage, London.

Diamond, J. (2005) *Collapse: How Societies Choose to Fail or Survive*, Penguin, London.

Dinham, B. and Sarangi, S. (2002) 'The Bhopal gas tragedy 1984 to? The evasion of corporate responsibility', *Environment and Urbanization*, vol. 14, no. 1, pp. 89–99.

Distaso, A. (2007) 'Wellbeing and/or quality of life in EU countries through a multidimensional index of sustainability', *Ecological Economics*, vol. 64, pp. 163–80.

Doane, D. (2005) 'Beyond corporate social responsibility: Minnows, mammoths and markets', *Futures*, vol. 37, pp. 215–29.

Dobson, A. (1998) *Justice and the Environment: Conceptions of Environmental Sustainability and Dimensions of Social Justice*, Oxford University Press, Oxford, UK.

Dobson, A. (2003a) 'Social justice and environmental sustainability: Ne'er the twain shall meet?', in J. Agyeman, R.D. Bullard and B. Evans (eds) *Just Sustainabilities: Development in an Unequal World*, Earthscan, London, pp. 83–91.

Dobson, A. (2003b) *Citizenship and the Environment*, Oxford University Press, Oxford.

Dobson, A. (2010) 'Democracy and nature: speaking and listening', *Political Studies*, vol. 58, no. 4, pp. 752–68.

Doppelt, B. (2000) 'Overcoming the seven sustainability blunders', *The Systems Thinker*, vol. 14, no. 5, available at: www.greenleaf-publishing.com/content/pdfs/systhink.pdf.

Doppelt, B. (2003) *Leading Change Towards Sustainability*, Greenleaf, Sheffield, UK.

Douthwaite, R. (1999a) 'The ecology of money' (revised 2006), available at: www.feasta.org/documents/moneyecology/contents.htm.

Douthwaite, R. (1999b) *The Growth Illusion*, Green Books, Totnes, UK.

Dowie, M. (2009) *Conservation Refugees: The Hundred Year Conflict Between Global Conservation and Native Peoples*, MIT Press, Cambridge, MA.

Downey, J. (2007) 'Participation and/or deliberation: The Internet as a tool for achieving radical democratic aims', in L. Dahlberg and E. Siapera (eds) *Radical Democracy and the Internet*, London, Palgave, pp. 108–27.

Downey, J. and Fenton, N. (2003) 'New media, counter publicity and the public sphere', *New Media Society*, vol. 5, no. 2, pp. 185–202.

Downton, P.F. (2009) *Ecopolis: Architecture and Cities for a Changing Climate*, Spring, Dordrecht.

Doyle, T. and McEachern, D. (1998) *Environment and Politics*, Routledge, London.

Draper, S. (2006) 'Key models for delivering sector level corporate responsibility', *Corporate Governance*, vol. 6, no. 4, pp. 409–19.

Drayton, W. (2003) 'Social entrepreneurs: Creating a competitive and entrepreneurial citizen sector', available at: www.changemakers.net/library/ readings/drayton.cfm, accessed 1 June 2006.

Dryzek, J.S. (1990) 'Green Reason: communicative ethics for the biosphere', *Environmental Ethics*, vol. 12, no. 3, pp. 195–210.

Dryzek, J.S. (1996) 'Strategies of ecological modernization', in W.M. Lafferty and J. Meadowcroft (eds) *Democracy and the Environment: Problems and Prospects*, Edward Elgar, Cheltenham, UK, pp. 108–23.

Dryzek, J.S. (2000) *Deliberative Democracy and Beyond: Liberals, Critics, Contestations*, Oxford University Press, Oxford.

Duffy, R. (2010) *Nature Crime: How We're Getting Conservation Wrong*, Yale University Press, New Haven, NJ.

Duffy, R. and Moore, L. (2010) 'Neoliberalising nature? Elephant-back tourism in Thailand and Botswana', *Antipode*, vol. 42, no. 3, pp. 742–66.

Dunaway, F. (2005) *Natural Visions: The Power of Images in American Environmental Reform*, University of Chicago Press, Chicago.

Dunbar, R. (1995) *The Trouble with Science*, Faber & Faber, London.

Dunn, C.E. (2007) 'Participatory GIS – A people's GIS?', *Progress in Human Geography*, vol. 31, no. 5, pp. 616–37.

Dunphy, D., Griffiths, A. and Benn, S. (2003) *Organizational Change for Corporate Sustainability*, Routledge, London.

Durham, P. (1992) *The Aim and Structure of Physical Theory*, trans. P. Wiener, Princeton University Press, Princeton, NJ.

Durning, A.T. (1992) *How Much is Enough? The Consumer Society and the Future of the Earth*, Earthscan, London.

Dwivedi, R. (2006) *Conflict and Collective Action: The Sardar Sarovar Project in India*, Routledge India, Delhi.

Dyer, A. (2007) 'Inspiration, enchantment and a sense of wonder . . . Can a new paradigm in education bring nature and culture together again?', *International Journal of Heritage Studies*, vol. 13, no. 4, pp. 393–404.

Dyer-Witheford, N. and de Peuter, G. (2009) *Games of Empire: Global Capitalism and Video Games*, University of Minnesota Press, Minneapolis, MN.

Earley, P. C. and Mosakowski, E. (2004) 'Cultural intelligence', *Harvard Business Review*, October, pp. 139–46.

East, R. (2007) 'Holding out for a hero: Green leaders for 2008', *Daily Telegraph*, 28 December, available at: www.telegraph.co.uk/earth/earthcomment/3320057/Holding-out-for-a-hero-green-leaders-for-2008.html.

Eckersley, R. (2004) *The Green State: Rethinking Democracy and Sovereignty*, MIT Press, Cambridge, MA.

Eckersley, R. (2005) 'Ecocentric discourses: Problems and future prospects for nature advocacy', in J.S. Dryzek and D. Schlosberg (eds) *Debating the Earth: The Environmental Politics Reader*, Oxford University Press, Oxford, pp. 364–81.

The Ecologist (1993) *Whose Common Future? Reclaiming the Commons*, New Society Publishers, Philadelphia, PA.

Economy, E.C. (2004) *The River Runs Black: The Environmental Challenge to China's Future*, Cornell University Press, New York.

Economy, E.C. (2013) 'China's environmental future: The power of the people', *McKinsey Quarterly*, June, available at: www.mckinsey.com/insights/asia-pacific/chinas_environmental_future_the_power_of_the_people.

Egoyan, A. (2002) 'Janet Cardiff', *Bomb*, no. 79, pp. 60–7.

Egri, C.P. and Herman, S. (2000) 'Leadership in the North American environmental sector: Values, leadership styles, and contexts of environmental leaders and their organizations', *The Academy of Management Journal*, vol. 43, no. 4, pp. 571–604.

Ehrlich, P.R. (1968) *The Population Bomb*, Ballantine Books, New York.

Ehrlich, P.R. and Ehrlich, A.H. (2009) 'The population bomb revisited', *The Electronic Journal of Sustainable Development*, vol. 1, pp. 63–71, available at: www.populationmedia.org/wp-content/uploads/2009/07/Population-Bomb-Revisited-Paul-Ehrlich-20096.pdf.

Ekins, P. (2000) *Economic Growth and Environmental Sustainability: The Prospects for Green Growth*, Routledge, London.

Eliasoph, N. (1990) 'Political culture and the presentation of a political self', *Theory and Society*, vol. 19, no. 4, pp. 465–94.

Eliasoph, N. (1998) *Avoiding Politics: How Americans Produce Apathy in Everyday Life*, Cambridge University Press, New York.

Eliasoph, N. and Lichterman, P. (2003) 'Culture in interaction', *American Journal of Sociology*, vol. 108, no. 4, pp. 735–94.

Emirbayer, M. and Mische, A. (1998) 'What is agency?', *American Journal of Sociology*, vol. 103, no. 4, pp. 962–1023.

Emmott, S. (2013) *10 Billion*, Penguin Books, London.

Ereaut, G. and Segnit, N. (2006) *Warm Words: How are We Telling the Climate Story and Can We Tell It Better?*, Institute of Public Policy Research, London.

Escobar, A. (1995) *Encountering Development: The Making and Unmaking of the Third World*, Princeton University Press, Princeton, NJ.

Escobar, A. (1996) 'Constructing nature: Elements for a poststructural political ecology', in R. Peet and M. Watts (eds) *Liberation Ecologies: Environment, Development, Social Movements*, Routledge, London, pp. 46–68.

Escobar, A. (2006a) 'Difference and conflict in the struggle over natural resources: A political ecology framework', *Development*, vol. 49, no. 3, pp. 6–13.

Escobar, A. (2006b) 'Places and regions in the age of globality: Social movements and biodiversity conservation in the Colombian Pacific', manuscript accepted for publication by Duke University Press, Durham, NC.

ESRC (Economic and Social Research Council) Global Environmental Change Programme (2001) 'Environmental justice: Rights and means to a healthy environment for all', *Special Briefing* (University of Sussex), no. 7, available at: www.foe.co.uk/resource/reports/ environ mental_justice.pdf

Fairlie, S. (1996) *Low Impact Development: Planning and People in the Countryside*, JCP, Charlbury, UK.

Fernandes, E. (2006) 'Updating the Declaration of the Rights of Citizens in Latin America: Constructing the "Right to the City" in Brazil', in UNESCO *International Public Debates: Urban Policies and the Right to the City*, Paris, UNESCO, pp. 40–53.

Fishman, R. (1982) *Urban Utopias in the Twentieth Century*, MIT Press, Cambridge, MA.

Fixico, D.L. (2003) *The American Indian Mind in a Linear World*, Routledge, New York.

Flannery, T. (2005) *The Weather Makers*, Penguin Books, London.

Fleming, P. and Jones, M. (2013) *The End of Corporate Social Responsibility?*, Sage, London.

Flyvbjerg, B. (1998) *Rationality and Power: Democracy in Practice*, University of Chicago Press, Chicago.

Foley, J.R. and Polanyi, M. (2006) 'Workplace democracy: Why bother?', *Economic and Industrial Democracy*, vol. 27, no. 1, pp. 173–91.

Folke, C., Colding, J. and Berkes, F. (2003) 'Building resilience and adaptive capacity in social-ecological systems', in F. Berkes, J. Colding and C. Folke (eds) *Navigating Social-Ecological Systems*, Cambridge University Press, Cambridge, pp. 352–87.

Forum for the Future (2007) 'The sustainable cities index', Forum for the Future, London, available at: www.forumforthefuture.org.uk/files/ sustainablecities07.pdf.

Foster, J.B. (1999) 'Marx's theory of metabolic rift: Classical foundations for environmental sociology', *American Journal of Sociology*, vol. 105, no. 2, pp. 366–405.

Foster, J.B. (2000) *Marx's Ecology Materialism and Nature*, Monthly Review Press, New York.

Foster, J.B. (2002) *Ecology Against Capitalism*, Monthly Review Press, New York.

France, L. (ed.) (1997) *The Earthscan Reader in Sustainable Tourism*, Earthscan, London.

Frank, R. (1999) *Luxury Fever: Money and Happiness in an Era of Excess*, Princeton University Press, Princeton, NJ.

Fraser, N. (1990) 'Rethinking the public sphere: A contribution to the critique of actually existing democracy', *Social Text*, no. 25/26, pp. 56–80.

Freire, P. (1996) *Pedagogy of the Oppressed*, Penguin, London.

Friedmann, J. (1992) *Empowerment: The Politics of Alternative Development*, Blackwell, Oxford.

Froehlich, J. Dilahunt, T., Klasnja, P., Mankoff, J. Consolvo, S., Harrison, B. and Landay, J.A. (2009) 'UbiGreen: investigating a mobile tool for tracking and supporting green transportation habits', proceedings of the SIGCHI Conference on Human Factors in Computing Systems, pp. 1043–52.

Fuchs, R. J., Brennan, E., Chamie, J., Lo, F.-C. and Uitto, J. I. (eds) (1994) *Mega-City Growth and the Future*, United Nations University Press, Tokyo.

Fukuda-Parr, S. (2002) *Human Development Report, 2002: Deepening Democracy in a Fragmented World*, Oxford University Press for the UNDP, New York, available at: http://hdr.undp.org/en/ media/hdr_2002_en_complete.pdf.

Fukuda-Parr, S. (2004) *Human Development Report, 2004: Cultural Liberty in Today's Diverse World*, Oxford University Press for the UNDP, New York, available at: http://hdr.undp.org/en/media/ hdr04_complete.pdf.

Funtowicz, S.O. and Ravetz, J.R. (2001) 'Global risk, uncertainty and ignorance', in J.X. Kasperson and R.E. Kasperson (eds) *Global Environmental Risk*, Earthscan, London, pp. 173–94.

Gablik, S. (2000) 'Art for Earth's sake', *Resurgence*, no. 202, available at: www.resurgence. org/magazine/author10-suzi-gablik.htm.

Gablik, S. (2002) *The Re-enchantment of Art*, Thames & Hudson, New York.

Gallagher, J. (2010) *Reimagining Detroit: Opportunities for Redefining an American City*, Wayne State University Press, Detroit.

Gallagher, J. (2013) *Revolution Detroit: Strategies for Urban Reinvention*, Wayne State University Press, Detroit, MI.

Gardner, H. (1993) *Frames of Mind: The Theory of Multiple Intelligences*, Fontana, London.

Gardner, H. (2006) *Changing Minds: The Art and Science of Changing our Own and Other People's Minds*, Harvard Business School Press, Boston, MA.

Garside, J. (2013) 'Nasdaq crash triggers fear of data meltdown', *The Guardian*, 24 August, available at: www.theguardian.com/technology/2013/aug/23/nasdaq-crash-data.

Geoghegan, T. (2013) 'Post 2015: Framing a new approach to sustainable development', IRF/IIED, available at: http://sustainabledevelopment.un.org/index.php?page=view&type=400&nr=874&menu=35.

Georgescu-Roegen, N. (1994) 'The entropy law and the economic problem', in H.E. Daly and K.N. Townsend (eds) *Valuing the Earth: Economics, Ecology, Ethics*, Cambridge, MA, MIT Press, pp. 75–88.

Gerber, P.J., Steinfeld, H., Henderson, B., Mottet, A., Opio, C., Dijkman, J., Falcucci, A. and Tempio, G. (2013) *Tackling Climate Change through Livestock – A Global Assessment of Emissions and Mitigation Opportunities*, Food and Agriculture Organization of the United Nations (FAO), Rome.

Giddens, A. (1986) *The Constitution of Society*, Polity Press, Cambridge.

Giddings, B., Hopwood, B., Mellor, M. and O'Brien, G. (2005) 'Back to the city: A route to urban sustainability', in M. Jenks and N. Dempsey (eds) *Future Forms and Design for Sustainable Cities*, Architectural Press, London, pp. 13–30.

Gilchrist, A. (2004) *The Well-Connected Community: A Networking Approach to Community Development*, Policy Press, Bristol, UK.

Gillis, J. (2013) 'Climate panel cites near certainty on warming', *New York Times*, 19 August, available at: www.nytimes.com/2013/08/20/science/earth/extremely-likely-that-human-activity-is-driving-climate-change-panel-finds.html?pagewanted=1&_r=1&src=me&adxnnlx=1377029122-olLP3nIPAdlkPrb/xm7M2Q&.

Gilman, R. (1991) 'The eco-village challenge', *In Context*, no. 29, available at: www.context.org/ICLIB/IC29/Gilman1.htm, accessed 1 August 2007.

Ginsburg, F.D., Abu-Lughod, L. and Larkin, B. (eds) (2002) *Media Worlds: Anthropology on a New Terrain*, University of California Press, Berkeley, CA.

Girardet, H. (1996) *The Gaia Atlas of Cities: New Directions for Sustainable Living*, Gaia Books, London.

Girardet, H. (2010) *Regenerative Cities*, Hamburg, World Future Council, available at: www.worldfuturecouncil.org/fileadmin/user_upload/papers/WFC_Regenerative_Cities_web_final.pdf.

Girardet, H. (2012) 'Regenerative Adelaide', *Solutions*, vol. 5, no. 3, pp. 46–54.

Girardet, H. and Mendonca, M. (2009) *A Renewable World: Energy, Ecology, Equality*, Green Books, Totnes, UK.

Gladwell, M. (2010) 'Small change: Why the revolution will not be tweeted', *New Yorker*, 4 October.

Glenn, J.C. and Gordon, T. J. (2007) *State of the Future*, United Nations, New York.

GlobeScan/SustainAbility (2013) *The 2013 Sustainability Leaders: A GlobeScan/SustainAbility Survey*, available at: www.sustainability.com/library/the-2013-sustainability-leaders#.UitKG-A3SvS.

Godin, S. (2002) *Unleashing the Ideavirus*, Simon & Schuster, London.

Godrej, D. (2002) 'Eight things you should know about patents on life', *New Internationalist*, no. 349, available at: www.newint.org/features/ 2002/09/01/keynote.

Goldsmith, E., Allen, R., Allaby, M., Davoll, J. and Lawrence, S. (1972) *A Blueprint for Survival*, Penguin Books, Harmondsworth.

Goleman, D. (1996) *Emotional Intelligence*, Bloomsbury, London.

Goleman, D. (2002a) *The New Leaders*, Little Brown, London.

Goleman, D. (2002b) 'Leading resonant teams', *Leader to Leader*, no. 25, available at: www.pfdf.org/leader-books/l2l/summer2002/goleman.html.

Goleman, D. (2009) *Ecological Intelligence: The Coming Age of Radical Transparency*, Penguin Books, London.

Goodin, R.E. and Dryzek, J.S. (2006) 'Deliberative impacts: The macro-political uptake of mini-publics', *Politics and Society*, vol. 34, no. 2, pp. 219–44.

Google (2011) 'Google Green – A better web: better for the environment', available at: www.google.com/intl/en/green/bigpicture.

Google (2013) Google Green website: www.google.co.uk/green/energy/#power.

Gorbachev, M. (2006) *Manifesto for the Earth*, Clairview Books, Forest Row, UK.

Gore, A. (2006) *An Inconvenient Truth: The Planetary Emergency of Global Warming and What We Can Do About It*, Bloomsbury, London.

Gottlieb, R. and Joshi, A. (2013) *Food Justice*, MIT Press, Cambridge, MA.

Gough, C. and Shackley, S. (2001) 'The respectable politics of climate change: The epistemic communities and NGOs', *International Affairs*, vol. 77, no. 2, pp. 329–45.

Govindu, V.M. and Malghan, D. (2005) 'Building a creative freedom: J.C. Kumarappa and his economic philosophy', *Economic and Political Weekly*, vol. 40, no. 52, pp. 5477–85.

Graedel, T.E. (1996) 'On the concept of industrial ecology', *Annual Review of Energy and the Environment*, vol. 21, pp. 69–98.

Grainger, A. (2004) 'The role of spatial scale and spatial interactions in sustainable development', in M. Purvis and A. Grainger (eds) *Exploring Sustainable Development: Geographical Perspectives*, Earthscan, London, pp. 50–83.

Grant, J. (2007) *The Green Marketing Manifesto*, John Wiley & Sons, Chichester, UK.

Grant, J. (2010) *Co-opportunity: Join Up for a Sustainable, Resilient, Prosperous World*, John Wiley & Sons, Chichester, UK.

Green, B. (2007) 'Q and A: C. K. Prahalad – Pyramid schemer', *Fast Company*, no. 113, p. 79, available at: www.fastcompany.com/magazine/113/open_fast50-qa-prahalad.html.

Green Belt Movement (2003) 'Special annual report', available at: http://greenbeltmovement.org/downloads/GBM_Annual_Report_2003.pdf.

Greenhalgh, L., Worpole, K. and Landry, C. (1995) *Libraries in a World of Cultural Change*, UCL Press, London.

Greenpeace (2012) *How Clean is Your Cloud?* Amsterdam: Greenpeace International, available at: www.greenpeace.org/international/en/publications/Campaign-reports/Climate-Reports/How-Clean-is-Your-Cloud.

Greenpeace International (2007) *How the Palm Oil Industry is Cooking the Climate*, Greenpeace International, Amsterdam, available at: www.greenpeace.org/international/Global/international/planet-2/report/2007/11/cooking-the-climate-full.pdf.

Greenpeace International (2013) *Licence to Kill*, Greenpeace International, Amsterdam, available at: www.greenpeace.org/international/Global/international/publications/forests/2013/LicenceToKill_ENG_LOWRES.pdf.

Greenpeace UK (1999) *GM on Trial*, Greenpeace UK, London, available at: www.greenpeace.org.uk/files/pdfs/migrated/MultimediaFiles/Live/FullReport/1766.pdf.

Gregory, P.J., Ingram, J.S.I. and Brklacich, M. (2005) 'Climate change and food security', *Philosophical Transactions of the Royal Society B*, vol. 360, pp. 2139–48.

GRI (Global Reporting Initiative) (2007) 'Reporting the business implications of climate change in sustainability report', GRI/KPMG, available at: www.globalreporting.org/NR/rdonlyres/C451A32E-A046-493B-9C62-7020325F1E54/0/ClimateChange_GRI_KPMG07.pdf.

Grober, U. (2012) *Sustainability: A Cultural History*, Green Books, Totnes, UK.

Grubb, M., Koch, M., Munson, A., Sullivan, F. and Thomson, K. (1993) *The Earth Summit Agreements: A Guide and Assessment*, Earthscan, London.

Grubisich, T. (2005) 'Grassroots journalism: Actual content vs. shining ideal', *USC Annenberg, Online Journalism Review*, available at: www.ojr.org/ojr/stories/051006.

Grubisich, T. (2006) 'What are the lessons from Dan Gillmor's Bayosphere?', *Online Journalism Review*, 29 January, available at: www.ojr.org/ojr/stories/060129grubisich.

Gruenewald, D.A. (2003) 'The best of both worlds: A critical pedagogy of place', *Educational Researcher*, vol. 32, no. 4, pp. 3–12.

Guan, D., Liu, Z., Linder, S. and Hubacek, K. (2012) 'The gigatonne gap in China's carbon dioxide inventories', *Nature Climate Change*, vol. 2, pp. 672–5.

Guha, R. (1989) 'Radical American environmentalism and wilderness preservation: A Third World critique', *Environmental Ethics*, vol. 11, no. 1, pp. 71–83.

Guha, R. (2000) *The Unquiet Woods: Ecological Change and Peasant Resistance in the Himalaya*, University of California Press, Berkeley, CA.

Guha, R. (2006) *How Much Should a Person Consume? Environmentalism in India and the United States*, University of California Press, Berkeley, CA.

Guinée, J.B. (ed.) (2002) *Handbook on Life Cycle Assessment: Operational Guide to the ISO Standards*, Kluwer, Dordrecht.

Gundersen, A. (1995) *The Environmental Promise of Democratic Deliberation*, University of Wisconsin Press, Madison, WI.

Gupta, A.K. (2006) 'From sink to source: The honey bee network documents indigenous knowledge and innovations in India', *Innovations: Technology, Governance, Globalization*, vol. 1, no. 3, pp. 49–66.

Gupta, A.K., Sinha, R., Koradia, D., Patel, R., Parmar, M., Rohit, P., Patel, H., Patel, K., Chand, V.S., James, T.J., Chandan, A., Patel, M., Prakash, T.N. and Vivekanandan, P. (2003) 'Mobilizing grassroots' technological innovations and traditional knowledge, values and institutions: Articulating social and ethical capital', *Futures*, vol. 35, no. 9, pp. 975–87.

Habermas, J. (1974) 'The public sphere: An encyclopedia article', *New German Critique*, no. 3, Autumn, pp. 49–55.

Hahn, R. (2009) 'The ethical rationale of business for the poor – Integrating the concepts of bottom of the pyramid, sustainable development and corporate citizenship', *Journal of Business Ethics*, vol. 84, no. 3, pp. 313–24.

Haiven, M. (2007) 'Privatized resistance: *AdBusters* and the culture of neoliberalism', *Review of Education, Pedagogy, and Cultural Studies*, vol. 29, no. 1, pp. 85–110.

Hall, P. (1996) *Cities of Tomorrow*, Blackwell, Oxford.

Halleck, D. (2002) *Hand-Held Visions: The Impossible Possibilities of Community Media*, Fordham University Press, New York.

Halpern, R. (1995) *Rebuilding the Inner City*, Columbia University Press, New York.

Hamdouch, A. and Zuindeau, B. (2010) 'Sustainable development, 20 years on: On methodological innovations, practices and open issues', *Journal of the Environmental Planning and Management*, vol. 54, no. 4, pp. 427–38.

Hamilton, C. (2003) *Growth Fetish*, Pluto Press, London.

Hampton, K. and Wellman, B. (2003) 'Neighbouring in Netville: How the internet supports community and social capital in a wired suburb', *City and Community*, vol. 2, no. 4, pp. 277–311.

Hansen, J., Sato, M., Kharecha, P., Russell, G., Lea, D.W. and Siddall, M. (2007) 'Climate change and trace gases', *Philosophical Transactions of the Royal Society A*, vol. 365, pp. 1925–54.

Hardi, P. and DeSouza-Huletey, J.A. (2000) 'Issues in analysing data and indicators for sustainable development', *Ecological Modelling*, vol. 130, pp. 59–65.

Hardin, G. (1968) 'The tragedy of the commons', *Science*, vol. 162, no. 3859, pp. 1243–8, available at: www.sciencemag.org/cgi/content/ full/162/3859/1243.

Harding, S. (2006) *Animate Earth: Science, Intuition and Gaia*, Green Books, Totnes, UK.

Hardoy, J.E., Mitlin, D. and Satterthwaite, D. (2001) *Environmental Problems in an Urbanizing World*, Earthscan, London.

Hardy, D. (2006) *Poundbury: The Town that Charles Built*, Town and Country Planning Association, London.

Harre, R. (1984) *Personal Being: A Theory for Individual Psychology*, Harvard University Press, Cambridge, MA.

Harris, K. (2003) 'Keep your distance: Remote communication, face-to-face and the nature of community', *Journal of Community Work and Development*, vol. 1, no. 4, pp. 5–28.

Harriss, R. (2007) 'An ongoing dialogue on climate change: The Boulder manifesto', in S. C. Moser and L. Dilling (eds), *Creating a Climate for Change: Communicating Climate Change and Facilitating Social Change*, Cambridge University Press, Cambridge, pp. 485–90.

Hart, S.L. (1997) 'Beyond greening: Strategies for a sustainable world', *Harvard Business Review*, vol. 75, no. 1, pp. 66–76.

Hart, S.L. (2005) *Capitalism at the Crossroads: The Unlimited Business Opportunities in Solving the World's Problems*, Wharton School Publishing, Upper Saddle River, NJ.

Harvey, D. (1996) *Justice, Nature and the Geography of Difference*, Blackwell, Oxford.

Harvey, D. (2011) 'The future of the commons', *Radical History Review*, Winter, no. 109, pp. 101–7.

Harvey, D. (2013) *Rebel Cities: From the Right to the City to the Urban Revolution*, Verso, London.

Haughton, G. (1999) 'Environmental justice and the sustainable city', *Journal of Planning Education and Research*, vol. 18, no. 3, pp. 233–43.

Hawken, P. (1994) *The Ecology of Commerce*, HarperBusiness, New York.

Hawken, P. (2007) *Blessed Unrest*, Viking, New York.

Hawken, P., Lovins, A.B. and Lovins L.H. (1999) *Natural Capitalism: The Next Industrial Revolution*, Earthscan, London.

Hayden, D. (1997) *The Power of Place: Urban Landscapes as Public History*, MIT Press, Cambridge, MA.

Heal, G. (2000) *Nature and the Market Place: Capturing the Value of Ecosystem Services*, Island Press, Washington, DC.

Healey, P. (1997) *Collaborative Planning: Shaping Places in Fragmented Societies*, Macmillan, London.

Heede, R. (2013) 'Tracing anthropogenic carbon dioxide and methane emissions to fossil fuel and cement producers, 1854–2010', *Climate Change*, November, available at: http://link.springer.com/article/10.1007/s10584-013-0986-y.

Heifetz, R.A. (1994) *Leadership Without Easy Answers*, Harvard University Press, Cambridge, MA.

Heifetz, R.A. (1999) 'Change: What's essential and what's expendable?', interview for the Society for Organizational Learning, available at: www.dialo-gonleadership.org/interview Heifetz.html.

Heinberg, R. (2004) *Powerdown: Options and Action for a Post-Carbon World*, New Society Publishers, Washington, DC.

Held, D., McGrew, A., Goldblatt, D. and Perraton, J. (eds) (1999) *Global Transformations: Politics, Economics and Culture*, Polity Press, Cambridge.

Henriques, A. and Richardson, J. (eds) (2004) *The Triple Bottom Line*, Earthscan, London.

Hester, L. and Cheney, J. (2001) 'Truth and Native American epistemology', *Social Epistemology*, vol. 15, no. 4, pp. 319–34.

Hines, C. (2000) *Localization: A Global Manifesto*, Earthscan, London.

Hirsch, P.D., Adams, W.M., Brosius, J.P., Zia, A., Bariola, N. and Dammert, J.L. (2010) 'Acknowledging conservation trade-offs and embracing complexity', *Conservation Biology*, vol. 25, no. 2, pp. 259–64.

Hitchcock, D. and Willard, M. (2006) *The Business Guide to Sustainability: Practical Strategy and Tools for Organizations*, Earthscan, London.

Ho, M.-W. (1998) *Genetic Engineering: Dream or Nightmare?*, Gateway, Dublin.

Hoffman, A. J. (2003 'Linking social systems analysis to the industrial ecology framework', *Organization and Environment*, vol. 16, no. 1, pp. 66–86.

Hoggett, P. (2001) 'Democracy, social relations and eco-welfare', *Social Policy and Administration*, vol. 35, no. 5, pp. 608–26.

Holling, C.S. (2001) 'Understanding the complexity of economic, ecological and social systems', *Ecosystems*, vol. 4, pp. 390–405.

Holling, C.S. (2004) 'From complex regions to complex worlds', *Ecology and Society*, vol. 9, no. 1, available at: www.ecologyandsociety.org/vol9/iss1/art11.

Holmberg, J. and Robèrt, K.-H. (2000) 'Backcasting from non-overlapping sustainability principles – A framework for strategic planning', *International Journal of Sustainable Development and World Ecology*, vol. 7, pp. 291–308.

Holme, R. and Watts, P. (2000) 'Corporate social responsibility: Making good business sense', World Business Council for Sustainable Development, available at: www.wbcsd.ch.

Holmes, N. (2011) 'The art of sustainability', *New Scientist*, CultureLab, 12 July, available at: www.newscientist.com/blogs/culturelab/2011/07/the-art-of-sustainability.html.

Homer-Dixon, T. (1999) *Environment, Scarcity and Violence*, Princeton University Press, Princeton, NJ.

Homer-Dixon, T. (2002) *The Ingenuity Gap*, Vintage Books, New York.

Homer-Dixon, T. (2006) *The Upside of Down: Catastrophe, Creativity and the Renewal of Civilization*, Souvenir Press, London.

Honey, M. (2008) *Ecotourism and Sustainable Development: Who Owns Paradise?* Island Press, Washington, DC.

Hopkins, M. (1999) *The Planetary Bargain: Corporate Social Responsibility Comes of Age*, Macmillan, London.

Hopkins, M. (2006) *Corporate Social Responsibility and International Development: Is Business the Solution?*, Earthscan, London.

Hopkins, R. (2005) 'Designing energy descent pathways – One community's attempt at designing a prosperous way down from the peak', *Permaculture Magazine*, no. 45, available at: http://transitionculture.org/essential-info/what-is-energy-descent.

Hopkins, R. (2011) *The Transition Companion*, Transition Books, Totnes, UK.

Horton, D. (2004) 'Local environmentalism and the internet', *Environmental Politics*, vol. 13, no. 4, pp. 734–53.

Hough, M. (1995) *Cities and Natural Process*, Routledge, London.

Howard, E. (1902) *Garden Cities of Tomorrow*, Swan Sonnenschein, London.

Hoyt, E. (2005) *Marine Protected Areas: For Whales, Dolphins and Porpoises*, Earthscan, London.

Hu, A. (2006) 'Green development: the inevitable choice for China (part two)', *chinadialogue*, 26 June, available at: www.chinadialogue.net/article/show/single/en/135-Green-development-the-inevitable-choice-for-China-part-two-.

Hu, A. (2011) *China in 2020: A New Type of Superpower*, HarperCollins India, Delhi.

Hughes, J.D. (2013) 'Drill, baby drill: Can unconventional fuels usher in a new era of energy abundance?' Santa Rosa: Post Carbon Institute, available at: www.postcarbon.org/reports/DBD-report-FINAL.pdf.

Hulme, M. (2009) *Why We Disagree About Climate Change: Understanding Controversy, Inaction and Opportunity*, Cambridge University Press, Cambridge.

Hunt, G. and Mehta, M. (eds) (2006) *Nanotechnology: Risk, Ethics and Law*, Earthscan, London.

Hutchby, I. (2001) 'Technologies, texts and affordances', *Sociology*, vol. 35, no. 2, pp. 441–56.

IBEF (2013) Automobile Industry in India (July update), available at: www.ibef.org/industry/india-automobiles.aspx.

ICLEI (2002) *Curitiba: Orienting Urban Planning to Sustainability*. Case Study 77. ICLEI, Ontario, available at: www.iclei.org.br/polics/CD/P2_4_Estudos%20de%20Caso/1_Planeja mento%20Urbano/PDF106_EC77_Curitiba_ing.PDF.

IEA (2012) *World Energy Outlook 2012*, IEA, Paris, available at: www.worldenergyoutlook.org/publications/weo-2012/.

IFDA (1980) *Building Blocks for Alternative Development Strategies, IFDA*, Zug, Switzerland.

Igoe, J., Neves, K. and Brockington, D. (2010) 'A spectacular eco-tour around the historic bloc: theorising the convergence of biodiversity conservation and capitalist expansion', *Antipode*, vol. 42, no. 3, pp. 486–512.

Ihde, D. (1997) 'Whole Earth measurements: How many phenomenologists does it take to detect a greenhouse effect?', *Philosophy Today*, vol. 41, no. 1, pp. 128–34.

Ingalsbee, T. (1996) 'Earth First! activism: Ecological postmodern praxis in radical environmentalist identities', *Sociological Perspectives*, vol. 39, no. 2, pp. 263–76.

International Labour Organization (ILO) (2012) *2012 Global Employment Trends*, International Labour Office, Geneva, available at: www.ilo.org/wcmsp5/groups/public/@dgreports/@dcomm/@publ/documents/publication/wcms_171571.pdf.

International Rivers (2012) 'China's Three Gorges Dam: a model of the past', Factsheet, available at: www.internationalrivers.org/resources/china-s-three-gorges-dam-a-model-of-the-past-2638.

IPCC (Intergovernmental Panel on Climate Change) (2004) 'Sixteen years of scientific assessment in support of the Climate Convention', WMO/UNEP, available at: www.ipcc.ch/about/anniversary-brochure.pdf.

IPCC (2007) *Climate Change 2007: Mitigation*, contribution of Working Group III to the Fourth Assessment Report of the Intergovernmental Panel on Climate Change, edited by B. Metz, O. R. Davidson, P. R. Bosch, R. Dave and L. A. Meyer, Cambridge University Press, Cambridge, available at: www.ipcc.ch/ipccreports/ar4-wg3.htm.

IPCC (2012) 'Summary for policymakers', in C.B. Field, V. Barros, T.F. Stocker, D. Qin, D.J. Dokken, K.L. Ebi, M.D. Mastrandrea, K.J. Mach, G.-K. Plattner, S.K. Allen, M. Tignor and P.M. Midgley (eds) *Managing the Risks of Extreme Events and Disasters to Advance Climate Change Adaptation*, a Special Report of Working Groups I and II of the Intergovernmental Panel on Climate Change, Cambridge University Press, Cambridge, UK, and New York, pp. 1–19, available at: http://ipcc-wg2.gov/SREX/images/uploads/SREX-SPMbrochure_FINAL.pdf.

IPCC (2013) Working Group I Contribution to the IPCC Fifth Assessment Report: Climate change 2013 – summary for policy makers, IPCC, Stockholm, available at: www.climatechange2013.org/images/uploads/WGIAR5-SPM_Approved27Sep2013.pdf.

IPSO (2013) 'The state of the ocean 2013: Perils, prognoses and proposals executive summary', available at: www.stateoftheocean.org/pdfs/IPSO-Summary-Oct13-FINAL.pdf.

Isaacs, W. (1999) *Dialogue and the Art of Thinking Together*, Doubleday, New York.

Isaak, R. (2002) 'The making of the ecopreneur', *Greener Management International*, vol. 38, pp. 81–91.

ITU (2012) 'Measuring the information society', Geneva: International telecommunications Union, available at: www.itu.int/dms_pub/itu-d/opb/ind/D-IND-ICTOI-2012-SUM-PDF-E.pdf.

IUCN (1980) *World Conservation Strategy: Living Resource Conservation for Sustainable Development*, IUCN, Gland, Switzerland.

IUCN (2007) 'Gender aspects of climate change', available at: www.iucn.org/en/news/archive/2007/03/7_gender_climate_change.pdf, accessed 14 June 2007.

Jackson, R.B. and Salzman, J. (2010) 'Pursuing geoengineering for atmospheric restoration', *Issues in Science and Technology*, Summer, pp. 67–76.

Jackson, T. (2005) *Motivating Sustainable Consumption*, ESRC Sustainable Technologies Programme, University of Surrey, Guildford, UK, available at: www.compassnetwork.org/images/upload/MotivatingSCfinal.pdf.

Jackson, T. (2009) *Prosperity without Growth: Economics for a Finite Planet*, Earthscan, London.

Jackson, T. and Marks, N. (1998) 'Consumption, sustainable welfare and human needs – With reference to UK expenditure patterns between 1954 and 1994', *Ecological Economics*, vol. 28, pp. 421–41.

Jacques, M. (2011) *When China Rules the World*, Penguin, London.

Jaiswal, A.K. (2007) *Fortune at the Bottom of the Pyramid: An Alternative Perspective*, Indian Institute of Management, Ahmedabad, available at: www.iimahd.ernet.in/assets/snippets/workingpaperpdf/2007-07-13Jaiswal.pdf.

James, S. and Satariano, A. (2012) 'Apple opens suppliers' doors to labor group after Foxconn worker suicides', *Bloomberg News*, 13 January, available at: www.bloomberg.com/news/2012-01-13/apple-opens-suppliers-doors-to-labor-group-after-foxconn-worker-suicides.html.

Jamison, A. (2001) *The Making of Green Knowledge: Environmental Politics and Cultural Transformation*, Cambridge University Press, Cambridge.

Jamison, A. (2003) 'The making of green knowledge: The contribution from activism', *Futures*, vol. 35, pp. 703–16.

Jarvis, H. (2011) 'Alternative visions of home and family life in Christiania: Lessons for the mainstream', in H. Thörn, C. Wasshede and T. Nilson (eds) *Space for Urban Alternatives? Christiania 1971–2011*, Gidlunds Forlag, Möklinta, pp. 156–80.

Jasanoff, S. (2010) 'A new climate for society', *Theory, Culture and Society*, vol. 27, no. 2–3, pp. 233–53.

Jencks, C. (1987) *Le Corbusier and the Tragic View of Architecture*, Penguin, London.

Jenkins, H. (2006) *Convergence Culture: Where Old and New Media Collide*, New York University Press, New York.

Jenkins, H. (2007) *Confronting the Challenges of Participatory Culture: Media Education for the 21st Century*, The MacArthur Foundation, Chicago, available at: www.digitallearning.macfound.org/atf/cf/ %7B7E45C7E0-A3E0-4B89-AC9C-E807E1B0AE4E%7D/JENKINS_WHITE_PAPER.PDF.

Jenkins, R. (2005) 'Globalization, corporate social responsibility and poverty', *International Affairs*, vol. 81, no. 3, pp. 525–40.

Jenks, M., Burton, E. and Williams, K. (eds) (1996) *The Compact City: A Sustainable Urban Form?*, Spon, London.

Jeong, H.-Y., Kim, Y.-I., Lee, Y.-B., Ha, K.-S., Won, B.-C., Lee, D.-U. and Hahn, D. (2010) 'A "must-go path" scenario for sustainable development and the role of nuclear energy in the 21st century', *Energy Policy*, vol. 38, no. 4, pp. 1962–8.

Johnston, A.K. (2007) *Earth from Space*, A. & C. Black Publishers, London.

Johnston, P. and Santillo, D. (2006) 'The precautionary principle: A barrier to innovation and progress?', Greenpeace Research Laboratories discussion paper, available at: www.greenpeace.to/publications/precaution-and-innovation.pdf.

Johnston, P., Everard, M., Santillo, D. and Robèrt, K-H. (2007) 'Reclaiming the definition of sustainability', *Environmental Science and Pollution Research*, vol. 14, no. 1, pp. 60–6.

Jones, P., Selby, D., and Sterling, S. (eds) (2010) *Sustainability Education: Perspectives and Practice Across Higher Education*, Earthscan, London.

Jordan, L., Stallins, A., Stokes IV, S., Johnson, E. and Gragg, R. (2011) 'Citizen mapping and environmental justice: Internet applications for research and advocacy', *Environmental Justice*, vol. 4, no. 3, pp. 155–62.

Juris, J.S. (2005) 'The new digital media and activist networking within anti-corporate globalization movements', *The Annals of the American Academy of Political and Social Science*, vol. 597, pp. 189–207.

Karghiev, V. (2006) 'Energy and sustainable development in the Russian federation', Helio International, available at: www.helio-international.org/reports/pdfs/Russia-EN.pdf.

Karpf, D. (2010) 'Online political mobilization from the advocacy group's perspective: Looking beyond clicktivism', *Policy & Internet*, vol. 2, no. 4, article 2, available at: http://davekarpf.files.wordpress.com/2009/03/online-political-mobilization-from-the-advocacy-groups-perspective-1.pdf.

Kasperson, J.X. and Kasperson, R.E. (eds) (2001) *Global Environmental Risk*, Earthscan, London.

Kasser, T. (2002) *The High Price of Materialism*, MIT Press, Cambridge, MA.

Kates, R.W., Parris, T.M. and Leiserowitz, A.A. (2005) 'What is sustainable development? Goals, indicators, values and practice', *Environment: Science and Policy for Sustainable Development*, vol. 47, no. 3, pp. 8–21.

Kates, R.W., Clark, W.C, Corell, R., Hall, J.M., Jaeger, C.C., Lowe, I., McCarthy, J.J., Schellnhuber, H.J., Bolin, B., Dickson, N.M., Faucheux, S., Gallopín, G.C., Gruebler, A., Huntley, B., Jäger, J., Jodha, N.S., Kasperson, R.E., Mabogunje, A., Matson, P., Mooney, H., Moore III, B., O'Riordan, T. and Svedin, U. (2001) 'Sustainability science', *Science*, 292, pp. 641–2.

Katsaliaki, K. and Mustafee, N. (2012) 'A survey of serious games on sustainable development', IEEE *Proceedings of the 2012 Winter Simulation Conference (WSC)*, pp. 1–13.

Katz, P. (1994) *The New Urbanism: Toward an Architecture of Community*, McGraw Hill, New York.

Keeble, J.J., Topiol, S. and Berkeley, S. (2003) 'Using indicators to measure sustainability performance at a corporate and project level', *Journal of Business Ethics*, vol. 44, pp. 149–58.

Keeble, L. and Loader, B.D. (eds) (2001) *Community Informatics: Shaping Computer-Mediated Social Relations*, Routledge, London.

Kelly, A. (2007) 'This is just the beginning', *The Guardian*, Fair Trade Supplement, 7 March.

Kemmis, D. (1990) *Community and the Politics of Place*, University of Oklahoma Press, Norman, OK.

Kemp, V., Stark, A. and Tantram, J. (2003) *To Whose Profit? II: Evolution – Building Sustainable Corporate Strategy*, WWF-UK, Godalming, UK, available at: http://assets.wwf.org.br/downloads/to_whose_profit__evolution__completa.pdf.

Kerschner, C. (2010) 'Economic de-growth vs, steady-state economy', *Journal of Cleaner Production*, vol. 18, no. 6, pp. 544–51.

Kester, G.H. (2004) *Conversation Pieces: Community + Communication in Modern Art*, University of California Press, Berkeley, CA.

Kideghesho, J.R. (2010) '"Serengeti shall not die": transforming an ambition into a reality', *Tropical Conservation Science*, vol. 3, no. 3, pp. 228–48.

Kimerling, J. (2001) 'The human face of petroleum: Sustainable development in Amazonia?', *RECIEL*, vol. 10, no. 1, pp. 65–81.

Klein, N. (2000) *No Logo*, Flamingo, London.

Klein, N. (2008) *The Shock Doctrine*, Penguin, London.

Klein, N. (2013) 'Interview: Green groups may be more damaging than climate change deniers'. *Salon*, 5 September, available at: www.salon.com/2013/09/05/naomi_klein_big_green_groups_are_crippling_the_environmental_movement_partner.

Knol, E. and De Vries, P.W. (2011) 'EnerCities, a serious game to stimulate sustainability and energy conservation: Preliminary results', *eLearning Papers*, 25, 1–10, available at: http://elearningpapers.eu/en/download/file/fid/23295.

Koltko-Rivera, M.E. (2004) 'The psychology of worldviews', *Review of General Psychology*, vol. 8, no. 1, pp. 3–58.

Kopnina, H. (2012a) 'Toward conservational anthropology: addressing anthropocentric bias in anthropology', *Dialectical Anthropology*, vol. 36, nos. 1/2, pp. 127–46.

Kopnina, H. (2012b) 'Education for sustainable development (ESD): the turn away from "environment" in environmental education?', *Environmental Education Research*, vol. 18, no. 5, pp. 699–717.

Korten, D.C. (1995) *When Corporations Rule the World*, Berrett-Koehler Publishers, San Francisco, CA.

Korten, D.C. (1999) *The Post-Corporate World: Life after Capitalism*, Berrett-Koehler Publishers, San Francisco, CA.

Korten, D.C. (2000) 'Civilizing society: The annual FEASTA Lecture, Dublin', available at: www.pcdf.org/2000/FEASTA%20Civilizing% 20Human%20Society.htm.

Kotter, J.P. (1996) *Leading Change*, Harvard Business School Press, Boston, MA.

Krasny, M.E. and Tidball, K.G. (2007) 'Civic ecology education: A systems approach to education for sustainable development in cities', available at: www.dnr.cornell.edu/mek2/file/Krasny_Tidball_Civic_Ecology_Education.pdf.

Krosinsky, C. (2012) 'Is Apple the model of a sustainable company?' *Bloomberg News*, 13 June, available at: www.bloomberg.com/news/2012–06–13/is-apple-the-model-of-a-sustainable-company-.html.

Kumar, S. (1992) *No Destination*, Green Books, Totnes, UK.

Ladkin, D. (2006) 'When deontology and utilitarianism aren't enough: How Heidegger's notion of "dwelling" might help organizational leaders resolve ethical issues', *Journal of Business Ethics*, vol. 65, no. 1, pp. 87–98.

Lam, M.E. and Pitcher, T.J. (2012) 'The ethical dimensions of fisheries', *Current Opinion in Environmental Sustainability*, vol. 4, no. 3, pp. 364–73.

Lama-Rewal, S.T. (2011) 'Women's right to the city: From safety to citizenship', in M.-H. Zerah, V. Dupont and S. T. Lama-Rewal (eds) *Urban Policies and the Right to the City in India*, UNESCO, New Delhi, pp. 31–8.

Lane, R.E. (2000) *The Loss of Happiness in Market Democracies*, Yale University Press, New Haven, CT.

Langhelle, O. (1999) 'Sustainable development: Exploring the ethics of *Our Common Future*', *International Political Science Review*, vol. 20, no. 2, pp. 129–49.

Langman, L. (2005) 'From virtual public spheres to global justice: A critical theory of internetworked social movements', *Sociological Theory*, vol. 23, no. 1, pp. 42–74.

Lanier, J. (2013) *Who Owns the Future?* Allen Lane, London.

Lansing, S.J. and Kremer, J.N. (1995) 'A socio-ecological analysis of Balinese water temples', in D.M. Warren, L.J. Slikkerveer and D. Brokensha (eds) *The Cultural Dimension of Development: Indigenous Knowledge Systems*, Intermediate Technology Publications, London, pp. 258–68.

Lasorsa, D.L., Lewis, S.C. and Holton, A.E. (2012) 'Normalizing Twitter', *Journalism Studies*, vol. 13, no. 1, pp. 19–36.

Latouche, S. (1997) 'Paradoxical growth', in M. Rahnema and V. Bawtree (eds) *The Post Development Reader*, Zed Books, London, pp. 135–42.

Latouche, S. (2004) 'Why less should be so much more: Degrowth economics', *Le Monde diplomatique* (English edition), November, available at: http://mondediplo.com/2004/11/14latouche.

Latouche, S. (2009) *Farewell to Growth*, Polity Press, Cambridge.

Latour, B. (2004a) *Politics of Nature: How to Bring the Sciences into Democracy*, Harvard University Press, Cambridge, MA.

Latour, B. (2004b) 'Why has critique run out of steam? From matters of fact to matters of concern', *Critical Inquiry*, vol. 30, no. 2, pp. 225–48.

Lavigne, D.M. (ed.) (2006) *Gaining Ground: In Pursuit of Ecological Sustainability*, IFAW/University of Limerick, London.

Lawn, P.A. (2003) 'A theoretical foundation to support the index of sustainable economic welfare (ISEW), genuine progress indicator (GPI) and other related indexes', *Ecological Economics*, vol. 44, pp. 105–18.

Leach, M., Rockström, J., Raskin, P., Scoones, I., Stirling, A.C., Smith, A. Thompson, J., Millstone, E., Ely, A., Arond, E., Folke, C. and Olsson, P. (2012) 'Transforming innovation for sustainability', *Ecology and Society*, vol. 17, no. 2, available at: www.ecologyandsociety.org/vol17/iss2/art11.

Leadbeater, C. and Miller, P. (2004) 'The pro-am revolution: How enthusiasts are changing our economy and society', Demos, London, available at: www.demos.co.uk/files/proamrevolutionfinal.pdf.

Lebrun, G. (2013) 'Is this the end of Yasuni National Park?' *The Ecologist*, www.theecologist.org/News/news_analysis/2066313/is_this_the_end_of_yasuni_national_park.html.

Lee, S. (Director) (2006) *When the Levees Broke: A Requiem in Four Acts*, feature-length documentary, HBO, information available at: www.hbo.com/docs/programs/whenthelevees broke/synopsis.html.

Lehrer, D. and Vasudev, J. (2011) 'Evaluating a social media application for sustainability in the workplace', Center for Environmental Design Research, UC Berkeley, CA.

Leigh, P. (2005) 'The ecological crisis, the human condition and community-based restoration as an instrument for its cure', *Ethics in Science and Environmental Politics*, vol. 5, available at: www.int-res.com/articles/esep/2005/E60.pdf.

Leiserowitz, A. (2004) 'Before and after *The Day After Tomorrow*: A US study of climate risk perception', *Environment*, November, pp. 22–37.

Leiserowitz, A.A., Kates, R.W. and Parris, T.M. (2005) 'Do global attitudes and behaviours support sustainable development?', *Environment: Science and Policy for Sustainable Development*, vol. 47, no. 9, pp. 22–38.

Leite, J.C. (2005) *The World Social Forum: Strategies of Resistance*, Haymarket Books, Chicago.

Leopold, A. (1970) *A Sand County Almanak*, Oxford University Press, New York.

Lerner, S. (2005) *Diamond: A Struggle for Environmental Justice in Louisiana's Chemical Corridor*, MIT Press, Cambridge, MA.

Lester, L. (2010) *Media and Environment*, Polity Press, Cambridge.

Lester, L. and Cottle, S. (2009) 'Visualising climate change: Television news and ecological citizenship', *International Journal of Communication*, vol. 3, pp. 920–36.

Lester, L. and Hutchins, B. (2012) 'The power of the unseen: Environmental conflict, the media and invisibility', *Media Culture Society*, vol. 34, no. 7, pp. 847–63.

Levitas, R. (2010) 'Back to the future: Wells, sociology, utopia and method', *The Sociological Review*, vol. 58, no. 4, pp. 530–47.

Levy, P. (1997) *Collective Intelligence: Mankind's Emerging World in Cyberspace*, Basic Books, New York.

Lewis, J., Williams, A. and Franklin, B. (2008) 'A compromised fourth estate?, *Journalism Studies*, vol. 9, no. 1, pp. 1–20.

Li, Z. (2006) 'Rapid growth of China's cities challenges urban planners, migrant families', available at: www.worldwatch.org/node/4148.

Liebes, T. (1999) 'Comments on Eliasoph's *Avoiding Politics*', available at: www.mtsu.edu/~seig/response_t_liebes.html, accessed 31 July 2007.

Livesey, S.M. (2003) 'Organizing and leading the grass-roots', *Organization and the Environment*, vol. 16, no. 4, pp. 488–503.

Lockward, C. (2006) 'Building the green way', *Harvard Business Review*, vol. 84, no. 6, pp. 129–137.

Lomborg, B. (2001) *The Sceptical Environmentalist*, Cambridge University Press, Cambridge.

Lomborg, B. (2006) 'Stern review: The dodgy numbers behind the latest warming scare', *Opinion Journal* from the *Wall Street Journal Online*, 2 November, available at: www.opinionjournal.com/extra/?id=110009182a.

Lomborg, B. (2007) *Cool It: the Sceptical Environmentalist's Guide to Global Warming*, Marshall Cavendish/Cyan, New York.

Loong, L.H. (2012) 'The people's garden: In our city in a garden. PM's speech, Prime Minister's Office, Singapore.

Lopez, A. (2012) *The Media Ecosystem: What Ecology Can Teach us About Responsible Media Practice*, Evolver Editions, Berkeley, CA.

Lovelock, J. (1979) *Gaia: A New Look at Life on Earth*, Oxford University Press, Oxford, UK.

Lovelock, J. (1995) *The Ages of Gaia* (2nd edn), Oxford University Press, Oxford.

Lovelock, J. (2006) *The Revenge of Gaia*, Penguin, London.

Lovins, A.B., Lovins, L.H. and Hawken, P. (1999) 'A road map to natural capitalism', *Harvard Business Review*, May/June.

Low, N., Gleeson, B., Green, R. and Radovic, D. (2005) *The Green City: Sustainable Homes, Sustainable Suburbs*, Routledge, London.

Low, S. (2003) *Behind the Gates: Life, Security and the Pursuit of Happiness in Fortress America*, Routledge, London.

Low, S. and Smith, N. (eds) (2006) *The Politics of Public Space*, Routledge, London.

Lowenstein, O. (2001) 'Sensual simplicity', *Resurgence*, no. 207, available at: www.resurgence. org/resurgence/issues/lowenstein207.htm.

Lowenstein, O. and Bridgood, J. (2007) 'Inspiring futures: European timber architecture for the 21st century', Centre for Contemporary Art and the Natural World, Exeter, UK.

Loyn, D. (2006) 'No easy answers', *Developments*, no. 33, pp. 16–17.

Lucas, K., Walker, G., Eames, M., Fay, H. and Poustie, M. (2004) 'Environment and social justice: Rapid research and evidence review (final report)', Policy Studies Institute, London, available at: http://admin.sd-research.org.uk/wp-content/ uploads/2007/04/envsocialjustice review.pdf.

Lueneburger, C. and Goleman, D. (2010) 'The change that leadership sustainability demands', *MIT Sloan Management Review*, Summer, pp. 49–55.

Luke, T.W. (2005) 'The death of environmentalism or the advent of public ecology?', *Organization and Environment*, vol. 18, no. 4, pp. 489–94.

Lund, H. (2007) 'Renewable energy strategies for sustainable development', *Energy*, vol. 32, no. 6, pp. 912–19.

Lupton, D. (1999) *Risk*, Routledge, London.

Luthans, F. and Avolio, B.J. (2003) 'Authentic leadership: A positive developmental approach', in K.S. Cameron, J.E. Dutton and R.E. Quinn (eds) *Positive Organizational Scholarship*, Barrett-Koehler, San Francisco, CA, pp. 241–61.

Lux, K. (2003) 'The failure of the profit motive', *Ecological Economics,* vol. 44, no. 1, pp. 1–9.

Lynas, M. (2005) *High Tide: How Climate Crisis is Engulfing our Planet*, HarperPerennial, London.

Lynas, M. (2007) *Six Degrees: Our Future on a Hotter Planet*, Fourth Estate, London.

Maathai, W. (2004) *The Green Belt Movement: Sharing the Approach and the Experience*, Lantern Books, New York.

Mabey, R. (2006) *Nature Cure*, Pimlico, London.

McCann-Erickson/UNEP (2002) 'Can sustainability sell?', available at: www.unep.org.

McCully, P. (1996) *Silenced Rivers: The Ecology and Politics of Large Dams*, Zed Books, London.

McCully, P. (2001) *Silenced Rivers: The Ecology and Politics of Large Dams*, Zed Books, London.

McCurry, J. (2013) 'Fukushima radiation levels 18 times higher than previously thought'. *The Guardian*, 1 September, available at: www.theguardian.com/environment/2013/sep/ 01/fukushima-radiation-levels-higher-japan.

McDonagh, P. and Prothero, A. (eds) (1997) *Green Management: A Reader*, Dryden Press, London.

McDonough, W. and Braungart, M. (1992) 'The Hanover Principles', available at: www. mcdonough.com/principles.pdf.

McDonough, W. and Braungart, M. (2002) *Cradle to Cradle: Remaking the Way We Make Things*, North Point Press, New York.

Macedo, J. (2004) 'City profile: Curitiba', *Cities*, vol. 21, no. 6, pp. 537–49.

Macedo (2013) 'Planning a sustainable city: The making of Curitiba, Brazil', *Journal of Planning History*, vol. 12, no. 4, pp. 334–53.

McGillivray, M., Weston, C. and Unsworth, C. (1998) *Communities Count! A Step by Step Guide to Community Sustainability Indicators*, New Economics Foundation, London.

McGinnis, M.V. (1999) *Bioregionalism*, Routledge, London.

McGirt, E. (2008) 'How Cisco's CEO John Chambers is turning the tech giant socialist', *Fast Company*, issue 131, available at: www.fastcompany.com/1093654/how-ciscos-ceo-john-chambers-turning-tech-giant-socialist.

McGonigal, J. (2012) *Reality is Broken: Why Games Make Us Better and How They Can Change the World*, Vintage, London.

McIntosh, A. (2004) *Soil and Soul: People versus Corporate Power*, Aurum Press, London.

McKenna, P. (2007) 'Renewable energy could rape nature', *New Scientist*, 25 July, available at: http://environment.newscientist.com/article.ns?id=dn12346andprint=true, accessed 24 July 2007.

McKenzie-Mohr, D. (2000) 'Promoting sustainable behaviour: An introduction to community-based social marketing', *Journal of Social Issues*, vol. 56, no. 3, pp. 543–54.

McKibben, B. (1995) *Hope, Human and Wild: True Stories of Living Lightly on the Earth*, Milkweed Editions, Minneapolis, MN.

McKibben, B. (2003) *Enough: Staying Human in an Engineered Age*, Owl Books, New York.

McKibben, B. (2012) 'Global Warming's Terrifying New Math', *Rolling Stone*, 19 July, available at: www.rollingstone.com/politics/news/global-warmings-terrifying-new-math-20120719.

McLaren, D. (2001) *Sustainable Europe and environmental space – Achieving sustainability through the concept of environmental space: A trans-European project*, Friends of the Earth, London.

McLaren, D. (2003) 'Environmental space, equity and ecological debt', in J. Agyeman, R.D. Bullard and B. Evans (eds) *Just Sustainabilities: Development in an Unequal World*, Earthscan, London, pp. 19–37.

McLaren, D., Bullock, S. and Yousuf, N. (1998) *Tomorrow's World: Britain's Share in a Sustainable Future*, Earthscan/Friends of the Earth, London.

McLennan, J.F. (2004) *The Philosophy of Sustainable Design*, Ecotone, Kansas City, MO.

McManus, P. and Haughton, G. (2006) 'Planning with ecological footprints: A sympathetic critique of theory and practice', *Environment and Urbanization*, vol. 18, no. 1, pp. 113–27.

McMichael, T., Montgomery H. and Costello, A. (2012) 'Health risks, present and future, from global climate change', *British Medical Journal*, *Spotlight*, 19 March, available at: www.bmj.com/content/344/bmj.e1359.

Macnaghten, P. and Urry, J. (1998) *Contested Natures*, Sage, London.

McNeely, J.A. (1996) 'Partnerships for conservation: an introduction', in J.A. McNeely (ed.) *Expanding Partnerships in Conservation*, Island Press, Washington, DC, pp. 1–7.

McNeill, J. (2000) *Something New Under the Sun: An Environmental History of the Twentieth Century*, Penguin, London.

Magnusson, W. and Shaw, K. (eds) (2002) *A Political Space: Reading the Global through Clayoquot Sound*, McGill-Queen's University Press, Montreal, Canada.

Maisonneuve, M., Stevens, M. and Ochab, B. (2010) 'Participatory noise pollution monitoring using mobile phones', *Information Polity*, vol. 15, nos. 1–2, pp. 51–71.

Maniates, M. (2002) 'Individualization: Plant a tree, buy a bike, save the world?', in T. Princen, M. Maniates and K. Conca (eds) *Confronting Consumption*, MIT Press, Cambridge, MA, pp. 43–66.

Manno, J. (2002) 'Commoditization: Consumption efficiency and an economy of care and connection', in T. Princen, M. Maniates and K. Conca (eds) *Confronting Consumption*, MIT Press, Cambridge, MA, pp. 67–100.

Mansfield, B. (2007) 'Neoliberalism in the oceans: "Rationalisation" property rights, and the commons question', in N. Heynen, J. McCarthy, S. Prudham and P. Robbins (eds) *NeoLiberal Environments: False promises and Unnatural Consequences*, Routledge, London.

Manzini, E. (2004) 'Scenarios of sustainable ways of living: Local and global visions', available at www.sustainable-everyday.net.

Manzini, E. (2005) 'Enabling solutions: Social innovation, creative communities and strategic design', available at: www.sustainable-everyday.net.

Manzini, E. and Jegou, F. (2003) *Sustainable Everyday: Scenarios of Urban Life*, Edizioni Ambiente, Milan, Italy.

Marks, K. (2007) 'Aboriginal health – A hundred years behind whites', *The Independent*, 2 May, available at http://findarticles.com/p/articles/mi_qn4158/is_20070502/ai_n1904 8445.

Marks, N. (2006) 'The happy planet index: An index of human well-being and environmental impact', New Economics Foundation/Friends of the Earth, London, available at: www.new economics.org/gen/uploads/dl44k145g5scuy453044gqbu11072006194758.pdf.

Marks, N., Abdallah, S., Simms, A. and Thompson, S. (2006) *The [Un]Happy Planet Index*. Friends of the Earth/New Economics Foundation, London, available at: http://s.bsd.net/ nefoundation/default/page/file/54928c89090c07a78f_ywm6y59da.pdf.

Marten, G.G. (2001) *Human Ecology: Basic Concepts for Sustainable Development*, Earthscan, London.

Martinez-Alier, J. (2002) *The Environmentalism of the Poor*, Edward Elgar, Cheltenham, UK.

Martínez-Alier, J. (2009) 'Socially sustainable economic de-growth', *Development and Change*, vol. 40, no. 6, pp. 1099–119.

Martínez-Alier, J., Pascual, U., Vivien, F.-D., and Zaccai, E. (2010) 'Sustainable de-growth: Mapping the context, criticisms and future prospects of an emergent paradigm', *Ecological Economics*, vol. 69, no. 9, pp. 1741–47.

Mason, P. (2013) *Why It's Kicking Off Everywhere* (2nd edn), Verso, London.

Massey, D. (1993) 'Power-geometry and a progressive sense of space', in J. Bird, B. Curtis, T. Putnam, G. Robertson and L. Tickner (eds) *Mapping the Futures: Local Cultures, Global Changes*, Routledge, London, pp. 63–70.

Massey, D. (2005) *For Space*, Sage, London.

Max-Neef, M. (1991) *Human-Scale Development: Conception, Application and Further Reflection*, Apex Press, London.

Maxwell, R. and Miller, T. (2012) *Greening the Media*, Oxford University Press, Oxford.

Mead, G.H. (1934) *Mind, Self and Society*, Chicago University Press, Chicago, IL.

Meadows, D., Randers, J. and Meadows, D. (2005) *Limits to Growth: The 30-Year Update*, Earthscan, London.

Meadows, D.H., Meadows, D.L., Randers, J. and Behrens III, W.W. (1972) *The Limits to Growth: A Report to The Club of Rome*, Universe Books, New York, available at: www.clubofrome.org/archive/reports.php.

Mellahi, K. and Wood, G. (2002) *The Ethical Business: Challenges and Controversies*, Palgrave, Basingstoke, UK.

Merchant, C. (1989) *Ecological Revolutions: Nature, Gender and Science in New England*, University of North Carolina Press, Chapel Hill, NC.

Metcalf, L. and Benn, S. (2013) 'Leadership for sustainability: An evolution of leadership ability', *Journal of Business Ethics*, vol. 112, no. 3, pp. 369–84.

Meyer, A. (2000) *Contraction and Convergence: The Global Solution to Climate Change*, Green Books, Totnes, UK.

Mezirow, J. (1991) *Transformative Dimensions of Adult Learning*, Jossey-Bass, San Francisco, CA.

Micheletti, M. (2010) *Political Virtue and Shopping: Individuals, Consumerism, and Collective Action* (2nd edn), Palgrave Macmillan, London.

Middleton, J. (2007) *Beyond Authority: Leadership in a Changing World*, Palgrave Macmillan, London.

Mihata, K. (1997) 'The persistence of emergence', in R.A. Eve, S. Horsfall and M.E. Lee (eds) *Chaos, Complexity and Sociology: Myths, Models and Theories*, Sage, London, pp. 30–8.

Mill, J.S. (1974) *On Liberty*, Pelican Books, Harmondsworth, UK.

Millennium Ecosystem Assessment (MEA) (2005) *Ecosystems and Human Wellbeing: Policy Responses, Volume 3*, Island Press, Washington, DC. available at www.maweb.org/documents/document.769.aspx.pdf

Mills, W.I. (1998) 'Identity, power and place at the periphery', *Development*, vol. 41, no. 2, pp. 38–43.

Mintzberg, H. (1987) 'The strategy concept 1: Five Ps for strategy', *California Management Review*, vol. 30, no. 1, pp. 11–24.

Mintzberg, H. (1994) *The Rise and Fall of Strategic Planning: Reconceiving roles for Planning, Plans, Planners*, Free Press, New York.

Mirvis, P. and Coocins, B. (2004) 'The best of the good', *Harvard Business Review*, vol. 82, no. 12, pp. 21–2.

Mitchell, G. and Walker, G. (2003) 'Environmental quality and social deprivation', R&D Technical Report E2–067/1/TR, The Environment Agency, Bristol, UK.

Mitchell, W.J. (1996) *City of Bits*, MIT Press, Cambridge, MA.

Mitchell, W.J. (2000) *E-topia: Urban Life, Jim – But Not As We Know It*, MIT Press, Cambridge, MA.

Mitchell, W.J. (2003) *Me++: The Cyborg Self and the Networked City*, MIT Press, Cambridge, MA.

Mitlin, D. and Satterthwaite, D. (eds) (2004) *Empowering Squatter Citizen: Local Government, Civil Society and Urban Poverty Reduction*, IIED/Earthscan, London.

Mol, A. (2009) 'Environmental deinstitutionalization in Russia', *Journal of Environmental Policy and Planning*, vol. 11, no. 3, pp. 223–41.

Mol, A.P.J. and Spaargaren, G. (2000) 'Ecological modernization theory in debate', in A.P.J. Mol and D.A. Sonnenfeld (eds) *Ecological Modernization Around the World: Perspectives and Critical Debates*, Frank Cass, London, pp. 17–49.

Monbiot, G. (2003) 'World [fair] Trade Organization', *The Ecologist*, available at: www.theecologist.org/archive_detail.asp?content_id=360.

Monbiot, G. (2004) *The Age of Consent*, HarperPerennial, London.

Monbiot, G. (2006) *Heat: How to Stop the Planet Burning*, Penguin Books, London.

Monbiot, G. and Goodall, C. (2011) 'The moral case for nuclear power', George Monbiot blog, available at: www.monbiot.com/2011/08/08/the-moral-case-for-nuclear-power.

Montague, P. (2004) 'Answering the critics of precaution, Part 1', *Rachel's Environment and Health News*, no. 789, 15 April, available at: www.rachel.org/bulletin/index.cfm?St=4.

Montague, P. and Pellerano, M.B. (2001) 'Toxicology and environmental digital resources from and for citizen groups', *Toxicology*, vol. 157, nos. 1–2, pp. 77–88.

Moore, S.A. (2007) *Alternative Routes to the Sustainable City*, Lexington Books, Lanham, MD.

Morozov, E. (2012) *The Net Delusion: How Not to Liberate the World*, Penguin Books, London.

Morphy, H. (1998) *Aboriginal Art*, Phaidon Press, London.

Morton, T.A., Rabinovich, A., Marshall, D. and Bretschneider, P. (2011) 'The future that may (or may not) come: How framing changes responses to uncertainty in climate change communications', *Global Environmental Change*, vol. 21, no. 1, pp. 103–9.

Muir, J. (2012) *The Yosemite*, Century, New York, available at: https://archive.org/details/yosemite00muirgoog

Muller, B. (2010) *Copenhagen 2009: Failure or Final Wake-up Call for our Leaders?* Oxford Institute for Energy Studies, Oxford.

Mumford, L. (1962 [1934]) *Technics and Civilization*, Harcourt Brace, New York.

Mumford, L. (1966a [1938]) *The Culture of Cities*, Harcourt Brace, New York.

Mumford, L. (1966b) *The City in History: Its Origins, its Transformations and its Prospects*, Penguin Books, Harmondsworth, UK.

Mumford, M.D., Zaccaro, S.J., Harding, F.D., Owen Jacobs, T. and Fleishman, E.A. (2000) 'Leadership skills for a changing world: Solving complex social problems', *Leadership Quarterly*, vol. 11, no. 1, pp. 11–35.

Mychajlowycz, M. (2010) 'Overview of logging in Clayoquot Sound: 2000–2009: Friends of Clayoquote Sound', available at: http://focs.ca/wp-content/uploads/2012/07/Clayoquot-Logging-Report-2009-w-Apr2010-update.pdf.

Naess, A. (1973) 'The shallow and the deep, long-range ecology movement', *Inquiry*, no. 16, pp. 95–100.

Naess, A. (1995) 'The deep ecology movement: Some philosophical aspects', in G. Sessions (ed.) *Deep Ecology for the 21st Century*, Shambhala, London, pp. 64–84.

Narayanan SR, S. (2013) 'Effective strategy for organisational development: With reference to Kautilya's Arthashastra', *International Journal of Management and Social Sciences Research*, vol. 2, no. 5, pp. 79–82.

Nattrass, B. and Altomare, M. (1999) *The Natural Step for Business: Wealth, Ecology and the Evolutionary Corporation*, New Society Publishers, Gabriola Island, Canada.

The Natural Step (2000) *The Natural Step Framework Guidebook*, available at: www.naturalstep.ca/resources.htm.

Neate, P. and Platt, D. (2006) *Culture Is Our Weapon: AfroReggae in the Favelas of Rio*, Latin American Bureau, London.

Neidjie, B. (1986) *Australia's Kakadu Man*, Resource Managers, Darwin, Australia.

Nekaris K.A.-I., Campbell, N., Coggins, T.G., Rode, E.J., Nijman, V. (2013) 'Tickled to death: Analysing public perceptions of "cute" videos of threatened species (slow lorises – *Nycticebus spp.*) on Web 2.0 Sites', *PLoS ONE*, vol. 8, no. 7, e69215.

Nelson, R.K. (1986) *Make Prayers to the Raven: A Koyukon View of the Northern Forest*, Chicago University Press, Chicago, IL.

Neuwirth, R. (2006) *Shadow Cities: A Billion Squatters, a New Urban World*, Routledge, London.

Newman, P. (2006) 'The environmental impact of cities', *Environment and Urbanization*, vol. 18, no. 2, pp. 275–95.

Nicholls, A.J. (2002) 'Strategic options in fair trade retailing', *International Journal of Retail and Distribution Management*, vol. 30, no. 1, pp. 6–17.

Nonaka, I. and Toyama, R. (2004) 'Knowledge creation as a synthesizing process', in H. Takeuchi and I. Nonaka (eds) *Hitotsubashi on Knowledge Management*, John Wiley & Sons (Asia), Singapore, pp. 91–124.

Norberg-Hodge, H. (2000) *Ancient Futures: Learning from Ladakh*, Rider Books, London.

Nordstrom, C. (2007) *Global Outlaws: Crime, Money, and Power in the Contemporary World*, California University Press, Berkeley, CA.

Norgaard, R.B. (1994) *Development Betrayed: The End of Progress and a Coevolutionary Revisioning of the Future*, Routledge, London.

Northouse, P.G. (2007) *Leadership: Theory and Practice*, Sage, Thousand Oaks, CA.

Norton, B.G. (2005) *Sustainability: A Philosophy of Adaptive Ecosystem Management*, Chicago University Press, Chicago, IL.

Oates, J.F. (1999) *Myth and Reality in the Rain Forest: How Conservation Strategies Are Failing in West Africa*, University of California Press, Berkeley, CA.

O'Byrne, D.J. (2003) *The Dimensions of Global Citizenship: Political Identity Beyond the Nation-State*, Frank Cass Publishers, London.

Odum H.T. and Odum, E.C. (2001) *A Prosperous Way Down*, University Press of Colorado, Boulder, CO.

Oldfield, J. (2001) 'Russia, systemic transformation and the concept of sustainable development', *Environmental Politics*, vol. 10, no. 3, pp. 94–110.

Oldfield, J. and Shaw, D.J.B. (2006) 'V.I. Vernadsky and the noosphere concept: Russian understandings of society-nature interaction', *Geoforum*, vol. 37, no. 1, pp. 145–54.

Ophuls, W. (1977) *Ecology and the Politics of Scarcity*, W.H. Freeman, San Francisco, CA.

Ophuls, W. (2011) *Plato's Revenge: Politics in the Age of Ecology*, MIT Press, Cambridge, MA.

O'Riordan, T. (1996) 'Democracy and the sustainability transition', in W.M. Lafferty and J. Meadowcroft (eds) *Democracy and the Environment: Problems and Prospects*, Edward Elgar, Cheltenham, UK, pp. 140–56.

O'Riordan, T. and Cameron, J. (1994) *Interpreting the Precautionary Principle*, Earthscan, London.

O'Riordan, T. and Voisey, H. (1998) 'The politics of Agenda 21', in T. O'Riordan and H. Voisey (eds) *The Transition to Sustainability: The Politics of Agenda 21 in Europe*, Earthscan, London, pp. 31–56.

Orr, D. (1992) *Ecological Literacy, Education and the Transition to a Postmodern World*, State Universities of New York Press, Albany, NY.

Orr, D. (1994) *Earth in Mind*, Island Press, Washington, DC.

Owen, P. (2012) *How Gamification Can Help Your Business Engage in Sustainability*, Do Sustainability, Oxford.

Oxfam (2002) 'Rigged rules and double standards: Trade, globalization and the fight against poverty', Oxfam, Oxford, available at: www.maketrade-fair.com/assets/english/report_english.pdf.

Oxfam (2007) 'Increased ethical concerns leave UK public unhappy with supermarket shopping', press release, 2 March, available at: www.oxfam.org.uk/applications/blogs/pressoffice/2007/03/increased_ethical_concerns_lea.html.

Paavola, J. (2011) 'Climate change: The ultimate tragedy of the commons?', Sustainability Research Institute Paper, no. 24, University of Leeds, available at: www.see.leeds.ac.uk/fileadmin/Documents/research/sri/workingpapers/SRIPs-24_-1/pdf.

Pal, A. (2006) 'Scope for bottom-up planning in Kolkata: Rhetoric vs. reality', *Environment and Urbanization*, vol. 18, no. 2, pp. 501–21.

Palacios, J.J. (2004) 'Corporate citizenship and social responsibility in a globalized world', *Citizenship Studies*, vol. 8, no. 4, pp. 383–402.

Palmer, J.A. (1998) *Environmental Education in the 21st Century*, Routledge, London.

Parkin, S. (2010) *The Positive Deviant: Sustainability Leadership in a Perverse World*, Earthscan, London.

Parks, L. (2005) *Cultures in Orbit: Satellites and the Televisual*, Duke University Press, Durham, NC.

Paterson, M. (2000) 'Car culture and global environmental politics', *Review of International Studies*, vol. 26, pp. 253–70.

Payaud, M.A. and Martinet, A.C. (2010) 'Stratégies RSE-BOP et soin des communautés humaines: Concepts et propositions génériques', *Management International/International Management/Gestión Internacional*, vol. 14, no. 2, pp. 31–51.

Pearce, D., Markandya, A. and Barbier, E. (1989) *Blueprint for a Green Economy*, Earthscan, London.

Pearce, F. (2002) 'Top scientist ousted', *New Scientist*, 19 April, available at: www.newscientist.com/article.ns?id=dn2191.

Pearce, F. (2006) *The Last Generation: How Nature will Take her Revenge for Climate Change*, Eden Project Books, London.

Pearce, F. (2013) *The Landgrabbers: The New Fight Over Who Owns The Earth*, Eden Books, London.

Pearce, J. (2003) *Social Enterprise in Anytown*, Calouste Gulbenkian Foundation, London.

Peeples, J. (2011) 'Toxic sublime: Imaging contaminated landscapes', *Environmental Communication: A Journal of Nature and Culture*, vol. 5, no. 4, pp. 373–92.

Pellow, D.N. (2002) *Garbage Wars: The Struggle for Environmental Justice in Chicago*, MIT Press, Cambridge, MA.

Pellow, D.N. and Park, L. S.-H. (2002) *The Silicon Valley of Dreams: Environmental Justice, Immigrant Workers and the High-Tech Global Economy*, New York University Press, New York.

Pender, J. (2001) 'From structural adjustment to comprehensive development framework: Conditionality transformed?', *Third World Quarterly*, vol. 22, no. 3, pp. 397–411.

People's Republic of China (2012) 'National Report on Sustainable Development', Beijing, available at: www.china-un.org/eng/zt/sdreng.

Pepper, D. (2005) 'Utopianism and environmentalism', *Environmental Politics*, vol. 14, no. 1, pp. 3–22.

Pereira, M.A., Kartashov, A.I., Ebbeling, C.B., van Horn, L., Slattery, M.L., Jacobs, D.R. Jr and Ludwig, D. S. (2005) 'Fast-food habits, weight gain and insulin resistance (the CARDIA study): 15-year prospective analysis', *The Lancet*, vol. 365, no. 9453, pp. 36–42.

Peretti, J. (2003) 'Culture jamming, memes, social networks and the emerging media ecology: The Nike sweatshop email as object-to-think-with', available at: http://depts.washington.edu/ccce/polcommcampaigns/peretti.html.

Perlman, J.E. (2000) 'Innovative solutions create urban sustainability', *Global Issues*, vol. 5, no. 1, available at: http://usinfo.state.gov/journals/itgic/0300/ijge/gj-04a.htm.

Perri 6 (1997) *Holistic Government*, Demos, London.

Pezzoli, K. (1997) 'Sustainable development: A transdisciplinary overview of the literature', *Journal of Environmental Planning and Management*, vol. 40, no. 5, pp. 549–74.

Pezzoli, K. (2000) *Human Settlements and Planning for Ecological Sustainability: The Case of Mexico City*, MIT Press, Cambridge, MA.

Phillips, B.J. and McQuarrie, E.F. (2004) 'Beyond visual metaphor: A new typology of visual rhetoric in advertising', *Marketing Theory*, vol. 4, nos. 1/2, pp. 113–36.

Pickard, V.W. (2006) 'Assessing the radical democracy of indymedia: Discursive, technical, and institutional constructions', *Critical Studies in Media Communication*, vol. 23, no. 1, pp. 19–38.

Pierre, K. (2007) 'The economics of fair trade coffee: For whose benefit? An investigation into the limits of fair trade as a development tool and the risk of clean-washing', HEI Working Paper No. 06, Graduate Institute of International Studies, University of Geneva, Geneva.

Pigem, J. (2002) 'Barcoding life', *New Internationalist*, no. 349, available at: www.newint.org/features/2002/09/01/ethics.

Pilar, M. del and Marin, U. (2003) 'Time for Utopia', *New Internationalist*, vol. 357, available at: www.newint.org/issue357/time.htm.

Pilger, J. (2013) 'Australia's boom is anything but for its Aboriginal people', *The Guardian*, 28 April, available at: www.theguardian.com/commentisfree/2013/apr/28/australia-boom-aboriginal-story-despair.

Pillinger, I. (2000) *Quality in Social Public Services*, European Foundation for the Improvement of Living and Working Conditions, Dublin.

Pilnick, A. (2002) *Genetics and Society*, Open University Press, Buckingham, UK.

Pindar, D. (2005) *Visions of the City*, Edinburgh University Press, Edinburgh, UK.

Pitcher, T.J. and Cheung, W.W.L. (2013) 'Fisheries: Hope or despair?', *Marine Polution Bulletin*, vol. 74, no. 2, pp. 506–16.

Pitkin, B. (2006) 'Community informatics for community development: The hope or hype issue revisited', in P. Purcell (ed.) *Networked Neighbourhoods: The Connected Community in Context*, Springer-Verlag, London, pp. 77–98.

Ploger, J. (2004) 'Strife: Urban planning and agonism', *Planning Theory*, vol. 3, no. 1, pp. 71–92.

Plumwood, V. (1996) 'Nature, self and gender: Feminism, environmental philosophy and the critique on rationalism', in K. J. Warren (ed.) *Ecological Feminist Philosophies*, Indiana University Press, Bloomington, IN, pp. 155–80.

Pontin, J. and Roderick, I. (2007) *Converging World: Connecting Communities in Global Change*, Schumacher Briefing no. 13, Green Books, Totnes, UK.

Porritt, J. (2005) *Capitalism as if the World Matters*, Earthscan, London.

Porter, M.E. and Kramer, M.R. (2006) 'Strategy and society: The link between competitive advantage and corporate social responsibility', *Harvard Business Review*, vol. 84, no. 12, pp. 78–92.

Porter, V. and Sims, M. (2003) *Environmental Change: Communicating the Issues (An Intermedia Special Report)*, International Institute of Communications, London.

Portes, A. (1998) 'Social capital: Its origins and applications in modern sociology', *Annual Review of Sociology*, vol. 24, pp. 1–24.

Potts, D. (1997) 'Urban lives: Adopting new strategies and adapting rural links', in C. Rakodi (ed.) *The Urban Challenge in Africa: Growth and Management of its Large Cities*, United Nations University Press, Tokyo, pp. 447–94.

Potts, D. with Mutambirwa, C. (1998) 'Basics are now a luxury: Perceptions of structural adjustment's impact on rural and urban areas in Zimbabwe', *Environment and Urbanization*, vol. 10, no. 1, pp. 55–75.

Prahalad, C.K. (2009) *The Fortune at the Bottom of the Pyramid: Eradicating Poverty Through Profits*, Prentice Hall, New York.

Prahalad, C.K. and Hammond, A. (2002) 'Serving the world's poor profitably', *Harvard Business Review*, vol. 80, no. 9, pp. 48–57.

Princen, T. (2002) 'Consumption and its externalities: Where economy meets ecology', in T. Princen, M. Maniates and K. Conca (eds) *Confronting Consumption*, MIT Press, Cambridge, MA, pp. 23–42.

Princen, T. (2005) *The Logic of Sufficiency*, MIT Press, Cambridge, MA.

Princen, T., Maniates, M. and Conca, K. (eds) (2002) *Confronting Consumption*, MIT Press, Cambridge, MA.

Proctor, T., Proctor, S. and Papasolomou, I. (2005) 'Visualizing the metaphor', *Journal of Marketing Communications*, vol. 11, no. 1, pp. 55–72.

Prudham, S. (2009) 'Pimping climate change: Richard Branson, global warming, and the performance of green capitalism', *Environment and Planning A*, vol. 41, no. 7, pp. 1594–613.

Purcell, M. (2008) *Recapturing Democracy: Neoliberalization and the Struggle for Alternative Urban Futures*, Routledge, London.

Putnam, R.D. (2000) *Bowling Alone: The Collapse and Revival of American Community*, Simon & Schuster, New York.

Putnam, R.D. (2007) '*E Pluribus Unum*: Diversity and community in the twenty-first century', the 2006 Johan Skytte Prize lecture, *Scandinavian Political Studies*, vol. 30, no. 2, pp. 137–74.

Quinn, M. (2006) 'The power of community: How Cuba survived peak oil', *Permaculture Activist*, Spring, available at: http://globalpublicmedia.com/articles/657

Raco, M. (2007) *Building Sustainable Communities: Spatial Policy and Labour Mobility in Post-War Britain*, Policy Press, Bristol, UK.

Radjou, N., Prabhu, J. and Ahuja, S. (2012) *Jugaad Innovation: Think Frugal, Be Flexible, Generate Breakthrough Growth*, Jossey Bass, New York.

Rahmstorf, S. (2007) 'A semi-empirical approach to projecting future sea-level rise', *Science*, vol. 315, 19 January, available at: www.pik-potsdam.de/stefan/Publications/Nature/rahmstorf_science_2007.pdf.

Rahmstorf, S., Cazenave, A., Church, J.A., Hansen, J.E., Keeling, R.F., Parker, D.E. and Somerville, R.C.J. (2007) 'Recent climate observations compared to projections', *Science*, vol. 316, 4 May, available at www.pik-potsdam.de/~stefan/Publications/Nature/rahmstorf_etal_science_2007.pdf.

Rakodi, C. (ed.) (1997) *The Urban Challenge in Africa: Growth and Management of its Large Cities*, United Nations University Press, Tokyo.

Randall, B. (2001) *Songman: The Story of an Aboriginal Elder*, ABC Books, Sydney, Australia.

Raskin, P., Banuri, T., Gallopin, G., Gutman, P., Hammond, A., Kates, R. and Swart, R. (2002) *The Great Transition: The Promise and Lure of the Times Ahead*, Stockholm Environment Institute, Boston, MA.

Rath, P.K. (2010) 'Gandhian Sarvodaya', *Orissa Review*, October, pp. 36–9.

Ratner, B.D. (2004) 'Sustainability as a dialogue of values: Challenges to the sociology of development', *Sociological Inquiry*, vol. 74, no. 1, pp. 59–69.

Ravetz, J. (2000) 'Integrated assessment for sustainability appraisal in cities and regions', *Environmental Impact Assessment Review*, vol. 20, pp. 31–64.

Rawls, J. (1999) *A Theory of Justice*, Oxford University Press, Oxford.

Raynolds, L.T., Murray, D. and Wilkinson, J. (eds) (2007) *Fair Trade: The Challenges of Transforming Globalization*, Routledge, London.

Redekop, B.J. (2011) 'Challenges and strategies of leading for sustainability', in B.J. Redekop (ed.) *Leadership for Environmental Sustainability*, Routledge, London, pp. 55–66.

Redford, K. (2011) 'Misreading the conservation landscape', *Oryx: The International Journal of Conservation*, vol. 45, no. 3, pp. 324–30.

Rees, W. and Wackernagel, M. (1996) 'Urban ecological footprints: Why cities cannot be sustainable and why they are key to sustainability', *Environmental Impact Assessment Review*, vol. 16, pp. 223–48.

Reich, C.A. (1970) *The Greening of America*, Bantam, New York.

Reich, Z. (2010) 'Measuring the impact of PR on published news in increasingly fragmented news environments', *Journalism Studies*, vol. 11, no. 6, pp. 799–816.

Reid, W.V., Berkes, F., Wilbanks, T.J. and Capistrano, D. (eds) (2006) *Bridging Scales and Knowledge Systems: Concepts and Applications in Ecosystem Assessment*, Island Press, Washington, DC.

Reusswig, F., Schwarzkopf, J. and Polenz, P. (2004) 'Double impact – The climate blockbuster *The Day After Tomorrow* and its impact on the German cinema public', Report No. 92, Potsdam Institute for Climate Impact Research, available at www.pik-potsdam.de/research/publications/pikreports/.files/pr92.pdf.

Rheingold, H. (2000) *The Virtual Community*, MIT Press, Cambridge, MA.

Ries, A. and Ries, L. (2002) *The Fall of Advertising and the Rise of PR*, HarperBusiness, New York.

Ridlington, E. and Rumpler, J. (2013) *Fracking by the Numbers: Key Impacts of Dirty Drilling at the State and National Level*, Environment America Research & Policy Center, Boston, MA, available at: www.environmentamerica.org/sites/environment/files/reports/EA_Fracking Numbers_scrn.pdf.

Rifkin, J. (2000) *The Age of Access: How the Shift from Ownership to Access is Transforming Modern Life*, Penguin Books, London.

Ritzer, G. (2000) *The McDonaldization of Society*, Pine Forge Press, Thousand Oaks, CA.

Robèrt, K.-H. (2000) 'Tools and concepts for sustainable development: How do they relate to a general framework for sustainable development, and to each other?', *Journal of Cleaner Production*, vol. 8, pp. 243–54.

Robèrt, K.-H. (2004) 'Natural step by step: An interview with Julian Gold', *Corporate Knights*, March, available at: www.corporateknights.ca/content/ page.asp?name=pushing_limits_kh_robert.

Robèrt, K.-H., Schmidt-Bleek, B., de Larderel, J.A., Basile, G., Jansen, J.L., Kuehr, R., Price Thomas, P., Suzuki, M., Hawken, P. and Wackernagel, M. (2002) 'Strategic sustainable development – Selection, design and synergy of applied tools', *Journal of Cleaner Production*, vol. 10, pp. 197–214.

Roberts, R. (1971) *The Classic Slum: Salford Life in the First Quarter of the Century*, Penguin, Harmondsworth, UK.

Robinson, J. (2004) 'Squaring the circle? Some thoughts on the idea of sustainable development', *Ecological Economics*, vol. 48, pp. 369–84.

Robinson, J. and Tinker, J. (1997) 'Reconciling ecological, economic and social imperatives: A new conceptual framework', in T. Schrecker (ed.) *Surviving Globalism: The Social and Environmental Challenges*, St Martin's Press, New York, pp. 71–94.

Rockström, J., Steffen, W., Noone, K., Persson, Å., Chapin III, F.S., Lambin, E., Lenton, T.M., Scheffer, M., Folke, C., Schellnhuber, H., Nykvist, B., De Wit, C.A., Hughes, T., van der Leeuw, S., Rodhe, H., Sörlin, S., Snyder, P.K., Costanza, R., Svedin, U., Falkenmark, M., Karlberg, L., Corell, R.W., Fabry, V.J., Hansen, J., Walker, B., Liverman, D., Richardson,

K., Crutze, P. and Foley, J. (2009) 'Planetary boundaries: Exploring the safe operating space for humanity', *Ecology and Society,* vol. 14, no. 2, p. 32, available at: www.ecologyandsociety.org/vol14/iss2/art32.

Rodgers, D. (2004) 'Disembedding the city: Crime, insecurity and spatial organization in Managua, Nicaragua', *Environment and Urbanization,* vol. 16, no. 2, pp. 113–23.

Rodrigues, A.S.L., Pilgrim, J.D., Lamoreux, J.F., Hoffmann, M. and Brooks, T.M. (2006) The value of the IUCN Red List for conservation. *TRENDS in Ecology and Evolution,* vol. 21, no. 2, pp. 71–6.

Rogers, E.M. (2003) *Diffusion of Innovations,* Free Press, New York.

Rolston III, H. (1996) 'Feeding people versus saving nature?', in W. Aiken and H. LaFollette (eds) *World Hunger and Morality* (2nd edn), Prentice-Hall, Englewood Cliffs, NJ, pp. 248–67.

Rolston III, H. (2011) *A New Environmental Ethics,* Routledge, London.

Romig, K. (2005) 'The Upper Sonoran lifestyle: Gated communities in Scottsdale, Arizona', *City and Community,* vol. 4, no. 1, pp. 67–86.

Roseland, M. (1998) *Toward Sustainable Communities: Resources for Citizens and their Governments,* New Society Publishers, Gabriola Island, Canada.

Ross, A. (2005) 'The UK approach to delivering sustainable development in government: A case study in joined-up working', *Journal of Environmental Law,* vol. 17, no. 1, pp. 27–49.

Ross, A. (2011) *Bird on Fire: Lessons from the World's Least Sustainable City,* Oxford University Press, Oxford.

Ross, P. and Cabannes, Y. (2013) *21st Century Garden Cities of Tomorrow: A Manifesto,* Lulu.com, Raleigh, NC.

Rost, J.C. (1991) *Leadership for the 21st Century,* Praeger, New York.

Roszak, T. (1969) *The Making of a Counter Culture,* Doubleday, New York.

Roszak, T. (1972) *Where the Wasteland Ends: Politics and Transcendence in Postindustrial Society,* Doubleday, New York.

Roth, L. (2005) *Something New in the Air: The Story of First Peoples Television Broadcasting in Canada,* McGill-Queens University Press, Quebec, Canada.

Roy, A. (1999) 'The greater common good', available at: www.narmada.org/gcg/gcg.html.

Roy, A. (2003) 'Confronting empire', World Social Forum, Porte Alegre, Brazil, available at: www.zcommunications.org/confronting-empire-by-arundhati-roy.

Rumming, K. (ed) (2004) 'The Hanover Kronsberg Handbook', City of Hanover, available at: www.sibart.org/pdf/handbook_big_en.pdf.

Sachs, I. (1999) 'Social sustainability and whole development: Exploring the dimensions of sustainable development', in E. Becker and T. Jahn (eds) *Sustainability and the Social Sciences,* Zed Books, London, pp. 25–36.

Sachs, J.D. (2005) *The End of Poverty: How We Can Make it Happen in our Lifetime,* Penguin Books, London.

Sachs, J. (2009) *Common Wealth: Economics for a Crowded Planet,* Penguin, London.

Sachs, J. (2013) 'The end of poverty, soon', *New York Times,* 24 September, available at: www.nytimes.com/2013/09/25/opinion/the-end-of-poverty-soon.html.

Sachs, W. (1999) *Planet Dialectics: Explorations in Environment and Development,* Zed Books, London.

Sachs, W. (2004) 'Environment and human rights', *Development,* vol. 47, no. 1, pp. 42–9.

Sahavirta, H. (2012) 'Showing the green way: Advocating green values and image in a Finnish public library', *International Federation of Library Associations and Institutions,* vol. 38, no. 3, pp. 239–42.

Saith, A. (2006) 'From universal values to millennium development goals: Lost in translation', *Development and Change,* vol. 37, no. 6, pp. 1167–99.

Saiz, A.V. (2005) 'Globalization, cosmopolitanism and ecological citizenship', *Environmental Politics,* vol. 14, no. 2, pp. 163–78.

Sale, K. (1991) *Dwellers in the Land: The Bioregional Vision*, University of Georgia Press, Athens, GA.

Sandel, M.J. (2013) *What Money Can't Buy: The Moral Limits of Markets*, Penguin, London.

Sandilands, C. (2002) 'Between the local and the global: Clayoquot Sound and simulacral politics', in W. Magnusson and K. Shaw (eds) *A Political Space: Reading the Global through Clayoquot Sound*, McGill-Queen's University Press, Montreal, Canada, pp. 139–68.

Sargisson, L. (2001) 'Politicizing the quotidian', *Environmental Politics*, vol. 10, no. 2, pp. 68–89.

Sarnsamak, P. (2013) 'Polar bear hunters promise restraint', *The Nation*, 10 March, available at: www.nationmultimedia.com/national/Polar-bear-hunters-promise-restraint-30201618.html.

Satterthwaite, D. (1997) 'Environmental transformations in cities as they get larger, wealthier and better managed', *The Geographical Journal*, vol. 163, no. 2, pp. 216–24.

Savitz, A.W. (2006) *The Triple Bottom Line: How Today's Best Companies are Achieving Economic, Social and Environmental Success – and How You Can do it Too*, Jossey-Bass, San Francisco, CA.

Schaper, M. (2002) 'The essence of ecopreneurship', *Greener Management International*, vol. 38, pp. 26–30.

Schiller, H.I. (1989) *Culture Inc.: The Corporate Takeover of Public Expression*, Oxford University Press, Oxford.

Schlosberg, D. (2004) 'Reconceiving environmental justice: Global movements and political theories', *Environmental Politics*, vol. 13, no. 3, pp. 517–40.

Schor, J. (1998) *The Overspent American*, HarperPerennial, New York.

Schudson, M. (1999) *The Good Citizen: A History of American Civic Life*, Harvard University Press, Cambridge, MA.

Schumacher, E.F. (1973) *Small is Beautiful*, Abacus, London.

Scott, W.A.H. and Gough, S.R. (2003) *Sustainable Development and Learning: Framing the Issues*, Routledge/Falmer, London.

Scott Cato, M. (2012) *The Bioregional Economy: Land, Liberty and Pursuit of Happiness*, Routledge-Earthscan, London.

Seabrook, J. (1996) *In the Cities of the South*, Verso, London.

Secretariat of the Convention on Biological Diversity (2012) *Cities and Biodiversity Outlook*, CBD, Montreal.

Semler, R. (2004) *The Seven-Day Weekend: A Better Way to Work in the 21st Century*, Century/Random House, London.

Sen, A. (1999) *Development as Freedom*, Oxford University Press, Oxford.

Senge, P.M. (1999) *The Fifth Discipline: The Art and Practice of the Learning Organization*, Random House, London.

Senge, P.M. (2008) 'Building learning organizations', in D.S. Pugh (ed.) *Organization Theory* (5th edn), Penguin, London, pp. 486–514.

Seyfang, G. (2005) 'Shopping for sustainability: Can sustainable consumption promote ecological citizenship?', *Environmental Politics*, vol. 14, no. 2, pp. 290–306.

Shand, H. and Wetter, K.J. (2006) 'Shrinking science: An introduction to nanotechnology', in L. Starke (ed.) *State of the World 2006*, Earthscan/Worldwatch Institute, London, 78–95.

Shellberger, M. and Nordhaus, T. (2004) 'The Death of Environmentalism', Breakthrough Institute, Oakland, CA, available at: www.thebreakthrough.org/images/Death_of_Environmentalism.pdf.

Shepherd, S.J. (2012) *Visualizing Climate Change: A Guide to Visual Communication of Climate Change and Developing Local Solutions*, Routledge-Earthscan, London.

Shiva, V. (1991) *The Violence of the Green Revolution*, Zed Books, London.

Shiva, V. (1993) 'The Chipko women's concept of freedom', in M. Meis and V. Shiva (eds) *Ecofeminism*, Zed Books, London, pp. 246–50.

Shiva, V. (2000) *Stolen Harvest: The Hijacking of the Global Food Supply*, South End Press, Cambridge, MA.

Shiva, V. (2012) 'Our hunger games', *Global Research*, 29 August, available at: www.globalresearch.ca/our-hunger-games/5302603.

Shuftan, C. (1996) 'The community development dilemma: What is really empowering?', *Community Development Journal*, vol. 13, no. 3, pp. 260–4.

Shulman, S. (2009) 'The case against mass e-mails: Perverse incentives and low quality public participation in U.S. federal rulemaking', *Policy & Internet*, vol. 1, no. 1, pp. 23–53.

Shutkin, W.A. (2001) *The Land That Could Be: Environmentalism and Democracy in the 21st Century*, MIT Press, Cambridge, MA.

SIGMA Project (2003) 'The SIGMA guidelines: Putting sustainable development into practice', available at: www.projectsigma.co.uk/default.asp.

Silverstone, R. (2007) *Media and Morality: On the Rise of the Mediapolis*, Polity Press, Cambridge, MA.

Singh, A. (2005) *One Planet, Many People: Atlas of our Changing Environment*, UNEP/Earthprint, Stevenage, UK.

Slikkerveer, L.J. and Slikkerveer, M.K.L. (1995) 'Taman Obat Keluarga (TOGA): Indigenous Indonesian medicine for self-reliance', in D.M. Warren, L.J. Slikkerveer and D. Brokensha (eds) *The Cultural Dimension of Development: Indigenous Knowledge Systems*, Intermediate Technology Publications, London, pp. 13–34.

Smith, D.M., Cusack, S., Colman, A.W., Folland, C.K., Harris, G.R. and Murphy, J.M. (2007) 'Improved surface temperature prediction for the coming decade from a global climate model', *Science*, vol. 317, 10 August, pp. 796–9.

Smith, J. (2004) 'The World Social Forum and the challenges of global democracy', *Global Networks*, vol. 4, no. 4, pp. 413–21.

Smith, R. (2011) 'Green capitalism: the god that failed', *Real-World Economics Review*, no. 56, pp. 122–44.

Smith, T., Sonnenfeld, D.A. and Pellow, D.N. (eds) (2006) *Challenging the Chip: Labour Rights and Environmental Justice in the Global Electronics Industry*, Temple University Press, Philadelphia, PA.

Soil Association (2007) 'Soil Association to ensure air-freighted organic food benefits poor farmers – And challenges UK Government to do same for all air-freighted produce', press release, 25 October 2007, available at: www.soilassociation.org/pressreleases.

Soper, K. (2005) 'Thinking the unnatural', *Capitalism Nature Socialism*, vol. 16, no. 1, pp. 129–34.

SOS Yasuni (2013) Open letter to the President of Ecuador, available at: www.sosyasuni.org/en/index.php?option=com_content&view=article&id=185:open-letter-to-the-president-of-ecuador-as-the-date-approaches-for-assessment-of-the-yasuni-itt-initiative&catid=15:campaign&Itemid=27.

Soulé, M. (2002) 'History's lesson: Build another Noah's ark', *High Country News*, vol. 24. no. 9, 13 May, available at: www.hcn.org/issues/226/11219.

Spaid, S. (2002) *Ecovention: Current Art to Transform Ecologies*, Contemporary Arts Center, Cincinnati, OH.

Spence, M.D. (2000) *Dispossessing the Wilderness: Indian Removal and the Making of the National Parks*, Oxford University Press, New York.

Stapleton, L.M. and Garrod, G.D. (2007) 'Keeping things simple: Why the human development index should not diverge from its equal weights assumption', *Social Indicators Research*, vol. 84, pp. 179–88.

Steele, C. (2012) 12 Green Apps for Earth Day, 20 April, *PCMag*, available at: www.pcmag.com/slideshow/story/296829/12-green-apps-for-earth-day (accessed 29 July 2012).

Stefanovic, I.L. (2000) *Safeguarding our Common Future: Rethinking Sustainable Development*, State University of New York Press, New York.

Sterling, S. (2001) *Sustainable Education: Revisioning Learning and Change*, Green Books, Totnes, UK.

Sterling, S. (2004) 'Systemic thinking', in D. Tilbury and D. Wortman (eds) *Engaging People in Sustainability*, IUCN, Gland, Switzerland, pp. 43–62.

Sterling, S., Maxey, L. and Luna, H. (eds) (2013) *The Sustainable University*, Routledge, London.

Stern, N. (2005) 'Stern Review: Report on the Economics of Climate Change', HM Treasury, London, available at: www.hm-treasury.gov.uk/independent_reviews/stern_review_econom ics_climate_change/stern_review_report.cfm.

Stewart, K. (2006) 'Designing good urban governance indicators: The importance of citizen participation and its evaluation in Greater Vancouver', *Cities*, vol. 23, no. 3, pp. 196–204.

Stiglitz, J. (2002) *Globalization and its Discontents*, Penguin, London.

Stiglitz, J. (2006) *Making Globalization Work: The Next Steps to Global Justice*, Penguin, London.

Stiglitz, J. and Charlton, A. (2005) *Fair Trade for All: How Trade can Promote Development*, Oxford University Press, Oxford.

Stone M.K. (2009) *Smart by Nature: Schooling for Sustainability*, University of California Press, Berkeley, CA.

Sudjic, D. (2006) 'Making cities work: China', BBC News, 21 June, available at http://news.bbc.co.uk/2/hi/asia-pacific/5084852.stm.

Sugranyes, A. and Mathivet, C. (eds) (2010) *Cities for All: Proposals and Experiences towards the Right to the City*. Habitat International Coalition (HIC), Santiago, Chile.

Sunstein, C.R. (2006) *Infotopia: How Many Minds Produce Knowledge*, Oxford University Press, Oxford, UK.

Supreme Court of India (2000) *WRIT PETITION (C) NO. 319 OF 1994: Judgement*, New Delhi, available at: www.narmada.org/sardar-sarovar/sc.ruling/majority.judgement.htm.

Suri, S.N. (2010) *Safe Cities Free of Violence Against Women and Girls Initiative: A Draft Strategic Framework for Women's Safety in Delhi 2010*, Delhi: Jagori, UN Habitat, UN Women, Govt. of NCT of Delhi, available at: http://jagori.org/wp-content/uploads/2006/01/Strategic_Framework.pdf.

Sveiby, K.-E. and Skuthorpe, T. (2006) *Treading Lightly: The Hidden Wisdom of the World's Oldest People*, Allen & Unwin, Crows Nest, Australia.

Swyngedouw, E. (2007) 'Impossible "sustainability" and the postpolitical condition', in R. Krueger and D. Gibbs (eds) *The Sustainable Development Paradox*, Guilford Press, London.

Sylvestre, P., McNeil, R. and Wright, T. (2013) 'From Talloires to Turin: A critical discourse analysis of declarations for sustainability in higher education', *Sustainability*, vol. 5, no. 4, pp. 1356–71.

Talen, E. (2002) 'The social goals of new urbanism', *Housing Policy Debate*, vol. 13, no. 1, pp. 165–88.

Tapscott, D. and Williams, A.D. (2007) *Wikinomics: How Mass Collaboration Changes Everything*, Atlantic Books, London.

Taylor, D.E. (1997) 'Women of colour, environmental justice and ecofeminism', in K.J. Warren (ed.) *Ecofeminism: Women, Culture, Nature*, Indiana University Press, Bloomington, IN, pp. 38–81.

Taylor, P.A. (2005) 'From hackers to hacktivists: Speed bumps on the global superhighway?', *New Media & Society*, vol. 7, no. 5, pp. 625–46.

Teather, D. (2007) 'Branded for life?', *The Guardian*, 25 October, available at: www.guardian.co.uk/g2/ story/0,2198430,00.html.

TEEB (2010a) *The Economics of Ecosystems and Biodiversity: Ecological and Economic Foundations*, Earthscan, London.

TEEB (2010b) 'The economics of ecosystems and biodiversity: Mainstreaming the economics of nature: A synthesis of the approach, conclusions and recommendations of TEEB', available at: www.teebweb.org/wpcontent/uploads/Study%20and%20Reports/Reports/Synthesis%20report/TEEB%20Synthesis%20Report%202010.pdf.

Teivainen, T. (2002) 'The World Social Forum and global democratization: Learning from Porto Alegre', *Third World Quarterly*, vol. 23, no. 4, pp. 621–32.

Terborgh, J. (2004) *Requiem for Nature*, Shearwater Books, Washington, DC.

Terry, G. (2009) 'No climate justice without gender justice: An overview of the issues', *Gender & Development*, vol. 17, no. 1, pp. 5–18.

Thompson, J.B. (2005) 'The new visibility', *Theory, Culture & Society*, vol. 22, no. 6, pp. 31–51.

Thussu, D.K. (2006) *International Communication: Continuity and Change*, Hodder Arnold, London.

Tilbury, D. (2009) 'Tracking our progress: A global monitoring and evaluation framework for the UN DESD', *Journal of Education for Sustainable Development*, vol. 3, no. 2, pp. 189–93.

Tilbury, D. and Wortman, D. (2004) *Engaging People in Sustainability*, IUCN, Gland, Switzerland, available at: www.iucn.org/dbtw-wpd/edocs/2004–055.pdf, accessed 23 July 2007.

Tilley, F. and Young, W. (2009) 'Sustainability entrepreneurs: Could they be the true wealth creators of the future?', *Greener Management International*, vol. 55, pp. 79–92.

Tinnell, J. (2011) 'Scripting just sustainability: Through green listing towards eco-blogging', *Environmental Communication: A Journal of Nature and Culture*, vol. 5, no. 2, pp. 228–42.

Tinsley, S. and George, H. (2006) *Ecological Footprint of the Findhorn Foundation and Community*, Sustainable Development Research Centre, UHI Millennium Institute, Moray, UK.

Tomlinson, J. (1991) *Cultural Imperialism*, Continuum, London.

Torgenson, D. (1999) *The Promise of Green Politics: Environmentalism and the Public Sphere*, Duke University Press, Durham, NC.

Trader, T. (2013) 'Google limits carbon footprint, funds climate change deniers', *Green Computing Report,* 19 August, available at: www.greencomputingreport.com/gcr/2013-08-19/google_resizes_carbon_footprint_funds_climate_science_deniers.html.

Tuan, Y.-F. (1977) *Space and Place: The Perspective of Experience*, University of Minnesota Press, Minneapolis, MN.

Turner, B.S. (1993) *Citizenship and Social Theory*, Sage, London.

Turnhout, E., Hisschemoller, M. and Eijsackers, H. (2007) 'Ecological indicators: Between the two fires of science and policy', *Ecological Indicators*, vol. 7, pp. 215–28.

United Nations (UN) (2000) 'Millennium declaration: Resolution adopted by the General Assembly', available at: www.unmillenniumproject.org/documents/ares552e.pdf.

UN (2002a) 'Report of the World Summit on Sustainable Development', available at www.johan-nesburgsummit.org/html/documents.html.

UN (2002b) 'Financing for development: Building on Monterrey', available at: www.un.org/esa/ffd/Documents/Building%20on%20Monterrey.pdf, accessed 14 June 2007.

UN (2006) 'The Millennium Development Goals Report 2006', available at: http://mdgs.un.org/unsd/mdg/Resources/Static/Pro ducts/Progress2006/MDGReport2006.pdf.

United Nations (UN) (2012) *The Future We Want: Rio+20 Outcomes Document*, United Nations, Rio de Janeiro, available at: www.uncsd2012.org/thefuturewewant.html.

UNDP (United Nations Development Programme) (1997) 'Governance for sustainable human development: A UNDP policy document', available at: www.pogar.org/publications/other/undp/governance/undppolicydoc97-e.pdf.

UNDP (2006) 'Governance indicators: A user's guide', available at: www.undp.org/oslocentre/docs04/UserGuide.pdf.

UNDP (2011) *Human Development Report 2011: Sustainability and Equity*, UNDP, New York.

UNDP (2013) *Human Development Report 2013: The Rise of the South*, UNDP, New York.

UNECE (2011) *Learning for the future: competences in education for sustainable development*, UNECE, Utrecht, available at: www.unece.org/fileadmin/DAM/env/esd/ESD_Publications/Competences_Publication.pdf.

UNEP (United Nations Environment Programme) (2005) *Talk the Walk: Advancing Sustainable Lifestyles through Marketing and Communications*, UNEP, Paris, available at: www.unep.fr/pc/sustain/reports/advertising/ Talk_the_Walk.pdf.

UNEP (2006) 'Gender mainstreaming among environment ministries', available at: www.unep.org/civil_society/PDF_docs/UNEP-survey-reportJan-07.pdf, accessed 14 June 2007.

UNEP (2007) *Sustainability Communications: A Toolkit for Marketing and Advertising Courses* (CD Rom), UNEP, Paris, available at: www.unep.fr/pc/sustain/advertising/events_specifics/Education%20Kit_EN.htm.

UNEP (2011) *Towards a Green Economy: Pathways to Sustainable Development and Poverty Eradication*, UNEP, Geneva, available at: www.unep.org/greeneconomy/GreenEconomy Report/tabid/29846/language/en-US/Default.aspx.

UNEP (2012a) *Green Economy: Employment*. Briefing paper, UNEP, Geneva, available at: www.unep.org/greeneconomy/Portals/88/EMPLOYMENT.pdf.

UNEP (2012b) *Green Economy: Valuing Nature*. Briefing paper, UNEP, Geneva, available at: www.unep.org/greeneconomy/Portals/88/VALUING%20NATURE.pdf.

UNEP/Futerra (2005) *Communicating Sustainability: How to Produce Effective Public Campaigns*, UNEP, Paris, available at: www.unep.fr/pc/sustain/reports/advertising/Communication_Guide/webEN2.pdf.

UNESCO (2005) 'United Nations decade of education for sustainable development 2005–2014', available at: http://portal.unesco.org/education/en/ev.php.

UNESCO (2006) *International Public Debates: Urban Policies and the Right to the City*, UNESCO, Paris.

Unger, R.M. (2004) *False Necessity: Anti-necessitarian Social Theory in the Service of Radical Democracy*, Verso, London.

Unger, R.M. (2007) *The Self Awakened: Pragmatism Unbound*. Harvard University Press, Cambridge, MA.

UN-Habitat (2000) 'UNCHS (Habitat) – The global campaign for good urban governance', *Environment and Urbanization*, vol. 12, no. 1, pp. 197–202.

UN-Habitat (2003) *The Challenge of the Slums: Global Report on Human Settlements 2003*, Earthscan for the United Nations Human Settlements Programme (UN-Habitat), London.

UN-REDD (2011) *The UN-REDD Programme Strategy 2011–2015*, United Nations, Genev, available at: www.un-redd.org/PublicationsResources/tabid/587/Default.aspx.

Van der Donk, W., Loader, B.D., Nixon, P.G. and Rucht, D. (eds) (2004) *Cyberprotest: New Media, Citizens and Social Movements*, Routledge, London.

Van Matre, S. (1990) *Earth Education: A New Beginning*, Institute for Earth Education, Greenville, WV.

Verburg, R.M. and Weigel, V. (1997) 'On the compatibility of sustainability and economic growth', *Environmental Ethics*, vol. 17, no. 3, pp. 247–65.

Vidal, J. (2007a) 'A better brew', *The Guardian*, 12 September, available at: http://society.guardian.co.uk/societyguardian/story/0,,2166745,00.html.

Vidal, J. (2007b) 'Welcome to the Isle of Wight: Yachting Mecca, tourist haven ... and eco trailblazer', *The Guardian*, 2 November, available at: www.guardian.co.uk/environment/2007/nov/ 02/isleofwight.

Vie, J.-C., Hilton-Taylor, C. and Stuart, S.N. (eds) (2009) *Wildlife in a Changing World: An analysis of the 2008 IUCN Red List of Threatened Species*, IUCN, Gland, Switzerland.

Viola, B. (1981) *Hatsu-Yume (First Dream)*, video produced as artist-in-residence at Sony Corporation, Japan, 56 minutes, now available on DVD.

Von Ravensburg, N.G. (2011) 'Economic and other benefits of the entrepreneurs' cooperative as a specific form of enterprise cluster, ILO, Dar es Salaam', available at: www.copac.coop/publications/2011-ilo-copac-entrepreneurs%20cooperative.pdf.

Von Weizsacker, E., Lovins, A.B. and Lovins, L.H. (1997) *Factor Four: Doubling Wealth, Halving Resource Use*, Earthscan, London.

Wackernagel, M. and Rees, W. (1996) *Our Ecological Footprint: Reducing Human Impact on the Earth*, New Society Publishers, Gabriola Island, Canada.

Wackernagel, M. and Yount, D. (1998) 'The ecological footprint: An indicator of progress toward regional sustainability', *Environmental Monitoring and Assessment*, vol. 51, pp. 511–29.

Wackernagel, M. and Yount, D. (2000) 'Footprints for sustainability: The next steps', *Environment, Development and Sustainability*, vol. 2, pp. 21–42.

Walker, B.H. and Salt, D. (2006) *Resilience Thinking: Sustaining Ecosystems and People in a Changing World*, Island Press, Washington, DC.

Wals, A.E.J. (2012) *Shaping the Education of Tomorrow: 2012 Full-length Report on the UN Decade of Education for Sustainable Development*, UNESCO, Paris, available at: http://unesdoc.unesco.org/images/0021/002164/216472e.pdf.

Wals, A.E.J. and Blewitt, J. (2010) 'Third-wave sustainability in higher education: Some (inter)national trends and developments', in P. Jones, D. Selby and S. Sterling (eds) *Sustainability Education: Perspectives and Practice across Higher Education*, Earthscan, London, pp. 55–74.

Wapner, P. (1996) *Environmental Activism and World Civic Politics*, State University of New York Press, Albany, NY.

Ward, B. and Lewis, J. (2002) *Plugging the Leaks: Making the Most of Every Pound that Enters your Local Economy*, New Economics Foundation, London.

Ward, C. (2002) *Cotters and Squatters: Housing's Hidden History*, Five Leaves Publications, Nottingham, UK.

Warner, K. (2002) 'Linking local sustainability initiatives with environmental justice', *Local Environment*, vol. 7, no. 1, pp. 35–47.

Warren, K. (1996) 'The power and promise of ecological feminism', in K. Warren (ed.) *Ecological Feminist Philosophies*, Indiana University Press, Bloomington, IN, pp. 19–41.

Warren, K. (2004) 'Sustainable development and sustainable development education: An ecofeminist philosophical perspective on the importance of gender', in J. Blewitt and C. Cullingford (eds) *The Sustainability Curriculum: The Challenge for Higher Education*, Earthscan, London, pp. 104–25.

Warren, S. (2004) 'Review of Pellow and Park (2002)', *Journal of Urban Affairs*, vol. 26, no. 3, pp. 401–3.

Warren, S. (2004) 'The utopian potential of GIS', *Cartographica: The International Journal for Geographic Information and Geovisualization*, vol. 39, no. 1, pp. 5–16.

Watkins, K. *et al.* (2006) *Human Development Report 2006: Beyond Scarcity – Power, Poverty and the Global Water Crisis*, Palgrave Macmillan for the United Nations Development Programme, London.

Watkins, K. *et al.* (2007) *Human Development Report 2007–2008: Fighting Climate Change: Human Solidarity in a Divided World*, Palgrave Macmillan for the United Nations Development Programme, London.

WCED (World Commission on Environment and Development) (1987) *Our Common Future*, Oxford University Press, Oxford.

Webb, T. (2007) 'Going green keeps tills ringing', *Ethical Corporation*, September, pp. 46–7.

WEDO (Women's Environment and Development Organization) (2007) 'Changing the climate: Why women's perspectives matter', available at: www.un.org/esa/ffd/Documents/Building%20on%20Monterrey.pdf, accessed 14 June 2007.

Weinberger, D. (2002) *Small Pieces Loosely Joined*, Basic Books, New York.

Welford, R. (1998) 'Life-cycle assessment', in R. Welford (ed.) *Corporate Environmental Management 1: Systems and Strategies*, Earthscan, London, pp. 138–47.

Wellman, B. and Haythornthwaite, C. (eds) (2002) *The Internet and Everyday Life*, Blackwell, Oxford, UK.

Wellman, B., Quan-Haase, A., Witte, J. and Hampton, K. (2001) 'Does the internet increase, decrease or supplement social capital? Social networks, participation, and community commitment', *American Behavioral Scientist*, vol. 45, no. 3, pp. 436–55.

Welsh Government (2012) *A Sustainable Wales: Better Choices for a Better Future*, Welsh Government, Cardiff, available at: http://wales.gov.uk/docs/desh/consultation/121203asusdev whitepaperen.pdf.

Wessel, D. (2007) 'Prizes for solutions to problems play valuable role in innovation', *Wall Street Journal Online*, 25 January, available at: http://webreprints.djreprints.com/16577700 67525.html.

Wharburton, D. (2006) *Community Learning and Action for Sustainability*, WWF-UK, Godalming, UK, available at www.wwflearning.org.uk/data/files/clasl-design-summary-web-383.pdf.

Wheatley, M. (1999) *Leadership and the New Science: Discovering Order in a Chaotic World*, Berrett-Koehler Publishers, San Francisco, CA.

Wheatley, M. (2001) 'The real work of knowledge management', *IHRIM Journal*, vol. 5, no. 2, pp. 29–33, International Association for Human Resources Information Management, available at: www.margaretwheatley.com/articles/ management.html, accessed 18 June 2007.

Wheatley, M. and Kellner-Rogers, M. (1999) *A Simpler Way*, Berrett-Koehler Publishers, San Francisco, CA.

White, M.M. (2011a) 'D-Town Farm: African American resistance to food insecurity and the transformation of Detroit', *Environmental Practice*, vol. 13, no. 4, pp. 189–211.

White, M.M. (2011b) 'Sisters of the soil: Urban gardening as resistance in Detroit. *Race/Ethnicity: Multicultural Global Contexts*, vol. 5, no.1, pp. 13–28.

Whitehead, M. (2010) 'Hollow sustainabilities? Perspectives on Sustainable Development in the Post-socialist World', *Geography Compass*, vol. 4, no. 11, pp. 1618–34.

Wielkiewicz, R.M. and Stelzner, S.P. (2005) 'An ecological perspective on leadership theory, research, and practice', *Review of General Psychology*, vol. 9, no. 4, pp. 326–41.

Wijkman, A. and Rockström, J. (2012) *Bankrupting Nature: Denying Our Planetary Boundaries*, Routledge, London.

Wilkinson, D. and Appelbee, E. (1999) *Implementing Holistic Government*, Policy Press, Bristol, UK.

Wilkinson, R.G. (1996) *Unhealthy Societies: The Affliction of Inequality*, Routledge, London.

Wilkinson, R.G. (2005) *The Impact of Inequality: How to Make Sick Societies Healthier*, Routledge, London.

Williams, K., Burton, E. and Jenks, M. (eds) (2000) *Achieving Sustainable Urban Form*, Spon, London.

Willoquet-Maricondi, P. (2010) 'Shifting paradigms: From environmental film to ecocinema, in P. Willoquet-Maricondi (ed.) *Framing the World: Explorations in Ecocriticism and Film*, University of Virginia Press, Charlottesville, VA, pp. 43–61.

Winner, L. (1989) *The Whale and the Reactor: A Search for Limits in an Age of High Technology*, University of Chicago Press, Chicago, IL.

Winner, L. (1997) 'Technology today: Utopia or dystopia?', *Social Research*, vol. 64, no. 3, pp. 989–1017.

Wolch, J. (1996) 'Zoopolis', *Capitalism, Nature, Socialism*, vol. 7, no. 2, pp. 21–47.

Wolch, J. (2007) 'Green urban worlds', *Annals of the Association of American Geographers*, vol. 97, no. 2, pp. 373–84.

Wolff, R.D. (2012) *Democracy at Work: A Cure for Capitalism*, Haymarket Books, Chicago.

Wolpert, L. (1993) *The Unnatural Nature of Science*, Faber & Faber, London.

Woolcock, M. and Narayan, D. (2000) 'Social capital: Implications for development theory, research and policy', *World Bank Research Observer*, vol. 15, no. 2, pp. 225–50.

World Bank (2003) *Sustainable Development in a Dynamic World: Transforming Institutions, Growth and Quality of Life*, World Bank and Oxford University Press, Washington, DC.

World Bank (2006) 'Governance and anti-corruption', available at: http://info.worldbank. org/governance/kkz2005/maps.html.

World Social Forum (WSF) (2012) *Seizing the Moment, Building Solidarity Social Movements in Action at the 5th World Social Forum on Migration*. Migrant Forum in Asia, Quezon City, available at: *www.dropbox.com/s/ydt5rx6yh0unlwy/WSFM%20report%20final.pdf*.

Worldwatch Institute (2007) *Biofuels for Transport: Global Potential and Implications for Energy and Agriculture*, Earthscan, London.

Wright, B. (2005) 'Living and dying in Louisiana's Cancer Alley', in R. D. Bullard (ed.) *The Quest for Environmental Justice: Human Rights and the Politics of Pollution*, Sierra Club Books, San Francisco, CA, pp. 87–107.

Wright, F.L. (1958) *The Living City*, Horizon Press, New York.

WWF-Int (World Wide Fund for Nature) (2006) *Living Planet Report 2006*, WWF, Gland, Switzerland, available at: www.wwf.org.uk/wwf_articles.cfm?unewsid=1222.

WWF-Int (World Wide Fund for Nature) (2012) *Living Planet Report 2012*, WWF, Gland, Switzerland, available at: www.wwf.org.uk/what_we_do/about_us/living_planet_report_ 2012.

Wynne, B. (1996) 'May the sheep safely graze? A reflexive view of the expert–lay knowledge divide', in S. Lash, B. Szerszynski and B. Wynne (eds) *Risk, Environment and Modernity: Towards a New Ecology*, Sage, London, pp. 27–43.

Yanarella, E.J. and Levine, R.S. (1992) 'Does sustainable development lead to sustainability?', *Futures*, vol. 24, no. 8, pp. 759–74.

York, R. and Rosa, E.A. (2003) 'Key challenges to ecological modernization theory', *Organization and Environment*, vol. 16, no. 3, pp. 273–88.

York, R., Rosa, E.A. and Dietz, T. (2003) 'Footprints on the Earth: The environmental consequences of modernity', *American Sociological Review*, vol. 68, pp. 279–300.

Young, M. and Willmott, P. (1957) *Family and Kinship in East London*, Routledge, London.

Young, W. and Tilley, F. (2006) 'Can businesses move beyond efficiency? The shift toward effectiveness and equity in the corporate sustainability debate', *Business Strategy and the Environment*, vol. 15, no. 6, pp. 402–15.

Zadek, (2001) *The Civil Corporation: The New Economy of Corporate Citizenship*, Earthscan, London.

Zhang, K.H. (2002) 'What explains China's rising urbanization in the reform era?', *Urban Studies*, vol. 39, no. 12, pp. 2301–15.

Ziff, L. (ed.) (1982) *Ralph Waldo Emerson: Selected Essays*, Penguin Books, Harmondsworth, UK.

Zigurs I. (2003) Leadership in virtual teams: Oxymoron or opportunity?, *Organizational Dynamics*, vol. 31, no. 4, pp. 339–51.

Zittel, W. and Schindler, J. (2007) 'The crude oil supply outlook', Energy Watch Group, Ottobrunn, Germany, available at: www.energywatchgroup.org/fileadmin/global/ pdf/EWG_ Oilreport_10-2007.pdf.

Index